CHARLES EDWARD STUART

CHARLES EDWARD STUART

A TRAGEDY IN MANY ACTS

FRANK McLYNN

Oxford   New York

OXFORD UNIVERSITY PRESS

1991

Oxford University Press, Walton Street, Oxford OX2 6DP

Oxford New York Toronto
Delhi Bombay Calcutta Madras Karachi
Petaling Jaya Singapore Hong Kong Tokyo
Nairobi Dar es Salaam Cape Town
Melbourne Auckland

and associated companies in
Berlin Ibadan

Oxford is a trade mark of Oxford University Press

First published 1988 by Routledge
First issued as an Oxford University Press paperback 1991

British Library Cataloguing in Publication Data
Data available
ISBN 0–19–282856–8

Library of Congress Cataloging in Publication Data
Data available
ISBN 0–19–282856–8

Printed in Great Britain by
Biddles Ltd.
Guildford and King's Lynn

Contents

List of maps

Preface

There has never been a comprehensive scholarly biography of Prince Charles Edward Stuart. That deficiency, is, I think, sufficient justification for the labour expended in a twelve-year Odyssey in the world of 'Bonnie Prince Charlie', a journey that also produced my first three books on the Jacobites. I have consulted nearly 100,000 individual documents in the Stuart papers and tens of thousands in other manuscript collections, especially in the Vatican archives. To the best of my knowledge, much of this material has never been used before. Yet a biography can never be purely a work of antiquarian research. I have benefited greatly from wide reading in the literature on childhood, and I have found many psychoanalytical studies and psychohistorical methodologies useful.

I must first of all thank Her Majesty the Queen for allowing me to work in her archives. Then I must explain two procedural decisions I have taken that may offend purists. While leaving eighteenth-century punctuation intact, I have taken the liberty of tidying up Charles Edward's eccentric spelling. He was an atrocious speller, and I personally find that his letters when reproduced in all their pristine orthography distract one from the content of what he is saying. The other decision I have taken is to switch from New Style dates to Old Style during the period of the '45 itself. In the mid-eighteenth century there was an eleven-day difference in the two styles, but since the great events of the '45 are all known by Old Style dates (e.g. 'Black Friday' as 5 December 1745 OS, not 16 December NS; Culloden as 16 April 1746 not 27 April), I have retained the traditional dates. All dates before and after the '45 are New Style. Since long sea-voyages provide natural intervals both as prelude and sequel to the '45, no confusion arises.

Anyone attempting to write a biography of this scope is bound to end up owing a considerable debt to dozens of (usually nameless) individuals, librarians and archivists of many different tongues and cultures. But there are some individuals who have helped me 'above and beyond the call of duty' whom I must mention by name. Over the years I have had many interesting conversations about the Jacobites and their world with friends. In this category I would particularly like to mention Jack Lindsay, Eveline Cruickshanks and Jeremy Black. Then there are the people who helped me by smoothing the ways to archives. Here a special mention is due to Mgr Charles Burns of the Vatican Archives, Father Francis Edwards SJ, curator of the Farm Street archive, and Dom Geoffrey Scott of Douai Abbey. I have spent many fascinating hours discussing the workings of the unconscious with the distinguished Australian psychoanalyst Dr George Christie. Sir Oliver Millar generously gave me his expert advice in finding suitable illustrations. Miss Jane Langton and her successor as Registrar of the Royal Archives at Windsor, Mrs Sheila De Bellaigue, went to extraordinary lengths to help me in my quest. I must thank also those scholars with whom I corresponded and who helped me by shedding light in their particular area of expertise: Professor L. L. Bongie (the Prince's ladies), Dr Rohan Butler (Choiseul), Dr J. Rogister (Louis XV).

My list of acknowledgments would not be complete without mention of my editor at Routledge, Andrew Wheatcroft, who was enthusiastic about the project from the very start and who, as both a writer and an editor himself, was uniquely placed to appreciate the problems involved in writing such a work. But lastly and mostly, I must thank my wife Pauline both for her 'in house' editing and for her tolerance in enduring a thousand and one days and nights of Charles Edward arcana.

Twickenham, January 1987

Chronology of the Principal Events in the Life of Charles Edward Stuart *(1720–88)*

31 December 1720   Born at Rome.

1725   Birth of his brother Henry.

November 1725   His mother, Clementina Sobieska leaves James for a convent.

1726–8   The prince at Bologna with his father, James, 'the old Pretender'.

1728   Reunion with his mother and return to Rome.

1734   Gaeta campaign.

1735   Death of Clementina Sobieska.

1737   The prince's tour of northern Italy.

1738   Death of 2nd duke of Berwick (Liria).

9 January 1744   Departs Rome for France.

February–March 1744   At Gravelines with French invasion force.

April 1744–June 1745   In France (Paris, Fitzjames, Navarre).

July 1745   Sails from Nantes and Belle-Isle for Scotland.

3 August (NS)   Lands in Scotland.

19 August (OS)   Raises the standard at Glenfinnan.

17 September   Enters Edinburgh.

21 September   Defeats Cope at Prestonpans.

21 September–1 November   In Edinburgh.

8 November   Invades England.

5 December   Council at Derby insists on retreat.

20 December   Re-enters Scotland.

17 January 1746   Defeats Hawley at Falkirk.

1 February   Retreat to the Highlands commences.

Mid-February–mid-April   The prince based at Inverness.

16 April 1746   Defeated by Cumberland at Culloden.

17 April–20 September   The prince in the heather.

10 October (NS)   The prince arrives at Roscoff.

October 1746–January 1747   The prince in and around Paris.

January–March   His embassy to Madrid via Avignon.

May   His brother Henry departs secretly for Rome.

July   The prince hears that Henry has been made a cardinal.

Autumn 1747–January 1748   Affair with Louise de Montbazon.

February 1748   Beginning of affair with the Princesse de Talmont.

10 December 1748   His arrest and confinement in the Chateau de Vincennes, followed by expulsion from France.

27 December 1748 He reaches Avignon.

February 1749 Leaves Avignon to begin the 'obscure years'.

May 1749 In Venice.

1749–52 The prince based in Luneville. End of the affair with the Princesse de Talmont.

1752–4 Based in Ghent and Liège. Renews liaison with Clementina Walkinshaw. Failure of the Elibank Plot. Birth of his daughter Charlotte (1753).

1754–6 Final break with Marischal and effective end of Jacobitism. The prince in Basle with Clementina.

1756–8 In Liège.

1758–65 The prince based at Bouillon.

1759 Negotiations with Choiseul over projected French invasion of England.

1760 Clementina Walkinshaw leaves him, taking Charlotte with her.

1765 The prince renews contact with Henry.

1 January 1766 Death of his father James.

1766 The prince returns to Rome but is not recognised as 'Charles III' by the Pope.

1766–74 The prince based in Rome.

1772 Marriage to Louise of Stolberg.

1774–86 The prince based in Florence.

1778–80 Louise of Stolberg's affair with Alfieri.

1780 Louise flees to a convent.

1783–4 Visit of Gustav III of Sweden.

1784 Recognises Charlotte as his legitimate daughter and makes her duchess of Albany.

1786 Returns to Rome with his daughter.

30 January 1788 Dies in Rome, aged 67.

Jacobite Europe

The route taken by Prince Charles

Introduction

On Christmas Day 1688 a tired and broken man arrived with his family at the French port of Ambleteuse, on his way to Versailles to ask Louis XIV for sanctuary. The man was James II, king of England, expelled from his kingdom by William of Orange in what was to be known to history as the 'Glorious Revolution'. With him was his queen, Mary of Modena, and a six-month-old son, James Francis Edward. Thus was born the Jacobite movement. Neither the infant James Francis nor his son Charles Edward was ever to regain the throne of the three kingdoms of England, Scotland and Ireland for the Stuart family. But both their lives would be dominated and ultimately destroyed by the effects of that fateful year 1688.

James Francis Edward Stuart grew up in the chateau of St Germain, which Louis XIV made over to the exiled James II. His early years saw the successive disappointment of all Jacobite hopes of restoration, whether by war of diplomacy. All Louis XIV's tireless efforts on the Stuarts' behalf came to nothing.[1] At the death of William of Orange (William III of England) in 1701, and again on the demise of James's daughter Anne in 1714, Jacobite aspirations soared only to plummet.[2] The end of 1714 saw the House of Hanover shakily ensconced on the throne of England. After the failure of the 1715 Jacobite rising, the Hanoverian tenure was more secure, though still very far from unshakeable.[3]

The one unquestionable stroke of good fortune young James Francis enjoyed in these years was to be recognised by Louis XIV as James III, *de jure* king of England, after his father's death in 1701. But how strongly personal was Louis XIV's attachment to the Stuarts soon became clear after 1713. The conclusion of the War of Spanish Successsion forced French interests to override the idiosyncraces of

Le Roi Soleil. The Jacobite court was politely moved on: James III became 'Jamie the Rover', doomed to a series of rebuffs and disappointments.[4]

There are two things to note about the young life of James III at St Germain (until 1713). One was his physical bravery. At the murderous battle of Malplaquet (1711) James distinguished himself by pronounced, almost reckless courage. The other was his stoicism. He came under the influence of Archbishop Fénelon of Cambrai, who inculcated a detached resignation to life's buffetings and a quiet acceptance of God's Providence. This 'quietism' was later to be the source of much friction with his son.[5]

But as a politician James was a disaster. He had no power to move men. He was utterly lacking in charisma. He seemed to be singularly ill-starred, almost as if he had the Midas touch in reverse. The Jacobite rising of 1715 was a chilling demonstration of this. Detained on the Continent by adverse weather, James arrived in Scotland early in 1716 to find that his cause was already lost. His attempts to rally the clansmen by the force of his own personality led to humiliation for him and accelerated ruin for his Scottish supporters.[6]

James's fortunes in Europe were no better. Expelled from St Germain by the 1713 Treaty of Utrecht, he moved his miniature court onwards, unable for years to find a satisfactory base. He was successively in Bar (Lorraine), Avignon and Urbino. Finally, after much acrimonious negotiation with the Pope, James took up permanent residence at the Palazzo Muti in Rome.

The Palazzo Muti was no architectural masterpiece. The exterior was unprepossessing, and put in the shade by the glories of the church of Santi Apostoli adjacent to it on the Piazza. The Palazzo Muti was built around a square courtyard with ochred walls overlooking a small fountain in the centre. A dark, steep staircase led up from the entrance hall to the *piano nobile* where some semblance of regal atmosphere was imposed on the unpromising raw material.

Even before coming to Rome from Urbino, James had combined his plans for another Jacobite rising with his hopes for a suitable wife. James had thought seriously of marriage ever since the failure of the 1715 rising and the decline into terminal illness of his mother Mary of Modena (she died of cancer in 1718). His first choice was Benedicta, daughter of the duke of Modena; she reminded him of his mother both in looks and titles. James claimed to love Benedicta passionately. The duke of Modena was made of sterner stuff. He weighed James's restoration prospects in the balance and found them wanting.[7]

James's quest for a wife now became less sentimental and more hard-headed. Charles Wogan, one of the heroes of the '15, whom James had employed as an agent in Russia, was a dashing cavalier, likely to impress the great ladies of Europe. James sent him on a mission to scour the courts of Germany for a likely bride.[8] Wogan saw no one who fitted the bill in Westphalia or Bavaria, but at Ohlau in Silesia he met and was deeply impressed with Maria Clementina Sobieska, youngest daughter of the Polish Prince James Sobieski. The Sobieskis were one of Poland's great families. It was Clementina's grandfather John Sobieski who had turned back the Turks at the gates of Vienna in 1683.[9]

Convinced that he had found the right woman for his king, Wogan returned to Italy. He described the sixteen-year-old Clementina to James. She was small and delicate, brown-haired, black-eyed and full of the spirited courage of the Sobieskis.[10] James sent to Silesia to ask for her hand. The Jacobite suit was accepted without demur.

There is something curious about James's headlong dash into matrimony at the age of thirty. It was almost as though, having rejected sentiment as the basis for marriage after his disappointment with Benedicta of Modena, he became indifferent about his future partner, provided she satisfied the necessary minimum requirements for a royal bride. No doubt the fabled wealth of the Sobieskis, who were major creditors of the Polish state, had something to do with it. But if James had exercised his usual caution, he might have probed more deeply into the background of his future queen. Had he done so, he would have discovered a far from auspicious heredity. James Sobieski was a depressive, probably from the burden of living in the shadow of a famous father. Clementina's mother, a daughter of the Prince Palatine, was beautiful and elegant but feather-brained and unstable. Already this legacy had tilted Maria Clementina in the direction of excessive piety.

None of this seems to have been considered at the time. After so many rebuffs in so many different areas of his life, James was over-joyed to have achieved acceptance. He prepared to receive Clementina in Bologna.

The future queen and her party set out for Italy, ostensibly on a pilgrimage to Loreto. But word of the real purpose of her journey leaked out. Determined to stop the marriage, which would breed fresh pretenders to his English throne, George I brought pressure on the Austrian Emperor to have the Sobieski party arrested. Because of Clementina's dilatoriness at Augsburg, the arresting troops caught up with her at Innsbruck in October 1718.[11]

All that winter Clementina was under house (or castle) arrest. Both James and the Sobieski family contemplated calling the marriage off. Eventually a saviour was found: none other than Wogan, the man who had first 'discovered' Clementina. With three companions (the 'three musketeers' of Jacobite legend: Messrs Misset, Gaydon and O'Toole), Wogan engineered a daring rescue. Travelling to Innsbruck, they snatched Clementina from the Schloss Ambrass (April 1719) after a six-month captivity. Braving dreadful weather in the Brenner pass, Wogan and friends brought her to safety in the papal states.[12]

When they arrived at Bologna at the end of April, James was not there to greet his queen. He had gone to Spain, hoping to take part in the Spanish expedition on his behalf that became the storm-tossed fiasco and military defeat of the '19.[13] Consequently, it was by proxy that Clementina was married on 9 May 1719 to 'James III, king of England', with James Murray standing in for James.

The full, solemn marriage ceremony took place on 2 September 1719 at Montefiascone, seventy miles north-west of Rome, after James's return from Spain. It was only on the very morning of the ceremony that James first set eyes on Clementina. The *de jure* monarch was impressed by what he saw. His queen was less so: she had been buoyed up by the romantic illusion that all Jacobites were of the swashbuckling stamp of Wogan and his 'musketeers'; the dour and uncharismatic James brought her down to earth with a bump. Many years later James ruefully conceded that the marriage had never really had a chance on that basis alone; the contrast between himself and Wogan was too cruel. At the time all that James could see was that Wogan had served him well. In gratitude James made the Irishman a knight baronet and praised him extravagantly.[14]

The royal couple returned to Rome where a papal guard was mounted daily outside the Palazzo Muti. The dark and gloomy Palazzo would not have been any princess's idea of a fairy-tale castle. To compensate the Pope gave the couple the Palazzo Savelli at Albano as a summer residence. This became a great favourite with James. The country estate at Albano where he spent his *villegiatura* (summer holiday) provided him with one of his few lifelines in moments of great stress. There were too many of these for the 'Old Pretender' in the future.

But there were no regrets at first. In the honeymoon period James counted himself fortunate in having such a queen. And the following summer his joy was unconfined when he learned that Clementina was pregnant. At last he would secure the Stuart line with an heir.

Neither he nor the queen could have had any idea that he had begotten a son who was to be one of history's legendary figures.

Who was this man Charles Edward Stuart who became known to legend as Bonnie Prince Charlie?

The exiled Stuarts were at the centre of a web of hopes and aspirations entertained by hundreds of refugee clients, the men who had served them in their ill-fated attempts to recover the throne of England. The prince would thus be heir apparent to an esoteric cult. He would be in one culture but not of it; he would be of another culture but not in it. He would grow up speaking, writing and thinking in three languages but in none of them well. His ambitions would be centred on three distant kingdoms that he had never seen. He would have to carry the role of prince without the power and deference a prince normally commands. The gap between appearance and reality would always yawn like a chasm.

Other exiles have doubtless shared the same fate. But the most famous victims of diaspora, the Jews and the Huguenots, had a religious and cultural cohesion that gave them solidarity in the face of the outside world. One of the problems about the Jacobites was that they had no such binding ideological cement. Often the reason for people's Jacobitism was spurious or adventitious. Because of their aristocratic connections, the Jacobites slotted easily into élite positions in the military and administrative cliques of Ancien Régime Europe. As their careers flourished, they became increasingly reluctant to jeopardise them on quixotic pro-Stuart insurrections in Britain.

The pressures on a Stuart prince who would come to manhood in the early 1740s were therefore immense. He was involved in both a race against time and, it seemed, against destiny itself. The race against time was pressing, since England would have had more than fifty years to settle down under the aegis of the 'Glorious Revolution'; and because it was already late in the day to prise the leaders of the Jacobite diaspora out of their comfortable career niches in France, Spain, Austria and Russia.

The battle with history seemed an uphill struggle because of the incredible, almost supernatural, ill-luck of the Stuarts. When the Stuarts were the Scottish house of Stewart, they could record that their first four king Jameses had died by murder or misadventure. When the Stewarts gained the throne of England also, their bad fortune attained legendary proportions. Charles Edward Stuart's grandfather James II had been driven into permanent exile. His great uncle Charles II had endured a long period of exile. His great-grandfather Charles I had been beheaded, as had his even more remote ancestor Mary Queen of Scots.

For all these reasons, the pressure on the young prince to succeed would be enormous. The peculiar milieu of his birth, the eccentric role he had to play as phantom Prince of Wales, and the weight of history pressing down on his royal house, meant that the cards were stacked against him even before he was born. These are facts we must never lose sight of as we follow him through life.

I

A Man Born to be King
(1720–6)

For a long time there was uncertainty over when the happy event could be expected. James admitted that the doctors had got the dates wrong: 'it is indeed a little singular to have mistaken so much as three or four months in her reckoning',[1] but he attributed this to the general excitement and the feeling that the wish for a royal pregnancy might be father to the thought. The consequence was that, just one month before the prince's birth, the expected date of Clementina's confinement was set anywhere between early December and mid-January.[2]

Clementina enjoyed unfalteringly robust health during the pregnancy. This allowed James to address himself to issues of protocol surrounding the birth. A royal childbirth in the eighteenth century was a public event in every sense: labour and parturition would be witnessed by a multitude of onlookers. This raised the question of who should be present. Naturally, all the exiled Jacobites in Rome clamoured for a place at the bedside. Since it was impracticable for the lying-in chamber to hold them all – and dangerous petty jealousies would arise between those invited and those excluded[3] – James announced that only existing members of the royal household plus selected cardinals from the College of Cardinals would be present.[4] In the event, nearly one hundred people were present at the lying-in chamber, including foreign ambassadors and the leading lights in the Roman nobility.[5]

By 9 December 1720 James was convinced that his queen was in her ninth month and expected her to be brought to bed at any time.[6] Yet it was Friday 27 December before the labour pains began, or rather the pains of a false labour. The throng of spectators arrived but retired after several hours when nothing happened.

For all that, the confinement was as difficult for the queen as the pregnancy had been easy. All Friday night the pain continued. On Saturday the surgeons were consulted. They reported nothing untoward despite the fact that the queen was 'delirious with pain'.[7] On Sunday the 29th the contractions ceased only to return in the evening. Thereafter the dolorous labour continued until Tuesday evening. Three-quarters of an hour after sunset on 31 December she gave birth to a son.[8] An hour later the Stuart prince was baptised by Bishop Bonaventura and given the names Charles Edward Louis John Casimir Silvester Severino Maria.[9]

The birth of a Stuart heir was received with very great joy in Rome. The Pope sent 10,000 scudi as a present. A carnival-like excitement ensued in the city. The wine ran freely, fireworks were let off, and the princes of the Church vied with each other in writing verses of congratulations.[10]

James hurried to announce the birth to the great European potentates who were (or might be presumed to be) sympathetic to the Stuart cause: Peter the Great, Philip of Spain, the Emperor of Austria.[11] In his great happiness James forgot the protracted labour.[12] Very soon the replies of felicitation came back.[13] Philip V and Elizabeth (Isabela) Farnese of Spain were particularly enthusiastic.[14] As Charles Wogan reported from Cartagena: 'I must do justice to the honest Spaniards, who swear that neither they nor their forefathers have ever been so much put out of their gravity by the birth of any prince of their own.'[15]

The birth of Charles Edward Stuart was thought by the Jacobites to be especially significant in two ways. Its occurrence at Christmastime and on the eve of the New Year gave it an obvious symbolic resonance.[16] And at that very moment, in England, the South Sea Bubble crisis seemed to confirm in detail everything Jacobite critics had said about Whig corruption. Thoroughly discredited by this financial fiasco, the Hanoverian regime appeared particularly vulnerable; conditions seemed propitious for another attempt at Jacobite restoration.[17]

For the first two months of Charles Edward's life the 'lusty child' did well, according to James's official reports.[18] Unfortunately we possess no detailed daily record of Charles's early months such as Héroards's classic account of Louis XIII.[19] However, some revealing scraps of information are extant. With the use of these enough can be built up from inference to provide a reasonably convincing picture of the prince's childhood.[20]

It was the near-universal practice of the time to employ a wet-nurse to suckle the infant.[21] The nurse was thought to be a figure of cardinal importance, because nursing experiences were held to be indelibly imprinted on the child. It was considered that, just as the mother's mental state could affect the foetus she carried, so could that of the nurse influence the new-born infant. It was even thought that temperamental traits could be transmitted from nurse to child: sloth, impiety, promiscuity. So the ideal nurse had to combine a number of attributes. Free from the dreaded syphilis, she had to lactate at just the right temperature; if the nurse's milk was too hot, for example, it was feared that an effeminate boy might be the result. Moreover, because of the 'transmission' factor, the soul of the nurse had to be 'beautiful'. Small wonder, then, that Madame de Sévigné was prepared to put up with the most insolent demands from her nurse's husband in order to retain the imagined paragon for her child.[22] And all this was quite apart from the most basic consideration of all, that a successful nursing bond was a prerequisite in an era of high infant mortality. Where this rate ranged between 25 and 75 per cent, depending on social class, the survival of an infant could never be taken for granted, but was regarded rather as a major achievement.

The first wet-nurse to be employed at Charles Edward's side was an Englishwoman for, as James declared: 'Our son, who is a brave, lusty boy . . . is looked after . . . in the English way, for though I cannot help his being born in Italy, yet as much as in me lies he shall be English for the rest all over.'[23]

But the relationship between nurse and prince did not prosper. Alarmed at the lack of progress and seemingly ailing physique of the young Charles Edward, James changed his nurse after two months.[24] In pique, the dismissed nurse revealed to the English some of the secrets of the Palazzo Muti.[25]

James's reaction may seem a panicky one, but the alarmingly high rate of eighteenth-century infant mortality has to be remembered.[26] At any rate, his judgment was soon vindicated. The new nurse, Francesca Battaglia, did everything James expected of her and more.[27]

Apart from wet-nursing, the salient child-rearing practices of the time were those of swaddling and cold-bathing. We know for certain that the infant Charles Edward was swaddled.[28] In the early eighteenth century the arguments for swaddling were thought to be conclusive. These were threefold: first, that the child needed to learn correct human posture; second, for self-protection, on the ground that limbs could be dislocated by random movement; third, for warmth, especially in cold climates.[29]

It is true that by the time of Charles Edward's birth the practice of swaddling was beginning to be questioned in the Anglo-Saxon world, notably by Locke,[30] but the outer ripples of this debate had not yet reached Rome in the early 1720s.

The other absolute value entertained in contemporary child-rearing was a conviction as to the desirability of cold-bathing.[31] This was so common a practice at the time and so much taken for granted that we should need conclusive evidence before deciding that this Spartan austerity was not visited on the prince.

Though there is some slight evidence that Charles Edward was a backward baby, he made good progress with his new nurse. He was teething at six months. As his father proudly remarked: 'there is all the appearance that he will breed them easily'.[32] On 12 April 1722 he was weaned, at the age of fifteen months.[33] Though this was relatively late by the standards of the time, the prince's father continued to express every satisfaction with his son's progress.[34]

But if the problem of a satisfactory nurse had now been solved, that of an appropriate governess still remained. On 21 April 1721 James wrote to the earl of Mar (Jacobite commander in Scotland in the 1715 rising) on the subject:

> The qualities of a person for so important a charge are obvious, the better born she be, the better, but what is above all requisite is prudence, a reasonable knowledge of the world and a principle of obedience, attachment and submission to me, which may put her above private envies or faction. I know by experience these qualities are rare, but without them all things will not be well managed, and with the last the case might happen the child might personally suffer by it, and his life and good ought to be only regarded by one that looks after him. Till he is a year old, our English woman will do and she doth mightily well, but after that she will not be big enough, I mean she will be *of too low a rank*. (Italics mine)[35]

The Englishwoman referred to seems to have been a Mrs Lelido.[36] By the time the prince was six months old, Mrs Lelido (whom James described as having 'taken a wonderful deal of care of him and has succeeded very well in the way she has taken') was taking him out every day in the royal coach.[37] But her 'low rank' told against the good lady. In March 1722 Mrs Sheldon was appointed as the prince's governess.

This appointment was to have momentous consequences. Sheldon was a daughter of one of James II's equerries and sister-in-law of

General Dillon, currently in good standing with James but soon, like the earl of Mar, to be cast into royal anathema. All the evidence shows Mrs Sheldon to have been a forceful, even domineering personality, not remotely answering the description James gave Mar. But she appealed mightily to Clementina, who was already chafing at the hold John Hay and his wife had over the king – an influence apparent ever since 1715.[38] None of James's appointments was ever particularly fortunate. This one was to be ill-starred even by the singular standards of 'Jamie the Rover'.

In the early days of her incumbency Mrs Sheldon's task was onerous enough. A letter prescribing treatment for rickets (June 1722) suggests that the young prince was suffering from this ailment.[39] In the same month there is even stronger evidence that fears were entertained about juvenile arthritis in the eighteen-month-old Charles Edward.[40] On 29 August 1722 Mrs Sheldon found herself called on to answer queries about the prince's health. The reply is informative both about Charles Edward and the no-nonsense governess herself:

He never was very lusty, but after the appearance of the bad symptoms, he grew sensibly thinner and continued so. The sutures of his head seem closed enough for his age, the head is a little large in proportion to his body, but not very much so. He has no crookedness in the bones of his limbs, neither are they sensibly thicker than they should be with regard to their length. The backbone is in no ways bent but a little weak. The joints of the knees come too much inward or meet too right when his ankles separate too much; the ligaments of his ankles some time ago were very close, and his own toes turned much out, but they are now sensibly mended. He suffers scarce so much as others do in the breeding of his teeth and what he had got of them are very sound. He has now but six, though the two last he had but a month ago, and we expect every day to see two more. He has had since the heats, upon his breast and arms, a small outbreaking which the French call 'La Miniature' that came and went away again by turns and now and then a few pimples upon his face, but this is common to children in this country. When he is led supported by things such as he is fond of, his head falls forward, but when he is in one's arms, he holds it up much better but not so erect as might be desired.[41]

Yet Charles Edward was soon making good progress. He threw off a bad cold around his second birthday without difficulty.[42] In April 1723 James spoke of his son's improving daily 'in mind and body'.[43]

Signs of the prince's later robustness and energy can be seen in an aside in John Hay's correspondence when he talks of Charles's 'running about from morning to night'.[44] The young prince was speaking well by the time he was two, and in his third year clear signs of a liking for music emerged.[45] An excellent description of the child's progress is given in a letter from Hay in May 1724:

> The Prince is certainly the finest, charmingest child in the world. He is a great musician, sings and plays on his violin continually. No porter's child in the country has stronger legs and arms, and indeed he makes good use of them, for he is continually in motion. He eats, sleeps and drinks mightily well. One can't see a finer child every way, neither can one wish him better in every respect than he is.[46]

By the age of three, then, with the problems of nurse and governess satisfactorily solved, the young Charles Edward seemed to have survived the worst dangers of childhood. It was time to think in earnest about his education. At first simple lessons had been entrusted to a Signor Anchini.[47] But it was clearly the moment to appoint someone with weightier credentials as the prince's tutor. Charles had already had a woman brought from England as an English language teacher, but the experiment was not a success and put James off the idea of further educational hiring in the land of which he was *de jure* monarch.[48] Under Hay's influence James's choice fell on Andrew Michael Ramsay.[49] Ramsay appealed to him as the protégé and biographer of Archbishop Fénelon of Cambrai, the great philosophical influence on James. It was from Fénelon that James had learned the stoical attitude of quietism that was so to infuriate his son in later years.

Born the son of a baker in Ayr in 1686, Ramsay had already made his name as a writer of politico-theological treatises, and was later to be a significant figure in French freemasonry in the 1730s. He had won James's favour by dedicating his latest work to him, flattering him as a potential royal patron. Yet in many ways the choice of Ramsay was imaginative. His educational thinking was in advance of his time: he believed in drawing out his pupils, not in learning by heart or rote.

Ramsay arrived in Rome from Paris in January 1724, but he was fated to spend only nine months with the prince. Ramsay was indissolubly associated with the Mar faction among the Jacobites, and it was in 1724 that James broke decisively with Mar, after the bishop of Atterbury had exposed Mar's secret double-dealing overtures to London.⁵⁰ By November Ramsay, no longer in James's confidence, was on the road back to Paris.

In recoiling from the protégé of a man he considered a traitor, James unwittingly went on to open a Pandora's box. His next solution to the problem of Charles Edward's education was to summon James Murray of Stormont from Paris as his governor, while recalling Thomas Sheridan from his duties as an emissary in Vienna to be under-governor.⁵¹

Since this action was to lead straight to the greatest crisis in James's life, it is worth asking why he felt impelled to take it. From the fact that James's correspondence is full of references to the need to remove the young prince from the company of females, dilettante critics have assumed that he was motivated by general misogynism or a vague distaste for the female sex. The truth is altogether more prosaic and more specific. It was an abiding fear of aristocratic parents in the eighteenth century that children left too long in the company of maids would be sexually molested. No less a person than Cardinal Bernis testified to having suffered such a fate as a child.⁵²

If James's motives were characteristically sound and conscientious, his handling of the prince's transition from female to male care turned out to be a disaster. To assess correctly the causes of the sensational marital rift in the Stuart household caused by this transfer of power, we need to retrace our steps in an attempt to chart the mental progress of Queen Clementina.

It is clear that James was misled as to the intensity of the queen's feelings for her first-born and judged by appearances alone. Clementina, it is true, did not give the appearance of being inseparable from her child, but sober reflection might have alerted James that there were good reasons for this.

The most important of these was Clementina's poor health and the uncertainty surrounding her future childbearing potential. There were repeated false alarms about a second pregnancy for Clementina, most notably in May 1721, June 1722 and November 1723.⁵³ Hopes of another Stuart child were so regularly disappointed that the English spy Stosch (codename Walton) reported to London that an 'obstruction' meant Clementina's childbearing days were already at an end.⁵⁴

In addition, Clementina's mother died in 1721, causing her great grief.⁵⁵ Moreover, there are solid grounds for thinking that Clementina very soon found James a disappointment. His dour, stoical, pragmatic approach to life failed to strike a chord in her romantic soul. To make up for her sadnesses and disappointments she turned for solace to her infant son. This process was camouflaged by her frequent absences from his side, whether on *villegiatura* at Albano or on more extended trips, such as that to Lucca in 1722.[56]

James for his part might well have underrated the queen's attachment to Charles Edward, since he himself was so besotted with the child. His pet name for his son, 'Carluccio', made its first appearance in May 1721.[57] On Charles's birthday James asked whether it was appropriate for one so young to be made a knight of the garter. He received the reply that (quite apart from the consideration that a monarch is not constrained in such matters) there were precedents in the honours given Edward, son of Edward IV, and Richard, duke of York, not to mention Henry VII's son Arthur.[58] James determined on the honour as Charles Edward's second birthday present. A letter on 27 December 1722 neatly encapsulates the joy of the doting father:

> I gave my son the Garter and the St Andrew on Christmas Day. He continues, thank God, very well except suffering now and then a little on pushing his teeth, and he is already such a lover of music that I shall be tempted to carry him one night to the Opera.[59]

Both the prince's parents, then, were in thrall to unusually strong emotions over their son. It has to be remembered that such strong bonding was by no means the norm at the time. One leading authority on eighteenth-century childhood has gone so far as to suggest that high infant mortality actually imposed a 'tenderness taboo' between parent and child and so kept such strong emotions at bay.[60] No such consideration weighed with James and Clementina. In retrospect their conflicting needs and requirements for their son had already set them on a collision course.

The departure of Ramsay in November 1724 coincided almost exactly with the announcement that the queen was again pregnant. This time the pregnancy was successful.[61] The imminent arrival of a second child concentrated James's mind. It was immediately after the birth of Henry Benedict, in March 1725, that James took the final decision to put Charles into the hands of Murray and Sheridan.

James's decision was singularly unwise on a number of counts. It failed to take account of the fact that the queen might perceive a causal link between the birth of Henry and the departure of Charles Edward from the care of the women. There is some reason to think that after bringing forth her second son Clementina suffered from a form of post-puerperal depression.[62] In this state, her imagination might have magnified the significance of James's move to regularise

Charles Edward's education. She could well have seen it as an attempt to drive a wedge between herself and her first-born.

Certainly the queen's confidante Mrs Sheldon did nothing to disabuse her of the idea. James had been unhappy with the governess's behaviour for some time. When it was announced that the prince was to be taken out of her hands, she struck back with a whispering campaign directed at the impressionable Clementina. Angered by her meddling, James tried to dismiss her.[63] This drew tearful reproaches from the queen. To placate her, James switched to praises for Sheldon's qualities and offered to soften the blow by putting Henry in her charge. But when it became clear that there was no going back on the decision to place Charles Edward with Sheridan and Murray, Mrs Sheldon, presuming on the queen's protection, flew into a violent rage and was openly impertinent to James.[64] James retorted by ordering Sheldon to leave Rome. The governess then successfully appealed to Clementina for reinstatement.

Charles Edward, meanwhile, is likely to have experienced feelings of double jeopardy. The birth of a sibling is always a traumatic event for a pampered only child.[65] To have juxtaposed the birth of a rival with an order expelling Charles from the care of the women was insensitive of James, to say the least. Charles Edward's natural feelings of resentment towards the fledgling Henry would have been compounded by a sensation of the 'end of Eden'. Such a transition was far too brutal.

In this single act of transfer to the male world (unexceptionable in itself) lay the seeds of the entire later family tragedy: Clementina's abrupt separation from her husband, the fatal rift between her and James and much else. Charles's dislike for his brother never abated. Clementina herself never displayed much affection for Henry. James too would later sense the truth that Clementina had preferred her son to her husband. Most important of all, the unconscious mutual antagonism between James and Charles Edward began at this point.

In part James's insensitivity to the superheated atmosphere within his own family may have been the result of his preoccupation with public affairs. The years 1721–5 had seen an alarming decline in Jacobite fortunes. The regular correspondence with Philip V of Spain had tailed off; the Atterbury plot of 1722 in England had failed disastrously; the traditional French support for the Stuarts had been put into reverse under the duc d'Orleans and the Abbé Dubois and later the duc de Bourbon. Most crushingly of all, in the very month of Henry's birth Peter the Great died, the Czar who had written to

James in his own hand assuring him that he would definitely send an expedition to England to restore the Stuarts.

Faced with this plethora of frustration, one unconscious motive in James's mind in bringing Charles Edward out of the hands of the women might have been a desire to accelerate the pace of Jacobite activity. His sense of impatience and frustration, particularly noted at this time by the spy Walton,[66] might well have led him to leave his domestic flank unguarded.

At all events, James remained unaware of the storm about to break around him. On 25 September 1725 he wrote blithely to Atterbury: 'The Prince has left the women without concern, and will, I hope, now improve faster than he could have done amongst them.'[67] To celebrate the event Murray was given the titular earldom of Dunbar.[68] Dunbar did not long enjoy his triumph. Clementina at once struck back. She ordered her women, and Mrs Sheldon especially, not to release the prince into Dunbar's tutorial care.[69]

This immediately drew an angry response from James. He at once dismissed Mrs Sheldon, accusing her of meddling beyond her proper sphere.[70] Clementina's response to this was massive retaliation. Taking Mrs Sheldon and all her retinue with her, the queen sought sanctuary in the Ursuline convent. Since she held the Hays responsible for Sheldon's dismissal, she informed James that she would return to the Palazzo Muti only when her *bêtes noires* were dismissed and Mrs Sheldon reinstated. Again James responded hamfistedly. Always at his worst when on his royal dignity, he wrote the queen a pompous letter which is, however, significant for the latent tensions it hints at in the Palazzo Muti.[71] After referring patronisingly to 'the weakness of your sex', he moved on to the real nub of her grievance: that with the importation of Sheridan and Dunbar she too was being edged away from contact with her son:

> It is true I have given a general order that the governor and under-governor should never leave him for a moment and they always accompany him to my chamber, even though they don't always do it to you, for example when you were dressing. The reason for this order is that he should not escape among the servants, where children learn nothing good.[72]

After assuring her that it was never his intention to deprive her of sight of her son, James went on to draw a clear distinction between the courtesies he was prepared to offer his queen and his unyielding resolution to exercise his rights as paterfamilias; these included the irrevocable dismissal of Mrs Sheldon and his equally inflexible deter-

mination to keep on John Hay and his wife. He concluded by asking
Clementina to admit that her dissatisfaction with life in the Palazzo
Muti did not just begin when he took his son out of the hands of the
women.[73] As for Dunbar, he had chosen him after mature reflection
and on the basis of a long acquaintance with his character and merits.
He found it incredible that Clementina should object to him.[74]

But Clementina was as adamant in her resolve as James in his.
Neither side would capitulate; neither would compromise. The
unsavoury row between Stuart king and queen became the sensation
of Europe. Untold harm was done to the Jacobite cause. James's
envoys had laboured hard to build up an anti-Hanoverian alliance
of Spain, Austria and Russia. All their hard work now lay in ruins.
Stuart credibility was totally lost. The Jacobites never recovered from
this crushing blow. The Whigs moved in for the kill. Their Roman
agent Walton spewed out the most scurrilous propaganda, to the
effect that the real reason for Clementina's flight was that Mrs Hay
was James's mistress.[75] This was nonsense, but some of the mud
stuck.

Meanwhile Cardinal Alberoni, ostensibly pro-Jacobite but really
in the pay of the English, was instructed to do his utmost to make
sure that Clementina stayed in the Ursuline convent. Small wonder
that Sir Robert Walpole in Paris declared himself publicly one of
Clementina's supporters.[76] English intelligence unaided could never
have pulled off such a stunning anti-Jacobite *coup* as this family
débâcle.

James – looking for the beam in Paris and not seeing the mote in
Rome – was still obsessed with the idea that the queen's flight was
some Machiavellian contrivance of his arch-enemy the earl of Mar,
and quickly revealed himself to be out of his depth. He continued to
take up a rigid posture, standing on his rights as paterfamilias and
insisting on Clementina's duty to obey him.

The most the Jacobites could achieve was to limit the damage.
The Pope was asked to keep Clementina in the nunnery at all costs
so that her poisonous allegations could be contained within Rome.[77]
But at this stage sympathy was overwhelmingly running with
Clementina. Alberoni had cleverly persuaded her to focus on the
issue of the education of her son. He knew that the Pope would not
support her against her husband on issues within the jurisdiction of
a paterfamilias, such as Mrs Sheldon's dismissal and the prince's
transfer from women to men. Nor would she be able to light much
of a spark with her personal animosity towards the Hays. The trump
card to play was the issue of religion. She should attempt to persuade

the Pope that Charles Edward's immortal soul was in danger, that it was James's intention to bring him up as a Protestant.

This idea was not of recent vintage and had long worried Catholics in Rome. Much of the disappointment among the Jesuits and *zelanti* over the failure of the Atterbury plot focused on this issue. The thinking was that unless James regained the throne before Charles Edward reached the age of reason, any Jacobite restoration might involve as a *quid pro quo* the prince's education as a Protestant.[78] The fact that Dunbar and John Hay were Protestants provided Alberoni with the ammunition he needed. He persuaded Clementina to concentrate on this issue in her protestations to the Pope.[79]

The tactic worked beautifully. The Pope became deeply concerned about a Protestant Charles Edward. The Papal Inquisition was asked to investigate the extent of Anglican practices in the Palazzo Muti.[80] The appearance on the scene of the Inquisition seriously alarmed James. One afternoon Charles Edward was just about to be taken out for his daily constitutional in a carriage when James issued orders that he was to be kept inside the Palazzo until further notice, for fear he would be kidnapped by the Inquisition and brought up in secret as a fanatical Catholic.[81]

The perception of being under siege at the Palazzo Muti was not lessened when the Pope, acting as intermediary, gave his verdict on the affair. He informed James that if Mrs Sheldon were reinstated and the Hays dismissed, the queen would return forthwith. Meanwhile, as Sovereign Pontiff he shared the view that it was undesirable that Dunbar be put in charge of the prince's education.

James exploded with rage at this 'impertinent' intervention. Loftily he answered that he did not need the Pope's advice or consent on matters concerning the private affairs of his family. His state of mind can be seen from the following letter to Atterbury in December 1725:

> It has been talked in town as if the Pope might take from me the pension he gave me, but neither threats of this kind, nor any want of regard the Pope might show me will induce me to alter my conduct and will only serve to afford me an opportunity of showing my subjects that nothing can make me alter a conduct which I think right or just.[82]

It has to be remembered that this was the selfsame Pope who paid the Stuarts the signal honour of christening Henry and then rebaptising Charles Edward earlier the same year.[83]

But for all his bluster, James was in an extremely precarious position. Not only had the Jacobites been turned into the laughing-stock of Europe and all their political hopes shattered; James could also count on no reliable allies in his struggle with Clementina. The queen was backed by the Pope, Alberoni and most of the cardinals. James had no one of countervailing weight. The problem was that even the Protestant Jacobites who might have supported him in a struggle against fanatical Catholicism had no time for Dunbar and the Hays. The 'old Jacobites' – Bishop Atterbury, the duke of Ormonde, Earl Marischal Keith – loathed and detested the Dunbar/Hay clique. While they supported the idea of a liberal and even Protestant education for the prince, they drew the line at entrusting it to Dunbar.

There was therefore a lot of covert support among the Jacobites for Clementina. It was felt that although she had not necessarily chosen the right issue to fight on, her political antennae were sharp, and at bottom her instinct of distaste for Dunbar and the Hays was correct. The only comfort Atterbury could offer James was to assure him that in the event of his sudden death, while Charles Edward was still a minor, Clementina would have no rights to the Regency. While advising him not to put anything in legal form, he assured him that the laws of England allowed him absolute prerogative of declaring who the Regent should be. Nor could Clementina have any say in the prince's education; that was a matter for the Council of Regents.[84]

For the moment that was the only solace James could derive. What of his son and heir during the protracted crisis? We can only infer the nature of the trauma he must have suffered at the sudden departure of his mother, but it was sufficiently manifest even for James to worry about the effect the loss of his mother might be having on the boy[85] – and this in an era when such insights would not be automatic.

Certainly one result of his mother's departure was a drastic change in the prince's daily routine. The frequent audiences with the Pope came to an abrupt end.[86] James still kept up appearances, attending the ceremony of the closing of the holy gates on Christmas Eve 1725 with his elder son,[87] but the break with the Pope was now complete. In the Vatican fears about the anti-Catholic impact of Dunbar had already reached paranoid proportions. It was alleged that Dunbar had taught Charles Edward to laugh at the Angelus bell as an absurd superstition.[88] Cardinal Gualterio went so far as to charge Dunbar with having taught the young prince by heart certain anti-Catholic incantations: 'I'm sick of priests; monks are great buffoons; the Mass cost my grandfather three kingdoms' was one alleged litany.[89]

Still in fear of the Inquisition, James kept his son close to him at all times, taking him for carefully supervised excursions around Rome.[90]

Charles Edward spent a wretched Christmas and fifth birthday. James made it clear he had no intention of bending to the papal will (or his wife's). He went out of his way to defy them by promoting Dunbar to be Knight of the Thistle to mark the prince's birthday[91] (ironically in view of future events, another recipient was the Earl Marischal) and by sending the prince to Albano with Dunbar for the spring *villegiatura*.[92]

By now pressure was being applied on James from another source. The fanatically Catholic Philip V and his termagant wife Elizabeth Farnese began to turn the screws on James, genuinely alarmed by the possibility that the prince might be brought up a Protestant.[93] Elizabeth Farnese went so far as to describe his behaviour towards Clementina as detestable, and warned that he should expect no financial or political aid from Spain.[94] So vehement was Spanish support for Clementina that it soon became a genuine obstacle to a marital *rapprochement*, since there seemed no way James could back down without a disastrous loss of face.[95] The good offices of the duke of Ormonde and the Earl Marischal (both Protestant and both in Spain) were enlisted to persuade Philip V that a Protestant governor was mere window-dressing to appease the Jacobites' English constituency; there was no question of the prince's not being brought up as a Catholic. One possible way out seemed the replacement of Dunbar by Ormonde, who was acceptable in Madrid, but James refused this suggestion, on the ground that Ormonde was too valuable where he was.[96] He was, however, induced by the intense Spanish pressure to allow Clementina to see her children. There was a tearful reunion between mother and two sons in April 1726, but Clementina went back on her promise to James by excluding Sheridan and Dunbar from her rooms in the convent and bringing in Mrs Sheldon to see them.[97] She asked for a second visit in July, but James turned this down on the grounds of her unsatisfactory behaviour the first time. He asked for a Bible oath that if he sent the two princes to the convent again, they would not be introduced to Mrs Sheldon.

Clementina held out for two months, then agreed to James's terms. The visit was just about to take place when Mrs Sheldon made her play. Flinging herself at the queen's feet, Sheldon begged her tearfully not to betray her in this way.[98] Clementina was unable to deal either with the tears or the iron will of her favourite, and the visit was cancelled. To reinforce the point that she had no intention of surrendering, Clementina had Charles Edward's portrait painted so that it could be put upon the wall of her apartments in the convent.[99]

By mid-1726 James was friendless. A four-hour conference with

Alberoni in April did not produce the hoped-for breakthrough. The Spanish cardinal's hold over Clementina was as strong as ever.[100] Even James's previous allies the Jesuits had turned against him; the Father-General now shared the Pope's religious concerns.[101] James was faced with a 50 per cent cut in his papal pension. Rather than come to heel, James decided to quit Rome and move to some more congenial spot. He thought first of Venice, but was swiftly turned down.[102] Eventually he hit on the idea of Bologna.

Even so, there was a price to be paid. Before the Pope would allow Charles Edward to continue under Dunbar's tutelage in a papal state, he wanted to be assured that the child was being brought up as a Catholic. At an audience on 16 September 1726 the Pope made Charles Edward recite several pages of catechism and then put several questions to him on Catholic doctrine.[103] Satisfied with the prince's answers, the Pope and James agreed on the polite fiction that the departure of the Stuart court for Bologna was simply an extended *villegiatura*. Dunbar's name was not mentioned.

Whatever the psychological toll on the young prince of this sustained rift in the royal household, to outward appearances he was still doing well. He had learned to ride, was considered a natural horseman, and deeply impressed those who saw him. 'The eldest is the most surprising boy in every respect that ever was seen,' reported James Edgar the royal secretary. 'He now behaves and talks like a man.'[104]

The 'hell-fire' duke of Wharton, newly arrived in Rome and soon to depart for Spain on a mission for James, concurred:

> The Prince of Wales is one of the finest children I ever saw and daily gives remarkable instances of wit and vivacity uncommon to his age. The beauty of his person and his genteel behaviour make him the idol of the people here.[105]

Yet the prolonged absence of the prince's mother must have bitten deep. So far from there being any signs of reconciliation between James and Clementina, the queen's acquiescence in the departure of her sons for Bologna seems to have hardened James's attitude.[106] The failure of a final face-to-face plea to her to return did not help matters.[107] If there were any doubts left, James proceeded to back himself into a cul-de-sac by raising the widely unpopular Hays to the peerage. They were now the titular Lord and Lady Inverness.

On 30 September 1726 the journey to Bologna commenced. Charles Edward and Henry departed from Rome with Dunbar and Lady Inverness. They spent the first night at Civita Castellana, then went on to Loreto,[108] proceeding more slowly than their father, who went on ahead post-haste. In Bologna he awaited the arrival of the princes, who took three weeks, in slow, leisurely stages, to complete the journey.[109] It was already cold when Charles Edward arrived in Bologna on 21 October 1726.[110]

2

Bologna and Rome

(1726–33)

A few days after the prince's arrival in Bologna, James put him on public view at a ball. Wearing a scarlet coat, the young Charles Edward, not yet six, danced with a young lady dressed in blue, while his father looked on indulgently from a throne surrounded by his courtiers.[1] Now at last aware of the possible effect on his son of a long separation from his mother, punctuated by the brief, lachrymose meeting, James exhorted Sheridan and Dunbar to divert Charles by all possible means. His love of horses was encouraged. He was already an accomplished rider ('as well as if he had fifteen years of age') and had a large stable, in which his favourite was a little grey colt.[2]

All who saw the prince spoke of his manly bearing and behaviour,[3] but this was the credit side of a nature that was already revealing wilfulness and obstinacy. As long ago as June 1724 the prince had shown that he had a mind of his own. When James and Clementina were received then by the new Pope Benedict XIII and ceremonially kissed his feet, the young Charles Edward could not be induced either by threats or cajolery to follow suit.[4] At this stage in his development it was probably a mistake, in retrospect, to indulge him, but James's humanitarian instincts must nevertheless be applauded.

Because of the continuing question-mark over Dunbar's future, the day-to-day education of the prince was largely left to Sheridan, the under-governor. His idea of pedagogy was the inculcation of a series of pious and devotional maxims, and the learning of the catechism by rote.[5] But Charles Edward relished his tutor's indulgence. In many ways Sheridan became his true father but he was a father without tears – it was all spoiling and pampering, no discipline and authority. Yet for good or ill a strong bond was forged. Charles

Edward ever afterwards entertained strong filial feelings for Sheridan.[6]

Much of the prince's training at this time was of the outdoor or physical kind, especially in the use of weapons. In marked contrast to his brother at the same age, Charles was always the aspiring warrior. Just before the marital break-up, in August 1725, when James and his family were in procession in the Piazza Navona, Charles Edward could have been seen, carried on a dais, from which he would 'shoot' at onlookers with his crossbow,[7] This was the shape of things to come. In Bologna he was taught accurate shooting with the crossbow and other weapons and proved to have a remarkably good eye. He soon settled into a vigorous masculine routine; only Lady Nithsdale as governess provided the feminine touch.[8] A report from the royal secretary James Edgar in March 1727 conveniently sums up his progress:

The Prince improves daily in body and mind to the admiration and joy of everybody. As to his studies, he reads English now currently (sic) and has begun to learn to write. He speaks English perfectly well, and the French and Italian very little worse. He has a stable of little horses and every day almost diverts him by riding. Chevalier Geraldin is his riding master. He is most alert in all his exercises, such as shooting, the tennis, shuttlecock, and a gentleman in town has prepared a *caccia* of pigeons and hares to be shot by him this afternoon. You would be surprised to see him dance, nobody does it better, and he bore his part at the balls in the carnival as if he were already a man.[9]

Meanwhile 1727 seemed to herald some brightening of James's fortunes. His half-brother Berwick's son, the thirty-one-year-old duke of Liria, was appointed Spanish ambassador to Russia. A fervent Jacobite, Liria assured James he would do all in his power to induce the Czarina Catherine to throw Russian might behind the house of Stuart. The one obstacle in his path was the continuing estrangement between James and Clementina that so damaged Jacobite credibility. Liria proposed to call at Bologna on his way from Madrid to St Petersburg to see if he could patch things up. He arrived at Bologna at the beginning of May 1727.[10]

James was by now softening in his attitude to Clementina. He at last appreciated the grave damage the rift had done to his own cause. He was willing to give Inverness an honourable discharge. Dunbar had promised to turn Catholic to please the queen. The only condition

James still held out for was the dismissal of the detested Mrs Sheldon.[11]

Liria asked permission to write to Clementina, exhorting her to return to her husband and family, arguing that no credible barrier to a reconciliation now remained. James agreed. Liria stayed in Bologna until 4 May, composing a carefully modulated appeal to Clementina. While he was in the papal state Liria struck up an immediate rapport with the young Charles Edward. Describing him as having a beautiful figure and almost supernatural cleverness, Liria was particularly impressed by the six-year-old's intellectual potential.[12] Charles Edward in turn responded well to this sensitive soldier-diplomat of a cousin. The seeds of his second successful relationship with an older male were sown.

Liria had originally intended to present his letter in person to Clementina in Rome, but this proved unnecessary. Suddenly James received word that Clementina was returning to Bologna. James vowed to let bygones be bygones.[13]

But 1727 had not exhausted its quota of surprises. Even as James digested the news of the queen's return, dramatic tidings were received from England. George I had died suddenly. This was an opportunity James could not afford to miss. Sending his children into the country, he despatched an express to the Pope, giving him the overall responsibility for the prince's education during his own absence. Then, at the end of June, he left Bologna for the north.[14] He was to be away for six months.

From being without a mother for nearly two years, Charles Edward now found himself fatherless while his mother returned. It is perhaps not without significance that at the precise moment of his mother's arrival in Bologna, the young prince should have been taken ill.[15]

We know little of Charles Edward's relations with his mother during the second half of 1727. Clementina's letters to the absent James about her children are curiously offhand and contrasted with the fussiness and overprotectiveness of James's enquiries about them.[16] It fell to Dunbar to reassure the absent king that Charles Edward still remembered him and continually asked about him, especially when the newspapers arrived.[17]

Meanwhile James's dash for the Channel coast had ended in failure. The French, at this time in alliance with England, refused to allow him to set foot on their territory and applied pressure to have him expelled from Lorraine. Disconsolately, James fell back on the relative sanctuary of the papal state of Avignon. Here he wrote to Clementina to come and join him, leaving the children in Bologna.[18]

To his fury she refused, alleging that she found it impossible to leave her children, but really because the French had threatened to arrest her if she tried to cross their territory en route to Avignon.[19] There was another reason too. Clementina had still not dismissed Mrs Sheldon from her service. James made it clear that if the queen arrived in Avignon with that personage, he would take it upon himself to dismiss her formally in the presence of the papal vice-legate.[20] But, such was the pressure being exerted on the Vatican by both England and France, it was already clear to James that he would have to return to Italy the following spring.[21]

It was time for James to return anyway. His absence led to a serious breach of hospitality by the Bolognese. Meeting the young Charles Edward on horseback at the gates of the city on a narrow road, a local priest refused to move over to the side of the road even when he saw the Stuart colours displayed. This insult was a serious embarrassment to the legate of Bologna especially after James had entrusted Charles Edward to papal care. The offending priest was immediately imprisoned.[22]

James returned to Bologna in January 1728, after tarrying for a few days sightseeing in Milan. The royal secretary Edgar, sent on ahead, found Charles Edward much changed (and to his mind greatly improved) after six months: 'almost a man in his behaviour and carriage and at least two fingers taller than when I left him'.[23] Yet, true to type, when his father arrived a few days later, his first instruction to his son concerned duty, not admiration: Charles was to write a letter of New Year's greeting to Cardinal Gualterio.[24]

But if James hoped for a reversion to normal family life on his return, he was deeply shocked at the change in Clementina. 'Neurotic' would be too mild a word to describe her behaviour; religious mania comes nearer the mark. This is how James described her:

> I proposed to her diverting herself in the Carnival, but she showed no inclination to it. She has taken no manner of amusement, not even taking the air, and when she is not at church or at table, is locked up in her room and sees no mortal but her maids and sons. She . . . fasts to that degree that I believe no married woman that pretends to have children ever did. I am very little with her. I let her do what she will.[25]

To cap all, Clementina persisted in seeing Mrs Sheldon, whom she had set up in an establishment elsewhere in Bologna, and would not listen to James's plea for the return of his own favourites the Invernesses, now banished to Avignon.

What seems to have happened is that those who pleaded and cajoled with the queen to return to her wifely duty did their work too well. Taking her cue from her beloved St Francis de Sales, Clementina decided that marriage with James was a cross she had been called on to bear. Very well, the crucifixion would be complete. She would fast and mortify the flesh. It would seem that Clementina never really recovered from the depression following Henry's birth. She was now in the grip of genuine mental illness. If ever the death instinct could be cited to explain human behaviour, it was surely the key to Clementina Sobieska from 1728 onwards.

Faced with this alarming development, James freely confessed himself out of his depth. It is clear that he resumed normal marital relations with Clementina, but after less than two months he found the strain too much. In the vain hope that Clementina could be argued out of her state of mind, he went to Rome to enlist the help of friendly cardinals.

The strain of living with a neurotic mother must have been considerable for an over-active child like Charles Edward. In May 1728, under Sheridan's guidance, he wrote a well-known and very sad letter to his father in Rome, promising not to upset his mother by jumping near her.[26]

On his return from Rome, James tried vainly on Clementina the arguments that had been rehearsed to him in Rome. Now there was a further complication. Clementina was pregnant again.[27] Fearful of the effect of this both on his wife and his sons, James sent his children to the country for the rest of the summer and left Bologna himself.[28] It was a wise decision. As expected, the pregnancy was a difficult one. The queen complained of excessive pain and became convinced that she was suffering from an ectopic foetus.[29] Hearing this, James returned to Bologna and hired the city's best physician to be in constant attendance.[30]

By now under considerable stress himself, James decided to take his eldest son on a tour of northern Italy. They arrived in Parma on 10 June 1728, spent the 11th at Colorno and returned to Parma that evening for the opera, which the young prince greatly enjoyed.[31] A few days later James sent Charles Edward out to Piacenza to pay a courtesy call on the veteran duchess of Parma, who was seriously ill.[32] All in all, the trip was a success, and James expressed himself very pleased with his son's behaviour.[33]

But he returned to depressing news at Bologna. The queen claimed to have miscarried at the end of July, hardly surprising given her way of life.[34] The stress of life with Clementina now began to tell on

James. Always prone to psychosomatic illnesses at times of extreme tension, he lapsed into a serious illness in October.[35]

The valetudinarian atmosphere in the Stuart court was contagious. In September Dunbar was given sick leave until spring 1729.[36] John Paul Stafford, already confirmed as Henry's governor, was given temporary charge of Charles Edward; the idea was that Stafford would get to know the younger prince while he tutored Charles.[37] As if to prove the point that there was something ill-starred about the Jacobite household at Bologna, Stafford too immediately went down with fever.[38] James, always one for taking the wrong decision at the wrong time, chose this moment to bring his two children back from the country.[39] Apprehensive about the epidemic at his court, he did, however, arrange for an experienced physician to be in permanent attendance.[40]

The perfervid atmosphere was not helped by an announcement that the queen was pregnant again. This time there was total confusion over dates.[41] Then in January 1729 secretary Edgar made the following report to one of his correspondents:

> I am sorry to have occasion here to confirm to you that the queen herself, the midwife and the doctors have all been mistaken in thinking Her Majesty to be with child. Now it is very certain she is not, nor has been at any time.[42]

When a sense of chaos so clearly impresses itself across the centuries, we may well speculate what life in this hothouse of illness, rumour and uncertainty were doing to Charles Edward. All we know is that he spent most of the autumn days of 1728 playing golf, at which he became expert.[43]

Still James dithered about how to resolve his personal affairs. He had ennobled his favourites the Hays – they were now Lord and Lady Inverness – but Clementina had insisted on their banishment. He longed to recall Inverness, but feared that this might precipitate a second flight by Clementina.[44] Yet since the Pope was now showing signs of greater friendliness after their dramatic quarrel over the queen, James began to nurture hopes that his affairs might take an upward turn if he took his court back to Rome and was publicly reconciled with the Pontiff. He decided on an exploratory visit to Rome. Such was James's indecisiveness still that he even found it hard to decide whether he should travel to Rome publicly or incognito.[45] Eventually he made up his mind and set off for Rome at the beginning of January 1729.[46]

On arrival at Rome, he had an audience with the Pope. It went well: Benedict even sent back a blessing for the prince who had refused to kiss his feet five years earlier.[47] James decided to resume residence in the Palazzo Muti, intending his family to join him there in the spring.[48]

Feeling more settled in mind, and doubtless a little guilty about the uncertainty and chaos he had lately visited on his eldest son, James took the opportunity to write one of his effusive letters to Charles Edward, full of praise for the prince's patience and his 'mighty well writ letters'.[49] Significantly, perhaps, the prince was at that moment once again in a low state of health. The departure from Bologna was delayed to enable him to get his strength up for the journey.[50] To Clementina meanwhile James gave a hint of what he expected at Rome by writing that what his health needed now was not drugs but an absence of stress.[51]

Arrangements were made for the royal family to move down in May.[52] 'Be sure you are very good to Sir Thomas [Sheridan had been knighted] on the road and to behave yourself so that I may have a good account of you when you come here,' his father wrote to Charles Edward.[53] The clear inference is that Sheridan had previously encountered behaviour problems. Given the sustained confusion of 1725–8, it is not hard to see why.

So, at the end of April 1729, after an absence of two and a half years, Charles Edward returned to the city of his birth.[54] His mother remained in Bologna, again convinced that she was pregnant, this time asking for the papal blessing on her expected third child.[55]

What kind of a place was eighteenth-century Rome, in which Charles Edward spent his formative years? It was a city of churches and palazzi that occupied about a fifth of the area of Imperial Rome and had about one-tenth of its population (around 150,000 in the 1730s). The limits of habitation were set by the Quirinal, the Porta del Popolo and the bend in the Tiber. The most densely populated areas were in the Trastevere district and around the baths of Diocletian. Rome was a tightly controlled, hedonistic society, marked by relative absence of class conflict and the absolute domination of the Catholic church.

Daily life for Charles Edward and his brother involved riding in the Villa Borghese, promenades in selected locations (the baths of Diocletian were a great favourite with James), formal appearances in the Piazza Navona and, always, frequent attendance at Mass, especially in the church of the SS Apostoli adjacent to the Palazzo Muti. In the evenings there would be visits to the great houses and entertainment by the great names in the Roman nobility. The same names recur in Walton's endless and meticulous accounts of the movements of the Stuart family: Villa Ludovici, Bolognetti, Patrizi, Palazzo Corsini.[56] Occasionally the odd distinguished visitor came to call on the family. On 25 June 1729 Clementina received Montesquieu at the Palazzo Muti while James was at Albano. The two princes were present and Montesquieu was very taken with them.[57]

During his active periods, Dunbar made a point of showing off Charles Edward's undoubted talents as a dancer.[58] And on special occasions there would be an audience with the Pope. Clement XII, who became Pope in 1730, took a liking to the prince and gave him presents of money over and above the papal pension paid to his father: 600 scudi in November 1731, 1,000 pistoles in March 1732, and 4,000 scudi in May of the same year, raised from a lottery in Genoa.[59] So embarrassed was Walton by these signal marks of papal favour that he concocted an absurd story whereby the Pope allegedly tried to space out visits from the Stuart family at long intervals, because of the cost of his own generosity!

The humdrum tenor of everyday life for the prince masked the continuing tensions in the Palazzo Muti. Even though mother and son were capable of conducting their own relationship by now, James's brooding presence lowered over everything. A series of letters passed between Clementina and Charles while the queen, pleading the cold weather, delayed her journey to Rome.[60] Fussily James oversaw the correspondence, explaining to his wife that 'Carluccio' was now capable of reading her letters without much help from Sheridan.[61]

Finally, at the end of May 1729, Clementina set off for Rome via Loreto, her letters to her son full of the prayers she was saying for him.[62] Her marriage with James was still extremely shaky. The king chose to travel up to Rome from Albano to meet her but his note describing the meeting to his favourite Inverness is eloquent: 'The very next morning she showed a little humour which she might have spared me.'[63] It was already quite clear that no true marriage any longer existed. The couple rarely ate or slept together.[64] Predictably, there was another report of a pregnancy, but this time the queen's physician remained sceptical.[65]

Finally in November James admitted the truth to John Hay (Lord Inverness). The queen's self-mortification and fasting was playing havoc with her menstrual cycle. After heavy bleeding, she went for five months without a period (thus raising the hopes of a pregnancy), only to fall ill to another bout of dysmenorrhoea.[66] Once more James collapsed with nervous exhaustion. Again he was very ill with a series of mysterious maladies.[67] For the most part thereafter, James chose to live with his sons at Albano while Clementina remained in the Palazzo Muti.

Although the turbulence of his family life continued, the eight-year-old prince was already coming into his own as a charmer. James made a point of showing him off to the nobility and Jacobite exiles of Rome, with such success that Stosch/Walton grudgingly conceded that it had been a propaganda masterstroke on James's part to return to Rome from Bologna.[68] The prince seemed to have put all health problems behind him. He was robust enough for James to make him keep Fridays as meatless days in accordance with strict Catholic practice.[69] His prowess as a hunter continued too. To his father's great delight he shot a bird on the wing during a *caccia* at Albano when he was still two months short of his ninth birthday.[70]

But 1730 brought a major health anxiety. Shortly after James's illness Dunbar, recently returned from an extended sick leave, went down again, this time a victim of a 'flu epidemic that was raging through Europe.[71] Charles Edward was kept well away from him. The royal household, Dunbar excepted, seemed to have come through the epidemic unscathed. Then in July the prince succumbed to smallpox.[72] Fortunately, it was a mild attack and left no disfiguring scars. The prince's recovery was aided by the exceptionally mild Roman summer that year. By August he was completely recovered.[73]

What of the prince's education during this period? By June 1730 he had sufficiently satisfied Sheridan as to his competence in Italian to be started on Latin.[74] Sheridan of course continued to spoil him shamelessly. The dour Dunbar could scarcely act as a counterweight for, apart from his frequent illnesses, his heart was not in the job. The sustained sniping at his suitability and competence by Atterbury, Lord Marischal and others finally wore him down. He offered James his resignation, pointing out that since he was apparently so obnoxious to the English Jacobites, this vitiated the original purpose of his being the prince's governor – which was to reassure the English on the religious issue.[75] He cited the dismissal of the Invernesses as the obvious precedent for his own departure and wound up his representation to the king by saying that he would remain only if he received an express order.[76]

James had accepted the departure of the Invernesses with great reluctance and was not prepared to make another concession to English Jacobite opinion, especially as he thought Dunbar's critics were being manipulated by Hanoverian agents. Rejecting Dunbar's analogy with the Invernesses, he gave him an express order to stay, on pain of forfeiting the royal favour.[77]

The year 1730 brought another significant development. Benedict XIII, so long a thorn in James's side, died in the great epidemic and was succeeded by Clement XII. The new Pope took an altogether more benign view of James and conceded that he had been in the right in the dispute with Clementina. The result was that the Stuarts became frequent visitors at the Vatican.[78] Yet the new Pope drew the line at James's wish to have the Innernesses back, correctly conjecturing that this would bring on another crisis with Clementina. Try as he might, James could not budge Clement on this issue, even after a solemn promise that his two sons would always be brought up in the Catholic religion.[79] To soften the blow, Clement backed James's application to the French court for a pension for Charles Edward, but this was refused.[80]

One unfortunate result of the new Pope's support for James was to entrench Clementina even more firmly in her self-imposed regime of martyrdom. There is real anguish in James's report to his French agent in November 1730:

> The Queen is not at all in a good state of health. Ever since her coming out of the convent, she has put herself on a footing not only of not taking any diversion but even of scarce ever taking the air, more than going from one church to another. She eats excessive little and does not allow herself to sleep what is necessary for her. All that has been said to her on those matters has yet had no effect, although besides its making it next to impossible her having any more children, it manifestly ruins her health and may, 'tis to be feared, soon call her into a decay of which she has even already some symptoms.[81]

James 'solved' the problem of his marriage by, in the main, living at Albano while the queen remained in Rome. She would come out for day trips to Albano to see the children and return to Rome at night.[82] Normal marital relations between James and Clementina seem to have come to an end after the final dénouement of the series of false pregnancies. The only sustained period Clementina spent with her children (or, which came to the same thing, at Albano) was when James was away on a sightseeing tour of Naples in May 1731.[83] For the most part, Charles Edward's relationship with his mother was carried on by letter.[84]

There was now an explosive combination of factors in the ten-year-old's life. He had parents who rarely saw each other, a mother in the grip of religious mania, and a father prey to melancholia and psychosomatic illnesses. His governor was in post under duress, his brother seemed to be overtaking him in matters intellectual and artistic, and there was already clear evidence that Henry was James's favourite son.[85] Only Sheridan's continuing devotion buoyed the prince up. The upshot was that the prince reacted with stubborn rage to his father's (and Dunbar's) regime. At Albano he frequently had his privileges withdrawn – 'in penance', as James put it, for his disobedience.[86] The prince's response to this was illness.[87]

His anxieties must have been exacerbated by the realisation that his brother Henry, more than four years his junior, was already his equal in French, Italian and English; only in Latin did Charles Edward have the advantage at this stage.[88] Fortunately the prince still retained his taste for music and the opera; yet even here Henry was challenging him.[89]

Only very occasionally did Charles Edward please his father by showing real flashes of wit and wisdom. One such occasion was when a French bishop was talking self-satisfiedly over table at the Palazzo Muti in February 1732 about how Louis XV had recently silenced the French *parlements*. The prince, who had been speaking in English (his first language) suddenly rounded on the cleric in a torrent of French: '*Mais, monsieur, à quoi peut donc servir un Parlement quand on lui défend de parler? Autant vaudrait-il en avoir un composé de muets?*'[90] ('But sir, what is the use of a Parliament if you don't allow it to speak? Wouldn't it be better, then, to have an assembly of the dumb?')

As James turned his attention increasingly away from Clementina and towards his two children ('for I cannot expect to have any more. The Queen has been six months out of condition of becoming with child and I fear it is but too probable she may always continue in that state')[91] he began to ponder Charles Edward's future. This reduced itself to three main issues: should he arrange a marriage for the prince at this stage: should he send him abroad; how should he plan for the rest of his education?

The first suggestion of a childhood marriage – to the Emperor of Austria's youngest daughter – had been made in March 1726.[92] Now, thinking back to the groundwork laid by the duke of Liria on his mission to Russia in 1728–30, James toyed with an alliance between Charles Edward and the Princess of Mecklenbourg, heiress presumptive to the Russian crown.[93] This would link neatly with the other scheme Liria had promoted during his three years in Moscow: the ultimate accession of the prince to the Polish throne.[94]

But other events conspired to abort this scheme. Having the prince in eastern Europe would take the Jacobites farther away than ever from a Stuart restoration. It was more expedient to think of opportunities closer to home. Throughout 1732 and 1733 James puzzled over what these should be. The king inclined to the view that Charles Edward's first trip abroad should be a preliminary reconnaissance in France.[95] The problem here was that France was bound by its treaties with England not to give support to the House of Stuart. Nor were the French ministers keen on the idea. The vehemently anti-English Chauvelin thought that the Stuart prince should be brought to France only when a genuine attempt at an invasion was about to be mounted. With the pacific and pro-English Cardinal Fleury at the helm in France, there was no chance of that. However, Fleury himself heard of the idea, claimed to see merit in the prince's being educated away from Rome, and suggested Switzerland as a venue.[96]

Yet it was clear enough that in that country Charles Edward's religious affiliations might wither. There was the even greater danger that a prince's party might form in opposition to the king's party.[97] Moreover, James was so closely associated with the papacy that his restoration in England could be achieved only through foreign invasion. But if Charles Edward lived in a Protestant country like Switzerland, he might even be called in to legitimate an internal revolution in England and thus be restored over his father's head.[98]

There was another factor that gave James pause. The person pushing hardest in France for Charles Edward's education was none other than the erstwhile Jacobite and turncoat Viscount Bolingbroke, in whom James had no confidence at all.[99] All in all, given the worries about his son's religion, the security risks in Switzerland, and the fact that the French were pressing for a Swiss domicile for the prince yet washed their hands of any consequences, James could see no advantages in the idea. His son would be a virtual prisoner even in a Catholic canton, surrounded by so many Protestant neighbours. Most of all, he suspected the motives of the Bolingbroke faction in promoting the idea.[100]

Then there was the personality of his son to be taken into account: 'The Prince is now in a critical age, he is mighty lively, and though he has a quick apprehension, yet he is a good deal thoughtless, so that it would be more dangerous to expose him to certain dangers and temptations than most children of his age.'[101] James decisively rejected the idea of Switzerland and held out for Paris (though this was clearly a forlorn hope).

The statement above by James to his agent O'Brien in Paris was the fullest utterence yet of his reservations about his son. The truth was that Charles Edward's educational progress had proceeded anything but smoothly. James's letters to Clementina are full of strictures on his eldest son's unsatisfactory behaviour.[102] His resistance to all forms of discipline, especially of the intellectual kind, was becoming more pronounced. A progress report from Dunbar in January 1733 is typical:

> The Prince grows tall, strong and is, I believe, the most beautiful figure this day in the world, but to be ingenuous with you, it is impossible to get him to apply to any study as he ought to or indeed in any tolerable degree, by which means the Latin goes ill on, but he speaks both French and Italian easily.[103]

One ray of hope was his liking for design, for which he had a decided talent.[104] Dunbar encouraged him in this, hoping it would lead him on to geometry and other mathematical subjects.[105] But tension between Charles Edward and authority soon surfaced again. Since the Prince could not strike at the obvious target (his father), he struck at Dunbar, James's instrument of discipline. In September 1733 a furious row erupted over the prince's studies. Dunbar attempted to chastise him. Charles Edward lost his temper and kicked Dunbar. He followed this up with a threat to kill his governor if he laid a hand on him.[106]

James's retribution was swift. The prince was locked in his room and kept there the best part of a week until he purged his contempt. What particularly troubled James was that his son had sworn revenge against Dunbar and refused to relent in his resolve for several days. Yet there are clear signs that James was already preparing to accept the inevitable with his truculent elder son. He was not temperamentally the sort of father who favoured beating his son – and childbeating was already going out of fashion in pedagogic circles anyway. He faced the problem with resignation. Two months after the fracas with Dunbar, he allowed his son for the first time to make the ride from Albano to Rome without him.[107]

That Charles Edward was a confused and rebellious boy as he entered adolescence cannot be doubted. What general account can be given of his relations within the troubled Stuart family? There can be no questioning the closeness of his relationship with his mother. It was Clementina's policy to stay away from Albano and James as much as was consistent with keeping up appearances, yet when she heard that her beloved Carluccio had a bad cold, she sped out there to comfort him (October 1732).[108]

Concomitant with this intensity between mother and son was a widening chasm between husband and wife. Even the normally humane James was finding Clementina's permanent ill-health hard to bear. In September 1731 she complained of violent headaches. James did not put off his trip to Albano on that account, but set off without her, taking the two children.[109] The queen's status as a chronic invalid was now a fact of life in the Stuart household. Charles Edward could do no other than look on anguishedly as his mother wasted away. Clementina refused to change her ascetic way of life and spurned all medical advice. No amount of pleading could move her.[110] By June 1734 dietary deficiencies had brought her to the brink of total collapse, 'being scarce able to walk at all with the humour of the scurvy, and I am sorry to say I see little human hope of a perfect recovery, since her stomach will not bear strong remedies and that she will not do all she can and is requisite in her case'.[111]

Clementina probably left Charles Edward with a confusing legacy. On the one hand, their early years together gave him the core of inner strength he always retained. On the other hand, the many and prolonged absences from her side after the age of five may well have led to feelings of despair and moods of aggression that seemed at times likely to overwhelm him. In extreme cases a child in such circumstances may increasingly withdraw its contact from the outside world. Yet it is clear that the prince progressively reached out towards it. The relationship with his mother was clearly an ambiguous one, at once debilitating and strengthening.

There remained the prince's younger brother Henry. Here a twofold consideration obtained. Henry was his father's favourite, and had the usual problems of relating to a brother five years older. Moreover, he bade fair to outshine Charles Edward intellectually. An incident in January 1733 highlights the tension between the brothers. Dunbar had long noted what he described as the prince's tendency to 'bear hard' on Henry. On one occasion Charles took his brother to task for spending all his time drawing coats of arms and heraldic insignia, alleging that this would impair any ability he had for creative design. Like a whiplash Henry retorted in French: 'As long as it does not impair my ability to draw a sword for my father, I don't care if I'm never a designer.' The general consensus was that Henry could always think faster on his feet than his brother.[112]

Such was the tight, oppressive world of the thirteen-year-old prince when Fate gave him the opportunity to appear in public on a larger stage.

3

The Prince over the Water
(1734–7)

The year 1734 began promisingly for the Stuarts. With the outbreak of the War of Polish Succession and the possibility that France might mount an expedition for the Jacobites, it seemed that the exiled dynasty night be emerging from the diplomatic desert it had been in since 1726, James appeared to have more money at his disposal and to be taken more seriously by the Powers.[1] Charles Edward himself was crossing the invisible divide between childhood and adolescence.

The dawning of a new period in the prince's life seemed underlined by two pointers. On his thirteenth birthday a magnificent feast was prepared for him at the Palazzo Corsini. Several English lords paid public homage to him here; some even kissed hands.[2] And in February 1734 Charles Edward went through the last of his childhood illnesses; the cutting of his last teeth gave his face a badly swollen appearance.[3] As if sensing that the prince was on the threshold of a new and decisive period in his life, James commissioned the singing of a Mass at SS Apostoli every 31 January in perpetuity in honour of his eldest son.[4]

The war between Spain and Austria – part of the general Polish Succession imbroglio – was creeping closer to the territory of the papal states. James was keen for his son to see something of the Spanish troops, and procured permission for them to view a body of *carabineros* on the march.[5] But this was only the start of his ambitions. His heart was now set on sending Charles Edward to Paris. In the existing tension between France and England, it was felt that the British could not hope to stay neutral much longer. James had waived his previous fears that the French might be merely using the Jacobites.[6] He felt confident enough in the prince's physical stamina to subject him to the full meatless rigours of a Lenten fast.[7]

The arrival of the duke of Liria in Rome at the end of March changed the king's plans. Liria had been appointed (together with counts Montemar and Charny) to a tripartite command of the Spanish armies in Italy, whose aim was the conquest of the kingdom of Naples. But since Liria commanded the second division of the army, in which the Infanta Don Carlos was serving, in effect and by common consent Liria was the presiding genius of the Spanish army. Immediately on arrival in Rome Liria suggested that James should apply to the court at Madrid for permission for Charles Edward to serve with him.[8] Liria had not forgotten the young prince who had so impressed him at the age of six and a half. Nothing he saw in Rome made him alter his high opinion of Charles Edward.

Great military vistas opened up. Liria intended to besiege the cities of Gaeta and Capua, then, the conquest of the Neapolitan territories completed, to cross with the army to Sicily.[9] Nevertheless, Liria cautioned James not to send the prince to the army until he had obtained Philip V's formal permission.[10]

James's euphoria ebbed somewhat at this. He knew of old the tortuous protocol at the Spanish court and considered the prospect of a speedy reply unlikely.[11] Liria departed for Naples, intending to lay siege to Gaeta first.[12] Having taken this decision, he then realised that the operation might well be concluded by the time the permission came through from Madrid. Stressing that 'this siege will be well worth seeing', he fired off an express to James advising him to anticipate the expected favourable response from Spain.[13] James, a stickler for protocol, insisted on waiting for the matter to be cleared through the usual channels.[14] Contingency plans were laid. James and his son went to an audience with the Pope, where they were given 4,000 scudi as campaign expenses. Charles Edward went into serious training, galloping his horses daily in the Villa Barberini.[15]

By 21 July James had given up all hope of getting the authorisation in time for it to be any use to his son. No sooner had he confided these thoughts to his favourite Inverness than, *mirabile dictu*, the permission arrived from Madrid.[16] The stage was now set for Charles Edward's first appearance in the world at large.

Careful preparations were made for displaying the prince to the world. Long conferences were held with cardinals Rivera and Corsini; with the pretender to the Moroccan throne, also bound for Gaeta; and especially with the French ambassador the duc de St Aignan.[17] The Pope, who had long had a soft spot for Charles Edward, was especially pleased with the turn of events. He granted his young favourite a plenary indulgence and an ample sum of money to cover his expenses. Clementina asked all the nuns in Rome to pray for her son's success.[18]

On 27 July the prince set out for Albano with a retinue of ten followers in five post-chaises. Headed by Dunbar, the party included a surgeon and a confessor. James joined them at Albano on the 29th. After a lavish dinner, the prince and party started south for Gaeta with the king's blessing.[19]

Charles Edward's entourage proceeded slowly through Velletri and Mola, partly out of consideration for the sudden appearance of a sore toe that prevented the prince's putting his shoes on.[20] It was four days before they came close enough to Gaeta for Liria to go out and meet them. The prince was now in perfect health. Immediately he gave signs of the special charisma that was to serve him so well in later life. Liria took him to see the Infanta, always styled by the campaigning Spanish 'the king of Naples'. At the Infanta's palace all the honours due to a Prince of Wales were laid on but Charles, officially incognito, displayed good sense by asking the court chamberlain count Estemar to dispense with these.[21]

When the Infanta arrived, the prince paid him a compliment with all the panache of a veteran courtier. In the 'king's' rooms Charles Edward chatted with him with extrovert ease. This was not as easy as it sounded. Don Carlos was a notorious cold fish.[22]

Next morning Liria's co-commander the count of Montemar took the prince aside and reiterated that the Spanish court was willing to treat him publicly as the Prince of Wales if that was his pleasure. Again Charles Edward asked merely for the treatment due a distinguished incognito.

On Wednesday 4 August (together with Dunbar and Sheridan) he dined with the Infanta. Already the prince's grace, wit and charm were making their mark.'*Il est vif,il est charmant*' was the comment of the normally dour Don Carlos. He invited the prince to dine with him every day. Dunbar cunningly took aside the royal physician Buonnoni to learn things about the 'king' that Charles Edward might introduce into the conversation to his advantage.

In the afternoon Liria conveyed Charles Edward to a house overlooking Gaeta bay, which was used by Don Carlos as a safe vantage point for viewing the siegeworks. The Infanta did not accompany them so as not to inhibit the prince. Since the siege of Gaeta was expected to be a protracted affair, the plan was that the prince would be taken down around 11 a.m. the next morning to inspect the Spanish batteries, at a time when the defenders usually did not fire on their oppressors because of the noonday heat.

Then they returned to the prince's own quarters. This was a house belonging to Cardinal Cibo that enjoyed a full prospect of Gaeta. From here the prince could see every shot or cannonball that was exchanged between the two sides.

Meanwhile Dunbar and Liria plotted how they could extract the maximum propaganda advantage from the Prince's presence at Gaeta. Since the Infanta Don Carlos cautiously refrained from entering the trenches of the besiegers, they had to be careful not to upstage him with Charles Edward's exploits. For all that, Liria was determined that the prince should be seen in the trenches for, as he pointed out, Charles Edward had to impress his personality on the world, 'having no fortune . . . but what he must gain by the point of his sword'. Liria reckoned that if the prince craftily went into the trenches at the right time of day, he could secure within a few days a great reputation for courage while incurring minimal risk.

Such was the strategy decided on. On 5 August the prince spent some six hours with Liria in the trenches during the siesta hours. He was mounted on a little horse. The excursion was not quite so risk-free as Liria had hoped, but the young prince showed remarkable coolness under fire, 'even when the balls were whistling about his ears'.[23]

At court meanwhile the Stuart charm was as pronounced as ever. On one occasion the prince's cockade fell from his hat and one of the courtiers replaced it wrongly. Seeing this, the Infanta fixed it in the correct position. Charles thanked Don Carlos and said he would keep the cockade for ever in memory of the incident.[24] Already the prince was learning the art of reading men and saying the things they wanted to hear.

The prince quickly made a lot of admirers. Dunbar admitted that his charge's diplomatic skills exceeded his expectations.[25] Don Carlos especially expressed himself surprised at his maturity. Liria confided to James that the said Infanta was completely outclassed by the young prince in every department; education, breeding, wit, repartee.[26] Moreover, Charles Edward was already a great favourite with the troops. Quickly mastering the art of being all things to all men, the prince impressed the soldiers by speaking French to the Walloons, Spanish to the Spaniards, and Italian to the Italians. The men flocked around him, crowding in to catch his attention or beg a word with him, amazed at such a phenomenon. The prince joked with them in a familiar way. To Liria's astonishment he was able to charm them as easily as he had charmed the Neapolitan court, and with all the aplomb of an experienced military officer. Liria commented to his brother: 'His manner of conversation is really bewitching, and you may lay to your account that if it were otherwise, I would not have kept it a secret from you.'[27]

Having scored such a hit on his one day in the trenches, the prince wanted to plunge deeper into the thick of the action. He plagued Liria to be able to take up station with the forward batteries. Liria was at his wits' end to know how to refuse him. The prince's great popularity with the troops, and the fact that he had already ventured into the trenches where the Infanta feared to tread, was already sufficiently embarrassing. It was a delicate situation. If Charles Edward went any farther into the press of the fighting, Don Carlos would be publicly humiliated.[28]

Fortunately for Liria, his problem was solved in the most unexpected way. On 6 August the defenders of Gaeta suddenly and unexpectedly gave up the ghost; whether through the treachery of their Catalan mercenaries, as was alleged, or because of the sheer destructive power of the Spanish floating battery, was uncertain.[29]

The sudden collapse of Gaeta left the prince free to explore Naples. On the Sunday after the surrender of Gaeta he was entertained on board the Capetano galley by Prince Campo-Florido's brother, the captain-general of Spanish galleys. Unfortunately Charles suffered sea-sickness from the rocking motion of the ship; he was never to be a great sailor.[30] When he got back to his lodgings, he needed ten hours' sleep to get over this malady. When he got up, he found he had regained all his old resilience. He ate more in one day in Naples than in two at Rome.

The round of social engagements continued: dinner with count Estemar one day, with the Grand Prior of France the next. The Infanta put his own private galley at the prince's disposal. Charles went to bed late every night. By the time he arose in the morning, the cool house he shared with Liria was full of distinguished company, waiting to pay him compliments.[31]

There can be no doubt that the Gaeta excursion, though it actually involved no more than one day in the trenches, was a propaganda triumph for the prince. Liria was ecstatic about his charge and cousin: 'In a word this Prince discovers that in great princes whom nature has marked out for heroes valour does not wait for the number of years.'[32] The Infanta was particularly impressed with him and gave a prestigious position in his army to a Jacobite officer as a mark of his regard for the prince. As Liria remarked: 'The king of Naples was struck with wonder to find in the dawn of years such ripe thought and so much prudence, which are rarely to be met with in Princes arrived at the full maturity of age.'[33] Moreover, Charles had success-fully refuted those who said he was too young as yet to make a mark on the world.

The prince decided to make the most of his few precious days of freedom before returning to James's oppressive regime. Despite the nagging letters he received from his father,[34] while in Naples he ate and drank whatever he fancied and put on weight. As the helpless Dunbar reported to James: 'He eats a great deal more and with less rule as to choice of it than he used to, which gives me some apprehen-sion, but this air is more favourable to the digestion than that of Rome.'[35]

Meanwhile the political consequences of Charles Edward's first campaign continued to reverberate around Europe. Keene, the British Minister in Madrid, protested vociferously to Foreign Minister Patiño about this 'unfriendly action' by Spain.[36] The Spanish initiative was considered particularly dangerous in that it seemed to set a precedent. It was felt that France could not after this very well refuse the prince a campaign in her own army.[37] Fleury, apprehensive of English reaction, was particularly concerned at this development. He started lobbying at Madrid to ensure that Charles Edward did not serve with the Spaniards in next year's Lombardy campaign.[38] But not even the Jacobites' enemies cared to deny the wonderful fillip given the prince's reputation by the Gaeta campaign. 'Everyone agrees he will be with time a much more dangerous enemy to the present regime in England than his father has been,' Walton reported grudgingly.[39] From all sides the plaudits for the prince's success poured in. Dunbar confided to James that the Neapolitan ministers would be glad to see the back of him, since in public opinion Charles Edward far outshone the Infanta Don Carlos.[40]

It was at this precise moment, when the prince was winning golden opinions on all sides and basking in the attention of the Neapolitan nobility, that James showed himself at his most crassly insensitive. The occasion was the two short notes his son had dashed off to him in the general excitement, and for whose brevity he had Dunbar's sanction.[41] Bridling at what he took to be lack of filial deference, James on 27 August sent his son a blistering letter of rebuke. He complained of the insolent curtness of the letters and the fact that they were incorrectly copied:

But what makes these particulars give me the more concern is that I am sensible these omissions proceed from your too natural aversion to all application and constraint and that if you do not get the better of yourself and endeavour to cultivate the talents which Providence has given you, you will soon lose that good character which your present behaviour is beginning to gain you. Your great youth at present makes the smallest things be approved of and even admired in you, but as you grow older, every year, may I say every month, more will be expected from you and that more will never come without some pains and application on your side . . . if you will not so much be at the trouble of writing a letter of reasonable length on indifferent subjects, what can be expected from you in greater matters? What a figure will you make in the world? And above all, how highly responsible will you be to God Almighty for burying the talents he has given you and for not making yourself capable of performing the duties he requires of you?[42]

This letter is more eloquent on the true state of relations between father and son than a dozen routine, formulaic letters about 'dearest Carluccio'. What can have induced James to send off such a hurtful screed at the height of his son's triumph? It is difficult not to see some resentment or jealousy at work here. Quite apart from the brilliant figure his son had cut in Naples – contrasting so strongly with the débâcle in Scotland in 1716, the only time James had attempted to put his own personal appeal to the test – the whispers James heard around him that the son was already supplanting the father would have revived the hurt feelings over the 1733 Bolingbroke scheme to use Charles Edward to edge out the 'Old Pretender'. It will be remembered that the peculiar cunning of Bolingbroke's idea was the insinuation that Charles Edward could be restored by Parliament or by internal unrest in England, whereas James's restoration would take a French invasion.[43] Moreover, James had recently received striking testimony of the desire of the English Jacobites to go over (or under) his head to Charles Edward. The disgraced Church of England parson Zeckie Hamilton (confidant of Earl Marischal and Ormonde) had, the month before Gaeta, surpassed all his previous mad insolence to the king by writing to Charles Edward to ask him to disavow his father's authority.[44] So strong were the pressures from certain factions of the English Jacobites to detach the prince from his father that Walton at first thought this, not the siege of Gaeta, was the true explanation for Charles's departure from Albano at the end of July.[45]

There is, moreover, a disturbing hint of 'I told you so' gloating in

James's response to the news that his son had fallen mildly ill at Naples at the end of August.[46] Nor did the tension end there, but carried on into the period of what should have been the triumphal homecoming. Dunbar planned to set out on 12 September, resting a night at Mola before putting in a bruising day's travel from 2 a.m. on the 13th until nightfall so as to get to Albano on the third night out from Naples.[47] The original intention was that Liria would accompany them; he was now the 2nd duke of Berwick, following his father the marshal-duke's death on campaign at Phillipsburg. Accordingly James went out to Albano on 14 September and pushed on to Genzano to meet the returning party.[48] But there was no Berwick with them. The 2nd duke lay ill at Naples, in the first stages of the consumption that would carry him off four years later. This was unfortunate for Charles Edward, since Berwick was one man capable of getting James to see sense. Dunbar and Sheridan were both too far in the king's debt to be capable of pointing out his insensitivity.

The upshot was a pointed contrast between the prince as the idol of Naples and the delinquent son of James's perception. Charles Edward returned home after being fêted and lionised in Naples, loaded down with honours. He brought back two fine horses, magnificently equipped, as a present from Don Carlos, plus gifts of diamonds and precious jewels.[49] He was already both rich and famous. The Pope was so pleased with his protégé that there was talk of making the prince a cardinal.[50] On the return from Gaeta the Pontiff provided a papal honour guard of fifty men to escort him.[51] All James could see, however, was an unruly and competitive son who had failed to live by the rules his father had inculcated in him for so many years. The stress caused by the chasm between these two views of him was almost bound to cause the prince to erupt. It is therefore not surprising to read in a letter from James to Clementina who had dragged her pathetic invalid body out to Albano on 16 September to see her beloved son,[52] very soon after the prince's return, that their son had twice been 'in penance'.[53]

James continued his sniping campaign against his son in correspondence with O'Brien, pointedly contrasting him with Henry to the latter's advantage.[54] Nor did Henry help his own cause with his brother. To add to the wound caused by James's obvious partiality for his second son, Henry rubbed salt in the wound himself. It seems that both princes had designs on a puppy that secretary Edgar had been given. Henry outwitted his brother by waiting in the inner room next to the chamber where Edgar was closeted with James, then waylaying the secretary and extracting a solemn promise from him that the puppy would be Henry's.[55]

Yet sibling rivalry and James's insensitivity faded into insignificance alongside the crushing blow that fell next. The queen's health had long given cause for concern. The first indication that she might be entering a critical new stage was the alarm sounded by James at the end of October, when he reported a cough, ominously at the start of winter.[56] By the first week in November Clementina was already seriously ill.[57] On the advice of her physicians, the queen stayed indoors for a month. It was now suspected that she was suffering from acute scurvy, but as ever Clementina would take no medical advice nor any preventive action.[58] She was very weak and skeletal in appearance, but persisted in regarding her sickness as the judgment of God.[59] It was in some anguish that James wrote on 20 December 1734:

> Her distemper is the scurvy, which affects one of her legs and her mouth and which she has been subject to these several years, but by neglecting of it is grown to a great height now, though she has no fever, but yet I reckon the doctors think her in a dangerous state and I know not well what remedies to apply, because she endeavours to conceal the ails and what she suffers, which is certainly a great deal.[60]

At the beginning of January 1735 the queen contracted a fever.[61] During the next week her state of health plummeted alarmingly. By 12 January she was described as 'at the last extremity, though in all her senses'.[62] The last rites were administered. Death was now regarded as inevitable. James spoke with resignation of seeing her for the last time.[63] On 13 January Clementina said farewell to her children, exhorting them piteously never to desert the Catholic faith, not for all the kingdoms of the world. On the 14th she saw them again to repeat the same exhortation.[64] After 15 January she was only intermittently conscious.[65] Death came at 5 p.m. on 18 January 1735.[66]

The Pope gave Clementina a royal funeral with full honours. Her body was first exposed in the royal robes in the parish church then carried in state to be buried at St Peter's. Public prayers were said in Rome. The city mourned her passing. The lamentation was said to be as great as if the Pope himself had died.[67] At St Peter's the royal robes were taken off and the body put into the coffin in a Dominican habit. On Monday morning, 24 January 1735, a solemn Mass was sung. The body was then taken down and walled up in one of the vaults.[68] On Wednesday the 26th a requiem was sung in SS Apostoli, attended by James and the two princes.

There is no direct documentary evidence that enables us to gauge the impact on the prince of his mother's death. Yet the absence of any reference to the behaviour problems James had been so exercised with before the queen's death is in itself significant. It suggests that the prince's grief was so profound that it could not manifest itself in normal lamentations or temper tantrums but had burrowed deep, waiting to surface as volcanic rage at a later date. A superficial reading of the Stuart papers would suggest that Charles Edward was unaffected by his mother's death, that if anything his behaviour and attitude improved.[69] Yet all indirect inferences suggest that it was a terrible blow, as might naturally be expected.

If Charles Edward's personality was warped by his relationship with his mother, so that he was ever afterwards consumed by guilt and depression, this was unfortunately not the only crippling legacy of his mother's early death. There are strong grounds for thinking that the prince's later notorious difficulties in forming satisfactory lasting relationships with women can also be traced to the 'disaster' of his mother's death. Modern psychoanalytical studies show Oedipal conflicts reaching a peak at two points: the age of five and at adolescence, when there is a renewed surge of genital desire, and when the original choice of mother as sex object threatens to become conscious once more.[70] In other words, the key moments for Charles Edward's heterosexual development were also the ones of greatest trauma. On his fifth birthday his mother had just fled to the Convent of St Cecilia. Immediately following his fourteenth birthday she died. One does not need to labour the point.

Yet another consequence of his mother's death might have been the prince's later contempt for religion. It would not be altogether surprising if Charles Edward had developed an aversion to Christianity. Not only did it hold in thrall his father and brother (accounting in the prince's eyes for much of what was wrong with them), the near-psychotic mania induced by the saints of the Catholic Church (especially Francis de Sales) had also been instrumental in sending his mother to the tomb. The association of ideas would not have been helped, either, by James's insistence, immediately after Clementina's death, that the prince should undergo the full rigour of the Lenten fasts once more.[71]

In the years 1735–6 these were psychological potentialities insidiously dormant. At the superficial level the prince was doing well in both the mental and physical spheres. He continued to impress visitors to Rome, such as the Scottish Jacobite poet Allan Ramsay who saw him in the Villa Ludovici in 1736.[72] Dunbar's hopes that his charge's talent for design might lead him on to geometry and mathematics seem to have been fulfilled. During 1735 the prince made great strides in this area.[73] An order for a whole new set of mathematical instruments went out from the Palazzo Muti in March 1736.[74] In September 1735 Dunbar reported that in nine lessons the prince had mastered the first book of Euclid.[75] Yet Dunbar's continuing ill-health itself posed a question mark against the prince's future. His geometry lessons were assigned to a monk called Father Rovillas. There was talk of the prince's being placed in the Clementi college to study under the Abbé Severa, a protégé of the duke of Berwick.[76]

Even more spectacular progress was made in the sphere of physical endeavour. The prince was consciously trying to turn himself into a warrior, taking constant exercise and revealing remarkable stamina.[77] His horsemanship and eye for a horse were admired even by his enemies. As part of his warrior's training he went to particular lengths to get his steeds used to the sound of gunfire.[78] He was already by common consent a crack shot and a mighty hunter, absenting himself from home for days on end on the track of quail and other small game.[79] He was visibly growing stonger and taller. Whatever misgivings there might be about his intellectual progress, there were no worries on the score of health and physique.[80] His appetite for the chase was insatiable: the tallies of hares, partridges and other birds he bagged seemed to increase in geometrical progression.[81]

Yet neither the physical nor intellectual development satisfied James, who continued to carp at his son.[82] Even Edgar, usually an admirer of the prince, appears to have caught the bug from his master on occasions, denying him even some of the attributes the king grudgingly conceded him. After describing Henry as more composed and thoughtful than his brother, he comments: 'The Prince is very strong and healthful, has a fine presence and countenance, but is not tall for his age.'[83]

To offset these disadvantages, the prince was still Berwick's cynosure and the favourite son of the Pope, whose financial generosity to him attracted widespread comment.[84] Berwick's main concern now was to find another campaign in which his beloved protégé could shine again as brightly as at Gaeta. Much of Jacobite diplomatic correspondence after Gaeta and until 1737 is concerned with finding a venue where the prince could give another illustrious performance. At first James was determined that his son would campaign again in 1735.[85] All Europe had been mightily impressed by the prince's exploits. Without doubt Gaeta had been a great propaganda coup, so successful indeed that the Hanoverians were said to be sending the duke of Cumberland (a few months younger than Charles Edward) on a voyage by warship so that he could emulate at sea what his Stuart rival had achieved on land.[86] James imagined the next step might be a French campaign, possibly again under Berwick's tutelage. But France quickly showed the way the wind was blowing in Versailles by forbidding any signs of mourning by French Jacobites on Clementina's death.[87] If any doubt remained of French hostility, the ministers made the point explicit to O'Brien the following month.[88]

Even Spain was drawing in its horns. Here the problem was not just the rapport being built up between Foreign Minister Patiño and British envoy Keene, but a personal feud between Patiño and Berwick.[89] Despite James's confident assurances that Spain would soon agree to another campaign for his son, Patiño delayed unconscionably in replying to his overtures.[90] After stalling shamelessly for nearly a year – and after James had made a second formal application for his son to accompany Spanish troops on their projected conquest of Lombardy – Patiño flatly turned down the request.[91]

Yet James was determined that the memory of Gaeta should not be allowed to fade. This was not easy to accomplish. Berwick's overtures in Spain on behalf of the Stuarts came to nothing.

James turned his attention to the Imperial domains and beyond. He had long been brooding on the need to get his sons naturalised as Polish citizens, so that they could inherit without let or hindrance the considerable wealth of the Sobieskis from their grandfather who now hovered near death.[92] James therefore instructed O'Rourke, his agent at Vienna, to secure the Emperor's permission for a visit incognito by Charles Edward to his ailing grandfather.[93] O'Rourke advised him that because of pressure from the English, it was most unlikely that the Emperor would give written permission for such a visit, but would turn a blind eye if the prince came into his dominions incognito. However, he advised James to get the French to permit the prince to travel through their country to Flanders. If the French agreed, this would set a valuable precedent. Charles Edward could then go 'island hopping' through the Electorates of Bavaria, Cologne and the Palatine on his way to the Empire, increasing his prestige as he went.[94] But, as James accurately saw, this whole ambitious scheme depended on Charles Edward's being allowed into Austrian Flanders openly. This was even less likely than a permit for a visit to Vienna, since the Netherlands were traditionally an area of the greatest military sensitivity in English eyes.[95]

While O'Rourke negotiated at Vienna, James proposed sending his son on a tour of northern Italy. If Austrian permission was given, Charles would then proceed to Poland. But there was something essentially negative in the way he spoke about his son that, once again, hints at the tension between them:

It is certain parents cannot take too much care to preserve their children from all vice and ill company, but with those I should propose to send with him, and his being to remain but a very short time anywhere except with his grandfather, I own I think I may be as easy in that respect during the few months he may be away as if he were actually under my eye. Besides that, he is, I believe, hitherto very innocent and extreme backwards in some respects for his age, though otherwise strong and healthy and very lively. He does not want either good natural parts necessary for his improvement, but has a great reluctancy to application and is a little childish, as sometimes happens at his age, so that a little motion and travelling will be of little inconvenience by way of interrupting his studies and will, I hope, wean him from little childish amusements and help to make him more manly.[96]

Yet even before Charles Edward set out on his Italian trip, it was obvious that neither France nor the Emperor would allow him on their territory.[97] Given that the tour was now actually of minimal practical importance, it was vital to extract the last ounce of propaganda value from it. James intended to prove that the House of Stuart was no broken reed and that in Charles Edward it had its most formidable champion yet.

4

'The breath of kings'
(1737–41)

The Stuart entourage cut a dash on the road to Loreto, which surprised those who imagined the Jacobite court to be decrepit and impoverished.[1] The truth was that the prince had received money for his journey from two sources. The first was the Pope. At an audience with his protégé on 24 April 1737 Clement XII gave him a sufficient sum to cover the expenses of his trip.[2] The second was from James's emergency store of 50,000 crowns (£12,500 approx.) on deposit with Belloni the banker.[3] This was a sum sufficient to cover pay and expenses (including horses, livery, bedding, linen and plate) in the event the prince was permitted to make a campaign against the Turks in Hungary.[4] James still obstinately clung to the belief that the Emperor would relent and receive Charles Edward in his dominions; in which case he would go straight on from Venice to Vienna.

The prince's party crossed the Appennines, still within the papal states, and arrived at Loreto shortly after three o'clock on the afternoon of 1 May. Cardinal Massei had invited the prince to dine with him next day; but his palace was three hours' ride out of town, so that Thursday 2 May was wholly taken up with that excursion.[5] They started early on the 3rd, hoping to get to Pesaro by dinner (i.e. lunch) time. They succeeded and were given dinner by Monsignor Lanti. That evening there was a poetry-reading contest or *accademia* at which various poetasters recited their compositions in praise of the prince.[6] There followed the performance of a tragedy, which lasted until 1 a.m., followed by a lavish supper ('a table with forty covers in the form of a St Andrew's cross'). At this supper the prince sat alone, surrounded by the fashionable ladies of the town.[7]

The 4th of May saw another hard day's travel. They had hoped to get to Bologna by 11 p.m. that night, but delays on the road meant that they did not get in before 1 a.m. on the 5th. The whole of the next day was spent in Bologna. In the evening the prince attended a ball at the Palazzo Fibbia and danced until 11 p.m. Dunbar was able to score points off the Catholic clergy who had given him so much trouble in the past by pointing out to James that neither of the Bolognese cardinals called on the prince. When the more well-disposed of the two, Prospero Lambertini (the future Pope Benedict XIV) tried to attend the ball in order to have an informal word with Charles, Dunbar managed to head him off (he was not, he claimed, going to allow Lambertini to apply by the back door for what he had been refused at the front).[8]

The late-night frolicking at the ball delayed the party's departure next morning. In addition, the prince insisted on making a tour of the walls of Modena, to show his appreciation of a compliment sent him by the Princess of Modena.[9] After sixteen hours on the road in driving rain, they arrived (again at 1 a.m.) at Parma, where the duchess had left the town gates open for him. One of her men was on hand to convey the prince by coach to the same convent where his father had stayed nine years before.

On the 7th, after sleeping late, the prince dined with the duchess of Parma and impressed her with his charm.[10] Given the continuing heavy rains, the prince accepted her invitation to stay until Thursday the 9th. He plunged into a whirl of balls, lavish suppers, tours of picture galleries. He made a day trip to Reggio. While in Parma he also made contact with an important Imperial representative Prince Lobkowicz, commander of the Austrian armies in northern Italy.[11] Lobkowicz put his grenadiers through their paces for him on the esplanade of the castle.[12] On the morning of the 8th the two princes held a long conversation together, then joined the duchess for dinner. Charles Edward needed all his tact, for the old duchess's words were difficult to understand. She spoke in Italian without her teeth.[13] Nevertheless, he impressed her sufficiently to be presented with a gold snuff box inlaid with diamonds (valued at 500 Roman crowns). Finally, on Wednesday evening there was a concert featuring a violinist billed as the best in Europe, better even than Tartini.[14] Here again Charles Edward maintained the good impression he had made on Lobkowicz.

On Thursday 9 May the prince pressed on to Piacenza. There the tight grip Dunbar had hitherto managed to exert on protocol dissolved. The duchess there disregarded the prince's incognito and insisted on giving him the honours due a Prince of Wales. Dunbar spent some uncomfortable hours dissuading the envoy from the governor of Milan from addressing him in the same style. The entire tour seemed in danger of getting out of hand. Dunbar was glad to shake the dust of Piacenza off their collective feet.[15]

The next two days, from Piacenza to Genoa across the Appenino Ligure, were eighteenth-century travel at its very worst. All the wealth and prestige of the Stuarts could secure nothing more than a second-class, uncomfortable inn at Tortona. The prince arrived in Genoa at 8 p.m. on the evening of the 11th, utterly exhausted.

In Genoa they were lodged at a monastery belonging to the Roman order of the Apostoli. The prince slept until 10 a.m., then set out for a day's sightseeing with the marquis of Grimaldi and Cardinal Spinola. There followed a crowded week. Every day he was dined regally by one of the Genoese nobility. In the evening there were parties ('assemblies') or the *Comedia* to go to. As on all ports of call hitherto, the prince's charisma dazzled his hosts. Sometimes there was a social price to pay for his personal magnetism. At the ball he attended on the night of Wednesday 15 May the salon was too small for the numbers who crowded in to glimpse him, so that the atmosphere at the dance was unbearably hot and stifling.[16]

It had originally been intended that the prince would visit Turin, but English pressure led to the visit's cancellation.[17] This hiccup in the plans accounts for the apparent ineptitude of the itinerary, involving as it did the partial retracing of their steps. On Saturday 18 May the prince's party left Genoa for Milan, arriving there at 10 p.m. that night. On Sunday there was heavy rain and the sky was overcast, so that the prince had to inspect the paintings in the Biblioteca Ambrosiana that afternoon by candlelight.[18]

There followed another leisurely week, similar to that in Genoa: concerts, balls, card games, sightseeing. The prince was a frequent visitor at the great Milanese houses of the Stampas and the Lucinis.[19] On Sunday 26 May they set out for the long ride to Venice, making a late start because the prince had been dancing until 2 a.m. at one of the endless balls (one a night was laid on for him in Milan). They had expected a tiring journey to Venice on account of the bad roads, but it was made even worse by the shortage of horses, largely monopolised by the Elector of Bavaria, who was then travelling from Verona to Vienna, and by the depredations to the muddy track made by his horses and carriages.[20]

The shortage of horses led directly to a singularly unpleasant incident, which revealed once again how heavily the exiled Stuarts depended on papal patronage. Arriving in Verona at 10 p.m. on 27 May, having endured bad roads and with tired horses, Dunbar's first task was to get his hands on the post horses, so that next morning the prince would be first on the road and could set out the moment the city gates were opened. It turned out that the postmaster had been bribed by one marquis de Bevilacqua to let him have first call on the horses. When the postmaster refused to heed Dunbar's call next day, the royal tutor soon guessed what was going on. He asked Colonel Terry, in whose house Charles Edward was lodged, to send a dragoon ahead to secure the horses at the first post for the prince.

When Bevilacqua got there, thinking he had outsmarted the Stuart party, he found himself outwitted and the horses spoken for. In a fury he waited for Charles Edward's valet-de-chambre to come up, slightly ahead of the main party. Denying the prince's right to the horses, Bevilacqua swore an oath that he for one did not recognise the Stuarts, that if they wished to exercise their royal prerogative, they should go to England to do it. The marquis's wife thereupon loosed a volley of fishwife abuse on the unfortunate valet-de-chambre.

Aroused by the yelling imprecations, the post-mistress came out to adjudicate. In a most unsolomonic judgment, delivered on the basis of the highest rank of those present, she overruled the valet-de-chambre and gave the horses to Bevilacqua. The upshot was that when the prince came up, his fresh mounts were gone. The remaining horses were so tired they could barely crawl.

In Venice the authorities offered to arrest Bevilacqua for the insult, but since he was a papal subject, it was thought best to refer the matter to Rome. In any case, once in the Most Serene Republic, the prince put such tribulations behind him. Venice was to be the highlight of his tour. The itinerary had been planned so that he would be there in time for the Ascension Fair. He was to spend almost two weeks in the great watery city of the Doges, to the consternation and fury of the English, who had always regarded the Venetians as their loyal allies.[21]

Arriving late on the evening of 28 May, hard on the heels of the Elector and Electress of Bavaria, the prince quickly made his mark. On his first day in the city of canals, he was visited by the papal nuncio, the French ambassador and the commander of French galleys in the Mediterranean.[22] On Wednesday the 29th the prince attended the opera, seated in Cardinal Davia's box. On Friday the 31st he was given a sumptuous reception on board a Venetian galley. The Elector and Electress of Bavaria came alongside in their craft and boarded the galley, each side maintaining the fiction of the incognito by wearing masks in the time-honoured Venetian fashion.[23] But since both parties had large retinues in tow, no significant conversation ensued. Nevertheless, Cardinal Davia was instructed to tell the prince in confidence from the Elector that the failure to hold a tête-à-tête was not by his choice.

Any annoyance the English might have felt about cordial relations between Elector and Pretender were as nothing to the anger they felt once the Venetians showed clearly how they meant to proceed with their illustrious visitor. English irritation began in earnest on Ascension Thursday, when the prince went to see the ceremony of the marriage between the Doge and the sea. Lady Gradenigo, who had invited Charles to the ceremony, then took him on to witness the Doge's feast. As the Doge passed the prince on his way to the public dinner, he made him a very respectful bow.[24] Since the prince was not wearing his mask, the fiction of the incognito could not very well be maintained.

On the following Sunday Charles Edward attended the Assembly of the Grand Council of Venice. Again, since he was incognito, there should have been no question of his receiving full honours. But, again to the horror of the English envoy, the prince was met at the stairs by the Doge's attendants as he alighted from his gondola. On his approach to the council hall, the door was opened for him. Wearing his sword, the prince then entered and was conducted to the bench reserved exclusively for princes, as opposed to the bench set aside for visitors or strangers.[25] Once again, when the Doge entered he made the prince a low bow.

The English envoy immediately went to the secretary of the Venetian Inquisition to protest at the honours done the prince. He asked that he be expelled forthwith. Disingenuously the secretary replied that the honours were merely those done to a private gentleman. He added frostily that he would of course convey English feelings to the Inquisitors.[26]

The English torment was not yet over. Later that same Sunday the Elector and Electress of Bavaria again 'accidentally' encountered the prince, this time in the library of St George's convent. In the presence of more than two hundred onlookers, the Elector and Charles Edward stood conversing for fifteen minutes. They were joined by the Imperial Marshal Shullingberg, who questioned the young prince on the siege of Gaeta and found him knowledgeable. The conversation caught fire; the three of them then retired into the convent grounds and talked for more than an hour.[27] The fiction that the meeting was accidental fooled no one.

The second week in Venice saw visits to St Mark's, trips by pleasure boat in the Muran canal, magnificent dinners at the nuncio's and the French ambassador's, and (on Tuesday 4 June) a visit with Lady Gradenigo to the Venetian Arsenal. The governor of the Arsenal treated the prince with every distinction (again the incognito was disregarded), a demonstration launch was made of one of the Doge's large barges, and a sumptuous collation laid on in the main hall.[28]

On Saturday 8 June (Whitsun-eve) an oratorio was performed for the prince at the Hospital of the Incurables by young ladies educated there.[29] Dunbar prevailed on his charge to stay in that night, preparatory to the journey to Padua planned for Monday, but this (coupled with a siesta on Sunday afternoon) backfired on Dunbar. The prince was so full of surplus energy that he danced until 5 a.m. at the great farewell ball given for him by Lady Gradenigo on the Sunday night.[30] All of Venetian high society was there. Lady Gradenigo and the other fine ladies glittered in their jewels. Charles Edward was at his very best, impressing everyone with his wit and charm and his skill on the ballroom.

This was the last straw for the exasperated English. Enraged at the consistent lionising of the prince (and the constantly reiterated pretence that these were simply the honours given to a private individual), the English envoy again made strong representations, this time through Foreign Ministry channels. What infuriated the envoy was that Whit Sunday was traditionally a day when no public functions of this kind took place, yet the whole of Venice had gone out of its way to honour one who was openly talked of as 'the Prince of Wales'.[31]

Without question the Venetians had treated the prince with extraordinary courtesy. Their reception of Charles Edward was both unexpected and, by common consent, far beyond anything given to other princes. Officially incognito, the prince had been given actual royal treatment. He had scored a palpable hit in Venice, especially with the women, who clustered around him wherever he went. It is not surprising that George II was so angered by the Doge's conduct on this occasion that he expelled the Venetian Resident in London.[32] The anxiety with which the British government had watched Charles Edward set out on his journey had changed to something very close to alarm.[33]

On Monday 10 June the royal party started for Padua very late in the day; they did not arrive until 10 p.m. On Tuesday evening the prince went to the opera, Wednesday morning he spent sightseeing.[34] The next leg of the journey was to Ferrara, accomplished on Wednesday afternoon and evening. In Ferrara too the prince was well received. He and his suite were lodged at the house of the Abbé

Rota, who had a chef famous for his cuisine. A *corso de barbari* was laid on for his entertainment. Once again he attended an evening ball and danced until 2 a.m.[35]

Rather than face another late start, and fearing a further possible post-horse clash, this time with the Elector of Bavaria, Dunbar elected to press on overnight on the relatively short stretch to Bologna. The prince slept most of the time in the coach and was then in bed in Bologna the best part of the day. In the evening Cardinal Lambertini came to pay his respects, careful to avoid the gaffe he had committed on the prince's outward visit.

They rested a week in Bologna, going most nights to the theatre or the opera. By now the strain of the tour was telling on the forty-seven-year-old Dunbar. The Bevilacqua business had shaken him badly. In addition, he became more and more tetchy about Charles Edward's late nights and increasingly critical of the prince. A letter to James from Bologna on 19 June is typical:

> As H.R.H. cannot enjoy the diversion of dancing with any degree of moderation but overheats himself monstrously on such occasions, I have refused a ball the public intended to give him here tomorrow night . . . the later he comes home and the more he has of sleep, he will sit the longer at supper, so that it is not possible to get him to bed after an opera till near three in the morning, though he be at home soon after one.[36]

This was telling James what he wanted to hear, since he had been nagging his son mercilessly by letter throughout the tour. James's tone was at best patronising and at worst downright insulting, considering that the sixteen-year-old was already shaving and wearing a wig.[37]

Moreover, the reluctant tutor was forced to be on his mettle at Bologna. The Elector of Bavaria was in the city at the same time. Since there was no need for Charles Edward to go about incognito in the papal states, any meeting between the two would oblige the Elector to recognise Charles publicly as Prince of Wales. It had therefore been agreed that the two parties would give each other a wide berth. But by a blunder the same house and balcony had been assigned to both for watching the Corpus Christi procession. Charles Edward was at the very threshold before Dunbar spotted the contretemps and led him away.[38]

After a week's rest, Charles Edward's party moved on to Florence, arriving at night on 22 June. The Grand Duke of Tuscany had offered to provide honours in the form of coaches, but the Jacobite agent in

Florence, Tyrell, insisted on a punctilious observance of the incognito. By now the English were so jumpy that the mere suggestion that coaches might have been offered to the Stuart party worked the British Resident Fane into a lather.[39]

Word of Charles Edward's love of dancing spread like a forest fire through the towns on their projected itinerary homewards. Dunbar had at one time toyed with a route taking them to Rome through Perugia. Hearing of the atrocious state of the Siena–Perugia road, he devised instead an itinerary to take them through Lucca, Pisa, Livorno, Siena and Caprarola. Even while the prince danced the nights away in Florence, Dunbar heard to his horror that similar balls had already been arranged in Lucca, Livorno and Siena.[40]

Florence rivalled Venice in the warmth of its welcome and the variety of entertainments laid on. The prince was given magnificent dinners by the nuncio and the Corsinis, saw a 'singular collection of pictures' at the Uffizi gallery, and attended a horse-race with coaches which he viewed from the balcony of the Casino Corsini and which 'seems to be a small remnant of the Olympic games'. There was a side visit to the Pope's nieces, both nuns. Other lavish dinners and feasts were provided at Villa Castello, Palazzo Antinoni and Palazzo Guadagni.[41] The prince's magnetic appeal for the fine ladies was again in evidence. Nearly one hundred of them crowded in to see him at the illuminated ball at the Villa Corsini on Sunday night 30 June.[42] Such was the prince's popularity in Florence that the ordinary people were said to have lamented their inability to elect a Grand Duke – for they would certainly have chosen Charles Edward.

There could be no doubting the success of Charles Edward's 1737 tour of northern Italy. Not only did James regard the expenditure of 5,000 crowns (£1,250 approx.) as remarkably economical, but the possibility of further such journeys was raised, especially to Spain.[43] As a propaganda exercise the tour was even more efficacious than the Gaeta excursion. It was absolutely clear that Charles Edward was already a charmer of the first rank; not even the cross-grained Dunbar cared to deny it.[44] As General Bulkeley later expressed it in his essay on the prince: 'The English travellers who then most disliked his cause may remember how much they feared it too at that time from the opinion which they had conceived of that young prince.'[45]

Why, then, was James's reaction to his son's triumph so grudging? Although he had earlier claimed, in a rare moment of self-knowledge, 'I should be sorry if the Prince resembled me in everything,'[46] that is precisely what, on the most charitable view, he was demanding. There was no praise for his huge public relations success, no appreciation of his obvious charisma, simply endless nagging and pedantic fussing. This time the prince tried very hard to keep up his correspondence with his father, even though the constant travelling did not make this an easy thing to do.[47] James began by expressing pleasure in the fact that his son was writing to him as promised.[48] But before long the predictable carping tendencies returned; James began to find fault with Charles's spelling, grammar and punctuation.[49] The inevitable happened. Faced with this nitpicking response to his efforts, Charles Edward found the incentive for frequent correspondence lacking.

Soon James was returning to his original tack. All the public success in the world, he told his son, was not enough if he failed to keep up his correspondence.[50] Not a word here about the things the prince had achieved, things that were clearly beyond James's own grasp; merely a remorseless chipping away at peccadilloes.

So far James's attitude could be considered merely narrow, blinkered and insensitive. But there soon came dramatic evidence that there was more to it than that, that James was motivated by unconscious jealousy. On 30 July, while the prince was still basking in the golden opinions he had won on the tour, James wrote to Inverness as follows: 'I am going to cut off the Prince's hair with which I know not whether he or Sir Thomas are best pleased.'[51] The symbolism of this is glaringly obvious. James already felt (and not just from the Italian tour) that he was being eclipsed by his elder son, that most credible Jacobites were now beginning to place their best hopes on Young rather than Old Pretender. For the older man, the symbolic gelding of the warrior returning home flushed with triumph served as a reminder that he was the one who cut not the one who was cut, much as if Cronos had beaten Zeus to the sickle. Charles Edward's reputation was now too high, and he had gained it too obviously by being unlike either James or Henry. At a symbolic level he had to be castrated and deprived of his power. The inclusion of Sir Thomas Sheridan as the other one, apart from Charles Edward, who would be hurt by the act is also instructive. It suggests that James was also unconsciously striking out at rival father figures.[52]

That James's action was contentious and controversial can be seen from Edgar's comments a week later. It was ever Edgar's role to pour oil on troubled waters and even to rewrite history for his master's benefit, but there is a definite air of protesting too much in his letter to Kelly on the subject.[53] Why else should he have found an apparently trivial matter so troublesome?

The anticlimactic and even depressing sequel to the prince's grand tour was reinforced the following year with the death from consumption of the duke of Berwick (June 1738).[54] Berwick was the only Jacobite of the first rank, both socially and politically, who was a genuine admirer of the prince, who both loved and respected him. Berwick made an admirable father/authority figure for Charles Edward and his loss was incalculable. He might have filled the gap that James could never fill. The inability of the prince to form a proper relationship with his father was to have profound and disastrous consequences in the future. Because he could not 'have it out' with aloof and forbidding James, the prince was unable to find a middle path between anger and submission. This meant that he was later incapable, at moments of crisis, of the patient argumentation and reasoning that might have won over doubters. As Derby and Falkirk were later to show, the prince had just two gears: rage or dumb capitulation. At moments of extreme stress it was usually the former that prevailed. Yet the prince can scarcely be blamed for his father's failure as a parent. Faced with the same sheer cliff wall of cold duty, Henry solved the problem by internalisation through religious mania.

Charles Edward continued to hone his physical faculties to a fine point against the day when he would be called on to play a great part in the world. His dedication on this point, amid the competing temptations of the Roman fleshpots, shows him at his strongest, almost the morality of strenuousness personified. According to the Jesuit Julio Cordara who knew him well, the prince disliked Rome precisely because only the arts of peace and pleasure were practised there.[55] This was no place for the aspiring warrior.

So the prince steeled himself for war by the rigours of the chase. He made it a point of honour to penetrate the densest wood or the most desolate heath in all weathers. At sunset he would return, scorched by the sun or frozen by the cold. In conscious emulation of the Ancient Romans, he trained himself to endure all hardships. So skilled did the prince become in woodcraft that later, while a fugitive in Scotland, he amazed his followers by being able to lure plovers within the range of his guns by imitating the bird's call.[56]

His companion on many of these expeditions was Father Vinciguerra, later Bendict XIV's secret chaplain. Vinciguerra encouraged the prince to believe that the Christian warrior had to undergo the hardships of wind, rain, snow, poor food, sleeping on straw, etc. to gain God's support for his mission.[57] One might be tempted to call Charles Edward's monomania a 'Galahad complex' but for the unwarranted connotation of virginity. Of the prince's sexual career during these years, or even if there was one, we know nothing. His private life in Rome is a total blank.[58]

So Charles Edward's late teens and early twenties dissolve into a succession of hunting parties: at Palo, at Lamentana, and especially on the duke of Caserta's estates at Cisterna.[59] Some of the tallies for the *caccia* make the prince seem a veritable Nimrod; certainly his ability as a marksman was never in doubt.[60] The only Achilles heel in this body of physical accomplishments was that the prince never learned to swim, much to his cost later in Scotland. This was wholly a cultural matter: sea-bathing had not yet come into vogue in Italy.[61]

There is no question but that Charles Edward thrived on his Spartan regime. James, proud of being taller than Dunbar, noted with a mixture of pride and misgiving that his son was already as tall as his tutor and bidding fair to overtop him.[62] When Lord Elcho (born 1721) came to Rome on the Grand Tour in October 1740, James made him stand back-to-back with his son; to his delight James found Charles Edward much taller.[63]

In view of the prince's later problems with his health, it may be instructive to ask at this point how his constitution stood up to this rigorous testing. In April 1739 James claimed that his son had inherited his weak stomach, but it is clear that the slight disorder suffered on that occasion was the advance guard of the virus that brought him and his brother out in chickenpox the following month.[64] Apart from minor ailments and a bad toothache in August 1741, the chickenpox comprised the sum total of illness in the period 1737–44.[65] Given the many illnesses the prince was to suffer during the '45, there is at least a *prima facie* case for saying that his physical constitution was naturally very robust, and that he succumbed to illness mainly in times of stress.[66]

But if the prince was keying himself to concert pitch in physicality, his mental life was not developing at an equal pace. After 1737 the sole reference to intellectual interests comes in the form of an order for a book of Ancient History, doubtless to read up on the heroes of antiquity he wished to emulate.[67] The sole 'civilised' pursuit in which Charles the mighty hunter took an interest was music, both as listener and performer.[68] He was an accomplished cellist. One of his favourite pieces was Corelli's *Notte di Natale* (the Christmas Concerto, Concerto Grosso No. 8 in G Minor) which he and Henry (on violin) played for the French traveller Charles de Brosses in 1740.[69] And the prince clearly enjoyed the theatre and the opera.[70] His theatre-going became particularly assiduous in the period 1741–3, after his majority, when his patronage of a particular theatre would help to make it popular.

One of his favourites (and Henry's too) was the Teatro Aliberti. Four operas there were dedicated to the Stuart princes and enjoyed great popularity.[71] More rarely, the Stuarts would commission fresh settings of an opera. This involved new arrangements and libretti, with original arias expressly written for the local singers, and the entire work adapted to fit local conditions; in extreme cases new music would be written to accommodate a famous prima donna or an idiosyncratic local conductor.[72] In addition, the exiled Stuarts were alone in Rome in enjoying the privilege of having an aria repeated during the opera, a privilege they exercised in the case of their favourite pieces at the Aliberti.[73]

Charles Edward's other much-loved social activity was dancing. The great reputation he had acquired on the 1737 Italian tour followed him to Rome. The early months of 1739, when the prince was eighteen, were a vintage period. Within a seven-day period Charles Edward attended two sumptuous balls, for the princes of Saxony and Poland (at the latter he danced until 6 a.m.).[74] The rest of the evenings in the same week he spent at the Clementi theatre.[75] In 1740 his terpsichorean skills were observed by a number of foreign visitors. On the 14th of May both Horace Walpole and the poet Thomas Gray attended an élite ball in Rome where James and his two sons were the guests of honour.[76] Music was provided by the contemporary celebrities La Diamantina, Giovanni and Pasqualini.[77]

Two months later Gray was at the Villa Patrizi for a ball given to Prince and Princess Craon.[78] Gray was impressed, rather against his will by both the Pretender's sons: 'They are good fine boys, especially the younger, who has the more spirit of the two, and both danced incessantly all night long.'[79]

But perhaps the prince's finest moment in Roman society was the great ball given in Cardinal Rohan's summer palace, the Palazzo Pamphili in the Piazza Navona, in February 1741. This was on a vast scale. The usual boundaries between the three drawing rooms and the three playing rooms were discarded. There was a sixty-piece orchestra; the Cardinal himself held court in a hall of mirrors.[80] Roman high society was out in force for the (literally) glittering occasion. Their fine ladies dripped with precious stones. Yet the show was stolen by Charles Edward, attired in Highland dress and sporting a cluster of jewels that dimmed the lustre of the many fine pieces already there.[81] These jewels were valued at 40,000 scudi and were alleged to have been part of a sumptuary courtship display aimed at winning the hand of the Princess of Massa. Jewels of this quality were unavailable in Italy, and there was a subtle symbolism involved in their display on this occasion, since it suggested that the Stuarts had access to wealth and craftsmanship beyond the reach of the Roman nobility.[82] Just as the jewels surpassed in beauty anything made in Italy, so were the Stuarts meant to overtop the local grandees. There could be no doubting their success that evening.

5

Falling backward
(1739–42)

Historical inevitability is a seductive doctrine. From the standpoint of the twentieth century it is easy to make the mistake of seeing the Jacobite movement as inevitably doomed, and the Jacobite risings as mere 'local difficulties' along the line of march of a triumphant Hanoverian succession. Both the 'Whig theory of history', championed by Macaulay and his successors, and the Namierite orthodoxy that supplanted it in the twentieth century, consigned Jacobitism to the waste bin of history, the former explicitly, the latter by implication. It is only in very recent years that scholars have come to appreciate the gravity of the threat posed to the Whig/Hanover system by the exiled Stuarts.[1]

The revisionist view depends largely on shedding preconceptions and judgments by hindsight and returning to the original sources. If we view the period up to 1750 not through the distorting lens of nearly two hundred and fifty years of later history but as seen by contemporaries, a very different picture of the importance of Jacobitism emerges. From politicians at the apex of the élite, like Sir Robert Walpole, Lord Chesterfield and Lord Chancellor Hardwicke, we discern an anxiety about the Jacobite threat amounting at times almost to hysteria. This is reflected in the work of the literary jackals who paid deference to these lions, especially Henry Fielding and Daniel Defoe.

The Hanoverian dynasty, and its unflinching ally in Parliament from 1715–61, the Whigs – the party of Walpole, the Pelhams and the elder Pitt – knew that it was vulnerable to the Jacobite challenge on a number of grounds. The German kings were widely unpopular, their culture alien, their interests continental. It was the received opinion of the time that English foreign policy was almost entirely a function of the interests of the German state of Hanover. Walpole's system of patronage – 'Old Corruption' – bought off some critics, but not nearly enough. Its benefits were restricted to a small élite. Excluded was not just the gentry but the mass of the 'middling sort' of people. The social basis of the Whig/Hanoverian ascendancy was tenuous and precarious.

Moreover, on ideological grounds the supporters of the Hanoverian *status quo* could not discredit Jacobitism effectively.[2] The Whig prescription of political quietism recommended to its critics was refuted by the behaviour of the founding fathers of the 'Glorious Revolution' in 1688. The very powerful 'Country' critique of Whig corruption used by the Tories and other political dissidents inside England was endorsed and co-opted by the Jacobites. The Jacobites, too, had the attraction that they advanced beyond merely abstract denunciation of the Walpole political system and held out the hope that they might actually destroy it. The one trump card Walpole and the Hanoverian kings held was the Stuarts' religion. Anti-Catholicism was a powerful bugbear which Walpole's propagandists never ceased to exploit, even though one of the more ingenious black propagandists, Defoe, himself admitted that he knew of 'ten thousand stout fellows that would shed the last drop of their blood against popery that do not know whether it be a man or a horse'.[3]

The older historical view held that Walpole cynically played the Jacobite card for his own ends throughout the twenty years of his hegemony (1721–42), that he had no real fear of Jacobitism, that, moreover, the Whigs genuinely feared the 'popery' and 'arbitrary tyranny' of the Stuarts. The newer 'revisionist' view demonstrates that Walpole was not bluffing: he really did fear the Jacobites and all their works, and his fear had a much more solid basis than the religious scruples to which he and his acolytes paid lip-service.

Walpole's state was poised between an older landed class declining in power and a new rising aristocracy of money. It was thus in that limbo later memorably dubbed the 'half-state', not yet strong enough to beat off all challengers. The peculiar fear held by all beneficiaries of this inchoate capitalist system was that the Stuarts, if restored to power, would dismantle it in all three of its aspects, agrarian, financial and commercial. Not only would a triumphant Catholic dynasty have to do something about former church lands. It would surely also cancel the national debt, thus ruining fundholders, and would make commercial concessions to France in India and America as the price of Bourbon help in the Jacobite restoration.[4]

The fears entertained by the Hanoverian élite had a firm basis in fact. It was no secret that Scotland had been extraordinarily discontented ever since the 1707 Act of Union, especially since the expected benefits of opening colonial trade to Scottish merchants had not yet materialised. Ireland was a simmering cauldron, controlled by a mixture of carrot and stick: draconian penal laws whose importance was in their bite rather than their bark, since the Catholic gentry was co-opted by the very lax implementation of those penal laws.[5] Add to this the endemic riots and discontents of mainland England – disturbances which were often legitimised by reference to 'King James'[6] – and it can well be appreciated that Walpole and his followers often felt themselves to be perched on the edge of a rumbling volcano. Those who supported the Hanoverian dynasty genuinely feared the Jacobite threat, and they were right to do so.

But the Jacobites in turn threw away most of their chances. The failure of the 1715 rising was followed by an even greater fiasco in the rising of 1719. The year 1722 saw the failure of the important Layer/Atterbury plot in England. And any chance of constructing a grand European alliance against England was ruined for James in 1725 when Clementina left him. The credibility of the Jacobite movement was in tatters.

Then 1726 brought further problems for the Jacobites. France was always the key to restoration of the Stuarts, yet for seventeen years (1726–43) French policy was dominated by Cardinal Fleury, whose foreign policy can be summed up as 'peace at any price'. André Hercule de Fleury, bishop of Fréjus had been the infant Louis XV's tutor since 1715. The astute restraint with which he opposed the duc de Bourbon during the latter's tenure of supreme power in France (1723–6) assured his succession as first minister, as also his elevation to the purple. Fleury's pacific policies were echoed across the Channel by Walpole's cautious approach to foreign affairs. After 1727 there was no longer any hope for the Stuarts from Austria, or, after 1730, from Russia.

Yet, though moribund, Jacobitism did not die. In the years when Charles Edward was growing to manhood, it performed three extremely important functions. For the Tories in England it provided a countervailing ideology and source of inspiration. The proscription of the Tory party after 1715 and the barring of office-holding to its luminaries produced a sense of desperation that could be assuaged with hopes of a Stuart restoration. Walpole's branding of the Tory party as crypto-Jacobite became a self-fulfilling prophecy. Increasingly the English Tories saw Jacobite rescue as the only way out of an apparently endless sentence in the political wilderness.[7]

Second, in the first half of the eighteenth century it was the Jacobite movement that provided the checks and balances against the Whig/Hanoverian system. Curiously, in this way Jacobitism may have helped to head off revolution in England. With no internal brake, French absolutism careered unchecked towards catastrophe at the end of the century. The Hanoverian state, at least until 1760, had to rein in the worst excesses of executive power for fear of the political alternative across the water.[8]

Third, Jacobitism as an international force provided the 'ultimate deterrent' by means of which continental powers could obstruct British expansionism. It was bad luck for the Jacobites that France was unwilling to confront England during the 1720s and 1730s because England was not yet clearly perceived as the major threat to French global interests.[9]

Yet by the late 1730s rumours of war abounded. At the same time, for quite other reasons, discontent began to build in the Highlands, always the Jacobites' military nucleus. Charles Edward undoubtedly seemed to be the right man in the right place at the right time.

The Glenbucket mission to Rome in 1737–8 is sometimes credited with being the first cause in a chain of events that eventually precipitated the 1745 rising.[10] John Gordon of Glenbucket brought James word that the Highlands were in a ferment, that now was the time for a combined operation: a Jacobite rising in Scotland and a French invasion of England. James responded by sending one of his aides, William Hay, to Scotland on an intelligence mission. Hay was introduced into Scottish Jacobite circles by John Murray of Broughton (who had met Charles Edward in Rome in 1737 and was later to be his secretary during the '45). An association of Scottish Jacobites was formed, including Lord John Drummond senior, the duke of Perth, Lord Lovat, Lord Linton (later earl of Traquair), Donald Cameron of Lochiel and William MacGregor of Balhaldy. In the early 1740s the most important of these was Balhaldy, for on instructions from James he went to Paris to work in harness with the Stuart agent Lord Sempill.

James, who had always complained bitterly about Jacobite factionalism, helped to compound it by employing O'Brien and Sempill as parallel agents, now confiding his most secret dealings with the French to one, now to the other. But it is clear that Sempill and Balhaldy, largely by 'expedient exaggerations' forced the pace of Jacobite negotiations with Fleury along more forcefully than the sobersided and diplomatic O'Brien. Under their prompting, Fleury's first instinct was to trigger a Jacobite rising in the Highlands, using Spanish troops.

Spain and England had been getting ever closer to warfare in the 1730s over British contraband commerce with the closed trading area of Spanish America, and Spanish use of its *guardacostas* to intercept British smugglers. In 1739 this tension broke out into open warfare, the 'War of Jenkins's Ear'. In the early stages of the conflict, in the Caribbean, the Spanish held their own. They lost Portobello to Admiral Vernon, but when Vernon attacked Cartagena they beat him off with heavy losses. It made sense, then, for the Jacobites to co-ordinate their plots with Spain.

The most obvious way to do this was to send Charles Edward to Madrid. But at this juncture James, who had been pressing hard the year before for such an invitation, became circumspect. The ghost of the failure of the 1719 rising, engineered by Spain, haunted James.[11] It was quite clear that any Spanish enterprise would have to be directed against Scotland. But what James really wanted was a foreign invasion of *England*. This could come only from France. Moreover, James was not even certain that Spain was in earnest over a Scottish expedition: might they not simply be intending to use Charles Edward as a scarecrow? And the Pope was far from convinced that the Spanish would press hard enough for a Catholic restoration in England.[12]

This papal angle soon became crucial in more ways than one. Clement XII had promised a large sum of money to back the proposed Hispano-Jacobite scheme, but before the financial details could be ratified he fell dangerously ill. It was thought best to wait and see whether the Pontiff would pull through and, if not, who would succeed him, before committing Charles Edward to Spain.[13]

The winter weather of 1739–40 was singularly harsh. Not only did it carry off the ailing Pope, but it meant there was no question of the prince's leaving for Spain before the spring. When spring came, James took one of his rare firm decisions. His elder son's going to Spain was no longer even discussed. There were three main reasons for the decision. The first was the negative reports James was receiving from his representatives Ormonde and Marischal in Madrid. The count of Montemar ordered the two Jacobite emissaries to leave Madrid for the coast of Galicia, where they (and later the prince) would join an expedition to Scotland. Neither Ormonde nor Marischal believed the Spanish were sincere and asked for further assurances. Montemar became angry and tried to browbeat the Jaco-

bites – precisely the wrong tactics with proud and obstinate men like
Ormonde and Marischal.

A series of acrimonious meetings took place, at the end of which
Marischal reported to James that the court at Madrid was patently
insincere.[14] The last thing Elizabeth Farnese wanted was a military
stroke that would bring a quick end to the war with England. Moreover, the openness with which Charles Edward's advent was talked
about in Spain meant that the military project must be bogus. The
Spanish were so contemptuous of the Jacobites and so cavalier in
their tacit admission that they were merely using the Stuarts that
they could not even tell a consistent story. While the line being fed
to Ormonde and Marischal concerned an expedition from Galician
ports to Scotland, the rumours being put about by Spain in France
were to do with a descent on Ireland from Cadiz, using the prince.[15]

The second factor that gave James pause was the uncertainty over
the new Pope. The conclave that eventually produced Benedict XIV
was one of the longest in the history of the papacy. Clement XII
died in February 1740 and his successor was not chosen until
August.[16] Until he was sure he did not have another Benedict XIII
to deal with, James did not want to take any momentous decisions.

Third, anti-Spanish feeling engendered by the capture of Portobello
was running so strongly in 1740 that the time did not seem propitious
to James to launch a rising with Spanish help. The widespread hatred
for Spain in England meant that a Spanish bid to restore the Stuarts
at this juncture would be counterproductive.[17] It would be all too
easy for Whig propaganda to convert the social discontent that in a
time of peace would work in favour of the Jacobites into anti-Stuart
feeling by playing on this theme. Moreover, after the loss of Portobello
the Spanish themselves laid aside all ideas about invading the British
Isles. They remained on the defensive, building up their strength for
a counterattack in the Americas, It was clear that there had been no
co-ordination between Spain and France; as James clearly saw, the
trouble was that France could restore him without Spain but not vice
versa.[18]

The emphasis therefore shifted back to France. There was no more
talk of the prince's going to Madrid. It was now Paris that was the
favoured destination.[19] The obvious problem here was that, whereas
Spain and England were in a state of declared war, France was
still carrying on overt hostilities against England under a guise of
neutrality. Such a pretence would be impossible to maintain if France
made an open invitation to Charles Edward.

Yet the outbreak of general European war in 1740 did bring one advantage to the prince. The new Pope was friendly to the Stuarts. Fleury was under great pressure to declare war on England. A new Jacobite era seemed to be taking shape. Mindful that his son's political experience had been limited so far, to say the least, James finally made Charles Edward a full member of his council and had him present at all meetings.[20]

By now the prince's thoughts were concentrating strongly on Scotland. He wrote to the clans in September 1740, pledging that he would soon put into execution a project for their deliverance from the Hanoverian yoke.[21] It can thus be seen that his choice of Scotland as a launching pad for a rising in 1745 was no mere spur-of-the moment affair. Indeed the volume of traffic between Rome and Scotland at this time convinced Horace Mann, the English agent in Florence, that a descent on the northern kingdom, possibly to coincide with Charles Edward's majority, would not be long delayed.[22]

It was already an open secret that France would bring the prince to Versailles as soon as war was declared on England.[23] But when would that be? Some further means had to be found to turn the screws on Fleury. James was at this time in close touch with Cardinal Tencin, French representative in Rome. Unfortunately, James always overrated both the influence and ability of this prelate. Tencin was basically a nonentity who had risen to a position near the top of the French hierarchy through his sister's influence. The real talent in the Tencin family was Claudine Alexandrine (1681–1749). By this time she was well past the peak of her influence, but in her day, as notable beauty and novelist, she had dazzled France. Her lovers had included Louis XV's regent the duc d'Orleans and his partner in the sordid French politics of 1715–23 Cardinal Dubois. She had even served time in the Bastille, when one of the legion of her lovers shot himself in her house (1726).[24] Tencin had been elevated to the purple on James's nomination and was already being tipped as a future successor to Fleury as *de facto* Prime Minister. On his advice James began to look around for suitable marriage partners for the prince, to increase his credibility in French eyes and make an alliance with the Stuarts seem politically more desirable.

The first candidate proposed, in August 1740, was his cousin the Princesse de Bouillon. Such a match would have given Charles Edward a secure base in Poland, but would have taken him rather far from the main cockpit of political action.[25] More promising was the Princesse de Conti, then aged fourteen and in a convent, but said to be charming in both mind and body.[26] There were obvious advantages in a marriage with a Bourbon princess. O'Brien was willing to press Fleury for the match, against the competing claims of the duc de Chartres, but James decided that since it was still realistic to hope for a Stuart restoration, he could aim higher.[27] At the moment his sights were set on a princess of Spain or France.

At the beginning of 1741 Tencin suggested to James that the Princess of Massa, said recently to have broken off her engagement to the Prince of Modena, would be a suitable partner for his son. This princess was extremely wealthy and the marriage would give the Stuarts a territorial base on which they could, if necessary, live and drill their own army. Moreover, the match would have important political sponsors. The grand duke of Tuscany was fearful that the duke of Modena had plans to build a road between his duchy and Massa and install internal customs barriers in competition with those of Tuscany. The failure of the Massa/Modena dynastic alliance would effectively scotch this plan. Finally, he, Tencin, was prepared to guarantee that Spain and France would make over Corsica to the prince as a wedding present.[28]

While James dithered over this proposal, the duke of Modena, alerted to the danger of a Stuart competitor, dropped the previous conditions he had set for marriage to the Princess of Massa and pressed ahead rapidly with the union.[29] Despairing of a successful outcome there, Tencin suggested the duchess of Turin, a millionairess; but James's appetite for minor Italian principalities and duchies had never been keen.[30]

Throughout 1742 and early 1743 James took exhaustive soundings to determine whether there was any possibility of a marriage with one of Louis XV's young daughters.[31] The project had the backing of Stanislas of Lorraine (ex-king of Poland and Louis XV's father-in-law) and of the Jesuits. A favourite idea was that the French king's second daughter could become queen of an independent Scotland.[32] The death of Fleury in January 1743 raised James's hopes, but it soon became clear that, whatever France's future plans for the Stuart prince were, they did not include such a dynastic union. Before any further marriage projects could be set on foot the prince had left Rome for good.

It was always unlikely that the French court would entertain a marriage proposal from the Stuarts, since they could not even make up their minds to invite Charles Edward to campaign with their armies. After the Spanish venue for the prince had been dropped, three tiresome years passed in sustained lobbying by the Stuarts at Versailles, answered by equally assiduous French stalling.[33] There were frequent rumours that Charles had left Rome for France, which were as frequently denied.[34]

These rumours reached a crescendo on Tencin's recall from Rome in the spring of 1742.[35] It was feared that Tencin's departure could be used to mask the sudden disappearance of the prince.[36] There was no foundation in any of these rumours. In fact so dejected was James by the French court's repeated prevarications that he even toyed with sending his son to serve with Frederick of Prussia.[37]

Yet if there was nothing but disappointment for the Stuarts from the French as the War of Austrian Succession pursued its tortuous course, Charles Edward personally could congratulate himself on two counts. In the first place, the new Pope Benedict XIV seemed as impressed by him as his predecessor.[38] This was not simple continuity of policy. Benedict (Prospero Lambertini) was the outstanding Pope of the eighteenth century. His erudition, wit and humanity easily qualified him for the title of philosopher-king.[39] To win such a man's approbation was not easy. Anyone who has ever doubted the charisma of Charles Edward Stuart should ponder the impression he made on such a Pope. There can be no doubting the Pontiff's genuine warmth towards the prince. The frequency of their meetings alone is a salient pointer.[40] Indeed, on many significant indices Benedict showed himself even more committed to Charles than Clement had been. On his twentieth birthday the prince was given a present of 4,000 scudi in gold coins.[41] In June 1742, when the Stuarts went for their *villegiatura* at Albano, the Pope sent them an armed guard as a sign of his esteem, and on the 18th of that month came out to the Palazzo Savelli to visit them.[42] Benedict was also deeply involved throughout 1743 in the protracted negotiations to try to get Charles Edward to Paris.[43]

The other development was the prince's central and ever increasing role in the Jacobite movement, especially after he had passed his majority. Once Charles had been given a seat on James's council, he routinely read dispatches from foreign agents and ministers, even the highly confidential ones, as from Fleury. Whenever James held private meetings with important contacts (such as Tencin's nephew Bailli de Tencin), Charles Edward would be summoned immediately afterwards and given a summary of the meeting. It was customary for father and son to visit the Pope together. In the early days Charles Edward would depart from the meeting early, leaving James in private conclave with the Pontiff. Yet by early 1743 he was not only remaining the full hour with his father, but was actually staying on longer while James retired early.[44]

On 30 December 1741 Charles Edward attained his majority. He celebrated by giving a grand ball for the nobility of Rome.[45] James received the compliments of the pro-Jacobite cardinals. Although the prince was still a virtual prisoner in Italy and lacked a wider arena in which to exercise his talents, the year 1742 saw him very much as he would appear in Scotland three years later. What general picture can we provide of the prince as he stood at the threshold of his high adventure?

That he already possessed all the physical attributes of the warrior has already been demonstrated. A crack shot and superb horseman, his one deficiency was a lack of real military experience. For all the enthusiasm over his behaviour at Gaeta, it remained the case that he had seen just six hours' active service, and not even in the front line at that.

Intellectually, too, the prince had not kept pace with his achievements as marksman and hunter. His early life demonstrates an impatience and lack of concern with academic learning.[46] This is not to say that he was unintelligent (it is in any case an elementary error to confuse 'intelligent' with 'intellectual' or even vice versa), but simply that at this stage in his life the importance of reflective study had not been borne in upon him.[47] James emphasised its importance; therefore, in Charles Edward's eyes, it must be suspect.

Dunbar proved singularly useless as the prince's governor. His attentions were largely elsewhere, brooding on the threats to his position in the Stuart household and the rival claims for the king's affection of the absent Inverness and Marischal. That left only Sheridan, and his mode was shameless pampering. One result of this defective education was that Charles Edward was always an indifferent letter-writer in the formal sense.[48] His true mental qualities emerge more clearly in his own jottings and aide-mémoires. As we shall see, this inability, except on rare occasions, to communicate his sharper insights to others, is an important clue to his psychological make-up.

Too much should not be made, however, of the prince's notoriously bad spelling. Charles's quasi-italic impersonal handwriting doubtless offended nineteenth-century sensibilities more than it does those of the twentieth, where legibility is prized above 'character'. As for his eccentric orthography, one does not need to bring in the late twentieth-century diagnosis of 'dyslexia' to appreciate that poor spelling, though an irritant, need not necessarily be the final consideration when it comes to assessing a person's intelligence. Frederick the Great and Napoleon were also affected by this literary deficiency.

Against these defects can be set the prince's rare personal qualities. There is so much direct and indirect evidence of his charisma and ability to charm when he so chose that it is pointless to deny that he possessed personal magnetism of a rare order. This is an elusive and indefinable quality, all the harder to pin down since none of the extant portraits of the prince as a young man show him as conventionally handsome, either by eighteenth-century standards or our own. His features were somewhat spoiled by a sloping forehead and a long chin with a button point; the fact that the nape of his neck was bull-like did not recommend his looks to contemporary taste either. Like most of the Stuarts (Mary Queen of Scots is a well-known example) Charles Edward was well above average height. He was about five feet eleven inches tall, was long-faced, high-nosed, possessed the distinctive sensual Stuart lips, and had a ruddy complexion, large, melancholy rolling brown eyes and reddish hair. A description of the prince by Murray of Broughton in 1742 is useful as it makes exactly the point that it was not Charles's individual features that made the physical impact but rather the whole personality:

Tall, above the common stature; his limbs are cast in the most exact mould; his complexion has in it somewhat of uncommon delicacy. All his features are perfectly regular and well-turned; and his eyes the finest I ever saw. But which shines most in him and renders him, without exception, the most surprisingly handsome person of the age, is the dignity that accompanies every gesture. There is indeed such an unspeakable majesty diffused through his whole mien, and such as it is impossible to have any idea of without seeing; and strikes those that have with such an awe as will not suffer them to look on him for any time, unless he emboldens them to it by his excessive affability.[49]

In view of his later difficulties with women, it is worth noting that there is little sign of an 'objective' problem here. The problem lay in the prince's mind. All evidence, now and later, suggests that women were deeply attracted to him and that he reciprocated, at least superficially.[50]

A comparison with his brother Henry is instructive. Opinions were divided among contemporaries as to which prince was the more impressive. The consensus was that although Henry was superior in cunning and took to academic pursuits more easily, Charles Edward was actually the more intelligent of the two.[51] An observer in 1742 summed it up well: Charles Edward, he claimed, had a quicker mind than Henry but Henry, conscious of this, bridged the gap by hard work. Although both were well-bred and good-natured, Charles Edward had the edge in intuitive knowledge and understanding of the world, was considerate and reasonable in conversation and never spoke without thinking.[52] Moreover, all but zealot observers contrasted favourably the prince's lukewarmness about religion with Henry's increasing religious mania, already very evident by 1742.[53] It was also clear that Henry tried to emulate his brother and tried his hand at anything at which Charles was successful. This extended even to the game of *trucco in terra*, of which they both became devotees.[54]

Another contrast, written in November of the same year, comes from secretary Edgar:

> He [the prince] fatigues at that diversion [hunting] so much that nobody here can keep up with him, even a servant or two that are clever fellows have more than enough to do it, and if he were where we wish him, I doubt if I could find many that would not tire with the constant fatigue and exercise he takes. His brother takes a great deal of exercise also. Sometimes he goes out a'shooting, but has not such a delight in it as the Prince and sometimes he takes the air on horseback. At night, after a day's strong fatigue, the Prince sits down and diverts himself at music for an hour or two as if he had not been abroad, and plays his part upon the bass viol very well, for he loves and understands music to a great degree. His brother does not understand it as well but he sings, when he pleases, much better.[55]

Perhaps the reason Henry, a much lesser personality than the prince, attracted so many favourable opinions was simply that as a boy he was better-looking. The word used by so many travellers to Rome in the 1730s to describe James's second son was 'merry'. His features were more regular than Charles Edward's and his demeanour more smiling. His portraits show him to have been a very pretty child with wide, sparkling hazel eyes. He was shorter and more delicately built than his brother, But like so many pretty children, he turned out plain as an adult. The sunny disposition vanished to be replaced by a kind of dour narcissism. Charles Edward always retained his fair, reddish colouring but Henry in middle age looked dark and swarthy.

Henry is a key figure in the understanding of Charles Edward's psychological development, and to some extent represents 'the road not taken'. This is a complex skein to unravel, but, simplifying, we may say that the Henry solution – the way in which a given genetic inheritance interacted with the unique experience of the Stuart family context – was that of submission and internalisation. The later emergence of the 'Cardinal-King' as a homosexual personality reflects the disaster of his childhood.

Charles Edward's experience, and therefore his solution, was different. His precious first five years with his mother were enough to give him a predominantly heterosexual personality. But the ensuing years of trauma and her early death left him with a reservoir of unconscious guilt. This in turn produced the cluster of psychological near-relations of guilt which undoubtedly informed the prince's later behaviour: depression, rage, paranoia.[56] The lack of a satisfactory family life left Charles a dreadful legacy. Ever afterwards he evinced clear signs of an unstable ego, a self in danger of fragmentation, an uncertain identity, and a general sensitivity and vulnerability.[57]

Another aspect of such a personality is compulsive secretiveness. The refusal to expose oneself totally for the inspection of others bespeaks an excessive vulnerability, a refusal to run the risk of being hurt. Secretive Charles Edward certainly was, as we shall see later. At this stage in his career, the tendency manifested itself in a secret correspondence carried on with the English Jacobites – a correspondence that came to light only when James sorted through his son's effects two years later.[58]

From 1742, the one clearly discernible strand in Charles Edward's personality was the total lack of any mechanism for dealing with authority, and hence a fatally blurred distinction between his own will and reality. In February of that year cardinals Tencin and Acquaviva found James seriously despondent over Charles Edward's inability to take direction and over the possible consequences of the prince's overdeveloped willpower.[59] But James could scarcely escape responsibility for the way his son had turned out. Repressive in the areas where he should have been indulgent, weak where he should have been strong, manifestly preferring Henry to Charles, James elicited in the prince a deep contempt, whose dimensions were to be seen only later when father and son were geographically separate.

Most significantly of all, James had never acted the true role of parent, so as to enable the prince to reach adulthood. He had never shown him that authority could have a caring, healing and therapeutic aspect. The consequence was not only that the prince had to look for a replacement father, but whenever he found suitable 'father-figures' (like Lord George Murray or the Earl Marischal), he was forced to quarrel with them all in turn (i.e. to 'kill' them symbolically) in order to reach maturity. Such was the prince on the eve of his great adventures.

6

'Father's Sorrow, father's joy'
(1743–4)

The year 1743 brought a dramatic upsurge in Jacobite fortunes. The death of Fleury in January at the age of 90 removed the principal barrier to outright French support for the House of Stuart. At first Jacobite hopes seemed dashed once again when Louis XV announced that henceforth he would be his own Prime Minister; the expectation in the Palazzo Muti had been that Tencin would succeed Fleury. But Louis's own inclinations and the tide of events in the war, especially in Germany, soon led him to contemplate seriously a descent on England.

A decisive prod in this direction was Sempill's memoir to the French court in spring 1743, in the name of the leading English Jacobites, asking for a French invasion to restore the Stuarts.[1] This was a highly significant development. At last the French seemed to be hearing about conditions in England from the horse's mouth. This was a very different matter from the formulaic and predictable assurances that England was ripe for revolution, delivered periodically to Versailles by James.

Much encouraged by this new Jacobite bearing, Louis XV sent his master of horse James Butler on a fact-finding mission to England – the pretext was buying horses for the royal stables. Butler spent August and September 1743 in England. He returned to Versailles in October with a glowing report on the strength of Jacobitism in the British Isles. That was good enough for the French king. He now had both motive and opportunity for an invasion.

Full-scale planning for the project was set in train in November. Louis XV demonstrated his seriousness by writing to Philip V of Spain in his own hand to put him in the picture.[2]

What was James's position in all this? It has to be remembered that at the beginning of 1743 all talk of Charles Edward's departure still concerned possible service in the French army in Flanders or Germany. At this stage the Jacobites' best hope was that the prince would take part in an invasion of Hanover.[3] But as 1743 wore on, and whispers began to be heard in Rome that the French were contemplating some bold stroke against England, James's eagerness to send his elder son to France gave way to circumspection and indecisiveness. Always determined that Charles Edward should not be in France simply as a French dupe or to act as a 'scarecrow' against the English, James now raised a further query with Tencin (since 1742 a minister of state on Louis XV's great council of state): if a serious French project was on foot, would not the prince's presence in France alert the English and put them on their guard?[4]

James faced two major problems. First how serious were the French and what role in their schemes did they envisage for the prince? Second, assuming he could be reassured on French sincerity, there was the mechanical or physical problem of how Charles Edward got from Rome to Paris. The stumbling block here was the great Mediterranean plague, which was cutting a swathe through the Latin countries in 1743. As a result of its ravages, a *cordon sanitaire* had been thrown around the papal states. A strict quarantine was in force. There were alarming rumours that the virus had reached as far as Reggio in Calabria. Even communication with the outside world by letter was difficult. Rome in 1743 was to a large extent cut off from the rest of civilisation.[5]

A letter from James to Lord Sempill in September 1743 succinctly shows James's state of mind:

I never solicited the prince's coming into France in this juncture, for though I have long wished that he should be out of this country, and that he might have leave to make a campaign, yet I feared any motion of his at the present would give an alarm to the English government, who ought to be kept asleep and without suspicion till all be ready to attack them in good earnest. But if with all that the French should be really serious to have him in France, I think it would be wrong not to comply with their desire, whatever may be their view in it. Though should his removal from hence and his presence in France be never so necessary, I don't see how I could send him thither at this time with tolerable prudence and precaution for his safety unless the French themselves can fall on some method for that effect, since the quarantine by land makes all passages impracticable for him by that way, and that the English fleet render it extreme hazardous by sea.[6]

There was some easing of the situation by September, when it was found that the plague seemed to have been halted in its tracks in Calabria, but the basic problem remained.[7] James received conflicting advice on the proposed journey. Tencin recommended travel in small Maltese boats. Jacobites like O'Brien, on the other hand, argued that only in extreme emergency should the prince's person be hazarded at sea; the most he risked on land was arrest.[8] James at this juncture inclined to sending his son on a roundabout route via Switzerland.[9] It is clear that James would only have released his son for the journey to Paris after a pressing invitation from the French court. One of the puzzles surrounding the years 1743–4 has always been that, after the failure of the 1744 invasion attempt, Louis XV tried to lay the blame for the débâcle on Charles Edward's sudden appearance at Versailles in February 1744, at the most critical moment of the enterprise.[10]

The French had to balance security considerations against the desirability of quickening the Jacobite fifth column in England. The English Jacobites had promised to meet any French invading force landing in Essex with their own raw levies, provided Charles Edward arrived with the king's manifesto and the powers of regency. Only thus could the French descent be presented to the English people as an attempt at Stuart restoration rather than an invasion proper. On the other hand, since France intended to invade England without warning and without a declaration of war, the mere presence of the Stuart prince on French soil would alert the English to what was afoot.[11] How to square this circle was one of the principal subjects of discussion in Versailles in the second half of 1743.

A further complication affecting the investigation into who invited Charles Edward to France is that the discussions in the council of state on this topic were held on a hypothetical or contingency basis only. Louis XV, for whom duplicity was almost a conditioned reflex, did not confide the true details of the 1743–4 invasion project to all his ministers of state.[12] Foreign Minister Amelot and Navy Minister Maurepas were closely involved in the day-to-day planning, but Finance Minister Orry, Minister of War comte d'Argenson and Minister without Portfolio duc de Noailles were informed of the project only at the last minute. Even the pro-Jacobite Tencin, the last of the six ministers of state, was held at arm's length.

The exclusion of the royal favourite Noailles is particularly surprising, but Louis XV knew he would be opposed to a pro-Jacobite venture and did not wish to hear views differing from his own. The issue of whether to invite Charles Edward to France was largely discussed by the ministers in a vacuum, as if it related merely to military service on the Continent.

But by the time Butler returned from England with his mission successfully accomplished, the devious Louis XV had hit on a solution to the Charles Edward conundrum. The trick was to acquire the Jacobite manifestoes and declarations to the people of England without having Charles Edward in tow. By a sleight of hand Louis could contrive it so that the prince arrived in Paris only after the expedition's commander-designate, the comte de Saxe, had captured London. Charles Edward would then cross the Channel to ratify the French conquest. In this way the forces of the Jacobite fifth column would be successfully energised. while full secrecy was maintained right up to French landfall.

Accordingly Louis summoned Balhaldy and requested him to go to Rome on a confidential mission. His instructions were to travel to the Eternal City via Switzerland, bearing a letter of invitation for the prince addressed to James. Balhaldy made ready to depart. Eight days later he was informed that there would be no letter. Although his mission to Rome was still on, he was to discourage Charles Edward from setting out for Paris until the invasion was launched. Smelling a rat, Balhaldy asked for some form of written assurance for James.[13] He was told this would be forthcoming and ordered to hold himself in readiness for a sudden departure.

On 23 November, at Fontainebleau, the day before he was due to depart, Balhaldy received the king's instructions that he was to set out without a letter; the letter was deemed 'inadvisable for security reasons'. At the final briefing session with Amelot, Balhaldy asked how he was supposed to convince James of French good faith without a letter from the king. Amelot assured him that this would be sent once the expedition had set sail. Balhaldy realised that Louis XV was manipulating him (he claimed that the king had learned artfulness and cunning from Fleury, 'Old Papa Fréjus, as the king named him'), but felt it impolitic to insist on a letter.

He tried one last time for some documentary evidence of French *bona fides*. Amelot produced a passport for the prince.[14] At the conclusion of the interview Balhaldy asked Amelot for some specific date of departure he might mention to James. Amelot plucked the date of 12 January 1744 out of the air. In this one specific date lay the undoing of Louis XV's carefully nurtured piece of arch-cunning.

The dimensions of Louis XV's subterfuge are now plain. He sent

Balhaldy to Rome to get 'legitimating' material from James, informing him that there was a serious invasion project in hand, and that
France would call Charles Edward to join in later. Louis thus hoped
to get all he needed from James but still to keep the prince at Rome,
relying on James's characteristic trait of doing everything by the
book. He had reckoned without two things: the prince's stubborn
determination to get out of Rome; and Amelot's careless slip of the
tongue.

Balhaldy arrived in Rome on 19 December 1743 after a nightmarish
journey through the snows of Switzerland.[15] He found Charles
Edward straining at the leash, with everything ready for a swift
departure. James's declarations for England and Scotland and his
commission of regency for the prince had been printed.[16] After shrugging off an attack of 'flu earlier in the year,[17] Charles had brought
himself back to a key pitch of physical fitness through hunting.[18]

Balhaldy spent six days in Rome, until Christmas Day, reporting
French thinking to James.[19] He pointed out that the only specific task
assigned to him by Louis XV was to bring back the manifestoes and
declarations, but that there was a definite expedition afoot. James
was puzzled. If the French king had wanted to send him a message,
why a verbal one through Balhaldy? Why not through the established
channels via Tencin and his nephew Bailli? James still did not have
the measure of Louis XV's duplicity. He did not realise that Tencin
was not privy to the king's secrets.[20] Moreover, Machiavellianism of
this kind in a brother monarch would not have been suspected by
the ingenuous James.

The Jacobite monarch's every instinct told him to get a definite
written commitment from the French king. He dashed off a letter to
Louis, thanking him for Balhaldy's message and telling him he had
postponed Charles Edward's departure until he got a clearer light
from France.[21] Here was another error. If James had written directly
to Amelot, he might have received an express from the Foreign
Minister, telling him on no account to send the prince. But this letter
to Louis was never answered, either through the king's indolence or
because the missive got snarled up in French bureaucracy (either is
plausible).[22]

At this moment Charles Edward himself made a fateful entry into
the negotiations. Now thoroughly frustrated after years of prevarication from France, he pressed Balhaldy hard for evidence that the
French would welcome him on their territory. It is unclear what
Balhaldy said. Somehow mention of a departure date of 12 January

1744 seeped out. That was enough for the prince. Brandishing this evidence, he plagued his father to let him go.

James questioned Balhaldy further. It was obvious that this time there really was a French invasionary force poised to strike across the Channel; this was no feint. Balhaldy explained the strategy of a surprise attack: a bolt from the blue to redress the serious French reverses in Germany. Moreover, it was clear from the fact of Balhaldy's mission alone that the French were convinced of the strength of the English Jacobite party and wanted Stuart support. And there was the clinching factor of the date mentioned by Amelot as a likely one for the prince's departure. Suppressing his misgivings about the lack of a direct written invitation, James bowed to the combined arguments of Balhaldy and his son. He outlined his own objections, but left it to the prince to decide.[23] There could be only one choice. It was settled that Charles Edward would indeed depart for France in early January. All that remained was to decide the itinerary.

Here Balhaldy proved extremely helpful. The route he had just travelled, through Switzerland, was out, he told the king. So too was a wholly overland passage. Apart from the rains and snow, and the dreadful roads ruined by frost, all frontiers were being carefully guarded because of the plague. Every traveller was rigorously examined on who he was, where he was from and where he was going to. In Genoese territory a fifteen-day quarantine period was imposed on everyone, irrespective of rank. Moreover, the king of Genoa forbade embarcation on a *felucca*, effectively putting the Viareggio route out of the reckoning. And the coast road from Genoa to Antibes via Monaco was thronged and clustered with customs barriers and anti-plague quarantine posts. The sole plausible route was overland through Tuscany and Genoa and thence by sea to Antibes.[24]

James agreed that travel through Lombardy – where his son might be examined before the governors of various towns and his identity discovered – was too perilous. There was not the same risk in Tuscany. The going would be tough, but he relied on his son's stamina to see him through. The one thing neither James nor Balhaldy foresaw was the quarantine regulations in force at Antibes.[25]

Balhaldy departed from Rome on Christmas Day. Travelling at great speed through Tuscany and northern Italy, he reached Paris on 3 January 1744.[26] In Rome final preparations were pushed ahead for the prince's momentous journey.

The first task was to outwit the English spies in Italy. Sir Horace

Mann, the British Resident in Florence, maintained a formidable stable of agents, who dogged the prince's every move, reporting the trivia of his daily life. It was time to use their meticulous vigilance against them.

Foreseeing that the prince might some day want to make a swift getaway, James had obtained papal permission for the gates of Rome to be opened for his son at whatever hour of day or night he chose to go hunting. The usual bureaucracy surrounding the opening of the city gates was waived.[27] This meant that there should be no hold-ups in Rome itself.

Next a trial run into the country had to be essayed, to see if there were any snags that had been overlooked. On 4 January 1744 the prince sent out a two-man scouting party on the road to Massa.[28] His emissaries bore letters from the governor of posts, guaranteeing them horses. The reconnaissance mission soon proved its worth. The postmaster of Baccano, sixteen miles from Rome, refused the prince's men horses because they had not started 'post' from Rome.[29] This was a vital tip-off to Charles Edward not to start the journey with his own horses.

It now transpired that a most convenient cover story had presented itself. The prince had a long-standing invitation to go hunting on the duke of Caserta's estates in Cisterna. The season's hunting this year commenced on 9 January. Bringing his departure date forward three days, Charles Edward sent his household out to Cisterna on 7 January to make the usual preparations, oiling and cleaning his guns and setting up the cello in his chambers for the evening. Care was taken to bruit it about that the prince was looking forward to a good week's hunting.[30]

The final gossamer threads were then laid across the web of deception. The principals at this stage were the prince's groom François Vivier (a native of Tours), his aide Francis Stafford, Sir Thomas Sheridan and the Bailli de Tencin.[31] It was decided not to reveal what was going on to Henry. His highly emotional nature made him a poor repository for secrets of this kind, especially involving his brother.

On 8 January 1744 a poker-faced Charles Edward supped with his family as usual. Ostentatiously giving out to his brother that he was retiring early, the prince then made his way via a secret passageway to his father's chamber for a final briefing.[32] They talked together for an hour. James said farewell tearfully. Then, at 3 a.m., the prince set out. He would never see his father again.

The prince initiated the elaborate deception by getting into a post-

chaise with Sheridan. Stafford and Vivier the groom went ahead with
three black horses to the Porta San Giovanni.[33] The gate was opened
for the party without demur. Once outside the city walls, Charles
Edward and Sheridan staged a well-rehearsed charade. The post-
chaise came to a halt; the prince announced that he wished to go on
by horseback. Sheridan, warming to his part, strenuously disap-
proved. Charles Edward answered back vociferously in Italian,
making sure the postilion and servant on the chaise could hear him
saying that he was going to ride to Albano and then cut across
country to Cisterna.[34] Vowing that he would beat the querulous old
Sheridan to Cisterna, the prince galloped off down the Albano road
with Stafford.

Once they were sure they were not being followed, the prince and
Stafford changed clothes.[35] Stafford galloped on to Frascati. Charles
Edward meanwhile returned to the Porta San Giovanni and rode
around the walls of Rome. He crossed the Ponte Molle, took the via
della Storta, and arrived at Caprarola after riding for forty miles
(including the circuit of the city walls). At Caprarola he met up with
Vivier the groom. They found no difficulty in getting horses for the
onward journey to Massa.[36]

In the meantime Sheridan arrived at Cisterna, closely followed by
Henry. When Charles Edward failed to come in, there was a palpable
anxiety among the Gaetani entourage and the prince's own people
(except for Sheridan).[37] This was assuaged when Stafford arrived
with a story that the prince's horse had fallen near Albano, leaving
its master with a bruised rib. The consequence, Stafford explained,
was that the prince would be detained at Albano for three days.
In a brilliant circumstantial touch, Stafford handed Henry a note
purportedly penned by the prince at Albano. The note asked Henry
not to tell their father about the accident, since he had so often
nagged Charles about riding horses on precipitous roads; for this
reason, too, no servants should be sent to Albano.[38]

While this elaborate comedy was being played out, complete with
daily bulletins from Albano on the prince's progress, Charles Edward
and Vivier had pressed on to Massa.[39] They arrived there on 11
January and then survived a truly dreadful two days on roads smoth-
ered in ice and snow before struggling in to Genoa on the evening of
13 January. For five days the prince had barely slept, had not
undressed once and had had nothing to eat but eggs.[40] Yet even in
Genoa the dauntless prince did not slacken his pace. He pressed on
to the port of Finale to see if he could hire a *felucca*.

The severe rain and snow meant that no small craft were leaving that port. Refusing to take no for an answer, the prince rode on overnight to Savona. On his arrival there on the morning of 14 January, he managed to hire a *felucca* and to find a captain and crew willing to take him on. Ironically, they proved to be based at Finale. The captain arranged to return to Finale then come up to Savona the next day to embark the mysterious traveller for Antibes.[41]

But the winds were against the prince. Blowing from the south, they churned up the seas dangerously. Not even the most intrepid captain would take a small boat to sea in those conditions. For six days the prince prowled uneasily among the shipping at Savona, chafing at the delay.

The danger now was that Mann's spies might have cracked the façade of deception and alerted Admiral Matthews and the English Mediterranean fleet.[42] Yet to proceed overland was unthinkable. The land passes were guarded by the king of Sardinia, England's reliable ally.

On the sixth day the sea calmed a little, but it was still too rough for a normal sailor to venture out. Yet the slight break in the weather was enough for the prince. Rushing down to Finale, he offered the captain a substantial bonus if he would put to sea at once, regardless of risk.[43]

The captain agreed. At first luck was with them. They got to Monaco on the late evening of 21 January.[44] Next day the winds came howling back, stronger than ever. On the 23rd, with a slight lessening of the gale, they tried again. At daybreak the little boat was floundering so helplessly in the swell that it attracted the attention of Matthews's fleet as it cruised between Monaco and Antibes. A small boat was lowered by the English to give chase, but it failed to make headway in the heavy seas.[45] Nevertheless the English were alerted. Rumours of the prince's escape were now creeping up the Mediterranean seaboard. It was considered more than likely that the *felucca* did indeed contain the Young Pretender.

The danger from the English fleet became even more acute when the prince put in at Antibes on the evening of the 23rd. An English pinnace had been sent to intercept the boat; it came into port close on the *felucca*'s heels. Both sides asked permission to land from the harbourmaster. As they lay at anchor, the English craft was so close it almost scraped the stern of the prince's boat.[46]

The arrival of the two boats together in a quarantine port created a minor sensation. The commandant and governor of Antibes, M. de Villeneuve, was informed and came in person to investigate. Now was revealed a major consequence of the misunderstanding between

France and the Jacobites. Since Amelot and Louis XV had not expected Charles Edward to set out from Rome, no instructions had been sent to commanders of French ports. Villeneuve was completely in the dark.[47] According to his standing orders, he had to send back any boat arriving from Monaco or Italy or send it on to Marseilles or Toulon.

Things looked grim for the prince. Just when he was on the point of being expelled, he got a message to Villeneuve, stating that a great secret would be revealed to him if he would just find a pretext to be rid of the English pinnace. Villeneuve then pronounced his Solomonic judgment. Both boats must leave, he declared, but the English first, since he had further investigations to pursue with regard to the *felucca*.[48]

As soon as the English craft had cleared from the harbour, Charles Edward revealed his identity to an astonished Villeneuve.[49] Thinking quickly, the governor transferred the prince to another ship. This was a sane precaution, since Matthews did not seem disposed to take no for an answer. Even while Villeneuve was improvising arrangements for his unexpected royal guest, an English *chaloupe*, satellite of the great warships, came in and asked for supplies. Since no English ships had been seen for days before this, Matthews's game was clear to Villeneuve. He gave permission for revictualling on condition the *chaloupe* was gone that very night.[50]

While supplies were being loaded, Villeneuve played out yet another charade. Indignantly dressing down the captain of the *felucca* in public, he demanded that it leave forthwith. The Finale boat left before the *chaloupe* could give chase. When the latter's 'vital supplies' had been loaded on, it took up the trail and pursued the *felucca* all the way back to Monaco.[51]

The prince, of course, had meanwhile been transferred surreptitiously to a larger ship. Villeneuve pondered his next move. The presence of the Stuart prince obviously meant that great schemes were afoot of which he knew nothing. He dashed off an express to his superior, marquis de Mirepoix, Intendant of Ports, asking for clear directions.[52] He gave interim orders for the prince to be fed and housed with every courtesy on board the ship to which he had been transferred. When dusk fell on the evening of the 24th, he went down to the harbour and fetched the prince to his permanent quarters, a detached house in a secluded part of the town.[53]

There the prince waited until Villeneuve heard from Mirepoix. As the days passed and the governor chatted with Charles Edward, it came to Villeneuve that the affair was bigger even than he had suspected. Mirepoix might not have grasped the full implications of the prince's presence on French soil. Villeneuve accordingly sent a courier directly to Amelot, asking for explicit guidance.[54]

But Villeneuve had left it too late. The reply from Mirepoix came in. It stated that in the circumstances an eight-day quarantine should be enforced; after that the prince was free to leave.[55] There was no holding Charles Edward once he heard this. In vain did Villeneuve plead with him to stay in Antibes until the second courier, from Amelot, arrived. Faced with the prince's determination, Villeneuve could do nothing. Ostensibly expressing concern over the fatigue the prince had suffered and would again, he offered him a chaise, hoping perhaps to slow him down. The prince wanted none of it. He and his party galloped out of Antibes at full speed at 8 a.m. on the morning of 29 January.[56]

After an all-night journey, they arrived at Aix-en-Provence on the 30th. Even the prince was exhausted after the sixteen posts between Antibes and Aix, most of them on bad roads with inadequate horses.[57] Resting for a day, the party pressed on to Avignon, which was reached on 1 February. At Avignon Charles Edward discussed the implications of the French invasion project with the duke of Ormonde.[58] Ormonde was the Jacobite 'elder statesman'. Now nearly eighty, he had retired to Avignon in the 1730s after long service for James at the court of Madrid.

Then it was another gruelling ride, to Lyons, reached at 4 p.m. on 3 February. Leaving before dawn next morning, they spent four more weary days in the saddle.[59] Even the prince's great stamina was taxed. He arrived in Paris utterly exhausted ('rendu') on Saturday 8 February.[60]

What were the consequences of this heroic thirty-day journey in mid-winter?[61] The first thing to note is that everyone except the conspirators was taken completely by surprise. After years of crying wolf about Charles Edward's allegedly imminent departure for France, Mann was caught on the hop when it actually happened. The prince was in Lyons before that fanatical anti-Jacobite had word of his arrival in Antibes.[62] Even when it was known that the prince had escaped his agents' surveillance, Mann could not decide what his purpose was. Mann identified four possibilities; amazingly, not one of them was the correct one. These were: a descent on Scotland with the Brest fleet; a marriage with the king of France's daughter; a marriage with the Princess of Modena, then in Paris; service with France in the next campaign in Europe.[63] Mann then shot even wider of the target by postulating an invitation from the Emperor. We shall soon see the Young Pretender at the Imperial Court in Frankfurt, he assured Horace Walpole, prior to service in the Bavarian army.[64] This was supposed to be all part of a conspiracy by the powers (Austria, Prussia, Spain and France) to invade Hanover.[65] Never was Mann's anti-Jacobite paranoia more startlingly evinced.

Mann was equally wide of the mark when it came to assessing the papal role in Charles Edward's departure. He believed that the Pope had provided Charles Edward with 80,000 crowns plus a proclamation calling on all Catholics in the British Isles to rise and follow Charlie.[66] The truth was quite different. The Pope knew nothing of the plan to get the prince out of Rome and was as incredulous as anyone as news of his arrival in Genoa, Antibes, etc. came in.[67] As the witty Benedict XIV later remarked, if the British had offered a good price for his letters to Charles Edward on this affair, he would have sold and the British would have ended up, as their side of the bargain, with – precisely nothing.[68] The French representative in Rome was in no better case, sulkily reporting the escapade to Amelot as if it were a secret his superior had deliberately kept from him.[69]

Yet if everyone in Rome was taken completely unawares, their surprised reaction was as nothing to the consternation felt in Paris when the prince arrived like a thunderbolt from a clear sky.[70] Louis XV, realising that his Machiavellian game was up, sent a warm compliment to Charles on his arrival, hoping to rationalise the consequences of his own duplicity.[71] In reality the prince's arrival threw the French ministers into disarray. Security for the cross-Channel project was blown sky-high.[72] In order to assess the impact of Charles Edward's advent on the French invasion plans, we need to appreciate the stage Saxe's preparations had reached while the prince was on his thirty-day Odyssey.

Serious planning had been under way since the end of November 1743, but had already been bedevilled by grave disagreements between France and the English Jacobites. Although urged to ferry his army across in fishing boats, the comte de Saxe dared not take the risk and insisted on the protection of the Brest fleet.[73] The English Jacobites for their part decided to avoid the risk of arrest by asking for a postponement of the French landing until after Parliament had risen.[74] Both sides, then, were already showing signs of excessive timidity.

But worse was to come. The French strategy was to send the Brest fleet up the Channel to lure Sir John Norris's defenders to Spithead away to the west, leaving Saxe with an unguarded Channel to cross. Then 10,000 French troops would disembark at Maldon in Essex, to be joined by the English Jacobites and their levies. At this point both sides added complicating refinements to their plans. It was clearly impossible for the French to achieve total surprise *and* use the Brest fleet to convoy the invaders. Maurepas hit on a compromise. Roquefeuil, commander of the Brest fleet, was to decoy Norris or engage him in combat. While the Downs were thus left undefended, Roquefeuil was to detach five ships under Barrailh. Barrailh was to sail to Dunkirk to provide Saxe with the escort he had requested.[75] Such a plan greatly increased the possibility that things might miscarry. The English Jacobites compounded the complications by switching the projected landfall from Maldon in Essex to Blackwall, two miles from London.[76] This meant the provision of two sets of pilots to negotiate the treacherous Thames estuary: one to guide the French as far as the Hope; the other to take them to Blackwall.

The invasion project, then, already depended for its success on meticulous liaison, timing and co-ordination. The English pilots had to be in Dunkirk ready to take the French over the minute Roquefeuil decoyed Norris away from the invasion area. But the French still had secrecy on their side. Even with all the delays, the English government in the first two weeks of 1744 still had no inkling that their kingdom was about to be invaded.[77]

This was the situation when the exhausted prince rode into Paris on 8 February. By his untimely presence he immediately increased the risk that the English might divine the true scope of French intentions. It was still of course possible to argue, as Mann and others did, that the prince was destined for the French fleet, possibly for a descent on Ireland or Scotland.[78] But his presence on French soil clearly indicated that a formal declaration of war by France was not far off.

Moreover, there are circumstantial grounds for thinking that the discovery of the French invasion plan was triggered by the prince's arrival in Paris. Saxe's enterprise against England was revealed to the duke of Newcastle by his master-spy, French diplomat François de Bussy.[79] Bussy had known about the plan virtually since its inception. Why then did he not reveal it to his English paymasters earlier? The most likely answer is that, gambling for such high stakes when the future of kingdoms hung in the balance, he feared detection if he divulged the details of Saxe's operation. Yet Charles Edward's arrival could have placed him in an impossible situation. If Bussy continued to remain silent, and yet the project foundered, it would later be obvious to the English that their master-spy had suppressed vital intelligence. Bussy's credibility was now at stake.

The chronology of his leaking the Saxe project is intriguing. His cipher to Newcastle, revealing the entire operation, was decoded on 14 February, i.e. six days after the prince's arrival in the French capital. It could well be, then, that, albeit for different reasons, Charles Edward really did destroy the prospects for the restoration of his family in 1744 – as Louis XV and others later charged.

Naturally, none of this was apparent to the political actors at the time. All Saxe could see was further bungling by the Jacobites. After two requests for delays from Lord Barrymore and his associates across the Channel, here, to cap all, was the Stuart prince himself blundering on to the stage at the crucial moment, destroying the fragile fabric of secrecy Saxe had so painstakingly built up.

Not surprisingly, Paris erupted on all sides. As soon as he heard the news, comte d'Argenson, Minister of War, complained to Louis XV that this would ruin everything.[80] Recriminations flew thick and fast among the French ministers about who was responsible for inviting the prince. The blame was largely laid at Tencin's door though, as he truthfully protested, he knew nothing of the invasion project.[81] The English, too, seem to have scented something in the wind. The very next day after Charles Edward's arrival, British minister Thompson reported the possibility of a descent on the English coast, though not until 18 February did he know of the prince's presence in France.[82]

Something of the coolness of the French response to his arrival was borne in on the prince when the court informed him that he was to remain in the strictest incognito.[83] Lord Elcho went with the Earl Marischal to see the prince at Sempill's house on the Estrapade (where Charles was lodging). They found him alone, drinking tea, depressed about his incognito.[84] Conversation turned to the French invasion. The prince ordered Elcho and Marischal to follow him to Dunkirk. Yet within days these orders proved otiose. The French issued instructions of their own. Marischal and Elcho were to accompany the main invasion force at Dunkirk. Charles Edward himself was to embark with Saxe on the *Dauphin Royal*, Barrailh's flagship, but to remain incognito meanwhile at Gravelines.[85] Saxe showed just how much contact he wanted with the Stuart prince by stationing himself at Dunkirk, keeping Charles at arm's length and away from the open preparations.[86]

On 15 February Lord Sempill received from the French the first instalment of the prince's expenses, 10,000 livres.[87] Although the official stance at Versailles was that the young Stuart was an uninvited guest, they decided to make the best of things. An extraordinary payment, for the duration of the expedition only, was authorised. There was now nothing to keep Charles Edward in Paris. He journeyed up to Gravelines, confident that the hour of his destiny had struck.[88]

7

The New Byzantium

(March–September 1744)

Charles Edward arrived at Gravelines to find a situation very different from his sanguine imaginings. His own presence on the coast was now widely known.[1] Bussy's ciphered revelations had done their work all too well. The secret was out. Once the combined threat from Young Pretender and French invasion was realised, the English authorities sprang into action. George II addressed Parliament on the subject.[2] Wholesale arrests of the leading English Jacobites took place; troop reinforcements were ordered from Ireland and the Netherlands.[3]

All this was bad enough from Saxe's point of view, but the naval aspect was if anything even more discouraging. On 26 February 1744 Saxe wrote to d'Argenson and Amelot that he would already have landed in England if Barrailh had arrived.[4] Moreover, there was no sign of the promised English pilots that Henry Read ('Mr Red') was supposed to be bringing over to Dunkirk to guide the French flotilla to landfall.

On 27 February Barrailh arrived, having successfully detached from Roquefeuil. But there was still no sign of Read and the pilots. The unbelievable farce in which Read had become entangled only became clear later. It transpired that the English Jacobites had taken fright after George II's call to arms on 25 February. Fearing to entrust the secret of the expedition to English pilots, they sent Read on to France alone, with instructions to pick up suitable pilots in the Picardy ports.[5] Read arrived in France on 3 March. With little knowledge of French, and unable to find either the prince or any English contact, he wandered aimlessly around for a few days and then returned to England, his mission unaccomplished.[6]

By this time the French were already faltering in their resolve. On

6 March comte d'Argenson told Saxe that he should prepare for a possible abandonment of the expedition, since Charles Edward's arrival had ruined everything.[7] There was real bitterness in d'Argenson's letter: Louis XV, he said, wished to put it on record as strongly as possible that the secret enterprise was destroyed by the Stuart prince's contumacious folly in arriving in Paris at that juncture. What d'Argenson did not realise was that Louis XV, under pressure from those like Noailles who stressed the paramountcy of France's German policy, was already having second thoughts and looking for an excuse to abandon the English project without loss of face.[8]

The Roquefeuil part of the invasion project was an even bigger disaster. The French admiral left Brest with twenty-two ships of the line, but found no English squadron at Spithead – Admiral Norris had slipped out two days earlier.[9] After telling Saxe it would be safe to cross the Channel, Roquefeuil realised his error and followed Norris up the Channel. On 7 March the fwo fleets came in sight of each other, Roquefeuil at Dungeness, Norris at Hythe. Slightly outnumbered, with fifteen men o' war to Norris's nineteen (for by now Barrailh's seven vessels had been detached), Roquefeuil prepared to give battle.

But before the rival fleets could close, at about 3 p.m., the first of the two great storms of March 1744 swept upon the combatants.[10] All that night and next day the tempest blew, stripping masts and spars, driving ships into each other. Eighteen of Norris's ships were damaged, five incapacitated; one was accidentally rammed and went down with all hands. Roquefeuil meanwhile slipped anchor and ran before the wind to Brest, sustaining only minor damage.[11]

The real devastation came at Dunkirk, where the transports were already loading Saxe's troops. Loss of life was slight, but eleven transports and many smaller ships were smashed and six months' supplies and materiel destroyed, along with anchors and tackle.[12] It was now obvious that the expedition could not sail. Saxe wrote angrily to the War Minister on 8 March, lashing out in all directions: at Barrailh, the English Jacobites, at Charles Edward himself.[13] The last straw was when he discovered that Norris's battered ships had reformed in line on the Downs, without a word to him (Saxe) about this from Lord Barrymore and his friends.[14]

A second storm on 11 March, causing further damage, put the issue beyond doubt. That very day Saxe wrote to the prince to tell him that the expedition had been abandoned.[15]

By this single communication the French awoke the sleeping tiger. Charles Edward's communications to Saxe hitherto had been models of tact and charm.[16] That he was in good spirits can be seen from a letter to his father while he was waiting to see if Roquefeuil would successfully decoy Norris: 'The king would laugh heartily and be mightily diverted to see us often disputing the idiom of the French language and the proper turn of words to express the idea we would have them take.'[17]

The first sign of gathering clouds came on 5 March when the prince learned of Saxe's latest orders. Incensed by the incompetence of their English Jacobite partners, the French court sent the commander instructions that if he was not met at the Hope, he was not to proceed into the Thames but to return to Dunkirk.[18] After the storm on 7 March, Saxe threw out a broad hint that the expedition would not proceed, but used the supineness of the English Jacobites as the likely reason.

Immediately and in all good faith the prince sent an emissary to smooth Saxe's ruffled feathers.[19] This messenger crossed with Saxe's letter of the 11th, telling him that all was over. Angrily the prince returned to the fray. How was it, he asked Saxe, that the weather had so devastated the French yet left Norris unscathed? If the destruction was as great as Saxe now claimed, how was it possible for the English fleet to be still on station in the Downs? This must be a 'Protestant wind' with a vengeance, capable of inflicting selective damage.[20]

At the same time the prince wrote to Earl Marischal, requesting him to seek an interview with Saxe and lay certain facts before him. He was to point out that two of the captains in Norris's fleet had already been suborned by the Jacobites. Marischal should further urge the immediate use of the Brest fleet as the sole means of retrieving the situation.[21] In private remarks to Marischal, the prince expressed his anger clearly, accusing the French of incompetence and cowardice in the face of Norris.[22]

Saxe's reply to these representations was cold and ironical. After explaining that the second storm on 11 March had destroyed a further three transports and one warship, and had left the fleet without cables or anchors, Saxe commented tartly that he himself could neither command the winds nor be responsible for them. If the prince wanted to fasten the blame on someone, he should consider Dame Fortune as the candidate.[23] Further stung by Marischal's lobbying for action from Roquefeuil, Saxe claimed disingenuously (and self-contradictorily) not to know where Roquefeuil was, but that since he was certainly at sea on 11 March, the extent of damage to his ships could be readily imagined.

The prince riposted in similar ironical tone. He welcomed the fact that Saxe professed himself not discouraged and added that what was needed now was more adamantine spirit like the commander's. To make his contempt palpable, Charles Edward tried to reduce Saxe to the level of a banker; he asked for 500 *louis d'or* of the money the commander had been given for the Stuart prince's use.[24]

The cold exchange continued. Saxe claimed that Roquefeuil's fleet was *hors de combat*, having lost nine ships in the storm. He had no money available, since the only funds at his disposal were letters of credit on a London bank.[25] Then, in true *de haut en bas* style, he announced that the correspondence was closed, since he had been ordered to return to court.

The prince was left in a cold fury, with no focus for his rage. From this day on he was always to distrust and loathe the French. The débâcle, and the insensitive way Versailles and Saxe had dealt with him, tapped a deep vein of pain and rejection in the prince. It would have been better if someone in authority in France could have admitted candidly that there had been misunderstandings and problems on both sides, had frankly conceded that, whereas the French were annoyed with Charles Edward for breaching their secrecy and wrecking the invasion, they were scarcely blameless themselves. Such statesmanship called for the skills of a Benedict XIV; it was completely beyond the instinctively duplicitous Louis XV, quite apart from the consideration that he would have had to reveal his own chicanery over the Balhaldy mission.

The full force of the prince's anger comes across in his letters to his father. Inveighing against the incompetence of the octogenarian Roquefeuil, he asked, justifiiably, how it was possible for Norris to emerge from Spithead on 26 February and be on the Downs two days later if Roquefeuil's decoying tactic was meant to be the hinge on which the whole enterprise turned?[26] The prince added bitterly that but for the storm he would now be a prisoner in Norris's hands.

It was at this moment in his life above all that Charles Edward needed a true father, someone like his erstwhile protector the duke of Berwick, someone who could sympathise with his justifiable complaints while helping him to see the complex political situation steadily and in the round. What the prince got was the worst possible counsellor for him: the Earl Marischal. Aged fifty at the time of the invasion attempt, a veteran of the 1715 and 1719 risings, Marischal should have been the ideal guide and mentor for the prince. In reality the prince's worst enemies could not have provided a more ill-matched confidant. Proud, aloof and imperious, Marischal was like

Bolingbroke in that he wanted a Stuart restoration solely on his own terms. All Jacobite plots had to be under his direction, and he had in effect to be Jacobite Prime Minister, or he would react with sullen peevishness. He would serve in great affairs but never in small ones. These qualities had already led him into bitter clashes with James himself and were, ironically, precisely the reason James had not appointed him as his Secretary of State.

There were, moreover, more profound reasons for the irremediable personality clash between Marischal and Charles Edward that first became obvious in March 1744. Marischal managed to combine the patronising aspects of James that most infuriated the prince with personality traits similar to Charles Edward's; this especially made accommodation between them impossible, since they were in a sense in competition for the same space. Marischal disliked Charles on sight when he saw him in Rome in 1732. This kind of 'hate at first sight' is as difficult to explain as its existence is undeniable. The clash between the two men was now and later to yield bitter fruit.

What Charles Edward needed during the lonely days at Gravelines were qualities of empathy and understanding from a trusted counsellor, someone who would immediately appreciate the force of his criticism of the French. What Marischal provided was endless quibbling with the prince's opinions, infinitely elastic justifications of the French and, worst of all, gloomy and pessimistic jeremiads to counterpoint Charles's exuberance.[27] Where the prince could see only the opportunities Saxe and Roquefeuil were wasting, Marischal saw only the many barriers and obstacles to a successful French invasion.[28]

Besides finding copious excuses for Saxe and Roquefeuil, Marischal was amazingly quick to find reasons why the enterprise could not now succeed. He mentioned the suspension of Habeas Corpus in England, the withdrawal of troops from Ireland and Holland, and the unfavourable publicity given to the recent sneak French naval attack at Toulon, as reasons to hope for little from English Jacobitism. It was no wonder that the prince remarked acidly that Marischal made heaps of difficulties 'but is not of a mind perhaps to find remedies for them'.[29]

Even when the prince steeled himself to accept that the English expedition had been abandoned, and looked around for alternatives or palliatives, he found Marischal more than useless. What about sending the Irish brigade to Scotland, he suggested? Would Marischal undertake a mission to Scotland to keep the flames of Jacobitism alive and not lose the impetus engendered by the recent invasion fever? No, Marischal replied, he would not. He doubted French sincerity. Whoever told the prince that Louis XV was willing to press on despite the reverse to the Saxe expedition was telling him a pack of lies.[30]

Very well, the prince concluded, he would go to Scotland alone. The clans had assured him they would be willing to receive him on whatever basis. This would be singularly unwise, counselled Marischal. Scotland alone could not unlock the door to a Stuart restoration. And if the English Jacobites were chary about joining in a rising with the support of sixteen battalions of French troops, could anything seriously be expected of them if the prince went alone?[31] To round off his achievements, Marischal made a mess of liaison with the prince's second choice of emissary for Scotland, Nicholas Wogan.[32]

It seemed that to Marischal all paths to Britain were ineluctably barred, that the Hanoverian regime was as unassailable as the angel with the flaming sword who barred the return to Eden. Faced with this monumental defeatism, Charles Edward was fully justified in concluding bitterly: 'Nothing can ever gain my heart to a man who finds faults and difficulties in everything, but never removed any.'[33]

The bruising treatment the prince had received both from Saxe and Marischal made a profound impact on his fragile personal equilibrium. Charles Edward could only draw sustenance from success and forward momentum. Failure, particularly a débâcle when on the very brink of success, triggered the self-destructive side of the prince. A wise man would now have bowed to the inevitable. But Charles plugged away at his theme that sickness and weather could not have affected the French alone, that he therefore expected to see Louis XV take up the gauntlet again.[34]

Turning his back on Marischal as a hopeless pessimist, the prince addressed himself to Sempill. Urging him not to relax his efforts at Versailles, he proposed, if necessary, a switch of efforts from an English to a Scottish landing. For this he would need, in addition to the Irish brigade, two French battalions and a regiment of dismounted dragoons.[35] Predictably, the Earl Marischal poured cold water on this idea too when he heard of it. The news that he was returning to Paris was more than welcome to the prince.[36]

Fully convinced that the Scottish expedition would very soon take shape and hoping too to revive the cross-Channel project, the prince dispatched Buchanan (his old aide from Rome) to England to spy out the situation. Inevitably, Buchanan reported that the English Jacobites would not move a muscle until a French army had landed.[37] But he did recount a serious level of disaffection among the English

Tories. The prince was about to send this corroborating evidence to Versailles when he received the clearest indication yet of Louis XV's true intentions. Charles Edward was ordered to leave the coast and proceed, still incognito, to residence at the house of the bishop of Soissons.[38]

Only then did the floodgates of paranoia fully open. Charles Edward was left permanently scarred by French treatment of him. As he later remarked bitterly: 'A blind man could see that France was only making sport of him.'[39] The French, it now seemed, had never been serious. Saxe had been playing with him. Marischal had humoured him, secretly delighted at his failure. There had been collusion to prevent an excellent enterprise from being successful. None of the arguments put to him had been adduced in good faith. So be it, France would learn they had no pliant and deferential James to deal with this time. Pointedly Charles Edward ignored the summons to leave the coast. Instead, he wrote a long missive for Sempill to send to Louis XV, setting out in detail the reasons why the English enterprise should be revitalised. The implication was that he had no intention of leaving Gravelines.[40]

At this low ebb in his fortunes, the prince had to put up with his father's mournful and depressed letters, full of regret about the failure of the expedition, and once again chiding him for being a poor correspondent.[41] The gloomy atmosphere in the Palazzo Muti at this time was attested to by the Pope. Benedict XIV admitted that when the bad news came in, he avoided James for a week, unable to face him.[42] Putting on a bold front, the prince excused his failure to write on the grounds of a lack of a cipher.[43]

A week later he touched on more realistic issues, initiating the series of complaints about money that were to punctuate 1744: 'You would laugh heartily if you saw me going about with a single servant, buying fish and other things and squabbling for a penny more or less.'[44]

Meanwhile the French had somewhat played into the prince's hands. A memorandum from the comte d'Argenson to Saxe, demanding Charles Edward's removal from Gravelines to the bishop of Soissons's house, two leagues from the town of Soissons, arrived after Saxe had left the coast.[45] Even better, among the meticulously detailed instructions concerning the prince (including a specification that he should approach his new abode via Compiègne rather than Soissons) was a stipulation that Charles should have Marischal at his side as adviser. But Marischal, after a few days in his Boulogne house, had also departed for Paris.

So far was the prince from showing any signs of leaving the coast that he was talking of going to Scotland by canoe. He had also prepared a formal protest against the abandonment of the expedition for Sempill to present to Amelot.[46] From allegedly pro-Jacobite ministers like Tencin the prince was demanding a full explanation for French actions. Tencin was now under fire from two directions: from Louis XV for having allegedly invited the Stuart prince; and from the latter for being lukewarm in his interests. He could do no more than limply protest his continuing devotion to the House of Stuart.[47]

The French ministers were already under great pressure to do something about the prince's defiance. It was in vain that they protested, as they had earlier to the English, that the prince was a creature of whim, who was not under their control and who acted entirely on his own initiative.[48] His appearance in France was good enough proof for most people that he came there at the express invitation of Versailles. Although the earlier pressure from the British for his expulsion[49] had been shrugged off with the open French declaration of war on England (as soon as the invasion project foundered), there was German opinion to appease. For the time being France had to keep the prince under wraps, in a strict incognito.

It did not take long for the collective patience of the council of state to run out. The ministers at Versailles had never encountered a phenomenon like Charles Edward before. Maurepas expressed stupefaction that the prince had been written to three times with explicit instructions to proceed to Soissons, but had ignored all three letters.[50] This was only the beginning. France was to see much more such behaviour in the next four years.

The Jacobite representative Daniel O'Brien was prevailed on to write to James, stressing the serious consequences if the prince continued to snub the French court.[51] But James had already acted. Knowing his son of old and alarmed at his silence, he decided to send Sheridan, Stafford and two valets-de-chambre into France to join him.[52] At the same time he advised Charles to bow his head to the dictates of France.[53]

We know from his later correspondence the contempt the prince felt for his father on receiving this advice. It seemed to him, not for the last time, that his father was always prepared to side with his enemies and those who injured him; always to be polite, deferential and diplomatic, never to take a stand of principle. The conflation of his father with Marischal was too easy to resist: both automatically sided with France, took the easy *realpolitik* view, never contrasted what was with what ought to be. For the moment he was alone; he had not yet hardened himself to oppose his will to that of all comers. He had prepared to be stoical and enduring, expecting that James would support him, especially as he was about his father's business.[54] The disappointment at finding this was not so was acute.

Faced with the unanimous verdict of all around him that he should yield to France, the prince did so, but with a bad grace. Using the pretext of the duke of Ormonde's advice – that he would disgust his English friends if he was seen residing at the house of a Roman Catholic bishop[55] – Charles Edward did not go to Soissons. Instead he left Gravelines in disguise, making his way slowly to Paris.

For the first time he experienced the thrill of being a genuine incognito; he was later to acquire a taste for it, to the point where deception and subterfuge became second nature. As he rode south, he took delight in hearing the various rumours about the vanished prince's whereabouts: 'Some think him in one place, and some in another, but nobody knows where he is really, and sometimes he is told news of himself to his face, which is very diverting.'[56]

Yet if the prince was enjoying himself and saving face (sometimes literally), his father fretted anxiously about his 'invisibility'.[57] Believing, wrongly, that Marischal was now his son's closest adviser, James sent Sir John Graeme to Paris as a counterweight, in hopes of pulling Charles back on to the path of straightforward duty.[58]

At last, having teased his father and the French long enough, the prince threw off the mask and announced to the world that he was in Paris, disingenuously claiming that he was thereby obeying the king of France's orders.[59]

Anyone who queries why Charles Edward should eventually have gone to Scotland alone in 1745 should ponder the prince's nightmare experience in France in 1744. Proponents of the 'rash adventurer' theory should contemplate the chaos into which Charles descended, just weeks after expecting to enter London in triumph. It says much for the prince's willpower at this period that he did not crack under the strain.

On any analysis, French treatment of the prince during 1744–5 was despicable. They did not have the political excuses of the 1746–8 period. The ministers made promises and broke them; set deadlines and failed to meet them. They could not even agree on a settled location for the prince's abode.

Louis began by making a half-promise that the prince would be allowed to serve with the French army in Flanders, provided he agreed to remain incognito a little longer, perhaps six weeks in all.[60] Finance Minister Orry was made the chief conduit for Jacobite affairs.

In an interview with Charles, he confirmed that the incognito would cease at the end of July.[61] As a consequence the prince passed up an invitation from the Prince de Conti to serve on campaign with him.[62] This was an intelligent decision; at this stage Charles had to play for higher stakes.[63]

By the end of June the ministers had backtracked. Tencin told O'Brien there was almost no chance that the prince would be allowed to make a public campaign.[64] Charles expressed his impatience, ascribing French dithering to a mixture of stupidity, tight-fistedness and downright dishonourable behaviour.[65] The end of July came, but there was no lifting of the incognito. Sempill was told by Louis's personal secretary that the king wanted things to continue as before; the king again made a vague promise of future troop commitments against England.[66] Charles Edward replied with a request for a definite commitment: either a realistic pledge of another invasion of England or written permission to be allowed to campaign.[67]

Still Louis stalled, mystifying and obfuscating the issue by shunting the Jacobite emissaries from minister to minister, spokesman to spokesman, hoping to cover his disingenuous tracks under the mantle of the notoriously fragmented decision-making at Versailles. The Jacobites made it easier for him by their excessive factionalism, and by employing at least half a dozen different channels of communication. But the argument that it was divided counsels among the ministers of state that led to the unconscionable dithering and prevarication over Charles Edward's future will not hold up. Tencin was excluded from all influence and was reported to see the king only at council meetings. Orry was the minister delegated to deal with Jacobite affairs, and he was a faithful mirror of his master's deceit, procrastination and tergiversation.[68] Maurepas and comte d'Argenson were heard from rarely, but faithfully echoed the official line, that it was merely a matter of time before an enterprise against England was revived.[69] But it was always difficult to make physical contact with the Ministers of War and Marine, as they spent long periods in 1744 away from the court at the theatre of war.[70]

For all that, by September 1744 Orry had made his unsympathetic attitude sufficiently plain for Jacobite lobbying to be concentrating consciously on d'Argenson, Maurepas and Tencin.[71] On one occasion Orry's notorious parsimony led him into barefaced lies about the amount of money given by France to the Jacobites. Fortunately, the prince had chapter and verse to hand and forced the Finance Minister to retract. Orry created such animosity in Jacobite circles that Bailli de Tencin, no firebrand, advised the prince to allow him no respite and to continue bombarding him with memoranda even when the minister had retired to his country home.[72]

By October even Louis XV admitted that relations between Orry and the Jacobites were impossible. He put Tencin in charge of Stuart affairs.[73] This was exactly the pretext the other ministers needed to wash their hands of the prince. Comte d'Argenson sent back all Jacobite memoirs, with the terse comment that Tencin was now the one and only channel for their affairs.[74] Louis's Machiavellianism was evinced by this manoeuvre, since it was an open secret that Tencin had the least influence on the king of any of the six ministers of state.

French treatment of the prince provoked public incredulity and private anger in Jacobite circles.[75] Even the Pope, never one to rush to judgment, agreed.[76] In Rome James spent long hours puzzling over it. Could the apparent volte-face have something to do with Amelot's fall in spring 1744, since the former Foreign Secretary was the prime mover of the enterprise against England?[77] It was true that Amelot had been made the sacrificial victim after the English débâcle but, as Sempill reassured James, his disgrace followed a court intrigue and had no connection with the prince's fortunes.[78]

In that case, reasoned James, perhaps Charles Edward's failure to go from Gravelines to Soissons immediately had been a tactical error: if he had gone there, might it not have been impossible for Louis XV to insist on the incognito?[79] Charles Edward soon put his father right on that score. From the point of view of personal ease, Soissons would have been an ideal base, especially with its extensive hunting acreage, but it was an obvious snare. Too far from the centre of political gravity, Charles Edward would have been a permanent backnumber. The prince made the telling point that acceptance of Soissons made sense only if he had already concluded that the French were insincere; at the time he still believed their assurances.[80]

The more James worried away at French treatment of his son, the plainer became the dishonesty and duplicity of Louis XV. Balhaldy had warned him of this as early as June,[81] but it was not until December that, on receipt of correspondence from Tencin, James finally saw the full dimensions of the problem. Tencin put it to him that at bottom Louis XV disclaimed all responsibility for the prince, on the ground that he had never invited him to France.[82] For once James concurred with his son. Both men hit the nail on the head by agreeing independently to a cogent answer: if that was the case, they urged, what was Saxe doing at Dunkirk corresponding with someone who, according to his king, was on French soil illegally?[83]

It took O'Brien, long out of favour with James but now making a comeback as the star of Balhaldy and Sempill faded, to point up the real French motivation. In brief, they feared the impact on their German allies of too strong an association with the Stuarts. Although this fear should have lessened once Austria and Prussia were at each other's throats, the French, rightly, did not trust Frederick of Prussia and were determined not to sacrifice their German policy just for the Jacobites.[84] The other factor in French minds was the Dutch. France did not want to play the Jacobite card until the States General of Holland had committed themselves to an open declaration of war.[85]

Whatever the reasons for his treatment by the French, the prince remained in limbo throughout 1744. The uncertainty in his life even extended to where he lived. At the beginning of June he rented a house in Montmartre.[86] He chafed at his sedentary life, so different from what he was used to.[87] By September his crabbed existence was already intolerable to him. Moreover, the rental on the house was eating up his substance at an alarming rate. He began to prowl through Marly and Versailles in search of something cheaper and more convenient.[88] The upshot was vividly and bitterly related by the prince to his father on 14 September: 'M. Orry not having got a home for me, where I would not be obliged to be wet for to get to it, and where I would be more at my ease, I was forced to take a few rooms in town, which I hired and which is but a hole.'[89]

Yet already the incompatibility between his status as incognito and his frequent public appearances in and around Paris was irking Louis XV.[90] The French king decided it was time to keep Charles at a physical as well as diplomatic distance. While the question of his future abode was debated, the prince went into the country to stay at the estate of the archbishop of Cambrai, which that cleric made over to him for an indefinite period.[91] The prince, it seemed, had waived his objection to accepting hospitality from Catholic clergy. Then, suddenly, his cousin the bishop of Soissons added another twist to the clerical skein.

8

'Chaos of thought and passion'
(October–December 1744)

At Metz in September Louis XV fell dangerously ill and was thought on the point of death.[1] With his morbid fear of Hell, the king confessed all his sins to the bishop and promised to make a firm purpose of amendment if God spared him. The new-found surge of religiosity did not long survive the monarch's recovery, but meanwhile the bishop of Soissons had extracted an important concession from him. Soissons had been out of favour in Stuart circles and was anxious to reinstate himself.[2] He put it to the king that his treatment of Charles Edward had been unjust. Louis promised to regularise the footing on which his allegedly uninvited guest was in his kingdom.[3]

As his strength recovered, Louis XV pondered this pledge. He was not prepared to lift the incognito because of fear of alienating Prussia. But if Charles Edward would take up his abode well away from Paris, Louis would look into the tangled question of his finances, and also examine the plethora of Jacobite memoranda more closely. For the time being the prince was content to stay in the archbishop of Cambrai's house because of the good hunting.[4] When his financial situation eased, he still hoped to base himself somewhere within a day's hard ride of Paris.[5] Meanwhile, in order to fall in with the spirit of the promised 'new deal' with the court, he would reluctantly retire to Fitzjames, the bishop of Soissons's estate on the Calais road – the exact locale for which Louis XV had destined him in March. After nine months, the prince was in more senses than one back at his starting point.

To understand the prince's financial situation, it is necessary to go back a few years to the era of waiting and preparation in Rome. In principle, the death of the prince's grandfather Prince James Sobieski in February 1737 had left the House of Stuart wealthy. His father,

John Sobieski, the Polish hero, had made a fortune from his loans to the Polish crown. But like many rich men, he bequeathed more problems than benefits to his heirs. The kingdom of Poland had made over its crown jewels to the Sobieski family in return for a huge loan. Another massive sum of 400,000 Rhenish florins was raised by Poland from the Sobieskis on the security of the duchy of Ohlau. The Sobieski inheritance was thus a twofold one: the jewels themselves and the mortgage on the duchy of Ohlau.[6]

The jewels had been deposited at the Monte di Pietà in Rome, a deposit account bank, and redeemed by the Stuarts out of the sale of their undisputed property rights in Poland.[7] But the mortgage, the so-called 'Fund of Ohlau' proved a liability. In 1739 the two legatees (Charles Edward and Henry) were persuaded to deed the Fund of Ohlau to the Vatican. Because of the political situation, the Stuarts could not actually take possession of the real estate in Austria that was rightly theirs. It was thought best to process the sale through an intermediary, in this case the papal nuncio. The nuncio was just about to take possession of the real estate when the Prussian invasion of Silesia threw everything in Ohlau into confusion.[8]

The confusion did not end there. In 1741 the duchess of Bouillon, Clementina Sobieska's sister, disputed the Ohlau part of her father's will by making a claim on the fund. Although the Chancery of Bohemia decided in favour of the nuncio and against the Bouillons, complications over arrears in interest meant that there was no realistic hope of a settlement before a general European peace.[9]

That part of the Sobieski legacy, then, remained a dead letter. There remained the Sobieski jewels, both the Polish crown jewels at the Monte di Pietà, and Clementina's personal pieces. According to the terms of the will, these had to be divided equally between the two Stuart princes. This too was complicated, since part of the jewellery had already been sold, some was saleable, but most, including the Polish crown jewels, could not be touched for another fifty years, giving Poland the chance to redeem them or forfeit title for ever.[10] The jewels were given to Charles Edward to be held by him until Poland redeemed them (in which case the redemption money would be divided between him and Henry) or the redemption period elapsed.

The net result of all this was that when the division of the remaining assets between the two Stuart princes had been agreed, they possessed a paper fortune but little in liquid assets. Hence the disparity between the claims made by Mann and other Stuart-watchers that the denizens of the Palazzo Muti were as rich as Croesus and their own frequent protestations of penury. The fact was that in day-to-day terms James relied on his pensions from the Vatican, France and Spain, the last two of which were frequently in arrears.[11] When Charles Edward was sent into France in early 1744, it was in the confident expectation that he would soon be entering London in triumph. Only his campaign expenses needed to be thought of. Neither James nor his son had considered what would happen if Charles had to spend a long period of time in France.

As soon as the prince came to Paris, he alerted his father that he was penniless and would soon run into debt, whatever economies he exercised.[12] From the time of his arrival until October he was paid just 35,000 livres by the French court.[13] This sum, thought disgracefully low by his Jacobite associates, was the consequence of Orry's notorious frugality.[14]

This parsimony brought the inevitable results. While Orry doled out money in niggardly amounts of 3,000 livres a time, the prince's debts mounted.[15] The gap between income and outgoings steadily widened. In July 1744, the pension made by France to Charles Edward amounted, in English money, to the decidedly unprincely sum of £1,800 a year.[16]

The prince hinted to his father that he seemed unaware of the cost of sending couriers and envoys to Rome, Avignon and England. Since he knew James would suspect him of prodigality, he got other Jacobites like Sheridan to vouch for the truth of his statements.[17] Eventually, worn down by his son's constant lamentations, James asked for a detailed breakdown of Charles's debts, so that he could make informed representations to the French court.[18] The prince was often at fault for inattention to detail; but not this time. He had Sheridan produce the most meticulous accounting for his father. These confirmed the picture of indebtedness only too well.

The financial troubles of the prince were a real headache for the French court. After a good deal of difficulty persuading his reluctant colleagues, notably Orry, Tencin obtained a pension of 5,000 livres a month for Charles Edward. Yet by now the backlog of royal Stuart debts amounted to some 60,000 livres. Tencin was furious. How could he ask the king to clear such a mountain at a time when stringent war economies were being enforced? Moreover, Louis XV still maintained that he had no moral obligation to the prince, since he had not invited him to France. When these points were put to Charles, he shrugged them off: 60,000 livres was a great sum for an individual, true, but a drop in the ocean to the king of France.[19]

The other main factor in the prince's chaotic world in 1744 was his Jacobite followers. To say that factionalism was endemic would be mild.[20] The inability of the Jacobites in France to make common cause approached the pathological. Andrew Lang once spoke of the partisans of the House of Stuart at this time as being divided into a king's party (Sempill, Balhaldy, O'Brien) and a prince's party (Sheridan, Marischal, Kelly). Such a neat bifurcation might have presented a manageable situation. In reality there were at least four factions, within which each individual tried to down the others and so emerge as, in effect, the prince's chief minister. Some account of these factions and individuals and their dynamic interaction with the prince must now be given. Such a recital might appear tedious and esoteric at first sight, but much that is obscure about Charles Edward's later history becomes clear once we penetrate this labyrinth of personalities.

The four groupings we have mentioned were: first, the Balhaldy/Sempill clique; second, the coterie around Daniel O'Brien and his formidable wife; third, the motley assemblage of disparate individuals Lang identified as the 'prince's party'; fourth, a maverick group of Jacobites acting under the direction of the inveterate plotter Eleanor Oglethorpe, marquise de Mézières.

The Mézières group is the easiest to deal with. It was Pluto to the prince's sun, on the extreme outer edge of influence. Apart from La Mézières herself, its principal members were Thomas Carte and Father Cruise. Conducting independent negotiations in England and at Versailles, this coterie was frequently rebuked both by James and his son for unwarranted meddling.[21] Its principal significance was that it was the only Jacobite cadre that had contacts with Noailles.[22] It also had the best channel of communications to Maurepas.[23]

O'Brien's circle had received a crippling blow when James opened up a parallel diplomatic channel to the French court via Sempill and Balhaldy in the first years of the decade. James must take a clear share of the blame for Jacobite factionalism. In addition, O'Brien himself was personally repugnant to Charles Edward, as was Tencin, O'Brien's principal contact at the French court.[24] Yet the prince was forced to bend to the prevailing wind in October, when Tencin began to control his destinies at Versailles. Swallowing his dislike, Charles invited the O'Briens to sup with him and Bailli de Tencin.[25] But O'Brien, Tencin and their circle were always at best tolerated by the prince; in their circumspection and regard for protocol, they seemed to him all too much like chips off the paternal block.

That left the prince's immediate circle of advisers. Only the toughest survived the internecine struggle to be at his right hand.

The emissary sent by James to be a moderating influence, Sir John Graeme, made no impact at all and retired in disarray to Avignon after five months.[26] Avignon was also the destination of Earl Marischal, who had ruined whatever chances he might have had to influence the prince by his behaviour at Dunkirk. He had since compounded this error by persuading the French court that if Charles Edward campaigned in Flanders, this would 'disgust' the English.[27] Some of the prince's most bitter outpourings at this period were directed at Marischal, whom he rated second only to Tencin and O'Brien as an enemy.[28] For once James was inclined to agree with him: truly Marischal's record had been a discreditable one.[29] James had appointed Marischal captain-general of all Jacobite forces in Scotland at the time of Saxe's invasion project. For his behaviour towards the prince, Marischal came within an ace of having his commission rescinded.[30]

The most likely candidate to ascend to the position of premier counsellor to the prince was his old tutor Sir Thomas Sheridan, whom James had dispatched to Paris with Charles's effects.[31] Sheridan arrived in Paris in early June 1744, bringing with him among other impedimenta a complicated diet sheet for himself (he was something of a hypochondriac) and another for the prince.[32] Yet unaccountably he failed to slot immediately into the old cosy relationship with Charles. Part of the trouble may have been that Sheridan dared to tell the prince that he found Marischal whiter than he had been painted.[33] He also did not share the prince's contempt for the bishop of Soissons's behaviour. Understandably, Soissons was reluctant to alienate Louis XV by appearing publicly at the prince's side in Paris.[34]

The upshot was that Sheridan was soon markedly out of favour and even comtemplated leaving the prince's service.[35] The prince beat him to the punch. Once he saw how well Sheridan got on with the arch-enemies Tencin and O'Brien, Charles banished him from Paris.[36] The prince aimed to show he meant business: he who was not wholeheartedly with him was against him.

At James's intercession, the prince reinstated Sheridan and used him as a sort of roving ambassador.[37] At the end of September he accredited Sheridan to the comte d'Argenson and then sent him to Metz with a letter of complaint to Louis XV about the continuing incognito.[38] Sheridan, who was a depressive as well as a hypochondriac,[39] interpreted this as a demotion and fell ill.[40] Yet the prince insisted. Sheridan was to lobby all the ministers, especially Maurepas, Tencin and d'Argenson, about the incognito and his debts.[41] Sheridan's mission was a fiasco. He got as far as Strasbourg only to succumb to another of his mystery illnesses. The letters he sent on to the king and the secretaries of state were returned on the ground that Tencin was now solely in charge of Jacobite matters.[42] When Sheridan did get to see Tencin, he came away empty-handed.[43] Yet he had apparently done enough to reinstate himself. By the end of the year Sheridan was once more in the inner circle.

The man who had done most to cut Sheridan out, and was also responsible for ousting Balhaldy and Sempill from princely favour, was George Kelly, now and later the prince's evil genius. A Church of England parson who had been out in the '15, Kelly endured twenty years' imprisonment in the Tower of London until his escape in 1736. He had been secretary to the duke of Ormonde before Charles Edward summoned him to Paris.[44] Within a remarkably short space of time, Kelly neutralised Graeme and Sheridan, completed the disgrace of his (Kelly's) erstwhile associate Marischal, and began the process that would bring Sempill and Balhaldy to ruin.[45] His skills as a manipulator of the prince were superlative, but his was a purely destructive, self-regarding talent. His influence on Charles Edward was entirely baneful and negative.

It was Kelly who persuaded the prince and Sheridan of the desirability of a sudden withdrawal to Avignon, on the grounds that this would humiliate Louis XV.[46] Fortunately this wild scheme was confided to James, who at once saw its fallacy. Not only would the simultaneous presence of the prince and Marischal in Avignon lead to fresh ructions; such a move would also play straight into Louis's hands, letting himself off the hook on which he had impaled himself by his own duplicity.[47]

But Kelly's most guileful and devious accomplishment was to compass the downfall of Sempill and Balhaldy in the prince's favour. James had long fretted that his son was too much under their thumb and wished he would get out from under their dominance.[48] Kelly was now to fulfil the king's wishes, though Sempill and Balhaldy contributed substantially to their own doom through systematic duplicity.

The first thing to do was to contrive it so that the pair were seen to fail. The changing tide of opinion at Versailles helped materially here. Sempill and Balhaldy had put all their eggs into the Orry basket and openly snubbed Tencin, thinking he was finished as an effective force on the council of state.[49] When Tencin replaced Orry as minister in charge of Jacobite affairs, the star of Sheridan and O'Brien rose as Sempill's and Balhaldy's dipped. Yet even before this

Kelly had manoeuvred the pair into bad blunders. Kelly persuaded Charles Edward to send Sempill to Rheims to lobby Orry for a revival of the English invasion project. Kelly was sure such a mission would fail. Sempill took the bait and set out.[50] His mission was a flop. The prince was particularly disillusioned with the way Sempill accepted at face value French protestations that they had seriously intended another descent on England, which was prevented by unforeseen circumstances, and that it was their heavy commitments that prevented their offering the prince a campaign.[51]

Meanwhile Kelly intrigued with Tencin to increase the suspicion that Balhaldy had been either stupid or consciously mendacious in informing James in December 1743 that the French would greet Charles Edward with open arms.[52] Finally, when John Murray of Broughton came over from Scotland in April 1744 to co-ordinate a proposed rising of the Scottish Jacobites, two things became clear. One was that Sempill and Balhaldy had been negotiating with both English and Scots Jacobites behind the prince's back. The other was that the Scottish leaders did not trust Sempill and Balhaldy and would not co-operate with them. Lord Traquair was especially vehement on this point.[53]

The ultimate point in duplicity was reached in September when the prince made clear to his father that the two men were even capable of deceiving each other. Rebutting James's charge that it was owing to Sempill's and Balhaldy's influence that Sheridan had lost favour with him, he revealed that Sempill wanted the prince to show some secret correspondence to Sheridan but exclude Balhaldy.[54] By the end of the year Sempill was complaining that he had now been excluded from contact with the French court for five months at the prince's orders.[55]

Yet there were glimmerings of more auspicious signs, the merest hint that the prince might have turned the corner and that the worst was over. The year ended with Sheridan largely restored and Kelly as the prince's *éminence grise*.[56] The struggle within the Jacobite party was largely resolved. For better or worse, Tencin was the target minister at Versailles. The financial situation was on the point of being cleared up.[57] As the prince withdrew to Fitzjames for the winter, there were cautious grounds for hoping that the year 1745 might turn out more favourably. No one could have predicted that it would turn out to be the prince's *annus mirabilis*.

9

'Do or Die'

(January–July 1745)

If there was one thing that sustained Charles Edward during the dark days of 1744, it was the thought that Scotland might be the key to the door through which he would pass from the darkness into the light. A Scottish expedition became his talisman, his lodestone. Ever since the early 1740s, when he was still in Rome, the idea had inspired him. Murray of Broughton's mission in August–October 1744 seemed to bring the dream several steps closer to reality.

John Murray's embassy was a continuing link in the chain of intrigue that bound together France and the Scottish Jacobites. In 1743 when Murray came to Paris, he had crossed with Butler's English mission.[1] On that occasion he worked closely with Sempill and Balhaldy. But by 1744 their lies, exaggerations and double-dealings were common knowledge in British Jacobite circles. Murray determined to keep them at arm's length.

He arrived in Paris in August 1744 and begged immediate audience of the prince. The first meeting took place in the great stables of the Tuileries.[2] On this occasion the prince was accompanied by Sempill and Balhaldy. John Murray was bewitched by Charles Edward, as so many of his compatriots were to be later. He saw a tall young man with reddish hair, full of easy grace and charm, ostentatiously wearing the Star and Garter and Cordon Bleu.[3]

Yet Murray did not allow the prince's magnetism to seduce him into fantasy. He began the session uncompromisingly, pouring scorn on the number of Highlanders (20,000) said by Sempill and Balhaldy to be ready to meet the proposed French expeditionary force of 3,000 troops. You would be lucky to find 4,000, commented Murray tartly.[4] When Sempill and Balhaldy tried to pour oil on troubled waters,

Murray asked for a private meeting with the prince next day. This was granted.

While Balhaldy hovered in the next room, Murray poured out his bitterness about the supposed royal favourites. He revealed the many different ways in which they had duped their master. Charles Edward listened coolly and calmly to Murray's recital of their duplicity, merely remarking that everyone has faults. Murray was greatly impressed by the prince's sang-froid.[5] Charles salved his wounded pride by revealing his plan to retire to Avignon, which he had kept from Sempill and Balhaldy.[6] Encouraged by this to be really blunt, Murray went on to say that in his view the French military position was as weak as that of the clans in the Highlands; early assistance from Versailles was unlikely.[7] It was then that the prince made his momentous statement that he intended to come to Scotland next summer even if only with a single footman.[8]

Intense negotiations between Murray and Sheridan then ensued. Murray was given secret instructions from the prince to prepare the ground in the Highlands. An arms cache was to be built up in the remote Clanranald country.[9] All the Jacobite clan chiefs and the 'Associators' were to be put in the picture. The key figures in the lowlands were to be lords Elcho and Traquair.[10]

Murray returned to Scotland in October 1744. Both English and French spies had dogged his footsteps in Paris.[11] Charles Edward now turned this to his advantage. He wrote to Louis XV (then campaigning on the borders of eastern France) to say that he had just received the strongest possible assurances from the English Jacobites. If the French brought an army of 12,000 to England plus a reserve of arms, the Jacobites themselves could put a force of 30,000 men in the field. If this demand proved impracticable, the overthrow of the Hanoverians could be initiated in Scotland. Only 3,000 French troops (or conceivably even Spaniards) would be needed for this.[12] The prince was using good negotiating tactics, making an impossible primary demand in the hope that a compromise by the French king would secure the secondary one.

One of the problems about mounting a Scottish venture was that the prince was not a free agent. His father was vehemently opposed to an operation in Scotland alone.[13] The first stage was to sell the idea to James. Surely, argued the prince, if France offered him troops for Scotland alone, he would have to take them?[14] James was not easy to budge. His thinking was prophetic. Expressing grave doubts about the idea, he told his son:

It would, to be sure, be a melancholy thing for you to return to Rome without doing anything, but it would be certainly much more melancholy to return there, however, after an unfortunate expedition, and the ruin of a number of our friends, who might not be able to remain at home, while we might not be able to sustain them abroad.[15]

At this point Charles Edward received assistance from an unexpected source. O'Brien put it forcefully to James that the Jacobite choice was now Scotland or nothing. The reason the French wanted to begin operations there was that the Highlands would give them a line of retreat if their army was defeated. To be confident of success in England on the other hand, they would have to land troops in overwhelming numbers – out of the question at the present stage of the war.[16]

Grudgingly James acquiesced. The only certain path to a Stuart restoration was a simultaneous descent in Scotland and England. A small French army sent to Scotland alone made the project much more precarious. But if, in their wisdom, the French insisted on sending their troops to Scotland rather than England, he neither could nor would oppose it. It would be for the prince, on the spot, to decide what to accept and what to reject.[17]

Throughout the winter Charles Edward worked away on his Scottish inspiration. He even gave up the pleasures of hunting to sit in conference and refine his ideas.[18] Hope buoyed him up, enabling him to ride out the high seas of 1744. He professed to be untroubled by his exile from Paris: 'he would put himself in a tub like Diogenes if necessary!'[19] There was also the welcome prospect of some hunting once he had worked out a plan to his own satisfaction. The prince was worried about his declining physical fitness. He suffered from severe toothache in January 1745. As he confided to Edgar, as a result of the severe winter, he did not handle a gun for months.[20]

Yet the early months of 1745 made it clear that not even the tiny force of 3,000 men for Scotland would be forthcoming from Versailles.[21] The truth was that the French were by now disillusioned with the prince: he was dangerous and unpredictable, not at all malleable like his father. The settlement of the prince's debts by the marquis d'Argenson, achieved by Sheridan's bypassing of the normal channels, was the last straw for Tencin.[22] Nor did the prince win any friends by boasting that he had exaggerated the extent of his debts in order to force money out of the coffers of the tight-fisted Orry.[23] But Charles Edward was determined that his own patience would not snap. France would have to order him from its territory; it would never be able to claim that he left of his own accord.[24]

To cock a snook at the French, the prince decided to pay a number of clandestine visits to Paris, in defiance of the informal agreement. This was in any case a necessary safety valve. His life at Fitzjames on the Calais road (seven posts from Paris) had settled into a routine of intrigue and dull social life. Just before he left for Fitzjames, Louis XV had relented slightly on the incognito and allowed the prince to meet his French cousins, the Prince de Turenne and the duc de Bouillon and members of the Berwick family (such as the duke of Fitzjames and the bishop of Soissons himself).[25] It was at this time that he met the Prince de Turenne's sister Louise (duchesse de Montbazon), later to be his mistress.[26] The couple afterwards rationalised the meeting as *coup de foudre*. At the time, though, the prince's thoughts were firmly fixed on making war, not love.

Occasionally Jacobites like General Francis Bulkeley or Lord Clare would come out to spend a week or two.[27] In April the prince renewed his contacts with the Prince and Princesse de Conti.[28] But even this was against the strict provisions of the incognito, which stipulated a maximum of three visitors at any one time.[29] The incognito also required him to be called M. le Baron. Often Charles chose to assume a German name.[30] On paper, the French conditions for his continuing to remain in their land were stiff.[31]

The prince cared nothing for the protocol of perfidious France. The roads from Fitzjames to Paris were good; the journey could be made on horseback in six hours.[32] This encouraged Charles in his defiance. The pre-Lent days of 1745 were a halcyon period for masked balls, at Versailles, the Hotel de Ville, at the Opera. The prince made a point of attending the opera and theatre in Paris masked, but dressed in such a way that it was obvious who he was.[33] On one occasion he was publicly recognised by Madame de Mézières. On another he attracted the attention of the queen.[34]

Angered by this, Louis XV passed on via comte d'Argenson the message that the prince should not appear in Paris, even masked.[35] The prince's response was typical. He made a point of going to the capital in March and staying for a couple of weeks on 'urgent business'. While there he again ostentatiously attended the Comédie and went to a number of balls.[36]

The French riposte was to stall on the payment of his pension and to inform him that he would definitely not be allowed to campaign with their armies in 1745.[37] There is no question but that the prince was foolish to provoke the French at this time, even though James admitted that his son was being pushed to the limits of reasonable patience.[38] French attitudes to Charles Edward were by no means as uniformly hostile as the suspicious and prickly prince imagined. Roughly speaking, those ministers who wanted to prosecute the war vigorously saw a future role for the Stuart pretender. These were Tencin and the two d'Argensons, who had the influential backing of the royal favourite duc de Richelieu. Those who favoured a quick peace or disentanglement from continental commitments (Noailles, Orry, Maurepas) were unregenerate enemies of the prince and would like to have seen the back of him.[39]

Charles Edward was never one to be cowed. His response to French intransigence was to give another twist to the spiral of escalating tension between him and Versailles. On 17 April the prince returned to Paris for another sojourn, piquing the French by attending a masked ball at which all the ministers of state were present.[40]

Meanwhile the Fitzjames interlude was drawing to a close. The prince's preference for the duc de Bouillon and the Prince de Turenne irked the Berwick family, especially when Charles Edward wrote to his father to veto the award of the Garter to the duc de Fitzjames, on the ground that Bouillon was more deserving of the honour.[41] The sour state of relations with the Berwicks was underlined by petty meannesses practised by the duc de Fitzjames. Not only did he instruct his châtelaine to charge the prince's entourage Paris prices for all their needs but, knowing Charles's fondness for the chase, he had her hide away the extra bridles.[42] The prince was never one to take such insults calmly. He ordered his party to move on to the estates of a more generous patron, his uncle the duc de Bouillon. After spending Holy Week 1745 at the Bouillon estate at Pontoise, the prince's 'court' took up residence at Navarre, Bouillon's chateau near Evreux in Normandy.[43]

The superficial round of social life at Fitzjames, interspersed with frequent visits to Paris, gave an impression of quiescence. Nothing could be farther from the truth. Day and night the prince toiled away at his Scottish project. His thinking had now concentrated on two points. It was clear to him that the French would never invade England, nor even Scotland, without being given a powerful incentive to do so. It was equally clear that the English Jacobites would not (and conceivably could not) rise until a French army was actually on English soil. The only place where an unaided rising could be initiated was Scotland, where the tradition of the use of arms was still strong, where the Jacobite clans could provide an army. If

Scotland could be set alight with rebellion, the French would have to come over. It would be an opportunity too good to miss.

It is important to be clear that the prince never imagined a rising in Scotland *alone* would suffice to effect a restoration. The point was to induce France to send an army to Scotland. Since they would always find a reason not to make the first move, an incentive had to be offered. Even a small rising of the Jacobite clans might be enough to persuade Versailles to send, say, 3,000 men. A tiny French army would be an earnest of Louis XV's intentions. It would have a multiplier effect in the Highlands, drawing doubtful or wavering clans into the net of revolt.

Obviously the best way to arrange matters was to have a French landing in Scotland *followed* by the rising of the clans. But no serious problem arose if the sequence was reversed and the clans rose first, provided that the French then intervened. It did not occur to Charles Edward that, for various reasons, the French might not lend a hand and he and the Scots would be left high and dry. Only very late in the 1745 rising did this dreadful possibility dawn on the Jacobite leaders.

French reluctance to make the first move was, then, a key element in Charles Edward's thinking in the early months of 1745. There was a further problem. The excessive caution at Versailles meant that the ministers of state would never allow him to set out for Scotland alone to foment a rising. Moreover, if they would not send troops, they would certainly not entrust a large cache of arms to the prince either.[44] It followed that if Charles wanted to light the spark in Scotland that would eventually draw the French in, he not only had to go to Scotland without their foreknowledge; he had also to take his own arsenal for the arming and equipping of the clans. But how could he buy thousands of guns and broadswords if he was struggling to make ends meet on an inadequate French pension?[45] This was the principal problem he wrestled with in the crucial first six months of 1745.

The problem soon became urgent. The duke of Perth, one of the original 'Associators', wrote from Scotland to say that broadswords were urgently needed. Immediately the prince borrowed 40,000 livres from Waters, the Paris banker. To cover the debt he wrote to Rome to ask his father to pawn his jewels at the Monte di Pietà.[46] He explained that he needed the money to buy broadswords in case the French ever decided on a sudden invasion. The last time there was talk of a descent on Scotland, the French said they had no money for arms.[47] At the same time Charles Edward asked his father for an open letter of credit on the Waters firm.[48]

James proved singularly reluctant to help him. In a sharply worded letter on 13 April 1745 he reminded his son that his mother's jewels had been made over to him against the day of his marriage; he therefore urged him not to pawn them. If, however, he insisted, then he (Charles Edward) must find another agent to carry out the transaction. Reluctantly he sent an order to Waters to cover the 40,000 livres.[49]

One of the factors in James's lukewarm support for his son may have been a vague suspicion of what was running through his mind. By this time all James's agents (O'Brien, Sempill and Balhaldy) had been edged out of the prince's inner circle, so that James was in the dark about his son's thoughts and actions, dependent solely on what Charles told him. The 'prince's party' was now led by Kelly and Sheridan. Colonel John O'Sullivan was a new recruit to the growing 'Irish faction' and a rising star in the prince's entourage.[50] Sempill and Balhaldy had had the tables turned on them in dramatic fashion. They railed against the prince and his new cabinet with a venom only biters bitten can muster.[51]

Yet something must have leaked out, for in February we suddenly read the following in a dispatch from James to O'Brien:

As regards sending the Prince to Scotland without troops, that is something I will never agree to, for as the Scots as well as the English have repeatedly said, they can make no headway without foreign troops.[52]

James forgot that as a young man of Charles Edward's age he had been more than willing to travel to Scotland without foreign assistance to head a Jacobite rising.[53]

The pace of events was much too fast for the circumspect Old Pretender. In January he had refused to countenance a French expedition to Scotland alone, insisting on a descent on England. One month later he was having to face the possibility that not even a French landing in Scotland would materialise. But with or without his father, Charles Edward was making progress on the financial front. The payment of the original instalment of debt to Waters by James encouraged the former to extend further credit lines, and 120,000 livres were made available from the Waters firm.[54] Moreover, Charles Edward had now made contact with an expatriate Scot, Aeneas MacDonald, operating as a banker in Paris. MacDonald was prepared to gamble on the prince. At worst he had the security of the Sobieski jewels to fall back on. At best, his rewards in the event of a Stuart restoration could be incalculable. So the list of swords, saddles, bridles and spurs purchased at the firm of Geraldins and Bouques and sent on to secret storage at Nantes mounted steadily.[55] By June the prince had assembled in a warehouse at Nantes no less than 20 small field pieces, 11,000 guns, 2,000 broadswords, and a good quantity of powder. There was also a war chest of 4,000 louis d'ors in cash.[56]

The obvious questions arise. How could Charles Edward purchase all this without arousing the suspicions of the French authorities? And how did the prince propose to get himself and the matériel to Scotland without French foreknowledge? The answer lay in the contacts the prince had made with the expatriate Jacobite ship-owning clique: men like Walter Ruttlidge and, especially, Antoine Walsh. Based at Nantes and St Malo, these were men prepared to seek fortune and honours by all means possible: piracy, slave-trading, political intrigue.[57] They also possessed a most valuable attribute: years of experience in outwitting French bureaucracy plus a close knowledge of how the key French minister Maurepas's mind worked. Together the trio of Walsh, Ruttlidge and O'Heguerty concocted with the prince and his Irish advisers an ingenious scheme to secure an open channel of communication to Scotland.[58] Charles Edward did not yet reveal the full dimensions of his scheme.

This was the most secret part of the prince's preparations. Walsh and Ruttlidge specialised in privateering and buccaneering under letters of marque from the French government. They provided ideal cover for a cruise to Scotland. At Navarre, while the prince got himself back into peak physical fitness with hunting, he held extensive discussions with Walsh.[59]

The prince next applied to Maurepas for permission for Walsh and Ruttlidge to carry messages for him to and from England, in addition to their other official privileges, such as taking prize crews on the Downs.[60] The idea was that open passports or *laissez-passer* authorisations would be issued empowering privateers to act as Jacobite agents. This would give the privateers freedom from official checks at French ports and customs houses. Predictably, Maurepas turned down the request, on the understandable ground that if such passports came into the wrong hands, they could be used for their own purposes by smugglers and other adventurers.[61] Feigning openness, Charles Edward kept his father in the picture about all this.[62]

When the expected refusal was received, Charles Edward asked permission for a single ship, the *Elisabeth*, to cruise in Scottish waters,

acting as a go-between for French intelligence and the Scottish Jacobites. Having turned down the larger request, Maurepas was disposed
to grant this. The prince's plan worked.[63] To Charles's natural tendency to indirectness and even deviousness was added the skill and
cunning of professionals like Walsh and Ruttlidge. The whole scheme
had been carefully mulled over with them in April. On the 12th of
that month Charles Edward finally revealed the full scope of his plans
and asked Ruttlidge to secure Walsh's agreement in principle. This
was readily forthcoming. On 27 April the prince wrote to Walsh:
'What you have engaged to do is the most important service anyone
could ever do me.'[64] He immediately sent Sheridan to put Walsh
fully in the picture; Kelly meanwhile was to work closely with Walsh
on the task of loading the broadswords on board ship.[65]

The prince's plans were now progressing more favourably than he
had dared hope. Not a word of what was really afoot was breathed
to those outside the inner circle: James, Tencin, O'Brien, Marischal,
Sempill and Balhaldy were all expressly excluded.[66] The French had
not the slightest idea of what was going on.[67]

As the prospect of a voyage to Scotland ascended the scale of
probability, from dream to vague project to strong possibility, the
prince distracted himself at Navarre by hunting stags in the great
forest there. Now he had to decide whom he could take with him.

The Irish trio of Kelly, Sheridan and O'Sullivan had to be taken,
since they had been in on the secret from the very beginning. O'Sullivan further commended himself by some slight (though much-exag-
gerated) military experience in Italy.[68] The decision to take the old
and ailing Sheridan was controversial, but Sheridan had used all his
prima donna wiles on the prince: begging, weeping, cajoling.[69] James
never forgave the old tutor for this. The man he had sent into France
to restrain the prince's excesses had ended, as he saw it, by throwing
in his lot with a madcap adventure. Underlying James's feelings
for Sheridan was a resentment that Charles Edward preferred this
substitute father, who had never disciplined his charge like a good
and dutiful parent, but merely indulged him shamelessly.

The motive in taking Sheridan along was certainly in part a desire
on Charles's part to snub his father. And no other explanation is
possible in the case of Francis Strickland, the fourth Irishman to
make the trip to Scotland. Strickland, an old hunting crony of the
prince's, his brother Henry's ex-tutor, and friend of Dunbar, was
dismissed from James's service early in 1745. He promptly sought
out the prince in France and was taken into his entourage. This

further enraged James and incidentally finished off Dunbar's already faltering career at the Palazzo Muti.[70]

With four Irishmen in his party, but outward bound for Scotland, the prince felt the need to 'balance the ticket'. He had already decided to take the marquis of Tullibardine (the 'duke of Atholl' in Jacobite eyes) as a pretender to the key Atholl holdings in and around Blair Castle.[71] Aeneas MacDonald, who had contacts in the Clanranald country, was prepared to go along to protect his investment.[72] Finally, the prince chose Sir John MacDonald, a bibulous, cross-grained ex-soldier with contacts among the ship-owning fraternity, to accompany him on the basis of personal liking.[73] These four Irishmen and three Scots made up the far from magnificent 'Seven Men of Moidart' of later legend.

The prince also had to decide his strategy. This had been the subject of a veritable essay-writing contest between Scottish Jacobites in France and their counterparts in the Highlands. Old Lochiel, chief of the Camerons, had originally proposed making landfall at Inverlochy, but this was considered too far away from the main population centres.[74] Sir James Campbell of Auchinbreck, another of the many Jacobites by bankruptcy, proposed landing at Loch Fine, three days' march from Glasgow.[75] Lord Lovat had favoured a simultaneous seizure of Inverlochy and Fort Augustus.[76]

But Charles Edward had been greatly impressed with Sir Hector Maclean, who was in France during the winter of 1744–5.[77] Sending Maclean on ahead to prepare his clan, the prince made plans to land on the island of Mull.[78] In addition to the Macleans, the prince hoped to have under his standard within weeks the combined forces of Cameron of Lochiel and Cluny MacPherson, plus the MacGregors, Appin Stewarts, and MacDonalds of Glengarry, Glencoe and Clanranald.[79] The immediate target would be all the castles and forts in Scotland garrisoned by Hanoverian troops.[80] Unfortunately, the plan to land on Mull aborted when Sir Hector Maclean was taken prisoner soon after reaching Scotland and incarcerated in Edinburgh Castle.[81]

Last minute preparations were now made. The prince had given letters for Perth and Murray of Broughton to Sir Hector Maclean, but sent on separate messages for them in the changed circumstances, plus his manifestoes and Commission of Regency, with instructions that both be published together.[82] He next sent Sir John MacDonald secretly to Nantes to co-ordinate the shipping with Walsh.[83]

Immediately a major snag was uncovered. The *Elisabeth*, though having received her commission to cruise in Scottish waters, was being detained in Brest by the Marine Commissary, pending further orders about the future uses of the Brest fleet. Walsh knew what to do in such a situation. A bribe of 1,500 livres was paid over; the *Elisabeth* was released.[84] Ruttlidge weighed anchor to take the warship to the rendezvous at Belle-Isle.

At Navarre the prince laid down a smokescreen to cover his tracks. He informed O'Brien that he was going on a sightseeing excursion to the monastery of La Trappe, where his grandfather James II spent his last pious years; from there he and his party would stop over at Paris.[85] The departure of his entourage would not then occasion any surprise. He then sent Sir Thomas Geraldin to Spain to lobby for support. Letters explaining his actions were sent to his father and other Jacobites in Rome. The courier had instructions to make a leisurely journey and tarry awhile at Avignon, seeking support from Ormonde and Marischal, before proceeding to Rome, so that there could be no possibility of James's recalling them.[86]

The prince and his companions sped to Nantes, each taking a different route to conceal the design. When they arrived they lodged in different hotels and pretended to meet by accident.[87] The prince went down to the quayside in disguise. All 'Seven Men of Moidart' went under assumed names.[88] Joining up with Walsh and MacDonald, they left the city in two boats and proceeded down the Loire to St Nazaire.[89]

After a night spent at an inn, they embarked next morning (22 June OS; 3 July NS) in fine weather on the *Doutelle* (sometimes known as *Du Teillay*), a 16-gun frigate.[90] Contrary winds held them up at the mouth of the Loire, but eventually they stood away for Belle-Isle.[91] The prince was not a good sailor. Even on the short leg to Belle-Isle he suffered from sea-sickness.[92] There were other matters to make them all nervous. Two French ships, inbound for Nantes, crossed their track and recognised Walsh's colours. This increased fears among the nervous (Sheridan especially) that their secret would be out before they were properly seaborne.[93]

They made rendezvous with the *Elisabeth* on 12 July.[94] The *Elisabeth* was a 64-gun man o' war. Ruttlidge had done a superb job of fitting her out. In addition to the arms cache, 700 men from Clare's regiment (from the Irish brigade in the service of France) were on board as volunteers for an ostensible privateering mission.[95] The contemporary practice of taking ships out of regular commission into privateering and back again extended to men like those in Clare's, who on this occasion were to be used as marines.[96]

Ruttlidge was sent back to Paris with the prince's letters of explanation for Louis XV and the ministers of state.[97] With Walsh as captain, Charles Edward's party on the *Doutelle* settled into their quarters. Apart from the 'Seven Men', they included the prince's chaplain Abbé Butler, his valet Michele Vezzozi, Donald Cameron (one of old Lochiel's retainers) who was to act as pilot in Scottish waters, and Aeneas MacDonald's clerk Duncan Buchanan. On 16 July the two ships stood away into the open Atlantic.

What was in Charles Edward's mind as the shores of Belle-Isle merged with the horizon? What did he think he was doing? Why did he conceal his mission from his father and the French? Was his enterprise a rational one, or was it a mad, quixotic, juvenile scheme worthy only of a Polish blockhead?

We must look first at his own account of his motivation. The most extended version of this is in the long letter Charles sent his father from Navarre on 12 June, in which he revealed for the first time the true reason he wanted his jewels pawned. After complaining of the 'scandalous usage' he had had from the French for the past eighteen months, he went on to make the obvious and telling point that Versailles would never make the first move towards a Stuart restoration. Even when they seriously intended to invade England, they had merely wanted to use the Jacobites for their own ends. So the choice before the prince was clear. He could remain in misery in France, in permanent limbo; he could admit defeat and return to Rome; or he could force the French to act by giving them an opportunity too good to miss.[98] Only the last choice was a feasible one for the hero:

> I cannot but mention a parable here which is: a horse that is to be sold, if spurred does not skip or show some signs of life, nobody would care to have him for nothing; just so my friends would care very little to have me, if after such usage, which all the world is sensible of, I should not show that I have life in me.[99]

As for James's trust in patient diplomacy, this was a forlorn hope. Twenty-six years had gone by since the last Jacobite rising. All that time Jacobite diplomacy had beaten in vain against the cliff-face of the powers' self-interest. Spain, Austria, Russia, France, all had been courted with great skill and punctiliousness, and all with no result. Even now, when France was at war with England, the combination of Louis XV's fecklessness and the divisions among ministers of state meant that no firm, spontaneous decision to support the Stuarts would ever be made. The prince poured scorn on his father's hopes of Tencin: the cardinal was both useless and powerless; Louis XV despised and disliked him but, characteristically, was too lazy to replace him.

Finally, the prince pointed out, reasonably enough, that if he had alerted either Versailles or the Palazzo Muti to what he intended, he would have been prevented. The French would have taken particular delight in currying favour with the Hanoverians (with whom they intermittently contemplated peace) and in presenting themselves to James as statesmanlike in having scotched such a rash adventure.

In other correspondence the prince revealed the things he could not say to James. Here he laid bare his disenchantment with his father as well as with France.[100] There would have been problems even if France or Spain had sincerely wanted to help him. Because of his anomalous position as leader of the Jacobite movement but not its official head (in Bagehot's terms its efficient but not dignified aspect), he would have been compelled to go to Rome to get his father to sign a formal treaty. In the meantime the summer of 1745 would have slipped away while diplomats in Versailles and Madrid dickered and wrangled over the fine print. The opportunity would be lost. By the time all was ready, the power (or powers) could plead the advent of winter as an excuse to pull out from the enterprise.

Already we can see here the resentment against his father's seniority and the hatred of French supineness that the prince was eventually to conflate as one single oppressive authority. Yet the prince's reasons were cogent enough and, given his own premises of action or death, unassailable. The prince was driven onwards out of France by one set of powerful forces and drawn towards Scotland by another.[101]

Jame's reaction, when he eventually read his son's apologia, was one of shocked horror. To the public world he put up a show of bravado. The tenor of his correspondence to Louis XV and the French ministers was: the prince was wrong to go, but now that he has gone we must support him with all our power.[102] But in private he inveighed against Sheridan, Strickland and Dunbar, and commented bitterly on his son's penchant for bad company, wild amusements, and above all, his over-fondness for wine.[103] Those, like Benedict XIV, who saw him at really close quarters, were appalled at the physical and psychological deterioration in the Stuart monarch. Frantically, James asked the Pope for a loan of 100,000 crowns (£25,000 approx.) against the jewels in the Monte di Pietà.[104] Feeling genuine compassion for a man who 'bore his misfortunes like a saint', Benedict authorised the loan, even though the market value of the jewels had declined and they were no longer worth that much.[105]

If on the basis of outer propulsion Charles Edward had a strong case, did he have a valid one in terms of Scotland's own gravitational pull? One of the strongest indictments against Charles Edward Stuart has always been the charge that he sacrificed thousands of Scottish lives and destroyed an entire way of life on a mindless whim.[106] The hidden premiss of this argument is that the 1745 rising was bound to fail. Either, then, Charles Edward was extremely stupid in that he failed to see what everyone else could perceive clearly, or he was morally vicious in that he too perceived it but pressed ahead none the less, driven by who knows what demon.

But it is abundantly clear that none of the actors in the drama of the 1745 rising saw it as bound to fail. Such a view is the extrapolation of the historian working with hindsight and, in many cases, worshipping the god of historical inevitability. The indictment against the prince can therefore be dealt with at two levels.

All revolutionaries, especially failed ones, are liable to the charge that in pursuing their aims they throw up unintended consequences. This view has usually been received with rapture by the conservative or counter-revolutionary persuasion.[107] It has less often been seen that the argument leads logically to political quietism, in which any demand for change can be countered with the accusation that it may engender unintended consequences. It is strange how readily a political theory that amounts to a demand for guarantees for one's future actions has been embraced by people who would never dream of demanding the same standard of proof in any other sphere of their lives.

If Charles Edward is arraigned for not having foreseen all the possible consequences of his actions, one can only retort that nobody ever can. In this case there is the additional consideration that none of the available evidence warranted the conclusion that a failed Jacobite rising would lead to the ferocious and draconian backlash that actually transpired. The 1715 rebels had been treated mildly. Executions were few; the authorities had connived at the reacquisition by proxy of the forfeited estates of the great Jacobite families. Nobody in August 1745 could have predicted that another failure by the Stuarts would lead inevitably to the barbarities of 'butcher Cumberland', the savagery of 'hangman Hawley'; and still less to the abolition of the heritable jurisdictions, the banning of the plaid and the breakdown of social relations between chieftains and clansmen.

The 1745 campaign always looked winnable without enormous bloodshed. The ease with which the initial conquest of Scotland was achieved shows this clearly. Where Charles Edward can be faulted is in his too-ready assumption that France would be easily drawn in to administer the *coup de grâce* to the tottering Hanoverians. As we have seen, rebellion in Scotland first as an incentive to French invasion was every bit as rational an assumption as revolution first in Russia as a precursor to general European revolution after 1917. It was hardly Charles Edward's fault that he eventually confronted the equivalent of 'socialism in one country', i.e a Jacobite rising without the French. He could not have foreseen the singular French incompetence in response to the rising during 1745–6, nor the inept way they squandered a unique opportunity to disable their chief competitor for world supremacy.[108]

Could Scotland be detached from England? Many factors made it rational to assume that this conquest could be achieved. Widespread dislike of the Act of Union combined with economic grievances over the Malt Tax and the Excise (which had led to the notorious Porteous riots) kept the big cities of Edinburgh and Glasgow volatile. The ideological support of the Episcopalian Church was another important element in Jacobite support on which the prince could count. Meanwhile the much-diluted Jacobite loyalty of the Highland clans was stiffened by the attacks on the traditional system of land-holding essayed by the government after 1737.

The outbreak of a general European war was a necessary condition for the 1745 rising, but the peculiar circumstances of Scotland in the early 1740s made it much more likely that an attempt like the prince's would catch fire. These circumstances can be conveniently classified as military and political. In the military sphere two trends were noticeable: the denuding of Scotland of regular troops, and the military eclipse of clan Campbell. With the outbreak of a general European war in 1740, many of the regular army units were sent to fight in Flanders, leaving exiguous forces at the disposal of Sir John Cope, Commander in Chief, Scotland. Despite Cope's warnings on the appalling state of Scottish defences, the London government took no action. Meanwhile the 2nd duke of Argyll's attempt to switch from feudalism to capitalism by eliminating the tacksmen or Campbell gentry, and letting farms directly to their former tenants, bade fair to extinguish the Campbell fighting machine. The 3rd duke grasped the military implications of the demise of the tacksmen; the muscle and sinews of clan Campbell. By 1744 he had started to put his brother's policies into reverse.[109]

Politically, Scotland by 1745 displayed two ominous signs. The English government was vastly unpopular even among non-Jacobite Scots. This meant there would be little enthusiasm for rallying to the defence of the House of Hanover. At the same time a kind of political ossification had taken place among the élite as a result of the stalemate between the Squadrone faction, led by Lord Tweeddale, Secretary of State for Scotland, supported by George II and containing all the anti-Argyll nobility, and the Argyll faction, supported by the most powerful law officers, including Lord President Duncan Forbes, and backed by the Pelhams in London. To make matters worse, both factions disliked Cope, the Commander in Chief.

Scotland by 1745, then, presented many features favourable to Charles Edward's adventure: a virulent nationalism, opposed to the Act of Union; an Episcopalian and Catholic north-east committed *a priori* to the House of Stuart; and the Jacobite clans of the Highlands, determined to preserve their way of life but confronted with both a short-term and a long-term threat. The short-term menace was personified by the Campbells; the long-term by the growth of Scottish capitalism after the 1707 Act of Union.[110] The political leadership in Scotland was in disarray, although by 1745 Duncan Forbes and the 3rd duke of Argyll had repaired some of the damage of the late 1730s. It is unquestionable that their conciliatory policies kept loyal some of the Jacobite sympathisers who would have risen for Charles Edward if the Squadrone party had been in power.

To energise all this Jacobite potential and weld it into a Stuart Scotland that could then be reinforced from France does not at all look like the political programme of a madman, blockhead or rash adventurer.

One final piece of good fortune attended the prince's departure and seemed a singularly good omen both for his future success and for French co-operation. On 11 May 1745 the Jacobite Irish brigade snatched victory from the maw of defeat at Fontenoy. The result was a great triumph for Marshal Saxe and a serious reverse for the duke of Cumberland and his British forces. Although the prince at first claimed to find in Fontenoy an ambiguous result for his own future,[111] it was clear that its effects were twofold. More troops would be sent from England to Flanders, thus weakening the opposition to a rising in Scotland. Then, once the standard of revolt was raised, the London administration would be faced with a ticklish choice of Scotland or the Netherlands on which to concentrate their military resources.

In more ways than one, then, the key to the success of a rising in Scotland lay with France. This was to be a recurring motif in the prince's high adventures that now followed.

10

The News from Moidart

July–August 1745

Setting sail on a fair wind, the *Elisabeth* and *Doutelle* bore away on a north-westerly track. For two days the seas were moderate. Then came a brisk gale on the 18th, followed by a dead calm on the 19th.[1] At noon on 20 July there occurred a near-fatal blow to the enterprise. At latitude 47 degrees 57 minutes, one hundred miles west of the Lizard, they came upon an English ship that had the wind of them.[2]

This was HMS *Lion* under Captain Brett, secured for action. All afternoon the *Lion* and the *Elisabeth*, both premier class warships, tacked for advantage. By 5 p.m. they came to close quarters. A dreadful pounding battle ensued. The two warships tore each other to pieces; both sides took heavy casualties.[3] At sunset the grim combatants broke off the carnage. The *Lion* was dismasted and forty-five of her men were dead. She limped back to Plymouth, her captain wounded, her master-of-arms minus a limb.[4]

Technically the *Elisabeth* was the victor, but she had taken severe punishment and was in no state to continue the voyage. Throughout the combat the *Doutelle* had lain out of range of the big English guns.[5] Now, putting out lanterns to signal his position to the *Elisabeth*, Walsh conferred by loud-hailer with Captain Conway, who commanded the contingent from Clare's. Conway told him that there were so many dead and wounded aboard that there was nothing for it but to return to Brest. Knowing that on board the *Elisabeth* was the nucleus of the Jacobite army, plus 1,500 muskets with matching ammunition and 1,800 broadswords, Walsh offered to take the matériel on to the *Doutelle*. But he had reckoned without the severe damage to the *Elisabeth*. The warship was listing so badly that its captain dared not heave to for the transfer of arms and supplies to the *Doutelle*.[6] Bidding farewell to the stricken *Elisabeth* at 11 p.m., the *Doutelle* pursued its track to Scotland.

The loss of so many men and weapons was a bad blow to morale. This was tested still further in the following days by the notoriously treacherous seas around the British Isles and by a series of scares. On the 22nd the *Doutelle* was again spotted and chased by enemy warships.[7] Fortunately she was a fast and weatherly frigate and threw off her pursuers. But it had been a narrow escape. Thenceforth all lights were extinguished at night except for the compass.

Next came the battering by the storm winds. A two-day gale raged on the 26th and 27th.[8] Mercifully, this was followed by a period of exceptionally fine and calm weather. Yet the same serene sea brought its own dangers. The horizon was dotted with ships. As they passed the coast of northern Ireland, they could make out eight separate sail.[9]

August came in like a lion. At midnight on 31 July the seas began to make up again. By daybreak a full storm was blowing.[10] Fortunately this blew itself out with the short-lived fury of a typhoon. By now Walsh's dead reckoning told them they should be off the Outer Hebrides. They took soundings and struck the sea-bed at 108 fathoms. Shortly afterwards the Isle of Barra was sighted.[11]

Moving close in to land, Walsh lowered a boat so that Kelly and Aeneas MacDonald could reconnoitre. They quickly ascertained that the laird of Barra was not on the island. But even as the *Doutelle* lay off the coast, another ship came up. This proved to be a merchantman ferrying cattle between the islands. Walsh took off the pilot to guide him. They proceeded to Eriskay, which was reached on 3 August (NS).[12]

Why this particular approach to Scotland, it may be asked? With the capture of Sir Hector Maclean, Mull, the original destination, no longer made sense. But a landfall in the Catholic Clanranald country, remote, inaccessible and solidly pro-Jacobite, was a good bet from the security point of view. And although it would be difficult for government forces to reach Moidart quickly, clansmen could by forced marches easily get to the Jacobite heartland at the southern end of the Great Glen.

The green and grey island of Eriskay, with its blanched white sands, racked by violent winds and rain even in summer, would have daunted and demoralised ninety-nine out of every hundred men born and raised in Rome. The cruel climate alone would have been too much for the average Roman. Here too was poverty on a scale that would have shocked the citizens of the papal states, cushioned as they were against life's worst buffets by an advanced system of public doles. The impoverished clansmen lived on a diet of milk and whey, eked out with fish and sea food. The dark and dank bothies were windowless and suffused with smoke from the damp peat on the hearth.[13] If Charles Edward really had been the petty Italian princeling of Whig (and some later) propaganda, he would instantly have wilted under the impact of this most profound culture shock.

Yet the prince soon made good his boast that he had never cared for Rome, as a society too soft and decadent for a true warrior. If he could not yet exercise his devastating charisma, since the Catholic inhabitants of Eriskay spoke Erse or Gaelic, he could show that he was a hero. Bearded and unshaven, wearing the dress of a student for the priesthood at the Scots college in Rome, the prince settled down for his first night on Scottish soil.

It was a wet and windy night. They were lodged in the cottage of Angus MacDonald, a poor crofter. There was no bread, not even a grain of meal, but they cooked flounder over the peat fire.[14] It was by fire, or rather smoke, that the prince's first ordeal came. Since there was no chimney in the bothy, but only a hole in the roof, the lungs accustomed to the groves of Cisterna and the forests of Navarre soon protested. The prince was forced to make frequent trips to the door to inhale fresh air. Eventually Angus MacDonald, not knowing that he was dealing with his rightful prince and seeing only a scruffy cleric, burst out irritatedly in Gaelic: 'What a plague is the matter with that fellow, that he can neither sit nor stand still and neither keep within nor without doors?'[15]

The news of the prince's arrival had been taken across the strait to South Uist. In the morning there arrived Alexander MacDonald of Boisdale, brother of the chief of Clanranald MacDonalds. If the prince thought he had problems with smoky hovels and damp beds, these were trifles compared with the news Boisdale brought. The two great Skye chiefs, on whom the prince had depended for his initial strategy, Norman Macleod and Sir Alexander MacDonald of Sleat, absolutely refused to 'come out' in rebellion, on the grounds that the prince had not arrived with the promised French troops.[16] Sir Alexander was within his rights in refusing to rise, for he had indeed always made a French expedition a precondition of his appearing under the Stuart banner; Macleod had not.[17]

This was a staggering blow. Boisdale advised the prince to cut his losses and return home. 'I am come home,' the prince replied, a memorable opening to *Bliadhna Thierlaich* (Charlie's year, 1745–6).[18] After warning the prince that he would advise all other MacDonalds, including the Catholic Clanranalds, to do as Sir Alexander ('Lord of the Isles') had done, Boisdale departed.[19] At this the prince's followers took fright and urged an immediate return to France. Only Sheridan and, clinchingly, Walsh backed Charles.[20] Nothing daunted, the prince restated his case with vigour and clarity and sent Aeneas MacDonald over to the mainland by boat to sound his brother Kinlochmoidart.[21] Meanwhile he sent another message to Sir Alexander MacDonald, summoning him to the royal presence.

It was clear that the situation in Scotland was not nearly so promising even as in Murray of Broughton's 'realistic' estimate.[22] They could not remain on Eriskay. Apart from the lack of food, a Royal Navy vessel was now patrolling dangerously near the *Doutelle*.[23] Walsh proposed to give this unknown but dangerous snooper the slip at night. At dead of night on the evening of 24/25 July (OS) the *Doutelle* slid silently out of the loch and out on to the open sea. Walsh held a course for Moidart. At daybreak Skye was espied on the port side away to the north-east. To the south-east were Canna and Rhum.[24] Late on 25 July OS (5 August NS), they entered Loch-nan-Uamh and anchored at Lochailort in Arisaig.[25]

This part of the western Highlands – Arisaig, Moidart, Knoydart, Morar ('the highlands of the Highlands') – enjoyed a higher standard of living than the Outer Hebrides. With cattle bred in large numbers, and wild deer roaming free in droves, there was plenty of meat, at least for the Highland gentry and their royal visitor.[26] The prince was extended the spartan hospitality of a MacDonald farmhouse at Borrodale. For the next two weeks he remained at Borrodale, sometimes in the farmhouse, sometimes on board the *Doutelle*.[27] Here the local clan dignitaries came to meet him. Ranald MacDonald of Borrodale, who had met Charles in Rome eight years before, did not at first recognise the hirsute, shabbily dressed priest.[28]

On shipboard next morning (26 July/6 August), he was visited by young Clanranald, son of the chief of Clanranald MacDonalds, and by Alexander MacDonald of Glenaladale. Clanranald too tried to persuade the prince to return to France.[29] When he found his resolve firm, he agreed to take another message to the great Skye chiefs Macleod and Sir Alexander MacDonald.[30] Predictably, the pair again refused to have anything to do with an enterprise attempted without the minimum prerequisite previously stipulated: 6,000 French troops.[31]

Glenaladale meanwhile was sent to assemble Clanranald's clansmen as a bodyguard for the prince. Kinlochmoidart, Ranald MacDonald's brother, was dispatched to inform Lochiel, Perth,

Murray of Broughton and the other 'Associators' of the arrival of the Stuart liberator.[32] While the prince awaited the result of Clanranald's mission to Skye, further MacDonald luminaries came to visit him: MacDonald of Scotus (representing the chief of Glengarry), MacDonald of Keppoch, Alexander MacDonald of Glencoe, and Hugh MacDonald, brother of Morar.[33] Thus were assembled all the important decision-makers in the extended clan MacDonald, awaiting the final reply from the Lord of the Isles.

When young Clanranald returned with the Skye chiefs' adamant and depressing refusal to come out, even Sheridan and Walsh changed their minds about the wisdom of proceeding further. The prince was alone in his resolve to land.[34] Sheridan was further cast down by a disingenuous reply from Murray of Broughton, advising return; as Sheridan pointed out, Murray himself had explicitly agreed to the 'going it alone' strategy.[35]

Blithely confident, the prince ordered Walsh to land the arms and ammunition from the *Doutelle*. This was a key decision. There was no question of Charles's keeping the *Doutelle* cruising until he saw which way the Highland wind was blowing. This was Cortés burning his boats.[36]

And at this critical moment the prince's personal charisma came into its own. Charles Edward made a dramatic appeal for assistance, not to young Clanranald, whose refusal would have settled the issue, but to the headstrong young Ranald MacDonald. Bombastically Ranald replied that he would follow his rightful prince, even though no other man in the Highlands drew his sword.[37]

This was shrewd manipulation on Charles Edward's part. The code of honour put young Clanranald in an impossible position. How could he refuse where a lesser kinsman had accepted? Even so, he wrestled hard with himself before making his decision. His kinsman Sir John MacDonald (one of the 'Seven Men') related that Clanranald paced the room at Borrodale for half an hour, leaving it for consultations no less than three times, before he gave his consent. But when he gave it, it was wholehearted. Young Clanranald promised to raise his clan and defend the prince with his life, even if no other Highlanders joined the revolt.[38]

Once Clanranald decided to join in, Glencoe and Keppoch threw in their lot with him.[39] The prince was making progress, but he still needed a major accession of strength before he could form a credible Jacobite army. The turning point came with Donald Cameron, 'Young Lochiel'.

On receipt of the prince's letter, Lochiel made a more honest response then his fellow 'Associator' John Murray. He sent his brother Dr Archibald Cameron as his envoy to the prince, urging him to return to France. Charles Edward replied that honour and duty required that Young Lochiel say this to his face.[40]

Both Archie Cameron and his brother John Cameron of Fassifern, who accompanied him, quickly came under the prince's magnetic spell. Even so, the good doctor made no promises; he merely said that if he did join in, he would be the last to leave.[41] Fassifern met Young Lochiel on the road to Borrodale and warned him to beware the prince's spellbinding charm.[42] Lochiel arrived at Borrodale with his defences well prepared, determined not to be outwitted as Clanranald had been. No arguments would sway him from his self-imposed brief, which was to persuade the prince that he was embarked on a suicide mission.

The crucial meeting between Lochiel and Charles Edward at Borrodale remains a mystery.[43] No one knows exactly what was said, but the prince clearly excelled himself that day in powers of advocacy, refuting once again the canard that he was stupid. Lochiel was no man's fool, and only an exceptionally quick-witted individual could have demolished his arguments so successfully.

The main outlines of the interview can be inferred from hints and pointers given by the prince to his later biographers (such as O'Heguerty and Father Leslie). The prince did not make the mistake of lying about French assistance but strongly reiterated that it was inconceivable they would not send an army to Scotland once they saw a Jacobite rising fully launched.[44] The answer to the clan chief's question, why had he come without French troops, was obvious; if he had had them, he would not have landed in Scotland but in England.[45]

Lochiel saw an opportunity to blunt the force of the prince's telling point about France. Very well, he replied, if Your Royal Highness will not return to France, and what you say is correct, why not send an envoy to Versailles to tell them that you are safe and well hidden and will remain in the bosom of the clans, clandestinely raising a Highland army, until the French army arrives?[46] The prince was equal to the challenge. After eighteen months of dealing with the French ministers, he replied, he knew their minds. They would believe in the existence of a Jacobite army only when they saw it in the field. He reminded Lochiel of the many French projects for a descent on Scotland and how they had always foundered on the circularity of who should make the first move. It was now his role to cut the Gordian knot. French worries about landing troops would be removed if it could be shown that there was a bridgehead already in existence.

What impressed Lochiel was the calm, logical way the prince outlined his arguments. The combination of wit, charm and lucidity was a hard one to resist. While Lochiel hesitated, Charles Edward threw in the magic name of Earl Marischal, now negotiating at Versailles and destined as the ultimate Commander in Chief of Franco-Jacobite armies.[47] Marischal's reputation in the Highlands was enormous: his adherence gave the project a soundness and solidity it had seemed to lack. The prince added that he intended to raise the standard whatever the Camerons decided.

Lochiel was reeling, but he was not yet ready to give in completely. He would join the rising, he announced, if two stiff conditions were met. One was that the prince would give him security for his estates in the event of the rebellion's failure.[48] The prince, thinking of the Sobieski jewels, unaware that his father had already raised money on them, agreed. The second condition was that the chief of the Glengarry MacDonalds ('Old Glengarry') would undertake in writing to raise his clan for the prince.[49] This assurance, too, was given.

Lochiel's adherence was the turning point of the rising.[50] If there was any doubt of it, Charles Edward now sent Walsh back to France in the *Doutelle* with letters for the court and a recommendation to his father that the intrepid Franco-Irishman be knighted.[51] Arrangements were made to raise the royal standard at Glenfinnan on Monday 19 August (OS).[52]

The clan leaders departed to raise their tacksmen and tenants, leaving the prince under the protection of the Glengarry men.[53] He stayed at Borrodale until 11 August (OS), making this his headquarters. He continued to send out messages to all his friends and supporters in Scotland.[54] On Sunday 11 August the prince went by boat with the artillery and baggage to Kinlochmoidart, skirting the heads of Loch-nan-Uamh and Lochailort. The Clanranald men marched round by shore.[55]

From the 11th to the 17th the prince was based at Kinlochmoidart.[56] Here Keppoch joined him with three hundred fighting men of his clan. The prince, in good spirits, half-playfully suggested that all the clan leaders sign a bond of loyalty. There was, however, some serious purpose behind this proposal, since the prince was annoyed by the reports now reaching him that Aeneas MacDonald had tried to persuade his kinsmen to remain aloof from the rising. But Tullibardine reacted with wounded dignity, calling it a slur on his reputation and integrity. The other six of the 'Seven Men', who did not have Tullibardine's potentially lofty position in the world, decided to humour the prince's whim.[57]

The government in London, meanwhile, was slow to react to the prince's landing, largely through difficulty in believing in it. This was hardly surprising, since Whig ministers on the spot in Scotland were initially highly sceptical.[58] But by about 8 August (OS) disbelief was turning to alarm as reports came in of numbers of clansmen flocking to the Stuart prince's standard.[59]

It was fortunate for George II that at this juncture in Scotland he possessed a servant of high calibre. Born in 1685, Duncan Forbes, laird of Culloden and Lord President of the Scottish Court of Session, proved the Jacobites' most formidable opponent.[60] Successively Deputy Lord Advocate (1716) and Lord Advocate (1725), since becoming Lord President in 1737 Forbes had striven to reconcile the Jacobite clans to the Hanoverian regime and to get them to see the 1688 Revolution as an irreversible fact of life. He had kept the devious Lord Lovat out of Jacobite clutches[61] (though Lovat was eventually to be his greatest failure), settled Edinburgh after the Porteous riots, and effectively blackmailed Norman Macleod and Sir Alexander MacDonald into staying loyal to George II.[62]

In 1745 Forbes immediately tried to stop the contagion of rebellion from spreading. He rushed to Culloden House, near Inverness, where he rallied to the government side lords Sutherland and Mackay, the Grants of Grant, Lord Fortrose (Seaforth Mackenzie), Macleod and Sir Alexander MacDonald, plus the Munro clans, raising twenty companions for Lord Loudoun's regiment among Highlanders who might otherwise have followed Charles Edward.[63] There was little else he could do, since the 1725 Disarming Act meant that Jacobite clans had hidden their weapons, while pro-Hanoverian ones had surrendered theirs. Macleod and Sir Alexander MacDonald cunningly used their official lack of arms as an excuse to remain neutral during the crucial first few weeks of the rising.[64]

Despite his energy, Forbes at first experienced many disappointments. First there was the wholly unexpected defection of Lochiel; later the equally unlooked-for volte-face by Cluny MacPherson.[65] In August 1745 everything went Charles Edward's way. First blood in the rising was drawn by the Jacobites. Just before he left Borrodale on 11 August, the prince had made it clear to his chiefs how important it was to stop reinforcements reaching Fort William.[66] On 14 August Colonel Swithenham of Guise's regiment, on his way down from

Ruthven with sixty soldiers to take command at Fort William, was taken prisoner by Keppoch's men within twelve miles of the fort.[67] Two days later the Jacobites scored an even greater success. Keppoch's lieutenant MacDonald of Tiendrish, assisted by some of the Glengarry men, attacked two companies of the Royal Scots on the shores of Loch Lochy. These soldiers were also on their way (from Perth) to reinforce the garrison at Fort William. A running fight commenced at High Bridge eight miles from Fort William and ended at Laggan at the head of the Loch with the Royal Scots' surrender.[68]

At Kinlochmoidart things were also going well. Food shortages had been solved by Clanranald's capture of three barges loaded with corn and oatmeal.[69] At this Murray of Broughton finally decided to commit himself. He arrived at Kinlochmoidart on Sunday the 18th.[70] So far was the prince from holding his two-faced behaviour against him that, a week later, he appointed Murray to be his secretary. A shrewder man might have been alerted by Murray's foot-dragging, but Charles Edward was always of an excessively forgiving nature until the point where he toppled over into suspicion and hatred, when he became impervious to reason. Always in the prince's personality there was the lack of a middle path or a golden mean. He was too trusting and lacked normal shrewdness and suspicion when dealing with flatterers. When his suspicions were aroused, they quickly toppled into paranoia.

Yet all in all the omens were good when the prince set out for Glenfinnan. The only sombre note had been struck by the London government's putting a price of £30,000 on the prince's head. At this stage Charles was inclined to laugh this off.[71]

Leaving Kinlochmoidart, the prince marched to Loch Shiel and went by boat to Glenaladale, where he spent the night. There the first of the north-eastern lairds (distinct from the clan leaders) joined him: John Gordon of Glenbucket, a stooped man of fifty-eight who brought along Colonel Swithenham as a prize exhibit.[72] Swithenham thus enjoyed the dubious privilege (for him) of witnessing the raising of the royal standard at Glenfinnan next day.[73]

In the morning the prince, guarded by fifty of Clanranald's men, was taken by boat to Glenfinnan at the northern end of Loch Shiel. There he was met by Morar and the rest of the Clanranald clan.[74] The narrow fresh-water loch was beset by beetling hills and saw-toothed ridges. Rocky screes dotted with heather added to the sombre effect. It was a desolate location for a scene of high pageantry. No rebellious legion commander in Germany could ever have raised the standard of revolt against Rome in more remote surroundings.

This time it was the Spes Britanniae, come from Rome, that unfurled the banner. At the head of Loch Shiel on Monday 19 August 1745 the prince enjoyed one of his few days of unsullied happiness. The raising of the Stuart colours at the age of twenty-four was the culmination of all his childhood dreams and adolescent aspirations. At the side of the dark loch the prince waited with his three hundred Clanranalds for the gathering of the clans.

The rendezvous had been set for 1 p.m. but for two hours Keppoch and Lochiel did not appear.[75] One can only speculate at the anxious state of mind of a prince so plagued by fantasies of betrayal. Suddenly at 3 p.m. the distant skirl of the pipes was heard. Large numbers of Camerons began to descend to Glenfinnan out of the surrounding mountains, forming an 'agreeably bizarre' zigzag pattern as they did so.[76] Three hundred Keppochs and seven hundred Camerons, virtually that clan's full fighting strength, made the rendezvous.[77] Doubtless Lochiel refrained from telling the prince that raising them had not been easy, that he had had to threaten to burn bothies over their heads before they rallied to him.[78]

The prince made a short but inspiring speech, playing down his divine right, stressing instead that he had come to Scotland to make his beloved subjects happy.[79] At 5 p.m. he ordered the standard carried to the other side of the river Finnan and called his first war council for that very evening.[80]

At the council two things had to be decided: future strategy and a choice of military leader. The loss of heavy ordnance when the *Elisabeth* turned back meant the previous idea of first besieging Scotland's forts and castles would have to be abandoned; indeed, they would have to give Fort William a wide berth to avoid its cannon.[81] That being the case, the prince advocated a swift advance on Cope's forces as soon as the clan army was properly equipped and victualled. He was aware that Cope had no more men than he did, as a result of heavy troop withdrawals to Flanders, both before and after Fontenoy.[82] Lochiel and the other clan leaders also favoured another approach to the Skye chiefs, this time in their own names without mentioning the prince.[83]

Then they turned to the issue of the command. Lochiel spoke with due modesty, saying he knew nothing of formal military matters but would take advice from those who did. Sir John MacDonald then proposed O'Sullivan as major-general.[84] Strangely enough, considering his partiality at this time for the forty-five-year-old

Irishman, the prince deferred a decision. Perhaps at some level he knew O'Sullivan was a military dud. Only constant nagging by Sir John MacDonald over the next few days secured the appointment.

The prince passed that night in a little barn at the head of the loch. Next day he departed to spend some days with Lochiel at his estate at Achnacarry, between Loch Lochy and Loch Arkaig.[85] Then the small army began its march. They pressed on through mountain trails to the Glengarry country. From Kinlocheil, where Charles Edward jokingly offered £30 for George II's capture in response to the price on his own head,[86] he forged ahead to Moy, staying one night at Fassifern's house.[87] On the 24th the army made a detour to avoid being seen by a warship lying off Fort William in Loch Linnhe.[88] Not far from Fort Augustus the prince was met by five hundred Glengarry men and about three hundred Stewarts of Appin under Charles Stewart of Ardshiel.[89] Already the prince's mania for physical fitness was paying off. The clansmen actually complained that he set too fast a pace![90]

Monday 26 August was a critical day for the prince. He was now aware that Cope was marching by Dalwhinny towards Fort Augustus. He therefore sent part of his army by forced march to seize the head of Corriearrack pass before Cope could reach it.[91] Only one week after Glenfinnan the prince faced the prospect of a battle. He did not shirk it, even though sufficient excuse presented itself, in the surprising form of a communication from Lord Lovat.

On reaching Inverary Castle after a hard day's march by way of Letterfinlay, the prince was met by Fraser of Gortleg with a verbal message (naturally!) from Lovat.[92] Assuring him of his loyal services, Lovat asked the prince to direct his steps towards Fraser country. If he passed through Stratherrick to Inverness, clan Fraser would rise to a man; almost certainly such a march would also draw in the Grants, Mackenzies, Mackintoshes and Macleans, all of whom were Jacobite clans with unpopular Hanoverian or absentee leaders. In that case Macleod and Sir Alexander MacDonald would be cut off from their protectors; they would no longer be able to maintain their pro-Whig stance against the hostility of their own tacksmen.

This was a very tempting strategy. Even while Charles Edward pondered it, Tullibardine suggested another. This was to push south with all speed through Atholl country and swoop on Edinburgh. But not, the prince insisted, before he had dealt with Cope. Here, as usual, the prince's intuition was sound. His instinct was always for an early battle, and it was a good one in the early stages of the rising, when the best hope was a series of knock-out blows. Evasion of a battle in 1745 (as opposed to 1746) always brought misfortune to the Jacobites. The prince's conclusion was that he would take Tullibardine's advice once he had vanquished Cope.

On Tuesday the Jacobite army pressed on to Aberchalder, where the MacDonalds of Glencoe joined them, plus some of the Grants of Glenmoriston.[93] Ominously, though, there came the first signs of a problem that was to dog the prince throughout the campaign: desertion. This time it was a group of Keppoch's MacDonalds that absconded.[94] Yet, all in all, the prince felt his army to be in good shape for the coming clash with Cope.

The battle of the Corriearrack pass was, like the battle of Stone on 1 December, a case of a battle that never was which yet had momentous consequences. To understand the situation we must return to follow Cope's movements. The obvious government strategy was to keep the Jacobites penned behind the Highland line, waiting for lack of money and resources to dissolve the tiny rebel army. Cope decided otherwise. He quit Edinburgh on the day of Glenfinnan and was in Stirling on 20 August. His orders were to seek out and destroy the enemy before they could leave the Highlands – a rerun in effect of the strategy so successfully pursued by General Wightman in 1719. But it was a risky strategy, given the paucity of government troops in Scotland, for if it misfired the Jacobites could descend into the Lowlands and seize the great cities of Edinburgh and Glasgow. For success, Cope needed enemy leadership to be as supine as it had been in 1715 and 1719. Instead, this time he faced the driving, dynamic energy of Charles Edward Stuart.

Cope laid his plans carefully. Before leaving Edinburgh he strengthened the garrison there (and at Glasgow and Stirling) and left Colonel Gardiner's dragoons to defend the Forth at Stirling. Another company of dragoons was detailed to defend Edinburgh.[95] So far everything had been done professionally. But things began to go wrong for Cope when he was just one day out from his base at Stirling. At Crieff he found not a single pro-Hanoverian clan waiting to join him. His inclination was to proceed no further. But he had his orders.[96]

Advancing, he reached Dalnacardoch on 25 August, where he learned of the speed of the Highlanders' progress. The prospect of a battle in the Corriearrack loomed. Cope took his army to the closest possible base, at Dalwhinny.[97]

What he saw there did not reassure him. Corriearrack was an obvious spot for an ambush. A high pass through the mountains, separating Loch Laggan and the Spey valley from the Great Glen,

Corriearrack was in those days traversed by one of Wade's roads. A spectacular engineering feat, the road zigzagged up from the south side to a height of 2,500 feet. Then it descended more steadily to Fort Augustus on the northern side, passing through several glens and valleys with ample cover provided by dense heather.[98]

The negotiation of this pass would have been difficult enough for redcoats in full pack even with no enemy present. Convinced from his intelligence (though wrongly) that the Highlanders already controlled the north side of Corriearrack and had laid an elaborate ambuscade, Cope decided that any further advance would carry him into a death-trap. Cope concluded that the odds were against him. He ordered his men to make for Inverness by forced marches.[99]

The Jacobite army began its ascent of the pass before daybreak on 27 August, expecting, when they reached the summit, to see Cope's men strung out snake-like on the southern approaches.[100] The Highlanders gained the summit. There was not a single redcoat to be seen. On 28 August the prince advanced cautiously to Garvemore, in battle order, suspecting a ruse by Cope. From dispirited camp-followers of Cope's army they soon learned the truth. In jubilation they marched down the zigzags to Garvemore.[101] Here for the first time since Glenfinnan the army tasted bread, having eaten only roast meat on the road – a curious reversal of dietary fortune for most clansmen.

When the full army assembled. in high morale at the thought that Cope had fled rather then risk a battle with them, the prince called a hastily improvised council to consider pursuing the Commander in Chief, Scotland. A forced march through Strathclear might enable them to intercept him at Slochd Mor between Carrbridge and Tomatin. But it was decided that Cope had too long a start on them, and that the Highlanders were too fatigued to make success certain.[102]

The prince now wished to press south through the unoccupied pass of Killiekrankie to the Atholl country. Against his wishes, he was drawn into a diversionary raid. Hearing that Cope had fled pell-mell through Ruthven, doubtless demoralising the troops there, O'Sullivan saw a chance to set the seal on his oral appointment as major-general. The barracks at Ruthven looked an easy target. The prince, however, argued that with no cannon or scaling ladders, taking the barracks would not be worth the loss of life involved. Once again he was right.[103] Eventually O'Sullivan and Archie Cameron wore him down and persuaded him to let them have a small party of raiders for the attempt. O'Sullivan quickly revealed his military ineptitude. So far from being demoralised, the defenders at Ruthven beat off the High-landers with losses.[104]

More successful was the side trip to seize Cluny MacPherson at his house. Murray of Broughton had summoned the nominally Jacobite Cluny to the colours a second time on 26 August but there had been no reply.[105] The ambivalent chief was carried prisoner to the prince next day.[106] After Charles Edward gave him the same terms as Lochiel, i.e. security for his estate, he agreed to come out and raise his clan.[107] Disguising the hard-headed bargain he had struck, Cluny pretended it was loyalty to the Stuarts that had brought him out: 'an angel could not resist the soothing, close application of the rebels.'[108]

On 29 August the prince pressed on to Dalwhinny and on the 30th to Dalnacardoch. Here he had word from Robertson of Struan that the Robertson clan would be joining the army at Blair.[109] On the 31st the army proceeded to Blair Castle in Atholl. Here they received another important recruit in the form of John Roy Stewart.[110] The army was short of experienced officers, and John Roy had held a commission in the Scots Greys. The prince gave Stewart a commission to raise a new regiment in the north and if possible to bring in the Grants.[111] At about this time, too, good news was received from the MacGregors, who had surprised and captured eighty-nine soldiers at the barracks of Inversnaid.[112]

The prince spent a pleasant couple of days at Blair Castle. This was a different kind of Scotland, possessing the civilised trappings he recognised, and even some he did not. Two sensations he experienced here were totally new to him. One was the sight of a perfectly manicured bowling green.[113] The other was the taste of a pineapple, a fruit apparently unknown in Rome.[114]

With Tullibardine raising the Athollmen at Blair,[115] August ended very favourably for the prince. On 1 September he was joined by Lord Nairne and his brother Mercer of Aldie. With his army increasing daily, the prince moved down to Dunkeld on the 3rd.[116] On the evening of the 4th he landed his biggest catch yet. He entered Perth and proclaimed his father King James.[117]

II

'That sweet aspect of Princes'
(September 1745)

Man for man the Highlanders were more than a match for Hano-verian infantry. But hard fighting alone could not solve all the prince's problems. In the week Charles Edward spent in Perth (4–10 September), he addressed himself to the most serious of these: money, officering, and (crucially) what kind of image the Jacobite army should offer to the world.

Money had always been a headache. Charles Edward landed in Moidart with a war chest of £4,000.[1] By the time he got to Perth only one guinea was left.[2] At the entrance to the city the prince held the guinea coin ruefully in his hand and said to one of his officers: 'Behold my war chest!'[3]

The fallacy in Whig strategy was clear. By penning the tiny Jacobite army behind the Highland line, they could have throttled it. The only consolation for the prince was that the army in being had been paid for for the next fortnight. All future recruits would have to be enrolled on a promise of payment alone.[4]

Some slight relief was afforded by the collection of the public money (excise duty on malt and the cess) in Perth, and by anonymous donations from sympathisers, but the prince had to accept a loan of 1,500 guineas from Lord Elcho on 16 September just to tide him over immediate problems.[5] This injection of funds, however welcome at the time, was later to cause great bitterness, since the prince regarded it as a wager to be paid off at high odds if he regained the throne for the Stuarts; Elcho on the other hand regarded it as a commercial loan pure and simple.

Outriders were sent to Dundee and other towns within Perth's orbit to collect public monies and seize all available arms, ammunition and stores.[6] Yet the lack of pay for the considerable numbers who joined the prince at Perth led inevitably to looting and indiscipline. Lochiel had to mount his horse, fire warning shots over his clansmen's heads, and even wound one of them to drive home the point that casual sheep-stealing was not to be a characteristic of the Jacobite army.[7]

All the prince's problems in Perth were interconnected. The new influx of prestigious recruits meant that hard decisions had to be taken about the exact place of individuals in the Jacobite hierarchy. In Perth Lord Ogilvy, Lord Strathallan, the fanatically ideological Oliphant of Gask, and the duke of Perth himself joined the standard.[8] The most important recruit of all was Lord George Murray.[9] Fifty-one years old, a veteran of the '15 and the '19, Murray had been living peacefully on his estates for the past twenty years, a progressive and liberal landowner.[10] His joining the prince caused a sensation in Scotland and was a severe blow to Duncan Forbes's conciliation policy. It alerted many waverers to the real possibility that the Hanoverian position in Scotland might prove untenable.

As the rising was to prove, Murray was a military talent of a very high order. He was an incalculably valuable asset to the Jacobite army. Yet from the very first there was tension between him and the prince. Here was yet another of those unfortunate personality clashes between Charles Edward and a man of his father's generation. Murray was no courtier: he had no conception of how to charm or flatter to achieve his ends. He was a cold, aloof, blunt-spoken aristo-crat, who always told the truth as he saw it, regardless of the unpopu-larity of his advice.[11] Charles Edward was unused to such plain speaking. His only previous experience of it, with Lord Marischal, had left him with a distaste for that person. Marischal and Lord George Murray were, besides (along with his father), the only individ-uals in that age group who seemed to be impervious to his charm. The prince had charmed Lochiel at Borrodale, and Lochiel had seemed in many ways the ideal father-figure for him. Yet although Lochiel always had a soft spot for the prince, he was genuinely in awe of Lord George and profoundly respected his military judgment. Eventually Lochiel too would lose face in the prince's eyes for his deference to Lord George Murray.

The unsatisfactory relationship between the prince and the man who was to be his principal general would in other circumstances have possessed a psychological interest alone. In the context of the 1745 Jacobite rising, it was the cardinal weakness in the Highland army. Both men must share the blame for the disastrous lack of rapport that so vitiated the Jacobite effort.

The Seven Men of Moidart quickly spotted that Murray was not

the sort of man who would allow his great talents to be eclipsed
by their spurious authority. Instinctively the prince's sycophants
recognised the enemy. Sir John MacDonald regaled Charles with a
medley of insinuations against Lord George: he was a spy, he had
joined solely in order to betray the prince, he was Cope's fifth column,
a creature of Duncan Forbes, and so on.[12] The ease with which the
prince accepted these innuendoes right from the very start of
Murray's service with the Jacobite army would suggest extreme gulli-
bility, were there not a more profound psychological explanation for
his 'will to believe'.

One unfortunate effect of the disharmony between the prince and
Lord George was not immediately perceived. This was the gradual
split in the Jacobite high command between a 'prince's party' and a
'general's party', uncannily mirroring the division of French Jacobites
during 1744–5 into the prince's party and the king's party. The prince
had relished blunting his father's influence in this way. It was not
such a happy experience when he was on the receiving end. And this
split had a further unfortunate consequence in that it tended to follow
the lines of an Irish/Scots divide, with the Irish favourites (and later
military commanders) taking the prince's side while the Scots aligned
themselves with Lord George. This polarisation was to have disastrous consequences: at Derby, after Falkirk, at Culloden.

However, at Perth it was clear that Charles Edward could snub a
man of Lord George's experience and prestige only at the cost of
extreme prejudice to his cause. At first he appointed both Perth and
Murray as his two lieutenant-generals, alternating the command
between them.[13] Strathallan was made brigadier-general.[14] O'Sullivan
was confirmed as major-general and quartermaster. Sir John
MacDonald was given charge of the cavalry.[15] Other leading Jacobites, like lords Nairne and Ogilvy, were given regimental commands.

There remained the question of the Jacobite army's image. The
Irish, especially Sheridan and O'Sullivan, advocated a tough policy
when dealing with reluctant town councils or recalcitrant farmers.
Anyone not co-operating fully with the army should be dealt with
severely; only by showing they meant business would the Jacobites
command respect. Lord George, who had been startled at the prince's
words at their first meeting – 'it is the obedience of my subjects I
desire, not their advice' – fully expected Charles Edward to endorse
this foolish draconian policy.[16]

But at Perth Charles sided with Lord George in arguing that the
aim must be to win wholehearted Scottish support for the cause.
Everything must be paid for, all indiscipline stamped on. The Scottish

gentry must come to see that their rights were being fully respected, that for them a Stuart restoration would be all gain and no loss. Besides, the prince was not going to throw away the undoubted advantages brought by his own charisma. He had already tasted the delights of popular adulation at Dalnacardoch, when men, women and children came running from their houses for a sight of the Stuart prince.[17] Then there was the time at the house of Lude on 2 September (when he was travelling from Blair to Dunkeld). He had held the spectators spellbound by his dancing skills as he performed a strathspey minuet.[18] The prince possessed glamour and he knew it. A tough, repressive policy would throw away this precious asset.

By the end of his time in Perth Charles Edward was able to feel a guarded satisfaction about the condition and progress of his army. On 10 September he visited Glenalmond to inspect the newest additions to his army: Perth's regiment, Robertson of Struan's two hundred warriors, and assorted MacGregors raised by MacGregor of Glencainaig and Glengyle.[19] All eyes were now fixed on the capture of Edinburgh. All other strategies had been rejected.

When the prince heard that Cope had ordered shipping at Aberdeen to take his army by sea to the Firth of Forth, he held a council of war to see whether the Whig general's movements could be arrested.[20] This would mean a long and tiring march north to intercept Cope somewhere between Inverness and Aberdeen. There was a risk that, as on Cope's march north, he would move too fast for them. There was even an outside chance of ending up between two fires. If Cope stayed on his side of the Spey while the garrison from Stirling issued out to attack the prince in the rear, things might go hard for the Jacobites.[21] It was therefore the unanimous opinion of the prince's council to concentrate on Edinburgh.[22]

Before leaving for Edinburgh, the prince wrote a letter to his father which contains some important reflections on his dealings with the Highlanders so far.[23] Whereas his charm had worked wonders, his sophistication had been too subtle for them. His reaction to the £30,000 put on his head by George II was to reduce the gesture to farce by retaliating with his own offer of £30, demonstrating also that he was not prepared to stoop to the same barbaric level as the 'Elector of Hanover'. This immediately encountered stiff resistance from the clansmen. They queried why they should risk their own lives for a man who seemed so indifferent to his own. Faced with this outcry, Charles Edward had had no choice but to offer a matching £30,000 for George II.

But if the prince had misjudged the temper of the Highlanders, his physical robustness certainly did impress them. The spartan regime Charles had followed in Italy was now paying spectacular dividends. The frustrated man of action had truly come into his own: 'I keep my health better in the wild mountains here than I used to in the Campagnie Felice [sic] and sleep sounder lying on the ground than I used to in the palace at Rome.'

The sojourn in Perth ended. On 11 September the prince visited Scone, breakfasted at the house of Gask, dined at Lord George Murray's home at Tullibardine and marched to Dunblane.[24] Next day he proceeded to Doune and on the 13th crossed the Forth at the fords of Frew (Boquhan), wading through the water at the head of his detachment.[25] That night he encamped at Leckie House near Stirling while the army encamped at Touch.[26] The men of Gardiner's dragoons had boasted over their cups of what they would do if the Highlanders dared show their faces, but on their actual approach the gallant dragoons galloped off to Linlithgow.[27] There was no relaxing. The prince sat up late composing a letter to the Provost of Glasgow in which he demanded that city's arms and a contribution of £15,000.[28]

On the 14th the army marched past Stirling and was fired on by the castle garrison.[29] The clansmen showed their coolness under fire by not breaking step, even when the cannonballs whistled nearby.[30] Skirting St Ninians, they halted at Bannockburn, where the prince dined with Hugh Paterson (later to have great significance in Charles's private life). At night the army bivouacked at Falkirk while the prince spent the evening at Callander House, seat of his latest important recruit, the earl of Kilmarnock.[31]

That night Lord George Murray took eight hundred Jacobite troops encamped in Callander Park on the first of many raids in the darkness. Accompanied by Lochiel, Keppoch, Glengarry and Ardshiel, Lord George set out for Linlithgow, hoping to fall upon Gardiner's dragoons in their camp. This time Jacobite luck was out. Gardiner's men had already withdrawn to the safety of Edinburgh.[32]

Hard on the heels of the vanguard, the main Highland army came in at 6 a.m. and encamped to the east of Linlithgow. Pursuing his policy of conciliation, Charles Edward kept his men out of the town so as not to disturb the sabbath, and himself spent the day quietly in Linlithgow Palace.[33] In the evening the army bivouacked three miles to the east of town on the Edinburgh road; the prince slept at a nearby house. He was the sole exception to the egalitarian practice whereby, on bivouac, all officers from Lord George Murray down wards slept beside their men, without any covering but their plaids. The Jacobite aristocrats believed in the power of example.

The Highland army was now closing in on Edinburgh. On the 16th the prince marched through Winchburgh and Kirkliston. After halting a couple of hours at Todshall and sending out a reconnaissance patrol, he advanced to Corstorphine. From there he sent a summons to the magistrates of Edinburgh, calling on them to surrender to avoid bloodshed.[34]

Whether Edinburgh would put up a fight was now the burning question. Morale in the city had been grievously shaken by Cope's departure for Inverness, leaving the Scottish capital exposed. On the other hand there were 50,000 people in Edinburgh, enough to supply copious volunteers. It was protected by a garrison in the castle, and was surrounded by a wall on three sides and a boggy morass on the fourth.[35]

The earliest inclination of the city fathers had been to resist.[36] But Charles Edward moved too quickly for them. While the proposal to raise a defence regiment was plagued by the usual eighteenth-century legal pitfalls surrounding the association of irregular forces in arms, the authorities in Edinburgh failed to provide vigorous leadership; whether this was through incompetence or crypto-Jacobite sentiment is unclear. Gardiner's and Hamilton's dragoons were heavily outnumbered. General Guest, commanding Edinburgh Castle, would commit the dragoons to the town's defence only if the burghers provided infantry volunteers as back-up. Volunteers to face a Highland charge were naturally not plentiful. In any case, the Lord Provost advised the citizens that their best efforts should be concentrated on the defence of the city walls, not in meeting the clansmen in pitched battle.[37]

This was the confused situation when Charles Edward's letter, breathing fire and the sword, arrived. The prospect of an unsuccessful defence followed by wholesale pillage and plunder by the Highlanders did not appeal to the citizens. It has to be remembered that the eighteenth-century civilian mind was still heavily imprinted by the horrors of the Thirty Years' War and the dreadful fate meted out to cities taken by siege. Magdeburg then had the emotional charge that Dresden has today. Besides, the numbers in the Jacobite army were not known and were greatly exaggerated. The prospect of a holocaust of rape and butchery loomed.

It was while the people of Edinburgh dithered that the dragoons' nerve cracked.[38] Gardiner's men had retreated to Coltbridge, west of Edinburgh, where they were joined by Hamilton's dragoons, coming up from Leith. The combined dragoons stayed for no more than an exchange of shots with the Highlanders before bolting at full tilt through Leith, Musselburgh and Haddington. They did not pause until they got to Dunbar. This ignominious retreat, the third by the dragoons in the face of the Jacobite army, increased the panic in Edinburgh and virtually decided the authorities on surrender.[39] Their natural Jacobite sympathies had been given the excuse they needed. The magistrates sent a deputation to the prince, asking for time to consider the surrender. The time was approximately 8 p.m. on 16 September.

Suddenly news reached Edinburgh that Cope had reached Dunbar and was disembarking his army. This was the selfsame force that had turned aside at the Corriearrack. From Inverness it had marched to Aberdeen, where it was embarked on transports and sailed down the coast.[40] The news placed the Lord Provost and his cronies in a dilemma. If they surrendered Edinburgh to the prince now, and a battle was then fought which Cope won, they, the city fathers, would certainly be indicted for high treason. It was a race between Charles Edward and Cope. What the magistrates needed was more time.

Stalling, they sent a second deputation out to the prince's quarters – the miller's house at Gray's Mill in the parish of Colinton.[41] The time was 2 a.m. on the morning of the 17th. But the prince had heard the news from Dunbar too. The magistrates' game was transparent. Angrily Charles Edward sent back the deputation with a demand for immediate surrender or liability to the full rigours of martial law.[42]

There are conflicting accounts of exactly how the Jacobites took possession of Edinburgh, but the departure of the unsuccessful deputation was clearly a trigger. According to the usual account, when the hackney coach conveying the unsuccessful postulants entered the city at the Netherbow gate, the Highlanders stormed in. Jacobite sources tell a rather different story. According to them, the occasion for the opening of the Netherbow gate was the departure from the castle of an officer in a coach to rejoin his regiment at Leith.[43]

It seems that what we are witnessing here is another effect of the mutual recrimination between General Preston in the castle and Provost Stewart and the city authorities below. Preston testified that it was the blundering ineptitude of the peacemongering deputation that let the Highlanders in. The city fathers responded with a story of incompetence by the military. It is of course possible that both incidents took place. Perhaps the Netherbow gate was even left open a longer time than usual to accommodate two sets of traffic, outward and inward. What is certain is that the Jacobites had already identified this gate as a weakness and had foreseen that it would have to be opened for some such purpose.

Accordingly, the Camerons and MacDonalds (Keppochs, Clanranalds and Glengarrys) had already stationed themselves in the vicinity. They had even tried to introduce one of their number in the guise of a Lowland servant to try to open the gates from within, but the ruse had been spotted and the 'servant' fired on.[44]

When the gates were opened, a silent torrent of Highlanders poured in and secured the other gates. The burghers of Edinburgh awoke to find their city in Jacobite hands, All regular troops retreated to the castle or fled to Haddington.[45] Lochiel, Keppoch and O'Sullivan presided over the proclamation of James III in the market square.[46]

The stage was now set for one of the great showpieces of the prince's career: his triumphal entry into the capital of his ancestors' ancient kingdom. At noon he made his appearance, swinging in an arc via Prestonfield and King's Park so as to enter the palace of Holyrood from the south and avoid coming within range of the castle artillery.[47] Charles Edward had always had shrewd instincts when it came to propaganda or showmanship. He knew how to milk an occasion like this. The crowd wanted to see a fairy-tale prince; he would oblige them.

Trotting slowly, with Perth riding on his right-hand side and Elcho on his left (the reward for the 1,500 guineas he had loaned the prince),[48] Charles Edward cut a heroic figure. He wore a blue bonnet decorated with gold lace, topped with a white satin cockade. On his chest was the Star of the Order of St Andrew. His Highland dress consisted of a tartan short coat without the plaid, red velvet trousers and military boots. On his head he had a light-coloured periwig with his own hair combed over the front.[49]

At Arthur's Seat the army halted and the prince held a short review, so that the crowd could inspect him at close quarters. He made a very favourable impression, grudgingly conceded even by his enemies. Tall, handsome, with brown eyes and a fair complexion, clearly a magnificent horseman and at the peak of physical fitness, he seemed to combine the attributes of a perfect prince with the rougher qualities of a martial hero.[50]

There is no question but that the prince's entry into Edinburgh created a sensation. His reception was almost riotous.[51] Once again his personal magnetism proved itself. Everyone remarked that there were two sections of the crowd that were particularly enthusiastic: the so-called 'common people' and the women.[52] The soubriquet 'Bonnie Prince Charlie' was first used by the jubilant crowd on this joyous Tuesday.[53] High-born ladies clustered at the windows and threw their handkerchiefs into the street. When he continued to Holyrood, the prince was mobbed by prodigious crowds of enthusiasts.[54] On the steps of Holyrood palace Hepburn of Keith, who had made his reputation as an unregenerate opponent of the Act of Union, acted out a piece of theatre. He ostentatiously went ahead of the prince in a gallery touch meant to convey to the crowd both that Scotland took precedence over the House of Stuart and that to oppose Union with England was logically to be Jacobite. It had always been the principal aim of Charles's propaganda to equate Scottish nationalism with Jacobitism.[55]

The babel of excited voices continued all that night in the outer courtyard of Holyrood House, with the crowd huzza'ing and halloo'ing every time the prince appeared at the window.[56] Throngs of aristocratic ladies pressed into the palace to kiss his hand.[57] Tuesday the 17th was a day for euphoria and riotous excitement. And Charles Edward had indeed every reason for self-congratulation. Just twenty-eight days after Glenfinnan he was master of Scotland's capital. Within a month he had outdone all previous achievements in the Jacobite risings. Speed, mobility, success: these were the marks of Charles Edward's captaincy. Cope had been outmanoeuvred; Scotland's Hanoverian administration had been either intimidated or outwitted. The prince's campaign of rapid momentum and superior mobility convinced many waverers. Others who were ambivalent or neutral towards the Stuarts thenceforth became apathetic. Here seemed a striking vindication of the prince's view that revolutionary willpower was all.

Yet when the dust settled, Charles Edward knew he still had to settle accounts with Cope. The Hanoverian commander's disembarkation at Dunbar was now reported complete. He had been joined by the lacklustre dragoons.[58] Cope showed himself eager to erase the memory of the Corriearrack. On 18 September the prince ordered on pain of military execution 1,000 tents, 2,000 targes, 6,000 pairs of shoes and 6,000 canteens for cooking.[59] In Edinburgh 1,200 weapons had been found to arm the clans properly. Shortages of arms were always a problem in the Jacobite army: Lochiel had already sent some of his men home for lack of guns and swords. And now at the right psychological moment Lord Nairne arrived with two hundred and fifty men from the Atholl brigade, closely followed by MacLachlan of MacLachlan with one hundred and fifty of his clansmen. There was even a dribble of volunteers from Edinburgh itself; these were enlisted in Perth's regiment.[60]

On the 19th the army moved out to Duddingston to meet Cope, leaving guards only at Holyrood. It might have been expected that the garrison in Edinburgh Castle would have seized this opportunity to make a sortie in hopes of regaining the city. But the Highlanders had cunningly bruited it about, as if by drunken indiscretion, that there was a secret corps of three hundred clansmen in hiding, waiting for General Preston to make precisely that move.[61]

Cope moved up to Haddington on the 19th and to Prestonpans on the 20th.[62] A battle could not now be long delayed. On the 26th the prince received another important last-minute boost to morale in the shape of the arrival of one hundred Grants from Glenmoriston.[63] He was ready for his ordeal by battle.

12

'Wha widna' fecht for Charlie'

(September–October 1745)

Yet there were problems. One was to plague the Jacobite army all the way to Culloden. There was a running dispute between the MacDonalds and Lord George Murray's Athollmen as to who should have the place of honour on the army's right wing. This problem first surfaced just before Prestonpans and was solved only by Murray's statesmanlike decision to station the Athollmen in the reserve.[1]

Another headache was the prince's desire to lead the army from the front in the coming battle. Like his father, Charles Edward was always physically courageous. His desire was overruled: the prince was told firmly that his royal person was too precious to be risked in this way.[2]

On the night of 19 September mounted patrols were sent to reconnoitre the roads to Musselburgh. Lord George Murray put the army on maximum alert. He now had about 2,400 men under his command, though Cope imagined it was double that number. Cope himself had roughly the same number.[3]

On the morning of the 20th, at about 9 a.m., the prince addressed his army. Accurately gauging the mood, he kept his speech short, ending with the rousing words: 'Gentlemen, I have flung away the scabbard; with God's help I will make you a free and happy people.'[4] When these words were translated for the clansmen, they threw their bonnets in the air and set up a whooping cry of triumph. In high spirits the army set out eastwards for Musselburgh in a long column of threes, with Lochiel and the Camerons in the van.[5]

Hearing that Cope's forces were in the vicinity of Prestonpans, Lord George Murray determined to seize the high ground to the south and west, in particular Falside Hill. The Highlanders moved out on the double and secured their objective. When breasting the hill they came in sight of the enemy encamped below.[6] Despite his later reputation for incompetence, Cope had selected his battleground well. A flat plain, running east and west, about a mile and a half in length and three quarters in width, without any cover, provided the ideal field for his regulars.[7]

Covered in the stubble of a recently garnered corn harvest,[8] the field was very well protected. To the north was the sea, plus the covering line of the villages of Port Seton, Cockenzie and Prestonpans. To the west were the ten-foot park walls surrounding Preston House and grounds. To the east, flanking almost the whole of the south side of Cope's position, was a deep morass, criss-crossed by ditches (the largest eight feet wide and four feet deep).[9] Unless the Highlanders were to launch a suicidal charge down from the high ground through the morass, it seemed they could only approach from the west. It was therefore facing this direction that Cope drew up his troops.

At first sight, Cope's position seemed extremely strong. On their own admission, the Jacobite leaders grew despondent.[10] The tension and anxiety produced the first open breach between the prince and Lord George. Without informing his lieutenant-general, Charles Edward gave orders for the disposition of the Athollmen on the Musselburgh road. When he learned this, Lord George burst into a rage: 'he threw his gun on the ground in great passion and swore God he'd never draw his sword for the cause if the Brigade was not brought back.'[11] Faced with this outburst, the prince quickly ordered the Athollmen back.

Murray's highhandedness as commander soon manifested itself elsewhere. To the despair of the military men of Moidart (O'Sullivan and Sir John MacDonald), Lord George took a unilateral decision to attack from the east and marched the Camerons away in that direction. Seeing this manoeuvre in broad daylight, and noting too that the Athollmen were on the move on the Jacobite left, Cope conjectured that a simultaneous attack was to be launched on both flanks. He changed front to the south-west, keeping his artillery on the left, rather than in the centre where it would have done most damage.[12]

That evening Lord George Murray met the Jacobite leaders to discuss final plans for the dawn attack. The bold and simple stratagem of marching round the eastern end of the morass and falling on the enemy flank was adopted. But at midnight a crucial refinement was introduced. Robert Anderson, son of a local laird, came to Lord George after the meeting with intelligence of a less roundabout approach to Cope's position. He knew of a narrow track through the morass.[13] Murray immediately saw the value of this information. The battle plan was amended. Orders were issued to march at 4 a.m.

The Highland army moved out silently across the marshes before daybreak. Before the clansmen left, the prince repeated his set speech to them: 'Follow me, gentlemen, by the assistance of God I will make you a free people.'[14] This was standard rhetoric, yet by all accounts the prince was in good spirits and well recovered from the brush with Lord George the day before. The effect on morale of the intelligence brought by Anderson was incalculable.

Clanranald's, Glengarry's, Keppoch's and Glencoe's detachments were followed by Perth's, the MacGregors, the Stewarts of Appin and the Camerons. The van, or right, was commanded by Perth; the left, or rear, by Lord George.[15] The reserve under the prince and Lord Nairne, principally composing the Athollmen, was to follow at a safe distance. No cavalry was to be used lest the neighing and snorting of the horses alert the enemy.

The Jacobites got through almost the whole of the morass before they were picked up by Cope's scouts. As dawn broke and a cold morning mist hung over the marshland, the Highland vanguard entered the plain about 1,000 yards to the east of Cope's left flank, having crossed the final four-foot ditches by a plank bridge.[16]

Perth continued to strike north in the half-light before veering to form line, so as to leave room for the rest of the army to emerge from the morass. Everything had gone smoothly, except for a fall in the mud by the prince when he tried to jump over a ditch. The superstitious Scots in the rear regarded this as a bad omen. Fortunately, they were too far away from the front-line regiments to communicate their misgivings.[17]

On reaching the plain, the prince and the reserve drew up fifty yards in the rear of the front line. A short prayer for victory was offered.[18] As the sun rose the Highlanders attacked.

The Camerons fell on Cope's left. Throwing away their plaids, with their bonnets pulled low over their brows, Lochiel's men bore down on Cope's right with hideous shouts and yells, coming on at terrifying speed. The stubble of the recently shaven cornfields crackled and rustled under their feet.[19] They received one burst of shell-fire, at which they split into three groups. The crack troops of the Cameron regiment then made straight for the artillery and overran the guns.[20]

Then came the onrush of the MacDonalds. The fire from Cope's infantrymen failed even to break up their line formation. The combination of speed and discipline in the MacDonald formation demoralised Cope's low-calibre rankers. Swinging in towards Cope's left flank in an oblique direction, the MacDonalds directed an accurate long-range fire at Hamilton's dragoons.[21] Seeing that their colleagues in Gardiner's had already taken flight, the dragoons did not wait for more. Within minutes Cope's infantry had been deserted by its cavalry.

Attacked now both by Lochiel's clansmen and the MacDonalds, aware that their big guns had been captured and their horse had fled, Cope's foot succumbed to panic. Successive waves of Highlanders crashed into them from right and left. Abandoning their muskets, the clansmen hacked and stabbed with dirk and claymore at the human wall of redcoats.[22] Defeat turned to rout. The narrow gap south of Preston House, the one obvious exit from Cope's 'perfect' battlefield, soon became clogged with a mêlée of desperate, swearing, panic-stricken troopers and terrified, whinnying horses. Cope made a vain attempt to rally his dragoons at the far side of Preston village, but the contagion of fear had taken too strong a grip. The only way Cope could salvage anything from the rout was to ride off at the head of his fleeing horsemen, thus at least keeping them in one body.[23]

Trapped within Cope's 'unassailable' redoubt, the redcoats had just two avenues of escape: over the high walls or through the struggling sea of human flesh in the defile. As the hapless regulars tried to get out of their man-made prison, they were cut down in scores by the broadsword.[24] The savage cleaving cuts from the claymore produced a veritable charnel house. Limbs, trunks and heads littered the ghastly battlefield.[25] The spectacle of horror, real enough, was to lose nothing in the telling. It was only with great difficulty that Lord George Murray was able to restrain the Highland blood-lust.

The prince meanwhile had seen little of the fighting. No more than five minutes elapsed from the first impact of the Camerons to the breaking of Cope's front line.[26] Though little more than fifty yards behind the enfilading wings of his army at the start of the battle, when the prince came up to the scene of the fighting, he could see plainly the results of the dreadful carnage.[27] Nothing better illustrates the gulf between Charles Edward and William Augustus, duke of Cumberland than his reaction. Where Cumberland after Culloden was to regard the quality of mercy as the prerogative of 'old women', Charles Edward was immediately distressed by the butchery he saw. It was in his power to preside over a holocaust. Instead he did his utmost to call a halt to the slaughter. 'Make prisoners, spare them, they are my father's subjects,' he called out.[28]

Depressed by the moans and shrieks of the wounded and dying, the prince immediately ordered his surgeons to tend the enemy as well.[29] He even sent Oliphant of Gask back into Edinburgh for further medical aid. By his own estimate the prince thereby saved no less than thirteen Hanoverian officers from a lingering death from septic wounds.[30]

Despite the brief slaughter, Prestonpans was remarkable more for its psychological effects than its casualties. Perhaps three hundred of Cope's troops were killed and five hundred wounded (as against about two dozen Jacobites killed and some fifty wounded). The prisoners taken (at least 1,500), mostly broke their oath not to serve again against the prince.[31] Cope himself, broken in spirit, fled via Lauder and Coldstream to Berwick, where legend (but not fact) asserted that he arrived with news of his own defeat.[32]

On the other hand, the battle at once delivered Scotland to the Jacobites and had a devastating effect on people south of the border. The previous London attitude – that the rising was but a trifle and would soon be extinguished – was exposed as a severe misjudgment.[33] Apart from the Highland forts and barracks and the castles of Edinburgh, Stirling and Dumbarton, the prince was master of Scotland. It seemed that ties of blood, loyalty, courage and willpower could always defeat brute force and a soldiery that responded merely to the whip and the lash. Cope had had better weapons, fought on ground of his own choosing, and yet his force had been annihilated. There had never been a better demonstration of the superiority of the moral to the material.

This attitude brought the prince dangerously close to a fatal belief in the Highlanders' invincibility in battle. Yet there are no signs that the signal triumph of Prestonpans made him complacent in the ordinary sense. Always a humane and merciful man, he had been sickened by the slaughter. It grieved him, he claimed, to have to kill his own subjects just because they had been poisoned against him by Whig propaganda. When congratulated by an officer in the post-victory euphoria, the prince replied sadly that seeing his enemies dead at his feet did not give him any satisfaction.[34]

Moreover, he had no illusions about what he had gained at Prestonpans. In his mind, the conquest of Scotland alone would solve nothing unless complemented by that of England.[35] And still the loss of the heavy artillery on the *Elisabeth* irked him. It will be remembered that the prince's original strategy was to seize all Scotland's forts and castles first. Without heavy siege guns, he had to leave these garrisons undefeated. Even with Scotland in his hands he could not take them.

Yet how could he invade England if these dangerous gadflies remained on his flank?

It was therefore an elated yet cautious prince who returned to spend the night at Pinkie House while his army occupied Musselburgh. All opposition in Edinburgh was cowed. Feeling generous, the prince sent a message to the Presbyterian clergy, assuring them of religious toleration and inviting them to hold their Sunday services as usual.[36]

The prince soon consolidated his growing reputation for affability and magnanimity. On the morning after Prestonpans another Edinburgh deputation came to see him, to ask for more time to assemble what the Jacobite army had requisitioned. Protocol required that the burghers see the prince's secretary, but as Murray of Broughton was out, Charles saw them himself, saying he saw no reason why they should wait.[37] He then capped the gesture by allowing the period of grace asked for. This approachability, plus a total absence of gloating over the defeated, won the Jacobite cause many friends.

When the prince returned to Edinburgh on Sunday 22 September, his first task was to decide what to do next.[38] His own inclination was to press on into England at once. But at an improvised meeting of his officers it was put to him that the army was so weak and exhausted it could not even pursue Cope to Berwick.[39] Besides, they had just 2,300 men. inadequate provisions, no espionage or intelligence network in England, and no contact with the English Jacobites. The defection of the Skye chiefs was never more keenly felt than now. In the circumstances a proposal to invade England was nonsense. The best policy was to await the large-scale reinforcements which must now surely come from France. To ginger up the tardy ministers of Versailles, George Kelly was sent back to France, with instructions to exaggerate the prince's success and play down the unpromising aspects of the rising.[40]

Jacobite decision-making now had to be put on a sounder footing. The prince decided to set up a permanent cabinet or Grand Council. To this were appointed his Irish favourites Sheridan and O'Sullivan and all the leaders of clan regiments, viz. Lochiel, Keppoch, Lord Nairne, young Clanranald, Glencoe, Ardshiel (commanding the Appin Stewarts) and Lochgarry (commanding the Glengarry regiment). Perth and Lord George Murray qualified automatically as lieutenants-general. The Lowlands and north-east were represented by lords Elcho, Ogilvy, Pitsligo and Lewis Gordon, by Glenbucket and Murray of Broughton.[41]

This council met every day in the prince's chambers at Holyrood

House and reviewed not just policy and grand strategy but day-to-day administration. There was an enormous amount of the latter: public monies had to be raised in all the Scottish counties, marching shoes and equipment ordered in Edinburgh for the ill-equipped clan regiments; caches of arms secured; further troops raised.[42] There were also some hard political decisions to be taken. Almost the first action of the council was to advise the prince to make contact with the English Jacobites.[43] Unfortunately Charles Edward's emissary was taken prisoner just after crossing the border into Northumbria.[44]

The early days of the council's existence were not a happy experience for the prince. The familiar cross-cutting rhythms of Jacobite factionalism were soon in evidence. Lord Elcho made the extraordinary suggestion that Charles Edward be declared king and his father's formal abdication assumed. Even the prince, advised by Sheridan, baulked at this blatant attempt to drive a permanent wedge between king's Jacobites and the prince's party.[45] Next Lord George Murray, with his *bête noire* O'Sullivan in his sights, proposed that in the interests of propaganda all Catholics should be banned from the council. Charles retorted angrily that he would never be the one to ask Perth to give up his position, and besides there were too many Catholics on the council (himself included) to make this feasible.[46]

Soon the battle lines on the council were drawn in a way that was to become familiar. Two parties emerged: the prince's and Lord George's. The prince could count on the support of Sheridan, O'Sullivan and Murray of Broughton. Perth, Lord Nairne, Kilmarnock and Lord Pitsligo also deferred to him openly, whatever their private feelings. But such was Lord George's prestige that the others invariably sided with him, creating a natural majority for his party.[47]

This consciousness of being in a permanent minority on his own council was a source of great irritation to Charles Edward. It seemed like the Palazzo Muti all over again, with Lord George playing his father. Here was revealed one of James's most fatal legacies. If he had inculcated the virtues of collegiate decision-making into the prince, he would have prepared him for the ordeal by council in Edinburgh. But James's own natural autocratic bent (in reality a mulishness born of insecurity) had been spectacularly displayed in the wrangles with his wife. This, plus an unconscious resentment and sense of competition with his son, had led him to preach the virtues of 'he who is not with me is against me'. Elcho and others frequently accused the prince of autocratic behaviour on the council.[48] They could not understand the frustration of the young man who, at last out of the orbit of his father's constraints, found in Lord George merely another stern taskmaster, for ever opposing notions of 'duty' to the prince's will. To Charles Lord George was another James.[49] There were times when Murray seemed to see glimpses of the truth, occasions when he would play courtier and humour the prince. But always that cold, aloof, haughty temperament supervened. Lord George's patience would snap and his own overheated personality would take over.[50]

The uneasy atmosphere on the council was made worse by the prince's obvious distaste for anyone who disagreed with him publicly. He showed some political skill by forcing the opposition to declare itself. He made a practice of saying what he favoured before asking the opinion of the others in turn, thus flushing out contrary views and forcing his critics to go public.[51]

In his clashes with Lord George Murray the prince was secretly encouraged by Murray of Broughton, who seems to have harboured the ambition of becoming Fleury to Charles Edward's Louis XV – a prime minister in all but name. The evil genius of the Jacobite council, Murray of Broughton did most of his Machiavellian work behind Lord George's back, insinuating to the prince that his namesake was a traitor and had joined the Jacobite army with the sole purpose of betraying it when the right occasion presented itself.[52] These absurd accusations fell on fertile soil.

Lord George heard of the crazed accusations made against him by the other Murray, by O'Sullivan, by the drunken Sir John MacDonald. As a man who had been 'out' in the '15 and the '19 and was now risking life and property a third time for the Stuarts, Lord George treated the whispering campaign against him with the contempt it deserved.[53] But his lofty disdain served only to infuriate the prince further. He became convinced that Lord George's chief goal in life was to dictate to him and to humiliate him.

A divided council was the last thing the Jacobites needed, for even during the period of 'phoney war' in October 1745, they confronted serious problems. The most pressing was what to do about the castle garrison. On its return from the victory over Cope, the Jacobite army marched into Edinburgh and was billeted in the city and its suburbs. The role of Provost Marshal was given to Lochiel. He placed his Camerons on guard in the Cornmarket to prevent any sally from the castle. This meant a permanent bivouac in the Parliament House.[54]

Having sealed off the castle, the Jacobites next tried to starve out the garrison. But General Preston, commanding the castle, was one of those fire-eating octogenarians that earlier eras seemed to throw up. As soon as Charles Edward threw a ring of steel around the castle, Preston issued a threat that he would reduce the city to rubble with his big guns if the blockade was not lifted.[55]

Charles Edward mocked Preston's pretensions. Surely he could not be serious when he claimed to have only six weeks' provisions in the castle? Was this the treatment the Elector of Hanover meted out to his soldiers: 'if he looked upon you as his subjects, he would never exact from you what he knows it is not in your power to do.'[56] Sensing a bluff, the prince ended his message to Preston with a threat of severe reprisals once he was restored if any damage was done to the city.

To general incredulity Preston thereupon opened fire. The cannonade did a lot of damage and bade fair to do more. Some people were killed in the main street.[57] Panic spread through the city as the big guns blew away the sides of houses. Angered by this breach of all accepted rules of warfare, Charles Edward next threatened the confiscation of the estates of all officers in the castle if they did not desist. Preston replied with another salvo.[58]

The crisis with the castle escalated. On 3 October a party of General Guest's men climbed down on ropes for a commando raid and killed a Highlander.[59] Next day there was another cannonade followed by a further sortie in which some civilians were killed.[60] Preston sent an insolent message that if a single fence at his Fife house 'Valleyfield' was harmed, Wemyss castle (Elcho's seat) would be bombarded from the sea by an 80 gun man o' war.[61] On the 5th there was a further fusillade from the castle.[62]

The prince faced a dilemma. He could climb down in face of this barbarity and lose face. Or, in the interests of credibility, he could sacrifice further innocent lives to the castle cannon. Charles did not agonise over the choice. He sent word to the castle that the blockade would be lifted provided there was no more shelling of the city. Access to the castle for supply waggons would be by special pass.

In reply, Preston still reserved his right to open fire whenever he saw clansmen in the streets.[63] And even after the road blocks to the castle were removed, he continued intermittent shelling. If Charles Edward had only known it, he was getting his first exposure to the Cumberland touch. There were to be many more Prestons: 'Hangman Hawley', Captains Scott and Fergusson, the 'Butcher' himself. The Stuart prince consistently behaved to his enemies in a humane and courteous way. His chivalry was almost never reciprocated. The Hanoverian officers in general betrayed a frightening, sickening callousness in pursuit of their aims.[64] *They* did not believe in sparing civilians, pardoning deserters, conniving at insolent townsfolk or treating enemy wounded. They regarded the Scots in general as an inferior race, and the Highlanders in particular as benighted savages. For them the '45 was always a grim and bloody war to the death. When the moral balance sheet of the rising is drawn up, the prince's civilised and humane behaviour should always be remembered.

This remarkable quality of compassion and mercy manifested itself in two other ways during the prince's sojourn in Edinburgh. It was put to him that he ought to send an envoy to London to try to negotiate a cartel for prisoners of war. The advantages of such an arrangement for the Jacobites would be considerable. Their men would know that if taken captive they would be treated as prisoners of war, not traitors. Recruitment would burgeon, for the main deterrent to joining Jacobite ranks would have been removed.[65] The prince listened intently. What if the Whigs refused to deal with 'traitors', as was very likely? In that case, said his advisers, it should be made clear that the Jacobites would give no quarter, take no prisoners. The prince refused outright. He had no intention either of committing such barbarity or even of threatening it. If London called his bluff, he would either lose credibility or be reduced to becoming a cold-blooded murderer. Neither option was acceptable.

The prince's merciful nature was soon revealed in another context. On 9 October Strickland presided over a court-martial at Holyrood on six deserters from Lochiel's regiment. Condemned to die by firing squad at dawn on the 10th, they were reprieved and given a free pardon by the prince in consideration of their behaviour at Preston-pans. The only stipulation he made was that they should not desert again.[66]

Yet another instance in which the prince sacrificed his own best interests to his merciful nature occurred during the raid on Duncan Forbes's home by the Frasers on the night of 15–16 October.[67] Although the Frasers were beaten off, their chief Lord Lovat claimed that the raid would have succeeded if only Charles Edward's warrant contained the words 'dead or alive'. Again, such ruthlessness was foreign to the prince. And the seizure of Forbes at this moment could have had important consequences, as it would have prevented Norman Macleod from joining with the northern clans.[68]

Compassion was not the only positive quality in evidence during this brief period of success in the prince's life. He displayed a pleasing fondness for humour too. An English Whig in Edinburgh was asked if he wished to kiss the prince's hand and replied that he would rather kiss the Pope's toe. The prince was hugely taken with this, sought the man out and joshed him about the Pope's toe. The Whig

became a reluctant admirer and penned a useful portrait of Charles
Edward at this time:

> He is handsome, he is manly, sedate and quick, he has a good deal
> of cheerfulness but not many words, he likes better to hear others
> talk than . . . to engross the conversation to himself, he cares not
> for eating above once a day or for more than three hours sleep of
> a night. He does all his business and writes his letters while others
> are asleep. He is capable of any fatigue and is the first to wade
> through a river and get wet sho'ed all the day.[69]

While Charles Edward won golden opinions for his compassion,
humanity and moderation, his life in Edinburgh settled into a busy
and active routine. Preparations were made for an invasion of
England on the assumption that French aid was on its way. Messengers were sent again to summon the Skye chiefs. The third and lesser
chieftain, Mackinnon of Mackinnon, heeded the call. Sir Alexander
MacDonald confessed himself sorely tempted after Prestonpans, but
an opportune letter from Duncan Forbes kept him in the Hanoverian
fold.[70]

In general, the response from the clans who had earlier held aloof
was disappointing. The rich dividends expected from Cope's defeat
did not materialise. Lovat was still playing a double game. Kinlochmoidart and Barisdale were therefore sent north with urgent appeals
to him from the prince.[71]

Along with the shortage of men went scarcity of money. Hay of
Restalrig was sent to Glasgow to enforce the previous demand for
£15,000.[72] Everywhere Jacobite agents were scattered in search of
funds: loans, exactions, excise, the land tax.[73] Lord Ogilvy, who came
in with a regiment of Lowlanders in early October, was sent to collect
the excise in Angus.[74] But the great unsung hero of October 1745
was certainly the twenty-one-year-old Lord Lewis Gordon. His
importance came from his senior position in the Gordon family. It
was thought possible that he could act as a counterweight to the
duke of Gordon and raise the feudal levies.[75] Seeing clearly the key
role that Lord Lewis could play in the north-east, Charles Edward
appointed him lord-lieutenant of Aberdeen and Banffshire.[76] His
orders were to levy the public monies, borrow other funds and raise
a second Jacobite army in the north.[77]

The first army, meanwhile, was not proving easy to administer. It
was essential that enemy spies be prevented from discovering the
true numbers in the Jacobite force. It was therefore necessary to keep
the army constantly on the move, from billet to bivouac. The prince

could never review it as a whole, only in discrete portions.[78] A few days after the occupation of Edinburgh, all Jacobite troops, except the guards on the castle and at Holyrood palace, were removed to a camp at Duddingston, with outposts in some of the villages. Every day the prince went out to review and encourage the clansmen. Occasionally he spent a night among them.[79] In the middle of October, because of the cold, the camp at Duddingston was wound up, the tents struck, and the men billeted in Musselburgh and other villages around Edinburgh.[80] In this way the prince and Lochiel, another tireless worker, kept the men's morale high.[81] More importantly, they successfully camouflaged their small numbers, with the result that Marshal Wade, the new Hanoverian Commander in Chief, did not dare to enter Scotland and the Jacobites had ample time in which to build up their strength.[82]

The prince's sojourn at Edinburgh in October was in many ways the high point of his life. These were the great days, the ones he looked back on ever afterwards through a nostalgic mist. A typical day would see a council at Holyrood at 10 a.m., followed by a public dinner with his officers, where the crowds would be encouraged to come and view him. In the afternoon, escorted by Elcho's blue-coated Lifeguards, he would ride out to review his army, again watched by crowds. Then it was back to receive his hordes of female admirers before a public supper, followed by a ball or musical soirée.[83]

The great ladies of Edinburgh were in thrall to him, to a woman, it seemed. All Jacobite sources, even those hostile to Charles Edward (such as Elcho's) are in agreement on this. Lest it be thought this is simply an effect of Stuart hagiography, here is the prince's most formidable enemy, Duncan Forbes, on the subject: 'All the fine ladies, if you will except one or two, became passionately fond of the young adventurer and used all their arts and industry for him in the most intemperate manner.'[84]

But the more the women of Edinburgh set their caps at him, the more the prince remained aloof. He consented to have the most sumptuous dances put on, but declined to dance himself. When remonstrated with, he replied: 'I have now another air to dance, and until that be finished, I'll dance no other.'[85] His was the posture of chaste Galahad pursuing the Holy Grail. His decision to sublimate all his energies in order to attain his goal was sometimes misinterpreted. The well-known incident when he stroked the beard of one of his Highland guards, saying: 'These are the beautiful girls I must court now,'[86] has sometimes been interpreted as evidence of latent or repressed homosexuality. All conquerors are supposed to be rampant womanisers, but this proposition is simple-minded. And we shall see later, there was a clear-cut correlation in the prince's mind between sexual abstinence and success (and the reverse). He is only one of dozens of historical figures who have taken the same view. Nevertheless, the combination of regal authority, magical charisma and unavailability – making him a kind of priest-king – was an infallible formula for attracting an ardent female following.

A key day during the month at Holyrood was 10 October, when the prince issued his proclamations, principally a manifesto of future policy in both England and Scotland. Since the most damaging charge against the House of Stuart in the eyes of the aristocracy (and some of the gentry) was that they would dismantle the financial system introduced by the 1688 Revolution, Charles Edward attempted to reassure his audience by stating that he would refer the entire question of the National Debt to a future Parliament.[87]

An even more pressing issue for the Scots was the Act of Union. Here the prince hedged, promising that his first Parliament would revise it, but saying nothing about outright repeal.[88] This was a case of the prince's wriggling on the hook. In this instance French and Scottish interests coincided, but diverged from those of the House of Stuart. Since the 'natural' economic conflict between England and France would persist whoever was on the English throne (whether Stuart or Hanoverian), France generally preferred a Stuart restoration to Scotland alone, keeping the northern kingdom as a permanent thorn in England's flesh. And Scottish nationalism could be assimilated to Jacobitism only if it was clear that the Jacobites wanted repeal of the Act of Union and the creation of an independent kingdom of Scotia.

This did not suit the Stuarts. They always and undeviatingly wanted restoration to all three kingdoms. *'Rien de partage. Tout ou rien'* became the formulaic battle-cry of the prince in all his later jousts with the French ministers. This conflict between Stuart aspirations and the ambitions of the Scottish Jacobites finally found its disastrous resolution at Derby. For the time being the prince had to dissemble, to appear to promise what he had no intention of delivering. There was a terrible reckoning later. Ambivalence is fatal at decisive moments of history. French ambivalence over the Stuarts in 1745–6 cost them their best-ever chance to unseat their global rivals. Charles Edward's ambivalence on Scotland was to lead to the débâcle at Derby.

One can sympathise with his prevarications on this crucial issue. After all, all his education and upbringing had inculcated the idea that he was *de jure* heir apparent to the throne of England, as well as Scotland. The irony is that, if he had categorically refused to give any assurances about the repeal of the Act of Union in his proclamations, he would have been better served in the long run than by his actual hints and half-promises. For one thing, he would never have been able to carry the council with him on the decision to invade England. Lord George Murray was said to have found the prince's manifesto anachronistic.[89] It was hardly that; it was merely (and disastrously) studiedly ambiguous.

In his own mind Charles Edward was always clear that he would proceed to England once his numbers were respectable. From this viewpoint October 1745 was a month of mixed fortunes. The prince received various additions to his strength: from Lord Ogilvy, from Farquharson of Monaltrie, from viscount Dundee.[90] There were fresh levies from the Lowlands.[91] Glenbucket and Pitsligo brought in welcome recruits from Aberdeen and Banffshire.[92] The chief of Mackinnon brought in his clan.[93] One hundred MacGregors from Balquhidder came in.[94] Other notable recruits were Arthur Elphinstone (later Lord Balmerino) and the Master of Strathallan.[95] Tullibardine, jealous at the eminence attained by his younger brother Lord George Murray, pushed himself to the limit to raise a further contingent of Athollmen in his own right.[96] Finally, at the very end of October, Cluny MacPherson brought in his clan.[97] The Frasers under Lord Lovat were rumoured to be on the point of joining. The Mackintoshes, initially held in reluctant obedience to the authorities by their pro-Hanoverian chief, had been raised for the Jacobites in his absence by his wife Lady Anne ('colonel Anne' of Jacobite legend).[98]

But against this there were some grave disappointments and setbacks. The earl of Nithsdale and viscount Kenmure joined the prince, only to desert the next day when they learned of the exiguous numbers in his army.[99] Barisdale's recruiting drive in the north ended in fiasco. This ferocious and treacherous ruffian, one of the few really bad eggs in the Jacobite basket, had a very crude idea of enlisting men. This consisted of plying them with whisky until they were too drunk to know what they were signing up for. When they sobered up next day and found themselves in the Jacobite army, most of the 'recruits' promptly decamped.[100]

More seriously, Lord Lovat had still not committed himself.[101] Most ominously of all, the myth of the invincibility of the prince's Highlanders took a beating, albeit in minor engagements. A body of Macleans, on the march to Edinburgh to join the prince, was attacked, disarmed and dispersed by Lt-Col. Campbell and the Argyllshire militia (en route to join Lord Loudoun's anti-Jacobite standard).[102] The same Colonel Campbell struck again just as the prince crossed the border into England, this time checking MacGregor of Glengyle.[103]

The prince seemed to be barely holding his own. Then on 14 October came the event he had hoped and prayed for. Momentarily all his critics were silenced, all doubters dumbfounded. There arrived at Montrose, the marquis d'Eguilles, special envoy from Louis XV.[104] At last, it seemed, the French were coming.

13

Invasion!

(October–December 1745)

To explain d'Eguilles's sudden advent at Montrose, we must examine the impact in Europe of the prince's thunderbolt arrival in Scotland and his lightning successes thereafter. So totally unexpected was his landing at Moidart that all but the best-informed European sources remained incredulous for many months.[1]

The Pope knew better. From the very beginning of the '45, Benedict XIV followed the drama with avid interest.[2] Although his loyalties were divided – he feared that an unsuccessful Jacobite rising would lead to the full visitation of the Penal Laws on his flock in England – he decided to back the Stuarts discreetly with money.[3] Although reports of vast numbers of Roman crowns paid over in exchange for a pledge of the full restoration of Catholicism in England were pure fantasy,[4] Benedict did make money available to James over and above the cash raised in the Monte di Pietà.[5]

This extra sum was given to Henry Stuart when he left Rome for France at the end of August 1745.[6] At news of the prince's landing in Scotland, James prised the younger Stuart prince out of his hermit-like existence of prayer and asceticism and ordered him to go to Versailles to lobby on his brother's behalf. Thus began Henry's one and only venture into the world of secular politics. It was to be an ill-starred eighteen months, culminating in disaster.

When news of Prestonpans came in, and especially when Benedict was assured by Tencin that France intended to throw its weight behind the rising, the Pope sent a further sum of money to Henry.[7] Charles Edward's run of success in late 1745 amazed and delighted the Pope.[8] He began to allow himself to hope that he would live to see Catholicism restored in England, that sometime island of saints now occupied by demons, as he put it.[9]

French reaction was more circumspect. The initial reaction at Versailles had been stupefaction. Then, as the prince began to establish himself in Scotland and the Jacobite pressure groups got down to serious lobbying,[10] Louis XV and his ministers had to take firm decisions on what to do next. This, of course, was what Louis XV hated most. The divisions among his ministers gave him the excuse to temporise, always his natural reaction.

It was obvious that swift action was needed. An expedition should at once have been sent to Scotland to consolidate the prince's bridgehead. But Louis dithered. Although Tencin and the marquis d'Argenson urged an immediate troop landing in Scotland, the influential Saxe/Noailles clique favoured initiatives on the Continent, using the rising as a diversion.[11] The other problem about a Scottish expedition was that it meant using the Brest fleet. But Maurepas already had this earmarked for the projected reconquest of Louisbourg in north America.

Louis XV solved these conflicting demands by stalling and playing for time. He sent d'Eguilles on a fact-finding mission: his brief was to ascertain the numbers in the Jacobite army, sound the prince's intentions, and in general to gauge the strength of pro-Stuart feeling in Britain.

The ultimate downfall of all French efforts on behalf of the Jacobites in 1745–6 sprang from that one decision. By the time d'Eguilles's first dispatches reached Versailles, the prince was already embarking on his ill-fated venture into England. The only thing left for the French to do then was to mount a cross-Channel expedition. But an invasion of England was at once more hazardous and less consonant with French interests than a landing in Scotland. This is not to say that Louis was not serious in his desire to help the prince: he was, and his English invasion project of 1745–6 was no feint. But by his own incompetence as much as by the divisions between his ministers of state, he left himself with having to implement the far tougher option when a moment's decisiveness could have secured him the easier one.[12]

Yet whatever the ultimate consequences of the d'Eguilles mission, his immediate impact on arrival in Scotland was sensational. Here was the living proof of the efficacy of the prince's 'rolling strategy'. Everything he had said to the clan leaders appeared true. France was not just 'bound to' join in; now she could be seen to be already doing so.

This inference was strengthened by the number of small French ships that got through to Scottish ports in October. Louis XV began his support for Charles Edward with pump-priming: he ordered Maurepas to send all available privateers to Scotland with men and materiel. Between 9–19 October four vessels from France (including the one bringing d'Eguilles himself) landed at Montrose and Stonehaven with artillery and stores.[13] On the advice of James Grant, a siege engineer in French service who accompanied the big guns, the materiel was transported by the Athollmen and the MacPhersons to Edinburgh, then ferried across the Forth to Alloa.[14] Batteries were then erected on both sides of the river to secure the capital against any attempt by British cruisers to force passage. There were rumours that the Whigs would attempt an amphibious operation: a blockade running up the Forth combined with a sortie in force from the castle.[15]

D'Eguilles himself settled in well with the Jacobites. He was no dour Saxe, no pessimistic Marischal. Like so many others, at least at first, he fell under the prince's spell and allowed himself to be caught up in the general euphoria. Everything, then, combined to make the prince's prognostications of an impending large-scale French landing look sober and well-calculated.

The most significant factor in d'Eguilles's presence, adding even greater weight to the prince's blandishments, was that he had been sent to Scotland *before* Prestonpans. When news of that battle was received in Versailles, the French at last bestirred themselves. By the Treaty of Fontainebleau in late October they formally committed themselves to an alliance with the Jacobites.[16] This treaty has sometimes been regarded as a dead letter, but it did prevent the authorities in London from using Dutch troops against the 'rebels', since the Dutch were constrained by the articles of a previous capitulation to the French.

All of this helped the prince. The more evidence there was of French seriousness, the harder it would be for Lord George Murray and his natural majority on the council to resist the call for an incursion into England.

The moment of decision came on 30 October. That evening in Holyrood the prince forced a definite commitment, but not before the most acrimonious council debate yet had taken place, Charles Edward argued eloquently and cleverly for an invasion of England.[17] In the first place, he declared, it was now clear that the Jacobite army throve on activity and faded away in times of inertia or 'phoney war'. This was not just a question of desertions – though the desertion rate in Edinburgh in October had been alarmingly high – but of morale. A constant momentum had to be sustained if the shaky force of irregulars was to be kept in being. With the defeat of the regular

Hanoverian army and with all major Scottish targets in Jacobite hands, except for the forts and castles – impregnable in the present state of Jacobite artillery – where else could the Highland army meaningfully go?

It was well known, the prince continued, that the clansmen tended to lose interest if the prospect of hard fighting or good living seemed remote. The natural tendency to slink away to the glens and mountains was reinforced by the weeks of boredom and guard duty in Edinburgh. And the danger of wholesale desertion was compounded by another. The capture of Edinburgh and the defeat of Cope had delivered the Jacobites temporarily from financial embarrassment, but by now all the public monies had been collected, yet the Jacobite coffers were almost empty.[18] Their position was made no easier by Preston's previous removal of all silver coin to the castle.[19] It would soon be a choice between trying to collect the hated Malt Tax or leaving the army without pay. What would the desertion rate be like then?

Moreover, there was the not negligible point that clan reaction, even among supposedly Jacobite chieftains, had been a severe disappointment. A month after Prestonpans Lovat still equivocated, the Grants and Mackenzies were still divided, Macleod and Sir Alexander MacDonald still did Duncan Forbes's bidding. It was clear that a second victory was needed. It was necessary to seek out Wade and defeat him, in order to remove any doubt about the permanent mastery of Scotland.

Besides, the prince went on, d'Eguilles's presence showed that the French were in earnest. Yet it was equally clear that Louis XV had not finally decided whether to send his armies to Scotland or England. The victorious Jacobites in Scotland ought not to squeeze the French king for a definite commitment to a Scottish landing. Quite apart from logistical problems that might beset the French if they were forced to land in Scotland alone – here the prince postulated a scenario where it was relatively easy for a commander to cross the Channel but very hard to bring large numbers of men to Scotland – it was vital not to give Louis XV a plausible excuse for doing nothing. An invasion of England would allow the Jacobites to cover all options. The second army being raised in the north would control Scotland and secure the beachheads for any French landing. The first army in England would meanwhile act as an inducement to the French to make landfall in England if that was their inclination.

These were powerful arguments. Lord George Murray and the clan leaders hit back by calling for a retreat to the Highlands.[20] It was folly to enter England with 4,000 men to face 30,000 regulars plus large numbers of militia without definite cast-iron promises from France such as the marquis d'Eguilles was unable to provide. The Jacobites already had a sound base in Scotland; the task, Lord George argued, was to consolidate it. In this sense the greatest boon the French could give at present was heavy cannon and mortars to reduce the castles of Edinburgh and Stirling and pound the Highland forts into submission. Beyond this, the full fighting potential of the Highlands should be exhausted before any descent on England was made. Lord George called for a division of labour: Lochiel, Keppoch and the Stewarts of Appin should march to Glasgow and raise Argyllshire; the Athollmen would bring Breadalbane's levies out; the Glengarry and Clanranald men would return to MacDonald country to put the squeeze on Macleod and Sir Alexander MacDonald.[21]

The effort should not end there. The Mackintoshes and Frasers could raise the Mackenzies; the combined clans could attack the Munros and Sutherlands and take hostages for their good behaviour. It would be the task of Cluny MacPherson and John Roy Stewart to raise the Grants. Finally a general rendezvous should be held at Inverness. If the prince arrived there with the Lowland regiments, the combined army could amount to 24,000 men. Even a token reinforcement from France of, say, 3–4,000 troops would provide a large enough army for a confident and triumphant march on London, an army moreover elated with the knowledge that its rear in Scotland had been firmly secured.[22] As for the prince's objections about money, what was to stop the Lowland regiments making periodic raids into England to uplift the public money? And even if a cash shortage did develop, there was enough meal, beef and mutton in the Highlands to feed the army. Officers and men could be paid in IOUs meanwhile.

At this juncture the issue of the English Jacobites was raised. This was to be a running sore during the next two months. In 1743–4 the powerful trio of Lord Barrymore, Sir John Hynde Cotton and Sir Watkin Williams Wynn, the secret leaders of the English Jacobite party, had committed themselves to bringing their levies to support Saxe's French invaders once they made landfall.[23] Charles Edward assumed that what they had promised eighteen months earlier they would fulfil now, when conditions were far more favourable, with a Jacobite army already in being. The assumption was warranted, up to a point. As soon as they heard of the landing at Moidart, the trio sent secretly to Versailles to press 'loudly and vehemently for a body of troops to be landed near London as the most effectual means to support the prince, and the only method by which a dangerous and ruinous civil war can be avoided'.[24] What they did *not* want to do was rise in rebellion for the prince *before* a French army had landed.

The problem for the prince at the council in Edinburgh was that the Scottish leaders despised these English magnates. The prince maintained that his 'friends' in England would show themselves only if they could wrap themselves in the folds of an invading army. Lord George and the clan leaders dismissed the English Jacobites as paper tigers.

Which of them was right? There were circumstantial grounds for thinking that Murray was better informed on this particular issue. In 1743–4 the English Jacobites had not appeared to great advantage. Sir John Hynde Cotton had protested to the French about the original invasion date of January 1744 on the ground that the weather was too cold then. Aged fifty-seven at the time of the '45, Cotton was described by a contemporary as 'one of the tallest, biggest, fattest men I have ever seen . . . he was supposed to be able to drink as much wine as any man in England without being disgusted by it'. He escaped imprisonment in early 1744 during the French invasion scare, when Habeas Corpus was suspended, because a Hanoverian spy confused him with another Cotton (Sir Robert of Huntingdonshire).[25]

James, 4th earl of Barrymore was scarcely more impressive. Now aged seventy-eight he had been implicated in the 1743–4 invasion by a Hanoverian spy, arrested and examined by the Cabinet. Barrymore double-talked his way out of trouble on that occasion, and was released from house arrest in March after Saxe abandoned the descent on England, Yet Barrymore's words to the Cabinet in February contained more of his true feelings than he probably admitted even to himself:

> I have, my lords, a very good estate in Ireland, and, on that, I believe fifteen hundred acres of very bad land; now by God I would not risk the loss of the poorest acre of them to defend the title of any king in Europe, provided – it was not in my interest.[26]

The third of the English Jacobites was, by common consent, the most formidable. In his early fifties, Sir Watkin Williams Wynn was the most powerful territorial magnate in Wales. But his ultra-cautious credo comes out clearly in his statement of position in October 1745. He said he was 'languishing for the landing of troops' without which the English Jacobites 'don't find it in their power to make a step', although he added that they would certainly 'join the prince if H.R.H. could force his way to them'.[27] The problem with Wynn's stance was that he was in Wales while Barrymore and Cotton were still attending Parliament in London. The English Jacobite position thus amounted to a pledge that they would either join the prince in Wales – where he had no intention of going – or in London – in which case the prince would already have defeated his enemies. Lord George Murray was entitled to feel sceptical about 'commitment' of this kind.

Murray won the debate in the council over the English Jacobites. But the three issues of desertion, money and the French made a powerful impact on the waverers. Lord George found himself deserted even by some of his erstwhile allies. In the end he was left with just the rump of clan chieftains as support. A vote was taken. The prince's faction scraped home with one vote.[28] This narrow victory was attributable apart from the arguments advanced, to three special factors. One was that some of the council members were absent, away in the north drumming up men and money. The second was that John Roy Stewart, who would certainly have voted with Lord George, was, to his intense chagrin, the only regimental colonel without a seat on the council.[29] The third was that Perth and Elcho, who Lord George had thought committed to his Highland strategy, switched their votes at the last minute and sided with the prince.[30]

The interplay of personalities on the council at this crucial juncture is fascinating. Elcho was normally a Lord George man, but he was also a hothead, well capable of changing tack on a whim. He was a good cavalry commander, but it is doubtful that Lord George ever credited him with much *gravitas*. Lord George could bear his momentary defection with equanimity, confident that the next time the prince did something to annoy Elcho, the young Wemyss lord would be back on the side of the clan leaders.

Perth's opposition was more trying. As joint lieutenant-general, he seemed to be setting himself on a collision course with Murray. As a Catholic, he seemed to be aligning himself with the Irish 'Charles Edward right or wrong' faction. Yet, at thirty-two, James Drummond, 3rd titular duke of Perth, was no lightweight. 'A foolish horse-racing boy' one of his Whig critics had called him in the early 1740s, but Perth had deliberately cultivated a foppish façade to conceal the fact that he was a dedicated Jacobite plotter.[31] Perth was one of the 1744 Associators. After clandestine conversations with him that year, Murray knew that he could not be mistaken for anything less than a deeply serious devotee of the House of Stuart. Moreover, Perth had what Murray could never acquire: the gift of managing men, by appealing to their nobler, more heroic instincts. Murray realised that

Perth's opposition to him on this critical question of the invasion of England boded ill for the future.

The Jacobite army was also at this point running the risk of dangerous polarisation, not just in personalities, but in preconceptions and lack of liaison. Charles Edward was an inspirational commander, an intuitive opportunist. It was no accident that his youth had been largely spent as a huntsman, in pursuit of regular quarry. The slow methodical pace of eighteenth-century warfare was not his forte; he would have fitted better into a far different military framework. Murray, by contrast, was *par excellence* the soldier's soldier. What was needed to bridge the crevasse between them was a first-class staff officer. But no such person existed in the Jacobite camp. Despite his much-vaunted military experience, O'Sullivan was a tactical incompetent who disguised his deficiencies behind a smoke-screen of bluster. Perth was a fine diplomat, but knew little about the minutiae of soldiering. Lochiel, who commanded the confidence of both Murray and the prince, was on paper ideally placed, yet he was doubly handicapped for the role of staff officer through being overly deferential to both men.

In a sense, the dispute over the English Jacobites was profoundly revealing. Charles Edward, basing himself on the pledges given in 1743–4, took it for granted that he could pick Wynn, Barrymore and Cotton up where they had been left in March 1744. He made one half-hearted attempt to make contact with them while he was in Scotland, but his agent, one John Hickson, was apprehended by the enemy as soon as he crossed the border.[32] Thereafter the prince relaxed, buoyed up by his sycophantic followers among the Seven Men, especially the four Irishmen. Such complacency infuriated Lord George. He looked around for the staff officer who would arrange an efficient espionage system, who would establish definite contacts with the English Jacobites and generally tie up all the logistical loose ends. But in the prince's Jacobite army he looked in vain.

The fateful decision to invade England has often been considered a piece of mindless quixotry.[33] Yet, even apart from the compelling arguments put at the council which swung round the doubters, the decision contained a greater degree of rationality than it is usually credited with. To understand this we must turn aside for a moment to look at the enemy.

Throughout October the government in London was steadily building up its strength. On 1 October George II ordered a strong force of cavalry and infantry to prepare to march to Scotland under Marshal Wade.[34] This force assembled at Doncaster on 19 October and reached Newcastle on the 29th.[35] The English army in Flanders, recalled home to counter the rebellion, began to arrive in the Thames on 23 September and continued coming over until the beginning of December. Some of these troops were also sent to Newcastle and Berwick. By 29 September seven battalions of British troops and 6,000 Dutch had arrived as reinforcements for Wade.[36] General Handasyde arrived at Berwick as Wade's second-in-command; Ligonier was given charge of a second army; and the duke of Cumberland arrived in London from Flanders.[37] Most ominously of all, Lord Loudoun, who had fled to England after Prestonpans, returned to Inverness on 11 October and took over the forces Lord President Forbes had been raising.[38] Throughout England there were obvious signs of strengthened Hanoverian defences and clear hints of the counterattack to come.[39]

Wade had not yet been given the order to cross the border, but this could hardly be long delayed, especially since the longer the Jacobites remained in Edinburgh, the greater the likelihood that their true numbers would be discovered, or that the Whigs would finally conclude that it was paucity of numbers that was preventing a Jacobite invasion of England.[40] It was folly for Charles Edward to remain forever on the defensive, awaiting an onslaught that would be overwhelming when it came. Besides, the prince calculated that Scotland could never be raised in the way Lord George Murray suggested while Wade's army lay at Newcastle. Sea power – the selfsame naval hegemony that enabled the outwitted Cope to reappear at Dunbar from Inverness – meant that Wade could land troops in the Jacobite rear and catch the prince between two fires.[41] The only way to bring the recalcitrant Hanoverian clans (and the ambivalent Jacobite ones) to heel was to remove all hope of assistance from England. This meant defeating Wade. The prince, in a word, had to strike first before he was struck.

It can be seen, then, that there was some desperation as well as a good deal of rational calculation in the prince's invasion strategy. Time was against him, and he knew it.[42]

The prince was unable to carry the council with him on both halves of his strategy. Lord George Murray won the second round of the debate by persuading the council not to opt for an immediate head-on clash with Wade, but instead to enter England by the northwest. This would gain time and give the French an opportunity to act.[43] Lord George's arguments had a certain *ad hoc* force and appealed to men well aware of tactical realities.[44] But they effectively vitiated the prince's strategy in proposing the invasion in the first place. It was all very well Lord George's saying that a western itinerary would keep the Whigs guessing as to the Jacobites' ultimate destination: Wales or London. The duke of Newcastle and his advisers were not fools. The avoiding of Wade combined with a route that suggested a rendezvous in Wales strongly hinted at Jacobite weakness. If the Jacobites were a credible fighting force, it was madness for them not to advance on London by the quickest route.

Lord George's argument about sweeping up support in Catholic Lancashire was also bogus. These secret sympathisers would very probably declare for the prince *after* he had defeated Wade. It was most unlikely that they would appear in open revolt for a small army that had appeared to duck a pitched battle with Wade. In this way, the prince's grand strategic vision became lost in the detail of Lord George's tactical imperatives. Arguably, it was not the decision to invade England that was wrong so much as Lord George's excessive caution. The correct option was to attack Wade at Newcastle, as Charles Edward wanted to. His strategy was a gamble, admittedly, but once having agreed to it, however unwillingly, Lord George should have entered into its spirit. 'By the book' tactical circumspection has no place in such an enterprise. Brilliant as Murray was as military commander and tactician, he never fully grasped this, as Derby was to show.

But on 31 October the decision was taken: invasion, yes, but by the north-westerly route. Before setting out on this, the most spectacular episode of his high adventure, the prince made his dispositions in Scotland. The earl of Strathallan, already appointed governor of Perth, was to command the new army assembling there, with his deputy governor Oliphant of Gask as second-in-command.[45] MacGregor of Glengyle was appointed governor of Doune castle with a remit to conduct constant surveillance on Stirling castle. Other appointments were made to governorships of Aberdeen, Dundee and Montrose. Lord Lewis Gordon was already acknowledged as the key Jacobite figure in the north-east. Finally, young Glengarry was sent back to the Highlands to raise more MacDonalds.[46] In his absence Donald MacDonnell of Lochgarry would command the clan regiment in England.

As for France, a third envoy was sent to solicit aid. Father Gordon SJ had departed on 28 October. Hard on his heels now went Sir James Stewart of Goodtrees.[47]

Before we follow Charles Edward's small army across the border into England, it is worth examining the prince's legend and its relationship to sober history. Is it really true that Charles Edward conquered

Scotland on the basis of personal charisma and a plausible tongue? Were there really no dynamic elements of conflict in Scottish society that he was able to harness?

All historical figures ultimately depend for their position in history, as opposed to myth or legend, on their relationship with the social forces at play during their lives. Great men make history but not in circumstances of their own choosing. This alone makes it unlikely that the prince unaided, whatever his charisma, could have overturned a peacefully evolving social system in the Highlands, unless other factors were at work. This inference is strengthened when we examine those clan leaders who actually 'came out' for Charles Edward and those who did not. What is revealed is a pattern of big clans, co-opted into the post-1688 economic system, supporting the Whigs while the small clans, those excluded from the benefits of the 'Glorious Revolution', support the prince.

It would be a gross oversimplification to say that no one fought for Charles Edward out of loyalty, sentiment or ideological conviction. Clearly many of the great Jacobite leaders did just that: Lord George Murray, Perth, Pitsligo, Balmerino, Glenbucket, Oliphant of Gask.[48] Indeed, the solidly Episcopalian, properly so-called 'feudal' leaders, were largely actuated by ideological motives, forced their tenants out from a belief in divine providence and the Stuarts' indefeasible right, and were the major sufferers in consequence when the rising failed.[49] But since the cutting edge of Jacobite military strength lay in the clans, it is there that we must look for a more complete understanding of the deeper forces shaping the rising of 1745.

The Highland clans fell into four categories during the rising. There were those who were unwaveringly on the side of the government (Campbells, Munros, Mackays, Rosses, Sutherlands). There were putative Jacobite clans who took no part on the prince's side (Sinclairs, MacDougalls, MacDonalds of Sleat). There were the clans who did appear in strength for the prince (most of the branches of the Clan Donald, the Camerons, MacPhersons, Macleans, etc.). And there were divided clans who split in their allegiance, notably the Macleods and Mackintoshes.

When we turn to the subject of the clan leaders, a very different picture emerges. The motivation of the chieftains, whom legend has credited with unswerving loyalty to the House of Stuart against their better judgment, takes us into a twilight world of ambivalence. Even the legendary figures of the '45, like 'Gentle Lochiel', shrink to human size when their actions are analysed closely. Lochiel had both a cogent motive for rebellion, in that he was hard pressed by the

Campbells and had no clear legal title to his lands, and a unique opportunity to improve his fortunes, since Charles Edward indemnified him for future losses.[50]

The other clan leader with no clear legal title was Alexander MacDonald of Keppoch. Keppoch had an even more precarious hold on his lands than Lochiel, since his clansmen owed feudal duties to lords other than their familial leaders. Because Keppoch had no secure territorial base, his power over his clansmen depended mainly on sheer force of personality, and because such a hold was tenuous, the Keppoch MacDonalds had the highest desertion rate and the greatest reputation for indiscipline in the entire Highland army.[51]

Another clan chief, who merged his tiny force of 120 men with Keppoch's, was Alexander MacDonald of Glencoe who, though not a regimental commander, was given a seat on the prince's council by virtue of his nominal status. The decline of the Glencoe MacDonalds in the first half of the eighteenth century had been marked, as their scanty numbers indicated. Glencoe was motivated both by a desperate desire to arrest this decline and by the opportunity to settle scores with the Campbells, whose treachery in the 1692 Glencoe massacre was still remembered with bitterness.

Cluny MacPherson too fits the bill of ambivalence. In August 1745 he was working closely with Duncan Forbes, giving him information on Charles Edward's advance through the Highlands.[52] It was only after his capture by the Camerons that Cluny emerged as a Jacobite supporter, possibly after gauging the feelings of his own clansmen. Even then, he required to be given security for his lands before raising the MacPhersons.[53]

Apart from Mackinnon of Mackinnon, who saw the rising as a chance to escape from the shadow of the two great Skye chiefs, these were the only chieftains to take the field in person. This has been consistently overlooked by those who aver that clan leaders 'came out' for Charles Edward out of loyalty and against their own interests. And in each case examined above there was a compelling individual motivation for rebellion. No great Scottish magnate ever committed himself to the '45 rising.[54] Almost all clan chiefs hedged their bets to some degree, and this is true even of those who seemed to have more cogent motives and opportunities to rebel.

The Glengarry and Clanranald MacDonalds, for instance, were both Catholic clans. In the Highlands, unlike England, Catholicism and Jacobitism did go together.[55] At the same time, both clans were located in inaccessible areas of the Highlands, which meant that punitive action could be taken against them only by a genuine army of occupation (unfortunately, though no one could have foreseen it, especially if prognosticating from the aftermath of the '15, this is precisely what happened in 1746–7). Unlike the chiefs of Mull and Skye, the Clanranald and Glengarry leaders were immune to incursions from the Royal Navy. Even so these two MacDonald chieftains did not venture to appear openly for the Stuart prince. John MacDonell, patriarch of Glengarry's, sent his second son Angus to lead the clan regiment, while the Clanranald chief gave the command of his clansmen to his son Ranald.

This ambivalence among the clan leaders was a common phenomenon. Alexander MacDonell of Barisdale refused to compromise himself but kept his options open by sending his son Coll to head a contingent. The small unit of Chisholms from Strathglass was under the command of Roderick Og, fifth son of the chief Roderick, who stayed at home.[56] Alexander, chief of the Robertsons of Struan (who served in the Atholl brigade), gave ambiguous instructions to his kinsman Robertson of Woodshiel that his men could join Charles Edward 'if they please'.[57] The Farquharsons of Monaltrie were also led by a kinsman of the chief rather than the chief himself (in this case the head of the family, Finla, was a mental defective). Led by James Farquharson of Balmoral, this sept had been dubious about joining the rising and came out only after Lord Lovat had given a lead.

Lovat of course is the very epitome of the ambivalent Jacobite. A byword for cunning, the very fact of his joining the prince after years of playing off Whig against Jacobite indicated to more perceptive observers that the rising must be a very serious affair indeed and have a well above average chance of success.[58] For all that, although Lovat sent Charles Edward a message in August 1745, it was not until December, when all the omens for Jacobite success were propitious, that he sent out the Frasers under his nineteen-year-old son, Simon, master of Lovat. And so well were Lovat's tracks covered that it took the testimony of John Murray of Broughton, who possessed unimpeachable evidence of Lovat's complicity, to consign him finally to the executioner's axe.[59]

Another important clan, the Stewarts of Appin, were not led by their chief Dugald Stewart but by his kinsman Charles Stewart of Ardshiel. The latter, one of the more colourful leaders in the Jacobite army with a reputation as an expert swordsman, was in any case in a favoured position as a laird and suffered less than most non-chieftain clansmen when in exile in France. While paying their rents to the new incumbent on the Ardshiel estates, his tenants continued to send an equivalent amount across the water to their attainted lord.[60]

Where a clan had risen and the chief stayed at home, the commitment of those who served in the chief's name was not all that Charles Edward required. There was always some kind of a question mark about the reliability of the Glengarry men, whose indiscipline was second only to Keppoch's. Angus MacDonell, the nominal commander did not lead his regiment into England, but gave the command to his kinsman Donald MacDonell of Lochgarry.[61] Lochgarry was thus a proxy of a proxy. Although he had a seat on the prince's council, his voice counted for little.[62]

It is not true that the clans rose out of sentiment for the House of Stuart when it was against their interest to do so, despite the fact that it has become (through reiteration rather than sustained argument) the orthodox view of the '45 in Scotland. If it was loyalty to James and Charles Edward that brought out the clans, why did they not rise with a greater display of devotion to their rightful kings? Why is there not a single example of a major clan leader unequivocally committing himself out of ideological conviction to Charles Edward? Why, in the case of those who participated, can it never be demonstrated that participation was against a chieftain's interest? If we accept that the clans rose purely out of loyalty to the Stuarts, how was it that the principles of the chiefs overcame their interests to the point where they sent out their warriors but not to the point where they went out themselves?

All the evidence concerning the clan chiefs – and particularly in the case of ambivalent leaders like Lovat and Cluny, who weighed up with practised skill the likely outcome of the rebellion – demonstrates that the chieftains sent out their Highlanders because they were involved in a life-and-death struggle with the Whigs and their acolytes in Scotland. In this struggle they could score a devastating victory if the Stuarts were restored to the Scottish throne. At the heart of the struggle in Scotland was an irreconcilable conflict between the clan system of land tenure and the feudal – or in political terms between the Jacobite clans and the Campbells. Beyond this was the threat to the hereditary system in the Highlands posed by the mercantilist/capitalist influences spreading north from the Lowlands. The Jacobite rising of 1745 was the occasion rather than the cause of the destruction of the clan system that the pro-Stuart chieftains had felt to be in danger ever since the Revolution of 1688.[63] It is true that the heritable jurisdictions were anachronistic, but James had promised his followers that the old ways would be phased out only gradually, over generations.[64] In any case, the general expectation that the Stuarts would 'put the clock back' led to a feeling that the threat to the Highlands from incipient Lowland capitalism would be removed.

The failure of many chiefs to appear in the field themselves was more in the nature of an insurance policy, in case the rising, which truly did answer to their interests, ended in failure.[65] The fact that by and large the Jacobite clans committed their manpower but not their leadership is the clearest possible demonstration that their support was for the movement of revolt primarily, not attachment to the personality of Charles Edward Stuart. Calculation of this sort makes a lot of sense if we posit that the rising fulfilled 'objective interests'; it makes none at all if the sole motivating factor was loyalty to the Stuarts. Ideological principles are more likely to weigh with the leaders than the led, yet the notion that the clans rose out of dynastic sentiment would carry with it the implication that the tenants were more influenced by ideology than their lords.

This consideration helps to explain some of the paradoxical features of the rising. The most ideologically committed Jacobites, like Lord George Murray, Pitsligo, Glenbucket, Balmerino, experienced the most difficulty in raising men. Those who were clearly not committed, like the chiefs of Grant and Mackintosh, found their men defying them and joining the prince in large numbers.[66] Those who were ideologically pro-Stuart tended to be pessimistic about the outcome of the rising; those who had joined in purely for reasons of interest tended to be the optimists. On all counts, then, loyalty to the Stuarts alone, without consideration of interest, was likely to have produced exactly opposite results from those which obtained in 1745.

This can be seen most clearly in the attitudes of the clan leaders to the invasion of England, undertaken at Charles Edward's insistence to enable him to gain the English throne. To Charles the invasion of England was to be different in kind from anything undertaken from Scotland before. The clan leaders, though, could never entirely rid themselves of the instinct that any incursion south of the border had to be a raid, albeit in this case a large-scale one. Thus it had ever been in relations between England and Scotland. This attitude had a further implication. The Highland chieftains considered that their interests would be served quite well by a Stuart king in Scotland; Charles Edward's dynastic ambitions in England did not interest them. For this reason they entered on the adventure south of the border with reluctance and misgivings. Significantly, the only clan leader to advocate advancing on London from Derby was young Clanranald, whose position as his father's proxy absolved him from deeper consideration of his clan's interest.[67] Indeed, it can be argued that the entire rebellion of 1745 failed precisely because the Highlanders were motivated byunderstandable clan interests and not commitment to the aspirations of the Stuarts.[68]

It is clear that the differential attitude to Charles Edward of the territorial potentates in Scotland was not fortuitous. The pattern of conflict may not be a simple one of feudalists versus patriarchs, still less a direct one of capitalists versus traditional clansmen, but closer inspection does reveal a clear antagonism between big and lesser battalions.[69]

The only two clan leaders, who appeared openly at the head of their warriors and who did not have obvious *prima facie* economic motives, fit into this pattern of small clans versus big ones. Mackinnon of Mackinnon was struggling to hold his own against his two great neighbours in Skye.[70] And MacDonald of Glencoe was thought of so little significance in the political struggle in Scotland that after Culloden not even Cumberland thought him worth hounding. His abject letter of surrender and pitiful pleas for clemency were accepted by an administration not noticeably prone to leniency at this time.[71]

There was also a strong urban and proletarian element in the composition of Charles Edward's army. Artisans, shopkeepers, farmers and labourers made up a large part of the non-clan element of the army, many of them holding commissions of company rank.[72] Almost the whole of John Roy Stewart's regiment was recruited from the slums of Edinburgh.[73] The Manchester regiment was to contain a strong component of weavers, drapers and apothecaries. In all some 1,400 individuals from the working class (including agricultural workers) and the lower middle class (semi-skilled workers and tradesmen) served in the Jacobite army.[74]

The army that crossed into England in November 1745 was not a revolutionary force in terms of ideology or consciousness.[75] But in its unconscious representation of socio-economic conflict and the incompatibility of the interests of many of its members with the Hanoverian status quo, it stood for something much more than purely dynastic struggle.

14

A Second Anabasis

(November–December 1745)

On 31 October the prince left Edinburgh, scene of his greatest triumph, for Pinkie House, where he spent the night.[1] He was never to see Holyrood or the Scottish capital again. One good omen attended his departure. This was the arrival of a supply of money and arms from Spain.[2] All the indications were that it was the first of many such supplies. Assistance from Spain as well as France now seemed probable.

Rendezvous was at Dalkeith. From there the Jacobite army was to set off for the English border.[3] The plan was to advance in two columns. The main body under Lord George Murray (the Atholl brigade, Perth's, Ogilvy's, Glenbucket's and John Roy Stewart's) would proceed with the baggage and artillery via Peebles and Moffat before entering England at Longtown. The second division under the prince (Elcho's Lifeguards and the clan regiments) would make a feinting movement to Lauder and Kelso, as if making for Newcastle, and then sheer off via Jedburgh to meet up with Lord George's column near Carlisle.[4]

Even before the prince left Dalkeith, Lord George's words about the necessity of pacifying Scotland first came back to haunt him. At news of the departure of the Jacobite army for England, the town of Perth became 'fractious and insolent'. The prince had to tarry to write detailed instructions to Strathallan, Oliphant of Gask and Lord Lewis Gordon about the need to keep Scotland in an iron grip while he was away.[5]

There could be no turning back now. The prince marched down the Rule valley and Liddlesdale, forded the Esk and spent his first night in England on 8 November 1745 (OS).[6] Next day he linked up with Lord George's main column. The smoothness of this operation was, however, somewhat marred by two pieces of intelligence Murray gave the prince. One was that there had been considerable desertion during the passage through the Lowlands. No more than 5,000 infantry and 500 cavalry in the end crossed with the prince into England. The other was that tents, stores and ammunition had been 'lost' at Moffat.[7] It would be necessary now to billet the army in towns.

Nothing daunted, the prince ordered the siege of Carlisle to commence. Breastworks were opened on the 9th, but on the 11th the investment was broken off. The Jacobite army retired to Brampton to prepare for a battle with Wade, reported to be crossing the Pennines from Newcastle. It soon became obvious that Wade would not arrive quickly; in fact he was forced back to Newcastle by heavy snowdrifts in the mountain passes.[8] The Jacobites returned to Carlisle to commence the siege in earnest.[9]

Demoralised by Wade's failure to come to their aid, and with only a tiny garrison in the castle, the citizens of Carlisle decided to surrender. This time the prince was determined not to make the mistake he had made at Edinburgh: both town *and* castle had to capitulate before he would give terms; it was all or nothing.[10] Despite the pleadings of the castle commander, Carlisle accepted the inevitable. Both town and castle were given up. On Monday 18 November, riding a white horse, the prince entered Carlisle in triumph.[11]

The easy capture of the first obstacle on English soil augured well for the prince's future success, but a shadow was cast over his victory by another row involving Lord George. Murray peremptorily resigned his commission as lieutenant-general when the prince allowed the other commander, Perth, to negotiate Carlisle's surrender.[12] Lord George was on solid ground in pointing out the propaganda advantage the Whig government would extract from the surrender to a Catholic lord of the first town in England the Jacobites reached. It needed no special gifts of imagination to rehearse the likely parrot-cries of 'popery and arbitrary government'. But in regarding the task laid on Perth as a personal snub to himself, Murray ignored the fact that he had only himself to blame. He had declined to take command of the siege operations outside Carlisle, commenced when the citizens still had hopes from Wade. Perth, on the other hand, had thrown himself into the opening of trenches with gusto. In heavy snow and frost he worked in his shirt-sleeves alongside his men. The commission from the prince to accept the surrender may have been unwise on Charles Edward's part, but it was very understandable.

The resignation threw the clan regiments into consternation. Their leaders had faith in Lord George as a military captain, not in anyone else. The effect of the resignation on the clansmen's morale was so devastating that the prince, against his will, was forced to ask Murray to withdraw it. Perth magnanimously offered to accept what was in effect a demotion, in charge of the rearguard and baggage.[13] Thereafter Lord George was sole and undisputed field commander.[14]

The ease with which Carlisle had fallen might have made the Jacobites over-confident, but Lord George and his party on the council responded to it instead by arguing for a return to Scotland. The prince spiked their guns by bringing on d'Eguilles (who accompanied the Jacobites into England) and asking him to reveal his instructions from Louis XV.[15] When read out these made clear that the French king wanted to gauge the strength of the English Jacobites as well as the Scots. This could be done only by advancing into England. Reluctantly Lord George and the Highland leaders acquiesced. Snow and ice notwithstanding, they would have to penetrate farther into England.

Because of the loss of tents, the army had to spend every night of the march in towns. To solve billeting problems, the Jacobites advanced in two columns.[16] Lord George Murray led the first column, with Elcho's Lifeguards in the van. With Lord George were his Athollmen, plus Glenbucket's and Stewart's Edinburgh regiment. A day behind him came the prince with the main army. It was not planned to make a junction of the two segments of the army until the first sizeable town, Preston, was reached. Undoubtedly both Charles Edward and Lord George relished the days out of each other's sight.

The prince was in Penrith on 21 November, rested on the 22nd, and made the long trek to Kendal on the 23rd.[17] Despite the sleet, snow, bad roads and fatigue, he marched on foot at the head of his army. Only with difficulty was he persuaded to get up on horseback when crossing rivers.[18] On the twenty-seven-mile haul from Penrith to Kendal, he was so tired by the gruelling slog that he took hold of the shoulder belt of one of Ogilvy's men to prevent himself falling down in a faint.[19]

Resting on the 24th, the prince reached Lancaster on the 25th, hoping to confer with Lord George, but the lieutenant-general had already moved on to Preston. The speed of his advance irked the elderly Moidart Men (especially Sheridan, Tullibardine and Sir John MacDonald), who tried to influence the prince by saying that Lord George was stealing all the glory by being permanently in the van.

But, as Murray rightly pointed out to O'Sullivan it was not practicable to switch the order of march for the two columns before Preston.[20]

On the 26th the prince moved down to Preston. Cumberland and Westmoreland were well known to be hostile pro-Hanoverian country, but Lancashire had now been reached and this was where large-scale enlistment in the Jacobite army was expected. The response was disappointing: a mere dribble. One of the Lancashire volunteers, John Daniel, did, however, leave a famous description of the prince at this time:

> The first time I saw this loyal army was betwixt Lancaster and Garstang: the Brave Prince marching on foot at their head like a Cyrus or Trojan hero, drawing admiration and love from all those who beheld him, raising their long-dejected hearts and solacing their minds with the happy prospect of another Golden Age. Struck with this charming sight, and seeming invitation *leave your nets and follow me*, I felt a paternal ardour pervade my veins.[21]

Yet the underlying trend was worrying. There was no opposition to the Jacobites, but no enthusiasm for them either. When the two columns reunited in Preston, Lord George Murray insisted on another council meeting. Preston was psychologically important for the Highlanders, for it was the farthest south reached by any raiding Scottish army hitherto. It was also the scene of the Scots' rout by Cromwell in 1648 and of the Jacobites' second defeat (on the same day as Sheriffmuir) during the 1715 rising. Knowing well how the superstitious clansmen's minds worked, Murray worked hard to exorcise this ghost. He marched the vanguard through Preston and to the other side of Ribble Bridge so that the town would not be 'their *ne plus ultra* for a third time'.

There was further tension at the Preston council. Lord George's north-western strategy, based on his much-vaunted Stanley family connection which made him 'certain' they would find support in Lancashire, was already proving a failure. Murray would have liked nothing better than to cut his losses and retreat to Scotland. Again the prince produced d'Eguilles as his trump, again the Scots subsided, but there was a general feeling that the real issues had merely been shelved.[22]

The council turned to the question of itinerary. Since Warrington Bridge had now been broken down by the defending militia, the route the Jacobites had intended to take anyway (via Manchester) seemed all the more desirable, since the Whigs would still not be certain that the Jacobite target was London.[23]

The pressure on the prince was building up. He decided to write to Sir Watkin Williams Wynn: 'The particular character I have heard of you makes me hope to see you among the first.' He asked Wynn to join him with all speed and not to worry too much about numbers: 'it will be looked upon as a battalion if it come to the number of 4 or 500 men or upwards. But whatever numbers you bring will be acceptable, though they were below that and even though they were very small.'[24]

Napoleon used to ask of a general: 'Has he luck?' If we accept that this is a key attribute for a military leader, we can immediately infer something about Charles Edward from the fate of the letters he sent to the English Jacobite leaders. His first letter, sent to Lord Barrymore from Brampton on 11 November, was handed to his son, Lord Buttevant, by the prince's messenger, since Barrymore was at London in the House of Commons. Buttevant, who was violently opposed to his father's Jacobite sentiments, promptly burned it.[25] The prince's second letter, to Watkin Williams Wynn, was intercepted by one of Cumberland's agents.

The army pressed on to Manchester, through Wigan and Leigh. The road from Preston to Wigan was lined with onlookers, who stood at their doors and watched the Scots go by. Most of them wished the prince success but declined to fight when offered arms, on grounds of lack of training.[26] There was no opposition from the militia. The Jacobite commanders had correctly read them as 'small beer'. Whenever the prospect of a fight loomed, the militiamen dispersed or decamped. On the afternoon of 29 November the prince made another triumphal entry, riding to Manchester city centre by way of Salford.[27]

Manchester was another triumph in the style of Edinburgh though on a much smaller scale. Once again the prince captivated a town in which he had a lot of latent support.[28] Once again he made a particular impression on the ladies.[29] Here, too, as in Edinburgh, a regiment was raised from among the poor, dispossessed and socially precarious.[30] But for the clan leaders the similarities ended there. They were now deep in England, in the heartland of supposedly Jacobite Lancashire, and to show for it they had no more than three hundred volunteers. There was no sign either of the English Jacobites or of a French landing.

The council held on St Andrew's Day, 30 November, was the most acrimonious hitherto. The movement in favour of returning to Scotland had not yet become the earth tremor it was to appear at

Derby, but for anyone less confident and utterly sanguine than the prince, the rumblings would have been alarming. Once again Charles Edward got his way, just, but it took the intervention of Lord Nairne to sway the vote, plus some successful obfuscation on the prince's behalf by the Welsh Jacobite David Morgan.[31] A lawyer and former secretary to the Jacobite duke of Beaufort, Morgan was one of just two Welshmen who had joined the prince on his march south. So much for the legions of Watkin Williams Wynn. As Charles Edward later cynically remarked: 'I shall do for the Welsh Jacobites what they did for me; I shall drink their health.'[32] Lord George Murray agreed to give the English Jacobites one last chance. The army would march the length of Derbyshire.[33] If at the end of that time there was no sign of Lord Barrymore, Sir Watkin Williams Wynn or the other Tory squires, retreat would be the only practicable option. In the euphoria of the moment the prince heard only the agreement to advance, not Murray's ominous rider.

Crossing Crossford Bridge, the Jacobite forces marched through Stockport to Macclesfield.[34] At Macclesfield they took stock of the situation. It was clear that they had easily outpaced Wade's army of the north, but now they were in the orbit of the second army which General Ligonier had been preparing (and which had been transferred to the command of the duke of Cumberland). Twenty-four-year-old Cumberland, who had moved up from Lichfield to Stafford, was puzzled by the movements of the Jacobite army. The pointers were still ambiguous: the clansmen's destination could still be either Wales or London.[35]

Lord George Murray tried to make up the duke's mind for him. Feinting towards Congleton with 1,200 men, he then swung in an arc back to Ashbourne, planning to link up there with the prince and the main army. Convinced at last of Jacobite intentions, but in reality sent the wrong way by Murray, Cumberland selected a battlefield at Stone and placed his army athwart the route to Wales. The battle of Stone would have put the issue of the 1745 rising beyond doubt, but it never took place.[36] While Cumberland waited in vain for his enemy, the prince's army pressed on to Leek, linked up with Lord George's column at Ashbourne, and reached Derby on the evening of 4 December after a twenty-four-hour march.[37]

The prince was now ahead of Cumberland in the race for London. The clansmen were on a knife-edge of expectation. Everyone expected a battle with Cumberland in the next forty-eight hours. Instead, on 6 December, the Jacobite army was retreating to Scotland. How did this happen?

The blame for the débâcle at Derby must be shared equally by the prince and Lord George Murray. Both suffered for ever afterwards from the momentous decision taken at the council on 5 December 1745. For Murray the retreat meant ruin and exile. For the prince it was the beginning of the collapse of his own personality. What exactly went wrong?

Charles Edward was at fault for not taking seriously the repeated warnings from Lord George and the clan leaders, at Carlisle, Brampton, Preston, Manchester and Macclesfield, that the advance of the Jacobite army into England was provisional only: it was contingent on the ultimate appearance in the field of the French or the English Jacobites with their levies. A good politician would have found a way to conciliate Lochiel and the MacDonald regimental colonels long before the moment of truth was reached. By sedulous lobbying, the prince could probably have detached Lochiel, Keppoch and Clanranald at least. But Charles was on such a remarkable winning streak that it did not occur to him that not everyone saw him as destiny's darling or his army as invincible. Such was his blithe confidence that he opened the proceedings at the Derby council meeting by taking it for granted that he and his advisers had gathered merely to discuss the line of march for 6 December.[38]

Lord George Murray brought him down to earth with a crash. The situation, as he saw it from the vantage point of a sober field commander, was that they had two armies (Wade's and Cumberland's) behind them and another ahead of them at Finchley. Each of these armies was twice the size of the Jacobite force. At the end of their journey loomed London, with a million inhabitants. Even assuming they kept ahead of Cumberland all the way to the capital, and then defeated the army at Finchley, they would arrive in London exhausted and with depleted numbers. A determined and numerous militia would be able to eat them up in that condition. The only thing that could justify an advance was the definite appearance of the English Jacobites or the French. Neither had appeared, so that was that. Only a fool or a madman would advance in such circumstances.

Charles Edward made a spirited reply, arguing that one final push was needed to bring the Hanoverian dynasty toppling down.[39] The very boldness of their advance had the enemy puzzled and disturbed. The psychological initiative would swing violently to Cumberland and the Whigs if the Jacobite army turned its back on England now.

The trouble with this argument was that the council members had heard it all before, in Edinburgh, at Carlisle, in Manchester. This time the prince's word alone was not enough. They demanded proof. Where were the letters from Louis XV explicitly and unambiguously promising a landing in England? Where were the written promises from the English Jacobites? If they had pledged themselves to rise, they must have specified a time and place.

At this juncture it dawned on the prince's officers just how much of a gamble they had committed themselves to. The prince was forced to reveal that he had no specific pledges from Watkin Williams Wynn, Barrymore, Hynde Cotton and his other English supporters. To general incredulity it emerged that he had not made contact with them once since his landing in Moidart.

This would presumably not have mattered too much if the English Jacobites were a credible organisation, since they would have used their initiative to meet the prince at the Mersey with their levies. The fact that they had not done so tended to clinch the Scottish thesis that the English Tories were merely Jacobites of the mouth or the wine-bottle.

Lord George and his associates may have been right in regarding the English Jacobites as paper tigers but for the wrong reasons. According to Aeneas MacDonald, it was the old Tory/Whig conflict of land versus money that finally put the English Jacobites out of the reckoning. When the prince crossed into England, Sir Watkin Williams Wynn had just £200 in ready cash. As MacDonald, with a banker's shrewdness saw clearly, in an emergency what is important is not so much wealth (in land) but liquidity. Once again the fatal consequences of the prince's failure to co-ordinate his movements with the English Jacobites were underlined. Williams Wynn, if given sufficient notice, could have raised, instead of £200, the £120,000 he had spent on the previous two general elections.[40]

Further probing by the council members threw up the alarming intelligence that Charles Edward did not know what stage French planning for an expedition had reached, since he had no established channel of communication with them either. The third weakness in the Jacobite army's strategy was already well known to the Scottish commanders themselves: they had no proper espionage system and were thus in the dark as to the enemy's true numbers and location.

It was on this issue of credibility that Charles Edward conclusively lost his audience. The arguments between the prince and Lord George Murray had been heard before. By their willingness to come this far, the chiefs had shown a 'will to believe' in the prince, even though every extra ten miles they went without seeing the French or the English Jacobites increased their scepticism. Yet at this display of political ineptitude by the prince, they decided enough was enough. The canard that had been whispered among them – that the prince cared nothing for Scotland and its interests, that his sights were always set on England and England alone – now looked increasingly like the sober truth. Why else would Charles have abandoned a secure and promising base in Scotland, in pursuit of a chimera south of the border?

From this point on the prince could win no support. Even Perth, who was initially sympathetic, dropped out when he saw the prince's cavalier way with solid objections. In danger of being conclusively outvoted there and then, the prince adjourned the meeting until the evening. He spent the afternoon trying to drum up support for his increasingly isolated stance. But if anything the tide of feeling by late afternoon was running even more strongly against him.[41]

The council resumed its deliberations in the evening. The prince found that erstwhile supporters had abandoned him. Any lingering hope of being able to swing the council round by a bravura display of rhetoric or magnetic charm was dashed when the English spy Dudley Bradstreet was introduced into the chamber. Bradstreet barefacedly spoke of a third army, 9,000 strong and commanded by Hawley and Ligonier, barring the way at Northampton (there was no such army).

Bradstreet's intervention infuriated the prince. 'That fellow will do me more harm than all the Elector's army!' he bellowed.[42] The glib and plausible spy was hustled out of the chamber. A vote was taken. The prince was alone: 'he could not prevail upon one single person to support him,' he later testified.[43] He was like Alexander the Great at the Beas, convinced that it was his destiny to march on, but unable to get any of his officers to see his point of view. 'You ruin, abandon and betray me if you do not march on!' he raged at them.[44] The councillors sat impassive and stony-faced. Finding that he could not even get old stalwarts like Tullibardine to break rank with this solid phalanx, the prince sullenly agreed to retreat. But, he added bitterly, 'In the future I shall summon no more councils, since I am accountable to nobody for my actions but to God and my father, and therefore shall no longer either ask or accept advice.'[45]

The prince remained convinced to his dying day that an earth-shattering victory that would have realised his destiny had been snatched from his hands at Derby by the cowardice, defeatism and treachery of his officers. This attitude has often been dismissed as the delusion of a sick, autocratic mind. Yet once again, a close examination of the situation reveals much more rationality in the prince's position than his critics give him credit for. To disentangle all the skeins in the decision at Derby, we need to make an important distinction between the subjective perceptions of the actors involved, and the facts available to the later historian with a privileged Olympian overview.

The first point to note is that Lord George Murray and the Scottish leaders made their decision in the dark. They did not know what the military situation of their enemies was. It is not an unfair criticism of Murray to say that he postulated the worst-case scenario for his own army, while giving the benefit of the doubt to the Hanoverians. Murray's argument was that an army of 5,500 was in danger of being gobbled up by the three armies, each in close proximity and each of 10,000 men. But in fact there was no third army. As Bradstreet admitted: 'Observe that there was not nine men at Northampton to oppose them, much less 9,000.'[46] Wade was far to the north at Wetherby and posed no danger. There was an ill-trained rabble of perhaps 4,000 at Finchley. That left Cumberland.

The desperate situation that George II's second son was in cannot be better conveyed than in this dispatch, written to the duke of Newcastle on 5 December by his aide the duke of Richmond:

Are we all mad, that you don't send for 10,000 more forces, be they Hessians, Hanoverians or devils if they will but fight for us. . . . The whole kingdom is asleep. Our cavalry can't be here before February and the Pretender may be crowned in Westminster by that time.[47]

In London Henry Fielding spoke of 'a panic scarce to be credited'.[48] Even the incurably eupeptic Horace Walpole allowed himself a scintilla of doubt: 'There never was so melancholy town (sic) . . . nobody but has some fear for themselves, for their money, or for their friends in the army. . . . I still fear the rebels beyond my reason.'[49]

The military situation was grave enough to warrant these panicky reactions. By his own admission and that of the duke of Richmond, Cumberland could have got no more than 4,000 troops from Lichfield to Northampton to contest the passage to London.[50] There was no serious doubt about the outcome of a battle between 4,000 of Cumberland's exhausted soldiers and 5,500 eager Scots. The clansmen's morale had never been higher than at Derby.[51] In his obsession with the total numbers facing him, Lord George Murray forgot the vital military principle of concentration of force.

It is often said that the decision to retreat from Derby was 'the merest common sense'.[52] But even if we accept the sovereignty of common sense, Lord George's decision did not fall into that category; it could not have done, since he did not know the facts. Nor did the prince. However, his intuition was sounder than his lieutenant-general's.

The distinction between subjective perceptions and objective circumstance also illuminates the position of the Hanoverians and the French. The panic both of the authorities in London and of their field commanders is too well documented to be shrugged off or dismissed lightly.[53] Lord George Murray had used the seemingly telling point at the council that if the Jacobites raced Cumberland to London, the duke would pick up numbers all the time, while the prince's strength remained the same or diminished as a result of skirmishes. Knowing the uncertain temper of the common people and especially of the London mob, the Whig grandees were not at all certain that the fresh accession of strength would not accrue to the other side.[54] The Lord Mayor of London told Aeneas MacDonald later that if the Jacobites had advanced, no more than five hundred men in London would have volunteered for the Hanoverian militia.[55]

Naturally, great stress is laid by pro-Hanoverian historians on the copious professions of loyalty before the invasion of England. But there is not much evidence of this loyalty in the crucial month 8 November–5 December 1745. What is certain is that all 'loyal' forces set up to oppose the clansmen melted away with amazing rapidity once the prospect of a real fight loomed. The Cumberland militia, the Liverpool Blues, the Manchester militia, the Derbyshire Blues: the story was the same everywhere; reluctance to fight.[56] How else indeed could the Highlanders have penetrated to just 120 miles from London and then retraced their steps to Scotland almost without loss, if they had faced a determined and hostile population, irrevocably loyal to the House of Hanover?

Significantly, even George II, who at the beginning of the rising had been inclined to dismiss it as a trifle, by December acknowledged that Charles Edward was a deadly foe. He even toyed with asking for reinforcements from Maria Teresa of Austria to deal with the threat to his dynasty.[57] None of this suggests a rebellion 'inevitably' foredoomed and fighting vainly against the tides of history.

The calamitous effect on the French of the decision at Derby must also be considered. At Versailles Louis XV had finally ordered an invasion of England in support of the prince. His favourite, the duc de Richelieu, was put in charge of the project, 15,000 men were assembled in the Picardy ports, and theoretically the expedition was ready to sail at the end of December 1745.[58] Ironically, news of the retreat from Derby reached Richelieu just as he arrived in Boulogne to take command. Although he did not immediately abandon the projected Channel crossing, in a psychological sense Derby blunted Richelieu's appetite. The French in late 1745 were playing an opportunistic game, looking for an easy victory.[59] This is not to say that they were insincere, simply that like the would-be invaders who came after them they were neither willing nor able to throw all available resources into a descent on England.

The retreat from Derby obviously meant that Richelieu would have a much tougher fight on his hands. Most crucially, psychological superiority was thrown away. French expectation of success had been predicated on the jittery state of nerves in London, with the authorities hypnotised by the speed of the Highlanders' advance and imagining all the time that the prince and the French were acting in concert.

'Black Friday', 6 December 1745, gave the game away to the Whigs in spectacular fashion.[60] It freed Newcastle from his nightmare of having to fight on two fronts at once. Even more important, it alerted him that there had been no collusion between France and the prince. Lord George Murray failed to understand that the psychological fillip given to George II and his ministers by this intelligence was worth several brigades. As for the French, did it not now seem that all their forebodings about the English Jacobites, that they existed on paper only, were borne out? If there really was an English Jacobite party, the prince would not be retracing his steps to Scotland.

Having had his best cards snatched from his hands, Richelieu lacked a psychological incentive to rise above the problems that then beset his expedition: adverse weather, the leaking of his battle plan, the depredations of the Royal Navy. The project to invade England was finally wound up in early February 1746 (NS).[61]

Derby also made it plain that Lord George's strategy was more conventional than the prince's in another sense. The prince realised that the English Jacobites would not rise while there were powerful undefeated Hanoverian armies at hand. Not only had the use of arms fallen into disuse, so that any levies the pro-Stuart squires brought out would be untrained rabble; it was even doubtful whether such levies could be brought out in the first place.[62] Quasi-feudal bonds in England were by now so weak that it was difficult for the gentry even to raise a sympathetic, intimidating mob at election time. As for raising men to fight regular troops, the clan leaders themselves, with the power of life and limb over their kinsmen, had found this difficult enough.

It was clear that the English Jacobites would rise only when a French army had landed or when there was no longer any military threat from London. They had no confidence in the Highlanders, regarding them as mere militia and (wrongly) far inferior to Cumberland's regulars.[63]

In other words, while the prince was taking risks, the English Jacobites were playing safe. The open adherence of just one English Jacobite leader might have had a multiplier effect, perhaps causing significant troop desertions in the Hanoverian armies, perhaps snow-balling into a general revolution.[64] But no one was willing to take the risk. In the absence of gamblers in the English Jacobite ranks, there had to be secret co-ordination of their efforts. This never happened.

Even if such mobilisation had been attempted in advance of the prince's invasion, it is unlikely that it could have been kept secret. The only other theoretical possibility for the prince was to consolidate his position in Lancashire, systematically raising and training recruits. But this, even if possible, would have destroyed the momentum of his onward march. And it was this purposeful speed and thrust that so panicked the Hanoverians.

The invasion of England by the western route, then, only made sense from the beginning if all this had been foreseen and compensated for. The obvious way to cut the Gordian knot was to seek out Wade at Newcastle and defeat him there – exactly what the prince wanted to do. As he correctly foresaw, a victory on English soil was crucial, to make it safe for his secret sympathisers to show themselves. Failing this, the Jacobites had to seek out and destroy Cumberland. Yet Lord George's strategy was expressly based on the avoidance of battles, almost as if he thought the army could simply walk to London. When, naturally enough, the enemy armies appeared in force, all Lord George could think of was retreat. Doubtless, as he himself claimed, he feared the impact of large-scale casualties in such a small army. And in terms of eighteenth-century military thought, if he could have got to London by constantly outflanking the enemy, he would have attained his objective. In modern terms, of course, to leave *two* armies in the field behind him was the biggest risk of all.

The irony of Lord George's strategy was that if Wade had proved even half-way competent, he would have moved across the Pennines from Newcastle when the Jacobites moved south, and cut off their retreat.[65] After the return to Newcastle from the snow-bound passes of the Pennines, Wade commenced a ponderous southerly march through Yorkshire. Had he crossed the Pennines farther south to block the retreat to Scotland, Lord George and the Scots would then have been left with no choice but to march south from Derby. It says a lot for Wade's influence with the Whig élite of the time that, where lower-ranking generals and officials of all kinds were haled before court-martials and inquiries on slender evidence of cowardice or incompetence (Cope, General Oglethorpe, General Durand, commandant of Carlisle Castle, Provost Stewart of Edinburgh), the Marshal himself escaped censure for what can only be described as gross military ineptitude.

The panic in London on 'Black Friday' could conceivably have had other momentous consequences if the Highlanders had not turned back. Those who applaud the wisdom of the Derby decision usually concentrate very narrowly on the military situation on paper. Yet there is also the question of general political confidence to consider. One of the reasons the French cursed themselves in later years for missing a great opportunity in 1745 was that they came to realise the catastrophic impact Derby threatened to have on the financial system in London.[66] The index of Bank of England stock fell from 141 in October 1745 to 127 in December.[67] Because of the general uncertainty engendered by the rising, bank stock did not rise above 125 in the early months of 1746.[68] It was the French view that an advance from Derby could have had two possible consequences.[69] One was a total collapse of business confidence and the disintegration of the administration into chaos. The other possibility was that National Debt fundholders, seeing their investment in danger of annihilation, might have colluded with Charles Edward's London supporters, possibly supporting his restoration in return for a binding guarantee that the National Debt would not be cancelled. Such a deal might even have led to a *coup d'état* in London ahead of the arrival of the Jacobite army.[70]

Such speculation on the might-have-been may appear otiose, but is of supreme importance in the quest for historical causality.[71] Some ingenious critics of Charles Edward have suggested that even if the prince had reached London and been restored, the train of events would very soon have led to his unseating.[72] A coronation with Catholic rites, a few examples of autocratic behaviour towards Parliament: it would not have taken much to precipitate another 1688. All one can say in answer to this is that Charles Edward's most detailed political testament shows that he had anticipated these objections and planned to build a power base on the common man to offset the expected backlash.[73] All of this is doubtless in the realm of remote speculation. But it is a travesty of Charles Edward's character and intelligence to say that he had no conception of the problems he would face if restored.

The debate about Derby can never be satisfactorily resolved. The fact remains, as one historian of the issue has shrewdly pointed out, that in their actual state of mind, the Scottish leaders would never have agreed to continue to London, whatever the cogency of the prince's arguments.[74]

States of mind were to be all-important after Derby. 'It is all over, we shall never come again,' was Sheridan's despondent conclusion.[75] The prince, who had trekked at the head of his army on the way south, now rode depressed and sullen on horseback in the rear.[76] Where on the march south he went to bed regularly at 11 p.m., often sleeping fully clothed, and was up again at 3 a.m., on the retreat he slept late, drank a lot, and often delayed the day's march.[77] He never truly recovered from the trauma of Derby. There were to be other, in some ways greater, shocks to his psychic system, but after Derby the prince was never the same person again, except perhaps for a brief period when his very survival was at stake in the heather. Just as the journey south fuelled the positive side of his personality, so that like a sun-god he waxed stronger and stronger until the meridian at Derby, so on the withdrawal north the negative charges in his shaky ego seemed to increase exponentially. By the time he reached Scotland the prince was psychically exhausted.

He can hardly be blamed for this. Even men with the strongest core of personal identity were shaken by the retreat from Derby. Discipline among the clansmen, which on the way south had been so extraordinarily good that at Manchester the prince was able to forbid female camp followers (bona fide wives only!)[78] and have the order accepted, now broke down; never entirely, but to a worrying extent.

Once they realised they were heading back towards Scotland (for the march north had commenced in darkness), the clansmen's morale visibly plummeted.[79] Ululations and cries of despair rent the air; some clansmen threw down their guns in disgust and vowed to quit the army once safely across the border.[80] Murray of Broughton's wife was seen crying like a baby.[81] To assuage the men's feelings, their colonels distributed powder and ammunition as if for a battle with Wade.[82] To camouflage reality still further, a story was put out that the second Jacobite army, commanded by Strathallan, was coming into England and that Wade was trying to place himself between the two armies.[83]

As the clansmen's discipline declined, the insolence of the English townspeople increased. On the march south, the Jacobite army looked like a possible victor, the prince a possible future king. On the retreat no such illusions could be entertained. Cumberland and Wade now had the whip hand, and the onlookers knew it. As it trudged wearily back through Ashbourne, Leek, Macclesfield and Stockport, the army had to put up with sniper fire and the summary execution of stragglers. At Manchester the prince's patience snapped. He had protected recalcitrant citizens from the wrath of the clansmen, prevented Ashbourne being put to the torch, even pardoned Cumberland's ace spy Vere. But disloyalty in Manchester was too much. A levy of £2,500 was exacted from the town for its contumacious behaviour.[84]

Lord George Murray had feared that the greatest danger to the Jacobite army would come from Wade. In fact Wade once again made no attempt to intercept them. All he did was to send a squadron of horse across the Pennines under General Oglethorpe to harry the retreating Highlanders.

The threat, unexpectedly, came from Cumberland, who had originally intended to follow the Jacobites no farther north than Macclesfield.[85] False rumours of a panic-stricken rabble throwing down their weapons in a mad rush for the Scottish border encouraged him to press on with the pursuit.

News of this chase brought out all the stubbornness in the prince's nature. He had been forced to retreat against his will; that was one thing. But he would not accept this further humiliation of seeming to flee before Cumberland. To Lord George's alarm, the prince began to slow the march up.

He was narrowly persuaded out of spending a second night in Manchester.[86] But, quoting back at Lord George his confident assurances at the Derby council that the army would be safe once it crossed the Ribble, the prince dug in his heels at Preston and insisted on spending an extra day there.[87]

The danger now was that Cumberland would catch up with the retreating army well before the Scottish border. In fact he would have done so, had he not also lost a day attending to a false report that the French had landed on the south coast.[88]

Fuelled by arguments from both Perth and d'Eguilles, the prince was already increasingly inclined to turn and face his pursuers. At Lancaster his irritation at retreating so fast in face of 'the son of a usurper' came to a head.[89] Come what might, he decided that Saturday 14 December would see a battle.

Lord George Murray, Lochiel and O'Sullivan selected a battlefield outside Lancaster. All seemed set for an encounter with Cumberland.

Then Wade's advance guard under Oglethorpe blundered on to the scene. They had been dispatched across the Pennines by 'Grandmother Wade' in partial atonement for his earlier failures to intercept the Highlanders. There was a skirmish with Elcho's Lifeguards. Some of Oglethorpe's rangers were taken prisoner. Their intelligence seemed to suggest that both Wade's and Cumberland's armies were close at hand.[90] Even the prince did not want to call on such a hand. On the 15th the army marched on to Kendal. Lord George Murray could not resist a taunt as they quit Lancaster: 'As Your Royal Highness is always for battles, be the circumstances what they may, I now offer you one in three hours from this with the army of Wade which is only about three miles from us.'[91]

The prince made Murray pay for the jibe. Beyond Kendal loomed the dreadful Shap Fell, a dismal prospect of snow, ice and mud. At Derby Lord George had sugared the pill of defeat for the prince by promising always to be in the rearguard on the retreat and to oversee the baggage and the artillery. Now the prince took advantage of this. In the interests of the safety of the army, Murray proposed abandoning the big guns at Kendal. The prince refused adamantly: not a single cannonball must be left behind, he averred.[92]

The consequence was that while the van got to Penrith with some difficulty (it took two days and a stopover at Shap), Lord George and the Glengarry men, in the rear with the unwieldy baggage waggons, took the same time to get only as far as Shap.[93] Cumberland sent a flanking column under Oglethorpe (who had linked up with the duke at Preston) to get round in front of the Highlanders and catch them in a pincer movement. Fortunately for Lord George, Oglethorpe bungled his part of the plan.[94] Even so, Cumberland's vanguard was now close on Murray's heels.

The inevitable happened. On the 18th, while struggling along the dreadful road to Penrith, Murray and the Jacobite rearguard were overhauled by the first of Cumberland's dragoons and mounted infantry.[95] All afternoon a running fight raged in and around Lowther Hall and the approaches to Clifton village. As dusk fell and the Highlanders were in danger of being surrounded, Murray learned from a prisoner that this was not Cumberland's main force (which numbered some 8,000 men) but merely the first 2,000 of them, commanded by the duke.

Here was a great opportunity to apply the maxim of concentration of force. For once the Hanoverians were outnumbered. A severe defeat this night would tarnish Cumberland's image, perhaps irremediably.[96]

To the fury of Lord George and his faction, the prince would not hear of returning. All he was prepared to do was to send back sufficient reinforcements to prevent Murray from being engulfed. Piqued at his lieutenant-general's reluctance to fight pitched battles, the prince now paid him back in his own coin. As Elcho, already disenchanted with the prince, remarked: 'As there was formerly a contradiction to make the army halt when it was necessary to march, so now there was one to march and shun fighting when there could never be a better opportunity for it.'[97]

Cluny MacPherson's regiment and the Appin Stewarts raced back to Clifton on the double. In the early evening moonlight Murray drew up his men in strong positions in hedges on either side of the Clifton road. A roughly equal number of Cumberland's dragoons dismounted and advanced on foot. A short, sharp, furious fight took place. Accurate shooting by Cumberland's men merely had the effect of drawing the snake from its hole. At the cry of 'claymore!', Cluny MacPherson's, one of the prince's crack regiments, drove Bland's regiment out of the Clifton ditches. After half an hour's fighting Murray had done more than enough to secure an unpursued Highland retreat.[98]

Lord George joined the prince in Penrith. Next day the Jacobite army moved on to Carlisle. Cumberland, left in Clifton to lick his wounds, felt no inclination to follow them.[99] The prince expressed himself very pleased with the night's work. But in effect, consciously or unconsciously he had sabotaged what could have been a decisive check to the Hanoverians.

This was not the prince's first eccentric decision. The desire to stay in Manchester for a second day; listening to Perth and d'Eguilles's siren song about a stand in Preston; the extra days spent in Preston and Lancaster; finally Clifton: already Charles Edward was exhibiting clear signs of self-destructive behaviour. But all this faded into insignificance alongside the decision he took at Carlisle. At a council called to consider the next move, now that Cumberland had called off his immediate pursuit, the prince proposed and carried the idea that a garrison be left in Carlisle.[100] The Manchester regiment, some two hundred and fifty strong, plus about a hundred Jacobites in the service of France, were left in Carlisle Castle.

What was widely predicted came to pass. On arrival outside Carlisle, Cumberland summoned heavy cannon from Whitehaven, blasted down the defences, and compelled the unconditional surrender of Charles Edward's few English volunteers.[101] The ill-fated Manchester regiment was led away to trial and barbarous execution.

The prince's action in leaving behind a garrison has always seemed inexplicable. Such military justification as can be adduced is remarkably flimsy. To explain the inexplicable, Chevalier de Johnstone proposed a hypothesis that the prince left the English volunteers in Carlisle to a certain fate as a calculated act of vengeance against an England that had failed to rise to his standard.[102]

Johnstone was on the right lines in suggesting a pathological origin for the prince's behaviour, but his explanation is too pat and contrived. This egregious error, one of the prince's worst mistakes in the '45[103] is so out of character that it seems more convincingly explained by an unconscious impulse of self-destruction. It is noteworthy that, throughout the '45, the worst excesses of the prince's self-destructive behaviour occurred after bruising encounters with Lord George Murray. This is compatible with the notion that at an unconscious level Charles Edward consistently conflated Murray with James as parents who had failed him. At a conscious level, he simply hated being thwarted.

It was a sombre and despondent prince who crossed the Esk into Scotland. The Jacobite army had achieved great things. Its five-hundred-mile round trip to Derby and back would long be remembered as an outstanding military exploit. But the prince was numb to the positive side of what had been achieved.

15

'Mired in shallows'

(January 1746)

The prince crossed the Esk back into Scotland on his twenty-fifth birthday (20 December OS; 31 December NS). Immediately on gaining Scottish soil, the army split into two columns: Lord George and the Lowland regiments trekked up through Ecclefechan, Locherby, Moffat, Douglas and Hamilton, aiming for Glasgow.[1] It was the intention that the Lowland brigade would enter Glasgow one day ahead of the prince and make all ready for him.

Charles Edward meanwhile travelled 'over cruel roads' via Dumfries and Drumlanrig.[2] Marching up Nithsdale, he crossed the Mennock pass by Leadhills and spent the night of 23 December in Douglas Castle.[3] The next day he came to the castle at Hamilton. This pleased him so much that he halted for a day and went hunting.[4]

On the 26th the prince entered Glasgow.[5] The reason for this choice of rendezvous was mainly financial.[6] The Jacobites intended to levy contributions in cash and kind from these hostile burghers, who had already shown a spirit of defiance to the prince.[7] Charles remarked that Glasgow was indeed a fine town. But it was clear he had no friends in it; what was worse, the Glaswegians did not trouble to hide their feelings.[8]

During the week in Glasgow Charles Edward reviewed his entire army on Glasgow Green and brought himself up to date on Scottish developments in his absence. The general review showed that remarkably few men – no more than two dozen – had been lost during the invasion of England.[9]

Scottish developments, on the other hand, presented a mixed picture. Edinburgh had been reoccupied by the Hanoverians almost the second the prince crossed the border into England.[10] Cope's successor General Handasyde had marched up from Berwick and entered it without opposition. Then General Hawley had been appointed as Wade's successor and moved the army of the north across the border. Hawley despised the Highlanders as a rabble, and was so confident of an imminent victory over them that he erected gibbets in Edinburgh.[11] Meanwhile in the north Lord Loudoun still held Inverness for the Whigs.

On the other hand, a second Jacobite army had been assembled at Perth and Dunblane. Although Lord Lewis Gordon had experienced great difficulty in raising the Gordons, he had collected many men from Aberdeenshire as well as the Farquharsons of Deeside.[12] Lady Mackintosh had raised her husband's clan under MacGilvray of Dunmaglas. Another Jacobite wife of a pro-Hanoverian magnate – Lady Fortrose (Seaforth), whose husband was with Lord Loudoun – had herded together a few Mackenzies.[13] Lord Cromarty and Lord Macleod brought in the main Mackenzie regiment. MacDonald of Barisdale and young Glengarry had gathered reinforcements from the west. Glengyle brought in some MacGregors from Perthshire.[14]

The most dramatic developments had taken place in the north. At last Lord Lovat had committed himself to the prince. Lord Loudoun had finally forced the issue. On 3 December he marched a force to relieve Fort Augustus, then threatened by the Frasers under the Master of Lovat.[15] On 11 December Loudoun took Lovat in person to Inverness as his prisoner.[16] This ended the old fox's prevarication. Escaping from Loudoun's hands with contemptuous ease, he finally brought out his clan.

At about the same time Loudoun sent a strong force under Norman Macleod and Grant of Grant to relieve Aberdeen. Lord Lewis Gordon soon demonstrated that the prince had not entrusted him with high command for nothing. On 23 December he marched out from Aberdeen and routed Macleod at Inverurie, forcing him to retire across the Spey. As a result of Inverurie, Lewis Gordon held all the country between Aberdeen and Speyside for the prince.[17] In addition, following this reverse a large number of men in Loudoun's independent companies deserted.[18]

But the most heartening news of all was the arrival from France of Lord John Drummond with some 1,100 troops of the Irish brigade. Drummond immediately took over the Jacobite command in Scotland from Strathallan.[19] The psychological boost of this landfall at Montrose was immeasurable. Not only had Drummond warned the Dutch that their participation in the fighting would be an infringement of international law, but he published Louis XV's declaration, which made it clear that Drummond's contingent was only the first of many troops France intended to pour into Scotland.[20]

Since the prince had ordered that no more formal council meetings would be held after his humiliation at Derby, the chain of command began to fall apart at Glasgow. It was suggested privately to the prince that the Jacobites should proceed to a second occupation of Edinburgh, or at least a march to East Lothian to keep the new Hanoverian commander 'Hangman' Hawley guessing and so force him to bivouac his men out at night in the cold.[21] There was something in this idea, since the particularly cold weather would have taken a toll on Hawley's troops and sapped morale. But this action would commit the prince sooner or later to a battle with Hawley. For the moment he wanted to keep his options open. He had still not given up hope of a second invasion of England and hoped at any minute to hear that the French had landed with his brother.

So on 3 January 1746 Charles removed himself from hostile Glasgow to Chevalier Paterson's seat between Stirling and Bannock-burn.[22] Once again the army marched in two columns. Lord George's force (six clan regiments and Elcho's Lifeguards) travelled to Falkirk via Cumbernauld.[23] The prince took the rest of the army by Kilsyth. The purpose in taking up position on the Bannockburn–Stirling–Falkirk line was to link up with the new army under Lord John Drummond now marching down from Perth.[24] Drummond had been joined by Lord Lewis Gordon. Mackintoshes, Frasers, Farquharsons and Mackenzies now mingled with the Irish veterans of the battle of Fontenoy.[25] Elcho's Lifeguards were thrown out as far as Falkirk to make it look as though Edinburgh was the objective.[26]

While the troops were cantoned in the towns and villages round about (St Ninian's being a particular centre), the prince made his headquarters at Bannockburn House.[27] Now finally removed from stress into a safe haven, his health broke down. The prince's valetudinarian condition for most of the rest of the '45 campaign has hardly been commented on, but is surely significant. Nothing could impair his vitality while he took events at the flood, all the way to Derby. But once he was back in relative safety in Scotland, all the pent-up anger since Derby broke loose. The 'internal saboteur' in the prince's mind, responsible for his self-destructive behaviour on the march back through northern England, now manifested itself as illness. From 5–16 January Charles lay seriously ill with influenza and a high fever at Bannockburn House.[28]

The prince's three major illnesses in the months January–April

1746 surely have to be regarded as stress-related. It is more than a little curious that his health should have held up so well from August to December 1745, and again from April to September 1746 during the flight in the heather, only to dip so alarmingly into this trough during the first three months of 1746.

The prince had already shown signs of a changed personality. In Glasgow, in contrast to his behaviour in Edinburgh in October, he made a determined effort to exploit his undoubted appeal for the ladies.[29] He dressed in his most lavish French clothes, exhibiting finery that he had not been seen in before.[30] Every night he supped in public, making a conspicuous display of his sumptuary splendour.[31] Unlike at Edinburgh in October, he took part in the dancing. It was almost as though he was signalling the end of his period of heroic strenuousness, acknowledging that his warrior personality had failed.

The most significant event at Bannockburn was that Clementina Walkinshaw nursed him through his illness and became his mistress.[32] She was the daughter of John Walkinshaw of Barrowfield, a Jacobite who had been out in the '15 and escaped to join James Stuart in Bar-le-Duc.[33] John Walkinshaw was one of the party who rescued Charles Edward's mother from the Emperor in the famous Wogan escapade. He named his own daughter after Clementina Sobieska.

It is of the utmost importance to appreciate the significance of the open appearance of women in the prince's life. The contrast between his behaviour in Glasgow and his earlier indifference to the ladies in Edinburgh suggests an inner psychic drama – as does his later dancing at Inverness after the pointed abstention from the ballroom floor at Holyrood. We shall see later too the remarkable difference between his austere, monkish life in France in 1744–5 and his hedonism during 1746–8. We cannot assume, as has been done too readily, that Charles was a male virgin before the '45. But it is clear that in his positive phase, on the upward climb to the meridian at Derby, women were unimportant to him.

As the prince lay ill, pampered with the then fashionable cinnamon treatment, he was suddenly confronted with more immediate problems. Lord George Murray burst in on his retreat with a peremptory demand for a solution to the Jacobite decision-making process. Since the prince was not willing to summon any more full war councils, Murray proposed a committee of five or six regimental commanders who could take decisions in an emergency. That was reasonable enough. But relations between the prince and his lieutenant-general were so bad that Lord George could not resist throwing in a taunt. Collective decision-making was what had saved the army from destruction at Derby, he claimed. Had the council met at Lancaster also, the foolish decision to spend an extra day there would not have been taken.[34]

The prince's reply is revealing at several levels and is therefore worth quoting at some length:

When I came into Scotland I knew well enough what I was to expect from my enemies, but I little foresaw what I meet with from my friends. I came vested with all the authority the king could give me, one chief part of which is the command of his armies, and now I am required to give this up to fifteen or sixteen persons, who may afterwards depute five or six of their own number to exercise it, for fear if they were six or eight that I might myself pretend to the casting vote. By the majority of these all things are to be determined, and nothing left to me but the honour of being present at their debates. This I am told is the method of all armies and this I flatly deny, nor do I believe it to be the method of any one army in the world. I am often hit in the teeth that this is an army of volunteers, and consequently very different from one composed of mercenaries. What one would naturally expect from an army whose chief officers consist of gentlemen of rank and fortune, and who came into it merely from motives of duty and honour, is more zeal, more resolution and more good manners than in those that fight merely for pay: but it can be no army at all where there is no general, or which is the same thing no obedience or deference paid to him. Everyone knew before he engaged in the cause, what he was to expect in case it miscarried, and should have stayed at home if he could not face death in any shape: but can I myself hope for better usage? At least I am the only person upon whose head a price has been already set, and therefore I cannot indeed threaten at every other word to throw down my arms and make my peace with the government. I think I show every day that I do not pretend to act without taking advice, and yours oftener than any body's else, which I shall continue to do, and you know that upon more occasions than one, I have given up my own opinion to that of others. I stayed indeed a day at Lancaster without calling a Council, yet yourself proposed to stay another but I wonder to see myself reproached with the loss of Carlisle. Was there a possibility to carrying off the cannon and the baggage, or was there time to destroy them? And would not the doing it have been a greater dishonour to our arms? After all did not you yourself instead of proposing to abandon it, offer to stay with the Atholl Brigade to defend it?

I have insensibly made this answer much longer than I intended, and might yet add much more, but I choose to cut it short, and shall only tell you that my authority may be taken from me by violence, but I shall never resign it like an idiot.[35]

Anyone who still clings to the canard that Charles Edward Stuart was an unintelligent Italian princeling should ponder that letter: concise, lucid and shrewd. As if to reinforce the point that he still intended to command, he ordered the investment of Stirling Castle. This was eminently feasible now that he had been joined by his second army of 4,000 men.[36] While Charles convalesced in Clementina's arms, his officers bent their energies to this difficult task.

As ever, the town adjacent to the castle presented no problems. Stirling was called upon to surrender on 6 January and did so two days later.[37] The problem was the citadel. It would be a tough nut to crack even if Hawley stood idly by. He soon showed he had no such intention.

The Jacobites' initial problem was that they had to bring heavy siege artillery up the Firth from Alloa.[38] But Alloa itself was dangerously exposed. The river at that point was too wide to be commanded by a battery. Indeed an enemy sloop sailed beyond Alloa and landed a force that came close to capturing Lord Elcho.[39] If the Jacobites meanwhile erected a battery at a point farther up the river towards Stirling, so that they could command the whole river and blow enemy warships out of the water, it was conceivable that Hawley in turn could land forces at Alloa itself to destroy the Jacobite heavy artillery before it could be moved.[40]

This was in fact precisely what Hawley planned to do. At a crucial moment Lord John Drummond, guarding Alloa, received a stiffening from Lochiel's regiment. Hawley's landing force sheered off.[41] The Jacobites then transported their heavy guns to Stirling. They had a battery that commanded the Forth approaches, so could (and did) beat off any enemy probes made in that direction.[42] To relieve the castle, Hawley would now have to come overland.

But the siege of Stirling quickly lurched from difficulty to disaster. The so-called French expert on siege warfare, M. Mirabel (who had come over with Drummond), proved to be a spectacular incompetent.[43] The men conducting the siege were overworked and poorly fed.[44] There was particular strain on Ogilvy's regiment. Since clan regiments detested siege work, there was little relief for the Lowland battalions.[45] It was as much as Lord George Murray could do to get the Atholl brigade to guard the trenches.[46] And the whole operation was hampered by heavy, driving rain.[47]

At this point Hawley made his move overland. He sent ahead an advance screen of cavalry to Linlithgow.[48] Hearing this, Lord George Murray took five battalions of Athollmen with Pitsligo's and Elcho's cavalry to intercept them and deny them forage and provisions.[49] Arriving at dawn, they surprised an advanced patrol of Hawley's dragoons and took possession of the magazine and military supplies.[50]

Pursuing Hawley's outriders beyond the town, Elcho's Lifeguards collided with a further body of dragoons and chased them off. Yet it was obvious that the main force was not far behind. Retiring for the night to Falkirk, Murray's forces joined the rest of the army at Bannockburn on the 14th.[51]

Nettled by what he considered his own failure to achieve very much, Lord George gave vent to his irrational side. He complained to the prince that the Linlithgow operation could have been successful if he had had the Camerons along with him, forgetting that their presence at Alloa was necessary to force Hawley to come overland in the first place. He also complained that the prince's idyll at Bannockburn was a strain on manpower: it stretched his Athollmen thin, since they had to do guard duty both at Falkirk and Bannockburn.

Hawley's army marched from Edinburgh to Linlithgow on 15 January. The Hanoverian vanguard under General Huske was at Falkirk on the 16th, to link up with 1,500 Argyllshire militia under Colonel Campbell.[52] During these two days the Jacobite army stood to, drawn up in line of battle on a plain to the east of Bannockburn.[53]

On the 16th the Jacobites dispersed from the field at 3 p.m., again disappointed that the enemy had not come. Their dispersal was carelessly arranged. As Elcho pointed out, a better general than Hawley would have chosen this moment to attack; he could have picked the Jacobite regiments off piecemeal.[54]

On the morning of the 17th, the implications of this carelessness became clear. Despite precise orders issued the night before, it was almost midday before the entire Jacobite army was assembled. Such a state of affairs could not be allowed to persist into a third day. Since Hawley would not come to them, it was time for the Jacobites to take the offensive. Lord George Murray suggested seizing the high ground to the south-west of Falkirk, a ridge of moorland about a mile from Hawley's camp.[55] For once the prince agreed with Murray.

To camouflage the movement, Lord John Drummond and the Irish troops were sent along the main road from Bannockburn to Stirling. Marching by detours, side roads and across fields, the Jacobite army approached the high ground. It was now about 8,000 strong, roughly the same size as Hawley's. The only units of the prince's troops not engaged were the 1,200 men left with Perth to continue the siege of Stirling.[56]

The approach of the Highlanders was noticed by the enemy but, amazingly, Hawley considered it inconceivable that his army was in any danger of being attacked.[57] At Callendar House (his headquarters) he sat down to his dinner unconcerned, confident with the folly of arrogance.

Between one and two o'clock graver intelligence came through. It was clear that this was no feint. The entire Jacobite army was ascending the high ground. At last Hawley realised the seriousness of his position. Leaving the table in a fluster, he galloped hatless up to the head of his troops. Hurried orders were given to forestall the Highlanders in the occupation of the summit of the moor.[58]

Falkirk Muir rose steeply from the town. It was a moorland plateau of scrub and heather. Halfway up the hillside a deep ravine cut across the moor. The preliminaries of the battle resolved themselves into a race for the summit. The race was won by the Jacobite right, but Hawley's dragoons got to the plateau minutes behind them.[59] The consequence was that when both armies drew up they were in slanting formation.

The Jacobite centre and left extended down the hillside from the fairly level ground near the summit occupied by the right. Here were the MacDonalds in the front rank, with the Atholl brigade in the second line and Ogilvy's in the centre. Elcho's and Balmerino's horse provided the cavalry reserve in this sector.[60] The extreme left was posted near the mouth of the ravine. Here were the Camerons with Lord Lewis Gordon's cavalry in the second line and Kilmarnock's behind them. To the south was boggy ground, making encircling movements by Hawley impossible. To the north, towards Falkirk, the salient feature was the ravine or gully that separated the Jacobite left from Hawley's.[61]

Such terrain clearly ruled out complex military manoeuvres. But now the elements took a hand. As Hawley's infantry struggled up the hill, the overcast day turned to storm. A strong wind blew from the south-west and the icy rain beat directly into the faces of Hawley's troops as a result of the sloping ground.[62] They suffered the additional disadvantage of not being able to see all the clansmen above them on the skyline. As the dark of a stormy winter's afternoon descended, visibility was severely restricted on both sides. There was even doubt about whether powder could be kept dry. Hawley gave the order to fix bayonets.

Seeing that it was impossible to outflank the Jacobite right on account of the marshy ground, Hawley's dragoons tried to draw the Highlanders' fire and break up their formation by riding in among them.[63] But the MacDonald regiments had been well drilled by Lord George Murray. He had impressed on them that in no circumstances were they to open fire until he gave the word.[64]

Perceiving that there was no obvious way of shifting the Highlanders, and doubtless fearing that the clansmen would have the edge in confused night fighting, Hawley ordered his dragoons to attack. It was nearly four o'clock.[65]

Nothing more clearly demonstrated Hawley's incompetence than an order to 700 dragoons to charge a front line of 4,000 well-drilled clansmen.[66] Colonel Ligonier at the head of the cavalry found his orders incredible. But he knew better than to question the command of the savage 'Hangman' Hawley. Advancing on the Highland right, the three cavalry regiments came on at the trot.[67]

Waiting until the horses were a pistol shot away, Lord George Murray raised his musket as the signal to fire. The dragoons took a devastating volley at a ten-yard range.[68] About eighty of them fell dead on the spot. Watchers in Hawley's rear saw 'daylight through them' in several places.[69] Two of the cavalry regiments broke and fled, riding over their own infantry as they went. The third was all but annihilated in gruesome manner by clansmen playing the role of berserkers, hamstringing and disembowelling horses with the claymore, pulling and scything their riders out of the saddle.[70]

The MacDonalds' blood was up. It was impossible to maintain discipline. Two of the best Jacobite regiments dispersed to plunder the fallen dragoons or maul the weak Glasgow militia.[71] The Hanoverian foot was left intact. This created a potentially dangerous situation, for the heavy rain and the fact that they did not use cartridges left the Highlanders unable to return Hawley's fire. But this was when the clansmen were at their very best. Throwing down their muskets, they charged broadsword in hand into Hawley's left.[72] After a brief resistance four of Hawley's six front-line regiments on the left broke and fled.

This was the moment when defeat could have turned to rout. Two things conspired to rob the Jacobites of an overwhelming victory. On the Hanoverian right the three regiments under General Huske did not break but held up well.[73] And, though the prince had been asked by Lord George to appoint a commander on the left, he had neglected to do so.[74] The bad consequences of the Bannockburn/Falkirk separation now made themselves felt. To overcome the determination of Huske on the right, the Jacobites needed someone of Murray's verve. In fact, incredibly, there was no overall commander there.

To make things worse, the sloping battle line meant that the Jacobite left could hear the sounds of battle behind them. It was impossible in the gathering gloom to get a clear line on what was happening. The obvious conclusion from Huske's firmness was that Hawley must be winning the battle on the Jacobite right. The regimental commanders on the left did not therefore feel like trying conclusions with Huske.[75] In this way the opportunity for total victory was lost.

After twenty minutes, with dusk descending rapidly, and with a large part of both armies having already quit the field, Lord George decided that he no longer had enough men to deal decisively with Huske. But he was determined to occupy Falkirk at once, lest the enemy recover and make a stand behind gun emplacements.[76] The defeat suffered by Hawley and the consequent Hanoverian panic enabled Murray to do so. Falkirk was a victory, but it was not the crushing destruction of Hawley it could have been after the 'Hangman's' initial dreadful mistake. Jacobite losses had been about 50 killed and 70 wounded. The Hanoverians sustained casualties of some 20 officers and 400 men killed.[77]

The prince had once again not seen much of his victory. He had been in the rear of the second line with the Irish battalions and came up with Lord George Murray only in the closing minutes of the battle. At one stage it seemed that a detachment of dragoons had seen the royal standard and was attempting a snatch raid on Charles.[78] But the resolution of the Irish picquets soon dispersed them.

The problem was that in the driving rain and excessive gloom, everyone was dispersing, Jacobite clansman and Hanoverian regular alike. The prince tried in vain to rally his men.[79] Then he conferred with Murray. They agreed that it would be folly to make a night attack on Falkirk if Hawley was still there; if he was not, a pursuit on such a dreadful winter night was also out of the question. The prince's men had been stood to arms since 7 a.m. and were already soaked to the skin. The pools of water on the sodden ground were already hardening into ice.[80] In the end, they decided to enter Falkirk tentatively, Drummond from the east and Murray from the west.

The battle of Falkirk might have been thought likely to lift Charles's spirits, but never was a victory so much attended by gloom in the post-mortem. A great opportunity had been lost: this was the consensus on all sides. All that remained was to find culprits on whom to fasten the inevitable recriminations. It was plain that Hawley, though mauled, would soon recover. He had got away to Linlithgow with most of his troops; the new arrivals pouring into Edinburgh from London would soon more than make good his losses.

The Jacobites, on the other hand, had been handed victory on a plate and had failed to clinch the issue. They had had the advantage of the ground, the rain was blowing into the enemy's faces, Hawley had given his dragoons a suicidal order to charge; and yet the decisive victory that should have come had eluded the prince's men.[81] In the Jacobite camp accusations and attributions of blame proliferated. Lord George Murray alleged that it was clearly Drummond's job to take command of the left wing; Drummond pointed the finger at Murray for his caution and restraint in not allowing the clansmen full rein in pursuit, and even for fighting on foot.[82] The prince was also piqued by d'Eguilles's praise for Lord George's generalship at Falkirk. To 'set the record straight', he instructed Sheridan to write a letter to Versailles, balancing the French envoy's account by exaggerating O'Sullivan's role.[83]

The gloomy feelings in the Jacobite camp were accentuated next day. Charles Edward arose from his bed in Hawley's rapidly vacated quarters (where he was said to have eaten the dinner left untouched by Hawley)[84] to find that an event of singular ill-omen had occurred. Young Glengarry (Angus) had been accidentally shot dead in the streets of Falkirk by the careless discharge of a musket by a Keppoch MacDonald.[85] Despite Glengarry's dying pleas, the Keppoch clansman was executed forthwith as an example. This foolish decision merely alienated the Keppochs while doing nothing to restore Glengarry morale.[86] The immediate consequence was a string of desertions that was to set in train the Jacobites' ultimate disaster.

This was a moment when decisive leadership was called for. The Jacobites should have pursued Hawley to Edinburgh and reoccupied the city. Initially, of course, there could be no question of pursuit. The Jacobite troops were too tired even to harry Hawley as far as Linlithgow. But on the 18th there were calls for the reoccupation of Edinburgh and even for a second invasion of England.[87] Undoubtedly the prince should have opted for the former of the two, so as to prevent Hawley from recovering his balance.[88]

But the unsatisfactory result of Falkirk and the disarray among his officers that followed disturbed Charles Edward. He suffered a relapse

of his illness and returned to Bannockburn to Clementina's minis-
trations; the Lowland troops went with him as bodyguard.[89]

In the decision-making vacuum that ensued, during the crucial
days when the clansmen should have been pressing home their advantage and snapping at Hawley's heels, all that was done was to
accelerate work on the pointless siege of Stirling Castle.[90] This was
already a hopeless enterprise. Mirabel was by now adding drunkenness to his other deficiencies.[91] Even Lord George, who had been
inclined to defend the Frenchman against his detractors, eventually
admitted he was impossible.[92] And when the long-awaited Jacobite
battery was finally ready and directed its salvoes at the castle, it
was answered by a devastatingly accurate cannonade that very soon
silenced the battery, not without considerable loss of life.[93] Moreover,
morale among the Scots undertaking this thankless task was not
improved by the fact that Charles Edward saw fit to pay one visit
only to the trenches around the castle.[94] Finally, news came in that
Cumberland had arrived in Edinburgh to take over the command
from Hawley. He brought with him three new regiments.[95]

During this critical period, when the fate of the rising was virtually
decided, everything conspired to dampen morale in the Jacobite army
and to underscore the gloomiest prognostications of the growing band
of pessimists in the ranks of the officers. The prince's absence at
Bannockburn at this juncture was one of his most signal self-destructive acts. True, he was ill, but the illness itself was part of the internal
sabotage, increasingly in evidence since Derby. While he was closeted
with Clementina Walkinshaw at Bannockburn, a tide of opinion was
building up among the clan leaders that would prove impossible to
reverse.

The prince was finally spurred into activity by news of the presence
in Edinburgh of his rival and contemporary Cumberland.[96] Since it
was clear that George II's second son would immediately try to
relieve Stirling Castle – and it was equally obvious that Mirabel was
as far away from completing the siege as ever – the prospect of
another battle loomed.[97]

The prince's spirits lifted at the thought. He sent Murray of
Broughton to Lord George with orders to prepare to engage Cumberland at Linlithgow or Falkirk. Lord George appeared to accept the
command without demur. But on the evening of the 29th the lieutenant-general sent Hay of Restalrig to Bannockburn with a document
signed by Murray and six clan chiefs (Lochiel, Keppoch, Clanranald,
Ardshiel, Lochgarry and the Master of Lovat). This document
strongly urged retreat to the Highlands in view of the critical rate of

desertion taking place in the army.[98] Lord George's remonstrance claimed that 2,000 clansmen had already deserted, that the number of absconders increased not just daily but hourly. If they faced Cumberland now, it would be their 5,000 men pitted against twice that number under the duke's command. There was, however, an honourable alternative to continuing the siege of Stirling. If the Highlanders chased Loudoun from Inverness and captured the northern forts so as to open communication with Ross and Caithness, they could reasonably expect fresh accessions from Jacobites in those counties.[99] Together with the deserters, whom the clan chiefs would round up in their own country, it was reasonable to assume that an army of 10,000 could be put in the field for a spring campaign. Murray also sent a verbal message with Hay which said: 'We are sensible this will be very unpleasant, but in the name of God what can we do?'[100]

What caused this remarkable defeatism? Undoubtedly morale among the Highlanders had taken a severe blow in the limbo period after Falkirk. The failure to follow up the victory, the continued frustration of the incompetent siege of Stirling, the demoralisation of the MacDonalds after the shooting of Angus Glengarry, all played their part.[101] The key to it all was inertia. Clan armies needed cease-less momentum of a purposive kind or they tended to fall apart. In fallow periods, especially after a victory, the temptations to slip away to home and hearth with booty were irresistible. Fear of desertions, it will be remembered, was one of the key reasons for the decision to invade England.

Moreover, except in extreme cases, discipline could be maintained only by example, not by the lash or the firing squad. The incident that led to Glengarry's death in the streets of Falkirk is itself instruc-tive. Despite constant pleas to the clansmen not to fire off their guns on impulse, Lord George Murray had no real sanction to bring to bear if they disobeyed. Nor could the clan leaders do much about desertion. The usual fate of a deserter was simply to be coaxed, cajoled or shamed back into fighting.[102] Even if a clan chieftain was inclined to be draconian, the Highlanders knew they could rely on the prince's merciful nature to get them a reprieve – after all, he even refused to execute Cumberland's spies.

If the lax discipline in the Jacobite army gave the clansmen the motive to desert in droves, the aftermath of Falkirk gave them their opportunity. The decision to prosecute the siege of Stirling Castle was a disaster. The Highlanders detested siege work and particularly hated the menial duty of guarding the trenches.[103] There were other reasons, too, for their low morale after Falkirk. Within a few days, as their leaders failed to follow up, and as fresh enemy troops arrived at Edinburgh, the clansmen came to realise that the foe they had defeated at Falkirk was now stronger than ever.[104]

It was not entirely surprising, then, that desertions began to occur.[105] In retrospect, the empty ten days from 17 to 28 January was for the Jacobites the most ruinous period in the entire campaign. They did not so much lose the initiative as throw it away.[106] Some of the blame must be laid at the prince's door, as he dealt with illness, Clementina, and his own inner demons. But Lord George must also be brought into the dock. Why did he go along so lamely with the proposal to prosecute the siege of Stirling, knowing the likely consequences in the Highland ranks? The 'book' excuse about not leaving strongholds in the rear was a poor argument at this stage. Why did he not suggest to the prince that after driving Hawley out of Edinburgh, they should take the first step towards constituting an independent kingdom of Scotland, perhaps summoning a Convention of the Scottish Estates and making a public call to France for recognition and support?[107]

The time for remonstration was the 18th of January, not ten days later. Perhaps the strain Lord George was under was just too great. The prince preserved his equilibrium on the surface by his retreat to Bannockburn. His lieutenant-general had to exert an iron grip on the army night and day. As he wrote poignantly to his wife: 'What would I not give for a little rest! I have heard of a person being turned into a post-horse (by those who believe in transmigration) as the worst change that could happen. If I continue much longer in the way of life I am in now, a post-horse would be an ease to me.'[108]

There are some grounds, then, for thinking that Lord George was under excessive strain when he got the clan chiefs to sign his remonstrance. Certainly his nightmare estimates of mass desertions were very far from the mark, as later became plain. Lord George's demand for a retreat to the Highlands was a very bad mistake, on a number of counts, and his gross overestimate of the desertion rate showed an untypical tendency to panic. But the stress of the tough campaign, then (in his case) in its fifth month, should not be underestimated. Since early September the destiny of the Jacobite army had been in his hands. He was permitted no breather, no interludes. By contrast the Hanoverian captains benefited from fighting in relays. Cope, Wade, Ligonier, Hawley, all served their limited time and then handed on to someone else. Cumberland spent December in the saddle, took January off, returned to Scotland at the end of that month, and then spent six weeks relatively stress-free in Aberdeen. Only Lord George kept unceasing vigil over his army. He made a disastrous blunder in advising the retreat to the Highlands, but the context in which he did so should be appreciated.

When the fateful remonstrance arrived at Bannockburn, Murray of Broughton read it incredulously and then passed it to O'Sullivan for his opinion. The prince was asleep (this was late on the evening of 28 January). Realising that his rage would be terrible when he did read it, the two advisers decided not to wake him and to leave the storm until next morning.[109] Murray of Broughton rode back to Falkirk that night on a fruitless mission to persuade the chiefs to change their minds.

The storm next morning was every bit as bad as had been feared. When the prince read the document, it was as if all the rage he had ever felt in his life came gushing out in a single, highly significant act. The prince dashed his head violently against the wall, ranting and cursing about Lord George. 'Good God! Have I lived to see this!' he exclaimed.[110]

Eventually, conquering his irrationality, the prince sat down to answer the remonstrance. He began by pointing out the preposterous nature of the chiefs' demands. Had history ever recorded an instance where an army *retreated* after winning a victory: 'is it possible that a victory and a defeat should produce the same effects, and that conquerors should fly from an engagement whilst the defeated are seeking it?'[111]

Charles went on to point out the obvious flaws in Murray's argument. If morale was the issue, the existing psychological condition of the army would be made many times worse by a retreat. Moreover, Murray's arguments were nonsensical, since Cumberland would not simply leave them alone in the Highlands to regroup. The Jacobites would have to fight him sooner or later. Better to meet him now on terms more favourable than would obtain in a few months' time. By the spring the Jacobite army could well have shrunk to its Glenfinnan core. Cumberland, too, would claim that his name inspired such terror that the enemy ran away.[112] Most important of all, a retreat into the Highlands would finally destroy Jacobite credibility and kill off all hopes of help from France and Spain. 'For my part,' he concluded, 'I must say that it is with great reluctance that I can bring myself to consent to such a step, but having told you my thoughts upon it, I am too sensible of what you have already ventured and done for me, not to yield to the unanimous resolution if you persist in it.'[113]

The myth of Charles Edward the autocrat is not really compatible with that last statement. Indeed, if anything, the prince can be faulted for the mildness and feebleness of his reply. He should have rebutted some of Murray's specious arguments more vigorously. It was clear that Murray had not thought through his proposed strategy, that it had been plucked from the air and hurriedly improvised. There were solid grounds for arguing that an arithmetical rate of desertion would become a geometrical one in the Highlands, thus producing an exactly opposite result from that predicted by Murray. If it was acknowledged on all sides that population density in the Highlands already made subsistence precarious – and indeed was sometimes cited as being itself a precipitant towards Jacobite risings that would allow the clansmen to plunder 'in the plain' – where was the army to get its supplies? There were no magazines in the Highlands and certainly no food to feed an army of 10,000 men, given the marginal quality of existence there. Meanwhile, the areas of Scotland that *did* produce resources capable of sustaining an army – the Lowlands and the north-east – would have fallen to Cumberland without a fight.[114] But then it was Lord George's contention that in the struggle for those areas, sea power gave Cumberland a great advantage.[115] What he failed to see was that the logic of the decision to retreat to the Highlands entailed a withdrawal into the very locale where the army could not be adequately fed.

Charles Edward might also have asked Lord George how it was possible that an army that was thought capable of beating Cumberland on the 28th had suddenly become one in danger of imminent destruction on the 29th. But the prince had no middle gear. After his lurch to extreme irrationality, he swung back to a passive, almost deferential posture. There is no sign in Charles Edward's temperament of the psychology of the true autocrat.

The prince dispatched Sheridan from Bannockburn with the letter. Sheridan was now weak and ailing, and he crumbled too readily in face of the battery of arguments the chiefs brought to bear at Falkirk.[116] Acknowledging himself convinced by their advocacy, he asked them to send some of their number to Bannockburn to put the same points to the prince in person.

Cluny and Keppoch came back with Sheridan and reiterated to the prince with some force the arguments in the remonstrance. Their mulish doggedness during the meeting made Charles lose his temper. He quickly recovered and apologised, but showed a shrewd appreciation of the way the incident would be distorted by remarking in his second letter to the chiefs: 'I doubt not but you have been informed by Cluny and Keppoch of what passed last night and heard great complaints of my despotic temper.'[117]

Finding that he was unable to make any headway against the dogged clan chiefs, who were adamant for retreat, the prince in effect washed his hands of the whole affair. Prophesying that Stirling would become a second Carlisle through artillery losses, and that the trickle of deserters would soon become a flood, he concluded:

> After all this I know I have an army that I cannot command any further than the chief officers please, and therefore if you are all resolved upon it I must yield; but I take God to witness that it is with the greatest reluctance, and that I wash my hands of the fatal consequences which I foresee but cannot help.[118]

This exchange between Charles Edward and Lord George Murray is singularly revealing. The breakdown in communication between them was now total. Their incompatibility made effective co-operation impossible. Even if both men had not been under excessive stress, their collision was still inevitable. Their very styles clashed violently: Lord George's cold, aloof, aristocratic hauteur against the prince's flamboyant showmanship. Murray could survive Derby and Falkirk and still make something of what was left. It was the prince's tragedy that he could not.

16

'Climbing up the Climbing Wave'
(February–March 1746)

It was time to decide on the arrangements for the retreating Jacobite army. On 31 January Charles Edward and Lord George Murray finally came face to face. Lord George behaved tactlessly. He made no attempt to salve the prince's wounded pride, but launched into a complaint that his Athollmen were still being kept on siege duty at Stirling Castle. However, the prince kept his temper. The two men worked on the details of the retreat.[1]

They agreed that the combined forces should be drawn up at St Ninian's at 9 a.m. next day; Lord George would then select one hundred men from each regiment to form a strong rearguard. All cannon would be spiked and all surplus ammunition destroyed. Lord George would deploy the rearguard in such a way that Cumberland could not follow.[2]

But Murray made another bad mistake on this last day of January. Flushed with his triumph in the battle of wills with the prince, he refused to discuss the administrative details of the retreat with O'Sullivan and Murray of Broughton. The result was that no proper instructions were issued for the army's orderly withdrawal. In particular, not enough carts and horses had been requisitioned to convey the artillery.[3]

Even if efficient administration had been in evidence on 31 January, it is doubtful if the next day's chaos could have been much palliated. The problem, as Charles Edward had accurately foreseen, was morale. As soon as word of the retreat leaked out, large numbers of clansmen headed north without waiting for further instructions.[4] The result was that when the prince set out for Bannockburn next morning, he found only a skeleton army on the road.

At first he tried to bring back those who had jumped the gun by sending cavalry detachments after them.[5] But it was already too late. Even the troops at Stirling had taken alarm at sight of the general exodus and had quit the town long before the agreed hour.[6] Trying to make a virtue of necessity, the prince told O'Sullivan and Murray of Broughton to order a general retreat at once, without waiting for the 9 a.m. rendezvous at St Ninian's.

Unfortunately, Lord George Murray was asleep while all this was going on. He woke to find 'barely the appearance of an army'.[7] Everything was chaos and confusion. There was no question of saving the artillery. The Jacobites even left their wounded and prisoners on the road as they fled.[8] And because the agreed general review had not taken place, there was no infantry to support the cavalry patrols. Elcho's Lifeguards had been ordered to wait on the Bridge of Carron to cover the precipitate retreat. No further orders were sent to them. While they fumed impotently, they came within an ace of being caught in a pincer between Cumberland's van moving up from Edinburgh and Linlithgow and the garrison at Stirling Castle, now free to sortie at will.[9]

Lord George's own position was perilous. A sally from Stirling Castle at this point would have been devastating. Murray was left with so small an escort that he had no option but to gallop off northwards at great speed.[10]

While the army staggered north in disarray and confusion, the general shambles received its apotheosis at St Ninian's. The Jacobites had been using St Ninian's church as an ammunition dump. The prince ordered that all the gunpowder in the church there should be exploded on waste ground behind the church to prevent its falling into Cumberland's hands.[11] But the villagers were trying to secrete quantities of powder to resell it to Cumberland; pillaging was taking place.[12] Meanwhile, as the troops opened the casks and lugged them to the waste ground, casual powder spillage had taken place. One of the clansmen observed the pilfering and fired a warning shot over the villagers' heads. Unfortunately the colfing from his gun fell into the trail of gunpowder leading back into the church.[13] The sparkling snake of lighted gunpowder wound its way back, and the resulting explosion blew St Ninian's sky-high.[14] The blast was heard for miles. Lochiel, already suffering from a wound sustained at Falkirk, narrowly escaped serious injury. Murray of Broughton's wife was blown out of her chaise and left unconscious on the ground.[15] Fortunately, Charles Edward himself had left the church eight minutes earlier.[16]

Meanwhile Lord George Murray, riding furiously northwards,

came upon O'Sullivan vainly trying to drag some cannon over a bridge without horses. The sight of his *bête noire* once more revealing his ineptitude was too much for Lord George. His temper snapped. Reining in his horse, he began to berate O'Sullivan. In full hearing of the already demoralised clansmen, a furious slanging match took place.[17] Murray accused O'Sullivan of incompetently altering the orders that had been agreed the night before. O'Sullivan struck back furiously: they were only retreating in the first place because of Lord George's treachery.

The headlong retreat continued. The army crossed the Forth at the Fords of Frew and scattered for the night through Dunblane, Doune and the neighbouring villages.[18] The prince found a billet at Drummond Castle.[19] On the 2nd the cavalry and advance guard were ordered to Perth, while the clans and most of the other foot regiments made their way to Crieff. Once there, Charles Edward held a general review and found to his anger and disgust that there were far fewer desertions than had been reported to him by Murray. Jacobite strength had shrunk by only about 1,000.[20]

Then Lord George rode into Crieff and demanded a meeting of the full war council. It was by common consent the most acrimonious of all such meetings hitherto – and they had not been noted for their lack of harsh words and open antagonism.[21] Everyone's temper was frayed. The general black humour was not allayed by the anti-Jacobite party in Crieff, bitterly hostile to the House of Stuart ever since the earl of Mar burnt the town down during the '15.

Lord George began by making a violent attack on the prince and his supporters for changing the orders at Bannockburn. In this he was joined by Elcho and Lochiel, both furious at having come so close to capture by Cumberland.[22] O'Sullivan replied that all this was pharisaical: it was Lord George who had insisted on the retreat; the prince had pointed out the certain consequences; they had duly happened, therefore Murray had no cause for complaint.[23]

This simply lashed Lord George to new heights of fury. He demanded to know who was responsible for the pernicious order to retreat in such a chaotic fashion from Stirling at 6 a.m. on the morning of 1 February.[24] 'I am afraid we have been betrayed, for it is worth the government at London's while to give a hundred thousand pounds to any who would have given such advice and got it followed.'[25] O'Sullivan protested that he was not responsible. The matter was resolved only when the prince agreed to take all the blame on himself.

If there was a true instance of autocratic behaviour in the Jacobite army during the '45, it was provided by Murray's unconscionable behaviour at the council at Crieff. Pale with anger, he insisted that he and he alone was running proceedings; only those he named would be allowed to speak.[26] He treated his colleagues as witnesses in a court case where he was the prosecutor. He asked for opinions only and would not allow supporting reasons unless he so decided. Whenever the prince tried to speak, Lord George threatened to storm out. He told Charles Edward that he could speak only when everyone else had given their opinion. He was tired of the prince's tactics on the council; this time, if there was any leading of the witnesses to be done, he, Murray, would be doing it.

Lord Lewis Gordon protested at this impertinence: was Lord George mad that he could so humiliate the prince?[27] But Murray got his way. He pressed hard for general acceptance of a retreat through the Highlands to Inverness, via Wadebridge and the Tay.[28] But at this juncture the Prince dug in his heels. He wanted to march by the coast road. He still expected a French landing in the north-east. If the French sent an army, they would want to see the Stuart prince, not Lord George.[29]

To preserve harmony, Lochiel sided with the prince. Seeing Charles Edward's doggedness, Lord George became more conciliatory and offered to make a stand in the Atholl country if the prince would take the Highland route.[30] The prince refused.

At this point one of the Murray faction stormed out of the room in a glowering rage. Surprisingly, it was not Murray himself but his most successful military collaborator Cluny MacPherson.[31] White with fury, outside the room Cluny railed bitterly at the prince's self-destructive stubbornness. Realising the grave consequences of a continuing split on the council on this matter of the itinerary, Murray of Broughton prevailed on Sheridan to get the prince to reverse his decision.[32]

Still full of misgivings that once the clansmen were in their native hills, they would desert *en masse*, Charles Edward reluctantly agreed to accompany the clan regiments into the Highlands, while Murray, the cavalry and the Lowland regiments wound round the coast via Montrose and Aberdeen to Inverness.[33] The latter arrangement was a compromise to meet the prince's earlier objections and to provide him with a partial face-saver. A smaller third detachment of Ogilvy's regiment and the Farquharsons were allowed to make for Speyside via Coupar-Angus, Glen Cluva and Glen Muick, so that the men could visit their homes.[34] As a rebuke to Cluny for his intemperate departure from the council, the prince next day sent the MacPherson chief an order to use all methods of military execution, including the burning of houses, against those of his clan who deserted or refused to fight.[35]

The business of the council was now concluded. Later that same day Lord George Murray took his Athollmen on to Perth.[36] The prince stayed at Fairnton, Lord John Drummond's home, until the morning of the 4th.[37] Then he pressed on to Castle Menzies at Weem and spent a day there before linking up with his rearguard at Blair Atholl.[38] At Blair Castle he rested until 9 February.[39]

The dreadful winter weather ruled out any possibility of pursuit by Cumberland. After reaching Linlithgow on 1 February, Cumberland was detained when the old palace there was burned down through his soldiers' carelessness (truly 1 February 1746 was a great day for destruction in Scotland!).[40] He reached Stirling on the 2nd, Dunblane on the 4th, Crieff on the 5th and Perth on the 6th. There he halted, sending out garrisons to Dunkeld and Castle Menzies and strengthening the existing garrison at Fort William.[41] He had no intention of following the Jacobites into the Highlands until he had solved the problem of provisioning his army. He intended to follow Lord George Murray's column up the coast, meanwhile sending parties of irregulars into the Highland fastnesses.[42]

Lord George Murray proceeded from Perth through Cowpar-in-Angus and Glamis to Forfar.[43] Joined there by Cromarty and John Roy Stewart, he pressed on to Brechin and Stonerine.[44] At Stonerine Elcho's Lifeguards and the Edinburgh regiment were detached to oversee the delivery of carriages, horses, stores and ammunition to Stonehaven.[45] At Aberdeen (reached on the 10th), Murray paused for three days, waiting for the third column under Lord Ogilvy.[46]

Charles Edward, depressed at the turn events had taken, found himself at Blair having to boost the spirits of his dejected followers. Sheridan wrote to France to say that the Jacobite army was like the old man who felt fine but knew he had to die very soon.[47] Despondency found expression in internecine disputes. The prince had to step in to mediate in a dispute between Lochiel and Robertson of Struan.[48] With tongue firmly in cheek, he assured his men that they would surely be marching south in the spring with a larger army.[49]

A more positive sign was the capture of the barracks at Ruthven by Glenbucket.[50] After spending two nights at Dalnacardoch, a public house on one of Wade's roads, the prince took up his quarters in the Ruthven barracks at Badenoch on 12 February.[51] The weather was cruel and snow-ridden.[52] The going was so bad that horses were dropping dead of exhaustion on the road.[53]

After staying two days at Ruthven, the prince spent the night of the 15th at the house of Grant of Dalrachny. On the 16th he arrived at the Mackintosh seat at Moy Hall.[54] Here he was entertained by the beautiful Lady Mackintosh, that 'Colonel Anne' of Jacobite legend who had raised her clan for the prince in defiance of her husband.[55] The twenty-three-year-old Anne, a notable firebrand, provided a lavish supper for Charles Edward that night.[56] She also sent four men in charge of the Moy blacksmith Donald Fraser to watch the road from Inverness for any telltale movement of Loudoun's troops.[57] This chance surveillance gave rise to what was later known as the 'Rout of Moy'.

Grant of Dalrachny, the prince's unwilling Whig host of the 15th, sent word to Loudoun in Inverness that the 'Young Pretender' was at Moy with a very small bodyguard. Loudoun saw the chance to snuff out the rebellion and gain himself £30,000 into the bargain.[58] Without revealing the true nature of the target, he assembled 1,500 men in Inverness and threw a cordon around the town to prevent any warning from reaching the prince.[59]

Luckily, a fourteen-year-old innkeeper's daughter learned of the proposed raid on Moy from some officers she was serving in her father's Inverness tavern. She ran barefoot to the house of the dowager Lady Mackintosh and alerted her.[60] Lady Mackintosh sent a young lad, Lachlan Mackintosh, off to Moy with the warning. Evading the cordon and getting past the marching column proved difficult, but Lachlan got through to Moy Hall and raised the alarm.[61]

Young Lady Mackintosh and her guests had retired to bed and the boy's arrival threw the household into confusion. Waking from his sleep, the prince thought the enemy was upon him. Throwing a bonnet over his head, he escaped in a dressing-gown and night-cap, with his shoes unbuckled.[62] Lady Mackintosh was running through the house in her shift, 'like a madwoman', imagining the enemy was already within the house.[63] Eventually the Jacobites got a grip on the situation. The prince was sent off to skulk by the lochside a mile away, together with Lochiel and the Camerons.[64]

While the prince ran through the wood to the south-western end of Loch Moy, the most remarkable single incident in the entire '45 campaign was taking place. Donald Fraser, the Moy blacksmith, bluffed Loudoun into thinking that the clan regiments in their entirety were drawn up across the Moy road waiting to receive him. Fraser and his four men shouted out a series of orders to the phantom regiments of Clanranald's, Keppoch's and Lochiel's.[65] Keeping up a constant babel, they fired a number of volleys in Loudoun's direction.

In the utter darkness Loudoun took fright at the thought that he had wandered into an ambush.[66] Perhaps Grant of Dalrachny was a double agent. A chance shot, which killed Donald MacCrimmon, piper to the Macleods who were accompanying Loudoun, seemed to confirm the ill omens. Panic and confusion spread through the ranks of the men who had already been routed at Inverurie.[67] One of Loudoun's officers saw the men in front of him running and marched his troops after them on the double, thinking they were the Jacobites.[68] Finding his column in danger of breaking up, Loudoun ordered it back to Inverness.

The 'Rout of Moy' was a great psychological triumph for the Jacobites. Even d'Eguilles was caught up in the euphoria of the moment. He wrote back to France with a glowing testimony to Lady Mackintosh and her blacksmith.[69] One thing only soured the triumph. As a result of his midnight flight in dressing-gown and slippers, the prince caught a chill that later developed into pneumonia.[70] For the rest of February he was out of action.

The 17th of February was spent collecting 2–3,000 men for the assault on Inverness.[71] At the approach of the Jacobites, Loudoun fled and Inverness opened its gates.[72] Loudoun retreated in disorder. The prince's army was already entering the town as the Hanoverian rearguard was stumbling across the Ness bridge.[73] As this force withdrew, the Jacobites wheeled three pieces of cannon to Cromwell's old fort and bombarded them.[74] The salvo killed nobody, but it intensified both the panic and the desertion rate among Loudoun's men.[75] Loudoun's losses when he reached Tain in Sutherland were found to be considerable.

Major Grant of Inverness Castle was at first tempted to emulate his superiors Preston and Blakeney in Edinburgh and Stirling. But as soon as he saw Jacobite sapping and mining work commence, he surrendered.[76] Loudoun meanwhile continued his flight via the Kessack ferry to Black Isle.[77]

While the prince lay ill at Inverness, Lord George Murray and the Lowland regiments ran into the worst patch of weather yet in their trek across country from Aberdeen to Inverness. From Aberdeen they cut off the north-eastern corner of the Scottish coast by marching inland to Old Meldrum; their eventual destination was Banff.[78] The conditions they experienced on this march were well summed up by John Daniel:

When we marched out of Aberdeen, it blew, snowed and hailed and froze to such a degree that few pictures ever represented winter, with all its icicles about it, better than many of us did that day. For here men were covered with icicles hanging at their eyebrows and beards; and an entire coldness seizing all their limbs, it may be wondered at how they could bear up against the storm, a severe contrary wind, driving snow and little cutting hail bitterly down upon our faces, in such a manner that it was impossible to see ten yards ahead of us. And very easy it was to lose our companions; the road being very bad and leading over large commons, and the paths being immediately filled up with drifting snow.[79]

When they came out on to the coast road conditions improved slightly. They picked their way gingerly along the eastern shore route, through Cullen, Fochabers, Elgin, Forres and Nairn, before linking up with the prince at Inverness on 19 February.[80] Lord George visited the prince at his sick-bed in Culloden House the day before Inverness Castle capitulated.[81] He had satisfactory news about the conduct of the retreat. Garrisons had been left at Elgin and Nairn to prevent Loudoun from linking up with Cumberland.[82] The Lowland regiments were cantoned in the towns and villages of the north-eastern counties.[83] And just before Aberdeen was evacuated, a detachment of Berwick's cavalry had arrived from France, though without horses. The next move seemed to be Cumberland's.[84]

But Cumberland had problems of his own. He could not advance into the Highlands until he had secured adequate food supplies. Even to progress north of Perth carried with it the dangers of starvation.[85] He remained at Perth, building up his commissariat, until 20 February, when he began his march to Aberdeen via Montrose. The van of his army reached the town three days after the last Jacobite soldier had left, on 25 February. Cumberland himself came in two days later.[86]

Food and equipment were not the Hanoverian duke's only problems. His barbarism and insensitivity had already seriously upset his ally the Prince of Hesse, who arrived with his forces at Leith on 8 February.[87] The immediate issue was Cumberland's categorical refusal to agree to a cartel for prisoners, on the ground that he was dealing with 'rebels'.[88] The Hessians, for their part, refused to fight without one. Beyond that, Cumberland regarded having extra mouths to feed as a burden and was inclined to consider the Hessians a nuisance.[89]

There was also a clash of temperament between the two commanders, to some extent echoing the friction between Charles

Edward and Lord George Murray. The Prince of Hesse's civilisation and the barbarism of Cumberland and his henchmen had already been in collision.[90] The German prince hit back. While Cumberland was campaigning, the prince made a point of giving a number of balls in Edinburgh to which 'none but Jacobite ladies' were invited.[91] Cumberland's behaviour was not only insensitive but positively injudicious, since he could have had 6,000 Hessians with him at Culloden if he had been prepared to rein in his own savage instincts. Doubtless he did not want another 'old woman' (as he contemptuously dubbed Duncan Forbes) at his side when he put down the rebellion.[92]

The enforced stay at Aberdeen, while Cumberland replenished his supplies and built up his numbers to compensate for the absence of the Hessians, transferred the military initiative to the Jacobites. Their position was strengthened by a pact with the Grants. After long negotiations, the Grants concluded what was in effect a treaty of neutrality with Charles Edward.[93] With the prince lying ill at Culloden House, the way was open for the clan chiefs to pursue the specifically Highland strategy after which they had always hankered. Their approach was a fourfold one. They wanted to detain Cumberland at Aberdeen, retaining the coastal supply line for aid from France, while they besieged the Highland forts, dispersed Lord Loudoun's forces, and beat off any Hanoverian reinforcements coming up through the central Highlands. Lord George Murray was in buoyant mood. He claimed he could carry on the war in Scotland for several years and eventually force the English to come to terms; Highland cattle plus periodic raids into the Lowlands would provide the food.[94]

For a while the Jacobites achieved remarkable results with their new strategy. Maxwell of Kirkconnell rated the glorious late flowering of Jacobite military success in March 1746 as their finest achievement, ahead of Prestonpans, Clifton or Falkirk: 'The vulgar may be dazzled with a victory, but in the eyes of a connoisseur, the Prince will appear greater about this time at Inverness than either at Gladsmuir [Prestonpans] or at Falkirk.'[95] O'Heguerty, the prince's biographer in the 1750s, agreed with this assessment, as did some of the Whigs.[96] It seems not to have occurred to Maxwell or O'Heguerty to note the irony that this Indian summer took place while the prince was laid up with illness.

The first target was Fort Augustus. The capture of this fort was entrusted to Brigadier Walter Stapleton of the Irish brigade, who had come from France with Lord John Drummond. On 3 March trenches were opened.[97] Since Mirabel was in disgrace and no longer employed as chief engineer, the siege prospered. The new director of siege operations, Grant, showed how the job should be done. Aided by an explosion of the magazine inside the fortress, he compelled the surrender of Fort Augustus in just two days.[98] The fort was systematically pillaged by the Highlanders. According to Stapleton, the wholesale rapine surpassed anything he had seen in a long career of warfare.[99]

Two days later, on 7 March, virtually the same forces appeared outside Fort William.[100] Lord John Drummond was left as Jacobite governor of Fort Augustus. Motivation to compass the fall of Fort William was high, for this was Cameron country, and the Hanoverians' premier fortress had long dominated Lochaber. During the prince's invasion of England, the Fort William garrison had sortied to burn and plunder Lochiel's country.[101] Cumberland agreed with the Jacobites in their estimate of the fort's importance: 'I look upon Fort William to be the only fort in the Highlands that is of any consequence. I have taken all possible measures for the securing of it . . . for the preventing it falling into the rebels' hands.'[102]

Grant immediately set out to open trenches. With a good eye for terrain, he suggested establishing a battery on a hill to the southeast, dominating Fort William.[103] But by sheer bad luck he was killed almost immediately by a chance cannonball. Reluctantly, Stapleton had to send for Mirabel. Immediately jettisoning Grant's imaginative approach, the Frenchman soon showed that he had learned nothing and forgotten nothing since Stirling. Once again a Jacobite siege quickly settled into stalemate.[104]

At about this time, a courier arrived at Inverness for the prince, who was alternately staying at Castle Hill and Culloden House, still recovering from the pneumonia contracted on the night of the 'Rout of Moy'.[105] This emissary brought news that further units of the Irish brigade were on their way to Scotland. For a while it looked as if Lord George was right, and the Jacobites would very soon have an army 8,000 strong with which to face Cumberland.[106] The good news relieved the prince's worst anxieties. He was persuaded to accept the more relaxed convalescence provided in the Inverness home of the dowager Lady Mackintosh.[107]

After the Highland forts, the Highlanders' next objective was the persistent gadfly Lord Loudoun. Loudoun had foreseen the possibility of a seaborne Jacobite pursuit and had seized all available boats in the Cromarty and Dornoch Firths.[108] These, of course, were fishing vessels, not suitable for a sea-going voyage; for this reason Loudoun could not heed Cumberland's increasingly shrill summonses to join him in Banffshire.[109]

Following the capture of Inverness, Cromarty was sent with Glengarrys, Clanranalds, the Appin Stewarts, Mackinnons and some Mackenzies in pursuit. Having no boats, they were obliged to go round the head of the Firth. At their approach Loudoun retired across Dornoch Firth to Dornoch.[110] When Cromarty attempted to pursue him by land, Loudoun recrossed the Firth into Ross-shire.[111]

With all boats at his disposal, Loudoun appeared to be a very superior mouse dodging a lumbering and ponderous cat. Cromarty momentarily gave up and returned to Tain, upon which Loudoun again crossed to Dornoch.[112]

Cromarty's supersession by Perth as Jacobite commander in this theatre of war brought changes. It was quickly obvious to Perth that land operations were going to be impossibly protracted. He instituted an extended dragnet for fishing boats. Moir of Stoneywood got together an impressive flotilla at Findhorn, north of Forres on the North Sea coast.[113] These were then sailed across the Moray Firth during a thick fog which concealed them from Royal Navy cruisers.[114]

Knowing that there was no shipping for an army on the other side of Dornoch Firth, Loudoun felt himself secure. Suddenly, on 20 March, as if by sorcery, Perth's men were ashore and Loudoun's army surrounded. The Jacobites came in under a pall of thick wet mist that restricted visibility to one hundred yards. The operation ended with the total dispersal of Loudoun's forces.[115] Loudoun, Sutherland, Forbes of Culloden and the other leaders made their escape by sea to Skye.[116] Whatever Cumberland did now, the Jacobites could be confident of having no enemy in their rear.

The third Jacobite operation was the most spectacularly successful of all. On 15 March Lord George Murray marched south from Inverness with the Atholl brigade. At Ruthven he was met by Cluny MacPherson and his regiment, who had remained in Badenoch to guard the passes there.[117] At dusk Cluny and Lord George led their seven hundred clansmen from Dalwhinny to Dalnaspidal. There for the first time Murray let his troops into the secret of the operation.[118] There were thirty posts or blockhouses (some houses, some inns) scattered around the Atholl country: all were to be taken out simultaneously by thirty Highland detachments, the raids to be carried out before daylight. The thirty detachments would then rendezvous shortly after dawn at the Bridge of Bruer, two miles north of Blair.[119]

The operation was a brilliant success. Between 2 and 5 a.m. all the blockhouses were taken without the loss of a single Highlander.[120]

And Lord George himself pulled off another 'Rout of Moy'. While he was waiting for the commando groups to rendezvous, Murray was alarmed to see that Sir Andrew Agnew, commander of Blair Castle, had sortied in force to see what was the matter with the outer defence ring. At this point Lord George had just twenty-five men with him. Realising that if he retreated, the returning raiding parties would simply be captured one after the other by Agnew, Murray simulated the presence of a brigade by displaying regimental colours and playing the pipes from behind a turf wall near the bridge. This, coupled with the flashing of claymores in the first rays of the morning sun, convinced Agnew that retreat was the wisest course.[121]

Soon afterwards, Murray's raiders came in, bringing more than three hundred prisoners, with news of a total success.[122] Murray advanced to the siege of Blair Castle. Sir Andrew Agnew, a well-known Hanoverian fire-eater, indignantly rejected the summons to surrender. As he did not possess the big guns necessary to reduce Blair, Lord George tried to starve the garrison out.[123]

He found the garrison 'more obstinate' than he expected. The firing was so heavy that Murray had to send for fresh supplies of ammunition.[124] Nevertheless, there were only five days' provisions in Blair and hunger would soon procure for Lord George what he wanted.

Suddenly reinforcements arrived for Agnew in the form of the earl of Crawford and the Prince of Hesse. Lord George immediately sent to Charles Edward to let him have another 1,200 men, with whom he was confident of routing Crawford's dragoons and the Hessians. Such a victory would have compelled Cumberland to withdraw from Aberdeen.[125] In a controversial decision, the prince claimed not to have that number with him in Inverness.[126] Lord George had no choice, then, but to retreat slowly before the relieving Hanoverian force, hoping to draw them into an ambush in the pass of Killiekrankie.

The ruse did not work, mainly because the Prince of Hesse refused to allow his men north of Pitlochry without the properly negotiated prisoner cartel that Cumberland adamantly refused.[127] The Hessian prince once again proved his reasonableness by declaring publicly that he was not sufficiently interested in the quarrel between the houses of Stuart and Hanover to risk his subjects in a fight with men who had been driven to despair.[128] Yet Hesse's very reasonableness involved Lord George in a charge of treachery. Because Murray felt he could deal directly with such a man, he put out feelers to see whether a negotiated settlement of the rising was possible.

To Charles Edward this was treason, and not to be condoned.[129] He could not afford an open breach with his lieutenant-general, but he set a detail of picked men to watch Murray night and day and to seize him if he showed any signs of betraying the army. Surprisingly (since the Frenchman had so lauded Lord George after Falkirk), Charles Edward was encouraged in this paranoid delusion by the marquis d'Eguilles.[130]

For all the recriminations it would later engender,[131] Murray's raid into the Atholl country was everywhere recognised as a fine exploit. Jacobite spirits were noticeably lifted.[132] Cumberland began to complain about the rebellious spirit even of those areas of Scotland under Hanoverian occupation.[133] There was no longer any talk of the rising's petering out or of sending the Hessians back to Germany.[134] The triumphant Jacobites withdrew in good order, Lord George to Inverness, his infantry to Elchies on Speyside.[135] Cluny remained to guard the Badenoch passes.

The crucial battlefront remained that around the Spey. Here the duel between Jacobite and Hanoverian developed into probe and counterprobe. There were two routes that Cumberland could take from Aberdeen to Speyside, one via Meldrum and Cullen, the other by Kintore, Inverurie and Strathbogie. To keep his enemy guessing, Cumberland sent out detachments to secure both routes.[136] The Jacobite defence then moved up to cover the advance probes. Lord John Drummond, overall commander on the Spey, had his head-quarters at Gordon Castle near Fochabers. Strathallan was at Cullen. John Roy Stewart's Edinburgh regiment and Elcho's Lifeguards were on station at Strathbogie.[137]

No serious Hanoverian move was made until 16 March. Then Cumberland suddenly altered the pace and rhythm of his thrusts. General Bland, commanding the forces at Old Meldrum and Inverurie, was ordered to take four regiments and fall on John Roy Stewart's at Strathbogie.[138] Jacobite numbers were known to be no more than five hundred foot and fifty horse. Their cavalry had virtually ceased to exist. Kilmarnock's and Pitsligo's were no more; their men had been incorporated into the infantry regiments. Lack of forage and replacement horses had thinned out the once useful riders.[139]

As fortune would have it, the Jacobites were at that very moment trying to run to earth the Hanoverian chief of irregulars Colonel Grant. In Strathbogie their vigilant outriders spotted the movement of Bland's approaching vanguard. With supreme aplomb John Roy Stewart ordered an hour's rest for his weary troops, figuring that it would take the Hanoverian main column that long to come up to

Huntley.[140] Then the Jacobites retired in good order, their rear holding the bridge until their comrades were safely out of the town.[141] They crossed the river Deveron, then formed up again to face the enemy. Bland was not disposed to pursue beyond the river, as the mountainous path on the other side was narrow, rocky and precipitous.[142] The Edinburgh regiment then retired in good order to Keith and Fochabers. Their morale was sky-high at the thought that they had made a disciplined withdrawal in the face of a hugely superior enemy without breaking rank or losing a single standard.[143]

Next day they crossed the Spey, bringing news that Cumberland was on the march. It took time for the Jacobites to discover that the Hanoverian movement was merely a reconnaissance in strength.[144] Once they did realise this, Drummond counterattacked. Cavalry patrols were sent across the Spey to reconnoitre. The enemy seemed in complacent mood. Drummond decided to shake them.

Drummond sent Major Glasco on a daring raid. Jacobite infantry made its way silently along the road to Fochabers, while the cavalry arm headed for Keith.[145] Glasco's forces linked up and reached Keith at dead of night without being discovered. It so happened that a large body of Campbell militia was billeted in the church after an attempt to scout Gordon Castle.[146] Suddenly, at 1 a.m., they found themselves under fire. A fast and furious fight took place in the churchyard. Bullets whined and pinged around the headstones.[147] The sons of Diarmid kept up a brisk fire from the church windows and used up eight rounds before faltering.[148] Hearing that quarter would be given, the Campbells surrendered after perhaps half an hour's defiance. Their casualties were about 80 (including 9 killed) to the Jacobites' 12.[149]

After that bruising experience, the Hanoverians did not choose to spend another night in Keith. Bland withdrew to Strathbogie, from where he sent out daily probes. These frequently encountered Drummond's patrols. Skirmishing and guerrilla warfare became the norm. Glasco set several ambuscades at Keith but the enemy did not come near enough to fall into them.[150]

March 1746 was a month of uninterrupted triumph for the Jacobites. They had taken hundreds of prisoners.[151] Fort Augustus, Dornoch, the Atholl blockhouses, Keith: the string of successes seemed likely to go on and on. But just when Lord George Murray's forecast of a spring campaign seemed likely to come to pass, the Jacobites were hit by a succession of hammer blows. March 1746 saw the prince's fortunes at their highest. April was to bring utter disaster.

17

The Night March

(March–April 1746)

Throughout the remarkable run of Jacobite success in March, Charles Edward was out of the reckoning. Except for brief intervals, illness kept him confined to his quarters for the first three months of 1746. First there was 'flu at Bannockburn in January; then pneumonia after the 'Rout of Moy' in February; finally in March he was stricken by potentially the most serious malady yet.

After a week's convalescence at the dowager Lady Mackintosh's house, the prince set out for the north-eastern front (11 March), intending to make a tour of Jacobite defences on the Inverness side of the Spey. He spent a night in Forres, then pressed on to Elgin.[1] But in Elgin he was almost at once struck down by a violent attack of scarlet fever.[2] For ten days his aides watched anxiously as he tossed and turned in bed with a dangerously high temperature. As was customary in the eighteenth century, the response to this fever was to let blood. According to his physicians, this timely bleeding prevented a tubercular haemorrhage.[3] Whatever the truth of this, it is certain that for two days the prince's condition gave cause for concern. Finally the crisis passed and Charles made a good recovery.

On 20 March, against medical advice, he insisted on getting up. His physicians, fearing that he might after all have contracted typhoid fever, tried to keep him on light broth, but he quickly progressed to solid food.[4] Had the doctors' fears been justified, and the food taken before the lesions healed, perforation and swift collapse would have followed. But the prince typically declared that if he had to die, he would rather do it on horseback fighting Cumberland than in bed timidly sipping bouillon.[5]

The irony was that the prince was ill throughout the Jacobites' run of good fortune[6] and recovered only to face catastrophe. His recovery 'caused a joy in every heart not to be described'.[7] His aides rushed him back to Inverness, allowing only a short side-trip to Gordon Castle.[8] Once in Inverness, the prince did not stir from his twin bases in the town and Culloden House except for one brief visit to Lady Seaforth at Braan Castle.[9]

The Jacobites' joy at the prince's recovery was short-lived. As April began, a series of disasters rained on the Highlanders. The lifting of the siege of Blair Castle was attributable to superior Hanoverian numbers. But the débâcle at Fort William was the result of simple incompetence in siegecraft. Mirabel this time evinced fresh dimensions to his general uselessness: the disgruntled Highlanders nicknamed him M. Admirable with contemptuous irony.[10]

Seeing the inept way the siege was being conducted, and sensing the lack of determination among the attackers, the Fort William garrison determined on a sortie in force. On 31 March a clever sally resulted in the destruction of the Jacobite batteries and the capture of some of their guns.[11] The loss was irremediable. After a final face-saving bombardment on 3 April, the Jacobites abandoned the siege.[12]

This was a crushing blow to morale which had already started to ebb as the clansmen's successes brought them neither victory nor a breathing-space. Charles Edward's illness at Elgin had to be kept a secret from the rank and file for fear of its impact on their spirits. It was given out that he was staying at Elgin to link up with his brother Henry, daily expected with the long-awaited French army.[13]

The reasons for low morale in the Jacobite army were by now legion. In the ranks it was the lack of pay that bit most deeply. The prince received no further supply of money after Falkirk, except for £2,500 in Spanish funds landed at Montrose. He was not at first aware how parlous the situation was, for his officers concealed the truth from him during his illness. But on his return from Elgin to Inverness he was dismayed to see his troops being paid in kind and fed on oats.[14] Payment in meal might keep the army fed, but it did nothing to stem the desertion rate.[15] And even the provision of basic foodstuffs was becoming more and more difficult. The commissary-general fought a losing battle with the farmers of the north-east, trying to get them to pay the public money in meal when they claimed to have paid it time out of mind in barley.[16]

The clansmen's patience was at snapping point. Lord George strove valiantly to prevent them going on the rampage, as this would alienate the local population for good.[17] But what else could he do? All Charles Edward could contribute was the now tired and formulaic assertion that the French were coming and that Cumberland's men would not fight against their true king.[18] Eventually, morale in Perth's regiment reached such a low point that in desperation Charles Edward called in the Jacobite engraver Robert Strange and asked him to design and issue the Stuarts' own bank-notes,[19] but not before Sheridan had delivered an unjustified attack on the good faith of Perth's regiment. Rebutting the duke's complaints about sinking morale in his ill-paid regiment, Sheridan wrote sneeringly to Perth that it seemed his men never expected to have to fight for their lives but thought the rising was some kind of adventure.[20] The injustice of this jibe can perhaps be appreciated when it is remembered that throughout March Perth's regiment acted as the prince's bodyguard; in fact with the dispersal of his forces on four separate and simultaneous military operations, they were the only Jacobite troops left in Inverness.[21]

The crisis over money turned into catastrophe with the enemy capture of the *Prince Charles*. This was the Hanoverians' greatest success in the seaborne war to deny French assistance to the Jacobites. Careful preparations had been made in France so that this ship would bring the prince substantial succour.[22] Lord Clare had hand-picked the cream of Berwick's regiment.[23] Even more significant than the men was the money the *Prince Charles* was carrying: £13,600 in English gold and 1,500 guineas laden in five chests.[24] There were also 14 chests of pistols and sabres and 13 barrels of powder.[25]

The *Prince Charles* reached the coast of northern Scotland without difficulty. But on 25 March she was spotted by four English cruisers in Pentland Firth. After a five-hour chase, the *Prince Charles* ran aground in shallow water near Tongue while taking evasive action.[26] Lord Reay, who was in the vicinity, hurried to the spot, seized the treasure and took nearly two hundred prisoners.[27]

In desperation the prince sent a force to lay hands on Reay and force him to disgorge the money. The prince's hopes were slender, since in Sutherland Reay could easily decamp with his loot by sea to Skye.[28] Yet even Charles Edward cannot have expected the dismal sequel. Not only did Cromarty (to whom he entrusted the expedition) not regain the treasure, but he also failed in his secondary aim: to raise men and money for the Jacobites in Sutherland and Caithness. Even worse, Cromarty's battalion commanders were surprised on 15 April by the retainers of Lord Reay and Sutherland and taken prisoner to Dunrobin Castle.[29]

The loss of the *Prince Charles* was an extraordinarily grievous blow for the prince. There was now no prospect of paying his men and thus arresting the drooping morale and accelerating desertion rate.

Lack of money also prevented him from advancing to Aberdeen to meet Cumberland, as originally intended.[30] The prince had no room at all in which to manoeuvre. He had to seek the earliest possible confrontation with Cumberland but could not advance beyond the Spey to encounter him.

At this point yet another dreadful blow hit Charles Edward. As the prince recovered from his illness at Elgin, Murray of Broughton caught the infection and was laid low for the first two weeks of April. After Elgin the prince never saw his secretary again.[31] Whatever John Murray's many faults, he was a good administrator. As the prince's secretary he had always handled the provisioning of the army efficiently, as even his bitter enemy Lord George Murray conceded.[32] His successor, Hay of Restalrig, proved as incompetent in the job as Mirabel had been at siegecraft.[33] Conceivably the Jacobites could carry a bumbling director of siege operations. But to have an incompetent commissariat was a first-class disaster. The clansmen in the field starved and were on half-rations even while there were stores in abundance at Inverness.[34] By the end of the first week of April, Murray of Broughton's absence was already being felt and food shortages had become acute.[35] To the failure at Fort William, and the loss of the *Prince Charles*, with the financial disaster this brought, the Jacobites could now add breakdown in commissariat.

The prince's situation was clearly desperate. Only a French landing or a *coup d'état* in London could save him now, and both were fantasies. Early in April a courier from Versailles got through to tell him that all plans for a major expedition to Scotland had been laid aside.[36]

What was Charles Edward's demeanour in the face of looming disaster? His overt stance was one of cheerful optimism: 'HRH looks upon what has happened at Fort William as a flea bite and would not have anybody cast down upon it.'[37] He rationalised the rash dispersal of his army on the grounds that this made it easier for his men to live off the land.[38] And to demonstrate his unconcern the prince gave a number of balls at Inverness at which he danced himself, in contrast to his behaviour in Edinburgh in October.[39] According to his own account vouchsafed to O'Heguerty in the 1750s, he took this action purely to bolster morale.[40] He made a point of appearing in better spirits than ever.

But the difference between his actions in Edinburgh and now in Inverness was an important pointer to his state of mind. Contact with women in Charles Edward's case always meant touching the chords of failure. The measures he trod with the fine ladies of Inverness were not so much a question of fiddling while Rome burned as an unconscious admission that his cause was now hopeless.

The pattern of self-destructive signs and pointers was not confined to the ballrooms of Inverness. For the first time there is a scintilla of harshness in the prince's reactions to the sullen recalcitrance of Scottish Whig sympathisers, more of a tendency to condone burnings and draconian treatment through military execution of a foot-dragging population.[41]

The refusal to reinforce Lord George Murray at Blair is also instructive. If the prince did not agree with the strategy of forcing Cumberland to withdraw from Aberdeen, what exactly did he propose as an alternative? The answer seems to be, nothing.

The prince was unwise in his differential treatment of Scots and Irish officers. The favouritism shown to Irish cronies had long been resented by the Highlanders. There was particular pique about the fact that those chosen to go to Versailles as envoys were always the tame Irishmen (Kelly, Warren) who could be relied on to present the prince's version of events.[42] This was the moment when the prince should have jettisoned his sycophantic henchmen and used all his considerable charm to conciliate the clan officers. So far from doing this, he actually ordered his Irish favourites to shoot Lord George Murray if he showed any signs of defection to the enemy during a battle.

Charles Edward's paranoia was not limited to Murray. It seems that the Scots' reprehensible behaviour towards his ancestor Charles I had made a deep impression on him. Until his experience in the heather in 1746, he always tended to regard the Scots as potential traitors. What is interesting about this view is not its lack of rationality – for after all as a matter of historical record the prince was entitled to some uneasiness – but that Charles should have fastened on this as the key Scottish characteristic, ignoring the heroism and sacrifice they had already displayed on his behalf.

Matters in the Jacobite camp were already at a highly unsatisfactory pass when, on 8 April, Cumberland at last marched out from Aberdeen, making straight for the Jacobite jugular at Inverness. The weather had improved and the duke's food supplies were assured. Cumberland was always a plodder, but his preparations had been painstaking. At least his men would fight with full bellies.

As the Jacobites admitted, Cumberland's advance caught them unprepared.[43] It was a case of 'cry wolf'. The Hanoverian advance had been so often reported and then denied that it was at first hard to accept that this time Cumberland really was on the move. This rapid progress punctured the bubble of much Jacobite vainglory. Certain adherents of the House of Stuart in Aberdeenshire had boasted that Cumberland could not move an inch through their country without their knowing it. Yet the duke was at Old Meldrum, heading for Banff, before these Jacobite worthies dashed off a message for the prince.[44]

When the news sank in, the prince's superficial reaction was contentment that the issue would soon be decided.[45] But the orders issued to the scattered regiments indicate a certain alarm, like that of a sleepwalker awaking on the edge of a precipice. The truth was that in the strategic vacuum that persisted from early March, none of the Jacobite commanders had worked out a contingency plan in case the army was still dispersed when Cumberland advanced in earnest.[46] And now here he was, marching faster than expected. By the 11th he was in Cullen. Still the complacent Jacobites did not fully awake to the danger. Lord Nairne enquired lackadaisically of John Roy Stewart if the summons back to Inverness was really urgent, as he did not want to weary his Athollmen with an unnecessary forced march.[47]

It was imperative to get the widespread regiments back in one body at Inverness. Lochiel and Keppoch were still in the vicinity of Fort William, unable to accept the implications of the failed siege. They were now ordered back with all speed: 'The Prince would rather have you in three days with five hundred men than with a thousand three days after.'[48] There were anxieties that the Camerons would not leave their country exposed to reprisals from Fort William; but Charles Edward reckoned that without their chieftains, the men would have to follow. It is instructive, though, that even at this stage the prince should be trying to make use of his now much-tarnished image. 'Those that love me will follow me, those that will not will stay behind,' is a pure attempt at charismatic leadership.[49]

Beneath the brave words there was confusion and some apprehension. Sheridan's dispatch to Perth on 9 April begins jauntily but ends on a note of something close to despair: 'As to Cumberland's movements, he [the prince] thinks there is no great reason to be alarmed. He is making all the haste he can to gather his men in order to fight him ... he hopes his men will not abandon him at such a critical juncture.'[50]

The key question about the events in the week leading up to Culloden is why Charles Edward did not dispute the passage of the Spey. This was the obvious place to stand and fight Cumberland.

The Spey's width and fast-flowing currents made it a perfect place for a defence. When Cumberland approached its banks, Lord John Drummond and John Roy Stewart had 2,000 men on hand. The two men were breakfasting at the minister's house at Speymouth when a messenger rushed in with the news that the far side of the river was a 'vermine of Red Quites [redcoats]'.[51] Drummond and Stewart rode to the top of a hill and at first claimed only to see muck heaps. When they could no longer deny the truth, the order to retreat was given. First, however, there was a show of bravado. Cumberland reported seeing the rebels 'making a formidable appearance'.[52] Then, after firing a few shots and burning their magazines, they were gone.

Why was Jacobite resistance so feeble? There are several answers to this. The most fundamental is the misguided Jacobite strategy pursued in March. The string of successes achieved then was remarkable, but what in the end did it really amount to? The real threat was always from Cumberland and it is in that sector that the Jacobites should have concentrated all their efforts.

The villain of this particular piece was O'Sullivan. In March he went on a tour of inspection of the Spey and pronounced it indefensible, given Jacobite resources.[53] Because the river was fordable at several places, the clansmen would need to be at the Spey in force. But such numbers could not live off the country for long – they had no tents to sleep in and no reserves in the magazines. So concluded O'Sullivan. But his analysis missed several points. First, a concentration of all the forces already on Speyside would have been sufficient to fight a holding action until the main Jacobite army came up. There were a number of fords so that Cumberland's numbers would tell. On the other hand, their zigzag shape meant that the Hanoverians would take heavy casualties in trying to force passage.[54]

But any defence along these lines was vitiated by two things. Despite Lord John Drummond's plea for concentration of force on Speyside, the Athollmen and most of the Edinburgh regiment were away in Grant country, trying to 'force out' the neutral Grants. They were still there when Cumberland's army arrived.[55] The other point was that Perth and Drummond needed artillery to conduct a riverside defence against Cumberland's field-pieces. But the prince point-blank refused to release his cannon for this purpose.[56]

There can be no doubt that a delaying action with artillery would have inflicted considerable, even conceivably unacceptable, losses on the Hanoverian attackers. This would have given the prince the option either to support Perth and Drummond in divisional force and so provoke a decisive battle on very dangerous ground, or to slow the Hanoverians down considerably and so give the Jacobites the chance to bring their army up to full strength.

How can we explain the prince's failure to take his chances at the Spey? Various answers have been suggested: Perth's orders not to risk a general engagement, uncertainty about what would constitute such a risk, Jacobite desire to avoid casualties. The most likely answer is the absence of effective command. The absence of Lord George Murray was crucial, for he would surely not have let such an opportunity go. And only Lord George had the seniority and prestige to overrule O'Sullivan. Once again we may ask, why was Lord George in Atholl country, and Lochiel in Cameron country, pursuing narrow clan or family interests at such a crucial juncture? It was surely obvious that Cumberland would sooner or later make exactly the move he did make. Certainly it was not really open to clan leaders to use O'Sullivan's argument that the army could not live off the land, since during the altercation at Falkirk they had repeatedly assured the prince that this was possible.

The other potential answer was that Hay of Restalrig's incompetence was even more pervasive and significant than has been realised, that the prince did intend to move his army across to contest the Spey passage, but that commissariat problems prevented this. But if such had been Charles Edward's intention, he should have had his various regiments within easy call, not scattered to the Scottish winds.

The more one looks at the crucial decision not to fight at the Spey, the more it looks like another of Charles Edward's self-destructive acts, inexplicable in rational terms.[57] There is no evidence here of the 'blind optimism' and pigheaded confidence the prince's detractors usually impute to him at this stage of the campaign. It seems too as if Charles Edward's unconscious wish to be rid of the stress of an army that had betrayed him had combined with the real demoralisation in Jacobite ranks.

Whatever mystery attaches to the failure to dispute the crossing of the Spey, there was nothing mysterious about the sequel. Charles Edward now faced the prospect of a battle without many of his best regiments. Cluny MacPherson's men were in Badenoch; Cromarty, Mackinnon and Barisdale were still in vain pursuit of Lord Reay and the money from the *Prince Charles*. Only about half the Camerons were accompanying Lochiel back from Achnacarry. Keppoch's and Clanranald's were much reduced in numbers. Other absentees included the Lovat Frasers and many of the MacGregors and Mackenzies.[58] Out of a possible muster of 7–8,000, only 5,000 were present at the fatal field of Culloden on 16 April.

To give the absentees time to join the main army, the Jacobites tried to find ways to delay Cumberland. After crossing the Spey the duke quickly advanced through Elgin and Alves.[59] The task of holding Cumberland up fell to Perth's regiment and to Clanranald's and the Appin Stewarts, who had earlier been based at Elgin.[60] On the road to Nairn on the 14th these men, assisted by about seventy of Fitzjames's cavalry, performed valiantly, incidentally exposing the absurdity of Sheridan's earlier jibe at the courage of Perth's regiment. Perth would not have been able to buy time for Charles Edward by this manoeuvre unless his men were singularly intrepid.[61] First they tried to cut off Cumberland's advance guard. Cumberland blocked this move with a cavalry screen provided by General Bland.[62] A running cavalry skirmish developed, with the two sides exchanging shots. On the far side of Nairn, Bland pursued the Jacobites hotly for two miles before Cumberland recalled him.[63] The Hanoverian camp was then pitched at Nairn.

The prince, who had spent the 14th at Culloden House, was convinced that next day would see the decisive battle. He did not go to bed on the night of the 14th, but spent the time drawing up battle plans.[64] The army meanwhile lay out of doors on the hill above Culloden House. An elaborate set of orders was worked out by the prince and Lord George. All deserters were to be shot, there was to be no stripping or looting the slain until the battle was over; 'the highlanders are all to be in kilts and nobody to throw away their guns.'[65] Putting a brave face on it, he told his officers he had no intention of making contingency plans in the event of defeat. Here he undoubtedly overdid the gallery touch but, to be fair to him, all his officers shared his belief in the invincibility of their clansmen.[66]

Next day the Jacobite army was drawn up in much the same order as on the day of the battle itself (the 16th), except that on the 15th the lines were a little closer to Culloden House. But there was no sign of Cumberland. He chose to spend his twenty-fifth birthday, 15 April, resting in Nairn. This was a bad omen. It meant that Charles Edward had already read his opponent wrongly. He had assured his officers that the temptation to seek a victory on his birthday would be too much for Cumberland.[67]

The tired and hungry clansmen stood all day with just a biscuit each at midday, waiting for Cumberland to come.[68] Lochiel's Camerons suffered particularly, for they had arrived at Inverness only on the evening of the 14th, after a fifty-mile march from Fort William. The prince tried to lift their spirits by riding along the lines with words of encouragement. He was dressed in a tartan jacket and buff waistcoat, trying hard to get across the morale-raising point that he was the true heir apparent to the Scottish throne.[69] In the late afternoon the men were dismissed.

The choice of Drummossie Moor as the battlefield was the prince's own, for at last he intended to command his troops in person. It was bitterly attacked by Lord George Murray and the clan chiefs as unsuitable ground for their men to act on. Acting on the 'professional' counsel of O'Sullivan, who advised him that his left wing would be protected by a morass, Charles Edward insisted on drawing up his men on this strip of open moorland one mile to the south-east of Culloden House. He turned down Lord George's far better battlefield – a stretch of rough and open ground near Dalcross Castle, where Cumberland would not be able to make full use of his cannon. The prince was playing into Cumberland's hands, giving him exactly the sort of terrain he would have prayed for, rejecting the ground that favoured the Highlanders.

Having turned down his lieutenant-general's choice of battleground, the prince felt bound to support him in the wrangle that now broke out over who should have the right wing. The MacDonalds claimed this as their time-honoured right in clan armies. But Lord George Murray insisted that he must have the Athollmen with him on the right. The prince settled the argument in Murray's favour.

This was not the only problem that beset the 5,000 or so troops actually available to the prince. The Glengarry men were still smarting at the loss of Angus Og at Falkirk. The Macleans, deprived of the leadership of Sir Hector, were disputing over the military command of the clan. And above all other issues loomed that of commissariat. Hay of Restalrig protested to his critics that he had assembled a granary of corn in Inverness. He denied indignantly that he had not seen fit to convert it into bread, but was forced to admit he had not provided the waggons to bring the bread from Inverness to Culloden House.

With so many question marks against his army, it is not surprising to find the prince on the 15th developing an obsessive interest in a night march to surprise Cumberland. He was described as 'cajoling' the chiefs to fall in with a scheme for a dawn attack on Cumberland's camp at Balbair on the outskirts of Nairn.[70] At first the prince made little progress with his advocacy. The clan chiefs refused to consider the idea until reinforcements arrived. Lord George spent the time arguing for another battlefield which Brigadier Walter Stapleton and Colonel Ker of Graden had reconnoitred, on the south side of the river Nairn.[71] This was eminently suitable terrain for the Highlanders.

But neither now nor later would the prince entertain any scheme that smacked of withdrawal in face of Cumberland.[72]

The arrival of Keppoch from Lochaber late on the afternoon of the 15th, plus reports from spies that all was quiet in the enemy camp, changed the aspect of affairs.[73] A shift in attitude to the night march proposal became perceptible. The prince immediately called a council, his first since Crieff. At first there were still many solid objections to the proposal. Its feasibility was questioned: surely Cumberland's patrols would spot the oncoming Jacobites and alert the duke? And did they really have sufficient numbers for the enterprise? If the attack failed, it would be difficult to rally the clansmen in the dark. The retreat would be a shambles. They would have to carry off the wounded with cavalrymen on their heels. All in all, the prospect of a fatiguing march, a do-or-die assault and then possibly a twenty-mile retreat seemed daunting.[74]

The prince hit back at his critics. He asked them whether they could really doubt the outcome of a furious hand-to-hand engagement, clansman versus regular, in a situation where Hanoverian gunnery could not be brought to bear. And he adduced one of his favourite fantasies. Since, he alleged, there were large numbers of secret Jacobite sympathisers among Cumberland's rankers, the confusion of darkness would make it possible for them to sabotage the duke's efforts. At the very least, in pitch blackness their half-heartedness could not be detected.[75]

At this Perth and Lord John Drummond declared themselves in favour, provided the night march could be accomplished by 2 a.m. They pointed out that, if successful, the Jacobites could solve their food supply problems by pillaging Cumberland's stores.[76] The leader of the Mackintoshes supported the prince by claiming that their clansmen could lead the Jacobites across the moor all the way, shunning houses. This route, across Culraich Moor, also gave them the means of a secure withdrawal in case of repulse. Besides, the enemy would not dare to follow them until daylight, so, provided the attack was launched between 1 and 2 a.m., they would be safe. By dawn the retreating clansmen would have reached Culraich and the hilly ground on the south side of the river, where they could not easily be pursued.[77]

Lord George Murray then intervened to ask if the prince was still determined to fight on Drummossie Moor instead of crossing the Nairn to the Ker/Stapleton battlefield and waiting for the rest of the Highlanders to arrive. The prince said that the supply situation gave them no choice. If they did not engage the enemy by the afternoon of the 16th at the latest, the clansmen would have dropped in their tracks through starvation.

Regarding Drummossie Moor as a suicidal field of battle – for they could foresee the consequences if Cumberland's artillery got on to such easy terrain – Lord George and Lochiel reluctantly agreed to the night attack.[78] Since the prince would not agree to wait for his other units, anything was better than fighting on the open moor.

The final plan was elaborated. After encircling the town of Nairn, Lord George and the first Jacobite wave would attack Cumberland's camp on the east and north, in the rear. Murray intended to cross the river Nairn about two miles short of the town, march along the south bank to avoid Hanoverian outposts, then recross the river a mile farther on. From there he would fall upon the flank and rear of the English cavalry. The remaining two-thirds of the army were to keep to the north bank of the Nairn almost until they came to the camp. Then they would turn to branch off to the left, in a line extending to the sea, and launch a simultaneous attack on the infantry. This second wave, from the south and west, would consist mainly of Perth's and the Irish troops.[79] The prince would then support Perth's frontal attack with the reserve.[80]

It was an ingenious plan. No muskets would be used; the attack would be made with broadswords. The clansmen would fall silently on their sleeping foe, slashing guy-ropes, overturning tents, cutting into the human bulges within.[81] But there were still those who insisted that leaving Culloden at dusk and travelling eight miles across difficult moorland would not leave enough time for an attack before daybreak. Lord George Murray solved this objection peremptorily by saying that he would answer for the scheme's feasibility.[82]

Things began to go badly wrong before ever the columns set out on the night march. At 7 p.m. the clansmen, who were resting without tents on a dry hill near Culloden House, cold, hungry and dispirited, began to stream off in large numbers towards Inverness in search of food.[83] It proved impossible for their officers to recall them. The clansmen defied their superiors to shoot them, remarking that if they were to die, it were better by gunshot than from starvation.[84] When the prince learned this, he gave immediate orders to march. A good general would have abandoned the attempt at this point.

At the beginning of the march, the prince manifested distinct manic tendencies. An exploit like this touched the deep springs of Charles Edward's imagination. Bold, attacking strategy, this was ever the stuff to bring his positive impulses to the fore. The charm, so long dormant during the ordeal of early 1746, briefly surfaced again. His remarks to Lord George give a lightning flash of the Charles Edward of Moidart eight months before:

> 'Lord George, you can't imagine, nor can I express to you, how acknowledging I am of all the services you have rendered me. But this will crown all. You'll restore the king by it. You'll have all the honour and glory of it. It is your work. It is you imagined it, and be assured that the king nor I will never forget it.'[85]

In an effusive gesture of friendship, the prince placed his arm around Murray's neck. He then walked beside him a long way, charming and flattering. The response from the cold and aloof Murray was typical. He said not a word in reply, but stiffly took off his bonnet and made a low bow.[86] Even allowing for the deference due to the Prince Regent by indefeasible right, this degree of reserve by Murray was odd; he might at least have mumbled a homily in reply.

After firing the heather around Culloden to make the enemy think they were still there, the army marched out in a single column, the rear about a mile from the van. Lord George had the van, Lord John Drummond was in the centre. Perth was in the rear with Charles Edward and Fitzjames's horse.[87] The Mackintoshes were in the front and rear to prevent straggling. Small parties were sent out to seize all adjacent roads so that Cumberland could not be tipped off.[88]

It had originally been intended that three separate columns should approach Nairn by three different routes, but owing to the incompetence of the Mackintosh guides, only one route was followed. Inevitably, delays resulted. After only a mile orders were sent to the vanguard to slow down.[89] The Irish troops in the service of France were not used to the Highlanders' furious pace and could not keep up. Another serious bottleneck was caused by a wall in Culraich wood which the Mackintoshes had not taken into account in their optimistic estimates. This stone wall prevented the Athollmen from going three abreast. They were reduced to single file.[90]

By 1 a.m., when the attack should have been starting, Lord George Murray and the van had progressed just six miles and were still four miles short of their target.[91] Murray claimed he had already received 'one hundred' messages to slow down while crossing Culraich.[92] Apart from the heavy going underfoot and the thick fog, the Irish picquets and Royal Scots had proved useless at the kind of marching that was second nature to the clan irregulars. They even insisted on marching in full battle order.

There were other impediments. The bog on the moorland was splashy. The clansmen had to make frequent turns and detours to avoid houses. There were also two or three dykes that took a long time to pass.[93] It became quite obvious that the Mackintosh guides had never really had any true idea of how long it would take to march ten miles across this moor.

The last straw for Lord George was when Lord John Drummond came galloping up a mile before the intended river crossing with yet another message to slow down.[94] Murray sent Lochiel back to Charles Edward to suggest that time had already run out on them and the march had better be abandoned.[95] Lochiel added his own worries, telling the prince that many of his Camerons had deserted under cover of the fog.[96]

The appearance of Lochiel with Lord George's plea to retreat was too powerful a reminder of Derby, where these two men in his father's age group had ruined him, as he saw it. All the prince's positive impulses, in evidence at the beginning of the march, went into reverse. Struggling to control his rage, he rebuked Lochiel sharply and turned down all idea of a retreat: 'I'll answer for the men, but I am surprised that you are the man chosen to bring me such a message.'[97]

The prince ordered O'Sullivan and Perth to go back and talk to Lord George. Riding hard, they overtook him by the farm of Knock-buie or the Yellow Knoll, a little to the east of the ancient mansion of Kilravock, about a mile before the spot where Murray intended to cross the river.[98] The hopeless situation was immediately clear to Perth. He and his brother Lord John agreed that any further advance was impracticable. They could not possibly reach the enemy before daybreak. But O'Sullivan, knowing how his master's mind worked, repeated the prince's adamant orders, that the attack could be called off only if compelling reasons were shown.[99]

Knowing the storm that would follow, Lord George insisted on having the opinions of all the officers present canvassed and recorded.[100] Except for O'Sullivan, Sir John MacDonald and the officers who had volunteered for the first wave, they were unanimous for calling off the advance. To a man, the clan leaders pointed out that they could not conceivably attack in force before daylight. If the van pressed on, they could attack on their own. But what could 1,200 men do against 8,000, even with the element of surprise? Another consideration was that for three miles around Nairn the ground was open moor with hard dry soil.[101] The Jacobites were on the horns of a dilemma. If they waited for the whole army to come up and then attacked at daylight, they would be annihilated in such conditions.

If they attacked with just the van, they would be eaten up by superior numbers.

The volunteer Jacobite gentlemen who had been marching at the front with Lord George were all for pressing on, on the grounds that the redcoats would all be blind drunk after celebrating Cumberland's birthday.[102] This said a lot for their courage but not their insight. Cumberland had foreseen this possibility and deliberately rationed the supply of brandy to his men.[103]

O'Sullivan now had Lord George, Perth, Lochiel and Drummond ranged against him. Predictably he began to bluster. The discussion became acrimonious.[104] After a quarter of an hour of this, tragedy seemed likely to turn to farce with the arrival of Hay of Restalrig. Hay arrived to reiterate the prince's insistence on an advance, even if this meant an attack by 1,200 in the vanguard alone.[105] No more unhappy choice of messenger could have been devised at this juncture. Hay was already hated and despised for being responsible for the clansmen's starved and emaciated physical condition. Anything he said was likely to be greeted with derision. Overtly snubbed, Hay galloped back to the prince with the alarming tidings that unless he appeared at the van in person, retreat was irreversible.[106] Perth was close on Hay's heels. When he reached the second column, Perth ordered the officers to wheel about and march back to Culloden.[107]

Perth's men had not retraced their steps more than a hundred yards when they collided with the prince, now riding furiously towards the front column after receiving Hay's intelligence. 'Where the devil are the men going?' the prince called out distraught. 'We are ordered by the duke of Perth to return to Culloden House,' came the answer.[108]

At this the prince exploded. 'Where is the duke of Perth?' he raged. 'Call him here instantly!'[109] He went on in the same vein: 'I am betrayed! What need I give orders when my orders are disobeyed?'[110]

It appears that while the prince was waiting for Perth to present himself, he heard many seditious mutterings in the ranks: men vowing they would not fight once daylight came, others commenting on the general exhaustion of the army and the desertion rate on the march.[111] It was a more subdued Charles Edward who took Perth to task. Coldly angry, he asked Perth what he meant by ordering the men back. Perth answered that Lord George Murray and the van had turned off the trail three-quarters of an hour ago, heading for Culloden House.[112]

'Good God!' said the prince, reeling under this fresh blow. 'What can be the matter? What does he mean? We were equal in numbers and would have blown them to the devil. Pray, Perth, can you call them back yet? Perhaps he is not far gone?'

Seeing that this conversation was being conducted within plain earshot of his demoralised men, Perth asked for some private words with the prince. They drew aside. Patiently Perth explained the situation. Charles seemed crushed by what he heard. Returning to the army, he spoke aloud to his officers. 'There is no help for it. March back to Culloden House.'[113] To the troops he tried to speak more encouragingly. ' 'Tis no matter, then. We shall meet them and behave like brave fellows.'[114]

So ended the ill-fated night march to Nairn. Lord George Murray and the rearguard had already veered off to the left and taken a different route back to Culloden.[115] The retreat was the easy part. Now that the Highlanders did not have to shun houses, they were able to march very quickly, as the crow flies. The bulk of the army got back to the environs of Culloden around 6 a.m., in time for three or four hours' sleep.[116]

Why did the plan for a night attack, so promising on paper, end so disastrously? The truth was that it was always a much more risky enterprise than anyone admitted to the prince. It seems clear that the march did not get under way in earnest until 9 p.m. Even given the lengthening evenings in April and the need to preserve absolute secrecy, the Jacobites must have lost a good hour of marching time in the vain attempt to round up those clansmen who had decamped to Inverness in search of food. Then the Mackintoshes had absurdly underestimated the time needed to achieve the ten-mile march across Culraich and the river Nairn. The clansmen were tired and hungry and unlikely to match their best trekking efforts. Weather conditions and the inexperience of the French regiments in irregular warfare also told against the Jacobites.

But it seems that sycophancy among Charles Edward's inner circle of admirers also played its part. The prince was never warned of the very real risk that the enterprise might miscarry.[117] At this stage in his life, Charles was far too credulous and trusting towards his favourites, while being ludicrously suspicious of those not in the circle of initiates. The charm and affability of Charles Edward was the positive side of a mentality that was also distinguished by a marked anxiety to please those he considered his friends. This made him highly vulnerable to flattery and in thrall to those who had captured his confidence. All of these signs of a fragile identity were reinforced by a declining grip on reality. Charles Edward genuinely thought his clansmen were invincible, that Cumberland's troops were mesmerised and awestruck by them. He was obsessed with the desire not to appear weak and lose face before Cumberland. Now once again, as at Derby and Falkirk, he felt himself betrayed. This conviction led directly to the ultimate disaster at Culloden. For what sort of a remark is the following to be addressed by a field commander trying to rally his troops? On good authority, Charles Edward is said to have told his men with tears in his eyes on the march back to Culloden that he did not so much regret his own loss as their inevitable ruin![118]

18

Débâcle

(April 1746)

The army began to arrive back at Culloden at 5 a.m., but Charles
Edward did not return to his quarters until two hours later. Deeply
affected by the privations of the clansmen, he rode twelve miles to
Inverness and back in search of provisions.[1] His quest ended in anger
when he threatened to burn down Inverness unless the townspeople
got the necessary provisions out to Culloden House in waggons.[2]
With difficulty Perth, aware of the possibility of an immediate attack
by Cumberland (who had by now learned of the failure of the night
march), persuaded the prince to return to Culloden.

Almost the first person Charles met there was Lord George
Murray. The prince railed at him for his timidity. Murray stood his
ground, confusing the issue by shifting the responsibility for the
retreat to Lochiel, whom the prince deeply respected.[3] A fruitless
argument then took place as to who exactly had first spoken of retreat
and in what terms. When the abortive conversation petered out, Lord
George asked the prince if he still intended to give battle that day.[4]
The prince replied that there were no realistic alternative options.
His officers were too tired for a council to be called. In fact all ranks
had simply flopped on the ground, sleeping wherever they halted.[5]

Lord George answered that there were no fewer than three possi-
bilities. They could retire to Inverness where there were stores, and
defy Cumberland to winkle them out in a siege he could not
accomplish. The Hanoverians would take severe casualties if they
tried to storm a well-barricaded town.[6] They could melt away into
the Highlands and the shires of Aberdeen, Banff and Angus, ready
to reform in the spring. If Cumberland attempted to follow them
there, he would be drawn away from his supply lines, for his army
was being revictualled by shipping in the Sound of Nairn.[7]

Finally, if the prince was set on a battle, they should retire across the Nairn to the field that Stapleton and Ker had reconnoitred the day before. This hilly, boggy and mossy ground on the south side of the river was steep and uneven and ideally suited to the Highlanders' methods.[8] A meticulous three-hour examination by Ker and Stapleton had revealed that the ascent from the waterside was steep, that there were only about two or three places within a four-mile stretch of river where horses could cross, and that horses could not act on the terrain even if they did cross.[9] There was the further advantage that the Jacobites could fight a holding action if necessary, keeping Cumberland at bay until next day when Cluny's regiment and the other reinforcements would have come up. It also left the door open to another night attack on Cumberland.[10]

The prince dismissed all three suggestions. A siege of Inverness would merely postpone the inevitable battle. The Jacobites would be bottled up while Cumberland could be reinforced by sea.[11] A fighting withdrawal to the Highlands, on the other hand, was ruled out because of the clansmen's desperate hunger.[12] As for the field of battle on the far side of the Nairn, not only would this look as though the Jacobites were shunning Cumberland, but it would also mean abandoning Inverness with all stores, ammunition and baggage to the enemy.[13] Lord George replied that if they were defeated, as they were likely to be if they fought on Drummossie Moor, Inverness would be lost anyway.

Seeing the prince adamant in his determination to fight that very day and on terrain that would benefit Cumberland, the marquis d'Eguilles made a dramatic entry into the fray. He pointed out to the prince that his men were starving, that he was without a large number of them, and that those who were with him mainly no longer even possessed targes. D'Eguilles advocated the Ker/Stapleton battlefield or retreat to the Highlands. The Jacobites could still hope to receive aid from France via the west coast.[14] These exhortations made no impact.

D'Eguilles then asked for a quarter of an hour alone with the prince. Once in private, he threw himself at Charles Edward's feet and begged him not to give battle that day. The prince was immovable. As d'Eguilles commented bitterly afterwards: 'I saw before the end of the day the most striking spectacle of human weakness – the prince was vanquished in an instant, never was a defeat more complete than his.'[15]

With the failure of all entreaties to swerve him from his fixed purpose, Murray and the others left the prince alone. He flung himself fully clothed on the bed to snatch two hours' sleep, having been up all night on the 14th and 15th.[16] Murray was left to ponder this signal instance of the prince's obstinacy. Lord George was inclined to blame the Irish, especially O'Sullivan, for the insane decision to fight on Drummossie Moor.[17] He attributed this to their inability or reluctance to campaign in the rigours of the Highlands: 'we were obliged to be undone for their ease.'[18]

Lord George, a sober sceptic himself, underrated the element of blind irrationality in Charles Edward's decision. His refusal to make contingency plans, or to fight on the other side of the Nairn, his confidence that the other Jacobite troops would arrive in time were at best part of a process of whistling in the dark to keep up his spirits. This in itself gave an unfortunate impression of vainglorious thickheadedness, so that even if we allow that these were tactics on the prince's part, they were a failure.

Cumberland could have been defeated on the 17th on Lord George Murray's chosen field. Whether another Jacobite victory would have done more than delay the inevitable, whether it would not have been merely another Falkirk is uncertain. The crucial point is that a defeat against the particular army Cumberland brought to Culloden, *if the battle was fought on Lord George's choice of ground*, was by no means the inevitable outcome. It was the prince's self-destructive actions that made defeat certain and turned a single defeat into the demise of an entire way of life.[19] The obsession with the notion that a retreat before Cumberland would be an unacceptable loss of prestige suggests strongly the kind of fragile identity that means the fantasy self-image of an invincible warrior must be maintained at all costs.

Any lingering chance of persuading the prince to change his mind after his hasty nap was destroyed by Brigadier Stapleton's infamous jibe about the Highlanders: 'the Scots are always good troops till things come to a crisis.'[20] After that, Lochiel and the other chiefs were determined to go down fighting and cast the lie back in the Irishman's teeth. When the prince was aroused with the news that Cumberland's cavalry were now just four miles away, there was no longer any question of fighting elsewhere than where they stood (or slept).

In the utmost confusion orders were issued. Drums beat, pipes played and cannon were fired to recall the foraging Highlanders. Because the clansmen had scattered to find food or sleep, many took no part in the battle; some were cut down later as they slept.[21] Apart from the 2,000 Jacobite absentees, an estimated 1,500 slept through it.[22] Barely 5,000 Highlanders gathered on Drummossie Moor to oppose Cumberland's 9,000.[23]

These now hurriedly took up their positions. Lord George Murray and the Athollmen were on the right, Lord John Drummond was in the centre, and Perth with the sullen MacDonalds on the left.[24] The prince rode among the men, trying to encourage them, especially the MacDonalds whom he had overruled for the place of honour on the right in favour of Lord George. 'They don't forget Gladsmuir nor Falkirk,' he told them. 'You have the same swords. Let me see yours . . . I'll answer this will cut off some heads and arms today.'[25] Yet even as he spoke, O'Sullivan, who knew his master well, said it was clear that at bottom the prince had no great hopes.

On arrival at Drummossie Moor the prince soon revealed his incapacity as a battle commander. He began by refusing Lord George Murray's request for a close inspection of the terrain, which would have revealed a marshy hollow over which the Highlanders later had to charge.[26] Next, he overruled Murray's urgent plea to throw down the western walls of the Culloden Park enclosures. This dry-stone wall ahead of the Athollmen was directly in front and to the right of his men and was likely to impede their charge. The prince and O'Sullivan alleged that an advance to break down the walls would fracture the Jacobite battle line right under the enemy's gaze.[27] They ignored the fact that Cumberland was not yet on the field.

At eleven o'clock the two armies came in sight of each other, still two and a half miles apart. Cumberland's men came on in good order. A French officer told the prince 'he feared the day already lost for he had never seen men advance in so cool and regular manner'.[28] Lord George Murray was equally pessimistic. 'We are putting an end to a bad affair,' was his doleful reply to Elcho's query about Jacobite prospects.[29] Yet the clansmen themselves seemed to fetch a second wind once they caught sight of the enemy.[30]

Cumberland's first move was to send the Campbells with a body of dragoons to the river Nairn to outflank the Atholl brigade.[31] This carried the threat that the Jacobites would be taken in flank and rear if the Hanoverian cavalry advanced over the dead ground in Culloden Park. To do this they would first have to throw down the park walls that Lord George had earlier wanted to dismantle.[32] O'Sullivan was sure they could not do this in the thick of a battle, but Lord George did not share his optimism.[33] Perth, called over from the left to investigate, advised lining the park walls. Murray did not have the men to spare for such an operation. He ordered Ogilvy's regiment to guard the flank.[34]

Meanwhile Cumberland's artillery had become bogged down in marshy ground. This was the first flaw in the duke's streamlined arrangements. The prince had withdrawn to a small hill behind the gap in the centre of the second line. He cut a fine figure in the last moments of exhortation before the battle proper. He was mounted on a newly acquired horse and brandished a pair of silver-mounted pistols. His leather targe was embossed with a silver head of Medusa. Now from the 'eminence' he saw Cumberland's cannon sink into the swampy ground. The duke's right was temporarily uncovered. In one of his good decisions, the prince sent O'Sullivan to Lord George with orders to attack.[35]

Lord George demurred, probably because he did not yet have sufficient numbers to mount the operation. Jacobite troops were still streaming on to the field as the battle got under way. The other factor in Murray's hesitation was that the Campbells had already occupied some of the park houses to his right. Murray wanted Cumberland's first line to proceed as far as the Leanach enclosures before he launched his attack; he feared that otherwise his Athollmen might be flanked by the Campbells and the dragoons.[36]

The late arrival of the Highland regiments, particularly the MacDonalds on the left, caused very great confusion. They were still getting themselves into their assigned positions when Cumberland's artillery, now clear of the marsh, came within range.[37] On the extreme left the Jacobites came up against a similar obstacle to that facing the Athollmen on the right. The Glengarry regiment was pinned against the south-east corner of a wall surrounding the Culloden enclosures. The effect of park walls on both sides of the army was to funnel the Jacobite front line into a narrow space no more than three hundred yards wide.[38] Moreover, since the enclosure wall on the left did not end at the same point as the park wall on the right, the Jacobite front line became slanted, with the MacDonalds on the left much farther away from the enemy than the Athollmen on the right.[39]

This skew effect was multiplied when the Athollmen advanced beyond the park wall on the right. The MacDonalds on the left showed a reluctance to follow suit. They were still sullen because they had not been assigned their traditional place of honour on the right.[40] Since the only hope of victory was a simultaneous attack by the whole of the Jacobite front line, Perth, commanding on the left, was at his wits' end. He called out to the MacDonalds to promise them that he would ever afterwards bear their surname if only they would advance.[41]

Shortly after one o'clock the artillery cannonade began.[42] The prince's miscellaneous batteries in the Jacobite centre fired the opening shots from a range of five hundred yards. But his gunners had no professional ordnance training. Their aim was feeble and ineffective. Just for a moment Cumberland's dragoons seemed to stagger, probably from nervousness at the sound of the bombardment. They soon recovered when they saw the enemy salvoes going wide.[43]

Two minutes later Cumberland's more expert artillerymen replied with their ten 3-pounders. The opening volleys appeared to onlookers to be directed towards the Jacobite rear, almost as if they were seeking out the prince.[44] One of his servants, thirty yards behind him, was killed.[45] So many cannonballs fell around the Stuart standard that Balmerino's corps escorted the prince away from the immediate danger, but not before his horse had taken a hit in the flank.[46] The previously docile horse began to kick. Seeing the blood gushing from its side, the prince dismounted and found another.[47]

The salvoes from Cumberland's accurate gunnery did a lot of damage among the prince's hussars in the rear.[48] For the first time, and in the most unfavourable circumstances, the clansmen were exposed to rapid and accurate artillery fire. The Jacobite guns, by contrast, were largely manned by scratch crews and did little damage. A contributing reason for this was the varied calibre of their guns (1½-pounders, 3-pounders, 4-pounders) which complicated the ammunition supply.[49]

Lord George now contemplated a flanking movement on the enemy left but Cumberland spotted the danger and posted a regiment at right angles to his left to pre-empt such a move.[50] Things were already going badly for the Jacobites when a squall of rain sprang up. Heavy precipitation of hail and rain lashed into the Highlanders' faces, dampening their powder horns.[51] This was Falkirk in reverse.

The Hanoverian guns were then trained on the Jacobite front line. To his astonished pleasure, Cumberland found his cannon 'rapidly thinning the Jacobite ranks without experiencing any loss in return'.[52] The prince's post at Culchunaig had been singularly ill chosen. He could not see the havoc and mayhem being carried out in his own front line.

After ten minutes of this, Cumberland's gunners switched to grapeshot 'which swept the field as with a hail-storm'.[53] Because of the funnelling of the Highlanders in the front line, it was impossible for the Hanoverians to miss. They scythed great swathes through the ranks of the clansmen. In some places large holes were torn in the battle line.[54] Still no order to attack came from the prince.

It was clear that this situation could not be allowed to continue.

Lochiel and Lord George sensed that their men were only minutes away from headlong flight. Murray sent urgently to the prince for the order to attack. The prince gave it.[55] But the delay was not yet over. On his way back to Lord George with the prince's 'attack' order, MacLachlan of Inchconnel was decapitated by a cannonball.[56] The prince sent Brigadier Stapleton with a repeat order.

This was the moment for right and left to surge forward in a cloud. But while the Athollmen, their patience already exhausted, burst without waiting for Stapleton's authorisation, on the left the MacDonalds declined to move.[57] When Sir John MacDonald delivered the prince's order for an immediate charge, the MacDonalds refused. All the pleas of Perth and his brother Lord John could make no impression on them. The consequence was that the Jacobite right attacked alone.[58]

When the cry of 'claymore' was finally uttered, the bottleneck in the battlefield meant that it was clan Chattan in the centre who got to grips with the enemy first.[59] The Highlanders are sometimes said to have fought below their best on the day of Culloden, but there was nothing inferior about this charge from the viewpoint of heroism or courage. What did the damage was clan Chattan's sudden swerve to the right, probably caused by a desire to charge along the firm ground of the old moor road rather than through waterlogged terrain.[60] This swerve not only prevented hundreds of the prince's best men on the right from getting into the fight, but pushed many of them into the mouth of the deadly fire coming from Cumberland's centre.[61]

The charge continued in a turmoil of fire and smoke. Half-blinded by the smoke which the wind blew strongly into their eyes, the men of clan Chattan gradually narrowed the gap between themselves and the enemy. Survivors later described themselves as being caught up in a whirlwind of thick smoke without seeing where it was coming from.[62]

Within two minutes Lord George released the Athollmen to support them. But now the bad consequences of being penned in by the park wall and the Leanach dyke showed themselves. The tightly packed Athollmen became the victims of a 'most terrible fire' at pistol-shot range both from Barrel's and Munro's regiments in front and Wolfe's and Campbell's on the flank.[63] Winnowed by this raking fire, most armies would have faltered. But, taking terrible losses, the Highlanders completed their charge and fell like furies on Barrel's and Munro's regiments.[64]

Hacking and cleaving through the ranks of men, they would soon have cut the two regiments to pieces but for support from Cumberland's second line. The stiffening of Bligh's and Sempill's regiments turned the tide. Staggering through the inferno of thick smoke and the bloody bodies of their comrades lying four deep, the Highlanders were mown down in droves. The few clansmen who got through to the second line were skewered on bayonets.[65]

Finally the wild impulse of the charge petered out. Heavily outnumbered, having taken dreadful casualties, the Jacobites began to stream back in retreat. Five hundred penetrated Cumberland's lines. Very few of them came back alive.[66]

The Camerons behaved badly. Most of them fled without helping Lochiel, who had been wounded in both legs by the flanking fire of the Campbells.[67] But the men of clan Chattan, without any effective reply to the devastating fire power of the overwhelmingly superior Hanoverian regiments, defied their butchers. In their fury and despair they stood for two minutes and hurled stones at Cumberland's men before the general rout began.[68]

Yet even now the ordeal of the right was not over. As they retreated past Leanach dyke, the Campbells swarmed out on them, claymore in hand. Furious swordplay ensued. The Camerons took further casualties.[69]

The Jacobite left never got into the fight. Even while Perth and Drummond made frantic efforts to bring the MacDonalds into the engagement, the repulse of the right became evident.[70] Shamed by the cowardice of his men, Keppoch and his brother charged forward without their regiment. Keppoch fell dead from gunshot almost immediately.[71] Clanranald was severely wounded in the head just as he had finally persuaded his clansmen to charge. At once the attack was called off.

Cumberland's cavalry now advanced on the centre of the Jacobite second line.[72] The Royal Scots were saved from encirclement by the Irish picquets, who directed a steady fire on the Hanoverian horse. Stapleton's Irishmen were the heroes of the Jacobite left, for their flanking fire from behind the walls of the Culloden enclosures enabled the retreating MacDonalds to get off the field.[73]

But on the right Cumberland's horse came within an ace of encircling the Jacobites. Following an absurd confusion in orders, Ogilvy's regiment had been withdrawn from its position guarding the walls of Culloden Park. The Campbells now made a breach in the west wall, wide enough for cavalry to pass through three abreast.[74] Through this gap poured Cumberland's dragoons. They were already almost in the rear of the Jacobites, behind the prince at Culchunaig.[75]

At the last moment Lord George Murray spotted the danger, which O'Sullivan had discounted so cavalierly. He ordered the pitiful remnants of the Jacobite cavalry to face about to meet this new threat. Elcho's Lifeguards and Fitzjames's horse faced the dragoons on either side of a hollow near Culchunaig. There were barely a hundred of them, ill-mounted on starving horses. They confronted five hundred of Kerr's and Cobham's dragoons, well-mounted and well-armed. Yet so resolute was the demeanour of this Jacobite cavalry that it was ten minutes before Cumberland's men attacked.[76] When they did, Elcho's and Fitzjames's were forced to give way, taking heavy losses as they went. But they had bought precious time and saved the prince and the rearguard from being surrounded.

By this stage of the battle the extent of Jacobite defeat was evident. Of the regimental commanders, only Ardshiel, Lord Nairne and Lord George Murray were left unwounded. Murray bore himself with great bravery. He lost his horse, had several cuts from a broadsword in his coat, had lost or dented two of his own swords, and lost his wig and bonnet.[77] A third of all the men in the centre and right-wing regiments were already dead. Only three men survived among the Mackintoshes. It hardly needed O'Sullivan to come galloping up and tell the prince: 'You see, all is going to pot!'[78]

What of the prince all this while? During the cannonade he had been led away from his post by Lord Balmerino and John Daniel.[79] When the rout on the right began, Charles vainly tried to rally the regiments on the left. He called out that he would get down off his horse and lead them in a last charge.[80] According to one report, his wig blew off while he was imploring the Gaelic-speaking clansmen to return to the fray; they looked at him uncomprehendingly.[81]

After the valiant rearguard action at Culchunaig, O'Sullivan seized the prince's bridle and ordered Colonel Robert O'Shea, who had been commanding Fitzjames's horse there, to accompany him off the field.[82] The prince remonstrated. O'Sullivan yelled at him that he was in danger of being surrounded. 'They won't take me alive!' the prince screamed.[83] Yet he eventually let himself be persuaded to leave the battleground, guarded by Glenbucket's and John Roy Stewart's men.[84] Once or twice he turned his head to look back at the rout of the men he had considered invincible. But Sheridan, reading his mind, implored him not to sacrifice himself in vain. Lochiel's uncle Major Kennedy then seized the bridle and led the prince firmly away from the scenes of carnage.[85] As the prince later put it, 'he was forced off the field by the people about him'.[86]

Accompanied by Sheridan, Hay of Restalrig and a body of Scots officers, shepherded by O'Shea and his men, the prince rode towards the ford of Faillie on the Nairn.[87] He did not see the butchery of the Jacobite left as the fleeing MacDonalds, now deprived of Stapleton's covering fire, were ridden down and sabred on the road to Inverness. Hundreds more sleeping clansmen were slain in the bothies into which they had crept after the exhaustion of the night march, or in the ditches where they had slept through the battle.[88] Wounded men were given no quarter; those who took shelter in rude huts had them burned down around their ears. Cumberland's troopers were seriously out of control. They hacked and bayoneted at anything that looked like a clansman. This kind of blood-lust is not uncommon after a battle. Usually victorious commanders wring their hands in half-regretful impotence. Cumberland was unique in that he encouraged the butchery and threatened with reprisal any officers who would not do his bloody bidding. Fortunately for the prince's peace of mind, it was not until much later that he learned of these and subsequent massacres − the heinous carnage that was to fix the soubriquet 'the Butcher' to Cumberland's name for all time.

As it was, the prince was 'in a deplorable state' mentally.[89] Convinced that he had lost the battle through treachery, he seemed uneasy when the Scots were about him, as if they would deliver him up to Cumberland. Eventually he dismissed his Scots attendants, ordering them to meet him at a village a mile away for his further orders.[90] Left alone with him, the Irish pressed their advantage. They advised him it would be dangerous to try to rally his army at this juncture. Acquiescing, the prince ordered a general review at Ruthven in Badenoch on the 18th. With his Irish clique, he pushed on towards the Fraser country.[91]

The small party rode grimly onward, past Tordarroch, Aberarder, Faroline to Gortleg. With the prince were Elcho, Sheridan, O'Sullivan, Alexander Macleod, Allan MacDonald a Catholic chaplain, the servant Edward 'Ned' Burke and Captain O'Neill of Lally's regiment (in the Irish brigade), who had been sent to Scotland with dispatches just before Culloden.[92]

What general conclusions can we reach about the prince's behaviour on the fateful day of Culloden? There is first the question of his abilities as captain-general. It is quite clear that the prince was an indifferent field commander. It was true that he was beaten before he started at Culloden, with every conceivable advantage of numbers, gunnery, morale, food, terrain, even weather, on Cumberland's side. Not even Marshal Saxe could have beaten Cumberland in such circumstances at that time and place. But then it was the prince's own decision to fight on this ill-chosen field, against the advice of all his best officers.

Once battle was inevitable, the prince's greatest error was to take O'Sullivan's advice. Neither Charles Edward nor O'Sullivan had anything like Lord George Murray's eye for ground, yet on crucial issues such as the stone walls of Culloden Park they preferred their own ignorant opinion to his.[93] O'Sullivan declared that breaking down the walls would throw the Jacobite battle line out. What destroyed its effectiveness was *not* breaking them down. Again, O'Sullivan claimed that cavalry could not enter Culloden Park by a breach in the east wall and exit in the Jacobite rear. Yet this is precisely what the enemy did. Only Lord George's quick thinking saved the rear from encirclement.

Drawing up the army between the walls of Culloden enclosures on the left and the walls of Culloden Park on the right was another piece of almost criminal incompetence on O'Sullivan's part. The prince's post at Culchunaig was also badly chosen, so that Charles Edward was reduced to directing the battle blind.

The allocation of stations to the various Jacobite regiments was also inept. Even worse was the truly appalling system of communications. Charles Edward later testified that he sent the order to attack eight times to Lord George before his command was acted on.[94] The fiasco over the uncoordinated order to charge shows all the negative factors coming together to produce disaster. The centre charged before they had received the order. The left did not charge when they did receive it. No account was taken of the sloping formation, which meant that the MacDonalds on the left would have farther to run before falling on Cumberland's right.[95] A good general would have ordered the MacDonalds forward a minute before the Athollmen to compensate for this. If they had refused to move, the Jacobite right would then have been saved from the certain annihilation involved in a unilateral charge.

The worst single order of the day was the incomprehensible one to Ogilvy's regiment, previously detailed to prevent flank attack through Culloden Park. Not only were they ordered away from this crucial station, but they were then withdrawn to form a reserve, with idiotic instructions not to fire unless ordered to do so.[96]

On the other hand, there may be answers to some of the more common military criticisms levelled personally at the prince. One is that he should not have demoralised his men by allowing the reality of Cumberland's greatly superior numbers to sink in on them while both sides manoeuvred for flanking positions.[97] The prince was alive to this consideration, which was why he gave Murray the order to charge when he saw Cumberland's artillery floundering in the mud. He had earlier opposed the retreat across the Nairn for this very reason: that it would give the clansmen the opportunity to ponder pessimistically Cumberland's larger numbers.[98]

The second criticism is the most obvious. Why did he allow Cumberland's artillery to play uninterruptedly on his men for more than twenty minutes, first with cannon, then with case and grapeshot? Surely to stand by doing nothing was unforgivable incompetence? The answer here is that the prince was vainly trying to work out a Culloden Park flanking movement in reverse. He sent John Roy Stewart's Edinburgh regiment to cross the Nairn and work its way round to the rear of Cumberland's forces.[99] If he could contrive this, the Edinburgh regiment would then mount a diversionary attack in force with the advantage of wind and rain. When Cumberland's rear wheeled about to face this new threat, the Hanoverian battle line might then become hopelessly confused. But while Stewart and his men were vainly trying to find an unguarded way across the Nairn, terrible punishment was being meted out by Cumberland's artillery.

Yet the question of Charles Edward's military competence must ultimately go beyond his contingent actions on Culloden field. What happened there that afternoon between 1 and 2 p.m. was the end point of a long causal chain. Ultimately, the reason for Jacobite failure at•Culloden has to be sought in the relations between the prince and his lieutenant-general.

One of the prince's problems from the outset was that he did not possess among the 'Seven Men of Moidart' anyone of real military ability. Charles Edward himself had neither the innate aptitude nor the experience to be his own captain-general. Although history provides many examples of young men achieving military distinction, in most cases they had a single mentor or a core of battle-hardened veterans to lean on. Even Caesar had his Marius and Alexander his Parmenion.

But because of an intrinsic clash of personalities, the prince had to rely on a man he neither liked nor trusted. If there had been anyone comparable in military ability with Lord George, the prince would have discarded Murray. Yet Murray was by common consent far and away the most able Jacobite commander. He stamped his authority on the clan army from the very first. His military dominance was as clear-cut as the prince's personal one. Murray carried the council with him by reason of his military brilliance alone. Before the '45 he barely knew the clan leaders he won over to his point of view.[100] Murray was neither an active Jacobite nor a great territorial magnate.

Yet because the prince felt a visceral dislike for Murray, he followed the advice of the hopelessly incompetent O'Sullivan. This was almost an 'objective correlative' of the internal process whereby the prince's negative feelings triumphed over positive ones. Murray himself eventually came to glimpse the truth of this. During the period of 'skulking' after Culloden, he was filled with a morbid conviction that he had failed the prince, that his brusqueness, impatience and lack of deference had played into the hands of Charles Edward's evil geniuses among the Irish and had encouraged the prince's worse side to prosper.[101] The decision to fight at Culloden *was* a self-destructive act. Even so, the damage could conceivably have been limited if Murray had been given the command.

The experience of Culloden temporarily threatened to unhinge the prince. He was adamant that he had lost only because he had been betrayed.[102] Whereas the retreat on the night march was a genuine shock and might well have elicited cries of 'betrayal', it is difficult to see how any rational person could have responded in this way to defeat at Culloden. It was evident to everybody that, at the very least, defeat on Drummossie Moor was probable rather than possible. Why, then, the insistence on 'betrayal'?

The obvious answer is guilt. The prince was guilty because at some level he had willed his own destruction and with it that of hundreds of his followers.

But it is interesting that in propagating the idea that he was betrayed, the prince was unwittingly helping to build up his own legend. Here is a modern estimate of the genesis of such a legend in a very different context:

A hero who has only a small army with him, their enemy racial or national aliens sworn to destroy the hero's people and culture. As the one-sided battle becomes hopeless, and the hero is worn down by superior numbers, a last stand is called for and the hero is defeated. But it is part of the archetypal appeal that not even the greatest numbers of the enemy, it is felt, could have overcome the hero, unless he had been betrayed.[103]

The prince's disturbed state of mind explains the unhappy sequel to Culloden. After leaving the battlefield on the afternoon of the 16th, the prince and his party were guided by Alexander Macleod's servant Edmund Burke to the Fraser country, using the best roads.[104] At the house of Gortlick that evening the prince met the old fox Lord Lovat for the first and only time. Over supper they discussed what to do next. Sheridan urged the prince to return to France at once to bring back the long-promised aid. Elcho angrily dismissed this as a chimera: the only choice now was between utter ruin for all time for the Jacobite cause and guerrilla warfare in the mountains.[105]

Charles Edward was caught between advocates of his positive and negative sides. Like good and bad angels respectively, Elcho and Sheridan argued the case for guerrilla warfare or an immediate return to France. Lord Lovat, doubtless still feeling that he could cover his own treacherous tracks if he could but bundle the troublesome prince off to France, weighed in on Sheridan's side.[106] How, he asked, could a mountain campaign be sustained without money or food? The Jacobite army had been starving when it still possessed the threat of military execution. How could it do better without any enforcing sanctions?

If there had ever been any intention of fighting guerrilla warfare, a supply of provisions should have been laid up in readiness. Lord George Murray had proposed early in March that a food dump be set up in Badenoch to which supplies should be brought from Inverness ready for a campaign in the mountains, if the worst came to the worst.[107] Charles Edward had turned this down as timorous defeatism, and now the original self-immolating decision was used to provide the good reasons that answered to the prince's real desire. Yet at Elcho's prompting, the issue was left open pending further developments.

It was at this juncture that Lord George Murray's anger and exasperation led him in turn into a piece of self-defeating indulgence. There was considerable confusion about the arrangements for a rendezvous in case of defeat. Some Jacobite units were under the impression that it was *sauve qui peut* immediately after any reverse. Others understood that Fort Augustus was to be a rallying point.[108] Yet Ruthven in Badenoch had often been mentioned as the official mustering place. Accordingly, from 17–20 April units of the shattered Jacobite army began to drift in from Coorybrough, Balnaspiech and Aviemore.[109]

On Lord George's arrival at Ruthven on the 17th, he found that the prince had kept back for his own use a sum of money that was to have been distributed among the starving troops.[110] This seemed such a bizarre departure from the previously agreed arrangements that the rumour gained ground that the prince had no intention of keeping the rendezvous at Ruthven. The clans had been enticed there, it was alleged, to lure Cumberland after them while the prince made good his escape.

Angry at what he considered Charles Edward's duplicity, and in the hot-blooded frustration of defeat, Lord George Murray dashed off a furious letter, excoriating the prince for everything from arriving in Moidart without French assistance to his direction of the battle the day before. This coldly self-righteous letter, when received much later, destroyed whatever slim chance Elcho's advocacy might have had.[111] Even if the prince had gone to Ruthven, Murray's letter would have given him the pretext for doing what he wanted to do anyway: abandon the enterprise. Sheridan and the Irish had by now dinned it into him that it was dangerous to trust the Scots, since to save their own skins they would do to him what they had done to Charles I: betray him to the enemy.[112] Moreover, they insinuated that the losses sustained at Culloden were much greater than they were. The prince sincerely believed Lochiel had been killed as well as Keppoch. Besides, since Murray had virtually accused the prince of bad faith, he could hardly maintain that he stood in need of such a leader.

The prince therefore sent his final orders to the army at Ruthven. First there was a verbal message: 'Let every man seek his safety in the best way he can.'[113] Then came a formal written communication. He told them he was going to France to bring back an army; in his absence the Jacobite leaders should look to their own salvation: in other words, *sauve qui peut*.[114]

When this message was received at Ruthven, the wailings and ululations of the night after Culloden were rekindled. Dazed and staggered, the clansmen suddenly realised that they had been left to Cumberland's dubious mercies. They did not see things at all in the same way as the prince. They were confident the struggle could be continued, that a guerrilla campaign was feasible. Now it was their turn to feel betrayed. It seemed to them that the prince was deserting an army that was bigger than ever. The prince's reputation in Scotland never recovered from his message to his troops in Ruthven. Even stalwart supporters like John Roy Stewart became disillusioned at this point.[115]

Whether a guerrilla campaign was feasible at this stage is a moot point. About 4,000 men eventually assembled at Ruthven. On the other hand, only Ogilvy's and Cluny MacPherson's regiments were intact. And there were no adequate food supplies. But the prince, it was widely felt, had gathered his men together in Badenoch as bait for Cumberland while he saved his own skin.

The accusation that it was the instinct of self-preservation that led the prince to abandon his followers is a valid one, though true in a sense other than that normally used by his detractors. It was not cowardice or self-preservation in its ordinary sense ('saving one's skin') that led the prince to abandon his men, but a desire to be free of the strains of responsibility. It was stress and depression that placed him *hors de combat* for the first three months of 1746. It was the absence of stress that enabled him to bloom like the heather through which he was hunted as a fugitive for the next five months.

19

The Prince in the Heather

(April–June 1746)

After the conference with Lord Lovat, the prince did not tarry long in Fraser country, thinking it dangerous to rest so near the enemy the night after a battle.[1] He and his party pressed on to the Glengarry country. At 2 a.m., just after the setting of the moon, they arrived, exhausted, at Invergarry Castle.[2] Ned Burke, the guide, produced a scratch meal of two salmon and an oatcake. Then the party napped fitfully.[3]

At 3 p.m. on the 17th the prince set out again, with Ned Burke, O'Sullivan and Father MacDonald.[4] Riding along the north-western side of Loch Lochy, with the dark and steep mountains on their right, they swung west to Loch Arkaig. After locating the cottage of Donald Cameron of Glenpean at about 2 a.m., the prince lay down to sleep in earnest for the first time in five days and nights.[5]

The pattern of resting by day and travelling by night continued. It was 5 p.m. before the prince resumed his journey. After eating a meal of milk and curds, he waited to hear the latest news of his army.[6] The prince later disingenuously claimed that he waited until all hope of reassembling his forces was gone.[7] If it was gone, the reason why was clear! But he did receive a message from Lochiel, whom he believed dead. Lochiel informed him that after being carried from the field of Culloden by his clansmen, he was placed, wounded in both legs, in a crofter's cottage nearby. By mere chance, Cumberland's troops, who were on the point of entering the cottage in search of Jacobite fugitives, were called away on other duty by their officer.[8] Lochiel was then conveyed to Cluny's house in Badenoch.

After leaving Glenpean in the early evening, the prince and his companions confronted the Braes of Morar. The way ahead was so rough that the horses had to be left behind.[9] Walking by a winding path, they marched the eighteen miles to the glen of Meoble south of Loch Morar in darkness. They arrived at 4 a.m. on the 19th.[10] Here they were put up 'in a little sheal house near the wood'[11] by Angus MacEachine, sometime surgeon in Glengarry's regiment and Borrodale's son-in-law. The prince was so tired that he could neither eat nor drink and required the help of one of his party to get into bed.[12]

The prince slept most of the day. That night, under a moon 'four days from the full' he walked to Borrodale on the north shore of the sea-loch Nan-Uamh where he had landed nearly a year before.[13]

He remained at Borrodale for five days. For greater security he chose not to sleep in Borrodale's house but in a cottage in nearby Glenbeasdale. He was able to rest and recuperate from the exertions of the past few days. O'Sullivan recorded that the prince did well: he had lamb, meal and butter to eat and straw to lie on.[14] This was the prince's first regular food since the supper at Lord Lovat's the night after Culloden.

At Borrodale Charles made serious plans for the crossing to France. Still harbouring the illusion that the Skye chieftains were his friends, he asked Donald Macleod, a seventy-year-old loch seaman from Dunvegan, to carry a message to Macleod and Sir Alexander MacDonald, asking for their assistance.[15] Macleod (tenant of Gualtergill on Loch Dunvegan), who had been sent to the prince as a guide by Aeneas MacDonald, knew very well what the sentiments of the Skye chiefs were. Angrily he remonstrated with the prince for wanting to trust men who would deliver him to the Hanoverians as soon as look at him; he refused the commission. Instead, he proposed to take the prince over the Minch to the Hebrides.[16] There they should easily be able to find a ship bound for France or, failing that, a boat for the Orkneys, whence the prince could escape to Norway.

The prince fell in with this proposal. Macleod departed to find a suitable boat. Charles stayed on in the neighbourhood of Borrodale, holding daily conferences with young Clanranald and MacDonald of Boisdale.[17] It was probably at Borrodale that Lord George Murray's angry letter of 17 April caught up with him and confirmed him in his decision. This would explain his reiterated farewell to the clan chiefs.[18]

One event soured his stay in Borrodale. Hearing that Elcho was now at Kinlochmoidart House, the prince ordered him to seek out Lochiel and put himself at the Cameron chief's disposal. Elcho indignantly replied that he intended never to fight under the Stuart banner again.[19] His long vendetta with the prince, destined to last for forty years, had begun.

The Elcho message revived all Charles Edward's worst feelings about the Scots and their alleged potential for treachery. He wrote to Sheridan to say that one of the principal motives for his immediate departure for France was fear of betrayal. Because he suspected that there were traitors in his entourage at that very moment, the prince added, his location and planned departure must at all times be concealed.[20]

Donald Macleod returned with a stoutly-built, eight-oared boat and a crew of seven.[21] At nightfall on 26 April the prince embarked, together with Macleod, O'Sullivan, Ned Burke, O'Neill and Father Allan MacDonald.[22] Donald Macleod warned the prince not to put to sea at this time as he could sense a storm in the offing, but Charles was adamant.[23] By the time they were out in the Sound of Arisaig, about 9 p.m., one hour after putting to sea, a full gale was blowing with accompanying thunder and lightning.[24] Donald Macleod turned the boat to steer north-west through the Cuillin Sound. Their track would take them to Benbecula, with Eigg, Rhum and Canna on the port side and Skye to starboard.[25] The prince's original intention was to make for Eriskay. Had he gone there, he would have run smack into three English men o' war.[26]

Violent south-easterly winds beat against the boat. As they rounded the point of Arisaig, the bowsprit broke.[27] They were now making headway by dead reckoning, in the pitch-black and with no compass. Macleod suggested putting in to Skye, protesting that they would never reach the Outer Hebrides in such weather. But the prince insisted that landfall had to be somewhere on the Long Island.[28]

Macleod hoist sail and prepared to run before the wind. So good was his seamanship that they sighted the coast of the Outer Hebrides by daybreak. The prince, never a good sailor, had lived through a nightmare. He was too sick and dispirited to appreciate Macleod's skill in keeping them off the rocks of Skye, to admire the many times when he cried 'luff' to steer the craft temporarily into the wind.[29] Seasickness blotted out everything else. It was compounded by the 'bloody flux' from which the prince suffered throughout his time in the heather.[30] But characteristically Charles Edward hung on grimly and uncomplainingly. Lack of physical courage was never his problem. As the worst of the seasickness abated, he led the sailors in Highland songs and took his turn at bailing.[31] This was a crucial part of the trip: at one time the boat seemed to be filling with water faster than they could bail.[32]

Out of the early morning mist loomed Benbecula, between North and South Uist. Landing with difficulty in the midst of the gale, they hauled the boat on shore at Rossinish. It was about 7 a.m. on the morning of 27 April. In the teeth of the elements they struggled up the beach. The wind blew so strongly that they could scarcely put one foot in front of another.[33]

They found a deserted hut, made a fire and dried their clothes. The prince lent a hand in the fire-making. His help was necessary, for the rowers were all in.[34] The wherewithal to revive them was also lacking – all they had to hand was biscuit spoiled by the sea water.[35] A jug of milk was all they could procure from the local people. They guessed who their visitor was and feared the consequences if they helped him too openly.[36]

There were cows grazing on the island. The prince, always scrupulous in matters of property, ordered his men to shoot a few for food, saying he would compensate the owners on his restoration.[37]

The beasts were shot, the butchery commenced. While the beef was being prepared, it was noticed that there was a hole in the cooking pot. The hole had to be stuffed with rags before the pot was put on the fire. This greatly amused the prince.[38]

They remained on Rossinish until the evening of the 29th. The prince received a visit from Old Clanranald, one of the many chiefs who had sent his son 'out' to represent him.[39] Clanranald, seeing the possible demise of the entire clan system now looming as a possibility, urged him to stay and fight. The old chief's arguments powerfully impressed Charles Edward. For a while he dithered.[40] Almost on cue, a message arrived that shattered any prospect of a guerrilla war. Cumberland had taken Fort Augustus and Loudoun had arrived in Arisaig from Skye. Any guerrilla army would be between a pincer. In particular, the Camerons and MacDonalds would be cut off from the rest of the Jacobite clans. Immediately the prince returned to his resolution of getting away to France. On Clanranald's advice, he wrote a letter to all the clan leaders, asking them to maintain a skeleton force until he returned with French reinforcements.[41]

On the evening of 29 April they put to sea again, heading for Stornoway.[42] In Lewis the prince's party was to put about the story that they were shipwrecked natives of Orkney, anxious to charter a ship to take them home. The prince would pose as 'Mr Sinclair, junior'; O'Sullivan would take the role of his father.[43] But stormy seas and a strong south-westerly wind forced them ashore at Scalpay, also known as Glass Island.[44]

Scalpay proved another haven. The tenant Donald Campbell entertained the prince royally in his farmhouse. There were eggs, milk and butter to eat. There was also a bed and clean sheets. But it is significant of the prince's deep fear of betrayal that he insisted on sleeping with his clothes on.[45]

On 1 May Donald Macleod departed for Stornoway in a borrowed boat, intending to charter a suitable ship for the voyage to the Orkneys.[46] The prince remained on Scalpay until the morning of the 4th. There was one bad scare for him, a portent of things to come. On 3 May, quite by chance, Donald Campbell ran into a party of militiamen on the island. Reports that Macleod was in Stornoway looking for a ship to take him to Bergen fuelled other rumours that Macleod had stumbled on a Spanish treasure hoard from a wreck on Barra.[47] Fortunately, Campbell managed to talk the militiamen out of visiting his home. But the prince was now edgy, eager to be away.

At last they received a message from Macleod that he had managed to hire a brig. They made haste to join him in Stornoway. At daybreak the prince called for a hearty dram and gave everyone a glass before they put to sea.[48] They sailed nearly to the top of Loch Seaforth in Harris. Then the prince, with O'Neill, O'Sullivan and a local guide, set off to walk across country to Stornoway.

Only then did they realise the dreadful nature of the country through which they were passing. This part of Lewis was a maze of hills and small lochs. The desolate hills rose abruptly from sea-level to 2,500 feet. Many tiny lochs lay in open moorland, surrounded by soft, black bogs. It was a wet and stormy night, and there would be no moon until half past two in the morning.[49]

In such conditions, even the local guide lost his way. Predictably, the prince thought this was a deliberate attempt to betray him.[50] They floundered through the boggy country, skirting the dozens of lochs, all night long. In the morning, after walking in semicircles for some eighteen hours, they found themselves at Arrish, two miles from Stornoway.[51]

But if the prince thought his ordeal had earned him the right to a respite, he was soon disabused. For Stornoway, it now transpired, was up in arms against him. How they knew of his imminent approach is obscure. Some accounts blame Donald Macleod for indiscretion. He is said to have chartered a 40-ton brig for £100, which aroused the master's suspicion. When the master tried to renege on the deal, Macleod offered to buy the ship for £300. The master than asked for

£500. Since Macleod made no demur, the captain was able to guess who the new owner might be.[52] According to O'Neill, who is not always reliable, old Donald got drunk and blurted out the secret of his commission.[53]

Whatever the case, when the prince got to the outskirts of Stornoway at 11 a.m. on the morning of 5 May, it was to find that Aulay Macaulay, minister of Harris, had aroused his flock against him.[54] The townspeople were apprehensive of the possible loss of life if they tried to seize the prince.[55] They did, however, send word that he would be refused entry to the town, that no ship would be sold or chartered to him, and that they would not even let him have the services of a pilot to get to Seaforth's country in Ross-shire – which Donald Macleod suggested as a compromise.[56]

The prince meanwhile spent four dreadful hours in the rain.[57] Macleod then sent his son to take the waiting party to Kilden House. He also sent the bad news, together with a bottle of brandy, which the three men disposed of in short order.[58] After dining at Arrish with Mrs Mackenzie ('Lady Kilden'), on eggs, butter, biscuits, tea and whisky, they took stock. The prince was cold, tired and drenched; his feet were blistered. He refused to move on immediately. While his sodden shirt and worn-out shoes were replaced, he seized a few hours' sleep.[59] Mrs Mackenzie supplied them with meat, bread and brandy for the onward journey.

On the morning of the 6th they embarked with the six remaining crew members, intending to get to Poolewe in Ross-shire.[60] An argument broke out between Macleod and the crew about the feasibility of beating all the way to the mainland against strong contrary winds.[61] The argument was settled in dramatic fashion when they saw the sails of warships. The waters of the Minch were now teeming with British cruisers. To avoid them they put in at the tiny desert island of Iubhard (also called Evirn or Iffurt), at the mouth of Loch Shell, some twelve miles from Stornoway.[62] Any attempt to cross the Minch at this stage would have led to certain capture.

On this uninhabited islet they remained for four days and nights, cooped up in a 'low, pitiful hut'.[63] They had to spread the boat sail over the roof to keep out the rain. They dared not build a fire for fear of attracting warships to the island.[64] The one compensation was that they found food. By now they were down to a single oatmeal cake. It would have gone hard with them if they had not found a quantity of salted cod and ling.[65] The Lewis fishermen used this desolate spot to wind-cure their fish; a ready-made iron ration was therefore available.

On 7 May the prince climbed a hill to get an overview of the Royal Navy patrols. To his astonishment, he clearly made out two vessels he was able to identify as French from their rigging.[66] But this time not even Charles Edward's famous charm could induce the crew to row out to investigate.[67] A great opportunity was thereby lost, for these were the ships that took Perth, Elcho, Lord John Drummond and many others back to France.[68]

On 10 May they put to sea again, making for Scalpay. They landed there only to find that their former host Donald Campbell was now also on the run.[69] The hospitality he had shown the prince a week before made him a marked man, and he had gone into hiding. Alarmed by the approach of four strangers, they returned to their boat and rowed away southwards.[70]

Off Finsbay they were spotted by HMS *Furnace*, commanded by the notorious Captain Fergusson. Fergusson crowded on sail for the pursuit. They gave him the slip by steering into shallow water near Rodil Point.[71] On an ebb tide the shallow-draught boat could go where Fergusson dared not follow. The *Furnace* broke off pursuit.

They now fetched a westward course towards Benbecula. But at Lochmaddy another Royal Navy frigate lay at anchor.[72] Again there was an attempt at pursuit, but a brisk wind blew up which detained the frigate and wafted the prince's boat out of sight.

They spent a grim night at sea off the forbidding shore of North Uist.[73] In the morning the wind forced them in to land at a little island in Loch Uskavagh in Benbecula. In heavy rain they found shelter in 'a poor grass-keeper's hut or bothy'.[74] The entrance to the hut was so narrow that the prince had to fall on his knees and creep forward on his belly every time he went in.[75]

In this awful hovel Charles Edward remained for three nights. It was evident to his followers that the prince was in very low spirits, but no word of complaint came from him.[76] Old Clanranald paid the prince another visit here and brought welcome provisions in the shape of trout, biscuits and some bottles of wine. This was an important addition to the prince's diet, which he had hitherto eked out by a solitary duck shot on Loch Uskavagh.[77] More significantly, Clanranald brought word of a good refuge in Corradale in South Uist.[78]

Mightily relieved to leave the bothy, the prince and party set out at 11 p.m. on 13 May and walked to Corradale, where they arrived at 6 p.m. the next day.[79] In a crofter's cottage in a rough inlet in the rocky coast, with Hekla rising 2,000 feet to the north and Ben More to the south, the prince found a satisfactory respite. For three weeks he rested and recovered while the hue and cry in the islands went on around him. The cottage in which he lodged was, he said, like a palace after the hole he had just left.[80] On the first night he basked in the unwonted luxuries of bread, cheese and goats' milk. He had his feet washed, smoked a pipe, and went to sleep on a bed of heather and green rushes, so soft that he slept until noon the next day.[81]

For twenty-two days the prince lived in comparative comfort and safety. He settled into a routine of hunting and fishing, punctuated by visits from Jacobites of the islands.[82] His expertise as a hunter and the deadly accuracy of his shooting amazed even those who had already witnessed the prince as warrior.[83] South Uist was at that time considered the best part of Scotland for game. All species of wild fowl were found here in great abundance. There were many deer. For the prince it was the Romagna all over again. He shot dozens of moorcocks and hens, bringing them down on the wing with infallible shooting power. One day he shot a deer on the run from long range.[84]

His health continued excellent apart from the dysentery or 'bloody flux' which came on periodically and was exacerbated by drinking milk.[85] His voracious appetite was much commented on.

Apart from the visits by Clanranald and the coming and going of his messengers to and from the mainland, only two events worthy of note took place during the three weeks. One day, while they were cutting up venison joints, a starving vagrant boy came up and put his finger in the meat. Ned Burke went to chastise him but the prince rebuked him in the name of Christian charity and of 'Scripture which reminds us to feed the hungry and clothe the naked'.[86] According to the legend, the boy, after being fed, repaid the Christ-like action by playing Judas, running off to tell the militiamen of Uist, who refused to believe his story of the prince on Corradale.[87]

On another occasion, while the prince was sitting on the beach, a school of young whales approached the shore. Calling for his gun, Charles took a pot-shot at them. But this time his legendary prowess deserted him. Convinced he had killed a whale, he called out to Neal MacEachain to swim out and haul in the stricken Leviathan (it will be remembered that the prince himself could not swim). To humour him, MacEachain began to strip off his clothes to make the attempt. At this point the comatose (and unharmed) whale stirred itself and swam slowly out of range.[88]

It might be thought that the opportunity for the prince's companions to observe him at close quarters over a period of three weeks would yield valuable biographical data. So it proves.[89] All the evidence agrees on two things: the prince was subject to severe mood swings; and he was already developing into a heavy drinker.

When the weather was fine, Charles would sit on a stone in front of the door of the cottage, with his face turned towards the sun. While in these reveries, the prince would oscillate wildly between melancholia and merriment. At times he would show symptoms of hypermania, dancing alone for an hour while he whistled a Highland reel to himself.[90] At others, he would plunge into profound gloom, especially when the invariably bad news from the Highlands was brought in. He brooded particularly on the way Lord George had allegedly betrayed him. On one occasion Donald Macleod, who had been sent to the mainland, came back with news that he had met Lochiel and Murray at the head of Loch Arkaig. Murray sent the prince word that Eigg would provide a safe hiding place. Charles Edward was convinced that the advice was given to ensure that he was captured. Learning that Eigg was a narrow island, easy to comb through, increased his suspicion. As he recorded later in a memoir of his flight through the isles: 'Charles knew better than to follow that advice.'[91]

The oscillation between euphoria and despondency clearly had some sort of link with his drinking. As Neal MacEachain related: 'He took care to warm his stomach every morning with a hefty bumper of brandy, of which he always drank a vast deal; for he was seen to drink a whole bottle of a day without being in the least concerned.'[92]

Charles certainly had motive and opportunity. Macleod and the other emissaries rarely brought any other provisions back from the mainland than brandy.[93] And brandy was, for the prince, a proven antidote to the dysentery from which he suffered, doubtless exacerbated by lack of a balanced diet. Whenever he drank milk 'which was a nourishment always contrary to him',[94] he had another attack, which was remedied only with a further intake of brandy.

The prince's fondness for alcohol had been noticed by his father even before he left Rome in 1744.[95] But on the islands he began to give unmistakable signs of a fondness for drink that was exacerbated by stress. Already his capacity for strong liquor was as pronounced as his skills as a hunter. On one occasion MacDonald of Boisdale came to visit him. He found the cottage in turmoil, laid waste after a furious binge the night before. Charles Edward had been carousing with another visitor, Hugh MacDonald of Baleshare. Challenging his companions to a drinking contest, the prince had drunk them all under the table, wrapped the debauched bodies in their plaids, and then said a 'De Profundis' for their souls.[96]

The fact is that every messenger who returned brought a further instalment of gloomy and depressing news. By now the prince was aware of two things: the scale of suffering unleashed on the Highlands in the wake of the defeat at Culloden; and the scope of the dragnet being laid down by London to apprehend him personally. Cumberland's armies had already cut a swathe through the Highlands, killing, raping, burning and looting as they went.[97] There was no resistance. Lochiel and the MacDonalds talked about raising a clan army at Badenoch and carrying on the fight until the prince returned with help from France. But the numbers of men who appeared in early May at the rendezvous at Muirlaggan on Loch Arkaig were so disappointing that the attempt to organise another rising was abandoned.[98]

As the grip of Cumberland (and later his successor in Scotland, Lord Albemarle) tightened on the country, the hunt for the prince intensified. At first it was believed he had been captured at Culloden or that he had fled north through Inverness.[99] But soon it became clear that Charles had got clean away: 'apprehending the Young Pretender seems to be a thing much wished for just now', one of Cumberland's aides wrote to the duke of Newcastle on 26 April.[100] By the end of April his trail through Lochaber had been picked up, as also his departure for the Long Island.[101]

A seaborne pursuit was ordered. HMS *Greyhound*, *Baltimore* and *Terror* were first into the fray.[102] Almost immediately they collided with the French. The two privateers *Le Mars* and *La Bellone* sailed from Nantes in April with 40,000 louis d'or for the prince, unaware of his defeat at Culloden. Anchoring in Loch-nan-Uamh, the French began to unload the money (later to become notorious as the 'Loch Arkaig treasure'). They also took on board an assortment of Jacobite refugees, including Elcho, Perth and Lord John Drummond.[103] On 3 May, while these operations were going on, the three British warships came upon them. The French cleared for action. A ferocious six-hour slugging bombardment left the English ships dismasted.[104] They stood away to the Sound of Mull. But the French too had taken severe punishment. There was no longer any question of going looking for the prince.[105] *Le Mars* and *La Bellone* set course for France. As they departed, the prince espied them from his eyrie on Iubhard. This was the occasion when he was unable to persuade his oarsmen to investigate.[106]

The return of the two privateers to France with the full story of the Jacobite defeat, but without the prince, caused consternation among his supporters on the Continent. Stung by the accusation that he had left the Stuart prince to his fate, Louis XV ordered a massive rescue operation to be mounted by French privateers.[107]

In Rome meanwhile James and his close friend Benedict XIV went through agonies of anxiety. Their worry had been gathering momentum ever since the retreat from Derby; it was not only the prince who saw that as the cardinal turning point of the rising.[108] James's agony is well chronicled in his papers for the summer of 1746.[109] Benedict described the prince's reverses as a 'second Passion'; in his eyes it was the worst cross he had had to bear in five years of a difficult Pontificate.[110] In his private correspondence he bitterly condemned Louis XV for his failure to make an all-out effort on the prince's behalf: God and God alone commanded the Channel, said to be the insuperable barrier; therefore 'His Most Christian Majesty' ought to have more faith in him.[111] By June Benedict was reduced to shaking his head and remarking that the justice of the Just God was impenetrable.[112]

The battle of Loch-nan-Uamh – the most serious naval clash of the '45 – did at least buy Charles Edward some time. Cumberland was convinced that his cousin and rival had made good his escape in the two French privateers, along with Elcho, Perth and the rest.[113] Just to be sure, he strengthened the naval patrols in the western isles. The battle-hardened trio of *Greyhound*, *Terror* and *Baltimore*, having repaired the damage sustained in Loch-nan-Uamh, were joined by powerful reinforcements: HMS *Furnace* (under Captain Fergusson), HMS *Scarborough* and *Glasgow* and three sloops: the *Raven*, *Trial* and *Happy Janet*.[114] Cumberland now had nine ships of the Royal Navy to scour the Scottish coast. Most of their captains were of the Hawley stamp and as such recommended themselves to 'the Butcher'. The names of Lockhart, Ancram, Scott and Fergusson were soon to join the roll of dishonour.[115] Captain Fergusson showed how he meant to go on by burning down the house in Arisaig where the prince had lodged, together with a couple of neighbouring villages.[116]

It was this naval pressure that finally brought the prince's peaceful sojourn at Corradale to an end. Learning that troops had landed on the Long Island and threatened to hem them in, Charles decided that his hideout could not remain secure much longer.[117] He particularly feared the pincer movement of the Skye chiefs' men on South Uist and Fergusson on Eigg.[118] It was time to depart.

In the days to come the prince was to look back on his time at Corradale as a halcyon period. It was as well that he had no inkling of what was to come. He had been tired and hungry already during his flight. He was now to face new privations and to end up fighting for his life.

20

Over the Sea to Skye

(June–July 1746)

Hearing that the enemy were on Barra in force, the prince and his companions sailed in the opposite direction. They held on in a northerly direction and came to the island of Ouia (or Wiay), to the south-east of Benbecula.[1] Here they huddled for three days while the searching cruisers zigzagged the Little Minch around them.

It was as well for the prince that Cumberland's bloodhounds knew only that he was somewhere on the islands. At this stage they could not even be certain he was on the Long Island. Playing a hunch, Commodore Thomas Smith, Royal Navy Commander in Chief in Scottish waters, sailed the *Furnace, Terror, Trial* and a number of other ships to St Kilda. On that desolate rock they found no prince, only some benighted islanders, to whom Europe's wars were as remote as the Roman Empire to the Chinese. The bewildered people knew only that the laird of Macleod had been at war with 'a great woman abroad' and had been victorious.[2]

After three days of indecision, the prince crossed to Rossinish with O'Neill.[3] But things were no better there. Militiamen in boats were scouring the shores and coves while their comrades combed the hills above.[4] After three more anxious nights, O'Sullivan and Donald Macleod came over from Ouia to Rossinish beach in the boat. The prince had more bad news to give them. There was a very strong rumour that 5,000 Frenchmen had landed in Caithness; alas, further investigation had shown it to be untrue.[5] There was also a false report that the Brest fleet was heading for Scotland; in fact its destination was Louisbourg in north America.[6] After a hurried consultation, they decided to return to Corradale, reckoning that by now it would have been searched.[7]

On their way south a violent storm blew up. They were forced to scramble ashore at Ushinish Point, a couple of miles north of Corradale.[8] They found refuge a little north of here, in a cleft of a rock at Acarseil Falaich.[9] In this niche they were pelted with rain, but dared not stir, since patrolling warships were constantly passing to and fro.[10] A break in the bad weather enabled them to get to Kyle Stuleg.[11] It was night-time when they arrived. Neal MacEachain aroused a known Jacobite family and brought back butter, cheese and brandy for the prince. Charles was all in. 'Come,' he said wearily, 'give me one of the bottles and a piece of bread, for I was never so hungry since I was born.'[12] After the improvised supper, they finished off the remaining brandy and fell into a sound sleep.

On 15 June they stayed hidden during the day and sailed for Loch Boisdale at night, in hopes of getting assistance from MacDonald of Boisdale. They soon discovered that he had been taken prisoner.[13] Moreover, there were now fifteen enemy sail around Loch Boisdale and parties of militiamen in the neighbourhood. They entered a creek and camouflaged themselves among the rocks. The prince lay down inside the boat and a canvas was stretched over it.[14] So he spent the day of 16 June. At night they finally entered Loch Boisdale and took shelter in an old tower 'in the mouth of the island'.[15]

The game of cat and mouse was now on in earnest. General Campbell of Mamore, whom Commodore Smith had sent to St Kilda, returned with his forces, straddling the area from Barra to South Uist.[16] Fergusson meanwhile was preparing to scour the island from north to south. For a while the prince and his comrades tacked to and fro in the little boat, backwards and forwards to Loch Boisdale.[17] Since the enemy warships were far out to sea, and the smaller craft were farther inland, Charles was able for a while to cross the loch mouth unobserved.

But this tactic of manoeuvring, waiting for a chance to break out, brought him close to disaster. As they came in to land, the party was met by a wildly gesticulating Highlander, who told them the enemy was approaching. They backed water rapidly and got under way just as a party of militiamen came over the skyline, heading for the exact spot where they had tried to land.[18]

Further information about Boisdale's arrest at his home now came through via the network of Jacobite sympathisers strung along the prince's trail. The problem was that Boisdale was one of the principal organisers of this royal chain. His capture was a grievous blow, for it meant there was now no hope of remaining on the Long Isle. The heart of the Jacobite underground movement on South Uist had been cut out.[19] In a panic, the crew holed the boat and sank it. Begging only the sails from them, the prince dismissed them, with orders to meet him with another boat at the most northerly part of the island.

The prince and his companions skulked up and down the loch, sleeping in open fields at night, using the boat sails as shelter. In the daytime they would dart in and out of caves, dodging the militia patrols and living off the local bread which they all found nauseating.[20] The area around Loch Boisdale was the wildest part of South Uist, barren and parched, rugged and rocky: 'not a tree, not a dwelling place of any sort, not even a shepherd's hut was to be seen. None of the necessities of life were forthcoming.'[21]

The prince was already in a dreadful physical condition. He described himself later as living 'like a roe on moors and mountains'.[22] The reality was grimmer. He could bear having his legs cut open with briars while he skulked, but found the clouds of midges intolerable. Drawn to his pale skin and reddish colour, the insects bade fair to eat him alive.[23] The prince was unable to resist scratching at their bites; they became infected and flared up as boils and welts. Ever afterwards the prince bore scars from his encounter with the midges.

But there were worse perils than insects. The prince was in deadly danger now, with his living space becoming daily truncated as the Hanoverian net tightened. The last straw was the landing of Captain Caroline Scott – another of Cumberland's desperadoes in military uniform[24] – barely a mile from his hiding place. This was a moment of supreme jeopardy. Not surprisingly, there was further panic. The prince was convinced that he was surrounded.[25] According to the stories of hostile critics, it was at this point that he contemplated surrender to General Campbell.[26] This is unlikely. It does not square with the prince's personality. Much more authentic-sounding is O'Sullivan's tale that he refused to flee before he had packed up his meat supply and taken it with him – an echo of the obstinacy he habitually displayed over the artillery and baggage in the '45 campaign itself.[27]

It is difficult to exaggerate the peril the prince found himself in. He could not escape by sea, Scott was on top of him, and Fergusson was combing the island. There were redcoats to the south and black-coated militiamen to the north. The prince decided to head north, taking only O'Neill with him as companion and Neal MacEachain as guide. At first they would skirt the coast and risk being seen from the sea by the cruisers. Then they would strike inland, hoping to break through the cordon with the help of MacDonald sympathisers.[28]

Hugh MacDonald of Armadale, in command of the government militia in South Uist, was one of these secret sympathisers and had already engaged his stepdaughter Flora MacDonald to help the prince. In clandestine messages he had suggested to Charles Edward a possible means of escape to Skye.[29] Hitherto the prince had not thought himself to be in grave enough danger to fall in with Armadale's far-fetched proposal. Now it seemed to be his only chance.

The prince, O'Neill and MacEachain crossed the moor on the night of 21 June.[30] At this time of year in the Hebrides there were no more than five hours of darkness. This night there was also a full moon. At Ormaclett, three miles from Milton, on the west side of South Uist, they came to a summer shieling where the twenty-three-year-old Flora MacDonald was waiting.[31] The prince's identity was revealed to her. She set a dish of cream before him on the table. Then O'Neill explained her stepfather's plan to get the prince safely over to Skye. This involved his dressing up in women's clothes and pretending to be Flora's servant.[32]

It seems that Miss MacDonald was at first taken aback by the audacity of the scheme and declined to be involved. The prince won her round. Though the best efforts of romantic novelists have not been able to work up anything remotely sexual between Charles and Flora, it is clear that the famous magnetism once again did its work.[33] With wit and charm the prince patiently explained the sheer plausibility of the idea. Flora already had a passport to go to Skye and she was known to be returning within days. The authorities would certainly become suspicious if she asked for a passport for a manservant to accompany her, but would not jib at a female attendant. Finally persuaded, Flora set out for the Atlantic shore of Benbecula to enlist the help of Lady Clanranald.[34] The prince and his comrades meanwhile skulked on a hill three miles from Corradale.

The start of Flora MacDonald's errand of mercy did not augur well for its future success. She and her servant were stopped at a ford by a militia patrol and detained until morning for questioning by the senior officer. Since she knew this was her stepfather, Flora kept her head and waited patiently for his arrival.[35]

When Hugh MacDonald came to the ford, he immediately released his stepdaughter and made out the necessary passports, one for MacEachain, the other for a maidservant called Betty Burke. Flora then continued her journey and reached Lady Clanranald's. There she explained her mission. The two women set about preparing 'Betty Burke's' clothes.[36]

The delay at the ford meant that the message Flora had promised to send the prince did not arrive. Charles Edward grew anxious. At eight o'clock on the evening of 22 June he sent MacEachain to find out what was going on.[37] MacEachain was also detained at the ford and then released at MacDonald of Armadale's orders.

As he lay concealed under a rock, the prince's anxieties mounted. Finally MacEachain made contact with Flora. It was arranged that she would meet the prince at Rossinish.[38] MacEachain returned to the hideout. A mightily relieved Charles Edward broke cover and came running to meet him.[39]

The prince had not, as he feared, been betrayed. But now he faced the prospect of getting to Rossinish across closely-guarded country, with a price of £30,000 on his head. A small fishing boat in Loch Skipport took the prince and his two companions back to Ouia. Finding no one there, they spent an uncomfortable night, then persuaded the fishermen to row them at first light across to the nearest point of Benbecula.[40]

Once landed, the prince and O'Neill fell asleep from sheer exhaustion. Neal MacEachain took a walk and found that they had been landed on a tidal island; there was an arm of the sea between them and the rest of Benbecula.[41] In some alarm he went back to rouse the prince and give him the bad news. This provoked all Charles's latent paranoia. He raged at the boatmen who, he claimed, had deliberately marooned him on a desert island to die of starvation.[42]

MacEachain calmed him down and offered to swim across and bring back a boat. At this moment they spotted a rock protruding from the middle of the water, indicating that it was possibly shallow there. Just as MacEachain began to take off his clothes ready for the swim, with rain pelting down on him, the tide began visibly to ebb. In less than three quarters of an hour it was possible for them to walk across to the main part of Benbecula without even wetting the soles of their shoes. It is indicative of Charles Edward's state of mind that MacEachain describes him as being as pleased about his escape from the tidal island as if he had got clean away to France.[43]

They waited until nightfall before pressing on to Rossinish, taking temporary shelter in a hut, pushed to the extremes of hunger and tiredness.[44] They got some milk and cheese from some of Clanranald's tenants by telling them that they were Irish refugees from Culloden. The hut was singularly uncomfortable, so low and narrow that once again the prince had to creep into it on his belly.[45]

Once night came down, they started along the trail to Rossinish. The rain and wind were driving in their teeth, and they could see no more than three yards ahead. Charles himself lost his footing at almost every other step in some ditch or mire. He was forever losing his shoes in the boggy ground; the luckless MacEachain then had to fish them out.[46]

Their ordeal was not ended when they reached the rendezvous point around midnight. There was no sign of Flora and Lady Clanranald, but the countryside was stiff with militiamen. Again the prince raged at his bad luck. A cow-herd took pity on the dirty, bespattered figures and lodged them in his bothy a mile or so away. The prince sent O'Neill on to Nunton to find out what had happened to his two would-be female deliverers.[47]

At dawn they were rousted out by the cow-herd's wife with news that the militiamen were coming to the bothy to buy milk. The day that followed was one of the worst in the prince's life. All that morning he lay in the partial shelter of a rock, while the rain teemed on him and the midges gnawed at him. The prince emitted hideous cries of agony: 'it is almost inexpressible what torment the Prince suffered under that unhappy rock which had neither height nor breadth to cover him from the rain which poured down on him so thick,' MacEachain related.[48]

At the end of a long morning, the cow-herd's child brought word that the militiamen had moved on. The prince returned to the bothy. A roaring peat fire was made up. The prince was stripped of his clothes, which were hung up to dry. His spirits revived as he sat down by the fire in his undershirt, 'as merry and hearty as if he was in the best room at Whitehall'.[49]

The pitiful meal he now sat down to showed the prince in typical form: irascible, feeling victimised one minute, humorous and compassionate the next. The cow-herd's wife set before him something she described as cream but was in fact scalding milk. In his voracious eagerness, the prince burnt his hand on the hot liquid. Charles jumped up angrily, berating the woman for a vile witch who had burned him deliberately. MacEachain, still unused to the violence of the prince's mood swings, offered to paddle the woman with an oar that was lying handy. At this the compassion in Charles Edward at once surfaced, and he forbade MacEachain to do any such thing.[50]

While the prince slept on the floor in his plaid, a message arrived from O'Neill: rendezvous at Flora MacDonald's house in North Uist.[51] This plan was changed almost as soon as it was suggested because of the reluctance of her kinsman Baleshair.[52] Impatiently the prince summoned O'Neill to him. He promised to come next day with Flora and Lady Clanranald.

On the morning of 27 June two MacDonalds arrived with a boat.[53]

The prince set out for Rossinish. That afternoon he finally met up with the two Jacobite ladies, escorted by O'Neill.[54] In the bothy where he had stayed on his first night in the Long Island, the prince and the two young MacDonalds cooked hearts, liver and kidneys for their guests (also present were Lady Clanranald's daughter Peggy and Flora's brother Milton MacDonald).[55]

Half-way through supper the alarming news came in that General Campbell had landed not far from Nunton with a force of 1,500 men. With him were Captains Scott and Fergusson. The supper party fled to the boats in great confusion. Crossing Loch Uskavagh, they finished their meal at sunrise in another bothy.[56] At 8 a.m. Lady Clanranald went home to face the wrath of General Campbell.[57] Shortly afterwards she and her husband were arrested for harbouring 'the Pretender's son'.[58]

In the bothy on Loch Uskavagh, O'Neill – whose conduct had not been entirely pleasing to the prince – finally got his marching orders.[59] Flora's passport specified one manservant only. Since MacEachain knew Gaelic and O'Neill did not, the Irishman was the obvious choice to be dropped from the party.[60] Charles Edward went through the motions of pleading O'Neill's case, but Flora, who had apparently been the object of some effusive Irish gallantry, was adamant. O'Neill departed with the intention of rejoining the prince in Skye. In circumstances not entirely easy to follow, he fell into the hands of the brutal Fergusson. Lucky to escape a flogging at the barbarous captain's hands, O'Neill was taken prisoner to Edinburgh Castle.[61]

The party that departed for the legendary passage 'over the sea to Skye' thus consisted of the prince, Flora MacDonald and Neal MacEachain.[62] The prince donned his 'Betty Burke' disguise before they pushed off into the Minch. Stripping to his breeches, he put on a light-coloured quilted petticoat, a calico gown and a mantle of dull camlet, together with suitable shoes and stockings and a whig and cap to cover his entire head and face.[63] He wanted to carry a pistol under his petticoat, but Flora objected. If he was searched, such a weapon would give him away. To which the prince replied in high spirits: 'Indeed, Miss, if we shall happen with any that will go so narrowly to work in searching me as what you mean, they will certainly discover me at any rate.'[64]

There were last-minute alarums. While waiting for dark on this rainy evening, they were forced to put out their fire and dive into the heather when four patrol boats came into the loch. But no landing parties came ashore. At last, as the sun set, they put to sea.[65]

To begin with they had to row on a windless sea. The prince sang songs to the rowers to buoy up their spirits. Among this repertoire were 'The 29th of May' and, inevitably, 'The king shall enjoy his own again'.[66] Charles cradled the head of the sleeping Flora and protected her from being trodden on when one of the sailors clambered over her in the dark to trim the sail.[67]

Around midnight a westerly gale sprang up. There was heavy rain, followed by a thick mist that robbed them of the sight of land.[68] As the mist dissipated in the early morning sunshine, they found themselves off the point of Vaternish in north-western Skye. They pulled into a cleft in the cliff-wall to eat a breakfast of bread and butter, washed down with fresh water dripping from an overhanging rock.[69] They were unaware that this part of the island was infested with troops and militiamen. As they pulled round the point of Vaternish after the hour's meal break, a pair of sentries called on them to come ashore. The crew heaved strongly on the oars. The troops fired a volley. Other Macleods, as many as fifteen, came running. They too fired at the disappearing boat. Altogether the prince counted between twenty and thirty shots.[70]

This brush with the Macleods alarmed Flora MacDonald greatly. She was aware now, if not before, of what a grim business this manhunt was. Seeing her despondency, the prince spoke words of comfort: 'Don't be afraid, Miss, we won't be taken yet. You see it is low water, and before they can launch their boats over that rough shore, we will get in below those high rocks and they will lose sight of us.' The prince proved a good prophet. This was exactly what happened.[71]

After this episode they rowed across the bay of Loch Snizort to the longer peninsula of Trotternish. It was about 2 p.m. when they came ashore at a beach north of Kilbride.[72] Immediately Flora and MacEachain set off for Lady Margaret MacDonald's home at nearby Monkstadt, leaving the prince with the boatmen on the shore.[73]

Flora's arrival at Monkstadt threw Lady MacDonald into consternation. She was a convinced Jacobite herself, but could not compromise her husband Sir Alexander MacDonald, presently at Fort Augustus with Cumberland. In her house at that very moment was a Macleod lieutenant of militia. The prince was inches away from capture. If he was apprehended, it would be said that Lady Margaret had betrayed him. How to square the circle?

She sent for her faithful associate Captain Roy MacDonald and explained the situation to him.[74] With her factor MacDonald of Kingburgh they held a hasty consultation in the garden while Flora MacDonald kept the Macleod lieutenant talking inside the house.

The three MacDonalds in the garden decided that the only feasible escape route was across country to Portree; meanwhile the prince should be lodged at Kingsburgh's house that night.[75]

MacEachain set off for the beach to tell the prince that Kingsburgh was coming to take him to his house. Kingsburgh appeared on the beach shortly afterwards with a bottle of wine and some bread. After refreshing himself with the bread and wine, the prince set out with Kingsburgh to walk the seven miles to his house.[76]

On the road they were overtaken by a mounted party, consisting of Flora MacDonald and another MacDonald lady with her maid and manservant. This was the moment when 'Betty Burke' came closest to discovery. As a female impersonator, the prince left a lot to be desired. The way he moved, his long-striding walk, his very tallness of stature and the general gaucherie of the way he arranged his skirts would have given him away, had not the universal prejudice against the Irish worked in his favour. The prevalent notion that Irishwomen were tatterdemalion, hoydenish hobbledehoys predisposed the Scots to be satisfied with the outrageous story that this was an ill-bred female peasant from the bogs.[77] The MacDonald maid contented herself with a few derogatory comments on 'Betty Burke's' lack of feminine refinements before riding on.

Farther along the road, the prince and Kingsburgh ran into a crowd of people returning from Sunday services at the meeting-house. These god-fearing folk were also appalled at the ungenteel amount of leg 'Betty' displayed when lifting her petticoats to step across a stream. Eventually the tension became too much for MacEachain. 'For God's sake, sir,' he hissed at the prince, 'take care what you are doing, for you will certainly discover yourself!'[78]

On arrival at his house, Kingsburgh revealed to his wife that the 'odd muckle trallup' he had brought home was the prince.[79] At first his wife was shocked and dismayed. Then her concern shifted to the more mundane consideration of whether she had proper food to set before a prince, and whether she was worthy to sit at the same table as him.[80]

The prince's informality and charm soon put her at ease. After a supper of roasted eggs and bread and butter, the prince called for brandy: 'for I have learned in my skulking to take a hearty dram.'[81] After draining a bumper with a panache that would not have disgraced the most hardened toper, Charles took out a cracked pipe and asked for tobacco. Kingsburgh provided him with a clay pipe and a pouch of tobacco. The prince sat smoking and drinking with great cheerfulness and merriment. Kingsburgh reported that his attitude was not like that of a man in danger but more that of an amateur thespian who had put on women's clothes for a diversion.[82] That the prince was feeling cheerful again is clearly shown by his answer to a query from Kingsburgh. The MacDonald factor asked what he would have done if he (the factor) had not been at Monkstadt that day. Charles Edward replied: 'Why, sir, you could not avoid being at Monkstadt this day, for Providence ordered you to be there on my account.'[83]

The prince slept late. Next day Mrs MacDonald requested a lock of his hair as a keepsake. After some demure hesitation, Flora MacDonald sat at Charles's bedside and snipped the lock.[84] The prince assured his hosts this was only the first of many favours they would receive from him once he was restored.

It was late in the day when the prince set out for Portree. He dined, sipped tea, drank wine, and even asked for some snuff which Kingsburgh gave him but told him to keep in his woman's muff.[85] Flora and MacEachain had set out earlier to travel to Portree by road.[86]

Kingsburgh accompanied the prince part of the way on the cross-country trail. In a wood Charles changed out of the 'Betty Burke' outfit into Highland dress.[87] The gown and petticoats were burned by the Kingsburghs to remove incriminating evidence. For the rest of the route to Portree the prince had a lad called MacQueen along with him as guide.[88] They traipsed along the byways in pouring rain. At the inn in Portree he met up with Flora and MacEachain and Donald Roy MacDonald, the third conspirator in the garden.

Final plans were hatched for a pre-arranged crossing to Raasay Island.[89] The prince changed his shirt in the inn and sat down with his comrades to a meal of roasted fish, cheese, bread and butter.[90] After two hours in the inn, with the rain still flooding down, the prince was inclined to spend the night in Portree. His companions said this was too dangerous and argued him out of it.[91]

There was one last-minute hitch. The prince bought a roll of tobacco from the landlord for fourpence ha'penny. He paid with a sixpence and seemed disinclined to wait for his change. Donald Roy warned him that such aristocratic hauteur amid the poverty of Skye would attract immediate suspicion. The prince took up his three ha'pence change.[92]

Charles Edward was now leaving the sheltering custody of the MacDonalds for the uncertain care of the Macleods. There was both genuine emotion and some anxiety in his leave-taking. Not surprisingly, he, MacEachain and Donald Roy polished off a bottle of whisky before leaving the inn.[93] Then he bade a courtly farewell to his saviour Flora. 'For all that has happened, I hope, Madam, we shall meet in St James's yet.'[94] But they were not destined to meet again, in London or any other place.

At dawn on the first of July the prince left the shores of Skye for Raasay Island, accompanied by the leading Raasay Macleods, Murdoch, Malcolm and John. On Raasay the effects of Cumberland's devastation of the Highlands were only too plain to see. There had been three hundred cottages on the island. Not one was left standing. Cumberland's licentious soldiery had pillaged, raped and murdered their way from one end of the island to the other. When told of Cumberland's atrocities, the prince found them hard to believe: such actions were against all known laws of civilised behaviour.[95]

On arrival in Raasay, the prince slept for two hours in a small hut. Again it was of the variety where one had to stoop to enter.[96] Then he dined avidly on a meal of roast kid, butter and cream.[97] He was in euphoric mood, seemingly much taken with the idea of redemption through suffering: 'Sure. Providence does not design this for nothing.'[98]

But it was too early for self-congratulation. News of his presence on Skye was abroad almost as soon as he had cleared the island. The flight to Raasay already seemed like a false move. It was too easy to be trapped on this barren island. Next day the prince decided to take his chances back on Skye. While he was arranging this with his comrades, a lookout gave notice of the approach of a local pedlar, strongly suspected of being a Hanoverian spy. The Macleods at once decided to kill him. Immediately the prince's merciful and compassionate side was triggered. 'God forbid that we should take any man's life while we can save our own,' he expostulated.[99] Fortunately, the pedlar settled the argument by passing by at a safe distance.

At 9 o'clock on the evening of 2 July they put to sea again. It was a stormy night, the wind increased to gale force, and even on the short stretch between Raasay and Skye the waves threatened to overwhelm the boat.[100] They made landfall at Nicholson's Rock near Scorobreck, on the north side of Portree harbour.[101] After spending the night and the following day in a cow-byre, the prince set out on the evening of the 3rd for the Mackinnon country. Dismissing the boatmen Charles Edward took Malcolm Macleod alone with him and headed towards Strath. This time he took the alias of Lewie Caw, allegedly Captain Macleod's servant.[102]

To avoid Sligachan, then occupied by the enemy, they skirted the top of Loch Sligachan and made for Elgol by the circuitous route via Strath Mor. It was a hard night's marching, with difficult and treacherous conditions underfoot.[103] At one point the prince sank into a bog right up to his thighs. Macleod had to pull him out.[104] After more than twelve hours' dour marching, they reached Elgol in the early morning. It was as well that the prince, at Macleod's urging, had perfected his disguise, for outside the village they were stopped and questioned by three militiamen. Macleod and the prince had already decided to make a fight of it if the militiamen became suspicious.[105]

Their first port of call in Elgol was the house of Captain John Mackinnon, Malcolm Macleod's brother-in-law. Here they were fed and their clothes changed. With difficulty Macleod persuaded a servant girl to wash the feet of his 'servant'.[106] While the Mackinnons arranged for his onward journey, the prince dandled a young Mackinnon child on his knee and carried him on his back. 'I hope this child may be a captain in my service yet,' he remarked.[107] John Mackinnon's reply was to weep silently.[108]

Word of the prince's presence was brought to the old Mackinnon chief. Malcolm Macleod at once resigned the management of the prince's affairs to the Mackinnons and prepared to depart.[109] At about 9 p.m. Old Mackinnon, Captain John and four boatmen embarked with the prince for the mainland. Some enemy sails were seen on the horizon but Charles refused to delay his departure.[110] As if to confirm his trust in Providence, the wind veered and the ships stood away. They made the short crossing to Mallaig without incident.

The prince's devious circling path through the islands was over. From now on his flight would be through the burns and glens of the mainland.

21

His Finest Hour

(July–September 1746)

By now the authorities in London and their bloodthirsty acolytes were lashing themselves into frenzies of indignation and frustration at their inability to track down 'the Young Pretender'. Nearly three months had passed since Culloden. Ancram, Lockhart, Scott and Fergusson had spread fire and sword across the Highlands, yet still the major prize eluded them.[1] Cumberland himself stayed in Scotland until mid-July, vainly hoping to crown his triumph in battle with the capture of the 'Pretender's son'.[2] But although the Whigs were often hot on the prince's trail, they were always just short of catching him.[3]

Sometimes the Hanoverians rationalised their failure to capture their prey by alleging that Charles had already left Scotland. To the obvious objection that in that case he would have been seen in Paris, they replied that he must have escaped via Norway.[4] More often, they simply threw greater and greater resources into the chase.[5] If anything, after Cumberland's departure, his successor Lord Albemarle intensified the hunt, avid for the prestige of succeeding where his royal master had failed. On the mainland, in addition to the Campbell militia and Loudoun's regulars who made criss-crossing patrols, Albemarle placed a chain of sentries between Inverness and Inverary at the important passes, so that the chances of Charles's slipping through their fingers were considered remote.[6]

Whig money was firmly placed on the islands as Charles Edward's most likely hiding place. Almost Cumberland's last act before leaving Scotland was to order Albemarle to bottle up Skye, where the prince was now definitely placed (in fact he was already on the mainland).[7] Albermarle followed this up by sending search parties to every single Hebridean island.[8] He vowed he would not leave Fort Augustus until all hope of catching the Young Pretender was gone.[9]

Bit by bit Albemarle narrowed the gap between pursuers and pursued. Almost without exception, those who helped Charles Edward on his way were taken prisoner and questioned closely: Donald Macleod, O'Neill, Flora MacDonald, Kingsburgh, Malcolm Macleod, Old Mackinnon.[10] To a man (or woman) they testified that their motivation was common humanity and that they scorned the £30,000 reward on the prince's head. Flora MacDonald testified eloquently that she would have helped anyone so deeply in distress, not just the Stuart prince.[11] Kingsburgh spoke movingly of a fugitive without meat and sleep for two days and nights, whom he had come upon sitting dejectedly on a rock, beaten upon by the rain and, when that ceased, eaten up by flies. The fugitive was 'meagre, ill-coloured and overrun with the scab'.[12]

No threats of imprisonment (or worse) could shake the Highlanders' stories or drag from them a scintilla of useful information about the secret network of sympathisers that took the prince ever onwards out of the hands of his pursuers. As for the £30,000, that was looked on by the overwhelming majority with unconcealed contempt. Eighteenth-century Europe was much struck with this aspect of the prince's successful flight in the heather. Diderot, arguing for man's natural goodness, later cited the refusal of the Highlanders to give up the prince for £30,000 (a million-pound reward in our terms and the wealth of Croesus by any standards) as his most telling instance.[13]

The failure of the Whigs to locate and capture the prince during his five-month escapade has sometimes been set down to the London government's reluctance to apprehend him; a decision as to his fate would be fraught and embarrassing, the argument goes. Such a view cannot be sustained from the evidence.[14] It is true that the prince himself thought that if captured he would be in more danger of assassination by poison or 'accidental' death than public execution.[15] But in this he underrated the threat to his person. The London government had shown by its virtual suspension of due legal process in Scotland, and by the unleashing of Cumberland's military rabble, that it was determined to exterminate once and for all the hydra of Jacobitism. And what better way to do this than by burying the hydra's 'immortal head'? The execution of Charles Edward would produce a trauma from which the Jacobite movement could never recover. And precisely this consummation was both urged and expected by leading Whig luminaries. Horace Mann was asked by the Prince de Craon what would happen to Charles Edward if he was taken. 'He would be beheaded,' said Mann. 'Fie, fie, a king's grandson!' Craon remonstrated.'Well, Prince,' Mann replied, 'it is just that fact that would cause his destruction.'[16]

The first days on the mainland might have been a time for sombre reflection by the prince on his possible fate, since for three days and nights he and his party lay in the open air.[17] They could get no help or shelter because the presence of a militia encampment at Eansaig on the south of Loch Nevis intimidated their potential supporters. By the fourth day Old Mackinnon had had enough. He set off in search of a better refuge.

Chafing at the inactivity, the prince, John Mackinnon and the three boatmen launched the boat for an ill-advised reconnaissance of Loch Nevis. They were spotted by five militiamen on the shore and ordered to put in to land for identification.[18] The prince was all for making a fight of it, as they were roughly equal in numbers.[19] But John Mackinnon took command and ordered his men to pull away. He told them to have their muskets primed but not to fire unless he gave the word. If firing commenced, they could not leave a single militiaman alive.[20]

It did not come to that. They quickly outdistanced their pursuers and put in to a wooded shore. From a hill the prince watched the militiamen give up the chase and return to their station. Then he lay down on the hillside and slept for three hours.[21]

They re-embarked and rowed across to a small island on the north shore, a mile away from the house of Scotus, one of the luminaries of clan Donald.[22] John Mackinnon went ahead to sound Old Clan-ranald, who was known to be living there. The Clanranald chief was appalled to find the prince once again in his domains.'What muckle devil has brought him into this country again?' he cried, and went on to refuse all help.[23] The best he could suggest was refuge on Rona – an even more desolate island than Raasay. Both he and Mackinnon understood that this was code for an undeviating refusal to become involved. Rona was a green island with no cover; not a single sheep or goat could escape detection there, let alone a man.

Disappointed, the prince returned to Mallaig. With Captain John and Old Mackinnon, Charles walked by night to Morar Cross, a mile south of the bridge over the Morar river.[24] Here they found MacDonald of Morar, who was now living in a bothy, since his house had been burned down. The prince was fed on cold salmon and taken to a nearby cave to sleep.[25]

Morar meanwhile went in search of Young Clanranald. When he returned after an 'unsuccessful search', his entire manner was changed. It was clear that he had been 'got at' by Old Clanranald.[26]

At this point the prince became distressed. All the feelings of persecution and betrayal that had been palliated by the intense clan loyalty so far burst out anew. Plaintively he asked the Mackinnons not to behave to him as the Clanranalds had.[27] The two Mackinnons quickly reassured him and calmed him. Then they took stock. Perhaps a return to Borrodale was the best idea. The prince agreed. But he had not finished with the pusillanimous Morar. To show his contempt, he offered Morar a guinea to get intelligence from Fort Augustus. It would normally have been considered a gross insult to offer a clansman money. Nothing abashed, Morar replied that he could get a pedlar to carry out the assignment but that a guinea was too much to pay him. 'Well then, sir,' said the prince, summoning all his royal hauteur, 'if you think so, give him the one half and keep the other to yourself.'[28]

They reached Borrodale in the early morning of 10 July. This time their contact was Angus MacDonald – again a man reduced to living in a bothy after Cumberland's soldiers had burned down his house.[29] MacDonald of Borrodale was a fervent Jacobite. There was no Clanranald ambivalence here. He threw himself with gusto into the task of saving the prince. Seeing him in good hands, the Mackinnons took their leave.[30]

At Borrodale the prince lay hidden, first in a wood, later, after news of the capture of the Mackinnons, in a cave.[31] Meanwhile Borrodale sent for a man particularly trusted by the prince, Alexander of Glenaladale, a major in Clanranald's regiment.[32] Glenaladale joined the prince on the 16th at 'Macleod's Cove', his hideout on a high precipice in the woods of Borrodale.[33] From Glenaladale the prince heard for the first time the true story of his losses after Culloden – they were much less than he had been led to believe.[34]

Glenaladale was both a devoted Jacobite (he was still recovering from the wounds he had received at Culloden) and a highly efficient organiser. He had heard from Borrodale's brother-in-law Angus MacEachine that the prince's presence in the neighbourhood was suspected. The Hanoverians' relentless pursuit was paying off. They now knew the prince had slipped through their net in the Hebrides and had traced his devious trail through Raasay and Skye.[35] Accordingly, Glenaladale suggested a place of concealment he knew of near Meoble in the Braes of Morar.[36] He sent Borrodale's son to reconnoitre the place and report on its safety.[37]

Before this son, Ranald, had returned, Glenaladale and his son John were alarmed to see warships and a flotilla of small boats lying off the nearby coast.[38] Without waiting for Ranald to come back, the prince started for MacEachine's refuge. As Borrodale and Glenaladale and his son walked with the prince, they met up with MacEachine. He assured them that Young Clanranald was only a few miles away and advised them of a safe hideaway he had prepared for the prince. As it was now too late in the day to go to MacEachine's secret lair, they pressed on to Meoble.[39] During the night spent there, they laid future plans. Since General Campbell was in Loch Nevis with a large amphibious force, the first thing was to spy out his movements. Next, Borrodale would lay in a store of food for a prolonged concealment.[40]

The 18th of July was a black day for the prince. Borrodale returned earlier than expected with the news that they were surrounded.[41] Hearing that the prince was in Moidart, the authorities had acted quickly to establish a chain of military camps and sentry posts from the head of Loch Eil to the head of Loch Hourn.[42] Linking up with Young Clanranald was now out of the question.

Bold tactics were called for. They decided to skirt the line of forts and probe the cordon until they found a weak spot to break through. They would then head for a northern port, possibly Poolewe.

Safety dictated a reduction in numbers. The prince went on, accompanied only by Glenaladale and his brother and Borrodale's son.[43] By midday they had climbed to 1,800 feet and reached the top of Sgurr Mhuidhe, three miles north-west of Glenfinnan, where the Stuart standard had been raised nearly a year before. Here Glenaladale's brother went on to Glenfinnan for news. They arranged to meet that night on the heights of Sgurr Coireachan.[44]

The prince's party, now reduced to three, were at Fraoch Beinn to the north of Glenfinnan by 2 p.m. Falling in with some of Glenaladale's kinsmen, they discovered that the redcoats were already systematically criss-crossing the country around which they had tightened the cordon. They had reached the head of Loch Arkaig and would soon be athwart the prince's track.[45]

It was time for a quick change of plans. The local pathfinder Donald Cameron of Glenpean was sent for. If anyone could guide them out of Moidart, it was he. But events were moving too fast even for swift improvisation. The remorseless dragnet soon reached the foot of the hill on which they stood waiting. It was too late to wait for Glenpean.

Under cover of darkness they struck out in thick mist. By great good fortune, at about 11 p.m. they accidentally stumbled across Glenpean in a hollow between two hills at Coire Odhar in the Braes of Morar.[46]

All night they walked with Glenpean. At times they were so close to the guards along the cordon that they could hear every word they spoke.⁴⁷ They wound their way by precipitous paths to a hill overlooking Arkaig. There was a militia camp not one mile away, but the hill on which they lay had already been searched. Unbelievably, they were joined on the hillside during the day by Glenaladale's brother, whose mountain-man's instinct took him straight to them after the failed rendezvous at Coireachan.⁴⁸

At night they continued their trek to the north and reached Coire-nan-Gall at 1 a.m. Glenpean knew of a hideout at the head of Loch Quoich a mile away, so they holed up there during the daytime of 20 July while Glenaladale's son went to try to get some food.⁴⁹ They had nothing with them but a little oatmeal and dared not even light a fire to make oatcake.⁵⁰

This was the supreme moment of peril for the prince during his entire wanderings, more dangerous even than the predicament he found himself in on South Uist when Flora MacDonald rescued him. Albemarle's men were ranged in three parallel lines, ten or twelve miles apart: one from Fort William to Inverness; another running through Mull, Strontian, Glenfinnan and Loch Arkaig; the third from Lochleven through Rannoch to Fort Augustus.⁵¹ The cordon was particularly tight where the prince was just now. From Loch Eil to Loch Hourn there were camps at half-mile intervals and sentries posted within shout of each other.⁵²

The danger was not just something that would be encountered once they tried to break through the net. Glenaladale's brother returned at about 3 p.m. from his scout for food with two cheeses and the news that a hundred redcoats were swarming up the other side of the hill. There was nothing for it but to sit tight and hope that the searchers missed them in their 'fast place'.

So it turned out. Despite a meticulous search, the troops failed to uncover the hideout.⁵³ At 8 p.m. the prince and party were able to strike north again. At the top of the hill of Druim Cosaidh, they saw the enemy's camp fires ahead of them. Creeping close to the sentry posts, they passed by in silence, near enough to hear every word of their conversation.⁵⁴ They repeated the performance on the next hill in Glen Cosaidh.⁵⁵

They were now through the cordon. But having narrowly escaped Scylla, the prince was almost taken by Charybdis. He was walking between Glenpean and Glenaladale when he slipped on a narrow sloping path.⁵⁶ He tumbled down to the edge of a cliff, over which there was a hundred-foot drop. Breaking his fall by twining his legs around a bush after his body had hurtled past it, the prince hung over the edge for a fraught few seconds until help came.[57] Quickly the two Highlanders grabbed hold of him. Had they not pulled him up, he would have plunged over the precipice to certain death or fatal injury.[58] The prince described the look on Glenpean's face as one of 'mortal terror'.[59]

They took shelter in a steep glen at the head of Loch Hourn in 'hollow ground covered with long heather and branches of young birch trees'.[60] They were restricted to a daily ration of cheese and oatmeal, washed down with fresh water.[61]

By this time Glenpean the pathfinder was beyond the country he knew intimately and into the unknown, with only his woodcraft to guide him. To their alarm, they found that they had been perilously close to two more of the enemy's camps.[62] It was vital to find a new guide, one who knew the country from here to Poolewe. They set out at night under a full moon; for all that, the prince described it as 'the darkest night ever in my life I travelled'.[63]

In the early morning they found themselves near Glenshiel, scene of the Jacobite defeat in the rising of 1719.[64] This was Seaforth country. After crossing the Shiel, they spent the whole day on the hillside north of the glen. It was oppressively hot.[65] The rigours of the weather found some compensation in the cheese, butter and milk they purchased from a crofter called Gilchrist MacGrath.[66] But MacGrath disappointed them with his news about Poolewe: there had been a French ship there but it had now left.

After abandoning his plan to make for Poolewe, the prince found himself at sea in another sense. Glenpean confessed himself lost. Providentially, and almost on cue, Donald MacDonald, a Glengarry man, fell in with them and offered to guide the prince to a refuge in Glenmoriston.[67] No further use to the prince, Glenpean took his leave.

Meeting the Glengarry guide was only the first of two pieces of great good fortune the prince enjoyed on that sweltering 22 July. Striking east through Glen Cluanie at nightfall, they had gone no more than a quarter of a mile when Glenaladale announced that he had lost his purse, containing forty louis d'or. Glenaladale turned back for the MacGrath place, suspecting the crofter's son (rightly) of being the culprit. The prince was left with MacDonald of Glengarry, crouching by the trail in the dark. While he was there a Hanoverian officer and three redcoats went by. It seemed certain the two parties would have run into each other in the normal course of events but for the purse incident. There was not even any contact between the redcoats and Glenaladale as he returned with the restored purse; some instinct brought him back by another trail.[68]

They walked until ten o'clock next morning, then rested in another tried and tested bolt-hole on the hillside above Strathclunie. Again the midges proved troublesome. The prince got his followers to swathe him with heather from head to toe for protection.[69] They set out again in the afternoon.

They had not proceeded far when they heard the unmistakable roll and crackle of gunfire. Turning northward, they climbed a high hill between Loch Cluanie and Glen Affrich. The rain began to pelt down heavily. Unable to explore the provenance of the gunfire further, they took refuge in an 'open cave' – no more than a niche in the rock. Drenched to the skin, the prince endured another night of discomfort, unable either to lie down or sleep.[70]

This turned out to be the dark night before the fine day of changing fortune. The Glengarry men were as good as their boast. On 24 July they delivered the prince into the hands of the 'Seven Men of Glenmoriston' at Coiraghoth in the Braes of Glenmoriston.[71] They[72] were much more indicative of the true sentiments of the Grants than was the leadership, with its ambivalent response. After Culloden, these devoted Jacobites had taken an oath to carry on the fight by guerrilla warfare in the heather.[73] Their warrior credentials were impeccable. Three weeks before the prince came into their care, they had ambushed a party of seven redcoats, killed two and put the rest to flight.[74] The fact that they had drunk themselves senseless on wine captured from the redcoats particularly endeared them to the prince; as did their ruthlessness in shooting dead a Strathspey man who was among the Grants as a spy. Having stuck his head on a tree on the high road three miles from Fort Augustus, they were beyond the pale of Hanoverian mercy. The prince could therefore be at perfect ease among them, knowing they could not betray him.

The week that followed was a halcyon period in the prince's life. He was lodged in the kind of a cave that had some of the qualities of a fairy-tale grotto, in stark contrast to some of the caverns in which he had recently taken refuge.[75] Within this grotto a wimpling stream of clear water ran by his bedside.[76] The prince was 'as comfortably lodged as if he had been in a royal palace',[77] He was provided with mutton, venison, butter, cheese and whisky from the expert foraging of the Seven Men.

The only thing the Glenmoriston men insisted on was that they, not the prince, were firmly in charge.[78] This point was early made to the prince with some sharpness by the one man in their number who could speak English.[79] By this time the prince had mastered the elements of Gaelic.[80] But he could not follow all the nuances of his comrades' conversation. The Seven Men tried to limit their discourse to simple things, but when complex information had to be conveyed, Glenaladale acted as interpreter.[81]

The prince's new protectors were masters of their immediate environment. When, after three days, they learned that Captain 'Black' Campbell's militia was encamped just four miles away, they moved the prince to another grotto 'no less romantic than the former' for the next four days.[82] Finally, on 1 August, fearing eventual discovery because of the now dense infestation of the black-coated militia in the surrounding area, they moved north to the Braes of Strathglass, again travelling by night and resting by day. By this time the prince was determined to have another shot at possible French shipping in Poolewe. After three nights in a 'sheally hut', he sent two of the Seven Men forward to Poolewe to reconnoitre.[83]

The recent long waits, combined with lack of progress towards any specific goal, finally wore down Charles Edward's patience. While his two envoys were away, the prince's nerves, which had been stretched taut while dodging through the cordon, snapped. Stress brought with it the usual self-destructive behaviour. Suddenly he ordered his companions to march on, without waiting for news from Poolewe. They refused, both on the grounds that their two absent comrades to whom they had sworn an oath were depending on them, and, more relevantly to the prince, that they could not guarantee his safety without the intelligence the absent pair would bring back.

The prince blustered and threatened. But his royal prerogative cut no ice here. Then he threatened to go on hunger strike. The Glenmoriston men hinted at forced feeding if he would not see reason. At this the prince changed gear at his usual lightning speed and capitulated, exclaiming bitterly: 'I find kings and princes must be ruled by their privy council, but I believe there is not in all the world a more absolute privy council than what I have at present.'[84] Significantly, though, there were no further altercations between him and the Glenmoriston men.

On 5 August they moved on to their rendezvous point. At midday they reached Glencannich and spent the rest of the day in a wood. After getting shelter for the night in a neighbouring village, they made an early (2 a.m.) start on the 6th and climbed Beinn Acharain, north-west of Invercarrich; this was the most northerly point of the prince's wanderings on the mainland.[85] Following another night in a 'sheally hut', they were joined by their comrades from Poolewe. These brought back news that a French ship had indeed put in there recently, but had departed after landing two of Louis XV's officers.[86] The two Frenchmen were now scouring Lochiel's country in search of the prince.

This landing at Poolewe was the latest manifestation of a stubborn and determined French effort to rescue the prince, In mid-June Maurepas dispatched two of his most able privateer captains to Scottish waters: Captains Dumont and Anguier, masters respectively of *Le Hardi Mendiant* and *Le Bien Trouvé*.[87] *Le Hardi Mendiant* reached the north-west coast of Scotland early in July and brought back O'Sullivan. Had the prince remained on Raasay, he would have been taken off too.[88] *Le Bien Trouvé* meanwhile landed the French officers the prince now heard of, before being herself captured by HMS *Glasgow*.[89]

When the prince heard of the Frenchmen's presence on Scottish soil, he decided to strike south, hoping to meet them and learn their exact orders from Versailles. On the dark moonless night of 8 August, he and his companions set out for Strathglass and recrossed the Cannich. Once again the prince emerged from a night's march caked with dirt and mud. He could keep up with the doughtiest clansman in the daytime, but at night, not being used to the rough, plashy going underfoot, he often fell in holes and puddles. Since he was wearing a short kilt this left him with dirty thighs and mud-splashed belly.[90]

They reached Fasnakyle in the morning. There the prince remained for three days, well hidden in a wood, while the Glenmoriston men scouted ahead.[91] Hearing that the troops who had been searching for the prince had all been recalled to Fort Augustus, they pressed on in confident mood to the Braes of Glenmoriston, east of Loch Cluanie. It became increasingly clear that the all-out manhunt for the prince had been abandoned.

Why did the London government call off the hunt at this stage, after coming so close to success? Largely this was a triumph of Jacobite disinformation. The cell-like structure of the chain of helpers along the prince's trail preserved secrecy admirably, for very few people knew of his exact whereabouts, and fewer still knew his future intentions. But secrecy was not only preserved in this way. Those taken into custody for abetting Charles Edward played their part: they told plausible stories about his intentions which, however, departed from the truth in significant essentials. Both Flora MacDonald and O'Neill, for example, swore up and down that the prince had crossed to the mainland from Portree.[92] On 27 July he was reported at Badenoch, a month before he reached that spot.[93]

The most subtle form of disinformation was that which mixed genuine intelligence with false, gave a correct time but incorrect place, or vice versa.[94] So, for example, Albemarle was told in September that Charles Edward was hidden underneath the ground in a sort of cave (as he was, in Cluny's cage), but that this was in Mull.[95] A large-scale search party was then sent to Mull, at the very time the prince was departing for France from Loch-nan-Uamh.[96]

The other Jacobite tactic which worked very well was to pretend that the prince had already made his escape. When O'Sullivan arrived in Paris in August, the marquise de Mezières bruited it about that the prince was with him. This was untrue, but the English accepted the story and virtually abandoned the search in the Highlands.[97] Albemarle broke his camp at Fort Augustus and sent the main body of his army south, out of the Highlands.[98] Campbell's Argyllshire militia was marched to Inverary and disbanded. Only Loudoun's regiment and seventeen companies of militia were left north of the Highland line.[99] As to why there was no sign of the prince in France, the usual answer given was French desire to obfuscate.

General Campbell alone disagreed with this analysis. He argued that Charles Edward must still be in Scotland, since it was in the French interest to keep him there as bogeyman as long as possible.[100] The consequence of these divided counsels was that for a long time the Whigs could not make up their minds whether the 'Young Pretender' was still in Scotland.[101] It was 17 September before the authorities had really solid information that the prince was still in the Highlands.[102] But by that time the intelligence was three weeks old and the bird had as good as flown.

The worst danger was in fact over, as the Glenmoriston men surmised. But there were still scouting parties in the Braes of Glengarry. It was thought best to wait until the way ahead was completely clear. The prince spent the day on a hilltop, then moved down to a sheally hut at night. His worst foe at this time was lice. Since he changed his shirt just once a fortnight and slept with his clothes on, it was not surprising that he became louse-ridden.[103]

On the 13th, two of the Glenmoriston men were sent to Loch Arkaig to locate Cameron of Clunes, the pathfinder to the Lochiel country. Next day, finding the Glengarry country apparently clear of troops, the prince and his party strode out well, making excellent progress.[104] After an afternoon start, they passed through Glenmori-

ston, Glenlyne and Glengarry. The river Garry was engorged with
flood water and fording it was difficult. As night came on, the rain
intensified. They spent a miserable vigil in the open, on a hillside
about a mile from the river.[105]

In the morning it was still raining, but a graver problem afflicted
them. They had nothing to eat, and the land round about had
been laid waste and depopulated by Cumberland's marauders. They
pressed on six miles to the Braes of Achnasual. They sheltered from
the rain in another wretched hovel: 'it was raining as heavily within
as without.'[106]

A message arrived from Cameron of Clunes with instructions to
go to a wood two miles away and rendezvous with him there next
day. This turned the tide of their fortunes. As they made their way
to the wood, hunger pains gnawing at their bellies, they espied a fine
red deer stag.[107] This posed a quandary. If they fired at the deer, the
shots might be heard by enemy patrols. For once the prince was
decisive: better a quick death than a slow one, he urged. Fortunately,
the Glenmoriston men were easily as skilled in woodcraft as they
claimed to be. The deer was killed outright with a single shot.[108]

They dragged the carcase to the wood recommended by Cameron
of Clunes and found it an excellent hiding place. Convinced that luck
was running their way, they dispensed with the normal precautions
and built a fire, over which they roasted haunches of venison.[109]

Even as they were gorging themselves, Donald MacDonell of
Lochgarry – the same who had commanded the Glengarry regiment throughout most of the '45 – came in with two of his kinsmen.[110] Lochgarry informed Charles that Lochiel was still alive.
He was amazed by the prince's physical condition. He described him
thus:

> He was then barefooted, had an old black kilt coat on, a plaid
> philabeg and waistcoat, a dirty shirt, a long red beard, a gun in
> his hand and a pistol and dirk by his side. He was very cheerful
> and in health and in my opinion fatter than when he was in
> Inverness.[111]

Next day Cameron of Clunes joined them. With good food inside
them, they trudged on to Loch Arkaig. Here they hid in a wood. The
prince sent messengers to summon Lochiel.[112] Lochgarry had been
urging on the prince ever since he met him that the Stuart standard
should be set up again. Lochgarry guaranteed that his people would
be ready to rise at forty-eight hours' notice; their first objective should
be the surprise and capture of Fort Augustus.[113] The proposal was

not to the prince's liking but he stalled, saying he needed first to hear the opinion of Cluny and Lochiel.

Three days later the Cameron chief's answer arrived. He apologised for not coming himself, but sent his brother Dr Archibald.[114] With Archie Cameron, as well as his kinsman Reverend John, were the three French officers who had been landed from *Le Bien Trouvé*.[115] Next day, in the wood of Torvault opposite Achnacarry House (Lochiel's seat but now a charred ruin after being gutted by Cumberland's men), the prince, incognito as 'Captain Drummond', interviewed the three Frenchmen.[116] M. de Lancize, spokesman for the three, showed him his orders and described the full-scale French rescue attempt. It was clear that, however much Louis XV had disappointed the prince during the '45 itself, he was determined to have the last word by whisking Charles Edward from under the Hanoverian noses.[117] The meeting had positive results. It encouraged the prince to go into hiding in a secure frame of mind, confident that the French were doing their best for him.

It was important now to construct a secure chain of communication with the Scottish west coast, so that there was no repeat of the many missed rescue chances in the half dozen French ships that had already made landfall. Lochgarry, Clunes, Archie Cameron, young Glenaladale and young Borrodale were sent off to arrange this.[118]

Charles Edward seemed beyond harm's way. But complacency nearly led to disaster. At the eleventh hour, by a mere fluke, Albemarle's men came closer to capturing the prince than at any other time.

Two days later, at eight o'clock in the morning, the prince was awakened by one of the Seven Men with news that the enemy was approaching the hut where they lay in Torvault wood.[119] Racing out of the hut, the prince and his eight companions took up position on the hill of Meall-an-Tagraidh above the wood. Charles's immediate reaction was that he must have been betrayed by one of the party who had departed on the 21st. He was determined to make a last stand and go down fighting. He examined the Glenmoriston men's guns, pronounced them in good order, and was confident they would do a lot of execution: 'for his part he was a tolerable marksman and could be sure of one at least.'[120]

But there was no treachery afoot. What happened was that a party of Loudoun's regiment under Grant of Knockando came upon the hut accidentally. They saw the signs of recent habitation but could not have dreamed these were traces of the 'Young Pretender'. There would have been nothing surprising about Highlanders fleeing from the advent of soldiers in the summer of 1746. Soon Grant's men moved on, suspecting nothing. But the prince was shaken by the incident. He spent the night on the hills of Glenkingie Braes.[121] Next day he slept on a mountain top right through the afternoon in his wet clothes, wrapped in a plaid, even though it was an excessively cold day and the driving rain frequently turned to hail.[122]

For the next two days the prince and the Glenmoriston men stayed on the heights of Glenkingie. They killed a cow and roasted its meat over a fire that they kept lit for half-hour periods only. Their ordeal was relieved by the timely arrival at midnight of a party of MacPhersons sent by Cluny. They brought bread and cheese and, more importantly from the prince's point of view, whisky. 'We persuaded him to take a hearty dram,' the Rev. John Cameron recorded laconically.[123]

Finally, on 26 August the prince felt secure enough to return to the Achnacarry neighbourhood. Lochgarry and Archie Cameron met them there with word from Lochiel that the prince would be safe where he (Lochiel) was hiding, with Cluny in Badenoch.[124]

With the MacPhersons as escort, the prince no longer needed the valiant Seven Men of Glenmoriston. All except Patrick Grant were dismissed.[125] Having got rid of those who had dared to rein in his impulsive behaviour, the prince ordered an immediate march to Badenoch. The MacPhersons protested that Cluny's idea was that Charles should wait in Achnacarry until their chief chose just the right moment for the journey. The prince would have none of this. As they were not their own men like the Seven, but answerable to a superior chief, the MacPhersons dared not oppose him. The consequence of Charles's impulsiveness was that he then missed Cluny on the road.[126]

At night on the 28th the prince set out. At the river Lochy he said goodbye to Patrick Grant and gave him a purse of twenty-four guineas for the 'Seven Men'.[127] The faithful Glenaladale, too, who had been with the prince for six weeks, was now allowed to depart.[128]

The prince's party pressed on, sleeping by day, travelling by night. At Corrineuir, 'a shieling of very narrow compass' at the foot of Ben Alder, he at last met Lochiel and Cluny's inner circle. But not before another close shave. Seeing a party of strangers approaching, Lochiel's group had taken them for the militia and were preparing to open fire, since Lochiel was still too lame to run. At the last minute, as they primed their guns in the embrasures of the hut at Corrineuir, they recognised friends.[129]

Inside the hut the prince found plenty of meat. He took 'a hearty dram' and for the next few days indulged his taste for Scotch whisky out of the twenty-pint cask they had there. 'Now, gentlemen, I live like a prince,' he remarked euphorically.[130]

On 1 September Cluny rejoined them having missed the prince on the road. At sight of the prince he tried to go down on his knees but Charles prevented this, gave him the kiss of an equal, and joshed him about having looked after Lochiel so royally.[131] Immediately they discussed Lochgarry's proposal to raise the clans again. Both Lochiel and Cluny dismissed it as impracticable. The only remedy now was to seek sanctuary in 'Cluny's cage' on Ben Alder.[132]

On 2 September they penetrated deeper into Ben Alder. For three nights they waited in a 'little shiel superlatively bad and smokey' until his clansmen gave Cluny the all-clear.[133] On 5 September they moved two miles farther into the mountain into the famous 'cage' that Cluny had constructed.[134]

Concealed by a thicket of holly, the 'cage' had been cut in the face of a very rough and steep rocky spur on the south face of Ben Alder overlooking Loch Ericht. Commanding a superb panorama of the surrounding countryside and guarded by sentries, the 'cage' could not be surprised or approached suddenly, for there were no woods in Badenoch but only mountains and crags. Inside there was a rude shelter on two storeys, consisting of several large boulders tilted at various angles. The accommodation was not spacious, but it had been arranged so that the inhabitants slept in the upper 'room' and ate in the lower, which doubled as kitchen and larder.[135]

Cluny's men immediately started excavating a subterranean 'house' for the prince to spend the winter in, in case he could not get away to France.[136] Meanwhile he was entertained to Cluny's best. A nearby fountain provided water. There was plenty of whisky. There was no shortage of food. Cluny's country was rich in game, especially hares and moorfowl. In addition, he had managed to conserve large flocks and herds from the wrath of the enemy: it was his precious collection of brood mares that had been plundered after Culloden.

With the prince in Cluny's cage, safe from enemies, we are presented with an opportunity to assess his thoughts and personality as revealed during the five months on the run. Two things strike one immediately: the amazing physical health the prince enjoyed; and the clear-cut way in which stress produced mood swings and depression.

It was a staple of Whig propaganda that the prince in the heather dragged himself from hovel to hovel, looking like a leper: 'scabbed to the eye-holes' was a favourite cliché of the London yellow press.[137]

The truth was that, the 'bloody flux' apart, the prince enjoyed amazingly good health, all the more remarkable when one considers the appalling conditions in which he lived: sleeping in the cold in wet clothes, bitten by midges, eating an uncertain and unbalanced diet.[138] Charles Edward's apparently ox-like constitution strengthens the inference that it was not organic weakness that caused him to succumb to illnesses like those in the first months of 1746. Such injuries as he did sustain healed quickly. He was hurt badly while crossing the burn on the road from Glencoradale in South Uist: he fell on a pointed stone and bruised his ribs, but mended with remarkable speed.[139] And, although naturally sunburned – 'black, weather-beaten' was one description of him in Benbecula – that was the only sign of wear and tear after the summer.[140]

As for mental health, the prince showed for the most part the positive side of his psyche. In particular, there is ample evidence of humour, one of the great defences against depression.[141] Only in moments of great stress, such as on the tidal island at Benbecula or when nearly surprised in the wood of Torvault, did the old cry of 'I am betrayed' go up. This relative equilibrium was purchased at some cost. We have Malcolm Macleod's testimony that the prince's slumber was frequently violently disturbed, that he would talk in his sleep in English, French and Italian. One of his English utterances was particularly significant:'Oh God! Poor Scotland!'[142]

The prince has often been accused of not showing sufficient remorse for the sufferings of his subject and largely unwilling allies in Scotland. Even at the conscious level, this is a hard charge to sustain. We have the clear statement the prince made to Lochiel and the other leading Camerons: 'he regretted more the distress of those who suffered for adhering to his interest than the hardships he himself was hourly exposed to.'[143] But there may have been other forces working at an unconscious level. One of the keys is the prince's genuine and absolute incredulity that Cumberland's atrocities could have been as bad as they really were.[144] If the prince did not express a level of remorse for the Highlanders' plight that would satisfy his critics, it may well be that squarely facing this extra cargo of guilt might have overwhelmed him.

Of Lord George Murray the prince was critical without being, as later, unbalanced. He pointed out that Murray always wanted to be the one to give orders, not to receive them, but he scouted any suggestion of treachery on Lord George's part.[145] The contrast with his later statements is so great that some have postulated that the prince's henchmen only truly inflamed his mind against Murray once in France. A more likely explanation is in terms of the prince's own psychology. The absence of responsibility for others during the time in the heather allowed his positive side to burgeon. He was therefore capable of the sort of balanced assessment foreign to him later when he was again pitched into the pressures of the world.

At this stage, too, there was no hint of hostility to his brother Henry. Some of his statements about his brother are, admittedly, so lavish that a suspicion of protesting too much arises: 'one preferable to himself in all respects', 'few brothers love as we do'.[146] But as yet Henry had done nothing major to offend the prince. As far as Charles knew, he had been at the coast with Richelieu, urging the French expedition forward. Only on his return to France would the prince's attitude change profoundly.

The one notable absentee as a subject of Charles Edward's recorded observations was his father. His only reference to James during the '45 came on 3 September 1745. When asked whether 'the king' would not be worried about his adventures, the prince replied: 'No, the king has been inured to disappointments and distresses and has learnt to bear up easily under the misfortunes of life.'[147] Bearing in mind Benedict XIV's description of James's hyper-anxiety at the time, we may read this either as lack of perceptiveness or (more likely) simple indifference.

The final point in the prince's psychological profile at this time concerns his much-touted plans for marrying a daughter of the king of France. Charles felt himself (with much justification) to be entitled to the admiration of all Europe for his exploits. In that case, he wished to claim a high marriage as his reward. His toastings of the 'black-eyed beauty' – whom he explained was Louis XV's second daughter – are evidence not so much of wishful thinking as a kind of exultant hypermania.[148] And we know from later correspondence that the claiming of a well-born wife ran very much in his thoughts at this time.

The prince's stay in Cluny's cage was his third relatively secure interlude during his days on the run. First there was Corradale; then the cave provided by the Seven Men of Glenmoriston; finally the untraceable eyrie on Ben Alder. Here he waited for a week, drinking and talking with Cluny, Lochgarry, Lochiel and Archie Cameron, until the chain of listening posts stretching to the west coast brought him word that there were two French ships in Loch-nan-Uamh.[149]

On 13 September the prince started for the coast, travelling by night and resting by day. At Uiskchicra John Roy Stewart came to the hut where he was resting. The prince gave him the fright of his life by rising up from a pile of plaid in the middle of the room.[150] This high-spirited jape gives a good indication of the prince's state of mind at the time.

They pressed on, through the Ben Alder forest to Glenroy, crossed the river Lochy by night and reached Achnacarry. The crossing of the river in bright moonlight again showed the prince at his most positive. When Cluny offered to cross the swollen Lochy by boat first, he gave six bottles of brandy to Lochiel for safe keeping. 'Oh,' said the prince, 'do you have a dram there?'[151] There was nothing for it but to broach the bottles. After consuming three of them in a very short time the prince was finally ready for the crossing. They rowed across in relays, first Cluny and party, then the prince, lastly Lochiel. On the final crossing the leaky boat let in five pints of water.

There was low comedy on the other side. The prince wanted to unstopper the other three bottles. Lochiel had to confess that they had been smashed on the way across and that the clansmen had lapped up the liquor from the boat bottom as if it were punch.[152]

They next passed through Glencamger at the head of Loch Arkaig. Only one day's journey now separated them from the French ships. The prince decided to risk travelling during the day. For additional security, he reverted to his 'Betty Burke' period and dressed as a woman.[153] The precaution was unnecessary. They travelled without incident all day on 18 September to Borrodale. On their arrival they discovered that the two French ships were *L'Heureux* and *Le Conti*.

Commanding this, the last of several French seaborne attempts to rescue the prince, was Richard Warren, the Irishman he had sent to France after the 'Rout of Moy'.[154] Warren gave the prince a tale of almost unparalleled good fortune in dodging Royal Navy convoys.[155] *L'Heureux* and *Le Conti* had been at anchor in the loch since 6 September. In normal circumstances they could never have hoped to remain a fortnight without being discovered, but a ferocious gale had been blowing all that time, clearing the Moidart waters of cruisers.[156]

The prince congratulated Warren on his tenacity. A large number of his followers, including Lochiel, Lochgarry and John Roy Stewart, embarked to accompany Charles to exile in France.[157] Cluny alone remained in Scotland. His brief was to prepare for the Second Coming which all, including the prince, fervently hoped for and genuinely expected.[158]

The prince took a last look at the country in which so much had happened in fourteen months. Then, dressed in trews, philabeg and grey plaid, he went aboard.[159] When *L'Heureux* weighed anchor at

2 a.m. on the morning of 20 September (OS) and hoist sail for France, no one imagined that this was 'Lochaber no more.'[160]

22

'Fall like Lucifer'
(October 1746–April 1747)

The amazing good fortune that had attended the prince in the heather stayed with him all the way to France. Swinging out into the Atlantic to the west of Ireland, Warren originally intended to make landfall at Nantes. Had he taken *L'Heureux* to that port, he would have run straight into a British squadron then raiding L'Orient and the Atlantic coast of Britanny.[1] Some instinct made Warren head for the Channel coast instead. The prince came to secure refuge at Roscoff at 2.30 p.m. on 30 September (OS – 11 October NS).[2]

Charles Edward's safe return threw France into a turmoil of excitement. It is difficult now to appreciate the sensation his exploits both on campaign and in the heather had caused. 'He left France an adventurer and came back a hero,' was Bulkeley's comment.[3] Without exaggeration, in October 1746 the prince was the most famous man in Europe. The glamour that attached to his name was of an unusual kind for that era, and this explains his continuing following among the ordinary people of France long after he had lost standing at Versailles.

In October 1746, at any rate, Charles Edward's appeal was well nigh universal. Even Frederick the Great, who had earlier offered troops to George II to suppress the rising, momentarily fell under the spell. At Dresden in May 1746 he delivered a public encomium on the Stuart prince before a crowded dinner table.[4] He followed this up with an effusive letter of adulation to the prince, asking for his portrait.[5] In private correspondence he described Charles as the 'Trenck' of Scotland.[6] Even Marshal Saxe, no particular friend to the prince after their encounter in 1744, called him the 'hero of the century'.[7]

That this was not hyperbole can be seen from the statements of those who had everything to gain from denouncing him: the luckless Jacobite captives in England facing the gibbet or the executioner's block. Before mounting the scaffold, Lord Balmerino, taken prisoner at Culloden, spoke as follows:

I am at a loss when I come to speak of the Prince. I am not a fit hand to draw his character. I shall leave that to others. But I must beg leave to tell you of the incomparable sweetness of his nature, his affability, his compassion, his justice, his temperance, his patience and his courage, which are virtues seldom to be found in one person. In short, he wants no qualifications requisite to make a great man.[8]

Lest this be thought aristocratic solidarity by a perfervid divine righter, the testimony of prisoners lower in the social scale can also be adduced. The Manchester Jacobites contrasted the Stuart prince's unfailing mercy with Cumberland's barbarity.[9] And David Morgan, a weak man who had tried to lie his way out of execution and who might have hoped for mercy through denigration of the prince, said: 'His character exceeds anything I could have imagined or conceived. An attempt to describe him would seem gross flattery.'[10]

The truth was that for the most part during the '45 and its aftermath, the prince had shown the bright side of his ambiguous face to his followers. He had proved himself not just singularly compassionate but capable of humour and gentle self-ridicule.[11] In his darkest hour he had charmed the dour Highlanders. His preference for the native whisky and oatbread above the more palatable brandy and wheatbread on the grounds that 'these are my own country's bread and drink'[12] was fondly remembered. As Bulkeley commented on the flight in the heather:

Whatever his education had been before, in this trial he had surely learned what few princes can ever have been taught, he had learnt the worth of individuals, he had learnt to admire the disinterestedness of peasants as well as higher persons. He had learnt to love virtue in all orders of men and to know the temper as well as the power of his country.[13]

To date only Lord George Murray, the failed father-figure, had really seen the dark side of the prince's nature that was ultimately to destroy him.

The prince, then, was at his zenith in October 1746. His star had reached its apogee. He was the talk of Europe and the toast of every palace. Everyone, king to peasant, had heard of the fabulous 'Prince

Edouard'. Already his five months in the heather had attained legendary status.[14] The *philosophes* were drawn to this exploit, as illustrating supposed truths about man in the state of nature. Diderot's comments have already been noted. Helvétius was fascinated by the stubborn loyalty to the prince of Donald Macleod and the others. He felt this was a cultural matter: such sturdiness and independence of principle would not be practised among the Turks.[15]

It was therefore in a state of euphoria and high excitement that the prince arrived in Paris. The duc de Luynes, who saw him soon after his arrival, thought he detected signs of scurvy and remarked on his short hair. But for all that Charles had just emerged from a gruelling five months and did not look his best, Luynes had to admit that the tall prince with the noble figure irresistibly reminded him of Charles XII of Sweden, the archetypal model of warrior-prince.[16]

On the morning of 17 October (NS) Charles and Henry had their first meeting. The prince did not at first recognise his brother, and this fact nearly led to tragedy. Overjoyed to see his brother, Henry leapt forward to greet him. One of the prince's Highlanders, thinking this was an assassin, drew his claymore. Just in time the true situation was recognised.[17]

Henry found Charles broader and fatter, 'which is incomprehensible after all the fatigues he has endured'.[18] The reunion was joyful. There was no hint of the trouble to come. Henry professed himself ready to follow his brother to the ends of the earth.[19]

At first, too, the French seemed likely to cherish their hero-prince. On Wednesday 19 October the two Stuart princes arrived at Fontainebleau to begin a round of social engagements designed to show the esteem in which France held Charles Edward. There was an immediate audience with Louis XV, followed by receptions given by the queen and dauphin. The dauphin, in particular, immediately came under the prince's spell. There was a further three-quarter-of-an-hour interview with the king during their sojourn at Fontainebleau, and further informal talks with the queen and dauphin.[20]

There followed a succession of lavish dinners. On 19 October the two princes supped with the marquis d'Argenson. On the 20th they took dinner with Tencin and supper with Maurepas. On the 21st it was the turn of comte d'Argenson to treat them to dinner; supper was with the duc d'Huescar, the Spanish ambassador.[21]

By now, entertaining the princes was developing into a contest among the ministers of state as to who could lay on the most lavish spread. On 22 October the duc de Noailles gave a sumptuous dinner, attended by all the princesses and great ladies of the court. The duc de Luynes, their host that night, found himself upstaged. He professed himself mightily disappointed for the turn-out for his supper party. Of the notables, only Noailles, comte d'Argenson and St Florentin attended. But the prince, who was a consummate charmer when he chose, made up to his host by giving with Henry an impromptu concert on cello and harpsichord. Luynes found Henry a much better virtuoso, overlooking that the opportunities for cello-playing in the heather had not been abundant.[22]

The crowning achievement of the princes' visit to Fontainebleau came on the evening of 23 October. After a dinner earlier in the day with Machault, the Comptroller-General (he had replaced Orry in December 1745), they went in the evening to supper with Madame Pompadour. There was a splendid guest list including (on the French side) the dukes of Richelieu and Bouillon and the Princesse de Conti and (on the Jacobite side), Lord John Drummond, Tyrconnel and O'Brien. The king himself put in an appearance at 11 p.m. and stayed until 1 a.m. – an unwonted honour.[23] Louis spoke of his intention to lodge the prince in one of his own houses at Vincennes. On 24 October the Stuart brothers returned to Henry's house in Clichy until such time as the promised accommodation was ready for them.

At Clichy Charles Edward set up a miniature court. Lochiel, Kelly and Sir James Stewart were his most visible advisers at this time. Crowds of the French nobility flocked out to Clichy to pay court.[24] And on Friday 28 October the prince scored a social triumph in some ways greater than the reception at Fontainebleau. His attendance at the Opera was the occasion for the sort of public lionising he had never known before. The crowd at the Opera went wild with enthusiasm. The prince was clapped and cheered on entering and leaving and was obliged to take more bows at the end than the performers.[25] Charles Edward was the darling of Paris. Possibly from this incident dated the prince's mistaken notion that he could use French public opinion to mould Louis XV to his will.

The honeymoon period with the French court lasted just two weeks. At the beginning of November tension between Charles Edward and Louis XV and between the prince and his brother became evident. In retrospect the signs had all been there at Fontainebleau. Charles had informed Louis that he would not discuss high politics in front of his brother and asked for a secret meeting. Louis refused.[26] A peace conference was in session at Breda and the king wanted to await the outcome. Already his ministers of state had advised against the public reception of the prince that Louis in fact provided at Fontainebleau.[27]

The circumspect French king drew back at the idea of secret negotiations with the prince, in which Charles Edward might extract a
promise on which Louis could not deliver.

Doubtless this 'new realism' dictated the king's next move. There
was no more talk of Vincennes or any of the other royal residences.
Instead, the princes were to be given the use of the financier Paris
de Montmartel's house at Bercy plus a monthly allowance of 12,000
livres.

The prince was stupefied at the news, more especially as it was
not even conveyed to him by one of the ministers of state but by Le
Dran, *premier commis* in the Ministry of Foreign Affairs.[28] Charles had
assumed from the reception Louis had given him at Fontainebleau
that the bad old days of 1744–5 were over. Now he learned to his
horror that Louis was not after all prepared to acknowledge him
openly as an ally. Louis had been all sweetness and light at Fontainebleau. The Vincennes idea had come from him personally. Now, once
again, this neurasthenic ditherer had allowed himself to be overruled
by his ministers. Charles Edward was once more expected to keep a
low profile. What was barely tolerable before his great exploits was
certainly out of the question now that he was the toast of Paris.

The prince's reactions were typical. First the stress caused by the
bad news brought on a fever. Charles had to spring up from the table
at the archbishop of Cambrai's house, where he was supping, and
take to his bed, where he remained for three days.[29] Next he sought
a scapegoat. After no more than two weeks, the mask of cordiality
he had shown to his brother was cast aside. He began to chide Henry
for his lack of sparkle and forcefulness.[30] Why was it that he had not
been able to compel the French to do more for him during the '45?
Why had he alienated the duc de Richelieu and others with his
sickening piety?

The prince ran true to form in another way. As always when under
stress, his self-destructive side asserted itself. In the struggle for
supremacy between the good angel Lochiel and the bad spirit Kelly,
it was Kelly who won.[31] Lochiel could have been the good father,
succeeding where Marischal and Lord George Murray had failed.
But perhaps in the prince's mind he was always indelibly associated
with Derby, where he had supported Lord George in counselling
retreat. At any rate, in the struggle to influence the prince it was
Kelly who prevailed, Kelly who was one of the few truly evil men
among the Jacobites.

These three factors – the prince's disenchantment with France, the
friction between him and his brother, and the ascendancy of Kelly –

were to become intertwined in the months ahead. Kelly urged the prince on to greater and greater defiance of France; Louis XV became more and more disinclined to oblige the prince because of the 'low people' (principally Kelly) around him; Henry, who pushed James's line of diplomacy and conciliation towards France on his brother, was progressively discredited in Charles's eyes by Kelly's insidious whisperings and innuendoes.

At first James did not see that Kelly was the real threat to his son's future. All his efforts were bent to bringing Sheridan to heel. At the conscious level James was furious with Sheridan for having (as the king saw it) deserted Charles Edward in Scotland. At an unconscious level, it is likely that he resented Sheridan's too-obvious attempt to usurp the paternal role and play the loving father. At any rate, he curtly summoned Sheridan to Rome to explain himself.[32] The reprimand from his royal master was the last straw for the ailing Sheridan. He collapsed and died before he could make the journey to Rome. Since James's *bête noire* Strickland had also died in England during the '45, James chose to interpret the two deaths as God's judgment on the false prophets who would seduce his son from the paths of righteousness.[33] But the more James lectured his son, the more Charles despised him.

In the closing months of 1746 James made repeated efforts to get Charles to deal with France in a realistic way and to amend his criticism of Henry.[34] At this stage James was still receiving first-rate intelligence on his elder son from Daniel O'Brien. O'Brien predicted a major clash between the prince and Henry because of temperamental differences; he also warned that Charles would refuse to accept the pension from France until he received 'proper' treatment.[35] Further grievance was offered the prince by Louis XV when, against Charles's specific request, the king released the English Lady Morton from custody and refused to arrest her husband.[36] The prince wanted the Mortons incarcerated until the Hanoverian government was prepared to strike a civilised deal over the treatment of the Jacobite prisoners of the '45.

By December 1746, relations between the prince and the French court on one hand, and Henry on the other, had reached a very low point. The heady days at Fontainebleau in late October already seemed light years away. Charles Edward still retained his huge following with the Paris crowd. At Versailles it was a very different matter. To the bones of contention over the prince's residence and his refusal of the pension were added more specific discontents. France seemed to have no inclination for launching an expedition against Britain. In the prince's eyes, this meant that precious time was slipping away.

In mid-November he sent in a three-page memoir to Louis XV, in which he explained that the '45 had failed only through lack of money, supplies and troops. He asked for 18–20,000 French soldiers for an immediate descent on England.[37] Louis XV made no direct answer, but kept the prince dangling. The French king was entering that period of singular duplicity in his life when he ran a secret foreign policy parallel to the open one pursued by his ministers. This was the *secret du roi*. There are indications that Louis and Charles Edward did carry out some secret negotiations at this time unknown to the ministers of state and the other Jacobites.[38] The proof is that the prince on one occasion blurted the contents of an unknown letter from the French king that had displeased him.[39]

Yet it is possible to guess at the factors that gave Louis pause from the progress of official negotiations between the ministers of state and the Jacobites. One of these was a natural French reluctance to make a winter campaign. Another was the consideration that French interests might be better served by obtaining a favourable peace. The third, possibly most telling, barrier to progress was that Charles Edward was by now insisting that any French expedition on his behalf had to be aimed at England, not Scotland. The prince had perceived the fallacy, as he saw it, of a conquest of Scotland. He had been there and he had found the main task still before him. Only a descent on England made sense. Probably at this stage the French would have backed another rising in the Highlands, but they drew back from the scale of commitment needed for successful conquest of England. Yet anything short of that merely aroused the prince's suspicions.

Time was running out for the prince in another sense. Unless he could get another expedition launched very soon, his aristocratic Jacobite clients would begin to clamour for a fixed settlement in France. Charles Edward could make good his promises and moral responsibilities to the exiled leaders only by securing them regiments and other lucrative appointments. But as soon as he did this, their appetite for another Jacobite rising would be blunted. On the other hand, he could no more keep his own colonels in limbo indefinitely than Louis XV could keep him. One way or another, there had to be a swift resolution.

The prince cunningly solved the problem by applying first for a regiment for Lochiel, the least career-minded of the exiles.[40] Even with a regiment at his command, 'gentle Lochiel' would be willing to return to Scotland at a moment's notice. But Charles took Lochiel's advice and delayed processing Lord Ogilvy's application for a regiment.[41] If it became known that Jacobite leaders were settling down in ease and plenty in France, this would be a major disincentive both for Versailles to abet a new rising and for the clansmen in Scotland to rise.

The prince, then, was pressing for swift action at the very time the French, for reasons of their own, wanted to go slow. Charles Edward's wilfulness, and the poor opinion of his followers entertained at Versailles compounded French desire to tread carefully. Just before Christmas 1746 Louis proposed giving the prince money and 6,000 men for another attempt in the Highlands. The proposal was backed by Tencin and the marquis d'Argenson, but Noailles and Maurepas demurred: in their opinion, judging from the prince's headstrong behaviour, if restored he would be a more dangerous enemy to France than George II ever was.[42] The proposal was quickly shelved.

By the end of December, the prince had lost patience with France and, in the opinion of both James and Tencin, was on a collision course with Louis XV.[43] He was also on the worst possible terms with his father and brother. His attacks on Henry for his lacklustre personality and dismal piety continued.[44] 'You cannot believe what hard cards I have to play,' Henry complained to his father in December.[45] In despair he thought of going on a mission to Spain simply to escape his domineering brother.[46]

There were two sources of sorrow for Henry. One was the accusation, fomented by Kelly but taken up avidly by the prince, that Henry had not done enough at Boulogne in 1745–6 to force or cajole Richelieu into making the crossing of the Channel.[47] The other was Charles's life-style. The clique with which Kelly had surrounded the prince was singularly unsavoury – hence Louis XV's oft-repeated strictures on 'low people about the prince'. The one-eyed Lord Clancarty (he had lost the other in a tavern brawl with General Braddock), himself one of the inner circle at this time, noted: 'if he had searched all the jails in Britain or Ireland, he could not have found such a set of noted, infamous wretches as those H.R.H. had about him.'[48] Some of these were officers from regiments of exiles such as the Royal Scots, described by the marquis of Mezières as an undisciplined rabble with no interests except drinking or debauchery.[49]

Certainly the bills in the prince's household bore out this story. Within one month at Clichy he spent more than 20,000 livres on entertainment for this unprepossessing entourage, whereas the monthly pension France wanted to settle on *both* princes was only 12,000 livres.[50] The lavish expenditure itself would probably not have been enough to perturb Henry, but the fact that his brother's followers were 'bewitched with whoring'[51] certainly did. Later in Rome Henry complained bitterly of the orgies held in the Clichy house by his brother and compliant ladies.[52] Not content with finding a whoremaster who procured girls for the prince, Kelly openly suggested one day at dinner that Henry use his services as well.[53] O'Brien protested that the trade of pander was scarcely fit for an Anglican clergyman. But the prince encouraged the jibe and confided to O'Brien later that Henry's sanctimonious piety infuriated him.

There were a lot of irritants now: Louis XV, Henry, James, even the voice of Charles's conscience, 'gentle Lochiel'. The prince dealt with their unpleasant impact on him by hard drinking of the kind that had amazed the clansmen in the heather. When O'Brien protested about the prince's bibulous over-indulgence at his twenty-sixth birthday party on 31 December 1746, he was contemptuously waved aside.[54]

O'Brien was not the right champion of Henry and James, for his position with the prince was also becoming untenable. When he communicated with the marquis d'Argenson in James's name without clearing it with the prince, Charles Edward gave him a fearsome dressing down.[55] Did he not realise that the Prince of Wales still held the powers of Regent and was therefore James's plenipotentiary? O'Brien would go behind his back again at his peril. The reason for the prince's sudden hostility to O'Brien, apart from the latter's loyal support for James and Henry, was his growing conviction that O'Brien, like Henry, had not pushed the French court hard enough during the '45. Moreover O'Brien's wife, also mistress of the arch-bishop of Cambrai, had diverted to her own use sums of money collected from sympathisers during the rising and earmarked for the prince's use in Scotland.[56] She and her husband were now marked persons in the prince's eyes.

The culmination of the rift between Charles Edward and Henry came with their decision to live apart – virtually a public advertise-ment of their differences. Clichy, the prince decided, was too cold to spend the winter in. He moved in to Paris, to the Hôtel d'Hollande (formerly Hôtel de Transylvanie). Henry took the house next door, the *petit hôtel de Bouillon*.[57] At the marquis d'Argenson's urging, the princes decided to accept the French pension provisionally. The prince then went back on this agreement, for fear of appearing to his English supporters as a French stooge. The pension continued to be paid, but the prince did not use it. He maintained himself from contributions from the English Jacobites. O'Brien meanwhile held the monthly pension payments in a kind of informal trust fund.[58]

At the Christmas season the prince departed to hunt at Navarre while Henry remained in Paris.[59] On his return two significant events occurred. First, Louis XV ignored a second plea the prince made for a British expedition.[60] The reason for this soon became clear. The marquis d'Argenson, the Stuarts' great champion, was abruptly dismissed as Foreign Minister in January 1747.[61] His place was taken by the anti-Jacobite Puysieux, whose goal was a general European peace at any price.

Second, a heated altercation took place between Henry and Kelly at the prince's own table. Kelly virtually accused Henry of outright cowardice (again with reference to the 1745-6 Boulogne period) in his brother's presence. So far from rushing to his defence, Charles remained silent.[62] Two things were therefore clear to the prince. One was that he should look for nothing from Louis XV. The other was that Henry was becoming impossible. The prince suggested that Henry find himself a wife.[63] His brother recoiled in horror. Noting his embarrassment, Tencin privately advised Henry to return to Rome with all speed.[64]

Yet Henry had a plan to vindicate himself. He would go to Spain and succeed by patient diplomacy in wresting from Madrid the kind of concessions that Charles had failed to wring from Versailles. This scheme was unwittingly aborted by O'Brien. O'Brien tried to draw the prince out of the orbit of Kelly, Harrington, Clancarty and the others by encouraging Charles's friendship with the Spanish ambassador the duc d'Huescar.[65] Contact with the Spaniard brought on one of Charles Edward's bright ideas. He would go to Madrid himself and plead his cause. Philip V was dead and there was a new king on the throne. Perhaps the prince could persuade him to steal a march on Louis XV by sanctioning another project against Britain.

Charles also realised that if he went to Spain, he would wrongfoot Henry. This had become an important aim ever since James rushed to his favourite son's defence in a series of letters.[66] Deploring the rift between his sons, he suggested that the solution was to have Henry in Spain while Charles Edward stayed in Paris.[67] By February 1747 he was upbraiding Charles bitterly for his treatment of Henry: 'You are his brother and not his father.'[68] Through all the letters ran the motif of condemnation of Kelly, whom James at last identified as his son's Mephistopheles.

Finally, on 3 February, James reviewed his relations with Charles Edward since 1742. The pattern was one of the son's bucking against the authority of the father. Always Charles Edward was led astray by evil men: first it was Dunbar (in 1742); then Sheridan (in 1745); finally Kelly and Sir James Stewart. James found three main things to criticise: Charles's 'self-defeating' behaviour over the French pension, his living in a separate house from Henry, and his wild life ('however dissolute your life, people will still think of you as a Catholic'). The letter ended in typical style: 'Enfin, my dear child, I must tell you plainly that if you don't alter your ways, I see you lost in all respects.'[69]

Alas for James's good intentions, Charles Edward was no longer in Paris to receive the lecture. As soon as he heard that James intended to give Henry the go-ahead for his journey to Spain, the prince launched his own venture instead. Typically, he took no one except Kelly into his confidence but gave out that he intended to retire to Avignon as a gesture of protest against French niggardliness over the pension. Since he could not live in a fitting style in Paris, he would set up court in Avignon.

Although the Jacobites did not know that Spain was the prince's ultimate destination, they were horrified at the thought of his departure even to Avignon. O'Brien warned him of the unfortunate impression his departure would make at Versailles; it was against the rules of *congé* for a high-born guest to depart the king's domains without a formal royal leave-taking.[70] Charles loftily replied that he expected Henry to make up suitable excuses, since he conceded his younger brother plenipotentiary powers while he was away. This meant, of course, that Henry could not make his own Spanish trip until his brother had returned from 'Avignon'.[71]

But no arguments could swerve the prince from his purpose. In the small hours of Wednesday 25 January 1747 he departed for the south.[72] On the icy roads the journey to Avignon via Lyons took him a week.[73] In Avignon he rested a further week while he laid his final plans and revealed his true intention to his followers. To Henry he wrote that Spain had always been his destination but he had not asked James's permission for fear of a refusal.[74] To James he wrote with a clear statement of his motives. These had nothing to do with the pension but derived from the continued French refusal to reply to the two memoirs he had sent in, requesting an expedition. In sum, his aim in Spain was to get the new king to take up the mantle of Stuart protector that Louis XV had laid aside. More precisely, his aim was a Spanish version of the 1745 Treaty of Fontainebleau and marriage to one of the Spanish king's sisters.[75]

This showed how little the prince understood the changing political complexion of Europe. After Noailles's 1746 mission to Spain the two Bourbon powers acted as one. The dismissal of the marquis d'Argenson had happened partly at Spanish insistence.

Had they known the true scope of the prince's ambitions on his southward journey, the Jacobites would have been appalled. As it was, even the trip to Avignon caused severe flutterings in Jacobite dovecots. As soon as he heard of the journey, James wrote to condemn it, pointing out that only an expulsion from France could justify such conduct.[76]

Lochiel took the opportunity to deliver a stinging but dignified rebuke to the prince. The Avignon trip was singularly ill-advised, not just because the French might take the opportunity to conclude a quick peace while the prince was off their territory, but because he seemed to be putting his own pride and pique with France before the interests of Scotland. It behoved him to make some excuse, to say that he had gone to Avignon to throw off British spies who were dogging his footsteps. Finally, Lochiel pleaded, both morality and the prince's own reputation required that he forthwith abandon his suit at Versailles for a descent on England. He owed it to the Scots to settle for what France was actually prepared to grant: a small expedition to Scotland.[77]

It is interesting that in the struggle between the good and bad father-figures, it was Lochiel who consistently urged the art of the possible (an expedition to Scotland), and Kelly who encouraged the prince in his 'all or nothing' posture (an expedition to England alone).[78]

Lochiel's misgivings about the Avignon venture were shared by Benedict XIV, who condemned the prince as a firebrand. The prince had thrown himself into a well, and his father's friends, like those in the fable, would have to let down a rope.[79]

It was not just the prince's friends and supporters who were stupefied by his action. His departure was the talk of Paris.[80] That it was foolhardy all agreed. All that remained was to assign it a meaning. Did it portend another unilateral Scottish venture?[81] Or was it the prelude to his return to Rome? The almost simultaneous departure of Dunbar from Rome to Avignon seemed to lend credence to the latter conjecture.[82] The French ministers were so baffled that they decided to adumbrate contingency plans in the council in case the prince was already launched on another unilateral British venture.[83]

We have dealt at some length with the degree of stupefaction elicited by the first stage of the prince's journey in order to underscore the awed incredulity that resulted when Charles Edward continued on to Spain. If the Avignon venture seemed to be the action of a blockhead, the Spanish mission genuinely appeared to seasoned observers like the work of a madman. It was a particular mortification to the prince's supposed friend the Spanish ambassador. In all their time together Charles had not breathed one word about a mission to Spain. For once the dour and pessimistic O'Brien was not wrong when he reported to James that the prince had now lost all credibility as politician or statesman. He had left France without Louis XV's permission, then added insult to injury by going to a foreign court for things Versailles had refused him. Moreover, his attitude to Spain was no less insulting. He proposed to enter Spanish territory without official permission, cutting across all James's careful diplomacy on behalf of Henry. It was now clear to the most purblind Spanish grandee that there was a total lack of rapport between the prince and his father and brother.[84]

The prince was undaunted. As long as he had Kelly to play the sycophant, he heeded no other voices. With an aplomb completely unwarranted by all political realities, he set out for Spain, travelling by way of Montpellier, Perpignan and Barcelona.[85]

On 2 March he arrived in Madrid, accompanied by Colonel Nagle (one of Ormonde's old followers), Dr Cameron and William Vaughan, a Welsh Jacobite who had been out in the '45.[86] He had hoped to meet up with Sir Charles Wogan, long in Spanish military service, but Wogan was now governor of La Mancha and absent from the court. But Sir Thomas Geraldin was there, and the prince at once sent him with a message for Carvajal, the Spanish chief minister.

The prince's arrival was a deep embarrassment for Carvajal. He had not presented the letter for King Ferdinand that Charles had sent on from Barcelona. Carvajal still thought that he could persuade the prince to depart surreptitiously, before anyone knew he was in the kingdom. In the greatest secrecy he sent a coach to fetch the prince for a parley. This cloak-and-dagger approach excited Charles's scorn: 'I find all here like pheasants, that it is enough to hide their heads to cover the rest of their body, as they think.'[87]

The interview with Carvajal was difficult. The minister repeatedly urged the prince to go back. Doggedly Charles insisted that his letter to the king be delivered. Reluctantly Carvajal agreed. Next morning Carvajal appeared at the door of the prince's inn with word that Ferdinand and his queen would like to see him.

At the royal audience the prince received the treatment he already knew so well from Louis XV. The Spanish king and queen wished him well, spoke of their personal friendship for the Stuarts, even guaranteed the continuance of a Spanish pension, but stressed that this was not the time to be thinking of large-scale expeditions. In the circumstances, they trusted the prince would not take it amiss if they asked him to return to France as soon as possible.[88]

These polite courtesies masked the political realities at court. The veils of illusion were lifted to some extent when the prince was refused permission to see the queen dowager Elizabeth Farnese. The prince was bitter about these facile protestations of friendship that had no content. He commented acidly: 'One finds in old histories that the great proofs of showing such things are to help people in distress; but this, I find, is not now à la mode, according to the French fashion.'[89]

It was made clear to the prince that all his future dealings in Spain would have to be with Carvajal, a man he despised on sight: 'a weak man just put in motion like clockwork.'[90] That the prince was in a wounded, depressed state is clear from an incident when he was leaving the palace. The well-known singer Farinelli took him by the hand and said that they had met before in Italy. Outraged at this familiarity, the prince glared at the singer for his effrontery.[91]

The private session with Carvajal that followed was even more painful. The prince put a number of firm questions to the minister. What help would Spain provide if France mounted an expedition? Would Spain agree to store 30,000 muskets and 10,000 sabres for him until the need arose? Would Carvajal grant commissions for raising three regiments in Spain? Most important of all, would he send three large merchant ships laden with corn to Scotland to succour the starving Highlanders, now suffering untold privations after Cumberland's reign of terror?[92] Carvajal promised to consider these points carefully. But on the loftier pretensions he could offer no comfort. Carvajal wound up the interview by dismissing all the prince's grand designs as chimerical. He then asked him again to leave Spain. The prince insisted on another interview next day. Carvajal agreed, provided Charles left Spain the day after that.

But Carvajal proved just as unyielding at the next interview and again sharply requested him to leave Spain. The prince stalled, claiming that he was awaiting the arrival of his retinue. At this point Carvajal put his foot down. He would allow a period of grace for the 'retinue' to come up, but the prince must leave Madrid and wait in Guadalajara.[93]

Before he left Madrid, the prince visited the aged Lady Mary

Herbert, an elderly female eccentric who earlier in life had refused to marry the duc de Bouillon and instead went off to Spain on a madcap scheme to exploit the mines of the Asturias. The prince found her living in a garret, very ill and in rags. He gave her all the money he had with him and his own greatcoat, for she was so reduced in penury that she no longer possessed outdoor clothes.[94]

Charles Edward arrived in Guadalajara with Geraldin on 8 March and immediately nagged Carvajal for an answer to his four propositions.[95] On 11 March the minister's answer arrived. He made no reply to the prince's query about ancillary aid in the event of a French expedition. He dismissed out of hand the possibility of new regiments but agreed to provide the arms and provisions for Scotland.[96]

The prince replied by asking for Ferdinand's personal answer to the expedition query.[97] Not surprisingly, Carvajal ignored this. The writing on the wall was clear even for the prince. As a parting snub to Carvajal, he deliberately ignored protocol and wrote directly to Elizabeth Farnese to say how mortified he was that the dowager queen had not received him.[98] Then he sent Geraldin and Archie Cameron back to Madrid to make sure Carvajal did send the provisions to Scotland.[99] Finally, he shook the dust of Spain off his feet as fast as possible.

What had Charles Edward achieved in Spain? At a personal level, his charm had worked with the king and queen; even Carvajal admitted he had made a good impression at this level.[100] As for the reportedly large sums given to the prince by Ferdinand, the stark reality was that Carvajal gave the prince just 1,000 pistoles to cover his expenses – an obvious snub.[101] Ever alert to the nuances of humiliation, Charles Edward adroitly turned the tables on Carvajal by pretending to regard this as a loan. On his return to Paris, he sent Carvajal a banker's draft for the amount.[102]

But the prince's efforts at the instrumental level had been worse than useless. The promised supplies were never sent to Scotland.[103] At best he succeeded for a while in muddying the waters of international diplomacy. An earlier rumour that Spain was involved in another Jacobite project seemed verified.[104] When it became clear that the Spanish court was deeply embarrassed by his visit, a French plot to stir up trouble between Spain and England was suspected.[105] The chances of success for the prince's Spanish mission were always so slim and its likely consequences so disastrous that one is tempted to seek the true explanation for the prince's trip at the psychological level.

The way Charles excluded members of his family from his plans until it was too late for them to do anything about it is striking. The complete break between the prince and his father and brother, which was to occur later in the year, is already present in embryonic form. The Spanish trip seemed to express all the disenchantment with the patient diplomacy favoured by his father and brother that Charles had always felt. At last he no longer felt like dissembling and suppressing his criticisms. In the prince's mind, assiduous lobbying of foreign courts, working through channels of established protocol, never produced results. It had produced the desert of 1719–45, only ended when he himself took matters into his own hands. He had tried diplomacy with Louis and his ministers of state. He had given it three months, and could see it stretching out to three years, then a decade, without issue. Voluntarism was the answer.

Such a stance immediately separated him from his father and brother, but by now Charles Edward thoroughly despised them. He told the English Jacobites before he left for Spain that he wanted to be his own master, with his own ministers in France, and wished for a complete divorce from James and all his works.[106] If this meant alienation, then so be it. Naturally, the prince was unable to see that this programme, which contained a scintilla of rationality, in fact released his own unconscious self-destructive impulses.

From Guadalajara the prince sped back to Paris. For a time he stayed incognito at the archbishop of Cambrai's house, the Maison Blanche at the end of the Faubourg St Marcel on the Fontainebleau road.[107] Unaware of the disastrous collapse of his reputation and credibility, he once again began lobbying the king and his ministers for an expedition to England.[108] He had also, as he thought, another ace up his sleeve. He was now prepared to marry for dynastic reasons, but his choice was the most surprising conceivable.

To understand the prince's thinking about a dynastic marriage, we must return for a moment to late 1746. On the prince's safe return from Scotland, James thought that the time was ripe for one or both of his sons to marry.[109] Possible brides were canvassed. O'Brien suggested a Mlle de Mazarini as a suitable consort for the prince, but James wanted someone of higher rank.[110] His favourite candidate was the Princess Fortunata, third daughter of the duke of Modena, or possibly even Matilde, the duke's second daughter.[111] But the prince was adamant that he would marry none other than Louis XV's daughter. It was her or no one. James pointed out the absurdity of such an ambition: it was plausible, even likely, once the Stuarts were restored, but a pipe-dream until then.[112]

There the matter rested until the prince's return from Spain. Suddenly Charles announced a bright idea that he claimed had been germinating ever since his days in the heather. If France and Spain would not help him, it was time to look further afield. What better choice as his bride than the Czarina Elizabeth? His marriage portion would be an expedition of 20,000 Russian troops against England.[113]

Once again the prince revealed his lamentable ignorance of international politics. Russia was drawing ever closer to England. The long-serving Field-Marshal Keith had recently been eased out of the Russian service. His brother Earl Marischal had been refused permission to visit him. This was the context of Russo-Jacobite relations in which the prince proposed to bid for the Czarina's hand! Not surprisingly, James scouted the idea as another of his son's fantasies.[114]

The year 1747 also saw the vanishing of the prince's last realistic hopes of aid from France. James feared an early peace and advised Charles to stay put until the French expelled him. They would then have to find him a suitable wife to salve their conscience.[115] But James underrated the extent to which opinion at Versailles was swinging against the prince. Even his applications to serve with the French army in the coming campaign in Flanders were brusquely refused.[116]

The return of the marquis d'Eguilles from imprisonment in England, plus the scheduled departure of Louis XV for the seat of war in Flanders made it necessary for the ministers of state to make a final decision as to military support for the prince.[117] They assembled to hear d'Eguilles's final report and to question the envoy closely. They also had before them a report from marechal-de-camp Hérouville de Claye, who had been urging another expedition against England as a means of preserving French possessions in the Americas.[118]

In his report d'Eguilles paid full tribute to the prince's sterling qualities as manifested in the '45. But he deplored his lack of intellectual grip and 'lack of reflection', which led him often to adopt the last viewpoint heard or the one most vociferously expressed.[119] This chimed with the mood of the meeting. The comte d'Argenson claimed to have it from the duc d'Huescar that the prince understood nothing of politics and was not quick-witted enough.[120] A tentative suggestion was advanced that an expedition to Scotland be mounted to coincide with the 1747 dissolution of Parliament.[121] But Puysieux argued that the prince had forfeited any right to such consideration by his behaviour since returning from Scotland, and especially by his extraordinarily mindless journey to Spain.[122]

The subject of Kelly – always the bone that stuck in French throats – was raised. Kelly was blamed for the prince's unyielding posture and his insistence that any French expedition must go to England, not Scotland. It was recognised that among the Highlanders Kelly would be the cipher he had been for the first two months of the '45.[123] But to remove the obstacle of Kelly seemed an impossible task. James had done everything short of issuing a direct order for Kelly's dismissal, yet the prince had ignored him.

Louis XV intervened to say that there were two things he would never understand. One was why Charles Edward had rushed off to Spain. The other was why he insisted on an expedition to England, which required twenty-five battalions and was in any case impracticable, given the poor state of the French navy.[124] Puysieux suggested that the true reason for this was the paucity of Jacobite supporters in England. The prince had often claimed that with a few more French battalions he could have won at Culloden. Why, then, did he not make good his boast? The French court was willing to provide up to 6,000 men provided the prince went to *Scotland*. But this was precisely what he consistently refused to do.[125]

The council concluded that French interests were best served by fomenting disaffection in Scotland without regard to the prince, possibly with a view to the ultimate establishment of a republic in Scotland.[126] The prince had pushed things to the point where he was no longer regarded by France as a serious factor even in the land of his greatest triumphs.

It seems impossible that any one man could have botched things as perfectly as the prince had done in the six months since his return from Scotland. The obstinate refusal to consider another rising in the Highlands, against the wishes of the French and Lochiel and the clan leaders, seems so extreme that one wonders whether the single explanation of Kelly's bad influence is sufficient. It is true that the egregiously dreadful 'Trebby' (Kelly's nickname among the Jacobites) had suborned both Lord Ogilvy and Sir James Stewart against a return to Scotland.[127] But the prince's reluctance to return to the Highlands may have had deeper springs. Along with self-destructive impulses was a profound guilt that made it impossible for him to accept culpability for the sufferings of the Highlanders. This impulse may well have prevented him from taking another gamble that would put more lives and fortunes at risk. Certainly the prince's refusal to return to Scotland and his insistence that any future expedition had to land in England, when it was clear that France was only prepared to back him in Scotland, has no rational basis.

Whatever the reasons, 1747 seemed to be developing into a year of disaster. It was the duty of a true king to find a suitable marriage for his son, and this James had signally failed to do. After all, especially for a Catholic monarch, marriage was a once-and-for-all affair. James had compounded his private failures as a father with incompetence as a sovereign. Charles Edward's desire to marry royally was a rational ambition. His father's unsatisfactory alternative suggestions simply added to the prince's feelings of being slighted and demeaned.

But what the prince had suffered hitherto was a mere flea-bite compared with what was to come. Suddenly Henry and James together aimed a mortal blow at the prince and the aspirations of the House of Stuart.

23

Betrayal and Rebirth

(April 1747–February 1748)

Henry's feeling of being in a world of chaos had not been assuaged when his brother departed for Spain. Within days Charles had written from Avignon to reprimand him for corresponding with James behind his back.[1] And Henry's activities as his brother's plenipotentiary brought him no sustenance. A meeting with Maurepas was followed by an audience with Louis XV, at which the king's face clouded over every time Charles Edward's name was mentioned.[2] Yet Henry was nothing if not loyal. When the ministers hinted to him that he had their sympathies in his problems with his brother, he coldly and haughtily rebuffed them.[3]

It was abundantly clear to the duke of York that his brother's precipitate departure to Spain had finished him at Versailles. Never again would Louis XV and his ministers take the hero of the '45 seriously. What, then, did the future hold for Henry?

By going to Spain and pre-empting Henry's hope of a permanent niche in Madrid, Charles Edward unwittingly uncoiled a chain of events that led to disaster. If Henry could not endure the hectoring, censorious regime of his brother in Paris much longer, and the escape route to Spain was now closed, what remained? To his horror, Henry found that he had to confront his own homosexuality, for the alternative that both his father and brother seemed to be favouring was marriage.[4] Since Charles Edward refused to marry anyone less than a reigning monarch or king's daughter, it was left to Henry to carry on the Stuart line.

As soon as Henry saw this trap looming, he wrote to inform James that he had a deep repugnance to the worldly life, and especially marriage.[5] He was not exaggerating. One of the great events of the social calendar – which Charles missed by going to Spain – was the wedding of the dauphine, followed by a celebratory ball. Henry was called upon to dance with many fashionable ladies, especially the Princesse de Conti. Terrified that his father might misconstrue this as fondness for women, he at once dashed off a 'confession' to Rome.

James's reply was what one might have expected from a civilised and urbane father: 'It was indeed a great *galanteria* the Princess of Conti did you to dance with you, and there was no need of any apology being made to me about it, for had I been there, I should have been tempted to have danced with her myself to complete the frolic.'[6] The remarkable thing about this correspondence was that Henry should have thought it necessary to raise the matter at all. It illustrates the extent of his fear and mistrust of women.

Fortunately, James had already suggested a way out of his younger son's psychological impasse. In December 1746 James raised, almost as an aside, the idea – no more than a *jeu d'esprit* at this stage – that Henry might like to consider becoming a cardinal. Henry confessed at the time that the notion had never previously entered his head.[7] Yet this was not quite the first occasion the suggestion had been made. In 1742 France and Spain had together asked the Pope to give Henry a cardinal's hat, after which they would make him Cardinal Protector of France.[8] But at various times it had also been suggested that the prince himself take the purple. It is important to be clear that Henry's deliberations in early 1747 belonged to an altogether different dimension of seriousness.

Once the spark had been lit in Henry's mind, it quickly caught fire. He became an enthusiast for the idea. Realising the gravity of the step they were about to take, he and his father laid their plans carefully. It was essential that Charles Edward not be given the slightest inkling of their intentions.

As confederates in the plan James chose Tencin and O'Brien, both men at odds with the prince, and who had consistently demonstrated their personal loyalty. Knowing very well the likely consequences of his action, James began by putting it to O'Brien that he would like him back in Rome as his secretary of state.[9] Since O'Brien was in any case wilting under the sustained verbal lashings from the prince for 'disobedience' (i.e. obeying James rather than him), he was glad to accept.[10]

For a few weeks Charles Edward enjoyed a halcyon period, the calm before the storm. He even remarked on the improvement in relations with Henry since his return from Spain.[11] His letter to James on this subject was a classic of dramatic irony. Henry was being more congenial precisely because the boats were burned and his father committed.

In mid-April 1747 James put the next part of his plan into operation. He asked Henry to return to Rome, explaining to Charles that he needed him there for a few months 'for comfort and to diminish expense'.[12] It was intended that Henry would leave Paris as soon as that letter arrived, before the prince could smell a rat. There was still every possibility that Charles Edward might somehow get wind of the clandestine project. James admitted to being terrified that his elder son might see the incriminating correspondence with O'Brien.[13]

Henry now laid a trail of subterfuge and evasion. On the last day of April, he invited Charles Edward to his house for supper. He left the house in the early afternoon after giving instructions to his servants to make all ready for the meal.[14] The prince duly arrived. The house was illuminated, the supper ready, the servants at their posts. But there was no sign of Henry. With mounting irritation and fury Charles waited until midnight for his brother. Unknown to him, Henry had already been five hours on the road south by the time the prince arrived for supper.[15]

Next day the mystery continued, and the day after. On the third day, when Henry was safely beyond recall, one of his servants delivered a letter for the prince. The letter announced Henry's departure for Rome. He apologised for leaving without informing his brother, but excused this on the grounds of his keen desire to see James and the attitude of the French.[16] Here Henry had a circumstantial point. Not only had the ministers refused both brothers leave to campaign, but they seemed to have singled Henry out for especially discriminatory treatment. One incident highlighted this. It was a unique privilege of servants of princes of the blood to enter the Tuileries. No others were admitted. Suddenly, the French decided to treat Henry as incognito. The next time his servants arrived at the Tuileries, wearing the duke of York's livery, the Swiss guards turned them away.[17]

All this Henry explained, but not the real reason for his departure. On he sped to Rome. In the mountains of Switzerland there was a strange encounter when his path and Dunbar's crossed.[18] Dunbar had finally split with James. He had been in disgrace for some time, but the appointment of O'Brien as secretary of state was the last straw. While Dunbar headed for Avignon, Henry descended into the Italian plain and arrived in Rome on 25 May. Even then he did not reveal the true motive for his visit.[19]

Henry reached Rome to find that James had fully implemented

his end of the operation. The Pope had agreed to elevate the duke to the purple in the July consistory.[20] This final strand in the web of deception had been achieved in mid-May, while Henry was still on the road.[21] Benedict XIV was surprised at James's request but granted it out of personal consideration and an appreciation of the sufferings James had sustained through his unwavering championship of Catholicism.[22] There was general agreement among the cardinals Benedict consulted that the pious Henry had the makings of a notable prince of the Church.[23]

All stages in the deception practised on the prince were known to Louis XV, Tencin and Puysieux.[24] Neither Louis nor Benedict XIV used normal diplomatic channels for fear that Charles Edward would find out.[25] For two months the prince lived in a fool's paradise. Just after Henry's departure, he moved into a fine country house near Passy, given to him rent-free by an admirer, Madame de Sessac.[26] With a well-cultivated garden and beautiful prospect, this Passy residence was far more pleasant accommodation than any he had enjoyed in France so far. O'Brien's departure for Rome went almost unnoticed: angry at his collusion in Henry's abrupt departure, the prince refused to grant him a farewell audience.[27]

While his future was being (adversely) decided at Versailles, the prince contented himself with firing off letters of complaint about Henry's absconding.[28] It is clear that the younger brother by this action had already pushed the fraught relationship to breaking point even before the cardinal bombshell burst. In this twilight period, both James and Henry showed themselves masters of duplicity, the equal of Charles Edward when they chose, it seems. Until the full truth was revealed, Henry's tone continued to be that of injured innocence: 'what have I done?' is the burden of his letters to his brother.[29]

Meanwhile Tencin, Puysieux and O'Brien were laughing up their sleeves.[30] The prince's next audience with Louis XV was significant. The king archly asked the prince if he had seen anything of Tencin recently. When the prince said no, Louis looked enquiringly at the duc de Bouillon. Bouillon said that the secret of Tencin could be unlocked by Puysieux better than anyone else.[31] There was much mute shrugging of the shoulders, in retrospect a pointer to Tencin's treachery. And by now Louis had received from James a formal written request for approval of his younger son's cardinalate.[32]

The prince departed in mid-June for the Princesse de Conti's country house, where he went sightseeing in St Germain and environs.[33] He returned to find that his carelessness and ingratitude were causing him to move house once again. The prince forgot to write a thank-you note to Madame de Sessac. She retaliated by declaring that the Passy house had been loaned on a one-month basis only. Fortunately for him, the prince was now offered Cardinal Rohan's country seat at St Ouen, at a riverside location six miles from Paris.[34]

It was there that the fuse, originally lit three months earlier, finally licked to the end of the gunpowder trail and exploded. In time-honoured fashion, the prince was almost the last person to know of Henry's elevation to the purple. James planned it that way, for he knew what must surely follow. For all that, his announcement of the *fait accompli* to Charles Edward is some sort of masterpiece of bland double-speak:

> I know not whether you will be surprised, my dearest Carluccio, when I tell you that your brother will be made a Cardinal the first days of next month. Naturally speaking, you should have been consulted about a resolution of that kind before it had been executed, but as the Duke and I were unilaterally determined on the matter, and that we foresaw you might probably not approve of it, we thought it would be showing you more regard, and that it would be even more agreeable to you, that the thing should be done before your answer could come here, and so have it in your power to say that it was done without your knowledge or approbation.[35]

The arch insinuation in the letter is as astonishing as its illogicality is gross.

It is difficult to convey the anguish in Charles Edward's heart, and the general consternation in the Jacobite movement, produced by this thunderclap. The prince found himself struck literally speechless when he read the letter. He shut himself up for several hours before penning a brief reply, the gist of which was summed up in the second sentence: 'Had I got a dagger through my heart, it would not have been more sensible to me than at the contents.'[36]

By common consent James and Henry had struck a mortal blow at the entire Stuart cause.[37] For Henry to accept a cardinal's hat with James's connivance was tantamount to admitting that only a fool could any longer believe in a Stuart restoration. James and Henry had conceded that the quest was forlorn, the cause hopeless. Moreover, Henry's embrace of 'priestcraft' seemed to turn the cliché'd dross of Hanoverian propaganda into pure gold. All the insinuations about 'popish pretenders' were true after all. Had not the younger

Stuart just proved it? Moreover, Henry's celibacy seemed to condemn the Stuart line to extinction unless Charles Edward married, which he refused to do. Unless Henry was later freed by papal dispensation to renounce Holy Orders, the Stuart dynasty was a heart-beat away from oblivion. What a temptation to prospective assassins that was!

All these points were made with some force by Jacobite supporters. Significantly, the most severe critics of Henry's actions were members of the Catholic clergy themselves. Father Myles MacDonnell delivered a biting attack on a move he considered actuated purely by Henry's pique and spite against his brother.[38] An even more incisive critique was sent to James by the bishop of Soissons. It seemed to be ever the bishop's fate to lock horns with rulers, whether *de jure* or *de facto*. He pointed out that Henry's cardinalate was, in effect, a resignation of Stuart pretensions to the throne of England. If Charles Edward died, the English would never accept a cardinal, even an ex-cardinal, as king. Even if the prince lived, he would have the perpetual albatross of a cardinal brother around his neck. To be restored to the throne of England, the Stuarts needed to put as much distance between themselves and Rome as possible without actually abandoning the faith. James and Henry had done the precise opposite. In any case, being a cardinal was a worldly ambition, designed to secure benefices. Surely a duke of York could get these without becoming a cardinal? It followed that the action Stuart *père et fils* had taken was futile.[39]

James later admitted he was shattered by the depth and breadth of the opposition to making Henry a cardinal. His tactic was to put the blame on Charles Edward for 'causing' Henry's flight to Rome.[40] In later years he rationalised his disastrous action as a Machiavellian ploy to force Louis XV to show his hand and prove that he had no secret agreement with the prince, unknown to the Palazzo Muti.[41] In the short run, he wrote a number of disingenuous letters to the prince, of which the burden was that Charles had only himself to blame for what had happened.[42]

The prince treated these apologies with the contempt which on this occasion they genuinely deserved. He informed his father that thenceforth he had no brother and never wanted to hear his name mentioned again.[43] To the bishop of Soissons the prince lifted a corner of his thoughts to reveal the extent to which he despised Henry. He could have admired him grudgingly if he had turned Capuchin out of a desire for spiritual perfection.[44] But to become a 'redcap' surely excited the contempt of all reasonable men.

The ripples caused by the explosion of the sensational news soon carried beyond the inner circles of the Jacobites. All Paris was stupefied by the tidings.[45] The common opinion was that for the 'Elector of Hanover' to have scored such a *coup*, he must have bribed many of the principals, especially Tencin and the Pope.[46] Interestingly, Benedict XIV revealed that he had in fact been offered £150,000 by the English to subvert the Stuart cause by making Henry a cardinal, even before James approached him on the subject.[47] The scale of the bribe is significant. By their actions James and Henry had handed the Hanoverians a political advantage worth millions of pounds in present-day terms.

We shall often enough have occasion to remark on the prince's tendency to paranoid delusion. But on this occasion his conviction that he had been uniquely victimised surely has some foundation. Louis XV cynically colluded with James to sink the Jacobite cause at the very moment he was supposedly seriously considering Jacobite military options on the council of state. This is of a piece with his personality. His natural instinct for duplicity would have been whetted by the prince's refusal to toe his line. Like all genuine tyrants, what Louis XV most detested was someone with the strength of will to stand up to him.

Even Benedict XIV, normally a wise and sagacious pontiff, must be faulted on this occasion. His bland statement that Henry's becoming a cardinal need not prevent a Stuart restoration if that was what God really wanted[48] is exactly the sort of nonsense that has so often gained organised religion a bad name.

Yet the most interesting psychological study is that of the two principal actors in the tragic farce. It is hard to escape the conclusion that both Henry and James were motivated by bad faith. With James it was the desire to, as it were, pull up the drawbridge on Jacobitism, to ensure that his elder son could not succeed where he had failed. With Henry, not only was there general sibling rivalry at play, but there was also the issue of his sexual personality. It is not too much to say, when all the threads have been unravelled, that the *coup de grâce* to the Jacobite movement was delivered by Henry's deviant sexuality, which made the thought of marriage purely horrific. This of course always remained something impossible to say in Jacobite circles.

Charles Edward sank into a profound depression as the impact of Henry's defection sank in. To Edgar he spoke of making a bonfire of all his ciphers to assuage his drooping spirits.[49] To his father he mentioned that he was hunting with Prince Constantin outside Passy 'so as to dissipate as much as possible my melancholy thoughts'.[50] In

February the papal vice-legate in Avignon had reported the prince's depression and his consequent heavy smoking and drinking.[51] But that was nothing compared with the trough of despair into which Charles now sank. Hunting with the Rohans alternated with heavy drinking sessions.[52] Occasionally he would pen a trivial line to his father, or write a note of congratulation to Louis XV for his victories in Flanders.[53] The rest was black despondency.

Almost incredibly, it was a matter of days after the prince had received the 'dagger through his heart' that Lord George Murray arrived in Paris to seek a reconciliation with him. Murray had been in Rome with James and had received a magnificent reception.[54] James knew his son's opinion of Lord George and had tried to dissuade Atholl's worthy scion from courting certain humiliation at the prince's hands.[55] But Murray insisted. He was not to know that Kelly and others had worked Charles Edward up to a rare pitch of hatred against his old lieutenant-general. When news came in that Murray of Broughton had turned king's evidence in England to save his own skin, Kelly cleverly worked on the prince to persuade him that the frequent clashes between the two Murrays during the '45 had all been a charade. In reality, behind the false front the two men had been in concert; their aim had always been to betray the prince.[56] Charles had already reacted by threatening to have Lord George arrested if he came to Paris. He asked James to do the same in Rome.[57]

Yet even if the prince had not already been in a state of almost permanent cold fury whenever the name of Lord George Murray was mentioned to him, Murray's timing was singularly infelicitous. He could not have chosen a worse moment to arrive in Paris. When the prince learned of his presence in the French capital, he sent Stafford round to his lodging to say that he did not wish to see him, either then or ever, and that Murray would be well advised to quit Paris with all speed.[58]

The arrival of Lord George Murray at such a juncture was particularly infuriating to the prince. At the precise moment he was digesting his father's treachery, the most troublesome thorn in his side during the '45 reappeared. Charles knew his father had been treacherous; he was still convinced that Lord George had betrayed him at Culloden. The association of ideas was too powerful. Here in a matter of days was the conjunction of two hated authority figures, his father by letter, and the failed father-figure of the '45 in the flesh. Always, it seemed, there was this element in the prince's disappointments. Derby was the work principally of Lochiel and Lord George. Henry's becoming a cardinal was the work of Louis XV, his own father, and Benedict XIV, the 'Holy Father'. And just as Louis XV had colluded in James's treachery over the cardinalate, so would James later collude in French treachery when they expelled the prince in 1748. Already, for Charles Edward, Louis XV and James were birds of a perfidious feather. In his best scathing style the prince later compared and contrasted them: 'They are both "honest men". James is blinded by priests and Louis by whores.'[59]

Pitifully, the prince had not yet learned to discard the most treacherous of all the father-figures. Trying to rationalise the complete break between king's men and prince's men, in 1747 he tried to interest Earl Marischal in becoming his secretary of state.[60] Marischal, who detested the prince, trundled out his usual excuse of 'ill-health'.[61] It would be another seven years before Charles took the full measure of this man's hatred.

All through August and September 1747 the prince was in the company of the Rohan family. He expressed his contempt for authority by hunting in an area exclusively reserved for the king of France; not even the great nobility were allowed to venture there. Puysieux, delightedly reporting that Louis XV was very angry about the incident, lost no time in warning off the delinquent prince.[62]

The Rohans were still devoted to the prince and concerned for his future. Cardinal Rohan tried to arrange his marriage to a ten-year-old daughter of the Prince de Soubise, reportedly a millionairess.[63] But the prince wanted none of it; he wanted to be free to act at a moment's notice if the call came from Britain. With the collapse of French aid, all his hopes were centred on a power vacuum in England following George II's death. It was expected that there would then be a struggle for power between Cumberland and Prince Frederick, George II's detested eldest son. It was the prince's intention, once the two combatants were exhausted in civil war, to play duke William of Normandy to the two Harolds of 1066. When one or other brother emerged victorious, the prince planned to cross the Channel to snatch the prize.[64]

As he confided to Papal Nuncio Durini, the prince had yet another reason for remaining unmarried. The lack of a Stuart heir might eventually force James to order Henry to renounce his celibate vows and beget legitimate descendants. The refusal to marry continued to be one of the principal ways for the prince to manipulate his father.[65]

In the summer of 1747 the prince's depression was remarked on by all observers.[66] Suddenly there was a remarkable change both in his fortunes and attitude. A letter of congratulation to Louis XV on

Saxe's great victories secured an invitation to Versailles in early October. There at last the prince secured for Lochiel the regiment which he had promised as collateral for the security the Cameron chief had taken in Lochaber in August 1745 and for which Charles had lobbied assiduously ever since. The regiment, once obtained, was worth three times the annual income from Lochiel's holdings at Achnacarry.[67]

At the end of September, too, signs of the old compassionate prince were once more in evidence. Writing to James about the capitulation of Bergen-en-Zoom (he never wrote now on any but public subjects and never mentioned Henry), he said he was very glad, as the surrender had saved the lives of many 'honest men'.[68] After the low point of his mid-summer depression, the prince seemed to have experienced a spiritual rebirth. What had happened? The truth was that Charles had experienced the first sustained love affair of his life. In passionate intensity it was certainly his most significant relationship ever with a woman.

Marie Louise-Henriette-Jeanne de la Tour d'Auvergne was the daughter of the duc de Bouillon. By marriage she was duchesse de Montbazon and Princesse de Rohan. She was also Charles Edward's first cousin, since her mother was Clementina Sobieska's sister, Marie Charlotte.[69] At the time of her affair with Charles Edward, she was twenty-two and married to the Prince of Rohan-Guéméné, one year her junior, with whom she had had a son in 1745. The couple had been married in 1743 in a dynastic union between two Jacobite families, the Bouillons and the Rohans.[70]

The Rohan-Guéménés were staunch supporters of the Stuart prince. When Richard Warren announced his rescue attempt of the prince in summer 1746, his projected exploit brought him an immediate interview with Louise (duchesse de Montbazon) and her formidable mother-in-law the Princesse de Guéméné.[71] But although Charles Edward had met Louise before (their first meeting was in early 1745 during his first period in France), it was not until late summer 1747 that romance blossomed.[72]

Exactly when and where the affair commenced – whether at Navarre in early September or at St Ouen shortly afterwards – cannot be determined. But it is clear that once the liaison did begin, it was passionate and erotic. Louise was obviously a highly-sexed woman and Charles Edward had already acquired a strong taste for carnal pleasure. The first phase of the relationship was easy and had an idyllic quality. Louise's husband was away at the wars in Flanders. The lovers frequently spent nights together, either at the Guéméné residence on the place Royale or at St Ouen, which Louise could visit under a plausible pretext, since her great uncle the comte d'Evreux had a summer place there, next door to the prince's house.[73]

It was in October that Louise conceived the prince's first child.[74] But immediately afterwards difficulties in their liaison began. The ending of the summer season removed the pretext for Louise's visits to St Ouen. Thenceforth the prince had to go clandestinely to the Guéméné house for his nights of frenzied love-making. To keep the affair a secret, the lovers took elaborate precautions. A coach, heavily draped and guarded, took the prince at night to the rue Minimes in Paris. When the coast was clear, the prince got out and made his way by side entrances to the Guéméné residence in place Royale (the rue Minimes ran parallel to the place).

Since the coach was soon observed threading its way along the country lanes of St Ouen at the same time each night, the Paris police were alerted. At first lieutenant of police Berryer thought there was an English assassination plot against the prince. Then Daniel O'Brien, the prince's valet and the only man he ever really trusted, was stopped for questioning by the police, following an early-morning incident involving the coach. It became clear that the prince was involved in a clandestine affair of the heart. The name of the lady in question was not mentioned. Satisfied, Berryer called off his dogs.[75]

The tempestuous affair now absorbed most of the prince's energies. He was besotted with Louise: physical desire was compounded by the feeling that she too, like him, was a rebel and an outsider. The prince even proposed to give up his claim to the Sobieski inheritance on her behalf, much to James's irritation.[76] He showed a wholly unwonted indifference to affairs of state. That there was an element of '*épater les Français*' in his relationship is clear from the few moments in late 1747 when he was called upon to play a political role. He was at the duchesse d'Aiguillon's house with the *philosophe* Montesquieu when news of Hawke's victory at Cape Finisterre came in. Charles Edward at once spoke with pride of the skill of Hawke and Anson. Montesquieu protested: were these not victories by his enemies? 'That's true,' the prince replied archly, 'but it's still my country's fleet.'[77]

An even more pointed snub to France occurred one night when the prince was at supper with the duc de Gèsvres and some of the ministers of state. The English had just landed troops in Brittany for an extended raid. One of the ministers suggested that Louis XV should put the prince in command of the forces sent to expel them. The prince rejected the idea out of hand. On English soil he was prepared to fight those who resisted his claim to the throne but 'I can never think of fighting Englishmen in any other cause'.[78] The issue of how he would behave towards France if he were king of England was then brought up. The prince replied that he saw no necessary incompatibility between the interests of the two countries, but if this proved to be the case, naturally he would put English interests first.

Such moments were brief interludes only in the round of passion. For a time it seemed to the prince that he had found the meaning in life which had hitherto always eluded him. When Louise announced that she was pregnant, the delighted prince would lay his head down on her belly, listen to the unborn child and even talk to it.[79] And still both lovers' deep physical and emotional satisfaction persisted, even through the usual storms affecting all love affairs. On one occasion the prince had to leave Louise's bedroom in great haste to avoid being discovered. On another, after a lovers' quarrel and in a rage, the prince threatened to fire off both his pistols at dead of night in the place Royale.

None of this was very serious. But in December a more formidable obstacle to the young lovers than Berryer's police appeared. Louise's husband Jules returned from the wars. To conceal the truth about the pregnancy, Louise had to allow a brief resumption of conjugal relations. Then the lovers had to decide how to deal with the much deteriorated situation. Louise suggested that it might be better if Charles did not come to her bedroom until half an hour after her husband had settled down for the night in his own apartment. This meant that their tryst could not commence until well after midnight. At that rate the prince would be returning to St Ouen in broad daylight. He solved the problem by moving to a house in the rue du Chemin du Rempart near Porte St Honoré. This was to be his last open abode in Paris.[80]

Yet his own psychological problems could not be so easily dealt with. The return of the young husband brought on towering fits of jealousy. This was almost predictable, given the prince's fragile self-esteem. Once the masking of the pregnancy had been achieved, he made Louise swear to abstain from intercourse with her husband.[81] The jealousy extended backwards in time as well. Perhaps Louise was more experienced than Charles thought, perhaps she had had other lovers before him? The prince's insane possessiveness for another man's wife can best be gauged from the fact that, despite perennial pleas of poverty to his supporters, he put Mlle Carteret, one of Louise's confidantes, on a permanent pension in return for her discovering Louise's true feelings for him.[82] He need not have put himself to so much trouble. Mlle Carteret reported that Louise loved only him, that her passion for him was akin to madness, that she lived solely to be in his arms.

But there was a new serpent in paradise. The Princesse de Guéméné, Louise's mother-in-law, was a dominant matriarch. She now began to complain to Louise and Mlle Carteret of strange noises heard at night.[83] Louise grew alarmed. She asked the prince to space his visits out more and to exercise even greater caution lest they be discovered *in flagrante* and her reputation ruined.

As Louis XV, James and a host of others could have testified, the one thing the prince would not tolerate was somebody trying to 'give him laws'. He reacted to Louise's suggestion with rage. It was a straight choice. She could put her security and reputation first, or she could choose him with all the attendant 'inconveniences'. Which was it to be?[84]

Unfortunately for both of them, as it later turned out, Louise was essentially weak. She had no means of dealing with a dominant will like the prince's. She threatened not to see him again if he did not behave less recklessly on his nocturnal visits, but spoiled her ultimatum by revealing her true emotions in the last line of the letter.

The prince knew how to deal with this sort of thing. He called her bluff in spectacular fashion and threatened to cause a public scandal in the Guéméné household unless Louise did his bidding in every exact particular. More precisely, he threatened that if he was not allowed to spend the entire night in her bedroom when he felt like it, he would create a scene by skulking all night long in the place Royale below. Cowed and browbeaten, Louise gave in.[85]

But now came a dramatic new development. The Princesse de Guéméné had just been waiting for her son to go to Marly before confronting her daughter-in-law. For the Princesse de Guéméné, it now turned out, had long known about the affair. The reference to strange nocturnal noises had been in the nature of a wink and a nod. She had been hoping that the affair would burn itself out, but every day it seemed to be reviving. Now that her son was out of the house, the time had come for a showdown with Louise.

On Tuesday 23 January 1748 Louise was expecting her usual midnight visit from the prince. She sat in her room talking to Mlle Carteret about him. Unexpectedly, her father the duc de Bouillon arrived. Downstairs he and la Guéméné conferred. At ten o'clock the two of them appeared at her door. Mlle Carteret was asked to leave. Then the princess began her indictment. She had known about the

affair with the prince for a long time. The matter was now becoming
a public scandal. The liaison must end at once. If Louise promised
to write a letter to Charles Edward, ending the affair, all traces of
her indiscretion would be covered up.[86]

Louise collapsed into hysterical screaming, followed by steady,
uncontrollable sobbing. But she was no more a match for the strong-
willed Princess de Guéméné than she had been for the prince. She
was forced to write a letter to Charles at her father's dictation,
informing him that their sexual relationship had to come to an end.
However, to avoid scandal, it was necessary that the prince continue
to visit the Guéméné residence on a social basis.

The prince did not at first know the reason for this sudden termination. It was a full five days later before Louise managed to smuggle
out a tear-stained letter, explaining the dramatic events of the night
of 23 January.[87] The letter alone would probably have been enough
to awaken his basically chivalrous instincts and enable him to resume
the affair, despite the Bouillon/Guéméné interdict. But the prince
had already received an account of 23 January from Mlle Carteret
that effectively destroyed the relationship.

Puzzled by the startling dénouement to his affair evinced by
Louise's dictated letter, the prince asked Mlle Carteret for an account
of all recent events she had witnessed, omitting nothing. It was then
that he learned of the highly critical remarks made about him by the
duc de Bouillon during the highly emotional confrontation on the
night of 23 January. In the hothouse atmosphere of Louise's bedroom
– where all three principals had at one time been in tears together –
the duc de Bouillon had denounced the prince as an ingrate and
snake-in-the-grass. Bouillon declared that he had always supported
the prince through great difficulties and at great personal and political
cost. The prince's return for this, it seemed, was to dishonour his
daughter in her own house.[88]

This charge upset the prince more than Mlle Carteret could ever
have imagined, and, typically, his response was one of hostility to
Louise for being weak enough to submit to her father's authority.[89]
He failed to reply to her smuggled letter. Louise in desperation
deluged him with further missives. Why had he forsaken her? What
had happened to their great and undying love? How could the prince
be so lacking in compassion? If he cared nothing for *her*, surely he
cared about the fate of their unborn child?[90]

No answer came. At great risk, since all her servants were under
orders from the Princesse de Guéméné, Louise began to write to
Daniel O'Brien and others of the prince's servants. What had

happened to the great and loving prince? If love had mysteriously evaporated, was there no pity left? O'Brien brought back fragments of rationalisation from the prince. Louise had been unfaithful to him, she had had other lovers, she had shown her letter to third parties. At this, Louise began to hint that she might take her own life and destroy the prince's unborn child.

Still Charles did not reply. This was his punishment for the unsupportable accusations meted out to him by her parents. Louise saw just one way out of the impasse. She would have to arrange a meeting with the prince. But the awesome Princess de Guéméné stood like the angel with the fiery sword barring the return to paradise. She managed to block and thwart all Louise's schemes for arranging a rendezvous.

The failure of Louise to meet the rendezvous agreed on by secret correspondence simply fuelled the prince's self-justifications. It proved her essential weakness and timidity. Was she not mistress in her own house? Why did she not slay the dragoness, stand up to the fearsome Princesse de Guéméné and tell her straight that she intended to command her own destiny, scandal or no scandal?

Despite many setbacks, Louise persevered. Her pertinacity was rewarded when she finally met her lover again, for the first time in four months. On 18 May 1748, on the Pont Tournant at midnight, she and the prince again consummated their love in a closed carriage.[91]

The encounter left Louise as emotionally frenzied as ever. But the prince was lukewarm. He was the sort of person who, if he could not experience a sensation at the exact time he wanted, quickly convinced himself the desire did not exist. The high tide of his passion had passed, he told her. He loved her still, though not as much as before. And he had someone else.

We cannot be certain if, following the encounter on the Pont Tournant, there was not more cramped dalliance in closed carriages. It is even possible that Louise finally risked scandal and went openly to the prince's house. Whatever the case, from the prince's viewpoint the affair was now clearly on the wane. The events of 23 January had worked their evil too well. There could be no going back. At some stage early that summer the liaison petered out.

The prince even lost interest in his child. A son was born, christened and duly accepted as a Rohan. At the age of five months, the child died.[92] By that time the prince was disporting himself in the fleshpots of Avignon and had forgotten all about him. As for the luckless Louise, she was the originator and recipient of nothing more than dutiful correspondence with the prince (and later king) for the

rest of her thirty-three years of life. Crushed by the traumatic experience of love *à la folie*, followed by callous abandonment by the man
of her life, she relapsed stoically into the life of an unambitious
aristocratic matron.[93] If we wish to believe that she ever saw the
prince again, we have to take the unconfirmed word of British sources,
who reported a meeting with the prince in 1753 at the monastery of
St Anchin near Lille.[94]

But it was not yet quite the end of the story. The prince did not
bow out of Louise's life before he had taken his revenge on the Rohans
by provoking a social scandal. It will be remembered that the duc
de Bouillon and Princesse de Guéméné had requested that the prince
continue his social calls, so that no malicious tongues would be set
wagging. This was precisely what the prince was determined *not* to
do. He had hit on the perfect method of chastising the contumacious
Rohan clan. Pointedly, he stayed away from their social gatherings.

Two of the prince's most ardent female supporters were Madame
de Mézière's daughters, the Princesse de Ligne and the Princesse de
Montauban.[95] They made repeated efforts in the early months of
1748 to get the prince to call at the Guéméné residence, but in vain.
The prince was not content with simple snubbing. He toyed with the
Guéménés, promising to attend suppers, then crying off at the last
minute through 'illness' (at least he had learned something from Earl
Marischal!).[96] Eventually, even the devoted Princesse de Ligne gave
up.[97]

The affront to the Rohans' honour was taken up by the two most
formidable matriarchs of the day. First the Princesse de Guéméné
essayed her mettle. But the prince hated and detested her.[98] Her
overtures were brutally rebuffed. The sequel to this was a public
slanging-match between the two, so fiery and intemperate that the
marquis d'Argenson misinterpreted it as a lover's quarrel.[99]

Next the marquise de Mézières tried her hand. She had a much
better track record of deference to the prince, but she fared no better.
The old intriguer's hackles rose. Angrily she accused the prince of
betraying his old friends: 'this in good French is called throwing your
friends out of the window for amusement.'[100] She ended her irate
letter by heavily underscoring her letter, 'Eleanor, Marquise de
Mézières', as if to reassert the injured honour of the Rohans.

The prince was unconcerned. He was still *the* social catch in Paris.
It was still a seller's market for the prince's attentions. The arrogant
Rohans could stew in their own juice. That there were plenty of
buyers for his presence soon became clear when he moved on to a
new mistress and a new social set.

24

A New Mistress

(March–August 1748)

The political situation in early 1748 could hardly have been less promising for the prince. It was now certain that a general peace would soon bring the War of Austrian Succession to an end. Charles Edward was still locked in stubborn conflict with France. All hope of a descent on England was laid aside. The prince's best efforts with the comte d'Argenson were devoted to finding lucrative positions for his followers; Lord Ogilvy finally obtained a French regiment.[1] But the War Minister's personal animus towards Lally – after Kelly the Jacobite personally closest to the prince – meant that, though Charles's personal choice, he was unable to take over Lochiel's regiment when the gallant Cameron chief died of meningitis later that year.[2]

All the senior Jacobite officers of the '45, except Lord George Murray, were now settled in France with places or pensions.[3] Charles Edward himself still officially refused to accept the French pension, but the French had hit on a scheme to force his hand. They refused to pay anything for the relief of the starving Jacobite 'other ranks' on the grounds that the monthly sum paid to the prince was 'global' and included an element for the subsistence of his needy followers. Henceforth the prince would be paid 11,000 livres a month (8,000 livres for himself and 3,000 for his followers).[4] Charles Edward was thus forced into a choice between seeing Highlanders die and accepting the French pension. He found an ingenious compromise. The ministers would pay the pension money to the banker Monmartel, who in turn would pay it to Lally.[5] It would then be distributed as needed, but the prince could still maintain the fiction that he had accepted nothing from Louis XV. When James wrote to say how glad he was that his son had finally accepted the French pension, Charles Edward angrily denied that this was the case.[6]

The prince continued as uncompromising in all other political areas. He rejected brusquely a proposal to make him the next king of Poland:

A throne in itself, I assure you, is not the object of my ambition. I see that a private man may be happier than any sovereign, but I think I owe myself to my country. No other throne in the universe but that of Great Britain would engage my desires.[7]

It is not surprising, given his inflexible attitude to Louis XV and his ministers, that he should have been drawn into a social circle that was far from uncritical of the Ancien Régime. Anne-Charlotte de Crussol-Florensac, duchesse d'Aiguillon, was the hostess of the most brilliant salon in Paris. Every Saturday she gave a magnificent supper, to which were invited notable foreigners, ministers in office, former ministers, and men of letters. She adopted a deliberate policy of mixing ranks. Among her circle could be found the future Foreign Minister duc de Choiseul, president Hénault, Abbé (later Cardinal) Bernis, Maupertuis the polar explorer, and the *philosophes* Voltaire and Montesquieu.[8]

The duchesse d'Aiguillon lived an eccentric life even by the standards of Ancien Régime France. Now aged forty-eight, she connived at the open affair between her husband and the Princesse de Conti. In effect, the trio lived as a *ménage à trois*. Someone with such contempt for the proprieties was likely to be attractive to Charles Edward. It was not just in her intelligence and ability to speak four languages that she seemed a perfect complement to the prince. Montesquieu said of her that she was the woman in France who lived most fully and intensely in any given period of time, and that she was fonder of her enemies than her friends. Some observers, who had contrasted the prince's reluctance to criticise Cumberland with his harshness towards Henry, thought they had heard that story somewhere before. And Montesquieu's damning portrait of the duchess uncannily pre-echoed Louise of Stolberg's later strictures on Charles Edward: 'She has intellect, but it is of the poorest kind. She has the pride of a pedant and all the faults of a lackey.'[9]

Moreover, some of the duchesse d'Aiguillon's acidulous comments on the court of Louis XV would have struck a sympathetic chord in Charles Edward: 'This place [Versailles],' she once declared, 'is the vain land of the wind. There blow there waterspouts of ambition, jealousy and pride. Illusions abound there.'[10]

Sure enough, the duchesse d'Aiguillon and Charles Edward greatly took to each other at the temperamental level, though there seems never to have been any sexual element in their relationship. The prince became a constant visitor at her Saturday evening soirées.[11] She corresponded with him about her growing family of grand-children.[12] He confided to her his hatred of Tencin.[13] She replied by identifying his friends and enemies at the French court (the duc de Gesvres, later in the year to play a crucial role in the prince's life, was placed as one of the former).[14] Even after the prince went into exile and began his years as a wanderer, the relationship continued by letter.[15] There is a very touching exchange between the two at the time of the duc d'Aiguillon's death in 1750.[16]

The duchess was not the only one drawn into the web of the prince's admirers. Montesquieu, who had earlier written to Hume for information on the Highland system of heritable jurisdictions, was also very attracted to Charles Edward. The feeling was reciprocated. General Francis Bulkeley told Montesquieu in August 1748, when the *philosophe* was at Bordeaux, that the prince liked him immensely, missed him and spoke often of him.[17]

The relationship began with an exchange of literary productions, the prince's protest against the Aix-la-Chapelle peace preliminaries for *Décadence des Romains*.[18] Montesquieu proved an adroit courtier. Who better to send a book on Roman heroes to, he wrote, than one who had made them come to life by emulating their exploits?[19] Continuing to lay it on with a trowel, Montesquieu spoke of the prince's written declaration as having simplicity, nobility and eloquence. He said that if Charles were not a great prince, he and Mme d'Aiguillon would like to propose him for election to the Académie Française.[20] Amiably the prince replied, speaking of the 'trust between authors'.[21] Montesquieu confessed himself flattered by the attention Charles Edward paid him.[22]

The process of mutual admiration continued after the prince's expulsion from France. Montesquieu frequently expressed his indignation at French treatment of the prince.[23] The level of mutual regard comes out in an exchange in 1749. Charles Edward requested that each edition of Montesquieu's work be sent to him as it came out, even if he was at the Antipodes. 'Though I am in obscurity,' he went on, 'my mind is not, thanks to your works.'[24] Montesquieu replied in kind: 'We are all like the brave Scots in that we cannot hear of you without loving you. Whether you show yourself, or remain hidden, you will always have the admiration of the universe.'[25]

But the most important development in the prince's life resulting from his entry into the d'Aiguillon social circle was his acquisition of a new mistress. Marie-Anne-Louise Jablonowska, Princesse de

Talmont, was a cousin of the queen of France and had been in her time a fabulous beauty. When the prince fell in with her, she was in her mid-forties.[26] Like her friend the duchesse d'Aiguillon, she was a highly unconventional woman. In her time she had had many lovers, most notably ex-king Stanislas of Poland (exiled to Lorraine after the War of Polish Succession in the 1730s).[27] In 1730 Marie Jablonowska was married to the Prince de Talmont, a scion and second son of the La Trémoille family.[28] This was another dynastic marriage of convenience. While the Prince de Talmont, ten years his wife's junior, was a repressed homosexual who sublimated his leanings in devotional austerities,[29] the princess continued to live an emancipated life and took a string of lovers. She was intelligent, witty, cynical and worldly-wise, one who masked a failed or frustrated creativity under a veil of caprice and eccentricity.[30] She had an instant entrée to the court both through her kinship with the queen and her friendship with Maurepas, who shared her taste in caustic wit and cynical lampoonery.[31]

By the time of Charles Edward's return from Scotland, even her shaky marriage of convenience with the Prince de Talmont was on the rocks. Their public quarrels gave scandal even to the permissive court at Versailles. King Stanislas, who had gone on to take the Princesse de Talmont's sister Countess Ossolinska as his mistress, was asked to mediate and arrange an amiable separation.[32] He in turn chose two arbitrators, one to champion the husband, the other the wife. President of the Parlement Maupeou was chosen to represent the prince; Maurepas represented the princess.[33]

The terms of the separation allowed the prince, whose income was much less than his wife's, to sell their *hôtel*. Until that time, the two would share the same home for the sake of appearances. Thereafter, the couple would live apart.[34] The protracted negotiations while the Prince de Talmont bartered for the best possible price for his house later produced some interesting and unforeseen results involving Charles Edward.

Such, then, was the woman whom the prince now publicly avowed as his mistress. Part of the punishment Charles meted out to his former mistress Louise de Montbazon was to appear openly at the Opera at the end of April 1748 with his new mistress, knowing that Louise was also in attendance and would be watching.[35]

The prince switched from the passionate intensity of love with the twenty-two-year-old Louise to the calculated lubricity of an affair with the mature and vastly experienced Princesse de Talmont. The arrangement suited him better at the sexual level. In place of feverish

love-making of the honeymoon variety, he now enjoyed the practised
arts of an aristocratic courtesan. This freed him from any real
responsibility in the sexual relationship. The switch from a twenty-
two-year old mistress to one twice her age is abrupt enough to merit
further consideration.

All the evidence from the doomed romance with Louise de
Montbazon suggests that the prince relished highly charged carnal
relationships. What he did not relish was any sense of responsibility
or commitment to a woman. It was to be the Princesse de Talmont's
misfortune, as she reached the end of her career as upper-class adven-
turess, that she tried to convert the affair with Charles Edward into
something more permanent. The more one examines the prince's
personality, the more one sees it as one where sexual promiscuity, or
at any rate tempestuous short-term affairs, were its most appropriate
expression. The peculiarly unfortunate, truncated and flawed
relationship with his mother must bear much of the responsibility.
Where a son enjoying a sustained loving relationship with a loving
mother gradually learns to integrate love and sex, one deprived too
early, especially in tragic circumstances, may find his response to
women fragmented. It is certain that Charles Edward never enjoyed
a satisfactory, sustained, integrated relationship with any woman.
The nearest he came was with Louise de Montbazon. But as soon as
stresses impinged on the passion, the prince's fragile personality
began to unravel.

From the very beginning the new relationship was a stormy one.
The prince and Madame de Talmont were oil and water. She was a
woman used to satisfying her whims, indulging her intellectual,
aesthetic or carnal fantasies – a genuine *capriciosa*, in a word. The
prince by 1748 had reached the point where he would allow no one
to question his authority, where he (or she) who was not with him
was against him, where no one could speak a word of even the mildest
criticism about him – this was construed as 'giving him laws' – where
his will was paramount. The underlying trend in the relationship
with La Talmont was thus the collision of the irresistible force with
the immovable object.

These latent contradictions took time to work themselves to the
surface. At the beginning of the affair, to testify to her devotion,
Madame de Talmont wore a cameo of the prince in a bracelet, on
the other side of which was a picture of Jesus Christ. A contemporary
wag[36] pointed out that the same motto suited both personages
depicted on the bracelet: 'My kingdom is not of this world.'[37]

At first it looked as though the marquis d'Argenson was right, that

Madame de Talmont had a mesmeric hold on Charles Edward and encouraged him in all his worst excesses, distorting his vision and adding a moiety of madness and stupidity all her own.[38] More and more it seemed likely that the prince intended to defy the French to do their worst once a general peace was signed. So worried were the exiled Jacobites in France, who after all depended on Louis XV for their new careers, that a general meeting was called to discuss the looming crisis. Present were Glenbucket, Ardshiel, Lord Lewis Gordon, Lord Nairne, Lochiel and Sir Hector Maclean – a fair sprinkling of the prince's council during the '45.[39] It was decided that Lochiel was the only person at once capable of giving dispassionate advice to the prince and still with enough credit to be listened to.[40] Unfortunately, Lochiel fell ill with meningitis and died soon afterwards. All other Jacobites felt they did not have the credibility to breach the magic circle of Kelly, Lally and Harrington. Mostly they were reduced to wringing their hands in despair.[41]

The peace preliminaries at Aix-la-Chapelle continued. Eventually agreement was reached. The prince's position became increasingly grave. How could he defy the might of France? Charles Edward seemed to be basing his hopes on two things: a prestigious foreign marriage and his status as the hero of the Paris mob.

The prince had an immense popular following in Paris. Throughout 1748 he tried to build up this power base by showing himself in public as much as possible. The Opera, Comédie Française and other spectacles were particular targets.[42] He seems to have thought that fear of popular disturbance might force the court to stay their hand against him. The strategy was not entirely chimerical: the ministers of state *did* take seriously the possible reactions of the mob. But the political consciousness that would sanction a head-on clash with the Ancien Régime was still forty years in the future.

The *deus ex machina* of a foreign marriage seemed much more promising. As usual, the prince started his marriage prospect by aiming very high. He sent Sir John Graeme to Berlin to ask for the hand of Frederick the Great's sister.[43] Apart from the desire to cock a snook at France, the prince had a further aim. As he told Graeme, he wanted to show the world that he had done with 'popery'. To seek a Protestant bride was his answer to the chicanery of the 'Vicar of Christ' who had connived at the treacherous design to make Henry a cardinal.[44]

Once again we confront the utter cynicism of the prince in matters of religion. He despised the forms and trappings of organised churches and regarded all religious disputation as the theological writhings of medieval schoolmen. He was a modern figure in that he genuinely could not understand how rational men could be swayed by dogmas and belief in the supernatural. But it was a mistake to make his contempt so plain. Committed believers, especially those with political leverage, do not like to be told by wayward princes that their cherished beliefs are no better than the totems and taboos of benighted savages. But it was ever thus with the prince: he would embrace any dispensation, Protestant or Catholic, as long as it seemed likely to take him closer to his personal goals.

Predictably, Graeme's mission was a fiasco. Frederick sent word that he wanted Graeme out of his kingdom instantly: the emissary should think himself lucky he had not been placed under arrest.[45]

Graeme now wanted to abandon the hunt for a Protestant princess in Germany, on the ground that all the other princelings would take their cue from Frederick of Prussia. But the prince held him to his task. He stressed that he was engaged in a race for time against the peace negotiations. As for family solidarity among the Protestant princes in support of the 'Elector of Hanover', Henry had already shown how much that was worth.[46]

Graeme then proceeded to Darmstadt and entered into negotiations for the hand of Princess Caroline-Louise, daughter of the landgrave of Hesse-Darmstadt. The landgrave stalled, stressed his friendship for George II, and hinted that the proposal would have been welcome a year earlier.[47] But Graeme was under strict orders from Charles Edward. The marriage proposal was a once-and-for-all affair; if it was rejected now, there would be no second chances.[48] The landgrave left the decision to his daughter. Knowing her father's real wishes, she rejected the suit.[49] This part of the prince's strategy of thwarting France was already an abject failure by August 1748.

25

'A Great Prince in Prison Lies'

(August–December 1748)

The great traumatic crisis with France in 1748, that was to leave a scar on the prince's psyche greater even than Derby or his brother's defection as a cardinal, was already in prospect by August of that year. The Treaty of Aix-la-Chapelle was to be ratified on 18 October, but it was already clear from the preliminaries that England would make peace with France only if all members of the Stuart family were expelled from French dominions. Naturally the Stuarts protested.[1] This was to be expected, a mere ritualistic formality. What no one except intimates of the prince expected was that by the most blatant brinkmanship he would force France to reveal her own shame. There was already domestic discontent about the terms on which France was proposing to make peace: '*bête comme la paix*', 'stupid as the peace', became a proverb. Charles Edward, by his stubborn resistance, would force the reality of French politics into naked exposure: not only was the peace against the national interest of France; it also made nonsense of her official ideology.

What eventually became the scandal of the decade began innocuously enough. In the early stages of the struggle with Louis XV the prince was diplomacy itself. In July he entered his own protest against the provisions of the Aix-la-Chapelle treaty which had just been published.[2] At the same time he wrote to the French king to explain his position, which was that the preliminaries placed him in a terrible position. He seemed to imply that his protest was every bit as formulaic as James's but added, in a phrase that acquires an ominous significance in hindsight, that he would never forget Louis's protection 'whatever happens in the future'.[3]

Immediately, the three-way process that clouded the events of late 1748 made its appearance. Puysieux sent a polite letter to O'Sullivan informally requesting the prince's departure. The mere mention of this from O'Sullivan brought an angry rebuke from Charles Edward.[4] Meanwhile, on seeing the prince's personal protest, James wrote to him in August to ask him not to publish any more declarations 'in the king's name'.[5] Charles regarded his father with contempt. He knew he could expect no positive support from him in the ordeal that lay ahead. All his letters to James in this period say the same: nothing.

Yet it was not easy to ignore the French. They were as determined that the prince should leave their territory as he was to remain on it. At first they tried gentle prodding. In August an envoy was sent from Versailles directly to the prince to remind him that the preliminaries of the peace had been signed as long ago as April. Puysieux, who hated Charles Edward and resented the place he had in Louis XV's affections, went twice in person to see his *bête noire* and to request him to observe the clear provisions of the Aix-la-Chapelle treaty.[6] The prince replied haughtily that since he rejected the legitimacy of the entire treaty, it followed that he could not be bound by any articles that referred to him.[7] Moreover, he pointed out, the Treaty of Fontainebleau, signed in October 1745 between James and Louis guaranteed him a secure asylum in France. Puysieux replied that the guarantee applied only in wartime. Nothing had ever been promised the prince in peacetime. And it was a commonplace of international politics, understood by everybody, that when a new treaty was signed it annulled the provisions of old ones.[8]

Puysieux then made his personal position crystal clear. On his first visit to the prince, he referred to him as 'Your Royal Highness'. By the second visit, this had become 'Monsieur'.[9] Puysieux's bad opinion of the prince was confirmed when a source from within the Stuart household informed him anonymously that Charles Edward was determined to dig in his heels and defy the French to do their worst.[10]

As he demonstrated later, Louis XV liked nothing better than running parallel policies. In echelon with the official channel used by Puysieux, the king tried his own brand of diplomacy. On 25 August he wrote the prince a long letter. As father of the French people, he argued, he could not allow the prince's interests to override those of twenty million Frenchmen and, ultimately, of all Europe. But he was personally sympathetic to the prince's position. Knowing his reluctance to return to Italy, he offered to use all his influence to find a safe refuge in Friburg or Switzerland.[11] The number of crossings-out in the letter indicates Louis's indecision and nervousness about how to proceed.

It was not difficult for Louis to persuade Friburg and the Swiss cantons to agree to provide a secure home for the prince.[12] Predictably, the English protested to the putative hosts, but their attitude smacked too much of dog in the manger.[13] In any case, the English minister in Switzerland, John Burnaby, overreached himself by delivering a note to the magistrates of Friburg that was far too imperious in tone.[14] English attempts at bullying were counterproductive. Friburg and the other Swiss cantons expressed themselves ready and pleased to play host to the Stuart prince.[15]

But Charles Edward wanted none of it. As far as he was concerned, the clauses of the Aix-la-Chapelle treaty demanding his expulsion from France could not possibly be implemented by a ruler by divine right. Louis XV recognised James as king of England and Charles Edward as heir apparent. Were Louis to expel a fellow sovereign at the behest of the English, he would make a mockery of the entire notion of divine, indefeasible right. If Louis once admitted that the legitimate claimant to a throne could be expelled by another divine right monarch in the interests of expediency, he cut the ground from under his own legitimacy. The situation was different with George II. He was self-confessedly king as trustee. He reigned with the say-so of the English Parliament. Louis XV was constrained by no parliament. It followed that if he expelled a fellow-monarch by divine, indefeasible right, he would in effect be conceding that he himself could be expelled by *force majeure*, since that was ultimately the only sanction he recognised. Charles Edward argued that Louis was in a different position from the 'Elector of Hanover'; he could not allow the untrammelled sway of expediency, lest he diminish the mystique of monarchy itself. Once again we see that the prince's intellectual grip was stronger than his detractors would have us believe. The events of late 1748 have usually been presented as the obstinate refusal of a blockhead to face reality. In fact they represented a calculated gamble. Only at the very end of the struggle, when the balance of power swung decisively in Louis's favour, did the prince's self-destructive urges come into play.

The prince miscalculated because he had not got the measure of Louis XV's personality. Concepts of honour and morality, other than as verbal camouflage, meant little to the French king. Fundamentally amoral, he was constrained by religion only because it threatened divine punishment in the after-life. The law of love itself Louis would have regarded with contempt. He was not the sort of person who would be bothered by philosophical self-contradiction or ideological inconsistency. Moreover, the prince's tactics were precisely the wrong ones when it came to manipulating Louis XV. Indecisive, secretive, neurotic, Louis was likely to react with peculiar anger to anyone who backed him into a corner. The prince's tactic of revealing the contradictions between the king's actions and Bourbon ideology were always likely to miscarry in face of a personality like Louis XV. To the French king, prevarication, secrecy and duplicity were almost a way of life. His resentment against a man who tried to strip away the veils of obfuscation and mystification in which he wrapped himself can well be imagined. The conflict between Louis XV and Charles Edward was not that between two strong wills. It was rather a duel between a hunter and a singularly deadly animal whose lack of aggression right up to the moment of truth misleads the hunter as to the beast's ultimate ferocity.

October came and with it the signing of the treaty. Louis had given the prince a lot of rope, but it was clear that he was not going to allow him to defy the might of the French state. France was in danger of becoming the laughing-stock of Europe. It was time for Louis to deploy more formidable forces over a wider front.

One obvious tactic was to bring pressure on the prince through the numerous Jacobite émigrés in the service of France, men who owed their pensions, careers and futures to the patronage and generosity of Versailles. But Louis overrated their influence with the prince. Charles Edward had long operated on the principle that whoever was not with him was against him. Since most of the émigrés were either James's men – and had already been used unsuccessfully by him to attempt to moderate the prince's behaviour – or were French careerists first and Jacobites second, there was little leverage they could exert. The fate of General Francis Bulkeley's attempt at mediation showed how little could be expected from this tactic. Bulkeley penned a most adroit letter of compliance as from the prince to Louis XV. Charles refused to send it on. In a most striking clue to his state of mind, he rejected Bulkeley's efforts with these words, echoing Pilate: '*Quod dixi, dixi, et quod scripsi, scripsi.*' ('What I have said, I have said, and what I have written, I have written.')[16]

A more promising line of approach seemed to be to muzzle those ministers most obviously opposed to Charles Edward, like Puysieux and Maurepas, and bring in those courtiers with a proven record of being able to get on with the prince. Immediately after signing the ratification of the treaty on 18 October, Louis sent the duc de Gesvres, governor of Paris and first gentleman of the Royal Chamber, to reason with the prince.[17] Gesvres was an old favourite of Charles Edward's, even though he was described unkindly by one Jacobite as having no more brains than a sparrow.[18] The interview was cordial but abortive. 'Do you like the king of England so much as to give him so much pleasure?' Gesvres asked, insisting that Louis XV would arrest the prince if pushed to the limit.[19]

The prince struck back vigorously. 'What crime have I committed that I should be arrested?' he asked. He warned that he would rather die than submit to the laws of Hanover.[20] De Gesvres stayed with him for more than an hour, explaining the situation.[21] He also read him a long letter from Louis XV, a mixture of threat and cajolery.[22] It was left that the prince would come to see Gesvres at 8.30 p.m. next day to give a definite answer. But Charles Edward's reply was a severe disappointment to the French. He simply reiterated the sentiments he had expressed to Puysieux in August. Although the letter was courteously written, the pith of it was that the prince regretted that he was unable on this occasion to do Louis's bidding.[23]

At about the same time Louis XV wrote to James to ask him to put pressure on his son.[24] James wrote to Charles about his 'singular' behaviour and warned him that he was on a collision course.[25] He did not, however, explicitly ask him to desist from his actions: as he explained to Tencin, given the prince's history of ignoring him, such a command would be counterproductive and might push his son into open revolt.[26]

James's lack of firm action over the prince's intransigence in the autumn of 1748 has sometimes been considered odd, but his correspondence with Tencin reveals the reasons.[27] One of the factors that constrained him was a fear of deepening the rift between himself and his son. James was convinced that many ostensible Jacobites like Kelly were either Hanoverian double agents or had their own sinister reasons for wanting to widen the breach between Stuart father and son. Besides, James was shrewd enough to see that summoning Charles Edward back to Rome meant conceding that all Jacobite hopes were in vain. And since the prince would not go to Switzerland – Friburg had by this time withdrawn its invitation – James was practically powerless.[28]

Matters had now reached a desperate pass. The eyes of all Europe were on Louis XV and the prince, waiting to see which would crack first. Frederick of Prussia, who had earlier claimed that France's sloughing off of Charles Edward illustrated the cynicism of the times, changed his tune by the end of November. He said he could not understand how a sane man could so depart from reason as to want to stand 'Knut-like' against the tide.[29] By the beginning of December he was bored with the long-running saga and rebuked his minister in France Chambrier for wasting too much time on it in his dispatches.[30]

Benedict XIV was another incredulous observer. He claimed that Louis XV had done everything possible to get the prince out of France without violence. The Pope's main concern was to make sure Charles Edward did not return to Rome. He was convinced that the shock would kill James.[31]

In England the crisis was watched with a mixture of exasperation and incredulity.[32] Some saw the prince's obstinacy as a colossal blunder, ruining his reputation and destroying the Jacobite cause more completely than Culloden.[33] Others perceived it as a brilliant propaganda stroke. According to this version, the prince's elaborate charade was devised for English consumption. He was showing the English nation that he was his own man, the exact opposite of a French puppet.[34] The same strategy had been adopted by Charles II: humiliated by France, then restored to England. Some even wilder rumours were gaining currency, to the effect that the dauphin and the French queen were using Charles Edward as a weapon in their struggle to smash the influence of Madame de Pompadour.[35]

What was happening meanwhile at Versailles? From being an irritant and an embarrassment before the final signature of the Aix-la-Chapelle treaty, *l'affaire Prince Edouard* was now a major crisis. The credibility of the king and his ministers was at stake. The only question for the council was how to resolve the crisis. Forlorn Jacobites like Lady Clifford, who feared for their own future if the House of Stuart became a dirty word in France, hopefully intimated that it was all a question of money.[36] If the right financial incentives were offered to the prince, he would be prepared to depart. Puysieux, rightly, was sceptical. He thought the issue was greater than mere lucre. In any case, he alleged, Louis XV was already so angry that it was doubtful he would agree to a pacific solution at this late hour.[37]

This was not quite true. Louis still hoped to avoid a damaging showdown. Again he sent Gesvres to see the prince and make a final effort to get him to see reason.[38] In tandem with this, he wrote to James in strong terms, asking him to *order* his son from France.[39]

Gesvres's second interview with the prince was a tearful affair. Charles stressed that he was personally and emotionally very attached to both Gesvres and Louis XV, but that had nothing to do with it. Gesvres warned that the prince had no choice: he could either depart peacefully for Switzerland or he would be arrested and shipped out to Rome.[40] At this the prince became angry. If what Gesvres said was true, it indicated personal vindictiveness on Louis XV's part.

Would he really need to use so much force just to please George II?[41] After his conversation with Gesvres, the prince made the following note:

> I have always thought Louis was constrained by the Treaty of Aix-la-Chapelle and that he acted reluctantly. But after his sending Puysieux and Gesvres twice, I begin to think this is a personal thing, that Louis wishes to chase me from his kingdom for private reasons.[42]

It is easy to dismiss this as paranoia, but it may be too easy. Anything that forced Louis XV to reveal his hand clearly, without subterfuge or prevarication, was liable to provoke an angry backlash. At last the prince began to realise something of the slumbering ogre he had aroused by forcing Louis into the daylight. But he was too far sunk in his own project to back out now. As his trump card, he warned Gesvres that Louis's troops would never take him alive. If they attempted to arrest him, they would have a suicide on their hands.[43] Since the prince had made a point of receiving him with his hand on his sword-hilt, and the room in which they sat contained enough guns and swords for a long siege, Gesvres was convinced this was no bluff.[44]

Gesvres finally asked the prince in exasperation whether he seriously expected France to renege on its treaty obligations and go to war again just for him. Stung by this, the prince replied haughtily that from then on he would discuss his position only with the French king himself.[45]

The court next made an effort to bring pressure to bear on the Princesse de Talmont. Madame d'Aiguillon had dropped out of the prince's circle once she saw him in head-on collision with Louis, but la Talmont was still at his side.[46] Some said she was encouraging him to fight to the bitter end; others claimed she was trying to turn Charles away from his desperate project. The truth was that she *had* originally encouraged the prince in his defiance. But once she saw how things were developing at Versailles and realised that she was on shifting sands herself, she changed tack and began to advocate bowing to the inevitable.[47] Maurepas, Talmont's chief contact at court, let it be known that when the prince was finally expelled, there would be a reckoning for those who had encouraged him to defy the king.

But this was not a good time to ask the Princesse de Talmont to exert influence. The hotel Talmont had still not been sold, and as part of the 'civilised' separation arranged by Maurepas, the Talmont couple took it in turn to live in the house. Unaware that it was the husband's turn to be in residence, the prince one afternoon went in search of his mistress. To his great consternation, he found the way barred by Talmont's butler and informed there was no one at home. Talmont had decided to heed Maurepas's warning by denying the troublesome Charles Edward his house.[48]

Thinking that it was his mistress who was excluding him, the prince returned next morning with tools for forcing the doors of the *hôtel*. A major scandal was brewing when General Bulkeley hurried to the scene and persuaded the irate prince to desist.[49]

The context was thus not propitious for the Princesse de Talmont to exert a restraining influence. First she had to make abject apologies for her husband's 'mistake'. Then she had to query the wisdom of the prince's posture towards Louis XV. The moment she chose was a dinner given by the Irish brigade officer Colonel Beauchair. She begged and implored the prince to see reason. Charles Edward's response was typical. In a singularly brusque manner he cut across her words and changed the subject.[50]

The only hope for the French now, short of violence, was a direct order to the prince from his father. When James received Louis XV's request, he agonised before complying. He told Tencin that it had cost him a lot to send the required order. The sole consideration that swayed him to act in concert with Louis XV was the thought of the fiasco that might ensue if the prince were returned to Rome under armed guard.[51]

Nevertheless, the letter James eventually sent could not have disappointed Versailles. After revealing that he had followed his son's struggle with the French with mounting anxiety, James concluded:

> I see you on the edge of a precipice about to fall in, and I would be an unnatural father if I did not do my best to save you. I therefore here and now order you, both as your father and your king, to obey without delay Louis XV's order to you to leave his dominions.[52]

There are two things to note about this letter. In the first place, if James was sincere in his avowed intention of playing no further part in public affairs, he should not have written it. For one thing, it gave the French the opportunity to say that any action they took against the prince was being taken not on their own account but in the name of King James.[53] Second, the prince was certain to regard this letter as the ultimate betrayal. By plotting to have Henry made a cardinal, James had already pushed his relations with Charles Edward dangerously near the limit. By writing this letter, in effect an act of collusion with Louis XV, James confirmed his status as evil genius in the prince's mind. It was bad enough that Louis XV should break his word and act as the creature of the 'Elector of Hanover'. But it was scarcely to be borne that the prince's own father should abet him in his nefarious actions.

Such an unambiguous and clear-cut order to the prince to leave French territory might have seemed the end of the affair for Charles. How could he deny his father, the source of his own legitimacy? But the prince had prepared for this eventuality. He had it bruited about that James had written to him secretly, warning him that he might have to indite a formal letter in such terms for reasons of diplomatic protocol, but advising him to ignore all such instructions issued under duress.[54]

The French ministers were determined to provide the prince with no loophole. The duc de Gesvres was sent on his third mission to Charles Edward, bearing a copy of James's letter. He also took Louis XV's ultimatum: the prince had three days to leave Paris and nine to quit France.[55]

True to his resolution to speak to nobody but Louis XV, the prince refused to see Gesvres. The governor of Paris was reduced to taking an affidavit from the prince's followers (Kelly, Graeme and Oxburgh) that they had received both the letter from James and the orders from Louis XV.[56]

The trio then reported to the prince. Kelly began to read out James's long letter. When he came to the words 'I order you as your father and king' the prince walked away and would not listen to any more.[57]

The next move in the battle of wits was for the French to publish James's letter in the newspapers and gazettes so that the people of Paris might know the true situation.[58] This seemed a trump card, but the prince was equal to this development too. James had copied the letter to his son in French for Louis XV's consumption and it was this version that was published. This gave the prince his opportunity. He declared that the letter was a forgery. The proof of this was twofold. In the first place, no king of England would ever write to the Prince of Wales in French, but in English. Second, the alleged letter had been delivered by Gesvres and had not arrived through the proper channels.[59] Naturally, the prince concluded, if the letter really was genuine, he would obey it; but he was certain it was a piece of imposture.

The prince followed this up with a piece of effrontery. He sent a message to Louis XV, asking for time to write to Rome to verify that the letter *did* proceed from his father. Charles claimed to be convinced that the letter was forged – either that or his father had been imposed on.[60] The clinching proof of this, the prince argued to Louis, was that his father had not withdrawn the commission of Regency. This was a nuance that a forger would not have been aware of. If it was really James who had written the letter, the very first thing he would have done was to revoke the powers of Regent.

Charles's stalling tactics served only to make the king still more angry. His rage moved up another notch when the prince once again raised the stakes. Two could play at the game of publishing confidential documents, Charles decided. He let it be known that he had private letters from Louis XV, couched in unambiguous terms and guaranteeing him life-time asylum in France.[61]

It was now clear to the French ministers that all normal measures had been exhausted. They either had to acquiesce in the prince's remaining in France, in full defiance of the king's orders, or they had to use force against him. After Louis XV's ultimatum delivered by Gesvres, anything other than the use of force would involve too great a loss of face by the French crown. The question then became, how exactly to proceed.

Divided counsels in the king's council (*conseil d'en haut*) were nothing new, but this time the differences over how to proceed were particularly pointed. The comte d'Argenson was against all violence, fearing the damage it could do the king's reputation.[62] The duc de Noailles agreed that the prince should be arrested, but felt that this should be a 'kid-gloves' affair.[63] Cardinal Tencin's position was the most ambivalent. As James's confidant, he had no particular liking for Charles Edward, who hated him. He was aware that he was being blamed in the council for the disastrous consequences of five years of pro-Jacobite policies, and wanted to distance himself from the prince so as to safeguard his own position as minister of state. At the same time, he realised that his position with James would be jeopardised if Charles Edward was treated humiliatingly. As Tencin saw it, the prince had pushed Louis XV into a corner.[64] The only way out was some eleventh-hour initiative from Charles's friends Richelieu and Belle-Isle. The trouble was that neither of these sat on the council of state.

But there can be no doubt that the two hardliners on the council were Puysieux and Maurepas. Puysieux had loathed the prince with incandescent intensity ever since the intellectual drubbing he had taken from him in August.[65] Noting the depth of his rancour,

Maurepas cunningly tried to evade responsibility for the prince's arrest by suggesting that Puysieux was the man with the right credentials for the job. This was too obvious a ploy even for a man of Puysieux's limited abilities to miss. He was adamant. Paris was Maurepas's responsibility as director of the city's police; it was therefore Maurepas who had to carry out the arrest.[66]

The devious and subtle Maurepas devoted much thought to the delicate task laid upon him. Foreign ambassadors were consulted. They opined that Louis XV was within his rights to arrest and expel Charles Edward, provided he was treated with respect.[67] But Maurepas's real problem was how to avoid the risk that the prince might make good his threat to kill himself. The course he favoured was to arrest Charles in his own house rather than in the open. A large body of old and reliable musketeers should surround the house and effect entry at 7 a.m. All other occupants of the house would be allowed to leave, but no one would be permitted to enter, by formal interdict which prescribed the Bastille as the penalty for non-co-operation. When the prince was left alone in the house with the musketeers, he would then be escorted to the prison at the Chateau de Vincennes.[68]

The other ministers considered that this was too risky. The prince would still have time to kill himself before the musketeers got inside the house. There was also the awesome possibility that the prince might persuade a band of fanatical Jacobites to fight to the death. Charles had also boasted (falsely) that his house was a veritable arsenal, chock-full of guns and gunpowder, and that anyone trying to storm it would be blown sky-high.[69] The prospect of a bloody siege and final storming of the house by musketeers, possibly involving heavy loss of life, conjured a vision of chaos too frightening to contemplate. Besides, it is abundantly clear from the evidence that the ministers feared that the Paris mob might make such an attack on the prince's house the occasion for a general street uprising.[70] Bloody revolution indirectly caused by the prince was the last thing Louis XV wanted.

The consensus formed for a street arrest. When Tencin saw the way the wind was blowing, he became more hard-line even than Puysieux and Maurepas, doubtless to impress the king with his commitment. It was apparently Tencin who first suggested that the prince be bound after the arrest.[71]

It was now just a question of time before the inevitable happened. This was the point, in these early days of December 1748, when the prince should have conceded defeat. He could have won the admiration of Europe for his defiant stand coupled with outstanding gifts as a diplomatic brinksman. The title of hero-statesman would have been his. But the prince redoubled his efforts even as he was losing sight of his aim. He told Bulkeley on 7 December that he would leave Paris only to depart for the other world.[72] Bulkeley, like all other Jacobites, detached himself from the prince once the contents of James's letter were known. Jacobite careers and positions depended on unquestioning obedience to the (rare) direct and explicit orders from James.[73]

What was going through the prince's mind in these last crucial days of freedom in Paris? Clearly the strain was intense. As early as September the papal nuncio reported that Charles was depressed, had lost weight and had an unhealthy colour.[74] Yet he bore himself outwardly as if he had not a care in the world. From August to December he continued to show himself in public and to frequent the opera.[75] On 30 November he attended the Comédie Française. Everyone in the audience stood up, as was the custom for princes of the blood.[76] So much for Puysieux and his 'monsieur'!

The contrast between the prince as seen in public and as seen by Nuncio Durini hints at the struggle going on within him. By now Charles had developed an obsession about French perfidy. His rational programme, as he later explained it to Bulkeley, was to force things to the bitter end, so that Louis XV would have to throw off the mask and sign an expulsion order in his own hand.[77] Then Louis would be exposed to the world as the perfidious charlatan he was.

Yet it is clear that the prince's struggle with France, fought against impossible odds, was also an externalised projection of an inner psychic drama. He had been beaten (betrayed, in his terms) at Derby, betrayed by his father and brother over the cardinalate. If he could just achieve this victory over France, the positive elements in his personality would once more gain the upper hand. The tragic irony was that the prince had chosen a scenario which could not but play to his negative, self-destructive impulses. We may say that France deserved better of Charles Edward. It is also plausible to argue the reverse. Yet there was in Charles Edward a perverse, almost suicidal, refusal to deal properly with the French court. Why could he not take the time and trouble to charm the French ministers – he was well capable of it? Instead, his self-destructiveness led him to express his disdain and contempt for them openly. He was outraged that such men controlled his destiny. He was not prepared to play by the rules of diplomatic protocol. He would not grovel before people for whom he had no respect. The unrealistic, self-destructive side of him seemed to conjure up a malignant demon or imp of the perverse that forever whispered in his ear: why should I truckle to these people?

On 10 December the prince's nemesis came at last. The French plan was governed by two considerations. The prince had constantly warned that he would carry out what Charles XII of Sweden had merely threatened: in other words, there would be a bloody siege followed by suicide. That ruled out house arrest. In the case of open arrest, the question was where to carry out the operation. It was the prince's insouciant frequenting of the opera that provided the clue.

The task of effecting the arrest was given to the duc de Biron, colonel of the French grenadier guards. With his most senior major M. Vaudreuil, Biron planned the coup with meticulous detail.[78] At Vaudreuil's house an operational committee was set up, consisting of the guards' battalion commanders and their sergeants. The ambush was to be laid in and around the Palais Royal. Altogether 1,200 men were deployed, in alleyways, courtyards, houses, and even kitchens in the vicinity. It was known that carriages conveying the nobility to the Opera set down in the cul-de-sac hard by the Opera building. This was where the élite grenadier sergeants, hand-picked for their intrepidity, would be waiting.

The duc de Biron himself planned to wait nearby in a carriage, in disguise. All the way from the Palais Royal to the Chateau de Vincennes troops of musketeers were standing by, ready to spring to horse. Just in case Charles Edward managed to elude his captors and take refuge in a nearby house with his retainers, with the intention of standing off a siege, locksmiths, ladders and a supply of axes were at hand. There were even three surgeons waiting to tend the wounded. The most famous doctor in Paris, M. Vernage, was told to hold himself in readiness at his house between 6 and 7 p.m. and to come without question if he was summoned.[79] Most controversially of all, Biron ordered up ten lengths of red silk cord, with which he intended to bind the prince hand and foot.

On the morning of the 10th, rumours of what was afoot reached the prince. The marquise de Mézières gave him an explicit warning that the ministers intended to arrest him.[80] For his own reasons, or possibly because he still thought Louis would not dare to arrest him, Charles disregarded the warnings. Even as he drove to the Opera, the warnings continued. As he passed the Tuileries and came out on to rue St Honoré, someone called out: 'Go home, prince, they're going to arrest you!'[81]

It was between 5 and 6 p.m., already dark, when the prince arrived in the Opera cul-de-sac. With him were Harrington, Goring and

Sheridan.[82] As soon as he entered this miniature box-canyon, all gates and thoroughfares of the Palais Royal were closed. No one could get in or out.[83] The prince must have suspected something was afoot when he saw the press of people in the cul-de-sac. But, dauntless as ever, he stepped out of the carriage. A throng of sergeants flocked around him, dressed in hodden grey, like servants anxious to catch a glimpse of a great man. Then a uniformed sergeant approached as if to clear a way through the crowd. This was the signal for his disguised comrades to act.[84]

One of the sergeants, who had assumed the *nom de guerre* of Sergeant Fortune took the breath out of the prince with a blow in his back from the knee.[85] Two other sergeants seized his arms and two more his legs. It all happened so fast that the prince at first thought he was about to be murdered. Shrieking loudly, he was frog-marched away to the bottom of the cul-de-sac, through a door, and into a house belonging to a M. Marsulan, chief surgeon to the duc d'Orléans.[86]

At the other side of the door was Vaudreuil with other guards officers. The prince was still jabbering away excitedly in French.[87] Vaudreuil addressed him calmly. 'Monsieur, I arrest you in the name of the king.'

They took the prince deeper into the house. Vaudreuil asked him to hand over his weapons. The prince refused but said he would not resist if they disarmed him. The officers relieved him of two loaded pistols, a sword and a double-bladed knife. Vaudreuil looked questioningly at the pistols. 'Don't be surprised at them,' said the prince. 'I've had them on me every day since I returned from Scotland.'[88]

Vaudreuil next asked the prince to give his word that he would not attempt to take his own life or anyone else's. Charles consented. But he continued to berate Vaudreuil. 'You carry on a vile trade,' he reproached him. 'I would not have been treated any worse by the Hanoverians.'[89] Vaudreuil lamely replied that he was merely carrying out the king's orders.

As soon as he had recovered from his initial shock, the prince began to taunt his captors with cowardice: they would not have dared treat him like this if he had had his Highlanders at his side. Then he switched the thrust of his attack, trying to confuse Vaudreuil with points of etiquette. He asserted that a mere major of the guards could not arrest a prince of the blood; it had to be done by a senior officer of the musketeers.[90]

While the prince raved on, Vaudreuil sought out the duc de Biron, still sitting in disguise in his carriage. Vaudreuil evidently felt ashamed at the work he was carrying out, for he asked Biron if he could dispense with the silken cords. The prince, he pointed out, had been disarmed and had put up no resistance. But Biron was adamant. If anything went wrong he, not Vaudreuil, would be blamed. He insisted that the prince had to be tied hand and foot for his own safety, to stop him attempting suicide.[91]

Vaudreuil returned to the prince and reluctantly explained his commission. As they bound him, the prince protested vociferously at this unwonted and unwarranted treatment. Again he asked Vaudreuil to accept his word that he carried no more weapons and would offer no resistance. Vaudreuil lamented his own shame. 'The shame is not yours, but your master's,' the prince assured him.[92] But relations between captor and captive turned sour when Vaudreuil, having trussed his arms and legs, added a final cord. The prince asked sardonically if they intended putting him in cross-garters.[93] 'I think you've done enough,' he added. 'Not yet,' said Vaudreuil. This answer gained him a coldly hostile stare.[94]

Next they took the prince outside to a waiting two-horse carriage. Vaudreuil sat beside Charles in the carriage with two of his captains. There was a mounted officer on either side of the coach. Six mounted grenadiers with fixed bayonets followed behind. A number of other soldiers milled around the carriage on foot.[95] As soon as Biron saw that the arrest had been successfully completed, he departed to report to Maurepas.

During the first stage of the journey, the prince continued to complain bitterly about his treatment and about the falsity of France, which had offered him a permanent refuge. 'As for me, I would share my last piece of bread with my friend,' he went on bitterly. When no one attempted to interrupt the flow of his recriminations, the prince began to warm to his theme. 'I am not so vicious as is believed,' he declared. No, the true viciousness had been shown by France. Was this the civilised and cultivated country he had heard so much about? 'I would not have got this treatment in Morocco,' he complained. 'I had a better opinion of the French nation.'[96]

In the Faubourg St Antoine they stopped to pick up an escort of musketeers and switch to a six-horse carriage.[97] The halt seemed to alarm the prince. 'Where are we going, Hanover?' he called out, half in sardonic jest, half in earnest. Vaudreuil explained soothingly that they were simply changing carriages to make the journey to Vincennes swifter.[98] But the prince continued to be suspicious. Half-believing himself the victim of an elaborate English assassination plot, he called out: 'I thought myself among Frenchmen, but I see English guineas have made you Hanoverians.'[99]

For the rest of the journey Charles Edward did not speak. It was between 7 and 8 p.m., just two hours after the arrest, that they arrived at the Chateau of Vincennes.[100] The drawbridge was lowered to admit the carriage, then hurriedly raised. Inside Vincennes the governor marquis de Châtelet came to greet him. Châtelet had just received orders to confine the prince in a dungeon and to cede his authority to the duc de Biron and his men.[101]

The prince was determined to squeeze the last drop of pathos from his predicament. 'Come to me, my friend!' he cried. 'You see I can't come to you.'[102] Châtelet was horrified to see the prince bound and ordered him untied. With trembling hands the deeply embarrassed governor took part in the untying. Together the prince and Châtelet then mounted the first fifty steps to his cell.[103]

The cell was furnished with a straw-backed chair and a truckle bed. '*Ce n'est pas magnifique*,' the prince remarked caustically. 'What are these?' he went on, pointing to a row of symbols on the wall. Châtelet explained that it was the handiwork of a priest who had made a long stay in that room.[104]

Vaudreuil intervened to point out that the prince had not been strip-searched. Châtelet asked the prince if he had anything else about his person. Charles gave his word that he had not. Vaudreuil motioned Châtelet aside. They huddled together a long time in whispered conversation. Then they returned and searched the prince so thoroughly that Vaudreuil even groped around his genitals. The prince riposted with an indignant look but said nothing. The search produced nothing but a wallet.[105]

The prince then remonstrated about the size of his cell. He was a man used to taking exercise, yet he would have to face four ways just to walk up and down. Was it the French intention, he wondered aloud, that he should fall ill from foul air, claustrophobia and lack of exercise?

Châtelet indicated that there was a large cell next door which he would assign to the prince if he gave his word of honour not to escape. Coldly nodding in Vaudreuil's direction, the prince said that he had given his word once and it had not been accepted.[106] He did not intend to court humiliation twice. Nevertheless, Châtelet took it upon himself to move Charles Edward into the larger cell.

Vaudreuil departed. Once he was left behind with Châtelet, the prince relaxed a little and the atmosphere became lighter. Châtelet had tears in his eyes. 'I am in despair. This is the unhappiest day of my life,' he lamented. Displays of overt emotion always had an effect on the prince. 'You are known as my friend,' he reassured him. 'Be certain I'll never confuse the friend with the agent of government.'[107]

Vaudreuil had left instructions from the duc de Biron that there were always to be two officers with him in the cell and half a dozen sergeants in the adjoining room.[108] After refusing supper, the prince took to twitting his captors. 'I hope you didn't tie up my English supporters like this,' he said. 'If you treated Sir James Harrington as you treated me, he must have suffered, being so fat.'[109] The officers did not reply. They were under orders not to discuss his case. After a bit of pacing to and fro, the prince threw himself fully clothed on the bed. He found it difficult to get off to sleep. When he did, he slept fitfully, with much tossing and turning.

He awoke at 6 a.m. It was still dark. 'It seems the nights here are on the long side,' he remarked, essaying a jest.[110] He then talked freely with his guards on general subjects and waited for his next meeting with Châtelet.

Throughout Wednesday the 11th the prince reviewed his position. Louis XV had tried to make the issue one of whether he or the prince was sovereign in France. The prince had tauntingly replied that he was willing to accept French laws but not those dictated by the Elector of Hanover.[111] But surely now the prince's defiance had run its course. The news that came in during the day convinced Charles that some compromise was inevitable. His home had been thoroughly searched by lieutenant of police Berryer, and his followers Goring and Harrington sent to the Bastille.[112] He had a moral responsibility for their welfare also.

After an attempt at levity with Châtelet, when he asked how the singer Jeliotte had done at the opera, in the performance he had missed,[113] the prince got down to serious business. He asked Châtelet to make discreet enquiries as to how he could extricate himself and his followers from their plight.

Châtelet sent a note to Puysieux. Puysieux consulted with Louis XV. As a hardliner, Puysieux wanted the king to stick to his original resolution of delivering the prince to Civitavecchia under armed guard. But Louis felt he had made his point and did not want to push relations with the Stuarts to breaking point. Once Charles Edward had agreed in writing to leave French territory, he was free to go wherever he wished, either beyond the Alps or to Lorraine or Avignon. The only proviso was that he would have to be accompanied to the French border by a body of French musketeers who would then report his definite departure to the king.[114]

This was good enough for the prince. On 12 December he wrote to Louis to say that he was ready to leave his domains immediately and was only sorry that he could not explain his position in person.[115] But even now there was a Parthian shot of defiance. The prince wrote to Louis XV as from monarch to monarch in an easy, almost patronising style.[116]

Instructions were then issued to the marquis de Perussi, maréchal de camp of the 1st company of musketeers, to escort the prince to Pont de Beauvoisin on the borders of France and Savoy.[117] The prince was meanwhile asked to swear out a statement in the presence of Châtelet and four other officers. This made clear that the prince would be taken to Pont de Beauvoisin, accompanied only by persons mentioned on the escort warrant. Moreover, the prince would be pledged not to stay at Lyons or any other large city en route, not to re-enter Paris on his way from Vincennes, nor to seek sanctuary in Avignon at the end of the journey.[118] The prince gave his word of honour publicly.

Not everyone was happy with these lenient terms. Puysieux thought that Louis was too soft: the prince should be taken all the way to Civitavecchia, not just Pont de Beauvoisin.[119] Maurepas agreed, pointing out that if the prince went to Lorraine or Avignon, in defiance of his parole, French problems would begin anew.[120] Perussi too stressed that there was nothing he could do about it if the prince decided to proceed to Avignon.[121]

Charles prepared to leave. But on the evening of 13 December, at the agreed departure time, he fell ill. There was severe coughing and vomiting.[122] In this the prince ran true to form. Long periods of stress, followed by defeat, as after Derby, invariably produced this reaction.

On the 14th the prince's faithful servants Stafford and Sheridan were taken to Vincennes to accompany their master on his journey.[123] The prince was still vomiting, unable to eat anything except bouillon.[124] Nevertheless, he decided to attempt the first leg of his journey, as far as Fontainebleau. It was a decision he regretted. He was violently ill all the way there. On the night of the 14th he ran a high temperature and barely slept.[125]

Perussi was keen to press on and exerted as much leverage as he could on the prince to mount up again on the 15th. But Charles wanted to stay at Fontainebleau until he was completely recovered. A compromise was hit on. They would leave at 5 a.m. on the morning of the 16th.[126]

During the day of grace allowed him, the prince tried to put his affairs in order from his sick bed. General Bulkeley and the Princesse de Talmont asked permission of Maurepas to visit the prince in

Fontainebleau. Maurepas referred the request to Puysieux. Puysieux replied curtly that if the pair had anything to say, they could say it in writing.[127]

There was another worry for the French about the prince's stay in Fontainebleau. General St Clair, on his way back from a military mission in Turin together with his secretary the philosopher David Hume, arrived to occupy the room above the prince's at the Cabaret de la Poste inn.[128] The advent of the man who had landed troops at L'Orient in Brittany at the precise moment in September 1746 when the prince was coming to safe haven at Roscoff looked like too much of a coincidence to be true. This 'synchronicity' could be explained more rationally either as some anti-French plot between the prince and the English or, more plausibly, as a British attempt to assassinate him. Perussi's pressure on the prince to move on became more insistent.

On 16 December, at 3 a.m., Perussi and the prince headed south again. The first night's stop was at Joigny.[129] Then they passed through Auxerre to another resting place at Vermenton.[130] By the 20th, after exhausting riding, they had got as far as Beaune.[131]

It took until the 23rd to get to Pont de Beauvoisin. Here Perussi's task was complete. He bade a formal adieu to the prince.[132] But curiosity led him to send one of his men after the prince to see what he did next. The spy reported that after crossing the Pont de Beauvoisin, the prince bought three horses and then rode hard to Chambéry. Leaving the exhausted horses there, the prince disguised himself in a uniform lent to him by an Irish officer in the service of Spain. Then he, Stafford and Sheridan took the post to Orange.[133] They arrived exhausted, not having slept since the 23rd. From Orange they took a coach to Avignon. It seemed that Maurepas's prediction was coming true. The French had scotched the snake, not killed it. The prince in Avignon would be a continuing headache to the ministers at Versailles.

26

The Prince in Fairyland

(*January–February 1749*)

It is difficult nearly two and a half centuries later to convey the sensation caused in Europe by the arrest and imprisonment of the prince. In 1748 Charles Edward was arguably the most famous, and certainly the most glamorous, man in Europe. The French ministers expected a breathless reaction both from foreigners and their own citizens. Even so, the violent response of public opinion must have taken them by surprise.

The indignation flowed in parallel lines towards Versailles. In élite circles, the view was that by binding the prince hand and foot like a common criminal, the French ministers had violated international law.[1] The marquis d'Argenson thought the '*garrottement*' of the Stuart prince – the legitimate heir to the English throne – put France on a par with Cromwell for infamy.[2] These misgivings were widely shared among the nobility.[3] Even the Abbé (future Cardinal) Bernis, no friend to the Stuarts, said that Louis XV's advisers ought to have reminded him that Charles Edward was a descendant of Henri Quatre and that the French crown traditionally provided an asylum for unhappy princes.[4]

Within his own household too Louis XV had his critics. When he heard of the arrest, the dauphin burst into tears and reproached his father bitterly.[5] Almost the only supporter for the king in the upper echelons was Frederick the Great, who felt that the prince had gone too far and was an '*extravagant*' personality.[6]

The opinion which would most have disgusted the prince was his father's. When the new French envoy to Rome arrived in the Eternal City on 13 January, James told him that he would never forget Louis XV's wisdom and moderation in this unhappy affair.[7] D'Argenson had feared that the arrest of the prince would lead to a total rupture with the Stuarts, involving the withdrawal of the Irish brigade from France and many other consequences no one had thought through.[8] He did not know James as Charles did.

These were isolated opinions. The 'middle sectors' of Parisian society were incensed at the treatment of a popular hero, coming so soon after the humiliating peace.[9] The unrest reached the point where Louis XV issued a police edict forbidding the discussion of the topic in cafés – since such conversation inevitably ended in condemnation of the king.[10] This did little to halt the volume of criticism. The French public, which before the arrest had been divided between annoyance that the prince was flouting French authority and admiration for his heroic stand, now came down unreservedly on his side. A veritable explosion of lampoons and satirical verses burst on the capital.[11]

The ridicule for Versailles and admiration for the prince spread across Europe, as Charles had hoped it would. Not even Mann could disguise the near-universal contempt for the French action in Italy.[12] In England the prince's reputation soared. It was the common talk there that Charles Edward would never have surrendered Cape Breton once he had taken it.[13]

For a while Louis and his ministers were stunned at the Pandora's box they had opened.[14] They hesitated about how to react, lest the situation be made worse. One obvious move was to banish the Princesse de Talmont by *lettre de cachet*.[15] She had compounded her malign influence with insolence. When Berryer's men searched the prince's house, they found the princess's valet there with a *billet doux*. In the intemperate aftermath of the arrest, Mme de Talmont did not choose her words carefully. With icy hauteur she wrote to Maurepas that, since her lackey could not add to the king's glory, she would like him released from the Bastille. Louis XV wanted to exile her for her impudence, but her friend Maurepas pointed out the embarrassment that might arise in Louis's own household, since the princess was the queen's cousin.[16] In any case, it was thought best at Versailles to keep a low profile for a time and let the general storm of vituperation break over the ministers' heads.

While the ministers squirmed under the lash, each trying to fasten the responsibility for the binding and imprisonment on someone else, an attempt was made to strike back at the prince through black propaganda. The French tried a campaign of denigration: particular attention was paid to Charles's alleged cowardice at Culloden.[17] Furthermore, sustained efforts were made to falsify the record and rewrite history. It was now alleged that the prince had been bound only when he tried to jump out of the carriage on the way to Vincennes; also that he had given his word of honour that he was unarmed, only to be discovered by Vaudreuil with weapons about his person.[18] These scurrilous attempts to discredit the prince reveal the mental state of ministers who had not properly calculated the effect of their actions.

Yet the French were not finished with the prince, nor he with them. Contrary to the final terms of his sworn agreement with Louis XV, Charles Edward came to rest in Avignon. The carriage from Orange delivered Charles, Stafford and Sheridan at the Somme gate of the papal city at 7 a.m. on the morning of Friday 27 December.[19] The porter immediately directed them to Dunbar's house. Dunbar was told that an Irish officer wanted to see him: this was Charles Edward, still wearing the disguise he had donned at Chambéry. In Dunbar's words, 'I was never more surprised than to see him at my bedside.'[20]

The arrival of the prince in Avignon took the papal authorities by surprise. It was widely expected that Charles would now settle in one of the papal states, but the Pope had Bologna principally in mind.[21] Avignon, on the other hand, meant trouble with both France and England. But these were matters of high politics, for the Pope to decide. The vice-legate in Avignon at first saw only the glory that would redound to the papal enclave in making Europe's great hero welcome. When Charles Edward demanded identical treatment to that recently meted out to the Prince Infanta of Spain, the vice-legate did not demur. He had the prince taken out of one of the city's gates in a carriage with drawn curtains, then brought in officially through another one, accompanied by a retinue of local Jacobites and other carriages occupied by sympathetic local nobility.[22] Then Charles made his way to the Apostolic Palace where he was to be lodged. Cannon fired a salute. Three congratulatory poems were printed.[23] The vice-legate made a speech at the Apostolic Palace, referring to 'your heroic actions, source of the peace we now enjoy'.[24]

After three years of snubs, defeats, failures and humiliations, this unexpectedly warm and lavish welcome must have come as a bracing tonic to the prince. He was not to know that he was living in a fool's paradise, that the vice-legate was acting entirely on his own initiative. As soon as it was known that the Vatican had a cuckoo in its Avignon nest, Secretary of State Cardinal Valenti warned the vice-legate to make no further promises to Charles Edward, pending a final resolution of the matter.[25]

The Pope was caught unprepared. He was not disposed to blame the vice-legate. True to his sterling character, Benedict XIV took all the blame for this new development on his own shoulders. His mistake, he confided ruefully to Tencin, was in not having forewarned Avignon; he had taken it for granted that the prince would not break the word of honour he had given the French not to settle there.[26]

Benedict braced himself for the storm of protest that would erupt from France and England once the prince's presence in Avignon was known. He sent an express to the vice-legate to warn him that the prince should be prevented from making a permanent base in the city, and still less in the Apostolic Palace.[27] Quite apart from international repercussions, the Pope was worried about the expense. Even when he was prepared to welcome the prince to Bologna, this aspect of things irritated him. It seemed to Benedict that the prince had haughtily turned down a good pension from Louis XV, and then expected the Vatican to pick up his bills. The Pope was determined that this would not happen.[28]

So far Benedict had sent no message directly to the prince. He was sceptical that Charles intended to make a permanent home in Avignon, and considered that with someone as stubborn as the Stuart prince the line of least resistance was likely to be more efficacious in the short-term.[29] But the dispatches from the vice-legate soon convinced him that sterner action was called for. The prince had demanded that a festival be held in his honour. There would be balls, dinners in the Apostolic Palace, and carnival in the streets, all to be paid for, naturally, by the vice-legate. The prince had put it to him that this would be a sort of therapy for the trauma of his arrest and expulsion by France. The legate, noting the enthusiasm of the population for Charles and his proposals, did not care to argue the point.[30]

All this was to be without so much as a by-your-leave to the Pope. The prince pointedly refrained from sending Benedict a compliment. He was still too angry over his part in making Henry a cardinal. His behaviour in Avignon was unquestionably designed to punish the saintly 'philosopher-king'.[31] When James remonstrated with his son on this point, Charles Edward bluntly replied that he had made a verbal compliment through the vice-legate. This transparent evasion fooled nobody.[32]

Already Benedict was angry about the prince's breach of established protocol and normal courtesy. But he did not want to take a strong line against him. To do so would increase anxiety and tension in the Palazzo Muti. Benedict had the greatest affection for James and Henry. He did not want to fall out with them over Charles

Edward. If the Pope ordered tough action against the prince, the king and Cardinal York would have to demonstrate family solidarity, whatever their private feelings. The result might be a rift between the Vatican and the Stuarts that neither side wanted.[33] So Benedict had to swallow the humiliation involved in the prince's pointed ignoring of him. And he had to sanction the continuing expenses of the 'Charles Edward festival', even though he fretted that they would eventually bring the papal state to bankruptcy.[34]

Yet on one issue he was prepared to dig in his heels. One of the amusements Charles Edward wanted to introduce to the festivities in Avignon was bull-fighting: not the sanguinary duel to the death between beast and *matador*, but the *corredo* or bull-running, as practised in Aix and Arles.[35] In this contest of skill and quick reflexes, there was no cruelty and little danger. The problem from Avignon's point of view was that Article 40 of Pius V's bull *Cum Praecelsa* forbade bull-fighting on pain of very severe sanctions. The archbishop of Avignon therefore refused permission. Angrily, Charles Edward appealed through the vice-legate to the Pope for a dispensation.[36] Hardly surprisingly, both on grounds of canon law and his personal relations with the prince, the Pope refused to entertain the plea.[37]

Yet the incident brought it home to Benedict that the prince's presence in Avignon would lead to an escalating set of demands and pressures. Reluctantly he conceded that his 'softly softly' approach might not be adequate. He decided to call a conclave of cardinals to advise him on the matter. On Tuesday 21 January, Cardinals Valenti, Spinola, Passionei, Riviera and Lanti conferred with him.[38] It was decided that an envoy be sent to Avignon to tell the prince that his presence in the papal enclave was undesirable, but that he would be welcome elsewhere on papal territory. Benedict drew attention to a good stretch of country between Terracina and Comacchio, more beautiful than Scotland, where he could stay.[39]

Meanwhile the news from the vice-legate continued to be disheartening. Charles Edward and seventeen Scots attendants were lodged in the Apostolic Palace, eating and feasting. A major ball was held at least once a week. The prince now definitely seemed to be thinking of settling in the city, and why not? He had been given his best welcome since Edinburgh in 1745 and was content to waste the papal substance indefinitely. The vice-legate confessed himself at his wits' end.[40]

Then came the development the Pope had long feared. Vociferous protests from France and England came thundering in on the Vatican. There was talk of the English retaliating by bombarding

Civitavecchia.[41] The French were annoyed on two counts: that the prince had broken his word, and that they were being held responsible by London for the task of dislodging him from Avignon.[42] The protagonist on the French side, predictably, was Puysieux. He handed the papal nuncio in Paris a note of protest about the vice-legate's behaviour and demanded that the prince be forced the other side of the Alps. Puysieux cunningly tried to play on the Pope's fears by referring to the huge debts the prince had left behind in France.[43]

Even if Puysieux had not been actuated by personal animus against Charles Edward, he and the other ministers of state would still have been under enormous pressure from England. London insisted that the prince's presence in Avignon contravened the 1717 Treaty of Quadruple Alliance – a curious argument to raise when a war had already supervened, and exactly the sort of logic they had castigated in the prince as 'quixotic'.[44] The legalistic British point was that Article Two of that treaty had never been repealed, and it required the French to ensure that the Stuarts were kept behind the barrier of the Alps.[45]

Versailles responded with a twin-track strategy. While denying its responsibility for Charles Edward – on the ground that the 1717 treaty spoke of James Stuart but not his successors – France secretly brought extreme pressure to bear on the Vatican.[46] In desperation, the ministers even promised London to seize the prince and take him to Civitavecchia.[47] But the British pressure did not relent. They would not rest until the prince was in Italy.[48]

It was one thing for the Pope to want Charles Edward out of Avignon. It was another to bow to French pressure. Benedict defied Louis XV to do his worst. Of course, if it came to a showdown, the puny defences of Avignon could not stand against the might of France, but was 'His Most Christian Majesty' really going to risk anathema by hostilities against the Pope so soon after the notoriety of the prince's arrest? Benedict thought not, and his judgment was confirmed. As for England, the Pope expressed his contempt: they did not even enter into his calculations.[49]

So the stalemate continued. The vice-legate continually stressed the problems accruing to the Holy Father as a result of the prince's sojourn.[50] The prince reacted with indifference. For once he was enjoying himself. On 12 February the festival at which he had hoped to introduce the bull-fighting was opened. There was no longer any question of a *corredo*, partly because the archbishop and vice-legate had worked on public fears about danger to life and limb, partly because they had made sure that neither Aix nor Arles would send any bulls.[51] But there was a shooting competition, lavish illuminations and a spectacular ball. The entire courtyard of the Hôtel de Ville was built over, floored with wood and adorned with tapestries. Free food and wine were distributed to all comers, and a present of a pound each of grain and rice given to each individual – nobody was refused. A fountain of wine was installed in the place St Didier.[52]

Such reckless expenditure of money that was not his seemed almost to anger the heavens against Charles Edward. The festival was originally scheduled for 11 February, but a storm, not unlike the 'Protestant wind' of exactly five years earlier, wrecked the decorations.[53] The fête was postponed to the 12th. When it took place, the fiesta staggered even those used to the hedonism of daily life in the papal states. At 6 p.m. the city fathers gathered. The vice-legate went to the house of Dunbar's sister Lady Inverness (Clementina Sobieska's old *bête noire*) to fetch the prince in the official carriage. Preceded by the light cavalry of the city, the prince then made a tour of the walls before proceeding to the papal palace. A vast supper had been prepared. After the groaning board had been swept clean by the city's free-loaders, the prince made the tour of the best-illuminated houses before going on to the Grand Ball.[54]

All his old talents as a dancer were in evidence that night. It was eight o'clock next morning before the prince retired. The other revellers kept going until 4 p.m. To commemorate this unique manifestation of the pleasure principle, the citizens set up an equestrian statue of Charles Edward (on 24 February) in the place St Didier, opposite the house occupied by the exiled James in 1716.[55]

This fresh drain on his resources – so obviously a calculated insult to His Holiness – brought Benedict as close to vindictive rage as any event in his life.[56] The great 'Charles Edward festival' brought the Apostolic Chamber close to bankruptcy. They had already been forced to ask for a supplementary budget of several thousand écus to pay for the junketings.[57] On top of this came the horrifying news that Charles Edward's baggage and effects had now all arrived in Avignon. It seemed certain he was set for a long stay.[58] Nor was the Pope's temper improved by a series of long letters from Dunbar, purporting to justify the prince's every action from leaving Rome in 1744 to his present sybaritism in Avignon.[59] The Pope's anger and frustration found an outlet in expressions of contempt for Dunbar's intellectual capacity and his 'pathetic' epistles.[60]

The Vatican now had to implement two strategies. The first was somehow to winkle the prince and his entourage out of the Apostolic Palace. The second was to persuade him to move on permanently.

Getting him out of the palace in the interests of economy was vitiated by the prince's insistence that the vice-legate pay the rent for any alternative accommodation.[61] But the prince was finally persuaded to move to an imposing house on the outskirts of Avignon.[62]

The strategy adopted for getting him to move permanently involved stressing the security problems of an open society like Avignon. Secretary of State Valenti advised the vice-legate to keep a constant drip-drip of disconcerting news going, stressing the many dangers of assassination and abduction in the papal enclave. He was to advance the argument that these dangers augmented geometrically as the number of balls increased arithmetically, simply because the revellers went masked.[63]

The upshot was curious. When the prince finally quit Avignon, not long after moving into his new house, all parties took the credit on themselves. The Vatican congratulated itself on its 'security' disinformation campaign.[64] The French felt that their unrelenting pressure had finally paid off. The British thought that the trick had been achieved by their threat to bombard Civitavecchia.[65]

None of this was the case. The truth was that the prince had all along wanted to cock a snook at France while humiliating the Pope at the same time. In this way the twin wounds of Henry's defection and the French expulsion could be assuaged. When the round of pleasure in Avignon became boring, the prince intended to move on to Phase Two of his defiance of Louis XV.

All of this was hidden at the time. Shortly after the erection of the statue there came a dramatic and mysterious sequence of events. The Pope was fretting about the approach of Lent, determined that the prince be prevented from flouting religious scruple by continuing his festivities into the season of penance.[66] Suddenly it was announced that Charles was ill and would not be seen in society for a while.[67] The vice-legate stayed with the prince until midnight on the first day of his 'cold'. On returning next morning, he was not admitted. The pretence was kept up that the prince was indisposed and, later, that he was out taking the air.[68]

March came, and still there was no sign of the prince. At last Dunbar admitted to the vice-legate that the prince would not be seen again, for he had left on 25 February, taking with him just a single gentleman and no servants. The story about his illness had been a fiction. No one knew where he was going or what his intentions were.[69]

The vice-legate set his spies to work. The prince was traced as far as Orange. He had taken a post-chaise there and asked the driver to wait to take him back to Avignon. Then he had vanished.[70]

At first the Pope and the vice-legate waited nervously for their scourge to return. But he did not. Gradually their confidence built up. God had heard their prayers and delivered them. But where was the prince? This was a question that was to baffle the whole of Europe for the next nine years.

27

'Imaginary Space'
(1749–51)

When the prince vanished from public view at Orange, he was very clear in his own mind what his next step would be. He had already told Kelly that the reason he was to stay in Paris was that he, the prince, would be seeing him shortly.[1] Now Charles made good his boast. Travelling via Lyons – where he was momentarily spotted by a papal agent[2] – the prince arrived in Paris in heavy disguise, less than three months after he had given his solemn word not to set foot on French territory.

The plan had been concerted closely with the Princesse de Talmont, who remained in Paris to put the final touches to the masterpiece of deception.[3] When the prince arrived in the French capital, he was hidden away in the utmost secrecy in the convent of St Joseph in the rue Saint-Dominique. The convent had long boasted a 'profane' quarter where ladies of quality could take refuge from the outside world at moderate prices. No proof of religious commitment was required. It was accepted that the great ladies came there simply to look for a quiet retreat.[4] The convent was a favourite haunt of the Princesse de Talmont and her friends Elisabeth Ferrand and the comtesse de Vasse (Antoinette-Louise-Gabrielle des Gentils du Bessay).

For the next two months – and intermittently for the next three years, whenever he visited Paris – Charles Edward lived the life of a fugitive, sometimes cramped in alcoves and niches no bigger than priest holes.[5] There were false walls behind the rooms occupied by Mlle Ferrand and the comtesse de Vasse. The routine was that the prince spent the mornings in the infra-mural hideout in the former's chamber, then transferred to the room of the latter for the afternoon. In the evening, when all visitors were locked out of the convent, the prince would descend from the comtesse de Vasse's by a hidden staircase to the Princesse de Talmont's bedroom below.[6] There the lovers would spend the night.

At first all went well. From his eyrie during the daytime the prince played eavesdropper, listening to snippets of gossip about the court and personalities of Versailles relayed to the ladies Ferrand and Vasse by their aristocratic visitors. On one occasion he was highly amused to overhear a long conversation about himself, which included 'informed' speculation on his whereabouts.[7]

But as time went on, the prince began to grow bored and to chafe at his cramped lifestyle. He began to row with the Princesse de Talmont. These were no ordinary rows. The prince by now was accustomed to fall into volcanic rages if people opposed their will to his, crossed him, or even disagreed with him. The small change of verbal sniping between intimate couples was conflated by the prince into part of the general mosaic of rejection the world had foisted upon him. His subsequent rage frequently took a physical form and he would beat his mistress.

The battered Princesse de Talmont's legendary wit and repartee availed her little against a man who was not ashamed to use violence if thwarted, or simply worsted in a verbal encounter. More to the point, the two ladies Ferrand and Vasse, who were bound together by gentle bonds (probably unconscious lesbianism)[8] were deeply shocked by the outbursts of physical violence and the ferocious altercations between the lovers which they could not fail to overhear.

Tactfully the two ladies put it to the prince that it might be time to move on.[9] After two months of huddled daytime privation, Charles Edward felt he had made his point. He had bearded Louis XV in his own lair and thrown all the assassins and secret agents of Europe off his trail. Besides, he had decided where he would make his permanent home. On 20 April the prince wrote to Earl Marischal, asking him to meet him in Venice.[10] Charles Edward was still absurdly hoping to recruit this man (who, unknown to him, hated him vehemently) as his secretary of state. In hopes of assembling a skeleton court, Charles also asked Harrington (then at Dijon with Graeme) to join him in Venice.[11] If possible, Graeme should accompany him.

There was no reply from Marischal. The prince wrote again to the same effect on 5 May. Back came the lame old excuse about 'broken health'.[12]

The prince set out in early May 1749, intending to avoid all French garrison towns. He was not a moment too soon. By now the French had got wind of his presence in their capital – probably because the prince told John Waters his banker that he would be 'calling' for his mail. The French instituted an intensive search. This time, if they found Charles, they were going to take him all the way to Civitavecchia and deposit him there.[13]

The prince's itinerary took him through Luneville and Lorraine. Then he headed south into Switzerland, passing through Lucerne, the Mt St Goddard pass and the vale of Bellinzona to Lugano. Then he crossed lake Como and rested at Bergamo before pressing on to Venice.[14]

On 17 May Charles Edward wrote in sanguine spirits from the Most Serene Republic to his father. He was very hopeful of being allowed to stay in Venice, 'a place that next to France is the best for my interest'.[15] He decided to use the papal nuncio as his go-between to the doge's council. The nuncio was deeply sympathetic to the prince, but warned him that the most consideration he was likely to receive was tacit consent to remain a few days incognito.[16] But at least this time the prince did send on a formal compliment to the Pope – the first time he had done so since leaving Rome in January 1744. Benedict wrote back by special courier to tell Charles that he was free to reside anywhere in papal Italy, but would not be welcome if he returned to Avignon. Bologna was proposed as a suitable haven. But Charles Edward told the nuncio that in an open town like Bologna he would go in fear of his life – a very neat twist on the Pope's own arguments about Avignon.[17]

It gradually became clear why the prince had chosen to make his base in Venice. The city of masked revellers and shadowy secret agents was the perfect milieu for a man to whom disguise and cloak and dagger had become second nature. The prince dismissed Benedict's countervailing argument: that a city based on the incognito, where so many went masked, provided the perfect locale for assassins and was thus the worst possible bet for the prince.[18]

The doge's reply took a long time to come. A week later, on 24 May, the prince reported himself still hopeful.[19] But on 26 May the predictable answer came. The Most Serene Republic would not risk the wrath of England again, as it had in 1737.[20] When the nuncio brought the reply, Charles Edward commented laconically, 'Then I'll leave.' The nuncio tried in vain to find out where he was going next. He offered him the hospitality of the papal states. The prince made no reply but departed that very evening.[21]

In private the prince was full of brooding bitterness. The Venetians, he noted, were 'rascals'. Who would have imagined that the

Venice which behaved so decently to him in 1737 would behave so shamefully now?[22] 'Now my friend [i.e. himself] must skulk to the perfect dishonour and glory of his worthy relations,' he jotted down gnomically, 'until he finds a reception fitting at home or abroad.'[23]

Benedict XIV wrote to warn the cardinal legates of Bologna and Ferrara that the prince might be descending on them at any moment. He was determined not to be caught napping again. Weekly expenses at Avignon incurred on the prince's behalf had amounted to upwards of 6,000 écus. The Pope was adamant that there should be no repeat of such financial madness; if the prince came into the papal states, it was to be made clear to him that the legates would not pay his expenses. Benedict felt strongly on this point. With another sort of personality it might be different, but not with a prince whom caprice and bad behaviour kept away from his father.[24]

The Pope need not have worried. The prince already regarded the Vatican and all its works with a peculiar horror. He had already laid contingency plans in the event of a Venetian refusal. In the short term he would go to Lunéville, to the Ruritanian domain ruled by ex-king Stanislas of Poland.[25] The prince had a long-standing invitation to seek refuge there. The invitation had a dramatic provenance. Stanislas was actually listening to a lecture by Voltaire (one of Charles Edward's strong admirers) on the misfortunes of the Stuarts when a courier entered with news of the prince's arrest in the Opera cul-de-sac. Stanislas immediately offered Charles Edward asylum in Lunéville.[26]

To Lunéville, then, the prince went. He lodged at first in the house of M. Mittie, the surgeon-general, before finding more spacious quarters where he could rendezvous with the Princesse de Talmont. Mittie's son became for a time one of the prince's most trusted agents. Yet it is clear that the prince always regarded Lunéville as no more than a convenient stopover.

What he wanted now was to make a permanent abode in Imperial territory. To this end he wrote to Choiseul (then marquis de Stainville) asking for help. On 13 July 1749 a double envelope, incorrectly addressed to the comte de Stainville, was left at the door of Choiseul's Paris residence. The significant thing about the letter, which requested permission to shelter on Austrian territory, was that it was written on 26 May in Venice, immediately after the nuncio's negative reply from the doge.[27] When Choiseul did not reply, the prince wrote again, in January 1750, reiterating his request.[28] This aspect of the prince's intentions soon became generally known.[29]

That the prince was not prepared to settle down in Lunéville was

evident from the advice he sought from senior Jacobites on a permanent base. Marischal recommended Friburg.[30] Bulkeley opted for
Switzerland or Bologna.[31] Charles himself had an inclination towards
Sweden and actually set about obtaining a six-month passport there
for himself and his effects.[32] 'What can a bird do that has not found
a right nest?' he wrote to Bulkeley. 'It will always wander and never
pitch on a branch.'[33]

Yet inexorably, as the Powers closed ranks against him so as not
to offend the formidable English, he found himself perforce hemmed
in at Lunéville. Fortunately, very few people had the least idea where
he was. While he fretted and fumed about the future, the prince tried
to find distraction. On 22 September he observed the Aurora Borealis
at Lunéville and wrote a precise description of it.[34] Earlier he had
jotted down a set of maxims: (1) If there is a Being, there is also a
destiny. (2) One should never judge others by oneself. (3) Never tell
a secret to a weak man because it might frighten him and cause him
to use it against you.[35]

In early November 1749 the prince was back in Paris at the convent
of St Joseph, thumbing his nose at the Paris police. He was in the
French capital at least ten days. Among others he visited Lally,
seeking support for his idea of a *coup d'état* in London.[36] Once again
the French picked up his trail just too late. The ministers were
indignant at his behaviour. In their eyes, Charles Edward lacked
self-respect, both because he had promised not to return to France
and because he seemed fatally drawn to the city that had ignomini-
ously kicked him out.[37] By this time Louis XV himself seemed
disposed to connive at his clandestine visits. But Puysieux and
Madame Pompadour felt angry at the implicit insult to France.
They thirsted to apprehend Charles and to send him packing to
Civitavecchia.[38]

Yet Charles Edward was always at least one step ahead of those
who sought him. His abilities at playing a Scarlet Pimpernel role
were pronounced. The prince would have made a perfect secret agent.
As with many spies, the notion of betrayal was a central one in his
psychic imagery. And the taste for disguise, first broached in 1744,
then honed to a higher point of expertise with 'Betty Burke' and
perfected during the affair with Louise de Montbazon, now came
into its own as a fully-fledged aspect of the prince's personality. The
predilection for secretiveness, originally a means to an end, became
finally an end in itself.

Techniques of disinformation, the art of disguise, the ability to
cover his tracks, all these came as second nature to Charles Edward.

This helps to explain, but does not diminish, the achievement involved in his 'invisibility' during the obscure years from 1749 to 1758. The plain fact was that for most of this time the combined espionage efforts of Europe could not get a proper fix on a man who was arguably the greatest celebrity of the time.

Some idea of the utter confusion sown by the prince can be obtained from the contemporary diplomatic records, which at any given moment were capable of locating the prince anywhere on a line from the Atlantic to the Urals! The most popular guess immediately after the departure from Avignon was Bologna.[39] The duc de Luynes reported him 'certainly' there.[40] A variant on this was that Charles Edward had agreed to live in northern Italy provided James dismissed O'Brien as his secretary of state.[41] Some years later d'Argenson provided a further gloss on this with a story of the prince's living peacefully in a small town 300 leagues (sic) north of Rome.[42] Later the prince was reported in Berlin, much to Frederick the Great's surprise and amusement; this particular rumour reached a head about the time Charles Edward was actually in Venice.[43] A surreptitious return to England was another favourite theory.[44] The analysts who wanted to play safe predicted an imminent return to Avignon.[45]

It was left to the more intelligent diplomats to try to make something of the Talmont connection. Since her brother was Palatine of Ravva, this principality was added to the swelling list of possible locations.[46] More likely was Poland, where both the Princesse de Talmont and Charles Edward himself had roots and strong connections. The prince cunningly started a hare in this direction by writing a document in which he claimed to have married the daughter of the landgrave of Hesse-Darmstadt and then asked permission of the king of Poland to settle on his territories.[47] Predictably, reports began to flood in to the respective foreign offices that the prince had been seen in Poland.[48]

But since it was easy to ascertain that the Princess of Hesse had not in fact married the prince, his letter referring to 'my wife' and addressed to the king of Poland was taken to be a blind, masking a Polish marriage. The most likely candidate was Princess Teofila Konstancia, daughter of Michael Radziwill.[49] The Princess Radziwill rumour seemed plausible and it persisted for years, even though James Stuart himself accurately dismissed it as nonsense on the ground that Teofila was only ten years old in 1749.[50] Despite James's disclaimers, the canard proved remarkably hard to dislodge; its tenacity was proved by its still being current in 1752.[51]

Only a handful of observers guessed at Lorraine and Lunéville, and most of these included it merely in a shopping-basket of conjectures.[52] Puysieux alone, inveterate and brooding Stuart prince watcher, was always convinced his enemy was holed up in Lunéville.[53] Hatred, like the prospect of hanging, it seems, concentrates the mind.

Students of the hilarious could do worse than sample the infinite variety of the imaginary adventures of the 'prince in fairyland'.[54] Even sober commentators were seduced into Arabian Nights fantasy. Barbier produced a tale of an extended tour of northern Europe on foot.[55] D'Argenson, while incorporating some true material in his sketch of the prince's movements in 1749, concocted an itinerary that would have taxed a modern 'shuttle' diplomat: between Avignon and Venice (less than three months) the prince was supposed to have visited Sweden, Berlin and Dresden as well as Paris and Lorraine.[56]

The farrago of nonsense written about the prince's movements in 1749 and after testifies to the superlative skill with which he threw off his would-be pursuers. James and Henry themselves were no wiser than the benighted foreign diplomats. Charles used a cell structure of agents, wherein only the immediate link in the chain (usually Goring, a veteran of the Austrian service, at this stage) knew where he was at any given moment. In the intelligence battle the prince and his enemies used many of the same disinformation techniques against each other. Charles encouraged his supporters to spread rumours that he was dead or gravely ill, especially when he was about to embark on some perilous venture (like the 1750 trip to England).[57] His enemies retaliated, trying to winkle him out of hiding by claiming that he was dead at moments when they wanted him to show himself.[58]

One inevitable result of all this chaos and illusion was that many 'false princes' arose, trying to trade on his name and reputation. Sometimes this was just a case of Charles Edward lookalikes or people mistaken for him being taken into custody or reported by spies.[59] There were false sightings in Spain and Bordeaux in 1751 and in Corsica in 1753.[60] But often the false Charleses were conscious charlatans. In October 1751 an escaped prisoner turned up in Seville, masquerading as the prince.[61] A bogus 'Charles Edward' swindled his way right down through northern Italy in 1753, leaving IOUs in the prince's name.[62]

Poor British intelligence was part of the answer to the prince's success in these years. One highly-paid agent, supposedly hot on the scent of the prince, produced an 'exclusive' report that gave his height as 5 feet 5 inches (6 inches too short).[63] British spies also wasted a lot of time on meticulous surveillance of people who turned out not to be Charles Edward.[64]

.But another part of the answer was the prince's genius for disguise. His favourite garb was that of a priest;[65] given his contempt for priestcraft, this is significant in itself. One of the few British agents who actually got close to him in the 'obscure period' – Pickle the Spy – dealt with this aspect of the prince at some length in a report to the duke of Newcastle in 1755:

> The Young Pretender has an admirable genius for skulking, and is provided with so many disguises that it is not so much to be wondered at that he has hitherto escaped unobserved. Sometimes he wears a long false nose which they call *Nez à la Saxe* because Marshal Saxe used to give such to his spies whom he employed. At other times he blackens his eyebrows and beard and wears a black wig, by which alteration his most intimate acquaintances would scarce know him, and in these dresses he has mixed often in the company of English gentlemen travelling through Flanders without being suspected.[66]

Hand in hand with the penchant for disguise went a taste for the use of aliases: Mr Benn, Mr Douglas, Dumont, Cartouche, The Wild Man, Mr Thompson, these are only some of the pseudonyms used by the prince in the first five years of his incognito in 'imaginary space' (to use one of his own expressions).[67] There was more to this than simple prudence. Taken together, the disguises and aliases point to something central in the prince's personality. If a man turns to disguise as a way of life, it suggests a savage dissatisfaction with himself. And the use of aliases and pseudonyms even in contexts where the person receiving the letter knew perfectly well who the writer was suggests once again a fragile sense of identity.

This is hardly surprising. The long years of being a prince without a throne, royalty without a kingdom, a man supposedly deriving his right from God but enjoying the devil's own luck, were now compounded by a further dimension of alienation. It was inexpedient for the prince to have a settled location or a traceable identity. To be a pretender who has to pretend not to be a pretender introduces a Chinese-box sense of chaos. For other men not blessed (or cursed) by a royal heritage, it was possible to choose an identity from a number of available roles defined by parents, teachers, mentors, religious leaders. In a very real sense Charles Edward, by contrast, had to make up his identity as he went along. What else could a defeated pretender who was not resigned to his fate do?

A proud and obstinate refusal to wear the mask painted by others is potentially a sign of greatness. But if this obstinacy is combined with a fragmented or crumbling ego, the ensuing identity problems can produce a morbid fear of intimacy. The binding nature of sexual love can then feed into these problems and produce an even greater sense of alienation.

A priori we should expect the three years of frustrated and embittered exile in Lunéville to have seen the stresses on the prince reach their height. To judge from the passionate, angry and violent relationship with the Princesse de Talmont, this is exactly what happened. Until the prince's expulsion, the relationship had not been conducted in maximum stress. Thereafter it was; the strain began to show.

The first half of the year 1749 was a frenetic, itinerant time for the prince. The second saw him a recluse in Lunéville. He and the princess saw each other only for brief periods. Not surprisingly, in this year there were many declarations of love and undying passion from both parties.[68] 'Oh my king, where are you?' Marie-Louise exclaims during the Avignon separation.[69] There were similar sentiments while Charles was at Venice.[70]

But already there are signs of tension. The princess complains of headaches which she cures by taking opium.[71] She asks the prince for a signed declaration of his love. But since the prince is now in thrall to pseudonyms at all times, he refuses the request: ask me anything but that, he writes.[72]

The tensions broke into the open once they were together in Lunéville. Elisabeth Ferrand warned the lovers that Talmont's Paris maid knew their secret and might be unreliable.[73] Marie-Louise's fear of the Bastille was morbid and profound. The contrast with the prince's insouciant attitude to the French authorities brought on the first clashes. So as not to attract spies or assassins, they occupied different premises in Lunéville. The prince was fond of making nocturnal forays to Marie-Louise's house at any hour that took his fancy. She insisted on greater circumspection and regard for security. It was Louise de Montbazon all over again. One night the princess refused to admit him. This threw the prince into a rage. He insisted on his right to call at her house at will. She replied that if he persisted in his obstinacy, she would solve the problem by leaving.[74]

In the relationship between the two lovers, there was violent oscillation between love and hatred.[75] There were times when each recognised the enemy in the other, when the struggle for power between their wills became explicit.[76] 'If you want to help me,' the prince snarled at her, 'stop maintaining that black is white and you are never wrong. If you don't, why are you meddling in my life?'[77]

The two manoeuvred for advantage, each trying to wrongfoot the other. The prince would insist on seeing her when she was indisposed. She would insist on a meeting when he was most busy with his political affairs.[78] There are indications that the princess's frequent illnesses prevented her always from fulfilling the role of mistress.[79] She claimed her lover owed her something for two years' fidelity. The prince responded by casual encounters with other women, 'by night and day'.[80] Marie-Louise, faced with the open boasting of some of these 'conquests', threatened in despair to reveal the prince's whereabouts to the courts of Europe.[81]

Yet there were clearly many tender moments. He called her *'ma reine'*, she called him *'mon roi'*. Two incidents around Easter 1750 revealed the ambivalence in their relationship. Marie-Louise threatened to leave Lunéville on Easter Monday if the prince did not make strenuous attempts to patch up their flagging relationship.[82] The reply showed Charles Edward at his most charming. He wrote that, since it was the custom to make wishes for friends and enemies on the stroke of midnight on Easter Saturday, he wished her all possible happiness. He went on to dub her the Queen of Morocco and a tormentress: 'Have pity on your faithful subjects. They don't deserve to die of chagrin and despair.'[83]

Such moments were more and more becoming emotional oases in the middle of a wasteland of mutual destruction. The princess hated the boredom of Lunéville and longed to be allowed to return to Paris for a short holiday; even a fortnight would do. The prince would not hear of it.[84] When she insisted that life in Lorraine was driving her to depression and melancholy, Charles compromised. He was prepared for her to take a trip to Vienna. While she was there, she could make herself useful and lobby the court to allow him to reside in the Imperial domains. The tone in which the prince announced her departure (in April 1750) suggested that he did not much care whether she came back.[85] It is clear that he did not entirely trust her. He insisted on inditing a letter to his father in the form of an affidavit, which gave the princess's departure as the reason for his own change of abode.[86]

It is not possible to follow all the stages of the relationship on a day-by-day basis, but it *is* clear that Marie-Louise did not after all make the trip to Vienna. Having secured the prince's agreement in principle to the idea of a parting, she hammered away at a return to Paris. She stressed how useless she had been to him at Lunéville. He asked her to stay on for another couple of months. What point was there in that, she asked? Would she not be just as useless as ever?[87]

The prince brooded. Then something happened to break the logjam. The princess's sister fell dangerously ill. Again she asked leave to depart. After five days sullen silence, the prince gave his reply.[88] She had sold her idea too well. He was agreeable, provided he too went with her to the French capital. She begged him to reconsider, pointing up the risks of capture in Paris. But Charles was adamant. By June 1750 the pair were back in Paris.[89]

Before she left Lunéville, the princess poured out a stream of complaints about Charles Edward to Goring. She expressed sadness, disillusionment and disgust with life. The burden of her charge against the prince was, as from so many others, ingratitude: ingratitude for the asylum she had provided, for her good offices with Stanislas, for the way she had neglected her own fortune and interests in France.[90] Anything that was done for the prince, she complained, he took as his due. He dwelt exclusively on his misfortunes, never seeing how much worse his plight could be.

Nothing in Paris caused her to change her mind. The prince spent the best part of two months there, frequently changing accommodation, now with Elisabeth Ferrand and the comtesse de Vassé, now incommunicado, pretending to have left.[91] For a short while he accepted the hospitality of Helvétius, '*le philosophe*',[92] but his paranoid fear of being trailed and apprehended never allowed him to stay long at any one lodging. He had serious business in Paris, discussing with emissaries from England his plan to visit London and organise a *coup d'état* there, but he never let the Princesse de Talmont in on the secret.[93] Yet he did not cease to torment her. The spectre of the Bastille loomed closer with every one of the 11 p.m. or midnight visits he paid to her house.[94] On one occasion she lost her nerve and had him turned away at the door, then apologised next day for her panic and asked him to try again.[95] Marie-Louise began to see herself as more and more of a victim. She later complained that she had not slept properly once during her three years' liaison with Charles Edward. Insomnia is a constant motif in her correspondence.[96]

The prince for his part despised her 'weakness'. He announced loftily that he would leave Paris and never bother her again.[97] This was later elevated to a formal break with her.[98] He did not reveal that he had his own reasons for wanting to be unencumbered in the next few months, but took the precaution of writing letters from Lunéville on his return there, and another from Mons,[99] so that if she ever did have a mind to betray him, her intelligence would be useless.

The princess knew nothing of her lover's trip to England, its failure and its sequel. She would not have been surprised to learn that the prince was once again negotiating a marriage, this time with the daughter of the duke of Daremberg.[100] There was no reason why a dynastic marriage should seriously interfere with their relationship. But she might have been on her guard if the prince had admitted that he suggested a renewal of their liaison only after yet another marriage suit had foundered. When the plenipotentiaries met at Basle to arrange the secret marriage with a German princess, the negotiations immediately broke down over the prince's quixotic demand for a dowry of 12,000 troops for the invasion of England.[101] Not a word of this found its way into the letters the prince wrote to Marie-Louise from Lunéville.[102]

The period October–December 1750, after the prince returned from his unsuccessful foray into England, is one of the most obscure stretches in the 'obscure years'. When he was not busy on his many political schemes (or fantasies), Charles Edward maintained a steady correspondence with Elisabeth Ferrand, conducted in an elaborate code. Ever since the early days of the St Joseph convent, he had written to her on average once a month, usually to ask her to perform some chore. Now he stepped up the correspondence, obviously revelling in the gossip from Paris. All their friends and acquaintances (and enemies) were given cant names that are very revealing of the prince's attitude to them: Mme de Mézières was 'the old lunatic' (*la folle*); the hated Puysieux was the imbecile (*l'imbecile*), and so on.[103] Ferrand called Talmont '*une femme méchante*' and added that she did not understand why the princess bothered to visit her, since all she seemed to want to do was lose her temper.[104]

It is perhaps indicative of the prince's general mental state and of his attitude to the Talmont relationship that he encouraged the mutual jealousy between his mistress and Ferrand and Vassé as they vied for his attention. He would egg on either side to keep secrets from the other and would connive at their petty criticisms. Ferrand was particularly critical of Talmont and frequently complained of her meddling in the commissions the prince asked her to perform.[105] But it was typical of the prince that he laid down no clear guidelines on the degree and nature of backbiting he would permit. He arrogated to himself the privilege of taking a high moral tone on this mutual criticism when it suited him. Having condoned Ferrand's animadversions on Talmont in July 1750, Charles decided to object to them in

November of that year, about the time he asked Marie-Louise to return to Lunéville.[106] This tendency to blow hot and cold was another of the less attractive attributes of the prince. There could be charm one moment, cold anger the next; small wonder that so few of his friends and agents knew from one minute to another where they stood with him.[107]

At this period in his life, the prince was particularly interested in the thoughts of Helvétius, *le philosophe*, as he is invariably referred to in the correspondence between Charles and Ferrand.[108] Whether Helvétius would have approved of the prince's literary productions is more doubtful. Charles liked to while away the dead days in Lunéville by composing epigrams and other doggerel. Some of these are thoughtful, if intellectually jejune. Given how difficult it is for a physician to know about the heart, Charles asks, how much more difficult is it to know about the soul?[109] Others of the *obiter dicta* are, to say the least, less memorable.[110] But some of the political maxims have a sharp Humean flavour: 'the people' is a meaningless term, the prince observes; religion is necessary for good government, but it does not matter which one.[111]

The boredom found a focus in imagined slights. Some time in the autumn of 1750 the prince temporarily suspended correspondence with Elisabeth Ferrand and the comtesse de Vassé, probably because they had queried one of his instructions, complained of his ingratitude, or failed to fulfil a chore to his complete satisfaction.[112] The rift with these two ladies seemed to the prince's paranoid imagination not unconnected with the Princesse de Talmont's presence in Paris. He composed a memorandum in which he poured out all his bitterness about her: she was false, low, ungrateful, lacking in respect, she put her own follies and those of her family before devotion to him: 'the thing is come to such a push [sic] that I am as much incensed at her as ever I loved her . . . my being accustomed to crosses makes me take this very easy.'[113]

Yet this was not the whole story. That the relationship was composed of love and hate rather than pure hatred became clear when at the end of 1750 Charles wrote to Talmont to ask her to return to Lunéville. This put the princess on the spot. There were two very good reasons, apart from the prince's uncertain temper, why it was unwise of her to return to Lunéville. In the first place, the death of her son from smallpox at the age of fifteen while she was in the thick of the affair with Charles Edward seems to have brought on continued attacks of a mysterious illness (almost certainly psychosomatic in origin) characterised by nausea, migraine and vomiting.[114]

This had been apparent at Lunéville in the early months of 1750; she spoke of her illness as being 'near mortal'.[115] From a vivacious, witty, cynical, amoral social butterfly, the Princesse de Talmont had become a valetudinarian, the former sparkle being doubtless choked off by feelings of guilt about her son. Talmont ought to have known Charles Edward well enough to realise that her semi-invalid state would not go down well if she did return to Lunéville.

The other reason was more immediate. In the wake of her near-exile from the court at the time of the prince's expulsion, Talmont had to tread carefully, especially since her protector at Versailles, Maurepas, was himself disgraced early in 1749.[116] When she originally applied for *congé* to visit Luneville, she was given three months' leave of absence. It was well over a year when she finally reappeared publicly in court life. Louis XV, suspecting the true nature of her 'urgent business' in Lunéville, was very angry at her 'impertinent' behaviour and complained vociferously to his father-in-law Stanislas. Her kinswoman the queen also took a dim view of her activities.[117]

There were the circumstances when a letter from the prince arrived, claiming that he was inconsolable without her. Talmont sought an audience with Louis XV to obtain another *congé*. The king raged at her for her insolence: if she went to Lunéville again, it was on her own head; she could return to Paris only on pain of total disgrace. The princess used all her wiles to make her absence palatable. Louis would not accept that her reasons were valid. Finally he relented to the point of allowing her a *congé* from January to May 1751.[118]

The princess wrote to Charles Edward to announce her return to Lunéville. But just as she was about to leave Paris, she was again stricken with her mystery illness. In Lunéville the prince fretted at the delay, then made final plans to journey to Berlin to meet Frederick of Prussia.

At the very last moment Talmont seems to have had a premonition that she would lose the prince altogether if she did not at once make the trip to Lorraine. Cutting short her convalescence, against medical advice, she set out early on 24 January 1751. A gruelling two-day journey brought her, by now dreadfully ill, to her chateau outside Lunéville on the evening of 25 January.[119]

Marie-Louise had hoped that her heroism in making such a journey in winter in her condition would finally get the prince to see the light and appreciate the extent of her sacrifice for him. She looked forward to a reconciliation. But the prince was now committed to his Berlin trip. Since he did not trust his mistress, he certainly did not intend to divulge his plans. One look at the decrepit, ailing princess in any case disabused him of any notion that they could travel together.

Next morning, to Marie-Louise's utter astonishment, the prince left her, complaining that the chateau was too uncomfortable to house two separate retinues. She did not see him again for two months. She received a couple of notes purporting to come from him in Lunéville, but obviously sent by Mittie junior during his absence. One was a complaint about her behaviour, coupled with a wish that she would make a New Year's resolution to reform it.[120] The other harked back to his old grievance about having doors shut in his face.[121]

At the end of March 1751 the princess wrote to him, using the channel of Mittie junior. The letter was in the form of an ultimatum. Since she had returned to Lunéville at great personal and political risk only at his urgent request, would he now at once have the goodness to come and see her? Otherwise she would return to Paris to placate Louis XV.[122] The prince, by now returned from another abortive mission, replied that he wished she had stayed in Paris in the first place. He relented sufficiently to spend one night with her, but then left suddenly the next day.[123]

After an interval he returned, this time exuding charm. When Talmont, who had been bitten twice, reacted coldly, he complained of her lack of commitment and flew into a rage with her. She confided to Goring that he could no longer hurt her as much as in the old days, when all her emotions were in thrall. She bore the irate squall with equanimity.[124]

The off-and-on relationship limped along until the expiry of the princess's *congé*. Marie-Louise then announced her departure for Paris. This angered the prince. He had no particular liking or even use for her any more, but *he* would decide when the relationship was over. This was the old business of someone else 'giving him laws'. Marie-Louise then promised to write to Louis XV to ask for an extension, provided Charles pledged himself to live with her and see her constantly. The prince promised. Talmont prepared for a resumption of their old passionate relationship.[125]

But on the very night the idyll was scheduled to recommence, Marie-Louise had another of her dreadful attacks of migraine and vomiting. The prince arrived to find his mistress a puking invalid. His reaction was cold fury. He knew how to deal with this imperious Queen of Morocco who seemed to make a career out of thwarting his will. He had brought her to heel before by promiscuous flings with other women. With supreme callousness, the prince spent the night with one of the princess's maids.[126]

At noon next day Charles announced that he was leaving for good. The princess fell on her knees and begged him at least to save her a public humiliation by waiting until she had cleared the ante-room of servants. At least he would then leave unobserved. But the prince was savouring his total victory over the woman who had so long opposed her will to his. Coldly he informed her that he was going to take another mistress. He would leave when and how he pleased.[127] As a parting master-stroke of cruelty, he demanded that she return his portrait, knowing that it was in her bureau in Paris. He ordered her to hand it over to Waters, his banker. She protested at the thought of having Waters as a witness to her indignity, but Charles was adamant.[128] Then he swept from the chateau.

That was the end of the affair. Marie-Louise spent another two months in Lunéville, vainly hoping he would return to her. She wrote a number of letters to him, which she described as being capable of melting the heart of a stone. His only reply was to say that he never wished to see her again.[129]

Such was the dismal termination of a liaison that had from the very first carried within itself the seeds of its own destruction. The most obvious problem was that both the lovers were strong-willed and thought themselves perfect beings, let down or vitiated by the flaws of others. In the prince's case, this masked a deep unconscious self-loathing that caused him to fail in crucial moments unless objective circumstances were overwhelmingly favourable. Not enough is known about the Princesse de Talmont, but Madame du Deffand alleged that her vanity went beyond all normal vanity into a realm where she genuinely believed herself perfect and expected everyone else to feel the same way about her.[130]

The prince had turned to Talmont in the first place as a reaction to the affair with Louise de Montbazon, in hopes that such a sophisticated woman would not cling to him or make demands. At first the relationship seemed to fulfil these hopes. But there was one factor he had not counted on. The Princesse de Talmont was now in her late forties, and it was likely that Charles Edward would be her last lover. She wanted to exit from her career of dalliance with a solid, durable relationship, so that she could feel her emotional life had not been totally vain and ephemeral.

Once the prince sensed that she wished to make of the relationship something more binding and committed, he reacted with coldness. Profound relationships with women were beyond him, as he demonstrated throughout his life. He needed women sexually, but anything deeper, more testing, stretched his resources farther than they would go. Badinage and repartee in a salon with witty blue-stockings was one thing; sexual promiscuity with maids and courtesans was another. But the ultimate horror for the prince was any demand that he integrate the two strands.

In retrospect, the three troubled years with the Princesse de Talmont seemed to have produced nothing but a hell of physical and verbal abuse. The only good fruit of these years was the dismissal of Kelly (he left the prince's service in November 1749).[131] It took Marie-Louise to persuade the prince that if he really wanted Marischal as his secretary of state – and Marischal was adamant that he would have no dealings with the prince while Kelly was at his side – then Kelly had to go. But the diabolical Kelly was not finished with the prince yet. It was a woman who dislodged him. Years later he would take his revenge by being instrumental in dislodging another woman from the prince's side.

The Princesse de Talmont stayed on in Lunéville until the beginning of September 1751, still vainly hoping that the prince would relent and return to her. How far the prince was from entertaining any residual thoughts of her can be seen from the fate of the letter she sent him on her return to Paris. On the back of the paper where Marie-Louise speaks of his memory's reign equally in her mind and heart, the prince proceeded to jot down some financial calculations![132]

Talmont's bitterness when the prince made no reply eventually found expression in a tempestuous altercation with Elisabeth Ferrand. Mlle Ferrand had been ill with a fever and did not respond to the letters the princess sent enquiring about Charles's health and whereabouts. The princess dashed off a string of accusations, many of them personal, which Ferrand described as 'blush-making'. Remonstrating violently against being accused of '*basesse*', Ferrand put the termagant princess firmly in her place.[133] Then she wrote to the prince, complaining ringingly of his former mistress. Talmont backtracked and apologised to Ferrand for a hasty letter caused by excessive stress.[134] Henceforth she adopted a softer approach in her relations with the 'sisters' (which was how Ferrand and Vassé invariably referred to each other).[135]

The new tack availed her little. When the prince paid his next flying visit to Paris (in December 1751), he spent time with the 'sisters' but did not communicate his presence to his ex-mistress.[136] Like James, like Louise de Montbazon, the Princesse de Talmont had gone the way of all flesh. There was further correspondence with the prince, but for the remaining twenty years of her life she never set eyes on him again.

28

The Elibank Plot
(1749–53)

During the years of his turbulent relationship with the Princesse de Talmont, Charles Edward's attention was by no means devoted only to his private life. He still hankered after a repeat of the '45 by other means. The years 1750–3 were full of plots and rumours of plots as the prince cast about for some ingenious means of overthrowing the Hanoverian dynasty. This time he would have to make the attempt without any help from France. And – another of the prince's *idées fixes* – it would have to be focused on England.

One of the problems about planning a *coup d'état* in England – and without foreign aid or an invading army a Stuart restoration could only come about in this way – was the lack of contact with either James or the Jacobites in France. This fact alone led to the abandonment of a number of promising schemes. In 1749 Sir Hector Maclean worked out an imaginative project for a new Jacobite rising with the duc de Richelieu and Paris de Monmartel, *éminence grise* of French finances. The plan was that 5,000 French troops would land on the east coast of Scotland while 4,000 Swedes disembarked on the west coast. A general rendezvous would be held at Inverness, where the Jacobite clans would join the two sets of liberators. But when Sir Hector Maclean went to Rome to get James's approval, the Stuart monarch vetoed the project, lest it clash with some other venture by the prince.[1]

The prince was indeed planning a scheme of his own, but its tenor was very different. By now he was convinced that the key to a restoration lay neither on the Celtic fringes nor with marginal religious groups like the Catholics. There was in England a solid rump of alienated people: not just Jacobites, but disaffected Whigs and extreme 'Country' ideologues at present attached to the rival

court of Prince Frederick at Leicester House, but chafing at its mild
reformist challenge to George II's supremacy.[2] Sir Watkin Williams
Wynn, doyen of the old English Jacobite party, had died in 1749.
The new Jacobite leaders seemed to be men of a different stamp,
especially the duke of Beaufort and Lord Westmoreland. Charles
Edward accordingly reverted to an idea long peddled by the marquise
de Mézières: that all attempts at Jacobite restoration should be based
on English Protestants alone.[3]

Moreover, by 1749–50 there were many straws in the wind that
indicated a revival of Jacobite fortunes in England after the disaster
of the '45. In 1749, at the dedication of the Radcliffe Camera in
Oxford, Dr William King, a prominent Jacobite of the university,
delivered a famous coded oration, punctuated at intervals with the
watchword *redeat* ('may he return!').[4] Everyone in the audience knew
that the 'Bonnie Prince' was being referred to.

Burgeoning Jacobite sentiment was not a prerogative solely of 'the
home of lost causes'. At the other end of the social spectrum, the
oppressed workers of England used pro-Stuart rhetoric as their legitimating ideology. In 1750 the striking keelworkers of Newcastle
proclaimed 'James III' as part of their political programme.[5]
Confirming all these pro-Stuart trends, a French agent in London
added further factors favouring the Jacobites. There was the burden
of land tax levied to meet the costs of the English role in the War of
Austrian Succession, plus the huge personal unpopularity of the duke
of Cumberland.[6]

Early in 1750 the prince took a firm decision to go to England that
year. He worked on a manifesto dealing with the National Debt and
sent secret messages to Lady Primrose (Anne Drelincourt, widow of
the 3rd Viscount Primrose), doyenne of the English Jacobites, to
enquire about his likely reception 'as the Prince is determined to
come over at any rate'.[7] Having satisfied himself on that score, he
assembled a minor arsenal at Anvers: 20,000 guns, bayonets and
ammunition plus 4,000 swords and pistols were to be loaded on one
ship, and another 6,000 guns and ammunition (but without bayonets)
on a second vessel.[8] Charles entrusted the work to his agents Goring
and Dormer. They were instructed to be ready to sail to England
with the arms as soon as he sent word.

Next the prince sent to Rome for a renewal of his Commission of
Regency. After much grumbling, James granted it.[9] Finally, Charles
laid a number of false trails to mask his risky journey to London. He
spread the rumour that he was ill and at the point of death.[10] And
he sent a package of letters to Elisabeth Ferrand, written as if on the

dates 15 September, 6 October and 24 October, with instructions that she was to post them on those dates.[11] Any spies intercepting and reading his letters would then conclude that he was still on the Continent. All was now set for his daring journey.

Why did the prince go to London in September 1750? Andrew Lang's judgment is this:

> There are no traces of a serious organised plan and the Prince probably crossed the water, partly to see how matters really stood, partly from restlessness and the weariness of a tedious solitude in hiding, broken only by daily quarrels and reconciliations with the Princess de Talmond and other ladies.[12]

But a close examination of the Stuart Papers shows that there was a much more compelling reason. What the prince feared was that George II would die before he himself was ready to act. In the ensuing maelstrom, unless he, Charles Edward Stuart, was on hand to make his bid, the initiative would pass to others. Charles's especial fear, shared incidentally by the Pelhams, was that in the event of the death of 'the Elector', Cumberland would seize power, either by a military coup or, more likely, through summoning Parliament and having his brother Frederick declared *non compos mentis*.[13] Cumberland would then be declared Regent until Frederick's children came of age.

The prince's visit to London was designed to prepare a pre-emptive strike. If George II died, the prince wanted to be able either to beat Cumberland to the punch or to manipulate Frederick into declaring a Stuart restoration. We may remark in passing that it was not the least of Charles Edward's misfortunes during the decade of the 1750s that the ailing George II clung to life until 1760, so that the expected power vacuum never took place. With hindsight, one can see all the prince's hopes in this decade blighted by two sovereigns who hung on until the age of seventy-eight: George II 'the Elector', and his own father James.

When all his preparations were complete, the prince left Lunéville on 2 September 1750, headed for Antwerp. He arrived at Antwerp on 6 September.[14] From there he went to Ghent to confer with the intermediaries from the English Jacobites, to check that it was safe for him to cross. Charles was provided with a list of names and contact locations. Among these were Theobald's Court in Theobald's Row; the Grecian coffee house near the Temple; and Simmons coffee house in Chancery Lane.[15]

Then the prince proceeded to Ostend.[16] There he met the man who was to accompany him to England, John Holker.[17] Holker was the very finest and most able type of Jacobite. Aged thirty-one, he had served in the Manchester regiment, was taken prisoner, but escaped to France, where he was already making a name for himself as a textile manufacturer in Rouen. He later became one of the key figures in the French industrial revolution.[18] Yet Holker never lost either his ardent Jacobite sentiments or his personal regard for the prince. It was a tribute to his sterling qualities that he was willing to accompany Charles on such a perilous mission.

On the morning of the 13th, Holker and the heavily disguised prince put to sea.[19] After landing at Dover, they arrived in London on 16 September.[20] Although the prince's plan to come to London was known to the English Jacobites in a general way, his coming caught them unawares. Fearing betrayal, he told no one of his detailed plans. The consequence was that his arrival caused a certain amount of consternation. When he was ushered in to Lady Primrose's house in Essex Street off the Strand under an assumed name, the mistress of the house was playing cards with some non-Jacobite nobility. Recognising him at once, she nearly dropped her cards in amazement.[21]

Recovering quickly, she set about devising a programme for him. Fifty of his partisans were invited to a secret meeting at a house in Pall Mall. Among those present were the duke of Beaufort, Lord Westmoreland and Dr William King;[22] also there was Robert Gordoun, henceforth an assiduous correspondent.[23] The prince addressed his followers and explained his aims. He needed just 4,000 men to achieve the restoration without foreign help. The English Jacobites became alarmed. They rehearsed to him all the old arguments used in 1745–6 to justify their non-participation in the rising. The gentry were unused to bearing arms, they could not raise a private army unobserved, they were short of cash, they could be arrested under general warrants at any time. It soon became clear to the prince that he had a wasted journey.[24] By inference from later events, it seems that the English Jacobites must have urged on him the desirability of some sort of foreign assistance and of a diversionary rising or raid elsewhere in the United Kingdom.

Disappointed in his main hopes, the prince made a tour of London strongholds with Colonel Brett, a veteran Jacobite agent who had acted as envoy between Fleury and the English Jacobites in 1739.[25] The Tower of London, the obvious target in any *coup*, particularly interested the prince. Like Cumberland with Carlisle Castle, Charles had no great opinion of its defensive potential. He remarked to Brett that one of the gates could be easily broken down with a petard.[26]

Frustrated in his primary intentions, the prince still had one essential task to perform in London. It had long been in his mind that the key to Jacobite restoration lay in England. If the work was to be done by English Jacobites alone, and this largely meant *Protestant* Jacobites, they had to be given a very great incentive. This incentive the prince now intended to provide in the form of a public abjuration of Catholicism and the embrace of Anglicanism.[27]

At a ceremony in an Anglican church in the Strand, the prince went through a formal apostasy from the faith of his forefathers.[28] With his contempt for organised religion, Charles Edward failed to understand what a sensation this change of allegiance would eventually cause. As an intelligent man, he found the tenets of Christianity either humbug or self-evidently absurd. He did not realise that religion was still life and death to many people.

It was clear, though, that the prince's hopes for a *coup de main* in London needed much more careful planning. It was time to depart to safety. Before he left, Charles spent an evening with William King, later to be an acidulous enemy. King found the prince naturally intelligent but lacking in formal education. At this stage in his career King was not in the business of rewriting history, so he freely admitted the prince's charm, remarking particularly on his handsome face and good eyes.[29] Only later did King rationalise his own disappointments in a character-sketch that was self-evidently absurd in its vindictiveness.[30] No such reading of a personality as King provided would have been available, even to a Freud, on the basis of a few hours' drinking tea in the good doctor's lodgings. Yet it *was* clear that the prince's decision to decamp was a prudent one. Dr King's servant remarked on the extreme likeness between the visitor and the busts of the 'Young Pretender' on sale in Red Lion Street.[31]

On 22 September the prince left London. He and Holker went by post to Dover, where they arrived in the small hours of the 23rd.[32] In the morning they crossed to Boulogne. Another stretch of hard-driving travel got them to Paris on the evening of 24 September.[33]

The prince remained in Paris until the 28th, then made for Lunéville post-haste, arriving on 30 September.[34] The entire excursion from Lorraine had taken just twenty-eight days. Apart from Dr King's perceptive servant, there had been no danger. The prince had been under the Whigs' noses without their having had the slightest suspicion.[35]

Yet the London trip, however superficially unsuccessful, had sparked in the prince ideas for a grand design within which a London *coup* could be carried out. His first task was to find foreign allies. He had vowed never again to collaborate with France. He had perforce to look elsewhere. One obvious possibility was Germany. The prince spent much of late 1750 scurrying from Lunéville to secret meetings with Goring in Worms and Mainz.[36]

As we have seen, the first notion Charles Edward toyed with was marriage to the duke of Daremberg's daughter in return for an army of invasion 12,000 strong, destined for England.[37] A secret meeting of representatives from both sides took place in Basle, but the proposal was not successful – hardly surprising, given the prince's premises.

Nothing daunted, Charles simply moved his sights higher. His next target was the daughter of Frederick of Prussia. Through the good offices of Earl Marischal, now Frederick's confidant, a meeting was arranged in Berlin in February 1751 between Charles Edward and the Prussian king.[38] Frederick would not entertain the prince's suit for his daughter's hand, but promised to think carefully about supporting another Jacobite rising. He advised Charles to live in the remotest part of Europe he could find – Silesia was mentioned. Meanwhile he should collect 6,000 Swedes, either as mercenaries or 'on loan'. When all the preparations in London were complete, the expedition should depart from Gothenburg for a landfall in north-east England.[39]

Charles Edward did not care for Frederick's suggestion that France be kept informed of all his plans. But he went away from the meeting animated with thoughts of a grand northern alliance, embracing Russia, Sweden and Prussia.[40] Finally, after much lucubration, he sent Goring back to Berlin to liaise with Marischal. The two of them were to lobby Frederick strongly for military assistance, stressing both the prince's personal esteem for the Prussian monarch and his determination to help the king's infant navy on to its feet if restored to the English throne.[41]

But at this point a number of dramatic events took place in quick succession. Early 1751 brought a crop of deaths. First there was the demise of the king of Sweden, which seemed to increase the likelihood of a general European war.[42] Then George II's son Frederick died.[43] If George II had succumbed at this time, the perennial Jacobite cliché about a 'favourable conjuncture' would at last have become fact.[44] Further Jacobite excitement was aroused by the false rumour that the duke of Cumberland had died. Alas for the Jacobites, further investigation revealed that it was a horse of that name, not the 'Butcher' himself, that had expired![45]

Any hopes of exploiting the new situation were unexpectedly dashed with the announcement that Frederick the Great was to send Earl Marischal as his minister to Paris.[46] Superficially, this seemed to favour the Jacobites. The development seemed particularly ominous to the jittery English, since Lord Tyrconnel, who had been 'out' in the '45, had just been appointed French minister to Prussia.[47] From the English point of view, France and Prussia were now represented in each other's courts by rebels. The dismissal of the notorious anti-Jacobite Puysieux from the post of Secretary of State for Foreign Affairs, and his replacement by the more pliable St Contest who, it was felt, would complement Marischal neatly, seemed to provide the clinching argument for a pro-Jacobite plot being hatched by France and Prussia.[48] English politicians in their private correspondence ruefully congratulated Frederick on a Machiavellian masterstroke.[49]

But Charles Edward, with the insight characteristic of cynicism, did not see things at all this way. Frederick had been Machiavellian, yes, but in a quite different sense. 'Lord Marischal's coming here [Paris] is a great politique [sic]: on one side to bully the Court of England, on the other to hinder our friends from doing the thing by themselves, bamboozling them with hopes.'[50]

The prince had always urged the English Jacobites to carry out an initiative on their own account. They had always insisted they needed a foreign ally. Now they seemed to have one. Yet Charles Edward knew from Prussian policy in the past and his personal acquaintance with Frederick that Prussia would draw back from outright Stuart restoration; they would, however, be quite happy to stir the pot betimes. If the English Jacobites handed Frederick a controlling interest in their affairs, they would be putting their heads in a noose. All the signs pointed to an anti-British alliance with France; yet he himself had sworn a mighty oath never to have anything to do with France.

Besides, there was the personality of Earl Marischal. Puzzlingly, however great his detachment from the Stuart cause and his general indolence on the Jacobite behalf, Marischal never lost credibility as he should have done. He, much more than either James or Charles Edward, was the high priest of the English Jacobite sect. They would not move a muscle without his approval. Yet the reality was that Marischal was already the type of 'Jacobite' – like Lord Clare in France or the old Marshal Duke of Berwick in James's heyday – who cared far more for his own career than for the restoration of the Stuarts.

Anyone who doubts this should look at Marischal's record. After the '45, every time James or Charles Edward asked him to undertake a commission on their behalf, he would decline on the grounds of 'old age' or 'broken health'. Yet in the service of Frederick of Prussia he exhibited the most remarkable vigour and enthusiasm. Charles Edward knew his man. He saw clearly enough that Marischal's appointment to Paris was in reality a disaster for his own plans. But because of Marischal's unassailable prestige with the English Jacobites, the prince had no choice but to work with him and through him.

Accordingly, Charles changed his instructions to Goring. Goring was told to seek out Marischal at Versailles; his brief was to wrest from him an assurance that his embassy had nothing to do with any Jacobite plots, and that the English should therefore look to their own salvation.[51]

But Marischal was determined to play dog in the manger. He had no enthusiasm for a *coup* in England. At the same time, he did not want such an enterprise to be undertaken by people not under his direction. He therefore decided to drag a red herring or two across the trail. Just before leaving Berlin, he wrote to Goring about the proposed northern alliance – which Charles Edward had now largely abandoned anyway, once he saw the way Frederick's mind was working. Marischal's point was that the prince's proposed alliance offended against balance of power considerations: if troops from Sweden were used against England, Russia would retaliate by occupying Finland.[52] Sweden knew that its best defence against Russia was Frederick of Prussia, so would take its cue from him. The deviousness of Frederick the Great thus comes through clearly. By encouraging Charles Edward to solicit Swedish help, while sending Marischal to Paris, Frederick aimed to control both ends of the Jacobite movement. He would keep his puppet dancing on the string until he had brought England to heel.

Charles Edward was already cynical about Frederick. As far as he was concerned, the only acceptable proof of the king's sincerity was to allow him to marry his sister and 'acknowledging me at Berlin for what I am'.[53] But he was now locked into an intolerable impasse. The English Jacobites would co-operate only if they received the go-ahead from Marischal. Marischal would give this only if he won the nod from Frederick. Frederick would make no move without France. Yet Charles Edward himself refused to work with the French. One of the most profound problems about the intrigues that went on during 1751–3 was that there was no way to square this circle.

When there was added to this the personal animosity entertained by Marischal for the prince, and the presence of a Hanoverian spy (Pickle) at the very heart of Jacobite deliberations, the recipe for disaster was complete.

The full extent of the deep endemic factors working against Charles Edward's designs was not immediately apparent. What later became known as the 'Elibank Plot' commenced with a series of meetings in Paris. Actually, the so-called Elibank plot is a portmanteau term for the entire class of very different projects that were adumbrated and discarded during 1751–3. After a lot of fussy pedantry from Marischal about the correct venue for their meetings,[54] the conspirators got down to business. Among those involved from the very beginning were Sir John Graeme, Goring, Lochgarry and Alexander Murray of Elibank.

Murray of Elibank was brother to the Lord Elibank who was a friend of Dr Johnson. He was typical of the adventurers attracted to the prince, and for whom he had a decided weakness. Early in 1751 he was charged with violence and intimidation in the Westminster by-election and was then imprisoned for refusing to beg pardon of the House of Commons on his knees.[55] This was not his only claim to notoriety. Though high-born, he possessed little money until a marriage of convenience secured him £3,000 a year, ironically all interest payments on bonds paid by the National Debt. A renowned miser and usurer, Murray lent the impoverished prince several hundred pounds at a high rate of interest. This secured him an entrée into Charles Edward's inner circles.[56] To the prince what counted was liquidity, not its provenance or the interest charged on it. In other respects, too, Murray was a nonentity. He had never risen above the rank of lieutenant in military service. But significantly, the man he had supported in the disputed Westminster by-election was a Whig. The prince was now close to making a fetish out of disgruntled Whigs as *the* pure type of English supporter he wanted.[57]

The first part of the plot, the *coup* in London, now took shape. The original idea of this part of the plan was that George II and other members of the 'Elector's family' be kidnapped and spirited away to France in a fast cutter waiting on the Thames. To this end, minute analyses of the sentry system at St James's Palace were undertaken. Two or three hundred hand-picked men were to assemble in Westminster. To avoid arousing suspicion, they would all take lodgings in different houses. On the night fixed for the abduction they would assemble at pre-selected locations. Then the Palace would be seized, the Tower gates thrown open, the guards overpowered, and the luckless scions of the House of Hanover taken to France, there perhaps to suffer a long house arrest in the same way as Mary Queen of Scots.[58]

Marischal listened glumly to the details of the plot. In his view, there was not the slightest chance that the conspiracy could succeed. The entire project was chimerical, worthless.[59] He later described the Elibank plot as being as impracticable as an attempt to seize the moon with one's teeth.[60] But, characteristically, Marischal did not veto the intrigue outright. He feared that if he did so, he would simply be cut out of the conspiracy. That would diminish his worth to Frederick the Great, and it was by the Prussian lodestone alone that Marischal now steered. So he expressed merely half-hearted opposition to the abduction. He did not full-bloodedly set his authority against the very principle of the scheme. This was read by the other conspirators as typical Marischal circumspection and defeatism. They went ahead, blithely telling their counterparts in England that Marischal had given the plot his imprimatur.

Gradually more and more pieces fitted into the complex mosaic. The circle of conspirators widened. Apart from Lady Primrose, the most important English Jacobite to be mixed up in the plot was Jeremy Dawkins, lately a Middle East explorer. In the City of London Jacobite movements were to be co-ordinated by Alderman George Heathcote.[61] Other aldermen mentioned as his acolytes were Benn, Blachford and Blakistoun.[62] Further names frequently encountered as the plot matured were Messrs Trant, Fleetwood, Charles Hepburn of Keith and Sir John Douglas.[63]

Much against Charles Edward's wish, French Jacobites were also drawn in. Dominique O'Heguerty, brother of the prince's biographer, drew attention in 1751 to the high level of unrest and tension in England, which could be turned to French advantage in an attempt to undo some of the damage of the 1748 Treaty of Aix-la-Chapelle.[64] Immediately the marquise de Mézières sent her trusted lieutenant Father Cruise to England. He confirmed O'Heguerty's analysis.[65] But he had further muddied the already turbid waters of the Elibank conspiracy.

The situation at the beginning of 1752, then, was this. There was a four-way traffic between Charles Edward and his clique, Marischal and the Prussians, the English Jacobites, and the French Jacobites of the diaspora. Lord Clare had been apprised in general terms that there was a project afoot.[66] Thomas Carte and the Mézières coterie were reluctantly accepted as conduits to the English Jacobites, since Mézières enjoyed the confidence of Marischal.[67]

The development of the Elibank plot is notoriously hard to unravel in detail. Hardly surprisingly in the case of such a desperate endeavour, most of the incriminating evidence was later destroyed. But there seem to have been three main stages. First, the abduction of the Hanoverian royal family, so as to create a power vacuum that Charles Edward could exploit. The difficulties in the path of the implementation of such a daring escapade were legion. So a second stage was reached in which the English Jacobites inclined towards a once-and-for-all solution that would not expose them to such grave risks. Alexander Murray of Elibank proposed that the Hanoverian family be murdered, possibly by poison. But the prince vetoed this suggestion.[68] He always felt repugnance towards schemes of assassination.

The third stage arrived when a compromise between abduction and homicidal action was proposed. The final version of the plot called for the seizure of the Tower and the Palace. The Hanoverian royals would be held as hostages. Once word of the *coup* reached the prince, who would be waiting on the Belgian coast, he would cross to consolidate the Jacobite position. Perhaps George II and his family would be forced to sign articles of abdication. Perhaps they would be shipped out to France as in the original plan. All these details are shadowy. But it *is* clear that the prince had lengthened the odds against himself by his morally commendable (if politically inex-pedient) refusal to countenance assassination.

Since the final version of the Elibank plot was an extremely perilous undertaking, the clamour grew for a diversionary project that would take some of the heat off the London conspirators. Various possi-bilities were canvassed. There was the old idea of landing Swedish troops from Gothenburg, but as no one had yet approached Sweden, this seemed the purest fantasy. More promising was the idea of using Irish malcontents to stage a diversionary 'invasion' of England. The Irish Jacobites felt guilty about their quiescence during the '45. Apparently some of their more vociferous spokesmen offered to land a force of between 11,000 and 14,000 either in north Wales or Scot-land.[69] This landing would be the signal for the London operation to commence.

But as 1752 wore on, it became abundantly clear that it was one thing to devise a complex and intellectually satisfying intrigue on paper; it was quite another to carry it out according to the plan. When it came to serious business, it transpired that there was no such Irish force as had been hinted at. Another part of the plot called for 8,000 swords to be delivered to Ogilvy's regiment at Dunkirk.

These would then be put ashore at the Firth of Forth.[70] But such an enterprise required the co-operation of both France and Russia. Now not only would Frederick not give his assent to this until he had finally decided with France what their real policy towards England was to be; even more importantly, the prince still refused to work with France.

The refusal to work with the French was only one of several self-destructive acts by the prince during 1752 that eventually precipitated the Elibank plot into débâcle. Another was his abrupt dismissal of Mittie junior. Apparently the reason for this was that the prince's anti-French sentiments had now hardened into phobia. Since the Elibank plot was supposed to be a purely English Protestant affair, Charles decided that none but Englishmen and women should be involved in it,[71] ignoring the fact that Mittie was already in the scheme up to his neck.

With characteristic self-laceration, the prince timed his hot-tempered sacking of Mittie for the very month when Lady Primrose was on the Continent to finalise the English end of the plot.[72] Goring and the prince's other advisers were aghast. Lady Primrose had always worked through Mittie, and now she was to be told that the man to whom she had confided all her secrets, and who knew enough to send the entire English Jacobite party to the gallows, had been dismissed from the prince's service![73]

Even more amazingly, in the very month of Lady Primrose's visit to Paris (May 1752), the prince decided to resume relations with Clementina Walkinshaw, his mistress from the days of early 1746. Since the English Jacobites suspected her of being a Hanoverian spy, they were dismayed when the prince refused to listen to their entreaties to send her away.[74] Security for the entire operation now seemed jeopardised.

The English Jacobites became confirmed in their suspicions when obvious intelligence leaks made it clear that there was a spy in their midst. The 'mole' was not Clementina but Pelham's agent 'Pickle'.[75] Yet the coincidence that Pickle's information started to become really effective immediately after Clementina joined the prince was just too great for the English Jacobites to form any other conclusion: in their view, Charles Edward was harbouring a spy and blindly refusing to do anything about this obvious fact.

It was Pickle himself who occasioned the fourth, and in some ways worst, of the prince's self-destructive actions in 1752. As early as May, the faithful John Holker had identified Young Glengarry as 'Pickle' and informed the prince accordingly.[76] Charles Edward simply refused to believe the evidence. As far as he was concerned, Glengarry had passed the only test that mattered: he had been to Rome but breathed not a word to James about the Elibank plot. There was no need to halt the planning. The scheme would proceed. The time to strike was at the end of October or beginning of November, when George II returned from Windsor to St James's Palace. A firm date of 10 November 1752 was agreed for the operation.[77]

The frenzied pace of activity can be appreciated from the many meetings in Ghent between the prince and English agents, and with MacNamara, Mittie's replacement, in Brussels.[78] Goring, increasingly Marischal's creature, was aware of all this, mentally shaking his head over the lack of clarity in the arrangements.[79]

Someone else who had passed the prince's 'ordeal by James' was the marquise de Mézières.[80] Following Lady Primrose's excursion to the Continent, la Mézières went to England to co-ordinate the final stages of the plot.[81] English suspicions were immediately aroused when she entered the country without an official passport.[82] The Pelhams already knew from Pickle that something momentous was afoot. The arrival of this inveterate but, at seventy, still deadly dangerous female intriguer put them on their mettle.

Hard on her heels came the principal architect of the project, Murray of Elibank. Murray entered England secretly in October 1752, hoping to improve on his previous meagre military reputation as a mere Hanoverian lieutenant by leading the assault on St James's and the Tower.[83] What he found appalled him. The promised diversionary raid evaporated once it was realised that its personnel were phantoms: there were neither Irish ready in Dublin nor Swedes champing at the bit in Gothenburg. Consequently the English Jacobites found themselves dangerously exposed. With a supremely perilous operation imminent, they suddenly realised that they had somehow been manoeuvred into the position all English Jacobites since 1688 had most dreaded: raising the Stuart standard when unsupported by foreign allies. In addition, the prince's wildly erratic behaviour was now causing deep concern. The much-vaunted conversion to Protestantism had backfired badly. It was felt widely, and correctly, that this was the merest opportunism. It confirmed the worst fears of those who thought Charles Edward had no genuine religious feeling but was an undeclared freethinker.[84]

The prince's stubborn refusal to send Clementina Walkinshaw away was a particular bone of contention for Lady Primrose, Dr King and the others. Their morale was badly affected. There were even some who suspected that they were already betrayed and that the Pelhams were lying in wait for them. All things considered, they lacked the stomach for the coming perilous enterprise. The contagion of defeatism infected Murray. He lost his nerve and announced a postponement of the operation;[85] 10 November 1752 would not, after all, be a red-letter day in the Jacobite calendar. Murray returned to Paris to give Charles Edward the bad news.

Ironically, the prince had already decided that the English Jacobites could not be left out on a limb. The question was where their support should come from. It is possible that the prince could have got a diversionary expedition launched from Paris, if only on an 'unofficial' basis using 'volunteers'. He had the powerful support of the duc de Richelieu, the comte d'Argenson and the financier Paris de Monmartel.[86] The regiments of the Irish brigade, especially Ogilvy's and Clare's, were mentioned as likely participants in any such diversion. But still the prince burned with unquenchable indignation against France. Until Louis XV and his ministers had apologised to him for the humiliating arrest in December 1748, he would have no dealings with them. Since the Irish, Swedes and Prussians had all turned out to be phantoms, that left just one possibility: the Highlands. This was precisely the direction the latest envoy from the clans (Ranald MacDonald, brother of Kinlochmoidart) was urging on him during their conversations in Paris.[87]

Accordingly, in the late summer of 1752 the prince obtained a *congé* for Dr Archibald Cameron and Lochgarry, releasing them from their regimental duties with Lochiel's at Douai. Then he summoned them to meet him at Menin, near Lille.[88] He ordered the two veterans of the '45 to go to Scotland immediately and prepare for a rising which would be timed to break out just before the London *coup*. Cameron and Lochgarry were to assure the Highlanders that both Marischal and his brother marshal Keith were ready to sail for Scotland at a moment's notice and that Prussia would send help.[89]

The prince has sometimes been accused of sending his two emissaries into the jaws of death on the basis of a blatant lie. The truth is more complex. At best the prince can be faulted for 'expedient exaggeration'. Frederick of Prussia had not finally made up his mind about the Jacobites. And although Marischal later complained bitterly about the misrepresentation of his position, he had only himself to blame. He was asked whether, in the event of a *coup* in London, the Highlanders should march to help the prince. Marischal jesuitically answered yes, meaning, as he later explained, that in such a hypothetical case, which was the merest fantasy, he would have said yes to the landing in England of 10,000 Janissaries or 6,000 Spahis.[90]

Marischal's donnish humour did nothing to help the cause. Cameron and Lochgarry went to Scotland convinced that they had the powerful support of the Keith brothers and, through them, of Frederick the Great. The English Jacobites' spirits revived. If there was a simultaneous rising in the Highlands, their *coup* would not be an isolated phenomenon. Even the Irish project was resuscitated. Although the existence of the mythical 14,000 Celts had still not been established, it was proposed to send 11,000 of them to north Wales and the other 3,000 to Campbelltown in Argyllshire, where they would be joined by the clans.[91]

In Scotland Lochgarry and Archie Cameron met Fassifern at Crieff.[92] Fassifern was to be the channel to Cluny MacPherson, still skulking in his cage on Ben Alder. Then they proceeded to Lochaber. They found morale among the clans high. Of particular encouragement was the news that the prince had converted to Protestantism and that help from the Keiths and the Prussians was on its way. Cluny promised that he could lay his hands on 5,000 'stand' of arms in the glens.[93] All seemed set fair.

Then the blow fell. Pickle's accurate information enabled Henry Pelham to close the trap. In March 1753 Archie Cameron was captured near Inversnaid by a redcoat patrol, acting on information from the highest sources.[94] Lochgarry narrowly escaped being taken with Cameron.[95] The prisoner was taken to Edinburgh, then on to London, and cross-examined closely and repeatedly. Stalling valiantly, Dr Cameron gave nothing away. He claimed to be ignorant of the prince's 1751 visit to Berlin, to know nothing of Lord George Murray's whereabouts, and not to have seen Marischal since 1716.[96]

In April he was condemned to death on the original attainder for having been out in the '45.[97] The sentence provoked a general outcry and was universally condemned for its barbarity.[98] But Pelham preferred a reputation for draconian severity to trying Cameron on fresh charges, as this would have meant blowing the cover of his priceless source Pickle.

For it was Pickle more than anyone who had dealt the *coup de grâce* to the Elibank plot. In a remarkably short space of time Pickle wormed his way to the very centre of the conspiracy. Shortly after Charles Edward gave his instructions to Cameron and Lochgarry at Menin for the rising in Scotland, Pickle, still posing as a loyal Jacobite, ran him to earth in Veurne (then Furnes).[99] Charles Edward, never thinking that a clan chief could be a traitor, revealed the plot in detail, and Murray of Elibank's leading role in it. It is clear that the decision to postpone the *coup* on 10 November 1752 was a lucky one for the English Jacobites. Armed with Pickle's intelligence, the Pelhams were just waiting for them to reveal themselves. Even when foiled of their principal prey on that occasion, they learned enough from Pickle to be able to trap Dr Cameron in the Highlands.

The arrest and execution of Archie Cameron put an end to all thoughts of a *coup* in London, no doubt to the relief of many English 'bottle Jacobites'. But the ferment aroused in the Highlands could not so easily be dampened down. In May 1753 Colin Campbell of Glenure, a powerful Whig magnate, was shot dead from behind a bush by Allan Breck Stewart of the Appin Stewarts.[100] Although narrowly interpreted at the time as a warning to non-Jacobites of the consequences of taking over the forfeited estates, the assassination can also be seen as an act of desperation by people frustrated almost to madness by the failure of the prince's great scheme for a Second Coming.

By a supreme irony, at the very time the extended Elibank conspiracy was faltering, Frederick the Great suddenly decided to take it seriously. It was Marischal who made the suggestion. Lukewarm and even privately hostile to the conspiracy so far, because it seemed to conflict with Prussian interests (which with Marischal always took precedence over those of the Stuarts), the Earl now saw a chance to use the Jacobites as a lever. Frederick was locked in dispute with England over a number of issues: debts in Silesia, ill-treatment of his merchant navy, the election of the 'king of the Romans'. Since Frederick could get no satisfaction through normal diplomacy, Marischal suggested playing the Jacobite card. He further proposed sending Dawkins, the explorer of Palmyra, to Berlin to firm up the scheme.[101]

Frederick asked for further details of the Elibank plot. It is clear from Marischal's letters to the king that he was very well informed. It is also clear that even in March 1753 Dr King and the earl of Westmoreland were still strongly committed to the conspiracy. Marischal's comment on the prince, however, is almost predictable:

> The Prince knows less of the affair than Dawkins does. The Prince's position, coupled with an intrepidity which never lets him have any doubts when he wants something, causes others to form projects for him, which he is always ready to execute.[102]

Although thinking the plot crude, Frederick agreed to stir the pot. He advised the Jacobites to try to suborn the army and navy. In

June 1753 he saw Dawkins in Berlin.[103] While continuing to think the plans for a *coup* crackbrained, he encouraged the conspirators to continue. He wrote complacently to his envoy in London that he had a trick up his sleeve which the London government would never guess.[104]

But the king of Prussia had left it too late. The execution of Archie Cameron in June was the last chapter in the ill-fated saga. Frederick was left to ponder other avenues for getting his way with England. Students of his methods were not surprised, however, to find him three years later a firm ally of England after the notorious '*renversement des alliances*'. It was a poor judge who put his trust in this particular prince, as Charles Edward had been shrewd enough to see.

The failure of the Elibank plot meant the end of the Jacobite movement as a credible political force. The prince's own public career effectively came to an end the following year after his violent breach with Marischal, Goring and the English Jacobites.

How to account for such a sensational débâcle? The weakness of the Elibank plot was a significant pointer to the desperate straits the Jacobite party found itself in by the early 1750s. But a plot that was unlikely to succeed was converted into one that was *certain* to fail by a number of different factors.

The Prussian attitude is especially revealing. Recent scholarly work has indicated that religious motives in the eighteenth century have been unduly neglected. In 1743–4 it was Frederick who was especially alarmed by the French attempts to restore the Catholic Stuarts. In Frederick's actions during 1751–3 we surely see an echo of this Protestant solidarity. At all points the natural interests of Prussia indicated an alliance with the Jacobites. Quite apart from Frederick's own maritime and financial quarrels with the English, London had drawn closer to the Empire since Aix-la-Chapelle. The ancient British ally, Holland, was Prussia's trading rival. Prussian designs eastwards were blocked by the formidable power of Russia. In return Prussia guaranteed the independence of Sweden against the Czarina. Frederick's only stable allies were Denmark and Sweden. The *rapprochement* with France was unreliable. The Austrians could, if they chose, always win over France by ceding her the Austrian Netherlands. In such a precarious international context, Prussian support for the Jacobites made a lot of sense.[105]

But still Frederick was reluctant. He could, it is true, have solved the problem at a stroke by occupying Hanover; this, however, would have involved him in a general European war. It is significant that he discarded this option even in 1753, when British intransigence seemed to leave him no way out of a diplomatic impasse. We are left, then, with a certain puzzle as to why he was reluctant to support Charles Edward, unless religious considerations were more important than is generally conceded. If this is true, irony piles on irony. Not only was Charles Edward actually a secret Protestant, so that Frederick's fears were groundless. But it would also be the ironical quintessence if religious scruples, for which the prince had such profound contempt, had actually contributed to his downfall.

However, even if the Elibank plot had still been alive in 1753 when Frederick finally decided to play the Jacobite card, the actual use of Prussian troops in England still seems inconceivable. The plain truth is that the Elibank plot could not have succeeded without foreign aid. The Stuarts' only truly reliable ally was France, yet Charles Edward adamantly refused to work with Versailles.

Lord Marischal must take a share of the blame for the fiasco. He never made it clear to the English Jacobite party that he was first and foremost a Prussian minister, and only secondarily a supporter of the House of Stuart. If Charles Edward was proving intractable, it was for Marischal, as the admired elder statesman, to use his influence and talk him round. Yet Marischal spent much of his time avoiding the prince and devising reasons why he could not meet him face to face. His skill as a politician is shown by the fact that not a scintilla of the mutual recrimination which burst out among the English Jacobites over the failure of the conspiracy was directed at him. He successfully managed to turn all the spleen of King, Dawkins and Westmoreland against the prince.

This should not be taken to imply that the prince was blameless. Pickle was not the only internal saboteur at work during the Elibank period. The prince's self-destructive urges were at full strength during this crucial time. His treatment of Goring was inept, his dismissal of Mittie junior senseless, his refusal to bow to English Jacobite pressure over Clementina Walkinshaw reprehensible. His resistance to sending her away would have been heroic and praiseworthy if he had loved her. He did not. It was the challenge to his will, and that alone, that he resented.

Finally, his understandable though excessive animus against France removed any chance that the Elibank plot could have had an international dimension. If he had been willing to work with the French, the Frederick/Marischal polarity could have been reversed. Instead of the manipulated, the prince could have become the manipulator. Pro-Jacobite pressure from Versailles on its Prussian ally would in turn have put pressure on Marischal and, through him, the English Jacobite party. As it was, both Charles Edward and Marischal pursued their own impossibilities. The prince had to satisfy the English Jacobites that they had reliable foreign allies while cutting himself off from the one power that fitted that bill. Marischal would truly consent to lead the English Jacobites only if he, not Charles Edward, were given supreme power, and then only if Frederick gave him *carte blanche*.

For all that, Charles Edward did secure some small triumphs in the Elibank years. Despite having a spy at the very nerve centre of Jacobite operations, the Hanoverians were as much at sea as ever as to the prince's movements and his location at any given time. Some of the intelligence reports from this period reach new heights of absurdity. In 1751 there was a ludicrous hue and cry following reports that the prince was at Borscheit in Germany.[106] Early in 1752 'the Young Pretender' was reported as being probably in Bordeaux but 'certainly' somewhere in southern France.[107] Later he was placed in Switzerland, intending (again!) to marry Princess Radziwill.[108] Some idea of the utter hopelessness felt by Hanoverian agents with the job of tracking Charles Edward can be seen from an intelligence report early in 1753, allegedly following the prince's itinerary successively through Prussia, Poland, Paris, Scotland, Denmark, Frankfurt, Strasbourg, Liège and Lunéville.[109] Simply by the law of averages, one of these 'sightings' was likely to correspond with fact!

The prince's other minor triumph was to direct a conspiracy without allowing any word of it to leak out to his father. After obtaining the renewal of the Commission of Regency in 1750, Charles Edward simply cut James out. His father's homily on the necessity of marrying, written on his son's thirtieth birthday, was ignored.[110] All James ever received was the occasional short note, without date or address, containing the inevitable 'my health is perfect'.

The failure of the Elibank plot also elicited two wildly divergent views of the prince from two of its principal participants. This is Dr King's version:

> I never heard him express any noble or benevolent sentiments . . .
> or discover any sorrow or compassion for the misfortunes of so
> many worthy men who had suffered in his cause. But the most
> odious part of his character is his love of money, a vice which I
> do not remember to have been imputed by any historian to any of
> his ancestors, and it is the certain index of a base and little mind.[111]

Here, by contrast, is what Dr Cameron had to say just before his execution:

I had the honour to be almost constantly about his person until November 1748 . . . I became more and more captivated with his amiable and princely virtues which are, indeed, in every instance so eminently great as I want words to describe. I can further affirm (and my present situation and that of my dear prince too can leave no room to suspect me of flattery) that as I have been his companion in the lowest degree of adversity ever Prince was reduced to, so I have beheld him too as it were on the highest pinnacle of glory amidst the continual applauses and I had almost said adoration of the most brilliant court in Europe, yet he was always the same, ever affable and courteous, giving constant proofs of his great humanity and of his love for his friends and country.[112]

In such a conflict of evidence, it is clearly preferable to accept the word of a man 'constantly about' the prince to one who had seen him briefly over a period of six days and later rewrote his testimony. This is to say nothing of one's natural preference for the word of the man whose mind the prospect of hanging, in Dr Johnson's words, concentrates wonderfully, rather than that of the embittered zealot who rationalises three years of wasted effort by outright apostasy.

But at another level the two wildly discordant judgments are interesting as denoting the two sides of the prince: purposive strength, willpower, perseverance, tolerance and humour on the one side; self-destructive guilt, rage and paranoia on the other. If Cameron concentrated solely on the light, King pointed up the darkness.

King's words were written after 1754, in the bitter aftermath of Elibank. King's evidence, selected and biased as it is, is of a piece with the psychological portrait we have offered. The constant action of the '45, the years of exile, the Elibank plot, all kept the prince's shaky mental equilibrium going. When the action ceased in 1754, and all realistic political hopes were laid aside, the hitherto contained suffering broke out anew. When Dr Cameron made his dying speech, the prince could still be perceived as the hero of the '45, his faults yet dimmed in the brightness of that golden memory. A year later little but a vague shadow of what he had once been remained.

29

Trust in Princes

(1752–4)

After the final break with the Princesse de Talmont, the prince's private life enters an obscure period. That he was still interested in women is clear, for in the years 1751–2 we find ample traces of secret amours. While his agent 'Grandval' (i.e. Dumont) was in Lille, the prince was smitten with *coup de foudre* for a beautiful unknown. He confesses that his head was completely turned at sight of her, that he was beside himself and that he was dying of love for her.[1] Unfortunately, no evidence exists as to the outcome of this liaison.

Suddenly, in 1752, the prince took a decision that amazed his contemporaries but has surprisingly not attracted as much comment as it deserves from later generations. He sent for Clementina Walkinshaw, his discarded mistress of January 1746. On any analysis this was an extraordinary thing to do, and it excited the stupefaction of Jacobites at the time. How can we explain it? What were the prince's motives?[2]

It is clear that by early 1752 the prince no longer felt safe in Lunéville. His enemies were closing in on him. If there is one thing that is bound to feed fantasies of persecution, it is circumstantial evidence of such persecution. By the beginning of 1752 the prince had plenty of it.

On 20 May 1751, while returning on horseback to Lunéville through the neighbouring villages, the prince was set on by three brigands. A man leading a horse by the fountain in the village of Enville gave the signal. It was just after 6 p.m. The three men then chased Charles Edward all the way to the village of Metz. Only the narrowness of the road prevented their coming at him three abreast. At Metz the attack was called off. The prince secured a guard from the post-horse *'syndique'* for the rest of the journey to Lunéville.[3]

The experience shook him profoundly. At first he raged at the incompetence of Stanislas for allowing such brigandage within his domains. Then he thought again about the peculiar circumstances of the attack. An altogether more sinister interpretation occurred to him. His fears seemed confirmed by a letter from Sir James Harrington three months later that spoke of an Alloa customs collector's having accepted a contract to assassinate him.[4] Further worry was caused by reports of an English spy called Leslie, said to have gone to Lorraine to worm his way into the prince's confidence 'in a country which it is strongly suspected H.R.H. has crossed and bordered on more than once'.[5] It seemed to the prince both that his enemies were out to kill him *and* that they knew roughly where to find him.

This reflection had another sombre implication. Charles Edward could no longer be sure that the seemingly casual encounters he had with beautiful women were not part of some Hanoverian web. His correspondence began to reflect this anxiety that his amatory conquests might be real spies rather than simple bedroom adventuresses.[6]

The prince therefore decided to change both his residence and way of life. He began by spending long periods away from Lunéville while he pondered the question of a more secure, permanent abode. He spent a good part of August and September 1751 at the waters of Spa.[7] He was in Paris in October 1751 and again in December.[8] In April 1752 he was seen at Middelburg on the Walcheren peninsula in Holland.[9] In May that same year he sent orders to Stafford and Sheridan to close down his household in Avignon. They were to stay in lodgings there until further notice; his effects were to be stored in the papal palace.[10] He himself moved to Ghent. His contact address there was the house of the lawyer Walwin (place de l'Emprereur, rue des Vasapelle, West Strata). All his precious books and collector's items were sent to his new home in Ghent.[11]

Immediately on arrival in Ghent, he sent to discover the whereabouts of Clementina Walkinshaw. At Bannockburn in January 1746 Clementina had promised him that if his great political ambitions came to nothing and he ever needed her, she would be his to command.[12] Six years later, out of clear-cut motives of expediency, the prince took her up on her pledge.

Who was this woman who was to be his mistress for the next eight years? She was the tenth daughter of John Walkinshaw of Barrowfield (born 1671), a man who had been out in the '15, been taken prisoner, and then escaped to join James at Bar-le-Duc.[13] When Clementina

Sobieska was detained at Innsbruck, John Walkinshaw was sent to remonstrate with the emperor. Later he was in Wogan's party that conducted James's bride to Rome.[14] An elaborate legend was later woven around Clementina Walkinshaw's allegedly being named after Charles Edward's mother.[15]

Nevertheless, there can be no doubt of the Walkinshaw family's real, if not sentimental, attachment to the House of Stuart. John Walkinshaw himself died in 1731. But one of his kinsmen was arrested in Scotland after the '45 on suspicion of having been one of the 'Young Pretender's' secret agents.[16] His real crime was having stuck to the ill-fated Lord Balmerino through his final days. Balmerino's last request was to have this Walkinshaw at his side in the hours before his execution.[17] And after the great and good Balmerino was beheaded, Walkinshaw took in Lady Balmerino and cared for her.[18]

Clementina, then, came from unimpeachable Jacobite stock. The other thing to note about her was that she was a Catholic. After the failure of the '45 and the departure of the prince from Scotland, she was left cocooned in the genteel poverty of Bannockburn. She determined to use her religion to break out of her prison. She applied to take the veil in convents in the Low Countries. Having convinced the respective prioresses of the suitability of her family background – for noble birth was all-important in the superior orders of nuns – she wore down the resistance of her family, who misunderstood her motives and scathingly called her a 'priest-ridden weak girl'.[19]

Clementina arrived on the Continent some time in 1751.[20] There was a choice of convents in the Austrian Netherlands, including those at Ardennes, Mons and Maubeuge, but Clementina based herself at Dunkirk and seemed in no hurry to enter any of them. Then in June 1752, by great good fortune, came the summons to join the prince in Ghent.[21]

It soon came to the ears of Charles Edward that the person who knew most about Clementina was John William O'Sullivan, major-general in the '45 and Lord George Murray's *bête noire*. Charles wrote to O'Sullivan for her address, indicating what he had in mind.[22] He suggested that Clementina be approached discreetly when she was on her own. That the prince felt some disgust about his cold proposition to a discarded mistress emerges in his (naturally unheeded) instructions to O'Sullivan to burn his letter.[23]

O'Sullivan received the prince's letter at Cambrai. After expressing his delighted surprise to be once again in touch with Charles, he advised the prince very strongly against renewing the liaison. To have Clementina with him 'would be too dangerous as well for Your Highness's safety as glory in the present juncture'.[24]

The prince reiterated his demands. O'Sullivan replied blandly on 3 June that he did not know where Clementina was exactly, but he was sure she would come out of her convent if the prince wished it, even though she had taken preliminary vows.[25] O'Sullivan's reluctance to be involved in this business was evident, but on the face of it his correspondence with the prince suggested no more than tepidity. The real significance of his reply to the prince (3 June) was that three days earlier (31 May), he wrote to Clementina; he was thus fully aware of her address. The tone was familiar but again that of a man acting under duress. Since, it appeared, she had neither entered the Convent of Poor Clares at Gravelines nor that at Arras, there could be no avoiding obedience to the prince's wishes.[26]

Clementina prepared to travel to Ghent by the roundabout route (via Paris) insisted on by Charles Edward. But no sooner had news of the prince's resolve become common knowledge in his inner circle than he found himself with a revolt on his hands. The official reason always given in Jacobite correspondence was that Clementina's sister Catherine was in the service of Augusta, Princess Dowager of Wales, mother of the future George III, at Leicester House.[27] The fear was that Clementina had been planted with the prince as a spy – a suspicion which the downfall of the Elibank plot shortly afterwards seemed to confirm.

Whatever the reasons for the peculiar distaste in which Clementina was regarded in Jacobite circles, its consequences soon made themselves felt. From Ghent Charles Edward rode to Lens to give Goring specific instructions about the route to follow when he brought Clementina from Paris. To the prince's utter amazement, he found Goring rejoicing that (as he imagined) Clementina could not be found and that the prince's 'sending for a bad woman had not succeeded'.[28] The prince lost his temper and bade Goring 'go to all the devils in hell'. Goring responded by resigning on the spot. At first Charles taunted him with taking his money for years for easy assignments. Finding his honour impugned, Goring offered to meet Clementina at Lille and stay with her for two days until another escort arrived, but on the strict understanding that she should be made aware that Goring was no longer in the prince's service.

The two men parted, When he had cooled down, the prince reflected on Goring's good service to him in the past. He wrote and offered to let bygones be bygones, but not without justifying his loss of temper: 'It is not surprising that I should not care to have one in

my family that pretends to give me laws in everything I do.'[29]
Thinking better of the assignment, the prince told Goring not to go
to Lille but to stay at Courtrai and await further orders.

This was not good enough for Goring. In a furious outburst he
reiterated that he could not remain in the prince's service if 'that
woman' was at his side. To have Clementina with him in Ghent was
inconsistent with the prince's honour:

> the man who keeps a mistress is indeed not so much liable to
> censure, but surely he that procures her for him, or bears the name
> of it, is no better than a pimp, which title no other title can cover,
> and a blue ribbon would not so much serve to cover as to expose
> his infamy.[30]

This outburst is puzzling from an eighteenth-century soldier who
had, moreover, witnessed without blinking Charles Edward's 'orgies'
in Paris in 1746–8. Once again, we are alerted to the fact that there
is something very strange and obscure about the whole Clementina
affair. What it was we shall shortly see.

Clementina was eventually conducted from Paris to Ghent and
took up her duties as mistress. The cold letter the prince addressed
to her in Paris showed that she could expect little in return.[31] So it
proved. The rest of 1752 saw an almost continual financial crisis,
with bankers complaining about overdrafts, and the prince forever
hurrying in to Antwerp to placate them.[32] There was a running
wrangle with Thompsons of Antwerp about a sum of £200 drawn on
the bank, which Charles Edward claimed never to have received.[33]
So serious was the prince's financial plight that even donations as
small as £10 were welcomed.[34] Charles's lamentations about shortages
of money became more insistent.[35] In the end, some temporary relief
was provided from an unexpected quarter at the close of the year.
Pointing out that no one at the Palazzo Muti had heard from him
for eighteen months, James Edgar reminded him that there was
a sum of 4,000 crowns waiting for him in Rome which could be
remitted.[36]

If Clementina had nothing but hardship and a seriously depressed
prince to deal with – especially when the Elibank plot aborted –
Charles Edward for his part had obviously not sufficiently realised
the price he would have to pay for having Miss Walkinshaw with
him.

The first consequence was the least serious. The relationship with
Mme Vassé became cold and then petered out once her 'sister'
Elisabeth Ferrand died in October 1752.[37] Once Ferrand was dead

and there was no one to moderate the contempt she felt for Clementina, Vassé moved quickly to terminate the relationship. Using the pretext of neurotic anxiety over what would happen to the prince's effects if she followed her 'sister' into sudden oblivion, Vassé cunningly prevailed on the prince to have his trunks and impedimenta removed. The prince's invitation to her to visit him at Ghent was turned down flat.[38] Charles took the hint and had his boxes transferred to the care of Waters the banker.[39] Vassé's bland assurances in April 1753 – that her worrying away about his possessions was merely a sign of her deep attachment to him – fooled nobody.[40]

To the prince the loss of such a friendship was of little importance. More serious were the continuing remonstrations from the English Jacobites about the security implications of his keeping Clementina as mistress. The prince rightly dismissed the rumour that she was a Hanoverian spy. It was not so easy to dispose of the argument that her 'high visibility' made the prince a much easier target for British agents and would-be assassins. Throughout 1753 the prince had to bear the brunt of both these sources of stress. As we have seen, part of the reason for the failure of the Elibank plot was the English Jacobites' fear of committing themselves to the prince while he shared his bed with a suspected Hanoverian spy.

The prince adamantly refused to listen to the entreaties from his friends on the other side of the water. There was no question of his dismissing Clementina, he informed them.[41] In January 1753 he told Murray of Elibank that he would grant him audience on the strict understanding that he did not mention Miss Walkinshaw's name.[42]

When the English persisted, the prince became even more angry and obstinate. William King and the earl of Westmoreland sent over an envoy to urge Charles to put Clementina in a convent where, if he truly loved her, he could carry on a clandestine liaison.[43] Marischal encouraged the envoy to make this demand bluntly to the prince. Charles Edward replied contemptuously that it was not for the English Jacobites to presume to advise him on this matter. He declared he would not put away a dog to please 'those people'.[44]

The prince's determination to hang on to Clementina was not based on sentiment. He cared little for her. But any overture that he could construe as 'giving him laws' was bound to be rejected angrily. This rejection of any form of authority other than his own will was one of the many consequences of his disastrous relationship with his father.

The other criticism of Clementina, that her presence made him vulnerable to abduction and assassination, affected the prince deeply.

He found himself unable to settle in Ghent, especially when Mari-schal, from whom he sought advice on his residence, warned him that it was dangerously close to Dutch territory.[45] Even his frequent trips to Brussels and Antwerp were now becoming fraught.[46] By April 1753 he was thinking of settling in Frankfurt or Cologne.[47] Pending a final resolution, he intended to be in Ghent as little as possible and to make frequent excursions to the waters of Spa and Aix.[48]

The prince's movements in 1753 denote a morbid fear of being seized by a Hanoverian snatch squad and the perennial terror of being betrayed. In February he made a fleeting trip to Paris, where he attended a Mardi Gras ball in disguise.[49] On 12 April he arranged to meet Dormer in Brussels. The next day he cancelled the arrange-ment and set out for Cologne, hoping to meet Marischal there.[50] The prince enjoyed himself, rummaging through the Cologne bookshops for works by Polybius and tomes on the French army.[51] But Marischal advised against his continued presence in Cologne on the ground that five or six men could seize him while he went for walks by the Rhine and then spirit him away to the Dutch territories.[52]

On receipt of this advice, the prince moved on to Coblenz, where he stayed at *Les Trois Couronnes* inn.[53] By the beginning of June he was in Frankfurt, intending to make a long stay. Once again he summoned Marischal.[54] Since Charles was staying at the *Emperor* inn, he suggested that Marischal put up at the *Rose* in the same street. But again Marischal warned that the presence of Clementina put Charles at risk in any part of the Rhineland.[55]

Frustrated, but still with a pathetic respect and trust in Marischal, the prince returned to the Netherlands. Passing through Luxembourg and then swinging in a wide arc to throw any pursuers off the scent, he made his way to Louvain and then doubled back to Liège.[56] The burgomaster of Liège, to whom Dormer made the introduction, found him a suitable residence.

Charles and Clementina settled in at their new house near the Pont Magen.[57] Almost the prince's first action was to order a crate of wine.[58] His state of mind at the time can be gauged from a series of jottings on 21 July that provide almost a textbook illustration of both the positive and negative sides of his personality. 'I aspire only to war and glory'; 'I am a man who believes in God but not in men': these 'uplifting' statements are followed by a paean of praise to drink. '*Le jeu, la chose est à boire.*'[59]

This turning to wine was very significant. Stress had built up again not just with the failure of the Elibank plot but with Clementina's pregnancy. First reported in June 1753, the pregnancy was a source of ribald and facetious comment in Jacobite circles. A remark from one of Edgar's Paris correspondents is typical. 'There is no news here at all but now and then some little talk of the Hibernian Princess who, they say, keeps her ground and begins to be sick in her stomach and pitches now and then of a morning.'[60]

But to Charles Clementina's pregnancy was no laughing matter. He had not summoned her to Ghent to produce unwanted infants, especially given his parlous financial position. The hostility to the pregnancy was no surprise; in psychological terms, it threatened to displace the prince as 'only child'. It is significant that although he and Clementina lived together for another seven years, there was no further issue. Predictably, too, at about the time of Clementina's confinement, the accumulated stress in the prince emerged as illness.[61] When the baby was born, he had 'such violent fluxions in the cheek that he is scarcely able to hold the pen'.[62] This is hardly consistent with Clementina's later statement that the birth of the child gave the prince great joy.[63]

Charles Edward's daughter Charlotte was born and baptised in the church of Sainte Marie des Fonts in Liège on 29 October 1753.[64] Her birth precipitated an outburst on the prince's part that no one has satisfactorily explained. Since the prince's conversion to Protestantism, he had taken it into his head to dismiss all his Catholic servants, at Avignon and elsewhere. Now, less than a month after Charlotte's birth, he suddenly added the following to these orders: 'My mistress has behaved so unworthily that she had put me quite out of patience and as she is a papist too, I discard her also.'[65]

In his instruction to Goring to get rid of all Catholics in his employment, the prince adds: 'She told me she had friends that would maintain her, so that, after such a declaration and other impertinences, makes me abandon her. I desire to know who her friends are, that she may be delivered into their hands.'[66]

Even more bizarre is the following note made by the prince at this time: 'A mark to be put on the child if I part with it – I am pushed to the last point and so won't be cajoled any more.'[67]

The usual explanations for these outbursts – financial worries, anti-Catholic bigotry, alcoholic rage – all fail to convince. They seem excessive even if we postulate the maximum in unconscious rage and resentment towards Clementina and the child. But they *are* explicable if we assume that at some stage during the pregnancy – possibly even during the delirium of childbirth – Clementina blurted out a hidden secret from her past. The prince's outbursts would then be a shocked recognition that this was no *ingénue* he had invited to share his life.

The English Jacobites had got it wrong. They suspected Clementina of betraying the cause. Charles Edward now suspected that the betrayal was of an entirely different kind and that it was his 'honour' that was at stake.

That there was something very mysterious about Clementina's life before 1752 has already been hinted. What it is we must now try to establish. The starting point must be her remark to Andrew Lumisden in 1760. 'I was bred to business about Whitehall and could be of use to him, were there not unluckily an obstacle in the way, which has done him no service and me great hurt.'[68]

This enigmatic sentence has been passed over as unimportant by all Clementina's biographers. Only Sir Compton Mackenzie, with his novelist's intuition, saw what a crucial statement it was:

> It is always assumed that the obstacle was her sister Catherine . . . but as this obstacle was perfectly well known to everybody, why write about it so mysteriously? The longer we ponder that letter, the more clearly we perceive a hint of something we know nothing about, something which perhaps was whispered in Jacobite circles and which created that overwhelming prejudice against Clementina. Had she been some great man's mistress already? Had she been used by him as a spy for his own ends? Had she even borne him a child?[69]

To produce a solution to this problem we must take account of a number of factors. First, there were persistent rumours of a second (or preceding) child borne by Clementina, so persistent indeed that the prince later swore an affidavit that he had had only one child with Clementina.[70] This would explain why the prince wanted a mark put on his own child. If Clementina departed and took up with a former lover, it might not then be possible for the prince to tell his own offspring.

Second, there is the uniform detestation of all the Jacobites for Clementina – a detestation that goes far beyond security considerations. Isabella Strange, most rabid of all female 'Prince Charlie' worshippers was quite willing to meet Louise of Stolberg in 1788, even though the prince's wife damaged him far more severely than Clementina ever did. But she contemptuously turned down a similar offer to meet Clementina Walkinshaw and Charlotte.[71] Why was this?

What is needed to make sense of all of this is a clear statement from a good source that Clementina had indeed had a lover before joining the prince in Ghent. To allow for the bias or unreliability of the source, we ought then to test the statement against circumstantial evidence from unassailable sources, especially the prince himself. Fortunately, there is such a source and it tells us who Clementina's lover was. It turns out that it was no accident that O'Sullivan alone of the Jacobites knew where to locate her, for it was he who was her lover and, probably, father of the mysterious 'other' child. But it is important to be clear that this is a judgment on the basis of probability rather than on the stronger criterion of 'beyond all reasonable doubt'. Cast-iron evidence on this point simply does not exist.

The only extant testimony unequivocally naming O'Sullivan as Clementina's lover before she came to the prince is that of the double agent Oliver MacAllester.[72] How reliable is MacAllester in general? There is no easy answer. Sometimes he is guilty of wild hyperbole. At others he is amazingly accurate and well-informed. Which is he in this case? At the very least, his 'fingering' of O'Sullivan is not inconsistent with all that we know of the Irishman and fits the rest of the circumstantial evidence.

Of the prince's fondness and almost ludicrous partiality for O'Sullivan during the '45 we have already provided ample proof. Why is it, then, that in 1756, among a list of Charles Edward's bitterest enemies that he sent to his father – and which includes the predictable names of Tencin, O'Brien, Clare and Pompadour – we find the name of John William O'Sullivan?[73] Between 1752, when he was on good terms with the prince, and 1756 O'Sullivan's name does not appear in the Stuart Papers. What had he done, or rather what had the prince found out about him, to merit such ostracism?

Again, a close reading of the letter O'Sullivan wrote to Clementina on 31 May 1752 throws up an interesting clue. O'Sullivan tells Clementina that she may have complete trust in Charles Edward's envoy but 'you must not, under any pretext whatever, confide in him as to the past'.[74] Since the prince's envoy would already have known about the 1746 liaison with Charles, why the fearfulness about the past?

But perhaps the most clinching piece of circumstantial evidence of all comes from Goring. Goring, it will be remembered, excoriated the prince violently for the proposal to bring Clementina to Ghent and resigned his service rather than carry out escort duties. Having stated that such a chore was fit only for a pimp, he went on: 'if you are determined to have her, let Mr. O'Sullivan bring her to you here.'[75] Presumably, the inference was that as a pimp enjoys his whore's favours, O'Sullivan was the right man for the job.

We are left, then, with the probable conclusion that the prince's apparently crazed behaviour at the end of 1753 derived from his discovery of Clementina's earlier liaison with O'Sullivan. The woman he thought would wait for his summons for ever, if necessary, had avenged the loss of her virginity to Charles at Bannockburn by having an affair with one of his favourites. This is entirely consistent with what we know of Clementina. She was nobody's doormat, as she was to prove. But the prince's realisation of the truth about her past altered his perception of her irremediably. From this date commences the long saga of rows, abuse and physical beatings that was to characterise their relationship thereafter. One early sign of his new contempt was a message sent to Dormer for 'my old mistress at Paris' (presumably the Princesse de Talmont).[76]

But, for whatever reasons, the prince did not send Clementina away. As 1754 dawned, he had fresh problems. Once again his enemies were closing in. The English had intelligence that he was somewhere in the Imperial territories. The most determined search yet was instituted by British agents.[77] The emperor's representatives in Brussels made it clear that they did not want the embarrassment consequent on the English finding the 'Young Pretender' on their territory, if that was where he was.

In some alarm the prince set out for Paris, leaving exact instructions with his servants about the guardianship of his daughter Charlotte.[78] His brief excursion yielded no results. The prince again failed to arrange a meeting with Marischal, whose opinion he had asked on the desirability of permanent residence in Orléans.[79] Charles decided on a more extended stay in the French capital. He returned to Liège to pick up Clementina and Charlotte and returned to Paris early in April 1754. This was the occasion when Clementina wrote a long memoir about the wardrobe she would need for a long absence from Liège, including a long cloak for Charlotte.[80]

It was in Paris that the full extent of the breakdown in the relationship between the prince and Clementina became clear. From 27 April they were lodging with a M. Florentin, a French supporter of the Stuarts, who however made a great fuss about the risk he was allegedly running in putting up the prince, for he was still officially barred from French territory.[81] Florentin was taken aback when on 29 April a furious row erupted between the prince and Clementina in his presence. It began with a commonplace of domestic dissension. Clementina was tired and wanted to go to bed. The prince, being a night owl, wanted her to stay up with him. Clementina lost her temper and railed at him, half in French, half in English. The prince's cold smirking fuelled her rage. She made use of several injudicious expressions that brought Florentin into the fray. He rebuked her both for her impertinence to the prince and for her careless use of expressions like 'Your Royal Highness', which gave the game away to the servants. At this Clementina stormed off to bed. To add to the confusion, Florentin's sister-in-law, who had overheard the row, was smarting from the 'humiliation' of not being allowed to dine with the prince. She threatened to walk out.[82]

The feuding couple continued to make public scenes, oblivious or indifferent both about indelicacy and security. A little later a 'devilish warm' dispute arose between them in the Bois de Boulogne. This became the talk of Paris and blew the incognito sky-high.[83]

The prince toyed with the idea of moving out into the country where he and Clementina could row with greater freedom. His departure was also necessary to permit the hue and cry over his much-bruited presence in Paris to die down.[84] Florentin rented them a house at Araneil. Characteristically, Charles changed his mind at the last moment. He took Clementina with him to another country village in the environs of Paris. There they remained until Pentecost.[85]

While the two of them were away, the Florentins had charge of Charlotte. On noticing a black spot on the child's body, they consulted an apothecary who diagnosed it as a bruise. They gave Charlotte a sleeping drug and called in a physician for a second opinion. The surgeon thought the 'bruise' was something more serious, possibly a tumour, and recommended an operation. It is entirely feasible that this was some sort of advance sign of the cancer that was to claim Charlotte at the age of thirty-five.

What happened next is unclear. The prince apparently agreed to the ministration of the surgeon, but whether he operated does not emerge. What is certain is that on their return from the country the prince and Clementina left Charlotte with the Florentins while they looked for new lodgings.[86] These they found at the Hôtel Pologne. Charlotte's parents returned to collect the child, now reported 'much better'. Florentin was mortified to receive just twenty-five louis d'or for all his efforts, plus a pledge from the prince that he would not forget him when he came into his own.[87]

Florentin did not show his displeasure then. But when the prince asked to move back to his house from the Hôtel Pologne, and Florentin refused, Charles put two and two together. He accused Florentin of fomenting a false rumour that there was a hot pursuit directed against him simply to get him out of his house (there was actually some truth in the accusation).[88] Not surprisingly, when Florentin in his poverty-stricken later years applied to the prince for relief (in 1767), he got short shrift.[89] Charles Edward Stuart was a man one crossed at one's peril.

All in all, the prince stayed in Paris from April to the end of September 1754. His presence there was not just to throw spies off his track and buy time until he decided what to do next. There were also financial considerations. The prince wanted to relieve his debts by selling off the bonds held by the House of Stuart in the Hôtel de Ville. As with all the prince's financial projects, this one ended in fiasco, with the banker John Waters advising him that the transaction would take a year to complete.[90]

But a much more important reason for the prince's presence in Paris was to seek a showdown with Earl Marischal. Ever since the collapse of the Elibank plot, Charles had been pestering Marischal for advice, and requesting meetings with him. In May 1753, when he was in Germany, he sent detailed instructions on the itinerary from Paris through Metz and Luxembourg to a rendezvous at Frankfurt.[91] Marischal ignored the invitation. Charles repeated the request through Goring.[92] Again Marischal prevaricated. Finally, on 18 September 1753 he wrote to the prince. In an irritatingly patronising communication, Marischal stated that as he was the only person fully trusted by the English Jacobites, the prince should copy all his correspondence with the English party to him.[93]

Perhaps Marischal thought he had shaken off his *bête noire*. But any hopes of parting on terms of cool politeness were shattered by the Goring affair at the beginning of 1754. Despite Goring's outburst over Clementina in June 1752, and his resignation from the prince's service, Charles Edward had treated him with kindness. When Goring complained to him in October 1752 that he was destitute, the prince, then changing lodgings in Ghent, wrote back: 'As long as I have a bit of bread, I am always willing to share it with a friend.'[94] Once the prince had completed the six-month rental on the new house in Ghent, he repealed the invitation.[95]

Goring, however, remained on the sidelines as a free-lance, carrying out the occasional commission for the prince. He was sucked back into acrimonious correspondence with Charles Edward at the time of the prince's severe depression in November 1753, just after Charlotte's birth. The prince's directive to dismiss all Catholic servants in his employ was triggered by anger at what he had just discovered of Clementina's past. Since Clementina was a Catholic, by association all Catholics were tarred with the same brush. A particular sufferer from this directive was the agent 'Grandval' (Dumont), whom the prince dismissed in November 1753.[96]

The failure of the Elibank plot, his refusal to send Clementina away, the dismissal of his Catholic servants: there seemed no end to the prince's capacity to alienate the English Jacobites. Finally he went too far. He sent an envoy to Marischal and Goring, as conduits from the English party, with a demand for more money. Since 1748 the prince had existed largely on contributions from his friends in Britain. The English Jacobites particularly resented paying their money for the prince's subsistence to the agent George Woulfe, as he refused to issue receipts or even acknowledgments. They were now insisting on a conduit through Earl Marischal in Paris. The prince's response to the proposed transfer was to ask for increased contributions. It seemed to Goring and Marischal that their countrymen had already done enough. When he received the new instructions from the prince, all Goring's pent-up resentment gushed out.

With Goring's angry outpourings, it seemed the magma of the English Jacobites' wrath had finally cracked its casing. In an immensely long letter, dated 18 January 1754, Goring inveighed against the prince across a broad front.[97] First, there was a denunciation of his unceasing demands for money. Second, there was a vehement attack on Clementina:

> Sir, your friend's mistress is loudly and publicly talked of and all his friends look on it as a very dangerous and independent step, and conclude reasonably that no correspondence is to be had in that quarter without risk or discovery, for we have no opinion in England of female politicians or of such women's secrecy in general.

Third, Goring denounced the prince for his sacking of Dumont; since Dumont knew so much, this was tantamount to blowing the entire network of underground Jacobitism in England, if the Hanoverians took it into their heads to co-opt Dumont into their service. Fourth, the dismissal of the Catholic servants was a bad error. Any hint of religious intolerance was counter-productive to the Stuart cause.

Without extensive quotation, it is difficult to do justice to the splenetic power of Goring's letter, but the personal animus it contains is evident in the closing remarks: 'To sum up, all these commissions you give me give me such affliction as will certainly end my life. They are surely calculated by you for that very reason.'[98]

The prince was stupefied by this verbal bombardment. After being told *ad nauseam* that the Catholic bugbear was the one thing that had blighted Catholic hopes, it now appeared that taking an overtly pro-Protestant stance was not acceptable either. He was damned if he did and damned if he did not. Charles cast about for an acceptable compromise. He would not budge on Clementina or Dumont, but he *was* prepared to reinstate his Catholic servants. As for the financial accusations, 'people should, I think, well know that if it was only money that I had at heart, I would not act as I have done and will do until I compass the prosperity of my country . . . but you know that without money one can do nothing'.[99]

What irritated the prince most about Goring's massive letter was not the substance of the accusation, but the frequent references to Earl Marischal as the ultimate arbiter and *éminence grise* of the English Jacobites.[100] He asked for a meeting with Marischal, adding (surely ironically), 'as I take you to be the best of my friends'.[101]

Marischal sent a brusque refusal, as well as the remaining money (7,200 livres) entrusted to him by the English Jacobites.[102] The prince responded by coming to Paris on his first 1754 visit in search of a meeting.[103] When this attempt failed he returned to Liège to bring Clementina to Paris for a longer stay, as we have seen. This time, to tempt Marischal to break cover, he wrote to him to canvass his advice on a possible permanent domicile in Orléans.[104]

If the prince was in any doubt about where he stood with Marischal, the Scot's chilling reply on 15 April soon disabused him. Marischal said he could not advise him where to settle permanently, and did not want to meet him as this would set up a conflict of loyalties between his Jacobite sentiments and the duty he owed to Frederick the Great. That would have been bad enough. But Marischal could not resist a final jibe. Arguing against Orléans, he mentioned the unmentionable (December 1748) by adding: 'you lie under a certain promise which nothing but absolute necessity can disengage you from.'[105]

Smarting under this lecture on duty from a fair-weather Jacobite, Charles rounded on Goring, whom he now saw as poisoning Marischal's Jacobitism. There is no such thing as an *honourable and unilateral* severing of contracts, he pointed out. Was Goring prepared to obey him or not, that was the only question.[106] Goring replied that he was not: 'I have twice been turned off like a common footman with most opprobrious language without money or clothes. As I am a bad courtier and can't help speaking truth, I am very sure it would not be long before I experienced a third time.'[107]

At this point the prince directed his anger back at Marischal. The tone of his next letter was sardonic. Since you can't be bothered to see me when I am in the same city, he writes, and since you consistently put Frederick of Prussia first, can you at least obtain for me a passport for Maria Teresa's Austrian dominions so that I can seek permanent asylum there?[108]

Marischal weighed in with the observation that he would not be prepared to deal with the prince through any intermediary other than Goring.[109] The prince replied that he was no longer prepared to tolerate Goring's impertinence, so Marischal would have to find another channel.[110] Marischal's riposte was that he did not trust anyone except Goring. Bitterly reproaching the prince for his treatment of his agent, he accused Charles of the height of infamy in having threatened to publish the names of all the English Jacobites, thus condemning them to the scaffold. Disingenuously pleading a broken heart ('my health and my heart are broke by age and crosses'), he declared that any further communication between them was now impossible.[111]

Charles Edward angrily denied the charge that he had threatened to publish names. He paid Marischal back in the same emotional coin: 'My heart is broke enough without that you should finish it.'[112] Making one final effort to bridge the yawning chasm between them, the prince sent Antoine Walsh to see Marischal.

Marischal treated Walsh with contempt. He insisted on writing out a verbatim account of the interview ('to ease his memory, as he wouldn't have been able to retain such a long conversation') and was even more uncompromising than before. After pouring extravagant scorn on the planning behind the Elibank plot, he made it plain that his overwhelming priority was the interest of Frederick the Great. If Frederick gave him *carte blanche* to pursue Jacobite interests, if there was a cast-iron guarantee of a foreign invasion of Britain, and if he, not the prince, directed the entire operation, then and only then would he reconsider. Marischal knew very well that such a scenario could never come to pass.

So ended all contacts between the prince and Earl Marischal, the man who could and should have been a father to him. Doubtless it was for precisely this reason that the prince's animus towards him was so great later on. What conclusion can we come to concerning this wretched episode?

It is clear enough that on this occasion the prince's fantasies of betrayal were fed by an objectively true instance. The plain fact is that Marischal let the prince down badly. The accusation that he had threatened to publish the names of the English Jacobites was absurd. It is possible, and even probable, that the prince threatened to do this in one of his rages. But anyone who knew anything at all about Charles Edward knew that he never carried out such insensate threats. The real or imaginary incident was simply used by Marischal as an excuse. This seems all the more pharisaical on the part of the Earl when we realise that he was already secretly preparing the ground for a pardon and restoration of his estates in Scotland (actually achieved in 1759).

Marischal has always been viewed most uncritically by historians, but there are elements in his personality that do not stand close scrutiny by a devil's advocate probing the reality of his much-vaunted 'goodness'. Why did he not try to reason with the prince in a fatherly way? Why was he always cold and aloof, forever singularly unhelpful and defeatist? Why did a man who managed to find good in Frederick the Great (when no one else could), and who achieved the distinction of being the only human being not to quarrel with Jean-Jacques Rousseau, fail to win round Charles Edward? If the prince's paranoia is cited as the barrier, what about the far greater paranoid delusions of Rousseau?

We are confronted at this point with one of those mysteries of the human personality. What *is* true is that the autocratic Marischal wanted always to command and to play the same leading role as the autocratic prince. Both men were tarred by the 'all or nothing' mentality. All the evidence suggests that Marischal intensely disliked the young prince at first meeting and never changed his opinion. If there is such a thing as hate at first sight, that is what Marischal felt for the prince.

The collapse of communications with Marischal shunted Charles Edward from limbo into the outer circles of hell. The events of 1754 finished the prince as a credible political force. He had now alienated France, Prussia and the English Jacobites. Apart from a few chimerical hopes entertained for Spanish assistance, he had nowhere to go politically.

Unconsciously, perhaps, he turned back to the few friends he had left. Chief among these was the faithful Edgar, with whom the prince reopened communication at the beginning of 1754 after a two-and-a-half-year silence.[113] In March the prince started to use Edgar as a confidant. That he was severely depressed is clear. On 24 March he wrote: 'I have nothing to say but imprecations against the fatality of living in such a detestable age.'[114] Rejecting all idea of marriage, he went on: 'Were it possible for me to find a place of abode, I think that our family has had sufferings enough that will always hinder me to marry, as long as in misfortune, for that will only conduce but to increase misery or subject any of the family that would have the spirit of their father to be tied neck and heel.'[115] It is not difficult to see this as an anguished cry against James for bringing him into the world.

The dreadful stress of 1754 did not abate. Unsolved financial worries, rows with Clementina, the rift with Marischal, all contributed to a depression that finally broke over Edgar in August with this chilling *cri de coeur*: 'My situation is terrible, the more that in reality I cannot see any method or appearance of its bettering . . . you can't imagine how many crosses I meet with, but never any shall hinder me from doing what I think for the best.'[116]

That the prince was seriously depressed can be seen from other pointers at the time. There was the Byzantine intricacy and cloak-and-dagger deviousness with which he arranged meetings with Waters and others.[117] There was his obsession over a watch. He had ordered this timepiece through Waters from Julien Le Roy, the famous Parisian watchmaker. Delays over its delivery infuriated Charles.[118] On one occasion he went to Le Roy's shop and made such a scene that one of the other customers penetrated the incognito and recognised him.

By the end of July 1754 the prince had had enough of Paris. He had achieved absolutely nothing on any front. He had been compelled to change his lodgings on at least three occasions. His incognito had been so thoroughly pierced that it was obvious that the French authorities by now connived at his presence in their capital.[119] But Charles was forced to wait until Charlotte's health was better before he could take her on a long journey.[120] At last, on 17 September, he told Waters that the air in 'this accursed country' did not agree with him and that he was going to live in Basle.[121]

Almost his last action in Paris was to summon Cluny MacPherson to Europe from out of the cage on Ben Alder where he had skulked for the past eight years.[122] All hope of another rising in the Highlands was over. In his heart Charles Edward knew he was already a beaten man.

30

Folly of Princes

1754–8

In Basle Charles and Clementina stayed at *L'Auberge des Trois Rois* while they looked for more permanent accommodation.[1] Getting their effects to Switzerland was troublesome, but not more so than the exorbitant cost of living in the cantons 'where money melts'.[2] But by March 1755 the prince reported the air and country to his liking and found a suitable permanent home.[3] He and Clementina settled in, using the alias of Mr and Mrs Thompson.[4]

The prince was in a bad mental state. He lived like a recluse, reluctant to see any of the few supporters that still remained to him. He warned Waters (now his principal channel of communication with the outside world) that he was not prepared to discuss Clementina with envoys from England unless they brought incontrovertible proof that she was a spy.[5] He reiterated the sentiments that had so angered Marischal, this time substituting 'cat' for 'dog'.[6] He honed his sense of being persecuted to a fine point, remarking about himself: 'it seems to be a wager who can fling the greatest stone at him.'[7] He continued to drink heavily, so much so that he even confessed himself worried about his own heavy intake.[8]

A good index of the prince's paranoia at this time can be obtained from his furious reactions over the watch he had purchased from Julien Le Roy. After an unconscionable delay the watchmaker finally sent the completed timepiece on via Strasbourg.[9] But the watch simply would not work properly, no matter what tinkering was done. The prince came to see it as a symbol of all his ills, as part of the conspiracy against him. It almost seemed now as though material objects had joined in the persecution.

The permutations and combinations of malfunction in the watch seemed legion. The timbre of the ringing mechanism was indistinguishable from that of the striking of the hours.[10] The watch stopped every quarter of an hour. A local watchmaker diagnosed faulty balancing.[11] Charles sent the intractable object back to Waters in Paris.[12] When the banker remonstrated with Julien Le Roy, the chronometrical virtuoso dismissed the malfunction as a trivial fault and suggested that the prince was overreacting badly.[13] Finally, in September 1755, the egregious Le Roy sent the watch back with the message – calculated to infuriate the prince – that there was nothing wrong with the piece but ill-usage.[14]

But, as so often with Charles Edward, his feelings of being persecuted had some slight basis in reality. Would-be assassins *were* on his trail. A 'contract' for £100,000 had been put out on him; the hired killer had already tried to poison his drinking chocolate with verdigris.[15] Luckily for the prince, the Hanoverian spymasters were as bewildered by his movements as ever. Whig secret agents consistently placed Charles Edward either where he *had* been in the past or where he was to be in the future, never where he actually was at any given moment.

In December 1753, when the prince was at Liège, there was a very strong rumour that he was in Paris under an assumed name.[16] In May 1754, when the prince was in Paris and there had been several good sightings of him, Lord Albemarle demanded that the French execute the relevant treaties and expel him.[17] But Albemarle was assured that the French knew nothing of his presence in their capital.[18] The new minister of state Rouillé denied all knowledge of him.[19]

In April 1755 the prince was again falsely reported to be in Paris by English agents.[20] By November 1755 he was described as appearing openly in the streets of Paris.[21] The correction of this bogus intelligence sowed wholesale confusion in British espionage. One report had the prince taking up the crown of Corsica.[22] Another claimed that he had been in England and visited Nottingham.[23] Yet another firmly placed him in Liège, where he was not to return until 1756.[24]

But if the stress the prince was reacting to in Basle was the blighting of his hopes – symbolised by the permanent malfunction of Le Roy's watch rather than the imminence of exposure by Hanoverian agents – the stress nevertheless produced very real symptoms. In September 1755 he was very ill with a mysterious malady, 'vapours mixed with spleen', which was almost certainly the result of heavy drinking, by now virtually the prince's conditioned reflex to stress.[25] Another permanent worry was money, especially in expensive Switzerland.

The number of servants thrown on the scrap-heap multiplied. Daniel O'Brien and Dobson joined Goring and Dumont on the list of cast-offs.[26] This is how the prince explained his situation:

> It is better that they should beg their own bread or go into other service than to let Mr. Thompson be obliged to sell drugs to gain his livelihood, which he is absolutely resolved to do if all fails him rather than ever to do the least thing that could anyways be against his real interest and honour.[27]

Others did not see it that way and interpreted his actions either as miserliness or eccentricity. Mittie junior sought relief at the feet of Lady Primrose, then visiting Paris. His pitiful tales hammered another nail into the coffin of Charles Edward's reputation with the English Jacobites.[28] The most ludicrous incident involved James in Rome. Five of the servants Charles had dismissed in Avignon made their way south across the Alps to the Palazzo Muti, after the prince told them to seek alternative employment there. James had a morbid fear of further clients attaching themselves to his payroll. After giving the men forty crowns each, he sent them back to France where, he alleged, there were more opportunities for work.[29] Subsequent tales of Stuart ruthlessness and ingratitude lost nothing in the telling.

The one event in the prince's life of any public significance in 1755 was his meeting with Cluny MacPherson. Unfortunately this relationship too turned sour. When Cluny landed in France after nine years of dodging the redcoats in Badenoch, he experienced a profound shock at many levels. There was culture trauma after a decade in the cage on Ben Alder. There was the shock of finding that events had moved on rapidly, that in Scotland he had been in a kind of time-warp. Most jolting of all was the change for the worse in Charles Edward. Once in Paris, Cluny expected an early conference with the prince as a matter of urgency. But the reclusive prince refused to budge from Basle.[30]

Cluny protested that he would feel naked if he made a trip to Switzerland, especially as he knew nothing of its language or culture.[31] But the prince insisted on Basle as the venue. He ordered Cluny and Henry Patullo (the messenger he had sent to Scotland the year before to fetch Cluny) to travel via Belfort to the *Le Sauvage* inn in Basle.[32] Then it emerged that Cluny was penniless.[33] This was a severe blow to the prince. He had called Cluny over precisely in hopes that the MacPherson chief would meanwhile have recovered the bulk of the Loch Arkaig treasure. Charles grumbled excessively about paying out fifteen louis d'ors for Patullo's and Cluny's travelling expenses:

In such straitened circumstances, anyone that has Mr. Douglas's interest at heart must make shift as well as they can . . . their zeal or credit seems very little not to have found some way of getting so little as to furnish for their journey hither.[34]

Cluny and Patullo finally made the trip, travelling via Compiègne and Strasbourg.[35] Their meeting with the prince in Basle was not a success. Charles was stupefied to hear that nothing remained of the Loch Arkaig treasure.[36] Even worse, Cluny had taken charge of a waggon-load of the prince's most treasured possessions after Culloden, including a family heirloom of jewels among the gold plate. He now claimed never to have seen it nor to know anything of it.[37] This lost plate and jewellery was to become a major obsession with the prince, dwarfing the neurosis over the Le Roy watch.

The prince was already angry when Cluny and Patullo added insult to injury by presuming to lecture him on his shortcomings, and in particular to discuss the recent calumnies spread by Marischal's protégé Jeremy Dawkins. The reason the financial supply from the English Jacobites had dried up, Cluny explained, was that Charles had lost all credibility. He would have to mend his ways.[38]

Charles Edward reacted with cold fury. Referring to a 'very surprising message delivered in a still more surprising manner', he repeated that he would not be bullied: 'Reason may and I hope always shall prevail, but my own heart deceives me if threats or promises ever can.' On his critics he remarked, 'I despise their low malice and I confess it below my dignity to treat them in the terms they merit.'[39]

Dismayed that he could make no more impression on the prince than Goring, Marischal or any of the others, Cluny saved his fire until he was well clear of Basle. After producing a detailed accounting of the Loch Arkaig money to vindicate his handling of the finances,[40] Cluny sat down with Patullo to make a final appeal to the prince to see reason. He should abandon his debauched life, agree to be guided by a cabinet of advisers, and vigorously rebut the slanders of Dawkins and Marischal. In particular, he should lay to rest the canard that, as a man ungrateful for the best services, but unforgiving and vindictive in face of the slightest offence, he combined all the vices of the Stuarts with none of their virtues.[41]

This was an ably constructed memoir, and it is just conceivable that the prince might have taken it to heart. Unfortunately Cluny and Patullo spoiled their own case by going over the top. Shocked by what they had seen of the prince's physical condition and his almost permanent inebriation at Basle, they now presumed to give him advice on his drinking: 'If you likewise would be prevailed on to use a little green tea mixed with cream, in place of beer, to abate thirst, you would soon be sensible of the happy difference.'[42]

Cluny had gone too far. To the prince, this was the rankest impertinence. Here was a man who could give no satisfactory account of his stewardship in Scotland, and who had lost the precious casket of family jewels among the plate, daring to lecture him like one of Wesley's temperancers. Cluny's homily merely succeeded in convincing the prince that he was being singled out for special discriminatory treatment. This feeling of being victimised that Cluny kindled in the prince had singularly unfortunate results. The character sketch adumbrated in the Cluny/Patullo memoir became a self-fulfilling prophecy. Forgetting all the services that Cluny had done him, the prince henceforth hounded the MacPherson chieftain mercilessly over the missing valuables until his death in 1764.

All overtures from normal mortals had proved unavailing. It remained to be seen whether his father could do any better. In 1755 hostilities broke out between Britain and France in north America. By common consent, a general European war could not be long delayed. This fact, plus the channel to the prince opened by Edgar in 1754, gave James motive and opportunity to begin a sustained correspondence with his son. It would be an exaggeration to say that relations between James and Charles improved after 1755, but at least they were now in touch with one another on a fairly regular basis.

The exchanges revealed a thinly-masked mutual hostility, common in such fraught relationships between father and son.[43] The correspondence opened with James's request (on 29 October 1754) for a letter setting out the details of his son's financial difficulties. At first the prince did not rise to the bait. He answered through Edgar that he needed no help with his 'lawsuit'.[44] James waited until his son's 34th birthday, on 31 December, before penning a homily in reply. He reproached Charles for taking it for granted that Providence had blessed the young Pretender more than the old. He himself had spent a lifetime hoping for a Stuart restoration, but it had never happened. It could well turn out the same for Charles, yet *he* was neglecting to provide an heir. He attacked the prince's so-called friends who 'have driven you into a labyrinth out of which it will be hard to extricate yourself'.[45] When the prince replied that he intended to do nothing contrary to his honour, James pounced again. 'Do you rightly understand the extensive sense of honour and duty?'[46]

James sweetened the pill in May 1755 by proposing that the two of them work together to get an alliance with France, now on the brink of declaring war on England.[47] The last of James's many messages rebuking his son for fecklessness at such a critical political conjuncture came at a bad time for the prince. He was already smarting under Cluny's criticisms. This time Charles struck back at his father with a stinging rebuke. Reverting to the question of heirs, he declared vehemently that he would never have any. James's own career, he added tartly, should have shown him the folly of begetting heirs. Why, all the world waited to see how James's son would turn out. The result was that from 1719 to 1745 the Jacobite movement was moribund.[48]

This nettled James. The hostility between the two was no longer kept under wraps. Returning to his son's financial problems, he asked what had happened to his much-vaunted friends. Finally he could not resist open sarcasm: 'What you gain by your present system I know not, but you fairly venture losing the advice and assistance of everybody that is not in that great secret.'[49]

James determined to tighten the screws on his son. Significantly, the episode of sending back the dismissed Avignon servants took place at the end of 1755. James followed this with an unsuccessful attempt to persuade Sir John Graeme to go as his personal representative to talk to Charles Edward.[50] But by a stroke of fate James was suddenly handed the most effective of entering wedges.

Out of the blue Waters made a bad mistake. Piqued by the continuing slanders about the prince from the English Jacobites, and annoyed with Charles for not deigning to reply to them, Waters set the situation before James. Without naming Clementina Walkinshaw, he laid the blame squarely at her door:

> There is a woman with the Prince who is the author of all this mischief, and unless she be got away from him without loss of time, it is only too apparent that H.R.H.'s reputation will be made very black over all Great Britain, so, with submission, there is a pressing necessity for the king to attempt a cure for this rising evil and to persuade the Prince to remove from the place he is in, for the government in England, I am persuaded, knows where he is.[51]

This was indiscreet and a bad error. Charles Edward had warned Waters that in no circumstances was he to divulge to James where he lived.[52] Now Edgar pounced. By return he conveyed to Waters the king's desire to know where his son was living, adding (just in case Waters had not got the point) that Waters himself must know, since he was so certain the English government knew where it was.[53] He further asked if the name of the woman in question was Clementina Walkinshaw and if there was a child.

This elicited something like a howl of pain from Waters. He was impaled on a hook of his own making. 'You pushed me too far, though I see you will say I brought it upon myself; theory told me there is no serving of two masters; experience convinces me.' Still wriggling on the hook, he tried to pretend that he corresponded with the prince only through a *poste restante*; his exact whereabouts were known only to a few intimates. But Waters did concede that the woman was Clementina Walkinshaw and that there was a female child of the union.[54]

With fulsome apologies, Waters apprised Charles Edward of his gaffe. Feeling himself cornered, the prince let Waters know his terms for a full reconciliation with James. He was to dismiss O'Brien (Lord Lismore) and to distance himself from Henry (Charles could not bring himself to mention his brother's name, but spoke of 'his young priest').[55] There, for the moment, the correspondence halted, brought to a sudden stop by another of James's severe illnesses.[56]

While all this was going on, and partly as a result of James's getting too close for comfort, the prince decided it was time to move on once more.[57] This was an abrupt *volte-face*, given his 1755 attitudes. Ill-health and lethargy kept him confined to Basle for the whole of that year. He flatly turned down all invitations to go to Paris, and lived as a recluse, penning the occasional reflection on contemporary events, such as the great Lisbon earthquake that famously aroused Voltaire from his dogmatic slumbers.[58] 'Too ill to travel' was the perennial refrain (too drunk, his enemies would have said).[59] The renting of a new home suggested a quasi-permanent residence in Switzerland.[60]

Yet in June 1756 Charles and Clementina quit Basle. Liège had been the cheapest place they had lived in so far. Therefore it was to Liège that they returned.[61] For the moment Charlotte remained in Basle.[62]

After leaving Clementina at their lodgings at Chausée St Gilles in Liège,[63] the prince immediately set out on another of his secret journeys. This time his destination was Lorraine, where he was to confer with ex-king Stanislas. Charles ordered his agent Colonel Hussey to meet him in Luxembourg, but Hussey failed to keep the appointment.[64]

The prince pressed on to Lunéville. He soon showed that, when he had a mind to, he had lost none of his old capacity to charm.

Stanislas was much taken with him and promised to promote his cause with his son-in-law Louis XV.[65]

On his return to Liège, Charles Edward was dismayed to hear from Waters that he and Clementina had already been observed in that town.[66] He considered moving on to another Flanders town, possibly Tournai or even Ghent – anywhere where it was cheap.[67] The nearby garrisons ruled out the two towns, as mature reflection soon revealed to the prince. France was out of the question for other reasons. For the moment Charles was at a loss.[68]

Then word came through that he had been seen in Calais and Compiègne.[69] The original 'sighting' in Liège, it transpired, was simply a lucky guess. Much relieved, the prince took a residence near the novitiate house of the Jesuits in Liège, on the rue de Sure de Hase.[70] It was settled that he would spend the winter there.[71]

But political business soon called him away to Paris. The Seven Years' War was now in full spate. Charles Edward was hearing a lot of encouraging stories about French intentions towards the Stuarts. An army, 50,000 strong, had already been assembled in the Picardy ports. Against his will, the prince felt constrained by the urgent pleas of his followers to go to Paris to take soundings.

In November 1756 he passed through Brussels *en route* to the French capital.[72] He took Clementina with him but left their child behind in Liège.[73] On the afternoon of 25 November he reached Le Bourget, and came into Paris later that night.[74]

In Paris he renewed acquaintance with his old ally the duc de Richelieu and discussed with him and Lally a possible descent on England.[75] The consensus seemed to be that for the moment the conduct of the war in Germany held France's exclusive attention. The time for a project to restore the Stuarts was not yet. In his best 'I told you so' mood, the prince returned to Liège.[76]

Until mid-1758 the prince thereafter scarcely stirred from Liège and its environs. He made one trip to take the waters at Spa in June 1757,[77] but otherwise increasingly sought solace in the bottle.

His tendency towards chronic alcoholism raises interesting questions about the relationship with Clementina. That the prince rowed with her, beat her and made her a scapegoat for his disappointments was now common knowledge, even though the wilder rumours of his behaviour towards her were false.[78] One of the marks of the true alcoholic – and the prince was already dangerously close to qualification for that description – is a rejection of sexual intimacy as a balm for the assailing troubles. From his heavy consumption of wine and spirits alone, we should be able to infer that, whatever merit

Charles had originally seen in Clementina as a mistress, he no longer perceived it. It is surely significant, too, that there were no more children of this ill-starred liaison.

For all that, he retained a touching faith in her fidelity to him (in all senses) and scoffed at rumours that she was trying to raise money to escape his clutches.[79] No doubt this residual fondness for her was at the root of the false rumour that he had married her.[80] But the prince's position was crystal clear. Although he would never marry Clementina, it was a point of honour with him not to cast her off at the behest of the English Jacobites.[81] The more the English party clamoured – and clamour they did, increasingly and vociferously, to the point of protesting that they would not co-operate in any French invasion until he had dismissed her – the more adamant the prince became.[82]

Ironically, the prince did have marriage on his mind at the time, though for quite other reasons. Although his official stance was that he would never marry until after a restoration, increasingly severe money problems tempted him to make a wealthy match as a way out of his financial morass.[83] His straitened circumstances made him particularly bitter towards Cluny, who now found his way on to the prince's short list of prime betrayers (along with O'Sullivan *et al.*) for his faulty stewardship of the Stuart plate.[84] When mention of Cluny coincided with a further malfunction of the dreaded Julien Le Roy watch, as it did in May 1757, the prince's rage knew no limits.[85]

While his supporters at Versailles lobbied the court for an invasion, and the ministers put them off with extravagant promises for the future, the prince's public life at Liège continued uneventful. In September 1757 he moved to a more private and secure country house just outside the town.[86] The drinking continued, as did the steady trickle of delegations from Jacobites in France urging more energetic pressurising of the French court.

But by now Charles Edward had more immediate problems. The years 1756–8 produced a determined attempt from James in Rome to get his son to 'see reason'. In a desperate efflorescence of eleventh-hour epistolary effort, James triggered a sustained debate by letter between Rome and Liège. To make sense of it, we must first place it in the context of the Seven Years' War and then examine the sombre psychological undercurrents.

The late 1750s saw a three-cornered relationship between James, Charles Edward and the French. Until 1759 French aims were simply to use the Stuarts as a scarecrow against England. James, on the other hand, was determined to force Louis XV bit by bit into giving more and more overt support for his cause. Charles Edward's position was one of detachment. He did not trust France and was willing to be involved only in a certain, guaranteed descent on England, *not* Scotland or Ireland.

The complicating factor was the prince's relationship with his father. Charles Edward refused to marry, as his father urged, or to give up Clementina Walkinshaw, as the English Jacobites demanded. This meant that France could not count on the support of the English Jacobites, even if they enlisted the prince on their side. It also meant that the kind of French guarantees the prince wanted would never be forthcoming. A firm and binding contract, in the form of a treaty of alliance like the Fontainebleau treaty of October 1745, could be made only between monarchs. Until James abdicated, Louis XV could not sign such a treaty for, if James was, in Bagehot's terms, the 'dignified' element in the Stuart dynasty, Charles Edward was the 'efficient' part. A treaty with James alone would not be worth the paper it was written on. But royal protocol prohibited a treaty with Charles Edward alone. James would have to abdicate and name his elder son as successor. But James in turn would do this only if Charles gave up Clementina Walkinshaw, promised to marry a suitable bride, and came to Rome to make formal obeisance and compose their differences.

The prince refused to do any of these things. The full extent of shadow-boxing, tail-chasing and vicious circling involved in French relations with the Stuarts in the late 1750s can thus be appreciated.

A prolonged examination of the correspondence between James and Charles Edward in 1756–8 would be a wearisome endeavour, but some account of their verbal duelling must be given. The thesis of unconscious resentment and hatred between the two cannot really be sustained without copious illustration.[87]

James opened his campaign in a curious way for one who claimed to want to conciliate his son. First he rebuked him for accepting a loan from Stanislas.[88] Next, he wrote to Louis XV to complain about his son.[89] This was an extremely curious thing to do for one who claimed to want to present a united Stuart front to France.

Charles replied to his father's overtures in his laconic quasi-heroic style: 'His situation is more than singular and had he not always Providence to favour him more than many, . . . he would long ago be drowned.'[90]

James never liked it when anyone other than himself played the stoic or martyr. Crisply he cut through this and urged the prince to work closely with France and to come to Rome to discuss with him a unified policy towards Louis XV.[91]

Feeling himself put on the spot, the prince consulted his Mephistopheles Kelly – now newly restored to favour. Kelly recommended neutralising James by spreading a story at Versailles that he had already abdicated in favour of Charles.[92] Kelly followed this up by another piece of arch-Machiavellianism. After making it clear that James's only importance to him lay in how soon he would die, Kelly recommended a campaign of attrition and procrastination. A euphuistic letter, full of filial submission, should be sent to Rome to shut James up.[93] Further stalling could be effected by the dispatch of an envoy to the Palazzo Muti to discuss common policy towards France.[94] Finally, when James had been played out far enough on the line, the prince should go to Rome as the dutiful son. By that time James would be so desperate for a *rapprochement* that he would give Charles anything he asked.[95]

The prince took the advice and sent the letter.[96] It was partly to talk over further ways of manipulating James that Charles went to Paris in the winter of 1756.

Predictably, James was delighted with what he read as a change of heart by the prodigal son.[97] Then Kelly callously played the prince's next card. The following communication to Rome embodied his poisonous advice. Before he made the journey to Italy, he wrote, there were certain 'outrages' to be cleared up. For instance, there was the 'overbearing and despotic' cardinal, his brother. And why, incidentally, had James told Charles Edward not to return to Rome after the imbroglio in Venice in 1749?[98]

Forewarned by his Jesuit contacts in Paris of what was afoot, James did not fall into Charles's (and Kelly's) trap. Ignoring the burden of his son's complaint, he turned his flank by blandly remarking that he understood that delicate diplomatic negotiations with France required his son's continuing presence in Paris.[99] Since substantive negotiations with the French were the last thing the prince had in mind, and by the time he got his father's letter he was back in Liège, the advantage had once again swung James's way.

James now moved over on to the attack. His first target was Charles Edward's cherished principle that he would not marry until a restoration. Was this not simply advertising Stuart pessimism and announcing to the world a lack of faith in God's providence?[100] French interest would be quickened in a Stuart prince with heirs; as proof of this, he revealed that Versailles had often in the past urged *him* to remarry.

Charles Edward's reply was lame. Suddenly, it seemed, the state of affairs in England and the pace of his negotiations with France were all-important.[101] That was the reason he could not go to Rome at present.

Ingenuously believing that serious negotiations between the prince and the ministers of state really were on foot, James agreed that by all means his son's trip to Rome should be postponed.[102] Then he revealed the oceanic depths of his lack of understanding of Charles Edward. Ever the stoical pessimist, James exhorted the prince to get an assurance of a high-born wife and a good pension out of France, even if the invasion project foundered.[103]

James had unwittingly touched a raw nerve. Stung by his father's constant emphasis on France, the prince revealed his continuing bitterness about his arrest in 1748. Too close an association with Versailles, he taunted his father, was inconsistent with true patriotism.[104]

James was deeply wounded by the aspersions on his patriotism. Peevishly he wrote back:

What I comprehend least of all is how you can bring in patriotism to support your opinion, while I think I can bring it in with a great deal of reason to support mine, and though I do not pretend to be a hero, I think myself as good a patriot as you and will not yield to you in that particular.[105]

The vast reserves of hostility are suddenly on open view in that letter, right down to the ironical taunt about heroes. The prince riposted with one of his favourite coldly contemptuous ploys. He wrote to Edgar the royal secretary, not to his father, requesting a renewal of the powers of Regent.[106] James granted the Commission of Regency[107] but continued on the attack, determined to bring his son to bay. Charles's way of life meant no permanent residence and no wife. If he, James, had embraced such principles, he would by now have been wandering the face of Europe for forty years. Was it not obvious that, however unpopular the Hanoverians were, no one would want to restore a dynasty whose leading scion had no heir? That would mean resurrecting the nightmare of a disputed succession on Charles's death.

James moved on to the arguments that had given him particular offence. When James had argued that all he had ever received from France he got because he had a son, Charles retorted that he did not want children who would be slaves to France and in a prison in Rome into the bargain. Rome was not a prison, James snapped back angrily, as witness his journeys to Spain in 1719 and to Lorraine in 1727. Moreover, 'if you call it slavery to be beholden to another prince, there are now few in Europe who might not be termed slaves in that sense, for you do not, to be sure, pretend to be self-sufficient and to want and depend on nobody, which are attributes of God alone'.[108]

The temperature of the exchange was rising. Smarting under this rebuke, the prince loosed his most deadly shaft at his father. His pointed reply, rejecting all idea of marriage, struck at James at his two most vulnerable points: his failures with his wife and with his son. In the first place, the prince purred maliciously, marriages were known to go wrong. In the second, history demonstrated that the Jacobites always waited to see how the son would turn out. That was why the Jacobite movement was moribund between 1719 and 1745.[109]

The prince had used this argument about twenty-six wasted years before and James had ignored it. Not this time. Since there was nearly a Jacobite rising in 1727, before Fleury got cold feet, it was simply not true to say that nothing happened between 1719 and 1745.[110] Still, James evidently felt himself the loser on points in this exchange, for in his next letter he asked sardonically what had happened to those famous English Jacobites who had supplied him with money since 1749 and led him into his 'painful and, I might say, ignominious life'.[111]

Charles Edward reverted to truculence. He insisted that if the French were serious about a descent on England, they must approach him, not he them.[112] Apparently he forgot that such a reply exposed the mendacity of his previous excuse for not going to Rome: that he was negotiating with the French. To James's horror, it now emerged that there had never been any negotiations.

The correspondence was now reaching into raw places. James inveighed against his son's favourite dictum 'all or nothing': 'What advantage has the Prince reaped hitherto from the maxims he has formed himself by?'[113] At last, James was coming close to the heart of the problem, which was located more in Charles Edward's psyche than in the corridors of Versailles. As layer after layer of the prince's defences were stripped away, he finally revealed himself in all his wounded despair. Charles Edward told his father he would never take the initiative in approaching the French court. *They* must first wipe out the infamy of the gross insult offered to him in December 1748. The only way they could do this was by undertaking a serious invasion of England on his behalf without his requesting it.[114]

At this point the exhausted verbal combatants paused for breath.

An interlude was provided by another of James's dangerous illnesses.[115] When he recovered, it was to find that circumstances had altered radically.

'Never to hope again'
(1758–60)

In mid-May 1758 the prince moved his abode from Liège to Bouillon. After travelling through Sedan, he took up residence at the Chateau de Carlsbourg, rented from the duc de Bouillon and nine miles from the town of that name.[1] Here Charles at last found a faithful friend. The president of the sovereign court of Bouillon, Monsieur Thibault, had been deputed by the duc de Bouillon to see that everything in the chateau was to the prince's liking. He became a close friend and great admirer.[2] This made up for the disappointing hunting and shooting Charles Edward found on the Bouillon estate.

In early July the prince rode south along the Meuse, through Verdun, to meet Stanislas in Commercy. Evidently he had expected something more concrete than the platitudes Stanislas proceeded to dispense. He returned to Bouillon disappointed.[3]

Now he began to hit the bottle harder than ever, despite the pleas from Murray of Elibank and others not to prove Lady Primrose's case for her by revealing himself openly as a drunkard.[4] In one of his inebriate rages the prince gave Sheridan (his servant from Avignon, fourteen years in his employ), such a verbal lashing that Sheridan resigned.[5] Lord Clancarty, another former toady of the prince but now openly critical of him, approved of Sheridan's action: 'whilst he drinks in that desperate manner, no man's life is safe.'[6]

This was the situation when James wrote to tell his son that he was sending Andrew Lumisden to Bouillon on a mission of reconciliation.[7] Lumisden, a Scottish Jacobite who had been out in the '45, currently held a position as under-secretary to Edgar and had the general trust of the Stuarts, both father and sons.

James gave Lumisden detailed instructions on the arguments he was to use on the prince. He was to impress on him the absolute necessity of co-operation with France, and of James's desire to abdicate in his favour as soon as possible, which was not yet. Thus far James's instructions did indeed seem conciliatory, but the king introduced a quite unnecessary element of tension by bringing up openly for the first time the subject of Clementina Walkinshaw: 'You will also explain to the Prince the comfort and satisfaction it has been to me to hope from some accounts I have received that Mrs Walkinshaw [sic] is, or will be soon, separated from him.'[8] There followed a homily on the extent to which Charles's mistress had prejudiced the Stuart cause and the Jacobite movement.

Once again James revealed the depths of his lack of understanding of his son. Even if Charles *had* been considering getting rid of Clementina – and it is quite clear that by this time the couple gave each other nothing but pain and were together only because of their shared love of Charlotte – such a message would have been counterproductive. The prince would never be seen to accept 'laws' given by someone else. He would immediately have stood his ground as a matter of principle. By this gratuitous intrusion into his son's private life, James doomed the Lumisden mission before it began.

The king's instructions to Lumisden could not have been worse conceived or more badly timed. That autumn of 1758 the prince seriously seemed to be considering visiting Rome.[9] Since winter ended any serious military initiatives by France, James was continually urging his son to take the opportunity for a quick trip to the Palazzo Muti.[10] At last it seemed that father and son, who had not seen each other for fifteen years, would meet. The arrival of Lumisden at Bouillon, conveying James's heavy exhortations on wisdom and duty, plus his unwelcome remarks on Clementina, ruined any chance of that. Nor were the prince's ruffled feelings assuaged when Lumisden began patiently to argue James's case to him. He could accept James's stricture that he was being unphilosophical about the perfidy of the French, since none of the same ministers who expelled him in 1748 remained on the council of state.[11] But the proposition that Charles Edward had pushed the French into the arrest merely reawakened in the prince the feeling that James and Louis XV could be seen as similarly oppressive authorities. Charles was disgusted, too, by his father's defeatism. James seemed more interested in the details of the financial settlement Charles could wrest from Versailles in the event of failure of a French descent than in the possibility that a restoration could succeed. The lecture on Clementina Walkinshaw simply made him angry.

The prince hit back. He demanded to know why James was jeopardising all his negotiations with the French by not abdicating. All Lumisden could do was parrot James's line that 'now is not the time'.[12] Charles pointed out the sheer destructiveness of this. Perfidious Versailles would, if it could, find a loophole to evade its solemn commitments, and here was James providing it for them. All the French had to do, whenever they wanted to jettison the Stuarts, was to say that it was impossible to deal with two separate parties, the prince's and the king's.

James's case was not helped by Lumisden's secret agreement with the prince on this point, nor by the fact that he got on remarkably well with the prince. Charles cajoled and charmed Lumisden and prevailed on him to stay on at Bouillon. This spiked his father's guns while he prepared a counterstroke. For recent events at Versailles seemed to be tilting the French court in his direction. He sensed a chance to cut his father out of the whole French connection.

Ever since the outbreak of the Seven Years' War, desultory Jacobite negotiations had gone on with one or other of the ministers of state, especially War Minister Maréchal de Belle-Isle. But while the Abbé (and from 1758 Cardinal) Bernis was Foreign Minister, the French concentrated on continental warfare. In December 1758 Louis XV dismissed Bernis and replaced him with the duc de Choiseul.

Choiseul saw clearly that the European cockpit masked the real struggle for mastery in the war and the true theatre where that struggle went on: north America. He estimated that Canada would very soon be lost to France unless drastic action was taken. Correctly identifying England as France's most deadly enemy, Choiseul threw resources into the most ambitious scheme yet devised for the invasion of the British Isles. The only question he had not answered in his mind was what role the Stuarts, and especially Charles Edward, should play in his great enterprise.[13]

With Choiseul's accession, the pressure on the prince to collaborate with France became intense. Stonewalling frenetically, Charles repeatedly asserted that both for security reasons and because of the pledges he had given the English Jacobites, he could not go to Paris to confer with Choiseul.[14] It was also his view that such a conference should come at the very end of French preparations, when their invasion fleet was ready to sail, not as a prelude to such preparations.

But Choiseul very soon backed Charles Edward into a corner. It was borne in on the prince by assiduous correspondence, especially from the special agent Colonel Wall whom he had sent to Versailles, that he could not pass up this opportunity and still retain a vestige of credibility.[15] With a man as stubborn as Charles Edward, even this might not have been enough to make him change his mind. But the thought of scoring a diplomatic *coup* over the French and cutting James out at the same time was too much to resist. After much adamant blustering that he would never go to Paris, the prince performed another of his lightning changes of mind. He prepared to avail himself of Choiseul's special offer: an apartment in the Hôtel Choiseul which he could enter by the garden and where he could maintain himself in the strictest incognito.[16]

The faithful Thibault was left to keep an eye on Clementina and Charlotte.[17] At the beginning of February 1759 the prince set out for his rendezvous in Paris. On the night of 5 February he arrived at Choiseul's house, very late and very drunk. There to confer with him were Choiseul and Belle-Isle.[18]

Choiseul assured him that Louis XV was deadly serious about an invasion of Britain and that he desired ardently to restore the Stuarts. The prince stated his requirements as to ships and men. Choiseul assured him that this created no problems; the French had already earmarked 50,000 men for the expedition. Having been bitten before by false French promises, the prince made it a point of understanding that the preparations had to be complete before he was summoned to join the embarkation. He wanted no repeat of 1744. He would never again be a mere 'scarecrow' to frighten the English.

Again Choiseul did not demur. He explained the complex French strategy for the invasion. The Prince de Soubise was to cross the Channel in flat-bottoms, while two separate expeditions made landfall in Scotland and Ireland. Since the Soubise preparations would take longest, Choiseul asked the prince if he would consider accompanying the forces invading Scotland or Ireland.[19]

All the prince's old suspicions about French duplicity were aroused by this proposal. Flushed by drink he became agitated and repeated that he was interested only in a landing in England. Fearing that he was in some subtle way being outmanoeuvred, the prince asked for the conversation to be minuted. This too was agreed.[20] The famous formula was concocted, to be repeated *ad nauseam* throughout 1759 in correspondence between Versailles and the Jacobites, that everything was to be done for and with the prince and nothing done without him.[21]

Without waiting to see the results of his other agents' (Murray of Elibank and Mackenzie Douglas) efforts to set up private meetings with Soubise and Madame de Pompadour, the prince sped back to Bouillon, travelling via Rheims.[22] He remained unconvinced by the sincerity of French intentions, but felt reasonably pleased with himself. As he saw it, his insistence that French preparations be complete before he joined the expeditionary force had backed Choiseul into a corner. In fact it had done precisely the opposite. It provided Choiseul with the opportunity to carry on with his invasion preparations without reference to the prince, while keeping the Jacobite fifth column alive by constantly pointing out to it that at the last minute Charles Edward would appear in the Channel ports as agreed.[23]

The truth was that the meeting at his house had disillusioned Choiseul with the prince. He could put up with the drunkenness and the security problems attendant on Clementina Walkinshaw's presence at Bouillon. But the sheer dogmatic inflexibility of Charles Edward in refusing to go to Scotland was a poor trading counter to set against the expected hostile Dutch reaction when they learned that Choiseul was involved in a scheme to restore 'the Pretender'.[24] From this moment on, Choiseul decided in effect to press on with his invasion schemes without taking the prince into serious account. If and when the invasion was successfully completed, it would be time enough for France to decide what to do about Charles Edward.[25]

Any doubts Choiseul might have had of his new policy of excluding the Stuarts were laid to rest when the prince sent him a highly querulous letter later in February. Consultation with Lumisden had prompted second thoughts. Charles now felt aggrieved at having to wait until August (Choiseul's target date for the Channel crossing). He claimed to have come to Paris on the understanding that the meeting was the last phase of the invasion process, not the first. He now felt that he had been lured to the conference on false pretences.[26]

The receipt of this missive more than ever determined Choiseul to press on with his preparations without taking the Stuarts into account.[27] This decision was reflected in the scale of the preparations. Where Richelieu in 1745–6 had intended to land in England with no more than 15,000 men, counting on massive pro-Jacobite support from the English Tories, Choiseul laid his plans on the assumption that he could expect nothing from the Jacobites. A fourth invasionary force under Chevert was added to the grand design. Altogether in the four separate expeditionary armies 100,000 men were assembled.[28]

The prince, in short, had overplayed his hand. For the moment he revelled in the deception he had practised on James by keeping him completely in the dark about Choiseul. James learned merely in general terms from Lumisden that his son had gone to Paris to talk to the French ministers (Lumisden could supply no details).[29] Partly in sorrow, partly in anger at the way his son had excluded him, James recalled Lumisden to Rome.[30]

The prince sent a message with Lumisden that he would be in Rome in May to see his father, once his negotiations with the French were complete.[31] Lumisden departed, still on good terms with the prince. He made his way back across Germany to Venice, then on to Rome via Ancona, Loreto and Macerata.[32]

But the contents of the letter he handed James in the Palazzo Muti stunned the Stuart king. There was nothing about the French, nothing about Clementina Walkinshaw, nothing about any of the substantive points he had put to Charles. Instead, there were long outpourings about his enemies (Aeneas MacDonald and Cluny MacPherson figured prominently) together with a detailed, meticulous account of the sins of Lord George Murray, with no incident of his imagined treachery going unmarked.[33] James had been eagerly awaiting Lumisden's return to learn of his negotiations with Choiseul and to see signs of the *rapprochement* he so hoped for. He was utterly devastated by this reply.[34] How utterly destroyed in spirit he was can be inferred from Lumisden's pithy and laconic dispatch to Charles Edward: 'when [the king] read your letter and heard the report he ordered me to make, it so disordered him that he finds himself unable to write to you at present.'[35]

The prince had crushed James for the moment, but the victory gave him little satisfaction. He was already beginning to realise with anger and despair how completely Choiseul had outmanoeuvred him. As the summer wore on, it became more and more evident that the French were making their invasion plans without taking any account of the Jacobite factor. The prince had only himself to blame. His friends and agents had urged further meetings in Paris with Soubise and Madame de Pompadour, but Charles showed an infuriating reluctance to stir from Bouillon.[36] His behaviour seemed particularly perverse in the light of past events. When the French expelled him from their dominions, he had seemingly not been able to resist the temptation to tread French soil illicitly. Now that they *invited* him to further talks, he refused to go. His perversity on this point recalled Elcho's military strictures during the '45.[37]

The truth was that the prince was locked in a trap of his own making. He had staked his credibility on not being willing to go to Paris until all invasion preparations were final and complete. But now that the seriousness of French intentions could no longer be doubted, it came to look as though Choiseul had turned the tables on him in a quite masterly way. French demand for a manifesto in his name conjured unpleasant memories of 1744.[38] Clearly Soubise and the other generals intended to land in England without him, while using the glamour of his name. He had cried wolf once too often. The penalty for obdurate refusal to believe in the seriousness of French intentions without overwhelming proof was that, when the evidence was clear to see, Charles Edward himself was to be excluded from the project.

The prince has been much criticised for remaining meekly at Bouillon in 1759 while the French assembled their armada.[39] But in his own terms he had no choice. To appear in Paris before everything was complete would involve a humiliating climb-down. France had already caused him too much pain for this to be feasible. Yet the consciousness that his own pride and honour were allowing Choiseul to make a fool of him activated the civil conflict within. Almost predictably, as the unbearable stress of his troubled relations with the French built to a crescendo, he fell badly ill.

The cycle of ill-health began in May 1759 with a bad case of influenza, which kept him in bed and obliged Thibault to answer all his correspondence.[40] This was followed by a peculiarly painful attack of piles.[41] Finally, his fingers became so sore that he could scarcely move his hand.[42] The overt cause of this organic breakdown was heavy drinking, but the drinking itself reached crisis proportions because of the stress of his duel with Choiseul.[43] On 14 May he wrote gloomily to Murray of Elibank: 'that cursed lawsuit gives both you and I [sic] more trouble than it is worth.'[44]

The prince's health had for some time been giving cause for concern. His devoted follower and admirer John Holker, now a successful industrialist in Rouen, met him during the February trip to Paris and recorded his impressions. He found Charles Edward much thinner than when he saw him last. 'I am truly chagrined to death when I think of his situation and would give the world, had I it in my power, to see him in another way, as it won't be possible for him to survive nor yet make old bones, was he to continue much longer.'[45]

By a bitter irony, James chose this moment to re-enter the fray. While the prince lay sick at Bouillon, James, now recovered slightly from the shock of the Lumisden mission, chose to attack his son in his two most touchy areas: religion and Clementina.

The first letter, written 29 May, revealed that James had long known about his son's switch to Protestantism. Given James's devoutness, the contents were no surprise. James managed a skilful balancing of dignity and sorrowful reproach!

Do not flatter yourself, my dear son, on this article there is no trimming, and you equally renounce your religion whether you conceal it, or embrace another. . . . I am far from dissuading you to seek a temporal kingdom . . . and it is manifestly for the good of our country that it should return under the dominion of our Family. But . . . what will avail to you all the kingdoms in the world . . . if you lose your soul. I am in agonies for you, my dear son, and you alone can free me from them.[46]

In a second letter of the same date he brought up the subject of Clementina Walkinshaw, of whom the prince had said nothing to Lumisden. He made a most strenuous plea to Charles to get rid of her and offered his assistance in getting her into a convent in France.[47]

The prince responded to both overtures with silence. His mind was on other, more important things. He looked on impotently as French invasion preparations took shape. There were to be three expeditions, one each to England, Scotland and Ireland. D'Aiguillon's landing in Scotland would precede Soubise's arrival on the south coast of England but was itself dependent on the escorting ability of Admiral Conflans's Brest fleet. But when Conflans came out of Brest in November to pick up d'Aiguillon's army at Quiberon, he was caught by Admiral Hawke and his fleet destroyed in one of the Royal Navy's most memorable actions. All Choiseul's invasion plans came to nothing, with or without the prince.

James was very ill throughout the winter of 1759.[48] As the spring of 1760 came and he recovered, it seemed to him that the abandonment of all French plans for invading Britain left his son free to come to Rome to see him. Accordingly, he issued the invitation.[49] He was still unaware of the resentment he had caused in the prince, both by his blundering intervention on the issue of religion and Clementina and by his inept refusal to stand aside in 1759, to abdicate and give his son full powers to treat with the French. Charles Edward replied that the state of his 'nerves' made such a journey impossible.[50] In truth, he was depressed and habitually drunk. At this point James revealed the depths of his unconscious resentment of his son. He made a decisive but self-destructive intervention in the affair of Clementina Walkinshaw.

3²

'Endless Night'
(1760–4)

By 1760 such picayune rewards as life with the prince held for Clementina had long since ceased to compensate for the cycle of drunkenness, verbal abuse and physical beatings. So violent were the prince's rages and so unpredictable and maniacal his behaviour during them that Clementina genuinely feared for her life – not so much that Charles would intentionally kill her as that he would be guilty of manslaughter in some moment of madness when he was beside himself.[1] His drinking had reached new heights of excess.[2] And the stress impelling him to almost permanent inebriation had found a new focus: once again he was visited by acute money worries.[3]

Things were so bad on the financial front that even the most poignant begging letter had no chance of eliciting a contribution from the prince. Clementina's feeling that she could not endure any more of life with Charles was brought to a head by one particular refusal of financial aid. In June a letter arrived from Boulogne from that selfsame John Walkinshaw who had taken in Lady Balmerino in 1746. He was now destitute and threw himself on the prince's compassion.[4] The prince could do nothing for him. This was the last straw for Clementina. She had long ago ceased to hope for anything for herself, but had kept going with the thought of at least being able to do something for her kin. Now this hope too proved illusory. How many more disappointments would there be? Would Charles turn on Charlotte next?

This was the point at which the prince's Mephistopheles played his evil hand. For some years now Kelly had oscillated in and out of favour. Now he saw a chance to avenge himself on his erstwhile master. He drafted a letter to James in Rome, as if from Clementina, telling him that she wished to leave the prince and would do so if only she could find a powerful protector.[5] James wrote back by a secret channel, encouraging her to take the plunge.[6]

Clementina had always given signs that she was not negligible when it came to willpower and assertiveness. Secretly she made preparations for her flight with Charlotte. On the night of 22 July 1760, while Charles was temporarily absent, she stole away from Bouillon with her child.[7] She left behind a note for the prince, stating that her principal reason for leaving was fear of losing her life. 'You have pushed me to the greatest extremity and that there is not one woman in the world that would have suffered so long as what I have done.'[8] She later amplified the statement, claiming that the prince had daily taken out all his disappointments on her: 'I was the victim of everything that disobliged you.'[9]

When the prince learned what had happened, he flew into a near-apoplectic rage. He cared nothing for Clementina, but he adored the six-year-old Charlotte ('Pouponne' was his pet name for her) and was sincerely grief-stricken to find that his little consolation had been whisked away from him.

Quickly the prince issued his orders. Since Clementina had fled, Charles was disposed to let her go. If she returned freely, he promised to forgive her. But at all costs Charlotte had to be returned to him. This was an unnegotiable demand.[10] Since Clementina was thought to be heading for Paris, he alerted his contact there, Abbé John Gordon. The instructions to Gordon were written by Thibault; in his own hand the prince added the following: 'I take this affair so much to heart that I was not able to write what is here above. Shall be in the greatest affliction until I get back the child, which was my only comfort in my misfortunes.'[11]

Gordon intercepted Clementina as she got off the Paris coach. He found her lodgings and gave her a stern talking-to.[12] He admonished her not to write to Choiseul and warned her in general of the consequences of her actions. He assured her there would be no problem about her entering a convent, but the child would have to be sent back to her father. Clementina promised to wait until Gordon received further instructions from the prince. Yet a more alert man than Gordon might have guessed what was in her mind when she asked him for money.

Gordon claimed not to have any. He thought he had outwitted her. But when he returned to her lodgings next day, Clementina had flown.[13] Patient enquiries threw up an address at the Hôtel St Louis in the rue des Grands Augustins. Gordon then addressed himself to Belle-Isle. After reading the prince's strongly-worded remonstrance,

Belle-Isle promised to put M. Cremilles, lieutenant of Paris police, on the job.[14]

But before Cremilles could act, the prince's recently reinstated valet John Stewart caught up with Clementina. The direct approach proved useless. Clementina would not listen to anything Stewart had to say. She claimed she would rather 'make away with herself than go back, and cut the child to pieces rather than give it back'.[15]

Stewart dogged her footsteps. At 10.30 p.m. on the evening of 30 July she went out with Charlotte. Stewart insisted on accompanying her. Clementina seemed not to mind. Then, at a prearranged spot, her coach stopped. Clementina got out and into another coach that was waiting. When Stewart tried to follow her, two professional bodyguards interposed themselves and told Stewart roughly to go about his business. Stewart tried to follow the coach but soon lost it in the maze of back-alleys.[16]

Following Belle-Isle's orders, for a few days the full resources of Cremilles's police department were thrown into the search for Clementina.[17] The 'wanted' posters contained Charles Edward's unflattering description of his mistress and child: Clementina, aged forty, blonde, average height, complexion marked by red blemishes; Charlotte, aged seven, white blonde, big eyes, full and round face, slightly flat nose, well-built and strong for her age.[18]

The days slipped by, the intensive search continued. Still there was no sign of the runaways.[19] Charles Edward raged at the incompetence of his agent who had let them slip through his fingers.[20] Though Belle-Isle was certain Clementina had left Paris, the prince, remembering his own experiences in 1749–50, was certain she was in hiding in some obscure convent in the capital.[21] With the obsessive energy of monomania, the prince prepared detailed lists of the people who might be sheltering the fugitives. Mrs O'Brien, Madame de Mézières, O'Heguerty, Walsh, Warren, Holker, Lady Ogilvy, Waters, Mme Ramsay: the daily lengthening list soon bade fair to embrace the entire body of Jacobites in France.[22] Nothing more clearly illustrates the prince's paranoia than the way in which trusted friends were progressively added to the list of potential betrayers. The prince revealed that at bottom he trusted no one.

At last a shaft of light penetrated the turbid fog of his persecution mania. He remembered O'Sullivan. More and more the prince became convinced that Clementina had returned to her former lover.[23] He sent out frenzied orders to track down the ageing Irishman. Yet, when caught up with, O'Sullivan had no more idea of Clementina's whereabouts than anyone else. The best clue came from Madame Ramsay. It was now certain that Clementina was in a convent.[24] But where?

By now the search instituted by Belle-Isle and Cremilles had petered out.[25] Charles Edward accused the French of not pulling their weight. How was it that the French were proving so incompetent at finding Clementina after the ruthless efficiency they had displayed towards him in 1748?[26] As so often, there was substance in Charles Edward's insensate accusations.

Suddenly Gordon found that Cremilles and Belle-Isle were 'out' or 'away' whenever he called to pursue inquiries.[27] The reason soon became clear. To the prince's indescribable fury, James revealed that he had taken the runaways under his protection.[28] This ended all French assistance for Charles Edward. They could not be seen to be supporting the son in defiance of the wishes of the father.[29] Quite apart from anything else, the affair was another nail in the coffin of the prince's reputation. Choiseul felt completely vindicated in his contempt.[30]

James had already committed a signal act of betrayal in the prince's eyes. But the king made things worse by writing to his son to try to justify his actions. His limp excuse that he had asked Clementina to get Charles's permission before leaving was a threadbare palliative. Once again James evinced his genius for getting hold of the wrong end of the stick. In an attempt to justify his decision to have Charlotte educated in a convent, he gave as his reason 'now that she is of an age incapable of being company to you or of giving you real comfort of any kind'.[31]

The prince had long suspected that Clementina could not have remained hidden so long without collusion by the French authorities.[32] He had always half-expected non-co-operation from Versailles. But he was deeply shocked to discover that this was the result of James's blundering intervention. The conflation of France and his father as oppressive authority became absolute. Absolute too was the veto on further searches for Clementina. Charles could not act on his own, since Gordon and the other Jacobites, once they realised that Clementina was under James's protection, declared that they could not serve two masters. In the hierarchy of commands from king and prince, James's will took precedence.[33]

Clementina's flight, followed by the disclosure that James had abetted it, precipitated the prince into total breakdown. He declared he would neither eat nor drink until the child was returned to him.[34] Nor would he answer any letters addressed to him, no matter who the correspondent, until France made reparation for the gross insult offered him. There can be no question but that the psychological blow of Clementina's desertion was comparable to other great traumata in his life: Derby, Henry's becoming a cardinal, his arrest in 1748. But before the prince withdrew into himself and maintained an almost catatonic silence towards the outside world, he took a resolution. James's treachery over Clementina had finished him for all time. Charles would never forgive his father.[35]

The débâcle over Clementina brought into the open the mutual unconscious hatred between father and son. What else, other than some deep-seated urge to get even with his son for the various ways in which Charles had supplanted him, can explain James's extraordinary meddling in his son's private life? Clementina Sobieska's overprotective instincts for her son had destroyed James's marriage. What more fitting than that the second Clementina should likewise flee to a convent, thus visiting on the son the humiliation the father had suffered thirty-five years before? Charles's jibes about his father's inability to manage his own marriage – which was why, he alleged, the Jacobites had waited to see how Charles Edward would turn out – could be neutralised if the son was also seen to be a failure in personal relations.

On the other hand, it is quite clear that James was prodded into this self-destructive act of unconscious revenge by the prince's steadfast refusal to take any notice of his advice. It is plain that, consciously or unconsciously (probably the latter), the prince never had any serious intention of visiting his father in Rome. Any chance of James's escaping the 'punishment' due to him for the 'horrors' of the prince's childhood (whether we see these as real or merely self-assigned by Charles) was almost certainly lost in 1747–8, after James's behaviour over Henry's cardinalate and the prince's expulsion from France. Neither the prince nor his father realised the strength of the bonds of unconscious hatred that linked them.

The two motifs, anger at his father's treachery and grief for the loss of Charlotte, accounted for the prince's subsequent actions, found inexplicable by his followers. They assumed that his emotions were affected primarily by Clementina. True, his pride was hurt. Although he cared nothing for Clementina, it was a matter of honour to the prince that *he* should decide when the relationship was to end. But the primary triggers that pushed him into breakdown had nothing to do with Clementina.

The prince's breakdown went through a number of phases. At first he was momentarily shocked into sobriety.[36] He could neither eat nor sleep.[37] Then he returned to the bottle with even greater vigour. He would get drunk by the early afternoon, sleep off the effects, then indulge in another heady round of hard drinking in the evening.[38] For a long time, too, he kept his crazed word, neither writing to anyone nor replying to any message. In his deranged state, he saw his threat to have no communication with the outside world until his child was returned as a kind of punishment, as if he as the source of light were withdrawing his shining beacon to leave the universe in darkness. His alcoholism had an integral relationship with this decision to make himself inaccessible. Alcoholism is one of the classic withdrawal routes from a world that seems to impose over-heavy burdens.

Clementina's place of refuge was, as he had suspected, a Paris convent – the convent de la Visitation de Sainte Marie in the rue du Bac. When he learned this, the prince's anger took the form of going out with his musket and firing potshots through the windows of the convents around Bouillon.[39] This obvious manifestation of mental illness was followed by a critical period of organic illness: a severe cold combined with an attack of haemorrhoids led to fever caused, in the language of the time by 'a plenitude of bile'.[40]

Bit by bit, as the prince recovered from this illness, his lucid intervals grew more frequent. Murray of Elibank had repeatedly argued that Clementina Walkinshaw was not worth the emotion he was wasting on her; since women were ten-a-penny, why did he not simply take another one?[41] In September the prince acted on the advice. He asked his secret agents Guérin and Jones to find him a girl aged 20–25, with good bourgeois sentiments. She must be *soignée*, of good health, and be prepared to look after his child and his linen.[42] In a second letter, dated 18 September, the prince amplified his requirements. The girl must be educated, without great property, have good teeth and an agreeable figure. A knowledge of music would be an advantage, and if such a person could be found, money would be no object. That the prince's thoughts were running on sexual lines is clear from his instruction to Jones, that the affair was to be a close secret and kept from Father Gordon.[43] We know little of the upshot, except that a girl answering this description was sent to Bouillon.[44]

While this piece of business was going through, Murray of Elibank was urging the prince to take up with one of his old mistresses in Paris.[45] It is quite clear that on his many clandestine trips to the French capital the prince had not remained faithful to Clementina. Murray had his hands full preventing this mystery woman from paying the prince a visit. 'I should not be surprised if she sets out for Bouillon, as her passion for you is beyond all manner of expression.'[46] This passion for the prince evidently endured well into 1762, but was not reciprocated.[47] By this time, not even a beautiful mistress could tempt Charles Edward out of Bouillon.

The prince's hermit-like existence in the Chateau de Carlsbourg, refusing to see or communicate with anyone, was now widely regarded as self-destructive. The English at long last knew exactly where he was and they were content.[48] They were delighted to find that, except when hunting, he was almost permanently drunk, forgotten by the French and regarded as hopeless by the Jacobite exiles in Europe.[49] Of particular satisfaction to the Hanoverians was his oft-repeated declaration that he would never marry, lest his children be exposed to miseries similar to his own.[50]

Charles Edward was the despair of his friends and admirers. The contingent absurdity of the world was summed up for Voltaire in 1763 by the thought that George II had deprived the French of Canada at the very time the Stuart prince was aiming kicks and blows at women.[51] For Voltaire the three great contemporary (1762) tragedies were the dethronement of the Czar by his wife Catherine, the death through grief of the king of Poland, and the fact that Charles Edward lived in obscure misery at Bouillon.[52]

The Jacobite Sholto Douglas put it even more trenchantly, directly to the prince: 'Your enemies now wantonly exult and express themselves as Peter the Great did of Charles XII of Sweden, that he kept his Swede chained at Bendar. They say they have you in a bottle at Bouillon and have the cork in their pocket.'[53]

Such exultation alone would surely by now have put paid to all the legends about subsequent visits by the prince to England, were he not already on the road to being a creature of myth rather than serious history. Even sober scholars have been seduced into accepting that the prince went to England in 1760 on George II's death.[54] And it was Sir Walter Scott who was responsible for popularising the similarly baseless rumour that the prince was present at the coronation of George III in 1761.[55] While it is not possible to state definitively that the prince never stirred far from Bouillon in the years 1760–5, all the evidence both direct and indirect – not least his alcoholism – works against the notion.[56] All definite 'sightings' of the prince outside Bouillon, such as that reported from Berne in 1762, were demonstrably untrue.[57]

Anyone doubting this should look at the volume of letters from his friends and sympathisers vainly urging just such forays on him. The most significant such advocate was his father. But the prince soon showed that he had been in deadly earnest when he declared that the Clementina affair had finished James for good. In April 1761 James wrote to ask his son what were his intentions when peace came.[58] Amazingly, he still seemed to have no idea of the damage he had done by sheltering Clementina. Charles Edward did not reply.

In January 1762 James tried again. Spain had just declared war on England and James offered to approach the king of Spain on his son's behalf to find a safe exile on the Iberian peninsula: 'My chief aim is to draw you if possible out of the hidden, and I may say, ignominious life you lead . . . if you make no reply to this letter, I shall take it for granted that . . . you are not only buried alive . . . but in effect that you are dead and insensible to everything.'[59] Again there was no reply.

In September 1762 James made his final effort. Upbraiding Charles for continuing to rebuff the English Jacobites until his daughter Charlotte was returned. James pointed out the impracticability and lack of Christianity in his son's project. As his long letter continued, James switched from logic to emotion. He ended with his final appeal, in which heartbreak and guilt seemed mixed in equal measure:

> Will you not run straight to your father? . . . There is no question of the past, but only of saving you from utter destruction for the future. Is it possible you would rather be a vagabond on the face of the earth than return to a Father who is all love and tenderness for you?[60]

If James had known anything of his son's stubborn will, he would have realised that such overtures were pointless. There was only one way James could restore himself to Charles Edward's favour and this was the one he would never take: the return of Charlotte to Bouillon.

Any further attempts at communication were in any case prevented by the onset of serious illness, from which James never fully recovered. In October 1762 an apoplectic fit and loss of speech led to extreme unction being administered.[61] Walpole overstated the case when he conjectured that on receipt of the news Charles Edward would probably get drunk to drown his sorrows.[62] Quite apart from Charles's indifference to his father's fate – for in his view James had effectively died once he protected Clementina Walkinshaw – the prince would never consent to go to Rome while the hated Cardinal York lived there.[63]

The wisdom or folly of the prince's attitude at the time was never tested, since James, amazingly, came through this illness too. Not until 1764 did he enter the terminal phase of his life. Then he took to his bed with a resolution that he would conduct no more business and read no more letters, but instead prepare himself for eternity.[64] In this twilight state, more dead than alive, he remained until his death in January 1766.

All James's appeals to his son were so much wasted ink. At first all other Jacobites fared no better. Murray of Elibank's taunt that he was fulfilling the prophecies of Marischal and Lady Primrose failed to stir him.[65] Nor did the suggestion (1761) that he approached the dismissed Pitt to act as his General Monk.[66] Frustrated at his inability to raise even a line of answer from the prince, Murray tried a new tack. He invented a rumour that the man living at Bouillon was not Charles Edward Stuart but an impostor.[67] Lord Caryll, a follower of the prince since Gravelines in 1744, was puzzled why Charles should be so concerned over an illegitimate child. Still, he offered the help of the dwindling English Jacobite party to get Charlotte back.[68] Even the duc de Bouillon wrote to say that Clementina Walkinshaw was not worth all the fuss.[69] Yet no answer came from the prince.

Finally, in January 1762, Charles relented a little. Walsh's brother the comte de Serrant was in touch about the possibility of the prince's settling in Spain. Charles broke his silence to inform the Abbé Gordon that it was still his intention not to enter into any political business whatsoever until his child was returned.[70] A year later the prince repeated the same sentiments to Serrant himself.[71]

At least he was now writing. A further chink in his iron defences came in 1762 when he allowed the first visit to Bouillon by an English Jacobite. The person chosen for this privilege was Lady Webb, who had already demonstrated a subtle line in charm and flattery.[72] Lady Webb, wife of Sir Thomas Webb and daughter and heiress of William Gibson, had a special niche in Jacobite tradition, since she was related to one of the great Jacobite martyrs, the earl of Derwentwater of the '15. Early in July 1762 she spent a week at the Chateau de Carlsbourg. The visit appeared to go well; Lady Webb spoke of the most precious seven days of her life. But on her return to Paris she did the unforgivable. She wrote to the prince, criticising his drinking.

> I observed several times while at dinner the blood rise and surround your neck and in an instant fly up to your head . . . there is but one remedy . . . cooling your stomach immediately by large draughts of water to which you have so great an aversion.[73]

That was the end of Lady Webb, at least on a face-to-face basis. The prince instructed Gordon to make use of her but on no account to allow her to visit Bouillon again.[74] It seemed clear to him that all the English Jacobites ever wanted to do was lecture him on his drinking without ever addressing themselves to the miseries that had brought on the drinking in the first place. His worst opinions of Lady Webb were confirmed. In May 1763 she delivered another homily. Referring to the prince's lack of exercise and fresh air, and his refusal to eat enough food to absorb his heavy consumption of wine, she predicted (accurately) the onset of dropsy.[75]

Lady Webb's gentle admonitions were nugatory alongside some of the broadsides directed at him by the Paris Jacobites. Money was again a problem. In January 1763 the banker Waters sent a splenetic letter to the prince:

> People to preserve their credit must pay their debts, it is the way to obtain more. The maxim holds equally with princes. The King of France borrows and pays and so do all other sovereigns, they know it is their interest. It cannot certainly be yours to ruin me.[76]

It took an iron constitution of a singular kind to stand up to the punishment Charles Edward inflicted on himself in the years at Bouillon.[77] A less robust man might well have succumbed to an alcohol-related disease. But as the prince entered his forties, intimations of mortality were all around him in the Jacobite movement. The royal secretary Edgar died in 1762. So did the baleful Kelly. Walsh died in 1763. Lally, disgraced in India, was marked down for execution (it took place in 1766). To reinforce the theme of *memento mori*, in November 1765 Lady Webb reported the death of the prince's old adversary Cumberland, who, she was certain, had gone straight to Hell.[78] Curiously the prince himself never shared the general Jacobite loathing for 'the Butcher'. He always found it hard to believe that a prince of the blood could really have been guilty of the cruelties after Culloden.[79] And he invariably vetoed all assassination attempts against him planned by the Jacobites. Moreover, he was personally magnanimous. The duchesse d'Aiguillon told Horace Walpole that when some of his friends abused Cumberland in her presence, Charles Edward replied that his brother Henry had hurt him more by turning cardinal than Cumberland ever could. The prince then recorded this eccentric verdict: '*C'est un prince très généreux, comme vous avez éprouvé, et vous ne devez pas parler contre lui, car il m'a vaincu.*'[80] ('You ought not to speak against him, for he beat me.')

Finally, the death of Cluny MacPherson in January 1764 reopened all the old wounds about the prince's lost effects.[81] Although Cluny declared on his death-bed that he knew nothing of the diamond rings and the seal whose disappearance the prince so lamented,[82] Charles decided to pursue his own enquiries. The trail led back to Cluny's elderly female relative in Badenoch. A correspondence peppered with mutual contempt went on between Gordon in Paris and Miss MacPherson in Scotland.[83] Eventually the acidulous MacPherson female promised to hand over what she possessed of the Stuart plate on production of an unquestionable holograph order from Charles Edward Stuart.[84]

It seemed there was no limit to the 'impertinence' the world was prepared to mete out to a 'man undone'. The prince's feelings of being fair game for all manner of quasi-aristocratic parvenus were emphasised by an unpleasant incident in Bouillon in 1764. This time the affront was offered by Major de la Motte, commanding the garrison at Bouillon Castle. Two army deserters got drunk, stole a pair of sheets, and were condemned to death. All the prince's old humanitarian instincts were aroused (and he might well have felt solidarity for the plight of some fellow drunkards). He sent his valet-de-chambre to de la Motte to plead for clemency, suggesting that the sentence be commuted to galley slavery and asking the favour on the strength of his royal birth.[85] Charles suggested that to save de la Motte's face, he should appear with his escort at the esplanade just before the execution and ask the boon of mercy.[86]

De la Motte was a man of the Hawley stamp. Not only did he turn the prince down, but he warned him brusquely of the consequences of interfering.[87] Not only did he *not* delay the executions so as to give the prince time to write an appeal to Paris; he rushed the hangings through and capped his defiance by making derogatory remarks about 'the Pretender'.[88]

The prince aroused his agents in Paris to seek satisfaction from Choiseul.[89] But Choiseul by now had no time for the prince. Charles's arguments were perfectly sound: he pointed out that he would not have interfered if the charge had been murder; it was the trivial nature of the offence that excited his compassion.[90] Yet he had lost all credibility in Choiseul's eyes. The upshot was that Choiseul conveyed informally to the prince's agents that he was prepared to discipline de la Motte only if he received a formal complaint from Charles Edward himself.

At this point the prince drew back. Such a supplication would breach his own rule that he would have no dealings with France until Charlotte was returned. Even worse, there was the possibility that Choiseul might turn him down as de la Motte had done.[91] Charles was not prepared to run the risk of being wounded in this way. His

informal suit in Paris to get de la Motte to purge his contempt
collapsed.

Bouillon was now soured for the prince. The man who had insulted
him and got away with it passed his chateau each day. But how to
get out of the impasse? He could not go to Paris, and had turned
down Madrid. Rome was out for obvious reasons. It was at this
juncture that a miraculous breakthrough occurred. On the eve of his
father's death, he was reconciled with his brother Henry. Even more
surprisingly, the agent of the reconciliation was Lady Webb.

33

'To the sunless land'
(1765–6)

Lady Webb was remarkably thick-skinned. The prince's obvious distaste for her strictures did not halt the flow of her admonitions and exhortations. With consummate cheek, she even dared to justify herself by reference to the prince's alcoholism, remarking that her resolution not to trouble him again was 'like those drunkards who make them in the morning and break them before night'.[1]

Her constant nagging, spiced with praise for the wondrous person that lay beneath the mask the prince chose to display to the world, even seemed to be paying dividends. At least the prince reverted to a semblance of normal life and went hunting every day.[2] Finally, Lady Webb's sheer relentlessness in the war of attrition produced its most spectacular result. She acted as the bridge between the ailing prince and Cardinal York at Frascati.

This achievement is all the more remarkable when it is remembered that at this precise time the prince's latent paranoia about his brother was being played on by Murray of Elibank. Referring to Henry contemptuously as 'Red Cap', Murray reported: 'he looks upon you as nobody and even says he believes you can't live long from your immoderate drinking.'[3]

This was the context in which Lady Webb informed the prince in December 1764 that his brother was eager for a reconciliation but did not venture to write, as he feared Charles would snub him and not answer his letters.[4] The prince replied through Thibault that although the row over Charlotte prevented his replying, he was in principle interested in such a reconciliation, especially given the state of their father's health.[5] Declaring that this reply 'gave me more pleasure than words can express',[6] Lady Webb conveyed the news to the Cardinal Duke. Henry was in conciliatory mood. He conceded

that the Clementina Walkinshaw affair had been badly handled by
his father, but now that James was virtually comatose, his attitudes
were no longer a barrier. James neither knew about the planned
reconciliation nor was in any mental or physical state to express an
opinion on it.

Henry went on to say that as a gesture of good will he was prepared
to make over the papal pension of 10,000 Roman crowns (which
James would have left to his cardinal son) to Charles.[7] In euphoric
mood Henry wrote a very warm letter to his brother. But he had
jumped the gun.[8] The prince was still not ready to abandon his
stubborn stance as incommunicado. Lady Webb rebuked him for
inconsistency. She pointed out that he already corresponded on business with Gordon. Surely an exception should be made for the
Cardinal Duke?[9]

The prince professed his attachment to his brother, but still did
not write to him.[10] Commendably, Henry then made another direct
approach (September 1765).[11] He followed with a small masterpiece
of diplomacy. Having heard that Charles in pique had abjured his
own abjuration when the prize of the English crown seemed finally
beyond his grasp, he praised him for returning to the faith of his
ancestors. He added that he quite understood the prince's distaste
about returning to Rome; he suggested instead some small town in
the papal states.[12]

At last, on 3 October 1765, the prince broke his silence and wrote
to his brother.[13] Lady Webb was triumphant: 'no words can express
the joy with which I received the honour of Your Royal Highness's
of the 3rd.'[14]

Yet the truth was that it was circumstance rather than sentiment
that produced the letter to the Cardinal Duke. At the eleventh hour
the prince suddenly saw the political abyss that yawned at his feet.
At the very last moment he realised that there was a real possibility
that he might not be recognised as *de jure* king of England when his
father died. Only Henry could help him now. But to appreciate the
dimensions of the problem Charles Edward faced on the *de jure*
succession, we must return for a moment to the reign of Benedict
XIV, the Vatican's philosopher-king.

Benedict XIV had steered a difficult course in his relations with
the Stuarts. Although in the excitement of the '45 he had momentarily
allowed himself to hope and believe in a Stuart restoration, the basic
tenor of Benedict's policies was to conciliate the British.[15] At the
same time, he had a very high personal regard for both James and
Henry, as evinced in the 1747 elevation to the cardinalate.

These good relations continued throughout the 1750s, until Benedict's death.[16] The Pope was particularly impressed with the fact that Henry had proved a happy choice as cardinal.[17] In the well-known rift in 1752 between James and Henry over the cardinal's close (possibly homosexual) relationship with the Abbé Lercari, Benedict acted as mediator and peace-maker.[18]

The curious thing is that in their official correspondence with the Pope, neither James nor Henry ever mentioned Charles Edward. The contrast between this official reticence and their domestic carping was clear, for in 1751 Henry complained bitterly of his brother's treatment of him.[19] Yet Benedict was statesmanlike enough to see the possibly disastrous consequences of an open rift between king and prince, especially if James made good his frequently intimated threat to cut Charles Edward out of his will, or at least out of the revenue from pensions and benefices.[20] Since the Pope was shrewd enough to realise that one of the causes of hostility between James and Charles was the king's obvious preference for Henry, he did his best to pour oil on troubled waters and to steer James away from over-reaction to his elder son's silences that the king might later regret.[21]

But Benedict did not need the doubts and reservations expressed by the prince's father and brother to make him disillusioned with Charles Edward. He achieved that condition unaided. In 1752 he raised with James the subject of the rumours then circulating that the prince had turned Protestant. When James promptly changed the subject, Benedict became convinced there was some foundation in the rumours.[22] Nor did he forget the disastrous months while the prince was at Avignon. In 1754, when the prince was in Paris seeking a permanent domicile, Benedict was informed that Charles Edward again considered Avignon an attractive prospect, especially since France would not oppose his settling there, unlike in 1749. The mere thought of a repeat of January 1749 filled Benedict with horror.

The thought of the prince's possible return to Rome was no more palatable. He would introduce 'libertinage' and 'civil war' into the Stuart household. If Avignon was preferable to that, there was still the virtual certainty that Charles Edward would once again treat the vice-legate as his servant and the enclave as his fief.[23] By now Benedict was contemptuous of the prince. In his heart he was already (1753) convinced that the prince was a lost cause and would never succeed in his designs.[24] Even so, this intellectual conviction was balanced by an emotional wish for Charles Edward's success, both because of Benedict's fondness for James and Henry and for the sake of the English Catholics. What the Pope dreaded most was that James would die suddenly and leave him the agonising choice of whether to recognise Charles Edward as king.[25] In such a decision, sentiment and ideology would pull one way, political expediency the other. Benedict prayed that such a choice would be left to his successor.

Benedict got his wish. The issue was still unsettled at his death in 1758. At the conclave to elect his successor, Cardinal York was already an important figure in the College of Cardinals.[26] Even Charles Edward saw the importance of electing a successor favourable to Stuart interests.[27] When Clement XIII was elected, after Cardinal Cavalchini, the front-runner, was blocked by the opposition of the French cardinals, the prince lost no time in sending him a message of congratulation.[28] But he rather spoiled things by asking for his compliments to be made secretly. As James waspishly remarked (hinting at what he already knew), only a Protestant prince would make such a request.[29]

The Vatican factor increased in importance as James's health faltered. Even Kelly could see that if the prince did not go to Rome before his father's death, he would suffer gravely from the omission.[30] If Charles were to appear at his bedside to receive James's blessing and be reconciled to him in a tearful and emotional finale to the king's life, it would be humanly and morally impossible for the Pope to refuse to recognise the prince as James's heir, the future Charles III of the three kingdoms.[31]

It was the mark of a bad politician to attempt to ask for recognition as *de jure* monarch after James's death. Charles Edward was no fool and at one level he realised this very well. Even if he had not been able to work out this obvious truth for himself, he was receiving precisely this advice from his friends. Murray of Elibank warned that if he went to Rome after James's death, the Pope would not acknowledge him. 'Not acknowledged by the Pope and deprived of your father's succession, your situation will be worse than when in the Highlands after the battle of Culloden.'[32] Lady Webb added that if he declared himself a Protestant, this would give the prince 'a unique loophole'.[33] As a half-hearted response to this, the prince in 1763 renewed his compliments to Clement XIII.[34]

The real problem was not the prince's lack of perceptiveness on the papal recognition issue. The trouble lay elsewhere. The flight of Clementina had opened a Pandora's box of self-destructive urges. As late as October 1765 Charles was planning to live in Paris after James's demise.[35] Such a course of action would have destroyed all chances of papal recognition. Yet after the Clementina affair the one thing the prince could never do was make obeisance to his father.

The opening up of the channel to Henry underlined the complexity of the situation. Clement XIII himself had suffered an attack of apoplexy in August 1765.[36] The one thing no one had bargained for was that James might die just after a new Pope had been elected or, even worse, during the conclave itself. But while communication with Henry revealed the labyrinthine implications of the *de jure* succession, it also offered hope. Henry suggested a way in which the circle might be squared. The task was to have Charles Edward recognised as legitimate successor to James without insisting on a formal bending of the knee by son to father. The fact that James was barely conscious provided a possibility of cutting the Gordian knot.

The critical four-month struggle for papal recognition began on 3 October 1765 when Charles Edward at last broke his silence with a famous overture to the Pope, hard on the heels of his first letter to Henry. After assuring the Pope of his veneration, the prince asked the Supreme Pontiff to procure for him the honours and titles his father had always enjoyed.[37] Meanwhile the *rapprochement* between the two brothers continued with a very warm letter from Charles Edward on 28 October, in which, anticipating success, he looked forward to embracing the Cardinal Duke in Rome.[38] The prince disregarded Henry's cautious letter, in which he warned Charles Edward that it would not be possible for him (Henry) to see the Pope for a fortnight.[39]

The tissue of confusions that characterised the next few months was immediately observable. The Pope's initial response was ambiguous. He promised to continue the pension of 12,000 crowns a year and to provide the Palazzo Muti as the Stuart residence, but said nothing about continuing to guarantee the marks of royalty, except that he would take his cue on this issue from the example of other sovereigns.[40] Henry meanwhile enlisted the aid of Cardinal Francis (Gianfrancesco) Albani, Protector of Scotland, to promote his brother's suit. Following an interview with Clement XIII, Albani was able to tell Henry that if Charles Edward came to Rome, the Pope would receive him with benevolence and paternal love.[41] Again there was no overt commitment to recognise the prince as Charles III, but at this stage Henry was well content and thanked Albani for his efforts.[42]

Henry's next move was to persuade Cardinal Albani to write to Charles Edward with these assurances and to invite him to Rome.[43] Albani then returned to the attack inside the Vatican. He successfully lobbied Cardinal Rezzonico and the ambassador of Malta. At his

next audience with the Pope, Henry brought letters of support for
Charles from these two. Again the Pope temporised. He said that the
question of recognising the Stuart prince as Charles III was so
complex that he would have to refer it to a special congregation of
cardinals. Albani pointed out that such a move would inevitably sour
relations with Charles Edward. The Pope remained unmoved.[44]

The reality of the situation in Rome was that prospects for Charles
Edward's recognition as Charles III were nothing like so propitious
as the prince himself assumed. Charles read Albani's letters as a firm
commitment from the Pope on this score. His mood was jaunty as
he prepared to quit Bouillon.[45]

Even so, he received enough warnings from his followers that he
was on shifting sands. Seeing the extent to which the Pope was
stalling, Henry thought it necessary to brief his brother on the tricky
political conjuncture. The crisis with the Jesuits made this a peculiarly bad time to approach the Vatican with a fresh political
conundrum. That was why it was essential for the prince to arrive
in Rome before James died. Clement's hand would then be forced:
he would either have to recognise the prince forthwith or expel him.
Henry ended by stressing the importance of getting the support of
France and Spain for the claim.[46]

Jacobites resident in France considered that getting the support of
Versailles would be no easy matter. The prince's past record did not
predispose the French court in his favour. Choiseul, especially, was
well known to be unflinchingly hostile to him.[47] Lady Webb suggested
that it might be better to try to win Spain over first, since the French
view seemed to be that they would recognise the prince as king of
England only when some other Catholic power had already done
so.[48] With this in mind, Charles Edward appointed the comte de
Serrant, Walsh's brother, as his minister in Spain and sent him off
to Madrid with a personal appeal to Charles III for recognition.[49]

So far the prince had acted with unwonted dispatch for this period
of his life. But he wasted valuable time winding up his affairs in
Bouillon and Avignon. He was in no doubt about his reception in
Rome. All boats were to be burned and all his effects transferred
there. To Stafford in Avignon he sent the unsentimental message:
'All the dogs to be disposed of, even the big one.'[50]

Yet, though he considered himself rushed and remained querulous
that he had to proceed to Paris without visiting Lunéville,[51] the
prince's preparations for the journey were stately and leisurely. An
apartment had been prepared for his use in Paris, but it was 12
December 1765 before he arrived in the French capital.[52] Then he

wasted further time, securing immunity from baggage checks and a multiplicity of *laissez-passer* documents before he departed southwards.[53] It was the last day of 1765, ironically the day before his father died, before he finally left Paris for Rome.[54]

Meanwhile in Rome events were moving too fast for him. On 1 January 1766, at 9.15 p.m., James finally gave up the ghost. Henry sent instructions through Andrew Lumisden that the prince should halt at the Albani palace at Urbino until he had secured recognition from the Pope.[55] Then he learned that the Pope intended to come to a definite decision on Charles Edward in early January. In a hastily-scribbled postscript, he asked the prince not to stop at Urbino but to come straight on to Rome.[56]

Then Henry sat down to compose a long memorandum to the Pope on the reasons why his brother should be recognised as king of England. He pointed out that five Popes had already recognised the Stuarts as *de jure* monarchs of England, Scotland and Ireland. Failure to recognise Charles Edward now would be to mock the memory of previous holders of the keys of St Peter. It would also be tantamount to denying that monarchs ruled by divine right.[57]

Henry accompanied his public memoir with a private letter to the Pope. The tone was mawkish. He expatiated on the bitterness of the blow of non-recognition to 'two orphan princes', a blow that would be delivered not by the enemies of the Church but by the Vicar of Christ himself. He ended with the somewhat injudicious quotation: 'if it be possible, let this chalice pass from me.'[58]

The memoir and the letter were delivered to the Pope by Cardinal Gianfrancesco Albani. The Pope read them and said he would seek further advice from the conclave. He asked Henry to make no further use of the memorial in the meantime. On the evening of 3 January Clement received Henry in audience. Henry pressed hard, but could get no concession other than permission to circulate his memoir to members of the Sacred College.[59] Dissatisfied with this response, Henry sent his paper to Cardinal Orsini, Minister of Naples; to Spanish Minister Asprus; and to the French ambassador the marquis d'Aubeterre.[60]

All three ministers obtained audience with Cardinal Secretary of State Torregiani and pressed Charles Edward's case. At the same time Henry wrote to the kings of France, Spain and Naples with supporting letters from their envoys.[61]

The Pope was already annoyed with Henry for, as he saw it, going behind his back to the French and Spanish. But now Cardinal York made an even more disastrous blunder. Alarmed at the Pope's foot-dragging, and afraid that the Pontiff might wriggle off the hook by claiming there was no clear constituency for recognising Charles Edward, Henry published the entire three-way correspondence between himself, the prince and Albani.[62]

This piece of consummate folly immediately alienated Albani. Justifiably, he protested that his efforts had been made in good faith and in confidence. Henry had no right to try to pre-empt the issue.[63] Henry lost a valuable ally. Albani was so angry at Cardinal York's faithlessness and duplicity that he was minded to denounce him publicly. His friends dissuaded him on the grounds that it was he himself who would look most foolish in such an exposure. Ominously, Albani proceeded instead to underline the distinction between a promise of welcome to the papal states – which he *had* made to Charles Edward – and the very different question of his recognition as *king*, which had never been promised.[64]

Henry had made powerful enemies. The Pope's selection of cardinals for the conclave that would decide Charles Edward's fate reflected this. The strongly pro-Stuart Cardinal Negroni was pointedly excluded.[65] Included was the notorious Hanoverian spy Cardinal Alessandro Albani, whose presence on the payroll of British intelligence was an open secret.[66] The other cardinals selected were either creatures of the Pope or dyed-in-the-wool supporters of the House of Austria. The full complement of the congregation held at the Quirinal on 14 January 1766 to decide whether or not to recognise Charles Edward as king was so weighted as to make the decision appear a foregone conclusion. Apart from Secretary of State Torregiani and Alessandro Albani, the others present were cardinals Rezzonico, Cavalchini, Ferroni, Antonelli, Castelli, Deprossi, Sorberoni and Stoppani.[67]

The conclave was immediately sworn to the secret of the Inquisition. Then Henry's long memoir was read out. This was generally considered very weak in its argumentation.[68] Once it had been read, the Pope proceeded to outline his objections to Henry's theses. His basic premise was that the interests of Catholicism in general must take precedence over those of the House of Stuart. At the moment the Catholic religion was tolerated in England. Large numbers of Catholics were emigrating from England to north America, holding out the hope that the Americas might some day be solidly Catholic. All this would be in jeopardy if the English were provoked into abandoning their policy of leniency.[69] Not only would Catholics be driven out of England, but English tolerance for Catholic missionaries in foreign lands, especially north America, would cease. Bringing the savages to God surely had to have a higher priority in the eyes of the Church than the interests of the House of Stuart.[70] Besides, the Pope pointed out, it was chimerical to hope for the restoration of Catholicism in England through the return of the Stuarts. It was now two hundred years since Pius V had excommunicated Queen Elizabeth.[71]

Summing up, the Pope pointed to a number of reasons why it was folly for the Vatican to recognise the Stuart prince as Charles III. The interests of Catholicism, the continuity of good relations between the Vatican and England, even the trade of the papal states depended on not provoking the English into retaliatory measures over the Stuarts.

Henry had lost the support of Cardinal Rezzonico through his treatment of Francesco Albani. But even Rezzonico was unhappy with this cavalier survey of the state of affairs. What about the fact that Clement had recognised James as king of England and his son as Prince of Wales?[72] If the Jacobite doctrine of divine right and passive obedience was jettisoned, what was the basis for papal recognition of the kingdom of Naples, or the duchies of Parma and Piacenza? In particular, if continuity was being stressed, how was it possible that Charles Edward had been recognised since 1720 as heir apparent to the English throne but now suddenly no longer was?[73] Moreover, if the Vatican recognised the House of Hanover as legitimate, it would also have to accept that any future actions, however draconian, that that regime took against English Catholics were justifiable; you could not logically recognise a regime as legitimate while repudiating its actions as illegitimate.[74]

Alessandro Albani tried to shift the argument back to practicalities. If the Pope recognised Charles Edward, the English would bombard Ancona and Civitavecchia.[75] Admiral Matthews had come close to this in 1745.[76] It was even conceivable that a military force would be landed on the territory of the papal states.[77]

At this point Charles Edward's one and only clear supporter in the conclave came forward to answer these and other points. Cardinal Stoppani scouted the idea that the English would take military action in retaliation for recognition of the prince.[78] This had not happened when the Vatican recognised James III, even though there were more compelling reasons then, as Jacobite rebellion was endemic in Britain. Was it really conceivable that the English would spend a vast sum of money sending warships against the papal states? Landing troops was a childish fantasy, since 'scorched earth' tactics could be used against the invader. Even a naval attack on the papal states was politically perilous, since it would look like an assault on the entire Catholic religion. In any case, Alessandro Albani's arguments could be turned on their head. If England was as stable as he claimed, the authorities there could afford to treat the recognition of 'Charles III' with contempt.

Stoppani then launched a strong attack on the other arguments so far marshalled.[79] It was absurd to argue that Catholics would be expelled from Canada if Charles Edward was recognised as king. Quite apart from the poor propaganda image presented to the world, the English had other factors to ponder. Many of England's most important trading partners were Catholic nations. Would England really jeopardise such commerce just because the Pope recognised Charles Edward? It was absurd, too, to argue that missionaries would be driven from north America. The civil authorities knew very well that the Indians there were held in check by the moderating influence of the missionaries. To expel them would be to remove an important element in the social cement of the American colonies.

Stoppani's arguments had a powerful effect on his audience. A consensus seemed to be emerging that the Pope should postpone any definite decision until he saw the line France and Spain were going to take.[80] Some of the anti-Stuart cardinals even advocated expelling Charles Edward when he came to Rome, simply to test the proposition that Spain and France would welcome him with open arms.[81]

But Clement XIII dug in his heels. It was for him to lead, not follow.[82] Again he brought his audience back to the question of political legitimacy: since England had a settled regime, it was absurd to pretend that some wandering prince was its rightful ruler. Besides, whereas there had been an equation between the interests of James and of Catholicism, this did not apply to his son. Both James and his father James II had actually sacrificed good chances of restoration to the English throne rather than abandon their Catholic faith.[83] Charles Edward, on the other hand, seemed to be a religious turncoat, an apostate twice over. Could he really be relied on to be a good Catholic monarch and, if not, did not the very foundation of Stoppani's argument collapse – that Vatican credibility depended on recognition of Charles Edward?[84]

Finally, the Pope pointed out that Stoppani's argument about the bombardment was too clever by half. It was precisely the domestic turmoil he had referred to that had stayed the British military hand in that epoch and created the context in which it was meaningful to speak of James III as a legitimate monarch.

It was time for a final decision. Aubeterre was known to be exerting tremendous pressure on the Pope for recognition, but was this Choiseul's own policy or merely Aubeterre's personal predilection?[85] It was common knowledge that Aubeterre had instructions to press the Pope hard to suppress the Jesuit orders but logically that should run counter to support for the supposedly pro-Jesuit Stuarts. Besides, Clement had good intelligence from Paris on British diplomatic pressure there.[86] He also knew that the Imperial court opposed recognition. Prince Kaunitz was actually lobbying other European courts not to support the Stuarts.[87] Clement felt that this was an occasion for boldness. He asked for a vote to be taken. With Stoppani alone opposing, it was decided not to grant the prince recognition as Charles III of England, Scotland and Ireland.[88]

It fell to Torregiani to convey the bad news to Henry.[89] The consequence was that when Charles Edward arrived in Rome, instead of being welcomed as Charles III, he found himself a virtual pariah.

The prince had a hard journey to the Eternal City, via Strasbourg, Innsbruck, Bologna and Florence. He was still suffering from a cold and a sore head when he set out from Paris to brave the rigours of winter.[90] In Italy the bad news came north to meet him. As a way out of his embarrassment, Henry suggested that the prince stay at the palace at Caprarola belonging to the kingdom of Naples. This would place the prince in a royal palace, outside the Pope's jurisdiction, yet no more than half a day's journey from Rome.[91]

But the prince insisted on pressing on to Rome. He argued that Cardinal Albani's famous letter of October 1765 *guaranteed* him papal recognition. Andrew Lumisden met him two posts beyond Florence, only to find that his royal master had just narrowly escaped death.[92] On the road one post out from Bologna his coach had overturned. Several passengers were hurt, but not the prince. The coach itself came very close to crashing over a precipice. Although Lumisden testified that the prince had lost none of his charm, he was in a bad way physically, with excessively swollen legs and feet.

Charles was pleased to learn that the queen's apartment in the Palazzo Muti had been prepared for him. He asked Lumisden to see to it that his baggage passed the Ponte Molle unexamined. Then he continued his journey, halting at San Quirico and Montefiascone. The trip was a terrible one. All the roads to Rome were sheeted in snow and ice.[93] Charles Edward had a cold coming of it in every sense.

On the evening of Thursday 23 January 1766 the prince entered Rome, a city he had last seen twenty-two years before.[94] Henry had organised a claque to call out '*Viva Il Re!*' when he entered the Piazza

S. Apostoli.[95] This was scarcely enough to assuage his brother's wounded feelings. Charles Edward felt that he had been lured to Rome under false pretences. He was bitter at what he considered Henry's incompetent lobbying of the Pope.[96]

The prince's supporters tried to encourage him, in three main ways. There had always been those in the Jacobite movement who considered that it was a mistake for the prince to go to Rome in any circumstances whatever.[97] These people now advanced the consoling argument that the estrangement of prince and Pope would work in his favour with English Jacobites worried about the bugbear of 'popery', and would appeal to the same constituency that had applauded his defiance of Louis XV in 1748.[98]

Another familiar comforting tenet was that Clement XIII could not live long and that the issue would have to be considered anew by his successor. As Lumisden put it: 'The government here is different from that of any other country. It is a continual flux that depends on the precarious life of an old man. As soon as this Pope dies, there is a total change of government. A new Pope produces a new Ministry, who lie under no obligation to pursue the measures of the former.'[99]

The third argument was that France and Spain could yet be mobilised to force Clement XIII to reverse his decision. Still in hopes, Charles Edward sent off letters to Louis XV, Charles III of Spain and Ferdinand, king of the Three Sicilies.[100] These hopes proved the most groundless of all. France took its cue on this matter from the Vatican; Spain in turn followed the French lead. As soon as Clement's decision was known, Choiseul and Praslin reprimanded Aubeterre for his pro-Stuart stance and ordered him to toe the line.[101] Similar orders to their ministers were issued at Naples and Madrid. Aubeterre became the laughing-stock of Europe.[102] Serrant's mission in Spain turned into an abysmal farce.[103]

Horace Mann was jubilant. France, Spain, the Vatican, all quaked at the might of the British.[104] This triumph, said Mann, was 'the most glaring proof of the submission to George III of the Court which excommunicated Elizabeth and all her descendants . . . if it is not sufficient, I will send the Pope to St. James's with his triple crown, that the king may tip it off with his foot'.[105]

Not surprisingly, the prince spent his first month in Rome in a state of even more acute depression than normal. For the first few days he got out of bed only for dinner and supper, under the excuse that he was recovering from the effects of the overturning of the coach.[106] So as to avoid meeting the Pope, he adopted the title of

Baron Douglas, while actually arrogating to himself royal privileges. The day after his arrival, Henry went back to see the Pope to renew his brother's claims. An acrimonious discussion took place. Henry was so angry at the Pope's unyielding posture that he decided to take matters into his own hands.[107]

Openly defying the Pope, he took to carrying Charles around the streets of Rome in his coach, with his brother on the right hand side, evincing a deference which cardinals were supposed to show to a crowned head.[108] Similarly thumbing his nose at his own court, Cardinal Orsini, the Neapolitan minister, visited Charles Edward and treated him like a king.[109] Cardinal Guglielmi also caused scandal by addressing Charles as 'Your Majesty'.[110] Finally, the Jesuits, then locked in a life-and-death struggle with the Papacy, saw a chance to use the prince as a wedge. The rectors of the Scots and Irish Jesuit colleges both recognised him as 'Charles III'.[111]

But Clement XIII was not the sort of man to be trifled with. He struck back vigorously. Another congregation of cardinals was held. It was decided that Secretary of State Torregiani should command the Cardinal Dean of the Sacred College, in charge of protocol, to require all cardinals to follow the line towards the Stuarts laid down by the Pope.[112] Recognition of the prince as Charles III became almost as much a treasonable matter in Rome as in England. The rectors of the Scots and Irish colleges were expelled from Rome together with the superiors of two Irish convents.[113] To cap all, while Charles Edward was away with Henry at Albano, the coat of arms of England was taken down from the door of the Palazzo Muti.[114] All signs of the Stuarts as a royal house were expunged from Rome.

It seemed that the prince had reached the nadir of his fortunes. He had now suffered the ultimate humiliation. He had returned to the city he swore never to see again only to find himself worse off than at Bouillon.

34

'King Charles III'
(1766–70)

There was just one small consolation for the prince as he settled in at the Palazzo Muti. His days of living from hand to mouth, one jump ahead of his creditors, seemed to be over, for in James's will considerable monies had been left to Charles.[1] In France James had income from town houses, investments in the Hôtel de Ville, and certain other real estate revenues which Dunbar and the dowager countess Inverness were enjoying in usufruct, but which would revert to the prince on their death. As a result of a series of trade-offs with Henry, the prince was the beneficiary of all Stuart income in France (apart from ecclesiastical benefices). In addition he owned the 100,000 Roman crowns (about £25,000) deposited in the Monte di Pietà, plus all the jewels and precious pieces held there.

On the other hand, James required his elder son to keep up all the pensions and payments to his vast army of dependants and clients.[2] And, now that the prince had inherited the so-called wealth of the Stuarts, Jacobite hangers-on who had not been heard of for a decade or more came forward with hard-luck stories, asking for money.[3] Mann waxed lyrically incredulous at the wealth of the Stuarts but, as Lumisden soon found out, the account books in the Palazzo Muti told a story not nearly so rosy.[4]

The prince set about regularising his household. Andrew Lumisden, who had been royal secretary since Edgar's death in 1762, intended to quit the service after the transfer of power, but Charles persuaded him to stay on.[5] Chief among the prince's other 'gentlemen' was John Hay of Restalrig, principally known for his disastrous failure over the commissariat just before Culloden. The prince appointed him major-domo and created him a baronet of Scotland on 31 December 1766.[6] There was the faithful John Stewart, who had accompanied the prince from Scotland, was imprisoned with him, sacked, restored to favour, and then led the private search for Clementina Walkinshaw in 1760. Stewart had sailed close to the wind with Charles Edward before, but had always remained just inside his master's favour. Two other veterans of the '45 completed the 'court' at the Palazzo Muti: Captain Adam Urquhart and Lachlan Mackintosh, who had actually commanded a clan regiment.[7]

There was one other of James's old retainers that Charles Edward thought worth keeping on. The Welsh clergyman, Rev. Mr Wagstaffe, formerly the Protestant chaplain, was retained by the prince as a wink and a nod to the English Jacobites that the Stuart heart was still really Anglican. The prince was always a trimmer when it came to organised religion. He did not oppose it with Voltairean intensity, merely despised it utterly.

Rather than bow the knee to the Pope, the prince preferred to remain incognito. This meant that he could not be received by polite society.[8] On the other hand, despite the attitude of their governments, he was frequently visited by the ambassadors of Spain, France and Malta.[9] At first Charles was content to be quietly defiant. He treated the Pope's absurd offer to recognise him as the Prince of Wales with the contempt its logic deserved.[10]

Once his legs were free of their dropsical swelling, he was out and about in Rome, now masked in the Corso, now at the opera in the French ambassador's box.[11] But he chafed at not being able to go hunting.[12] His attitude, as expressed to his brother at the end of March, was surely tongue-in-cheek: 'My health is, thank God, good, though my heart is not content, but my trust in the Being of Beings is my consolation.'[13]

The question remained: how long would he remain in Rome with such an uncertain and unsatisfactory status? Bologna was raised as a possible permanent residence. Aubeterre advised him to stay in the papal states until he had exhausted all possible diplomatic pressure on the European courts.[14] This meant keeping on in the Palazzo Muti pending further developments. Caprasola and San Marino remained as last-ditch sanctuaries. In the meantime Louis XV and Charles III of Spain would have to be pressurised to find him somewhere to live that afforded the same dignity James had enjoyed.

The chief problem here was that there was no hope for the prince as long as Choiseul remained at the helm in Versailles. Choiseul's anti-prince attitudes had, if anything, hardened since 1759.[15] Charles Edward's heavy drinking was well known to provide Choiseul with all the ammunition he needed to shoot down any overtures on behalf of the prince. Pointing out that massive consumption of wine was a slow but sure poison, Choiseul argued that it was senseless for France to lobby the Vatican for the Stuart cause, since the prince would soon die from drink anyway.[16] Choiseul added caustically that it was James's abstention from hard liquor that had contributed to his high reputation throughout Europe.

Frustrated at every turn, Charles took to spending as much time as possible outside Rome. After hunting at Palidoro in April, he paid a fleeting visit to the Palazzo Muti before departing for a long spell at Frascati.[17] In May he was at Albano for the *villegiatura*. There were many dinners with Henry, when Charles would try to broach his schemes for nominating cardinals off his own bat '*pour épater le Vaticane*'.[18] He complained to Thibault that the Italian hunting was not a patch on the shoots he had enjoyed in the Ardennes.[19] Most of all, there was the ever-increasing fondness for Cyprus wine.[20]

As 1766 entered its last months, Charles Edward's bitterness about the Pope remained unabated. The last straw was when Clement confiscated his carriage and horses for displaying royal colours. The prince acidly remarked that he thought he would go to Venice, where there were no horses but only boats.[21]

From the beginning of September until the end of November, Charles brooded at Albano.[22] He still sent no definite orders for the dispatch of the residue of his effects from Avignon and Bouillon.[23] He toyed with the idea of making a home in various localities, but as quickly discarded the notions. Valmonte, Cisterna, Venice, Avignon, Paris: the prince had only to think of them to find some compelling reason why he could not bear a permanent domicile in any of them.[24] In the end he admitted that the problem was insoluble and ordered Stafford to remove from Avignon, lock, stock and barrel.[25]

The prince remained at Albano, taking what consolation he could from playing the cello. But music and the chase did not compensate for the lack of good conversation and cultivated society, especially since the scarcity of game at Albano diminished the returns from hunting.[26] And always there was the constant throb of pain from his humiliation by Choiseul and the Madrid court.[27]

Rome, when he returned there in the New Year, was no better. There were visits to the Argentina and Aliberti theatres, but Clement XIII had cut back on Roman spectacles and the 1767 carnival was cancelled.[28] Charles Edward's depression and inebriation became acute. There exists a rambling, sprawling letter the prince wrote to Henry in February 1767, obviously written in a drunken state, in which Charles pours out his woes and frustrations while muttering darkly about his duty before God and men.[29] The prince's declining mental condition is also evinced by a maniacal insistence on secrecy in the matter of conveying his effects from Avignon to Rome, as if he were still the hero of the '45 and not a paper tiger and plaything of Mann.[30]

It may well have been the receipt of the shocking missive above, showing the extent of the prince's degeneration, that impelled Henry to try to patch up relations between his brother and the Pope. After conferring with Charles at Frascati in April, Henry implemented his plan.[31] In May 1767 Clement XIII and Charles Edward at last came face to face. On the evening of Saturday 9 May the Pope received the prince in private audience. Charles was supposed to be a private nobleman but went to the meeting quite openly, making no attempt at disguise.[32]

Clement had his own devices for putting the prince in his place. While Henry, as Cardinal York, was admitted at once to the papal chambers, Charles was kept waiting and then called for as 'the brother of Cardinal York'.[33] On entering the chamber, the prince was obliged to kneel and kiss the Pope's foot and to remain kneeling until the Pontiff commanded him to rise.[34] Recalling his mirth about the Pope's toe in the '45, we can see how low (literally) the prince had now come. This was reality. What he had refused a Pope as child was now forced from him as a middle-aged man.

An audience of a quarter of an hour ensued, with Henry working hard as go-between. The prince repeated his claims; the Pope reiterated that he could live in Rome on a proper footing only if he relinquished them. The prince in reply tried bluster. He said that Culloden had done him the sort of damage alongside which papal injustices were a mere trifle.[35] Both the Pope and the prince expressed themselves satisfied with the interview. Henry, however, complained privately of his brother's 'indocility and most singular way of thinking and arguing'.[36]

Henry no more understood his brother than James had. He could not cope with the violent mood swings, the rapid oscillation between charm and anger. It was characteristic of the prince to be angry with someone, then be charming and courteous to their face, then revert to rage. This was not insincerity or hypocrisy. The prince was a hopeless diplomat. He could not be firm with people while not alienating them. He had two modes: wit and charm, designed to cajole the opposition; and violent anger if such cajolery failed.

In July Henry offered to keep Charles Edward a place in St Peter's at his side, to watch the Pope's canonisation ceremonies. The prince declined; 'I think it improper for me to be present at any of the Pope's ceremonies until His Holiness shall do me the justice to receive me with all these distinctions that are due to me.'[37]

He proceeded to lay claim again to his father's prerogative of nominating cardinals.[38] Since 1767 was the year of the expulsion of the Jesuits from their utopia in the Paraguayan reductions, the Society of Jesus, with its own scores to settle with Clement XIII, were happy to support the prince. So too were the Benedictines. Their procurator in Rome castigated the head of the order for failing to give Charles Edward his proper title of Charles III.[39]

The ordeal continued. The prince spent a dreadful autumn at Albano in alcoholic despair, and with a protracted cold.[40] Henry wrung his hands over his brother's drinking but could see no light on the horizon until Clement XIII was dead.[41]

The year 1768 saw a further decline in the prince's fortunes. This time the occasion was the collapse of the miniature court he had installed around him. Andrew Lumisden had long been seeking an honourable exit from the prince's service. Under James he had been able to provide relief for many distressed Scottish Jacobites. Under Charles, the parlous state of finances at the Palazzo Muti made this impossible and removed Lumisden's principal motive for staying on.[42] But it was difficult to resign without seeming to abandon the prince – he had few enough 'gentlemen' around him as it was.[43]

So for three years Lumisden soldiered on beneath a crushing burden of duties. A letter to his sister in late 1766 reveals both his own despair and the futility of the prince's existence:

Almost from break of day to midnight I am employed about the king [sic]. Besides serving him as his secretary, I am obliged to attend him as a gentleman of the bedchamber when he goes abroad, both morning and evening, and after dinner and supper I retire with him into his closet. Add to this the time we sit at the table, and you will see I have not a moment to myself. I am never in my apartment but either to sleep or write. But this is not all. We have been five of the nine months since the king's coming into Italy either at Albano or other parts of the country, a' shooting, and which kind of wandering life is more likely to increase than diminish. . . . I have lived for many years in a sort of bondage; but I may name these past months a mere slavery. Yet I readily submit to every inconvenience, when honour and duty call on me to do so.[44]

The interdiction on polite company at the Palazzo Muti added to the strain. Moreover, it was not unknown for the prince to threaten his staff with physical violence when drunk.[45] All this for just twenty crowns (five pounds) a month plus board and lodging for Lumisden and the other 'gentlemen'. It was very quickly too much for Lachlan Mackintosh. But his fate showed what could happen to those who crossed the prince. Mackintosh threw up his post in 1767 but the prince promptly stopped his pension. Unable to eke out a living in France, Mackintosh crawled meekly back to Rome, cap in hand. The prince refused to readmit him to his service.[46]

The strains in the Palazzo Muti came to a head in December 1768. Apart from a visit to Viterbo early that year, the prince had done little but drink.[47] His supporters vainly tried to justify his alcoholism. Bishop Gordon in Scotland put it like this:

It was true indeed that the king had been in use for some time past to call frequently for t'other glass of wine at dinner and supper, not from any liking to liquor, but like one absent in mind when he met things that vexed him, as was too often the case.[48]

But Lumisden and the others close to him knew that this was a facile description of a very serious problem.

The prince was also bothered with an ominous swelling on the neck.[49] His drunken rages increased in intensity. Finally, on 14 December 1768, in a state of advanced intoxication, he ordered Lumisden and the other courtiers to accompany him to the theatre to hear an oratorio. To a man they refused. Almost expiring with fury, the prince dismissed them on the spot.[50]

Next morning he had sobered up and he regretted his hasty action. But it was already too late. He had provided Lumisden and the others with the pretext they had been looking for. In vain the prince called on Henry to get them to change their minds. Henry agreed with Lumisden that the prince was now impossible. Privately, he urged the dismissed gentlemen not to return to the prince's service. He even urged the valet John Stewart and the Rev. Mr Wagstaffe, who were not involved in the disgraceful dismissal scene, to quit his brother's employ. They, however, declined, for reasons that remain obscure. The places of Lumisden, Urquhart and Hay were taken by Italians.[51]

The prince retaliated for the 'insolence' of the dismissed trio by calling for their mail at the Roman post office, opening it and reading it. Henry was deeply shocked at this behaviour.[52] Lesser men might have been tempted to reveal all they knew to Hanoverian spymasters, but Lumisden refused even to censure the prince to the Jacobite inner circle. He accepted his sister's argument that excessive stress provided a reason, if not a justification, for the prince's behaviour. Lumisden refused to discuss his master's outrageous conduct even with Jacobite intimates.[53] Those who claim that the allegedly great and good Lord Marischal had no option but to respond to Charles Edward the way he did should ponder the example of the genuinely magnanimous Andrew Lumisden.

One beneficial, albeit short-term, consequence of the Lumisden débâcle was that the prince made an effort to give up drinking. Doubtless this accounted for the physical description the Scottish non-juring bishop Gordon was able to give of him in 1769:

> Not a blot, not so much as a pimple was in his face, though maliciously given out by some as if it were all over blotted; but he is jolly and plump, though not to excess, being still agile and fit for undergoing toil.[54]

But the received opinion was that the loss of his Scottish courtiers and their replacement by Italians was bad propaganda for the prince, as it seemed to suggest he was embroiled even more tightly in the coils of Rome. In 1771 Edmund Burke, while denying his own Jacobitism, pointed to the absurdity of being attached to a person 'when he is deserted by the whole world and by himself, when he has, as I am told, not so much as a single Scotch, English or Irish footman about him'.[55]

At long last, some relief was promised in 1769. The much-hoped for event transpired. Clement XIII, scourge of Charles Edward, died in April. The prince nervously awaited the election of his successor, knowing that this was probably his last chance of settling in Rome on anything like a civilised basis.[56] His hopes were pinned on Cardinal Stoppani, the man who had spoken out for him in the 1766 conclave.[57] But his strategy was unusually cautious. He advised Henry not to push the new Pope, whoever he was, to decide immediately on acknowledging him as Charles III; the best policy was to lead up to it gradually. The new Pontiff should be asked whether in all conscience he could recognise a usurper and whether Clement XIII's actions had not brought Catholicism into dispute. Most of all, Henry should stress that it was only the prince's steadfast embrace of Catholicism that had lost him the throne in 1745–6.[58] It is difficult to know whether the last point was conscious humbug or self-delusion.

All the prince's hopes for recognition were soon dashed. The new Pope, ex-cardinal Ganganelli, a Franciscan and the only member of the regular clergy in the Sacred College, had his hands full with the Jesuit crisis. He had no wish to introduce further complications into the international diplomacy of the Vatican by recognising a Stuart pretender.[59] Henry promised to do what he could, while stressing to his brother the almost insuperable obstacle posed by the (now anti-Stuart) representations of France and Spain. His advice to Charles was to stay out of Rome in the strictest incognito until the dust had settled.[60]

The prince reacted with a mixture of incredulity and self-pity.[61] The one positive statement he made was to ask for the earliest possible audience with the new Pope. The request was granted in mid-June 1769. The contrast with his previous papal audience was marked. Although certain Jacobites had affected to despise this jumped-up Franciscan who now bore St Peter's keys,[62] the prince found himself treated with every courtesy by Clement XIV. The Pope received him standing and would not permit Charles to kiss his foot.[63] After embracing him with affection, Clement reminded him of the time when he had served James as chaplain.

The Pope remained standing while he explained his position. He personally would like nothing more than to restore the prince to the titles and dignities formerly enjoyed by his father. But in matters of high politics, collegiate rule was the norm. There was the continuing crisis with the Jesuits, pressure from France and Spain, and the position of Catholics in England to consider.[64]

For once the tables were turned. The charmer was himself charmed. The prince agreed to Clement's suggestion that he appear freely in Roman society under an assumed name. After three years of banging his head against a wall, and after the sincere blandishments of the new Pope, Charles accepted that this was one struggle he could never win. It was agreed that the prince would appear openly in Rome as Baron Renfrew; the Vatican would attempt to make straight the social ways.[65]

But the prince soon found the taste of his new-found liberty turning to ashes. After a long period as a recluse, he found social engagements taxing. For the past three years he had leaned heavily on Henry, but now pastoral duties increasingly called Cardinal York out of Rome to his seat at Frascati. The prince decided to leave Rome for a while. In August 1769 he set out for Viterbo to take the waters.

At Viterbo he bathed, relaxed, ate a sensible diet and generally followed the directions of his surgeon Dr Martelli: 'I find him to be a sensible man and not a sophistical [sic] Aesculapius.'[66] In addition, the nobility of Viterbo treated him hospitably and there was a good

opera season in progress. The prince stayed on through the autumn.
He informed Abbé Gordon that he had taken a fixed and unalterable
resolution not to answer letters from his old contacts, even those he
had a high regard for.[67] It was in vain that John Holker and others
wrote to him about the agitated state of England after the Wilkes
disturbances, which they somehow, dimly, thought might help the
Stuart cause. The prince was now devoting himself to pleasure. If
anyone impaired this pleasure by their insolence – like the Sgr Carletti
who sat beside him unbidden at the duchess of Lanti's assembly –
he had powerful friends like Cardinal Marefoschi to whom he could
appeal.[68]

The sojourn at Viterbo seemed to reanimate the prince. There was
a temporary return of his old energies, and 1770 saw him pushing
forward a number of projects. As his fiftieth birthday approached,
he began seriously to think about marriage. His concern was neither
dynastic nor prudential. More mundane considerations weighed: the
prince was once again short of money.[69]

Wanting a moneyed wife was one thing; obtaining the right kind
of match quite another. Charles Edward's first choice, the daughter
of the duc d'Orléans, turned out to be already engaged to the duc
de Bourbon.[70] The prince instructed his contact in Paris, the duc
de Fitzjames, to take discreet soundings concerning Marie-Anne,
daughter of the late Prince Frédéric de Deux Parts, who was now
approaching her seventeenth birthday.[71] After securing French
backing for the match, Fitzjames sent his agent to Germany to ask
for the princess's hand. The agent was left dangling, and eventually
the suit died of inanition.[72] The prince began to regret that he had not
been able to compass a marriage with the daughter of the landgrave of
Hesse-Darmstadt, back in 1749.[73]

At the same time as his marriage overtures (and not unconnected
with them) the prince looked around for fresh sources of income. A
composition of the so-called 'Fund of Ohlau' had never been arrived
at, largely because of the Byzantine complexities arising from negotiations with the Austrian and Polish courts and the counter-claims
of the Bouillon family. Now, in a fresh attempt to cut the Gordian
knot, the prince sent his kinswoman Princess Jablonowska to treat
with the Bouillons in Paris. Since the princess was sister-in-law to
the duchess of Bouillon, she seemed an entirely suitable mediatrix.[74]

The new sense of momentum the prince was generating also found
a physical expression. On his return to Rome from Viterbo he found
he could not settle. Accordingly, in July 1770 he set out for a

prolonged tour of Tuscany, intending to take in the baths at Pisa *en route*.[75]

The trip started badly. Though a papal state, Bologna failed to welcome the prince. Instead, the Bolognese senate sent him an insulting brush-off, described by Henry as 'preposterous and, as Your Majesty justly observes, very Hibernian'.[76]

Charles Edward could not wait to shake the dust of Bologna off his feet. He proceeded to Florence, calling first at Arezzo and the fair at Sinigaglia. At Sinigaglia he was said to have lurched about the thronged streets, roaring drunk in broad daylight.[77]

Florence was the home of Sir Horace Mann. The elderly diplomat vainly tried to browbeat the authorities into refusing to receive the prince.[78] Yet Florentine reception of Charles Edward was cool. He cut a figure at the casino and the theatre, wearing the Garter and with the Cross of St Andrew at his buttonhole. As usual he was a hit with the ladies.[79] But his arrival did at least give Mann the opportunity to take detailed notes on the Italian staff that had replaced Lumisden, Hay and Urquhart in 1768. The two principals were the count Spada and the count Vegha, who were accompanied by two Roman gentlemen, one of them styled 'master of horse'.[80]

The prince made a point of finding out whether Horace Mann was to be present before attending a concert at the house of the ambassador from Lucca.[81] Then he went on to Leghorn before settling at Pisa for the waters. In Pisa he astonished onlookers by touching for the King's Evil.[82] The waters agreed with him. He reported on 27 August that the spa had produced an amazing effect in such a short time.[83]

From Pisa he proceeded to Lucca and Gricciano.[84] On his return to Florence, Mann scored a petty triumph when Charles Hadfield's English Inn refused to take Charles Edward's party in for fear of embarrassing the English guests. 'Foxes have holes and the birds of the air have nests, but I find the son of the Pretender could not find a place to lay his head in Florence,' jeered Mann's agent.[85] Never one to minimise his imagined achievements, Mann invented a story that the crowds surrounding the prince in Florence were less on his return visit. Not even the obvious rejoinder that there was no visible sign of this floored Mann; the Pretender, he claimed, was so thick-skinned that it was impossible to snub him.[86]

What Mann did not report to his superiors in London was that his diplomacy in Florence had largely been a failure. The chief Florentine minister Count Neri had shown Charles Edward such lavish courtesy that he was reprimanded by the Grand Duke of Tuscany in consequence.[87]

The prince remained in Florence until mid-October 1770. He then made a leisurely journey back to Rome, stopping again at the waters of Viterbo.[88] He arrived back in the Eternal City at the end of November.[89]

The six-month period from November 1770 is another 'black hole' in the prince's biography, or at least nearly so. All the evidence in this period points to an overall pattern of reclusive depression.[90] Yet it is evident that, with the new papal deal, the prince had already made some useful social contacts. In January 1771 the English traveller Lady Anne Miller was at the duchess of Bracciano's salon when 'Il Re' was announced.[91] Charles Edward then appeared, dressed in a scarlet coat, laced with broad gold lace. From his coat hung the blue riband, from which in turn was suspended an antique cameo as large as a woman's hand. To make his status as 'king' unmistakable to the English present, he wore the same garter, with the same motto, as that used by the 'true' order of St George in England.

The duchess confided to Lady Anne that it was the Pope's wish that no English travellers should speak to the prince and thus wreck the Vatican's tentative opening to the Court of St James. Lady Miller rightly decided that this was a fatuous interdiction. She made conversation with Charles, he asked her to speak in English, got to his feet when she left, and wished her goodnight.

A few nights later the two of them met at Princess Palestrina's, where the prince taught Lady Miller the card game *tarocchi*. Charles was evidently in good form that night, even finding time to make a joke at his own expense while he burlesqued Hanoverian clichés. Showing Lady Miller the *tarocchi* cards, he pointed to one and identified the figure as the Pope; then a second as the devil. With a laugh he turned to her. 'There is only one of the trio missing now and you know who that should be.'[92] The famous wit and charm could still be exercised when Charles wanted to turn it on.

Since we are now about to accompany the prince on a decade of steep decline, Lady Anne's description can serve as a fitting coda to his bachelor years. At the age of fifty, this is the physical picture the prince presented:

> He is naturally above the middle size but stoops excessively; he appears bloated and red in the face, his countenance heavy and sleepy, which is attributed to his having given into excess of drinking; but when a young man he must have been esteemed

handsome. His complexion is of the fair tint, his eyes blue, his hair light brown, and the contour of his face a long oval; he is by no means thin, has a noble presence and a graceful manner; . . . upon the whole he has a melancholic, mortified appearance.[93]

He was soon to have even more reason for his melancholia.

35

A Royal Marriage

(1771–4)

From the moment of his return to Rome in late 1770, the prince was actively planning his marriage. He sent Lord Caryll to Paris to begin negotiations with the French.[1] The prince's strategy was twofold. In the first place, he wanted a satisfactory financial settlement to arrest the pecuniary disorder in his own household. Dunbar's confused will (he died in 1770), leaving a legacy to Henry and the reversion of certain salt-mine revenues to Charles Edward, further compounded the chaos caused by the continuing squabbles over the Sobieski fortune and (later) the confusion resultant on the death of the banker Waters.[2] What the prince wanted from France, therefore, was a large, guaranteed annual subsidy.[3] Married with the encouragement of Louis XV, he then hoped to return to Rome with an unanswerable demand that the Vatican give him all the titles and honours granted to his father. Papal recognition was thus the second aim of his marriage.[4]

The first stage in the negotiations was entrusted to Lord Caryll. Born in 1716, Caryll first met Charles Edward at Gravelines in 1744 during the abortive invasion of England. An enthusiast ever since, in 1772 he was formally appointed to the position of secretary left vacant by Andrew Lumisden.[5]

Caryll began by talking to the duc de Noailles. Louis XV, smarting under the signal reverses of the Seven Years' War, still saw some advantages in maintaining the Stuarts as a gadfly on the English flank. If the Stuart prince produced heirs, the dynastic issue could be prolonged into the nineteenth century.

Before 1770 there had been a major snag. Choiseul, Britain's arch-enemy, who plotted tirelessly to redress the humiliations of the Seven Years' War, was also the prince's greatest critic at Versailles. His dismissal in 1770 cleared the way for French support for a Stuart marriage. Unfortunately, in the short-term his removal after eleven years at the helm increased political uncertainty, so that no firm decisions on great policy issues were being taken.[6]

After speaking to Noailles, Caryll enlisted the help of the duc de Fitzjames to get a passport for the prince. Fitzjames applied for one to the duc d'Aiguillon in the name of Douglas. After consulting Louis XV, d'Aiguillon replied that none was necessary. In their common interest, however, the prince should come to Paris in the greatest incognito.[7]

Meanwhile Fitzjames went ahead with the by no means subsidiary task of finding a suitable bride for Charles Edward. The prince had specified a German princess. This was designed as a means of keeping open the line to Protestantism which his residence in Rome might seem to have severed.[8]

Before his journey to Paris had been cleared with Versailles, the prince set out for Tuscany. His object was to disarm the suspicion that might arise if he left Rome suddenly. He gave out that he was travelling north to take the waters at Pisa.[9]

He left Rome in May 1771 and stayed two months in Pisa.[10] At the beginning of August he transferred to Siena.[11] It was there that Fitzjames's 'no passport needed' message reached him. On 17 August at 3 p.m., he suddenly left Siena, using the name of Stonor, Henry's private secretary.[12] Just outside the city walls a two-wheeled Italian post-chaise was waiting for him. Quickly the prince changed his clothes and put on a light round wig. To increase the confusion, when the post-chaise passed the Roman gate at Florence at midnight, he gave his name as Smith.[13]

By now Horace Mann's spies were on his trail. They followed him to Bologna, where they reported him keeping a handkerchief over his mouth to avoid recognition while the horses were changed. Then they tracked him to Modena. But at the foot of the Alps Mann's agents lost sight of him.[14]

The consternation aroused by the prince's disappearance in northern Italy testifies to the continuing power of his reputation and the morbid fear of him still entertained by the English government. Twenty-five years on the memory of Derby had still not evaporated. Those who had lived through Black Friday never really recovered from the shock. A drunkard the prince might be, but he was still considered a more dangerous enemy than a dozen sober Jameses.[15]

Speculation about the prince's destination became intense. The Pope himself was so anxious to know where Charles Edward was headed that he sent Secretary of State Cardinal Pallavicini to Henry, as if on a casual visit, to find out.[16] The more jittery English observers thought that his secret departure from Siena perhaps presaged a second coming in the Highlands.[17]

More sober analysts plumped for Poland. In 1771 the Polish confederation of Lithuania, Great Poland and Bar was opposing Stanislas II and was being secretly encouraged by France to declare the Polish throne vacant and expel the Russians. This 'confederacy of Bar' also had a religious dimension: it opposed the attempts of the 'dissidents' (Orthodox Christians and Protestants) to secure religious toleration in Poland.[18] The consensus of opinion was that Charles Edward was going to Poland to head the Confederates; less plausibly, it was also rumoured that he would join the dissidents.[19] Events that had a purely personal significance – such as Charles Edward's conferences with Princess Jablonowska in 1770 about the Sobieski money – were now reinterpreted sinisterly, as some grand Polish design.[20] Madame du Deffand's theory was that all the to-ing and fro-ing between d'Aiguillon and the Fitzjameses was to do with securing for the prince a Polish commission from Louis XV.[21] The Polish story became so well entrenched that the Polish minister at Rome (marquis Tommaso Antici) actually sent an express to Warsaw to warn the government that 'the Pretender' was on his way there.[22]

Reality soon broke through to smother all these fantasies. On the first day of September 1771 the prince arrived in Paris. He lodged at the Hôtel de Brunswick, rue des Prouvaines, near the rue St Honoré, under the name of Mr Douglas.[23] His arrival caught the Fitzjameses by surprise. The duke and marquis had been at Versailles and were obliged to 'wait on' the prince still in their country dress – a sufficiently serious breach of etiquette under the Ancien Régime for apologies to be necessary.[24]

Protocol also came to the fore in another sense. Since the prince was incognito, he could see no one but the Fitzjameses. All his negotiations with Louis XV were through the medium of the duc de Fitzjames (on his side) and the duc d'Aiguillon (representing the French king).[25]

The prince explained that he wanted French sanction for his marriage. It was imperative that the subsidies paid to James by Versailles, and discontinued on his death, be revived, so that he could make a credible marriage. In connection with the marriage itself, he asked Louis's permission to use the good offices of an Irish colonel in the French service.[26]

Louis XV replied that the marriage was agreeable to him, that he would settle all questions relating to passports and the furlough of the Irish officer concerned, and that he would settle the financial question with the duc de Fitzjames. The French king added that he would like to see similar subsidies forthcoming from Spain and the Vatican.[27]

Well satisfied, the prince employed Colonel Edmund Ryan of Berwick's foot regiment to make personal appearances at the various German courts to press his marriage suit.[28] The duc de Fitzjames would remain as the anchor in Paris while Charles Edward would take his son the marquis with him to Rome as liaison officer. The prince was pleased with himself. He wrote to his brother and to his great ally Cardinal Marefoschi of Macerata that he had secured all his aims in France. Then he gave Ryan a written power in his name to treat for the hand of the seventeen-year-old Marie-Louise Ferdinand, daughter of the Prince of Salm-Kyrbourg.[29]

In mid-September the prince left Paris for Italy, but not before he had revealed the other half of his strategy. He wanted to be treated like his father and have the incognito of Baron Renfrew discarded. Accordingly, he wanted Versailles to bring pressure on the Vatican, stressing French approval of the marriage and their renewal of a financial subsidy to the Stuarts.[30]

The prince returned to Rome with Caryll and Fitzjames. On the way back he ran into the black sheep of the Hanoverian family on the streets of Genoa. The duke of Gloucester had been virtually banished from England for his marriage to the dowager countess Waldegrave. He now spent much of his time wandering around Italy. The two men bowed graciously to each other and passed on.[31]

The prince spent four days with Caryll and Fitzjames at Pisa, taking the waters.[32] The rest of the journey was uneventful, except for a difficult passage of the flooded river Serchio near Pisa.[33] Charles Edward and party entered Rome on 12 October.[34]

The news he received there was a severe disappointment. His parting shot in Paris had been a bad miscalculation. Once the French realised that the prince intended to inveigle them into a wrangle with the Pope about recognising him as 'Charles III', they started to back-pedal on the question of a subsidy for the marriage.[35] The record is cloudy at this point, but the inference is that the prince, in a drunken rage, railed at the marquis de Fitzjames for having misled him.[36] Not wishing to stay any longer in the alcoholic miasma of the Palazzo Muti, the marquis offered to return to Paris to sort out the confusion.[37] But if the prince hoped for anything from his kinsman, it was a forlorn hope. Almost the first letter Fitzjames wrote on his return to

Paris was to inform Charles that the negotiations for the hand of the Princess of Salm-Kyrbourg had foundered.[38] This was a particular humiliation for the prince since, ever one to jump the gun, he had already announced his coming nuptials with this lady to the kings of France and Spain.[39]

Attention now switched to the Princess of Salm's first cousin Louise of Stolberg.[40] This was something of a soft option. So many marriage proposals had aborted that this time Ryan and Fitzjames were determined to net their catch. Louise's father was dead and she was one of four daughters in a family of reduced and, by aristocratic standards, straitened circumstances. The obstacles hitherto encountered with prima donna princesses were not likely to obtain this time.[41]

At this point the duc de Fitzjames took one of his convenient holidays. This was his invariable practice when under any kind of pressure. The prince's affairs were left to his son and Colonel Ryan. At the end of December 1771 Ryan arrived in Paris from Brussels with the news that his suit for the eldest Stolberg daughter had been successful.[42]

The duc de Fitzjames had shrewdly chosen his moment to exit. It fell to his son to write to Rome with exhaustive details of the Ryan negotiations. The Princess of Stolberg, senior, it turned out, had been so keen to marry off her girls that she offered the prince a choice of two: Louise, the eldest; and the third daughter, aged fifteen, described as 'big with a pleasant face'. The second girl was already married, and the fourth, of delicate health, was completing her education in a convent. Both on grounds of pulchritude and good sense Ryan and Fitzjames opted for Louise. She accepted the proposal without any hesitation or equivocation. After the vacillations and tergiversations experienced with other princesses, this matter-of-factness surprised Fitzjames.[43] Neither he nor the prince had any idea that they were dealing with a young woman of ruthless determination, shrewd and cunning beyond her eighteen years. The prospect of being 'a queen without a crown' did not disturb her. She was mature beyond her years, already a circumspect pragmatist.[44]

It remained to tie up the loose ends. Fitzjames sent on a genealogy of the Stolberg family. In return he requested a papal dispensation for the wedding and a marriage contract from Charles, plus a proxy for the actual ceremony. The prince got Caryll to write back, adding a few words in his own hand. He gave Ryan a proxy power to contract the marriage. The marriage portion to be settled on the princess was 40,000 livres a year, plus 10,000 livres pin money. The prince wrote to Fitzjames to specify the itinerary to be followed when bringing his bride to Italy. In a fateful decision he added: 'I have already informed you that I have chosen the eldest of the sisters. Her age is the most suitable for me, and what you have told me about the health of the younger confirms me in my resolution.'[45]

The preparations for the marriage show clearly that Charles Edward was a poor administrator. Ryan wrote back to query his instructions.[46] These spoke only of the financial settlement, allowances and jewels. But was the marriage contract to be governed by the laws of Flanders, France, Italy or even England?[47] Moreover, nothing had been said about an actual marriage ceremony in Paris. Was it the prince's intention that this should not take place?[48]

Ryan wanted no embarrassing scenes with the princess's family. Charles Edward was pressing for Louise to be sent to Italy as soon as possible.[49] But he did not seem to appreciate the delicacy of the steps Ryan and Fitzjames had to tread. So far the Stolberg family had co-operated admirably. They had seen the point of a private ceremony without notaries – since English spies could bribe notaries to let them have sight of the contract.[50] And the first instalment of money (36,000 livres) had been squeezed out of Versailles.[51] It was pointless, therefore, not to accommodate the wishes of the Stolbergs as far as possible. After all, without a formal *laissez partir* signed by the mother, technically the family could later plead duress or marriage by procuring.[52]

Charles Edward's inattention to detail may have been caused by the elaborate web he was now spinning to ensnare the Pope. His friend Cardinal Marefoschi had earlier advised him not to alienate Clement by trying to keep the marriage a secret.[53] Now Charles commissioned Marefoschi to insinuate the argument that his coming marriage changed everything. He therefore hoped that the Pope would receive him as his father had been received; even more, that his bride would be shown the same consideration as Clementina Sobieska. Marefoschi should stress to Clement that various cardinals (Calini, Canale, Corsini, Borghese, Orsini) already called him king. The coming nuptials gave the Vatican a chance to regularise the situation. A good outward symbol of the new relationship might be the restoration of the guard at the Palazzo Muti, and the provision of furniture for his wife, as in James's day.[54]

If these gentle persuasions failed, Marefoschi should bring pressure to bear on Cardinal Bernis. The argument should then be that France had insisted on Charles's marriage, but that the prince had only been able to find a suitable bride by promising her that the two of them would be on the same footing with the Pope as James and Clementina had been. Not to recognise him as king, then, meant that Louise could allege false pretences. Besides, Louis XV was just waiting for papal recognition of 'Charles III' before following suit himself.[55]

As a crowning touch, Charles Edward decided to time his overtures to the Pope so that he would be out of Rome when the hour of decision came. The Pope would probably wait until his return if he was going to reply in the negative. It would then be open for the prince to say that he naturally assumed the 'long silence' meant consent.[56] Just before he left Rome at the end of March 1772, the prince notified the Cardinal Secretary of State that he would no longer be known as Baron Renfrew, but expected henceforth to be addressed by the same title as his father.[57]

There was much cunning in this procedure, but, as so often with the prince, insufficient awareness of hard political realities. The truth was that Clement XIV had been engaged in secret negotiations with the roving duke of Gloucester. His aim was to better the conditions of English and Irish Catholics.[58] He did not intend to allow Stuart pretensions to stand in his way. Clement sent an invitation to the duke of Gloucester to visit Rome.[59] Gloucester arrived in the Eternal City on 25 February 1772, at the very time Charles Edward was bombarding the Vatican with his requests for recognition.[60]

Whether genuinely confident of a change of heart from Clement XIV, or merely self-deluded, Charles Edward pressed on with the preparations for his marriage. For months he had fretted impatiently. The prince was a man who wanted instant results. It seemed to him that Fitzjames and Ryan had been an unconscionable time finalising matters in Paris.[61] He was irritated and frustrated by the delays: 'moments are more precious than one can imagine in this affair.' He was especially infuriated by what he saw as legalistic nitpicking about the contract: the papers he had sent 'were as binding as words could make, both opposite to God and to man . . . approved by three people of logical mind, two of them cardinals'.[62]

But Ryan had run into fresh problems. The young lady earmarked as Louise's companion dropped out; a suitable replacement at short notice was not easy.[63] No sooner was this hiccup overcome than fresh problems presented themselves. The Stolberg party was due in Paris on 17–18 March to contract the marriage by proxy.[64] In the event, the princess and her mother did not arrive until the evening of the 19th. Immediately the princess, senior, gave clear signs of being the troublemaker she was. Not only did she object to the replacement companion found for Louise, but she and her relations insisted on inserting a written inventory of the wedding presents in the contract, even though Ryan pointed out that such insertions had no validity in law.[65]

Finally, on 22 March, the objections of the Stolberg matriarch were assuaged and the proxy marriage ceremony took place. Ryan and a M. de Betargh signed as proxies in the presence of the two Fitzjameses.[66] At long last, on Friday 27 March at 6 p.m., the proxy bride and her escort left the French capital. At the last minute one Mlle Power had been found to act as Louise's companion.[67]

The itinerary to Italy had been specified by Charles Edward with meticulous accuracy: Brussels, the Tyrol, Trentano, Bologna, Ancona, Macerata to Viterbo, where the marriage would be solemnised.[68] At some stage these arrangements were altered. It seems likely that Marefoschi, in compensation for the disappointment with the Pope that he saw looming, offered to marry the couple in Macerata, his own fief.[69]

But the prince's cup of frustration was not yet full. Ryan's party made slow progress after Strasbourg, mainly because the German roadmasters would allow only four-wheeled carriages on their highways.[70] The roads were in any case execrable. It took Ryan and his party until 6 April to get as far as Innsbruck.[71]

By the 11th they were in Bologna. Here the Stolberg family sent on a request that the marriage be solemnised on the day that the couple first met.[72] Macerata more than ever looked like the perfect venue.

Edmund Ryan's role in the entire affair is significant. The selection of an Irishman was a deliberate harking back to the bold Chevalier Wogan who accompanied the prince's mother, also from Innsbruck. Charles Edward might have thought the mimesis less appealing if he had reflected that Clementina Sobieska took no more than six years to seek refuge from his father in a convent, just as Clementina the less (Walkinshaw) did from him. It would have been stretching credibility too far at this stage if someone had suggested that a further flight and a further convent might lie ahead.

On 13 April the prince left Rome for Macerata.[73] On arrival there, he was informed that the Pope had granted him a dispensation to marry Louise and had allowed a nuptial benediction. He rode down to Loreto to meet his bride, then accompanied her back to Macerata. Louise was tired after being nineteen hours in the coach on Wednesday the 15th, but, two hours after reaching Macerata, she went through with the ceremony. At 2 p.m. on Good Friday, 17 April 1772, Cardinal Marefoschi solemnised the marriage in the private chapel of the palace of the Compagnoni Marefoschi.[74] Both bride and groom were sartorially resplendent; the prince wore a yellow-metalled sword specially for the occasion. The couple then spent their honeymoon in the Palazzo. Caryll's preparation of the bridal suite had been every bit as thorough as his arrangements in the chapel; Louise even had her own French-speaking maid.[75]

There is no doubt that the prince's first impressions of his bride were extremely favourable. On seeing her, he increased her pin money to 15,000 livres a year, 5,000 more than specified in the contract.[76] And that night he composed for her one of his couplets of doggerel:

> This crown is due to you by me
> And none shall love you more than me.[77]

The prince's reception in Macerata had echoes of that in Avignon nearly twenty-five years before. '*Viva Il Re!*', the crowds shouted. The governor of Macerata danced attendance on the newly-weds. An assembly of the local nobility in honour of the royal couple did not end until three in the morning. On Easter Sunday there was further lavish entertainment before Charles and his queen set out for Rome with eighteen post horses.[78]

The prince's wedding created a minor sensation in Europe, showing that he was still newsworthy. By the time of the solemnisation at Macerata, the news of the proxy marriage in Paris had already caused a ripple of excitement to run through Europe.[79] Frederick the Great saw the union as a significant development in the deepening Anglo-French hostility. It was quite clear to him that French desire to prolong the life of the Stuart scarecrow meant that a day of reckoning was not far off, when France would attempt to undo the 1763 Treaty of Paris.[80]

Yet those in the know realised how insignificant the match was in political terms. It was a matter of weeks rather than months before Charles Edward realised that neither of his hopes from the marriage was going to materialise. France intended to renege on its pension commitment; the Papacy would still not recognise him as Charles III.

It was the papal issue that impinged first on the prince's consciousness. Charles had never relaxed his pressure on the Vatican. He informed Marefoschi that he was bringing a queen back to Rome and the said queen would be mortified not to find a papal guard on duty at the gate of their palazzo.[81] But Clement XIV dealt with the prince's overtures by ignoring them. The only conciliatory step he took was to suggest to the duke of Gloucester that it might be politic for him to avoid 'Charles III's' triumphal entry. Gloucester took the hint and left Rome two days before Charles Edward's return on 22 April.[82] Clement had already secured the concessions he wanted from the English. One early result was that in 1774 George III proclaimed religious toleration for Catholics in Canada.[83]

On the prince's arrival in Rome, he decided to push matters to a conclusion. He called to see the Cardinal Secretary of State and announced the new era of king Charles III and his queen; this key event, he claimed, merited an immediate papal audience. The Secretary of State passed on the message. The Pope replied pointedly that he was glad to hear of the arrival of 'Baron Renfrew and his wife' and hoped soon to grant them an interview; this could not be in the near future, however, because of pressure of work.[84]

When he read the Pope's letter, the prince was thunderstruck. Reeling with shock, he ordered Caryll to return it to Marefoschi with the message that Charles declined to receive it. He then dashed off an angry letter to Marefoschi, full of the old 1766 arguments about scandalising European Catholics and truckling to the Elector of Hanover.[85]

There was no mistaking the Pope's negative intentions. For the third time, a determined bid to secure papal recognition for 'Charles III' had failed. The other prong of Charles Edward's strategy was also a lamentable failure. Despite their promises, the French made no further payments of the agreed pension.[86] At a political level, then, the marriage with Louise of Stolberg was already manifestly a failure, within months of the solemnisation at Macerata. What of the marriage at a personal level?

Here we have to deal with the difficult problem of Louise's personality and motivation. The swiftness of her acceptance of Ryan's proposals argues for an unsentimental woman of uncertain prospects with an eye to the main chance.[87] The alacrity with which she accepted the prince's offer was doubtless quickened by the consideration that her younger sister Karoline Auguste (the second daughter) had already married, at the age of sixteen, the marquis of Jamaica (later, in 1785, 4th duke of Berwick). There is no doubt that Louise found it a severe disappointment not, after all, to be received in Rome as queen of England. In her mind, this removed much of the point of the marriage.[88] Since Charles Edward's expedient reasons for marrying her had also come to nothing, the couple were thrown back on their own resources to make the match work. With an age gap of thirty-one years to bridge, this would have been a tall order for any relationship.

What do we know about Louise at this time? Contemporary

descriptions agree in finding her physically attractive without in any
sense being beautiful. The marquis de Fitzjames spoke of her medium
height and pleasant face.[89] Ryan drew attention to her good figure,
pretty face and good teeth.[90] The duke of Fitzjames found her on the
big side and a little thin, yet well-made with a good neck, outstanding
skin, vermilion-red lips, beautiful teeth and a pleasant face.[91] The
fourth of Charles Edward's quartet of negotiators (Caryll) agreed
about the remarkably fine teeth, the good complexion and trim figure,
and added some more closely-observed details: her eyes were dark,
her hair a fine light-brown and her nose well shaped.[92] All this was
confirmed by her admirer Bonstetten three years later. He spoke of
her deep blue eyes, retroussé nose and sensible expression that was
at once sparkling and guileful.[93]

The inner woman is more elusive. Her formal convent education
– which she claimed left her knowing nothing except how to pray –
had given her a strong distaste for organised religion.[94] She was
drawn to free-thinking and Voltairean modes of thought. This should
have provided some common ground with Charles Edward. There is
considerable dramatic irony here. Her uncomplimentary remarks
about convents would have chimed in well with his detestation of
such places following the Clementina Walkinshaw débâcle. Yet it
was a nunnery that was to play a key role in severing the links
between the prince and Louise.

Something of Louise's personality and character will emerge later.
In the first nine months of their married life, Charles Edward found
little to complain about. He confessed himself more than happy with
the charms of his young wife.[95] His problem in 1772 was not marital
but financial.

There was a three-way tangle involved here. First, there was a
running dispute with France about the promised but unpaid
pension.[96] Then there was a veritable mare's nest over Dunbar's will,
especially the salt revenues which he had enjoyed in usufruct but
which passed to the prince on his death in accordance with James's
will.[97] Finally, there was confusion over the French revenues from
the Hôtel de Ville, a confusion compounded by the death of John
Waters.[98] As for the Sobieski money from the 'Fund of Ohlau', that
remained as distant a prospect as ever.[99]

It was as well that the prince had Louise for company, for apart
from her in 1772 there was only Albano, the Argentina theatre, and
wine to distract his attentions from 'malice domestic' (the Vatican)
and 'foreign levy' (the French).[100]

The year 1773 brought an echo of the past. News of the marriage summoned Clementina Walkinshaw and the prince's daughter to Rome in hopes of a more favourable financial settlement. The two women had not completely vanished from Charles's ken. In August 1764 Clementina wrote with a progress report on Charlotte: she was tall, devout and good at music. Charlotte wrote her first letter to her father at this time.[101] Further letters followed in 1768. The burden of the correspondence was always the same: a plea for Charlotte's recognition.[102] This was backed by long screeds from Clementina herself.[103]

In October 1769 the two women wrote again, Clementina to explain her daughter's grave illness, an incipient form of the cancer of the liver that was eventually to kill her at the age of thirty-five.[104] The prince's answer to all these letters was the same: silence.

When news of Charles Edward's marriage reached the convent at Meaux where the two women resided, their different reactions were significant. Clementina recoiled with shock.[105] Charlotte redoubled her efforts. She showed every sign of having inherited her father's indomitable will, hammering away at the inalienable right owed to her by natural justice, whether she was deemed illegitimate or not.[106]

Lord Caryll took her side. He advised her that he could probably secure her a place in the 'king's' household, provided she broke with her mother. The greatest calamity of all would be if Clementina Walkinshaw were to show her face in Italy.[107] Charlotte now showed herself to be her father's daughter in more ways than one. After repudiating Caryll's advice to wait patiently for a more favourable moment, since her father was ill, Charlotte stepped up the pressure at the end of 1772, writing both to her father and to Cardinal York.[108] She also lobbied the French court intensely, painting a piteous picture of the plight she and her mother found themselves in.[109] When neither of these letters produced a response, she decided on a frontal attack. In May 1773 she and her mother travelled to Rome to press their claims. This was extraordinarily self-destructive behaviour.

The unwelcome duo arrived at a moment of maximum embarrassment for Charles Edward. By addressing themselves to the Vatican, Charlotte and her mother seemed to be increasing the possibility of further humiliation for the prince from Clement XIV. Caryll acted swiftly. Clementina Walkinshaw was ordered to leave Rome. At first, doubtless encouraged by Charlotte, she dug in her heels and refused to go.[110]

The Cardinal Secretary of State then issued a sombre warning of the possible consequences.[111] The unfortunate women were forced to retrace their steps: Genoa–Antibes–Aix–Avignon–Lyons, following almost the exact route taken by their oppressor in January 1744.[112] The sole concession Charlotte wrested from this ill-advised raid on Rome was permission to move convents, from Meaux to Paris.[113] It was to be another ten years before this indomitable young woman achieved her ends. But, like her father, she preferred constant action, even if it were self-destructive, to defeatist inertia. For the rest of the prince's marriage his natural daughter continued to be a thorn in his side.

The prince's attitude to his only daughter is at first sight bizarre. How could he act so coldly and callously to one whose loss had precipitated a nervous breakdown in 1760? The clue lies in his treatment of Louise de Montbazon a quarter of a century earlier. The prince habitually reacted to loss, especially loss for which he felt in some degree responsible, by pretending that there had been no loss. In other words, he dealt with guilt by a show of coldness that shocked and disturbed those (and in the eighteenth century that meant everybody) who could not fathom the deep unconscious springs of his actions.

By the end of 1773 it was apparent that Charlotte was not the only young woman destined to give the prince trouble. Louise found the restrictions of life in Rome as 'Baroness Renfrew' instead of the expected 'Queen of England' peculiarly irksome; even the newspapers from northern Europe arrived late.[114] For the first nine months of the marriage, by common consent, the prince behaved himself and kept off the bottle. Proudly he drove around Rome in an open carriage, showing off his young wife.[115] But when it became increasingly obvious that for Louise conception was going to be, at the very least, a difficult matter – it later transpired she was barren – the prince resumed his full quota of Cyprus wine.[116]

Seeing the storm clouds gathering, Lord Caryll determined to leave the Palazzo Muti at the earliest possible moment. Louise increasingly turned to books for comfort, and to the company of handsome young travellers. She was already being indiscreet, but had not yet got to the point of outright infidelity. The prince trusted her. When information was laid before him that Louise was physically attracted to his lackey Bernardo Rotolo and had confessed the attraction, he dismissed the report as idle rumour.[117] Provided his wife's admirers did not actually try to cuckold him, and provided they made themselves agreeable to him, Charles was prepared to tolerate Louise's flirtations. That she quickly became an accomplished coquette is clear from the soubriquet 'Queen of Hearts' very soon conferred on her by her suitors.[118]

Her first calf-love conquest was Thomas Coke, a young English Whig grandee on the Grand Tour. The culmination of this flirtation was a commission from the princess to the well-known portrait painter Pompeo Batoni to paint the youth and herself in the guise of Theseus and Ariadne on Naxos.[119] Coke returned to England from his travels besotted with the 'Queen of Hearts'; other young English travellers, too, returned glowing with her memory.[120]

But it was not Englishmen alone who were lured into Louise's tender trap. The Swiss Charles-Victor Bonstetten, later a well-known belle-lettriste, carried on a literary flirtation with her for two years, though this was a little later, in the Florence period.[121] Yet a remark made to Bonstetten by Louise early in 1775 shows the way her mind was working even during the dull days at the Palazzo Muti. She told him she approved of the basically polygamous instincts of men and felt the same principle should hold good for women: they should be allowed an intellectual companion by day and a carnal one by night.[122]

By early 1774, it seems unlikely that the prince was satisfying either the diurnal or nocturnal requirement. Even before the move to Florence, the danger signals were there for anyone who cared to read them. On the one hand, there was an angry, bibulous fifty-three-year-old, now disappointed even of the heir that would have perpetuated the Stuart line. Taken together with papal failure to recognise him as king, and French perfidy over the money, Louise's inability to become pregnant seemed to reduce the marriage to new levels of meaninglessness. For her part, Louise had to assuage her disappointed ambitions with physically unconsummated relationships with young men, and with incipient bibliophilia. Being Queen of Hearts was a poor substitute for the Queen of England she had hoped to be.[123]

The 'contradictions' in the marriage were already acute. Whether a change of locale could resolve them was doubtful. It was not long before the question marks against the marriage's viability became underscorings of the certainty of its failure.

36

The Queen of Hearts

(1774–80)

After a two-year lacuna since his disappointed entry into Rome with his 'queen', Charles Edward suddenly found his hands full both with pressing domestic issues and matters of high politics.

The year 1774 came in like a lion. The first piece of drama was Louis XV's sudden illness and death.[1] This aroused hopes of new bearings in French policy. The focus of attention again switched to Versailles.

Immediately Charles Edward ordered Lord Caryll to write to the duc d'Orléans, in tandem with the prince's formal condolences to the new king, twenty-year-old Louis XVI.[2] Under the pretext of welcoming the new reign, Caryll's letter protested at the non-payment of the pension promised by France on the occasion of the marriage with Louise of Stolberg. The prince's intention was to lobby Louis XVI on a twin-track basis. Along with the existing negotiations between the tardy duc de Fitzjames and the duc d'Aiguillon, the prince designed his fresh overtures as the opening of a second front.[3]

The forced resignation of d'Aiguillon in any case brought the first set of negotiations to a sudden halt, much to the relief of the Polonius-like duc de Fitzjames.[4] The prince pressed ahead through the supposed new channel. His arguments were threefold: kings by divine right owed a duty to each other; the French had done amazingly well out of the '45; and finally, the French had actually *promised* a subsidy when Charles was in Paris in September 1771.

But now the prince muddied his own waters. After putting out an initial feeler to the duc d'Orléans, he switched to lobbying Maurepas.[5] Charles Edward's old adversary from the days of the arrest and expulsion had been recalled by Louis XVI after twenty-five years in the political wilderness. Maurepas was now in his early seventies.

Louis installed him in rooms directly above his own at Versailles. Every morning, when the king heard his minister stirring, Louis would visit him to talk over the problems of the day.

On the face of it, then, Maurepas was uniquely well placed to promote the prince's cause at the French court. Yet the prince had discounted three factors. In the first place, it had been a serious blunder to contact Orléans, a known enemy of Maurepas.[6] If the prince wanted favours from Orléans, he should not have approached Maurepas, and *vice versa*. Second, Maurepas was retained by Louis XVI as Minister without Portfolio, so had no departmental resources to command, whatever his feelings for the prince. Third, and most importantly, the new king himself wanted to sever the French connection with the Stuarts. He regarded them as an unlucky, even accursed family, and felt they were an anachronistic impediment to proper relations with England, an unacceptable joker in the international pack.

Maurepas demonstrated that he had lost none of his old cunning. In his reply (indirect, using the excuse of protocol) to the prince, Maurepas expressed himself keen to help but unable to do anything: the spirit of divine right solidarity was willing but the ministerial flesh was weak (or non-existent). He suggested an approach to the new Foreign Minister comte de Vergennes.[7]

After another few ineffectual stabs in Maurepas's direction, the prince decided to take his advice.[8] By this time even Abbé Gordon, who had fancied himself as having the ear of the duc d'Orléans, regretted opening that channel.[9] Finding it quite useless for their purposes, the Jacobites shut it down and threw all their efforts into lobbying Vergennes.

But Vergennes had been appointed to retrench and make economies. At his first interview with the duc de Fitzjames, he overwhelmed him with fiscal detail, leaving him in no doubt that there was no money to spare for Jacobite affairs, not even in a case allegedly involving a moral obligation.[10]

The prince's impatience with the slow progress of negotiations at Versailles and his general paranoia about France began to feed into each other.[11] Brusquely, he informed his agents to go back to Maurepas and lay before him the entire correspondence with Orléans and Vergennes. This was a matter of deep embarrassment to the inept Jacobite negotiators. They knew only too well what Maurepas would make of such incompetence.[12] They counselled patience; but as usual the prince would not listen to such 'prevarications'.[13]

At this point Louise decided to lend a hand, on the ground that it was her queenly duty. She told the duc de Fitzjames that her husband would rather have an outright refusal than another two and a half years of double-talk.[14] The prince was desperate. There is a poignant quality to his appeal to Abbé Gordon in November 1774: 'It would be the last of cruelties were they not to give me a definite answer, for I cannot possibly stand it any longer. My debts augmenting so considerably every day puts me in the greatest of desolations.'[15]

Yet Vergennes and Louis XVI were determined to win the war of attrition with the Jacobites. At the end of the year Gordon told Caryll that Fitzjames was no farther forward than he had been when the new king came to the throne.[16] In exasperation (and not before time) the prince gave up on the feckless Fitzjameses and appointed Gordon to head the negotiations, adding the all but impossible remit that Gordon was to secure not a penny less than James used to receive.[17] The appointment of Gordon produced a quick answer from Vergennes, but it was not one the prince wanted to hear. Vergennes returned to the old stalling tactic used by d'Aiguillon: France would proceed only with Spanish collaboration, and liaison between the two courts would take time.[18]

Charles Edward then trumped Vergennes's ace, at least to his own satisfaction. Since Fitzjames and the other French Jacobites had not pulled their weight at Versailles, so that the French subsidy was not forthcoming, he, the prince, would cease paying out pensions to his followers in France.[19] Moreover, he was now in dudgeon with Spain. Since Madrid had meted out 'disgraceful treatment' to him, there was no question of his going cap in hand there. All the prince would allow was direct negotiations with Maurepas.[20]

This was self-destructive behaviour with a vengeance (quite literally!). Not surprisingly, the French negotiations fizzled out. Gordon ducked out by claiming that he lacked the personnel to go at the speed Charles Edward required. When the prince mentioned Father Welsh, Prior of English monks in Paris, Gordon simply passed the buck to him.[21] Maurepas, meanwhile, solved the Jacobite problem by not answering their letters.[22]

However, the French had a final card to play which, long-term, cannot have helped Charles Edward's marriage to prosper. They announced that since Louise of Stolberg had been so diplomatic and reasonable, in contrast to her husband, they were prepared to grant her a small personal pension of 60,000 francs.[23]

While this fiasco was resolving itself, the prince and his queen moved their tiny court from Rome to Tuscany. There were several motives for the move: Louise's discontent with Roman social life (or rather, its absence); Charles Edward's desire not to be in Rome while the hated Clement XIV celebrated his lustrum; and simple economy, since living expenses would be less in Tuscany.[24] Another telling consideration was the prince's health. Already he was complaining of severe piles and agonising pains in his leg.[25] His illnesses became more frequent and acute as the disappointments from the abortive negotiations with the new regime in France accumulated.[26]

The royal party travelled first to Siena, arriving in mid-July.[27] After staying there a month, they proceeded to Pisa to take the waters.[28] This interlude suited Louise very well; she enjoyed the spa atmosphere.[29] After a month in Pisa, they returned to Siena.[30] Then, in the middle of October, they moved on to Florence, intending to make only a short stay before returning to set up a permanent base in Siena.[31] But Louise liked Florence and prevailed on the prince to stay on. They rented the Villa Corsini, close to the walls of the town, until Lent 1775. The lease was taken out in the name of the count of Albany, Charles Edward's new pseudonym.[32] There, at No. 40 via del Prato, the prince was to live from 30 October 1774 until early July 1776.[33]

The prince engaged boxes in both theatres in Florence and again took up the heavy drinking he had temporarily laid aside while taking the waters at Pisa.[34] Within weeks Charles Edward was making news. His hatred of the French for the further humiliations they were now making him undergo led to an altercation with a French officer in his box. The prince made an insulting remark. Pompously the officer replied that perhaps the count was unaware who the man was whom he had insulted. '*Je sais que vous êtes français et cela suffit,*' Charles answered.[35] ('I know that you are French, and that's enough.')

Now came a fresh source of uncertainty and anxiety. Suddenly Clement XIV died. The conclave to elect his successor was by common consent going to be a difficult and protracted one. Perhaps someone favourable to the Stuarts would be elected, possibly someone like Stefano Borgia, who had close links with both Henry and Marefoschi?[36] At the very least, the prince would get his fourth chance to achieve papal recognition.[37]

The predictions of a hard fought papal election – since there was no obvious candidate to hand – were soon borne out. The conclave met in November 1774 and was still in session at the end of December.[38] It became obvious that none of the front-runners could secure the necessary majority and that a compromise candidate would have to be chosen. Charles Edward seriously considered that this 'dark horse' could be his brother: he admitted that Henry would have had no chance in normal circumstances but might just squeeze through this time, as he was not allied to either of the main factions.[39]

But Henry was not truly *papabile*. For one thing, to be elected he would have needed the support of the Spanish cardinals. Yet he was in bad odour at Madrid. The Spanish court remembered how he had abstained in the voting on the proposed beatification of the anti-Jesuit Spanish Bishop Palafox, a great favourite of Charles III and his then chief minister Ricardo Wall.[40] On the other hand, Henry had won no laurels from the Jesuit faction either, for he had also opposed the beatification of their favourite Robert Bellarmine.[41] What the Cardinal Duke saw as even-handed statesmanship his critics saw as systematic trimming, dictated by his dependence on French and Spanish benefices. The reality of the 1774–5 conclave was that Henry's name was never once mentioned as a serious contender.[42] Charles Edward's best chance turned out to be none other than his old friend Cardinal Marefoschi, who was at one time being seriously promoted as a 'dark horse'.[43] In the end, Cardinal Brasini, formerly Vatican treasurer, emerged as Pius VI. Almost his first act was to invite the duke of Gloucester to Rome again to press forward the policy of English conciliation.[44]

The prince went through the motions of applying for papal recognition as 'Charles III', but he must have known his quest was vain. He presented his compliments through the nuncio at Florence, promising to return to Rome if he were given his father's titles.[45] When the nuncio did not reply, Caryll was sent to see him as the bearer of a long palimpsest of complaints, going back to 1766. It is significant of the prince's state of mind that the events of that year were described as part of a Jesuit plot against the Stuarts!

But the prince was on firmer ground in his rebuttal of the argument that papal recognition would offend the English. On the contrary, the prince thundered, if I do not get it, I shall leave Italy. Then the English will really have something to be worried about, at the very time their hands are full of the rebellious American colonists.[46]

This was hardly the acme of statesmanship. Henry had to spend a lot of time in the Vatican undoing the effects of his brother's fulminations, just to make sure the papal pension to the prince was not cut off.[47] But the prince insisted on a categorical reply and he got it.[48] In no circumstances would the new Pope recognise him as 'Charles III'. The prince openly expressed his contempt for 'such low proceedings so contrary to the principles of their religion'.[49] He vowed never to return to Rome.[50]

This further bitter disappointment determined Charles Edward to remain in Florence. He extended the lease on the Villa Corsini beyond Lent 1775. But any hopes of a serene domestic situation to compensate for the run of diplomatic disappointments were shattered by two not unconnected events.

For a long time Lord Caryll had been disillusioned with the prince on a number of counts: for his drunkenness, his treatment of Charlotte, his unappreciative attitude towards Louise, and most of all, the extravagant nature of the tasks he (Caryll) was called upon to perform as royal secretary.[51] His appetite for his job cannot have been increased by the fact of its being unpaid. As John Farquharson, one of the dwindling band of Scottish Jacobites, remarked to Bishop Gordon in February 1775: 'He has not even dog's wages for his trouble but does all for stark love and kindness.'[52]

Matters came to a head in March 1775. Caryll had urgent family business to attend to in Rome. Charles Edward categorically refused him permission to make the trip, on the fantastic ground that none of his 'subjects' could be permitted to go there until the Pope decided to treat him as his father had been treated.[53] This was too much for the long-suffering secretary. He and Lady Caryll packed and decamped, provoking a great outcry from the prince about disloyalty, ingratitude and treachery.[54]

One result of Caryll's departure was to leave Louise more isolated inside the Palazzo Corsini. It was true that her band of admirers swelled in Florence. Following Coke, among Englishmen there was Henry Seymour.[55] Everywhere Louise won golden opinions. General Lockhart's wife described her as 'one of the prettiest and most agreeable of her sex I ever conversed with'.[56]

Another visitor to Florence to fall under her spell was Dr Moore, physician to the duke of Hamilton. The two Englishmen one day encountered the prince's suite on one of the avenues of a public walk near the city. Charles Edward, sporting the inevitable Garter, was with count Spada and his Italian courtiers and in deep conversation with the Prussian envoy to the court of Turin. Louise had Lucille de Maltzam, her new lady-in-waiting, with her. Maltzam was at this time carrying on a passionate affair with Bonstetten's travelling companion Scherer. Four liveried servants made up the entourage.

Moore and Hamilton yielded right of way and pulled off their hats. The Prussian envoy whispered something in the prince's ear. He looked very earnestly and steadily at the duke of Hamilton and returned the compliment. But what struck the visitors most was Louise. 'She is a beautiful woman,' wrote Moore, 'much beloved by those who know her, who universally describe her as lively, intelligent and agreeable.'[57]

Above all her admirers was the twenty-nine-year-old *literateur* Charles Victor Bonstetten who adored Louise just this side of madness. Charles Edward in general approved of all these gallants, especially when they were willing to listen to his long, rambling stories about the '45, as Bonstetten was. He was even prepared to overlook the quaint gaucheries of the Swiss in the Palazzo Corsini when he made hamfisted attempts to help Louise carve a roast turkey.[58] Adoration from afar, of the medieval chivalric variety, was fine, provided the legitimacy of any heir was not thrown in doubt.

But for all her conquests, Louise could not confide in any of these beaux her secret fears and misgivings. Caryll had provided her with a shoulder to cry on. He had dampened down her complaints about her husband and headed off marital crisis. Now he was gone, the safety-valve was removed. Significantly, immediately after Caryll's departure, Louise's first overt complaints are recorded. In a long letter she outlined her principal grievances. First, she had to traipse around the streets of Florence for one and a half hours in the excessive heat of June at midday, just because her husband was bored in his rooms. Then, there was the prince's insistence on waking her up at 7 a.m. when she did not get to sleep until two in the morning. In general there was his refusal to listen to reason.[59] 'Have you, who have always been a byword for gallantry, so declined that you do not want to stay just a few hours in bed with a pretty young woman who loves you?'[60] Perhaps already dimly perceiving the end of the road, Louise circulated this remonstrance to her friends.

Louise's spirits were farther cast down by having to share a bedroom with a man who snored excessively and whose health was already giving cause for concern. At the beginning of 1775, one of Glenbucket's descendants was granted a morning audience and found the prince looking 'old in complexion and pretty stout in person'.[61]

This was not the worst of it. Gluttony and excessive drinking were bringing even Charles's iron constitution close to the point of collapse. His body was attacked in two main areas. He developed asthma and heavy catarrh, which his Italian physicians diagnosed as apoplexy and treated with emetics and leeches.[62] At the same time the sore leg that had troubled him for the past few years began to discharge pus. When the doctors closed up the suppurating leg, this produced a slow fever with other complications. The pent-up purulence then threatened to break out in the other leg.[63]

The prince consulted an eminent physician in Paris. His explanation of the illness was piteous. He explained that his brain was being affected, that there were times when he could barely sign his own name. He could not remember proper names, wrote Gordon when he meant Caryll, and so on. The doctor poured scorn on blood-letting and recommended instead alkalines and a light, healthy diet. The prince should take exercise, use no drugs and abstain from all alcohol except a mere sip of the very finest vintages.[64] Since the prince was already in the habit of drinking six bottles of Cyprus wine a day, sleeping off one drinking bout and then getting drunk again, it can be imagined that this advice was not what he wanted to hear. Never-theless, his frequent consultations with outside physicians effectively turned him into a hypochondriac and amateur dabbler in medicines.[65]

For Charles Edward's medical progress we are largely indebted to Mann's spies. By September 1775, it was reported that the discharge from the leg had stopped, but that he now experienced violent stomach cramps after eating.[66] It gradually became clear that Charles Edward was suffering from aggravated dropsy. The suppurating leg acted as a conduit for the excess liquid he was retaining. He had two choices. He could either endure great pain from his swollen legs and thighs, which in turn produced severe fits of colic. Or he could have the opening in his leg sealed up, in which case he experienced general breathlessness and a panicky feeling of suffocation around his chest.[67] The severe stomach pains and indigestion gradually turned him against food, but he would never give up drink.[68] All in all, he preferred to suffer the pain of the discharging leg rather than the feeling of suffocation.

Absurdly, while resolutely refusing to abstain from alcohol, Charles Edward tried to put into practice the rest of the Parisian physician's prescriptions. He went out every day in his coach to take the air.[69] And he was an habitual frequenter of the theatre, where his normal mode was semi-somnolence. Gradually the drowsiness would turn to outright slumber. A bed was moved into his box at the theatre. When he had one of his bad attacks of stomach pain, he had to dash for the public passageway, where he was violently sick.[70]

This was a state of affairs that would have taxed the powers of an older woman, genuinely in love with her husband, who had the memory of better days to live on. Louise had none of these attributes to sustain her. She had problems of her own, quite apart from a drunken husband. Louise had long argued for residence in Florence, in preference to Siena, on the grounds that the latter city had not received her and her husband with proper respect.[71] But Florence soon showed itself no more willing than the other Italian city-states to offend the mighty English.

Louise began her stay in Florence by visiting all the great ladies of Tuscany. She was stupefied and appalled when the visits of the Florentine nobility to the Casino Corsini tailed off and then stopped altogether. Each side blamed the other.[72] But the net effect was a further narrowing in the social circle of the Queen of Hearts. Soon Bonstetten departed. Louise carried on a long-range flirtation with him by letter, but this was no substitute for the presence of the besotted Swiss.[73]

More and more Louise turned to books for consolation. This was her great bibliophile period. Her favourite pastime was reading a chapter of Montaigne in bed every morning. She announced that she would like to forget all pomp and be a republican. 'I measure the man and not his pedestal,' she said, 'and I prefer a loveable man, one I could love, to the greatest lord who bores me.'[74] It is not difficult to guess whom she had in mind!

The other great sadness in the princess's life was her increasingly obvious infertility. The Jacobite duke of Melfort's euphuistic message of June 1772, asking her to produce a son and heir,[75] now seemed like ironical mockery. In compensation Louise turned, as so many involuntarily childless women do, to the love of animals. She kept rabbits and quickly turned herself into something of an expert in their care and breeding.[76]

Such social interludes as there were had the appearance of snatched and furtive occasions. When they attended the same balls as the Grand Duke and Duchess, the Queen of Hearts and her consort were politely ostracised. Such snubs turned the prince even more in on himself. During the carnival he went everywhere in a mask; Louise chose always to appear *in propria persona*.[77]

It was a relief when one of the nobility broke the taboo and dined with them incognito, as the duke of Ostrogothia did in September 1776, using the pseudonym comte d'Oeland. Charles Edward was visibly touched. At the dinner table he remarked: '*Ah, M. le Comte, quelle consolation pour moi diner avec un de mes egaux!*'[78] ('Ah, count, it is such a consolation to me to dine with one of my equals!')

The prince's wounded sensitivity was such that he would go to extraordinary lengths to avenge insults, real or imaginary. When senator Guadagni's son (the Guadagnis were later to loom large in the prince's life) turned down a lunch (dinner) invitation with him and then appeared for a post-prandial coffee after lunching instead with the duchess of Chartres, the prince was so incensed that he planned an elaborate retaliation. He invited Guadagni to dinner again. Deliberately abstaining from drink so as to keep his head clear, he waited for the young man to appear, then hid himself behind the door. When Guadagni entered, the prince delivered a powerful kick on his behind. As Guadagni sprawled on the floor, Charles railed at him: 'That will show you I'm as good as the Duchess of Chartres. It will also teach you how to treat people of my rank. Notice, too, that I have not touched a drop of wine.'[79]

Charles Edward's one-man battle with the Papacy meanwhile came to an inevitable and ignominious end. His last fling was to attempt to get the Catholic bishops of England and Ireland to sign a document recognising him as Charles III. The Holy Roman Catholic Church would then have to confront the absurdity of a British flock who recognised Charles III as king while the Pope recognised George III. Fortunately, this hair-brained scheme was scotched by the prince's advisers as soon as mooted.[80]

Yet Charles Edward's humiliating climb-down before Pius VI did have one definite result. Since the prince had vowed never to return to Rome until accorded his titles, he now had to find a permanent home in Florence. To this end he energised his contacts in the city, the most important of whom was the marquis of Barbantane, French plenipotentiary at the court of the Grand Duke of Tuscany.[81]

Barbantane began by taking discreet soundings from Mann, to make sure the prince would not be embarrassed by a curt refusal if he attempted to rent an English house. Mann raised no objection, but Louise and the prince found fault with Barbantane's proposed accommodation themselves.[82]

In the spring of 1776 Louise found what she was looking for. In July 1776 the Stuart household moved from the Casino Corsini to the Palazzo Guadagni in the via San Sebastiano (now Palazzo San Clemente, via Gino Capponi).[83] The Palazzo Guadagni was a gem of late Renaissance architecture, with an enclosed portico for carriages, a spacious entrance hall, and suites of sumptuously decorated rooms on the first floor. There was a large garden, studded with cypress and ilex trees. Louise thought she had found her perfect haven.[84]

But almost immediately a rancorous law-suit developed. The Guadagni family had rented the palazzo to Charles Edward on an indefinite lease. Shortly after the Stuarts moved in, Lord and Lady Cowper came to Florence, took one look at the house, and decided it was for them. They agreed to the extravagant rental terms proposed by the Guadagni family; it seemed as though money was no object.[85]

But how to remove the Stuarts? Charles and Louise had found safe anchorage. They refused to budge. The matter was taken to a tribunal. There was frantic behind-the-scenes lobbying. The Grand Duke himself favoured the Cowpers, but most of the nobility felt sympathy for the prince. The dispute became the talk of Florence. Eventually the tribunal found in favour of the prince, much to the Grand Duke's irritation.[86] Lord Cowper considered appealing to a higher court, but was discreetly dissuaded.

Publicly Charles Edward fulminated against the 'rebellious opposition' of one of his 'subjects'. Privately, he conceded that the affair had taught him a lesson. The only way to achieve the security and peace of mind he needed was to buy the house outright. Purchase was beyond the Cowpers, whose assets were in England. Given that the price of the Palazzo Guadagni had shot up as a result of the litigation and resultant publicity, it seemed to be beyond Charles Edward's too. He took a brave decision. He would wind up all his affairs in Rome and withdraw every last Roman crown from the Stuart monies in the Monte di Pietà.

The years 1776–7 saw the prince obsessed with money. The reason was that he was scraping together all his finance to purchase the Palazzo Guadagni. All his best furniture and effects were brought to Florence from the Palazzo Muti.[87] The prince did not quite burn all his boats. He left a nominal retinue of servants in the house of his birth and refused all offers to rent it.[88]

At last, in December 1777, the prince had amassed sufficient funds to buy the Florentine palazzo. The sale was completed. For the last three years of their marriage, he and Louise enjoyed the security of being property-owners.[89] Ironically, the move into Louise's dream house took her into the darkest period of the marriage.

The first open quarrel, overheard by the servants, took place in the Palazzo Guadagni.[90] So did the first physical beating. Charles Edward was running true to form. Sooner or later, with all his women, when the first flush of excitement had gone, he would turn on them and use physical violence. So it had been with the Princesse de Talmont and Clementina Walkinshaw. So it was now with his wife.

What triggered the violence seems to have been increasing jealousy of Louise's admirers, compounded by his own flagging physical powers. He no longer trusted her. He had the approaches to her bedroom barricaded by a pile of tables and chairs to which were attached bells, whose tinkling would alert him to the approach of interlopers. Anyone wishing to get to Louise's bedroom would have to go through his room. To his advisers who remonstrated, he justified his actions as concern for the absolute legitimacy of any heir born in the palazzo.[91]

Yet, as so often with the prince, his delusions had a basis in reality. The fire behind the smoke this time was a twenty-seven-year-old poet and dramatist from Turin. When he first met Louise in 1776, count Vittorio Alfieri had a long career of lubricious libertinism behind him.[92] At the age of twenty-three, in Cadiz, he had contracted venereal disease. Though idle and dissolute, he was rich and strikingly handsome, with an undisputed literary talent. Alfieri had all the qualities Louise had sought in vain in her earlier admirers. Bonstetten was a pale foreshadowing of this answer to the Queen of Heart's dreams.

Alfieri and Louise later tried to turn their liaison into a story-book romance. The story of the *coup de foudre* when Alfieri first saw Louise looking at a painting of Charles XII in the Uffizi gallery has all the hallmarks of poetic licence.[93] But whatever the facts of their first meeting, by late 1776 Alfieri was a frequent visitor at the Palazzo Guadagni.

It was not easy for the lovers to achieve physical consummation in the confines of the palazzo, with the watchful prince ever at their shoulders. For the first two years of their relationship, they snatched kisses and held hands secretly while the prince dozed in the next room. In the evenings Alfieri would gaze, rapt and adoring, while Louise strummed on her guitar. In the daytime he devoted himself to the writing of the hagiographical *Maria Stuarda*, which he later repudiated.[94]

Increasingly Louise's reading reflected her new passion. It is surely significant that among the books she ordered from her favourite bookseller in Paris was an edition of Catullus.[95] At last, almost certainly some time in 1778, Alfieri and Louise became lovers in the full sense. The circumstantial evidence for this is fairly strong. It was in 1778 that Alfieri disavowed his Piedmontese nationality. The burdens of being a subject of the king of Sardinia were heavy. To travel abroad or to publish required the sovereign's permission. So did the transfer of capital out of Piedmont. Alfieri's most significant action in 1778 was to give up the rights to his property in Piedmont so as to be near his beloved and, as he put it, to make her free and independent as soon as possible.[96]

Alfieri was thus cutting himself off from his cultural and financial roots in a very important sense. That the relationship was taking a much more serious turn by 1778 is also shown by Alfieri's sustained efforts as a tutor that year, when he taught Louise to read and speak Italian.[97]

The years 1776–80 were a limbo period in Charles Edward's marriage. By now he and Louise were barely on speaking terms. The marital breakdown was attracting wide attention. In May 1777 a most extraordinary letter, written in London, reached the prince. It contained a vitriolic attack on him for his treatment of his wife, referring to his use of physical violence and his 'excess of wine'. The failure of Louise to produce an heir was laid squarely at the prince's door, being blamed on his doubtful health. Most of all he was taken to task for his tyranny towards his wife: 'a princess who is in every way your equal, descended from our ancient kings of Scotland and allied to all the great families of Europe. From these claims you derive your pride and fancy they give you authority to be wicked unpunished.'[98]

The provenance of this letter must have been the complaints Louise circulated to her friends. If so, the blundering intervention from England was counter-productive. It put the prince ever more on the alert *vis-à-vis* his wife and may have been instrumental in preventing her and Alfieri from becoming lovers until 1778.

While Alfieri and the Queen of Hearts were enjoying the raptures of true love, what of the prince? In his more lucid moments, in the interval between drinking bouts and slumber, he had but two interests: international affairs and his books.

By the 1770s it was apparent that a new era was dawning. In backward, deeply conservative Rome the new winds were blowing away some of the cobwebs. Even the Borgia family, quintessence of the old order, was raising its sights beyond the Eternal City. Captain Cook's voyage to the Pacific and Australasia in the *Endeavour* had fired the imagination of cardinals and prefects of the Congregation of the Faith.[99] Yet the most compelling focus for international attention was north America, where the colonists were locked in a life-and-death struggle with the mother country.

The Jacobites reacted with fascinated ambivalence. On the one hand here were the hated republicans of 'mob rule' seeking to overthrow monarchy. On the other, the detested Hanoverian regime was being stretched on the rack. The prince himself was always much more sympathetic to the latter view. The revolt of the American colonies was peculiarly fascinating to him, for in many ways the struggle seemed a rerun of his own battle with the House of Hanover in the '45. Many observers facilely extrapolated from the events of 1745–6 to the north American revolt: since the Jacobites had been worn down after some early successes, surely the same thing would happen to the rebels in north America? Charles Edward knew better. He was well aware how close to success he had been at Derby. Perhaps the American leaders would be made of sterner stuff than Lord George Murray and the clan chieftains.

There was another reason for the prince's interest in the war for America. Almost certainly, some kind of invitation was made by the Bostonians in 1775 that he should be the figurehead of a provisional American government. No clear documentary evidence remains, but Dutens, who was a reliable reporter, confirms the story, as do English sources.[100] In one version, the prince came secretly to Milford Haven in Wales to take ship for the New World.[101] Certainly this was the origin of the rumour that Charles was on the move in 1775, that he had been seen in Paris and England.[102]

What is beyond question is that the prince took an intense interest in the American war. In June 1775 there is a transcript in the prince's hand of a Salem newspaper report describing the battle of Lexington.[103] Another extract, again in his own hand, is a paraphrase of an article in the *New York Gazette* for 18 May 1775, dealing with the taking of Ticonderoga and Crown Point.[104] Another document details General Burgoyne's surrender to Gates at Albany in October 1777.[105] In 1781 the prince asked his agent Father Cowley of the Benedictines for a detailed map of north America so that he could follow the military operations, and also for maps and a historical précis of the whole American continent north of Panama.[106]

When France entered the war on the colonists' side, the prince made a copy of the relevant treaty.[107] By this time he was wholeheartedly behind the Americans, almost gloating over British reverses in the face of joint action by France, Spain, America and the Dutch (who joined in in December 1780).[108] French participation also conjured fleeting visions among the prince's followers of another pro-Jacobite descent on England.[109] In fact the French *did* attempt an invasion of England in 1779, in concert with Spain, but neither Jacobite personnel nor ambitions played any part in it.

Apart from international affairs, the prince's main distraction during the dark years of estrangement from his wife was his library. From the time of his 'obscure years' thirty years before, the prince had shown a great interest in books. In 1749–50 Charles Edward asked Mme Vassé to send him copies of Fielding's *Joseph Andrews* and of Montesquieu's *L'Esprit des Lois*.[110] Late 1750 was another rich period for reading in the prince's life.[111] It is true that at this stage reading tended to denote depression, an escape from an insupportable world. But as the years went on, Charles developed a taste for knowledge, especially philosophy and history. He had all the virtues and all the faults of the self-taught: omnivorous, eclectic but rather unfocused reading. At one time Leonardo da Vinci was a major interest.[112] This led him on to astronomy; there was a link here too with the prince of the Lunéville days, the prince who had meticulously recorded the Aurora Borealis in September 1749. Again, linking with the past, it seems that Charles sometimes kept up his cello playing and other musical interests. There exists a Florentine orchestra list in which Charles Edward, named as the count of Albany, is mentioned as the virtuoso on the *cimbalo*.[113]

If the prince's reading was sporadic and eclectic, the library he had built up in Florence by the late 1770s was impressive. There were works of political theory, history, military strategy, volumes of memoirs and travel diaries, scientific tomes, satirical pamphlets, and much else. Rousseau (especially *Emile* and *Du Contrat Social*), Voltaire, Montesquieu, Helvétius and Blackstone adorned the shelves. Caesar's *Commentaries* was a well-thumbed volume. Literature was represented by Swift, Milton, Pope and Fielding, *The Tale of a Tub*, *Paradise Lost*, *The Dunciad* and *Tom Jones*, in which the prince himself featured, being respectively particular favourites.[114] The prince often spoke of literature as a special interest.[115]

The effect of all this erudition was to make the prince a witty and urbane conversationalist. The notion of Charles Edward as blockhead dies hard, but it has no foundation in fact. Dutens relates that he once had a two-hour conversation with the prince during which Charles ranged effortlessly over a wide span of subjects, displayed a knowledge of several languages and showed himself expertly informed on European politics.[116]

Yet there was another side to Charles's interest in books. It was perhaps this other aspect that prevented him and his wife from finding a common interest in intellectual matters – apart from the fact that his taste ran to Enlightenment thought, while she preferred the ancient classics and their Renaissance counterparts like Montaigne. Even a cursory examination of the Stuart papers shows the prince's bibliophilia mounting in intensity as the 1770s wore on.[117] This suggests that a psychological motivation apart from intellectual curiosity was at work. We are irresistibly reminded of the neurotic fuss over Julien Le Roy's watch in the 1750s. Obsessive collecting can be a sign of a fundamentally authoritarian personality. In the case of the depressive, it is more likely to be a kind of *cri de coeur* against powerlessness. Amid his trophies, the collector can impose his own order and achieve the omnipotence the world denies him.[118]

But nothing the prince learned from his books kept him away from the bottle. Rather, the two streams started to feed into each other; he began to collect books on Burgundy and other wines.[119] The pain in his chest and his retention of water proved beyond doubt that he was a chronic sufferer from dropsy. Yet the prince refused to alter his routine. He insisted on going out every day in his coach and visiting the theatre every night, 'though of late [1779] with a strong fever upon him and so weak that he has to be supported by two servants from his coach to his box, where as usual, he laid [sic] on a couch'.[120] The excessive liquid on his chest caused him to cough continually. He lay awake most of the night, alternately coughing and puking, yet still insisting that Louise share his bed.[121] This was how she knew that he kept under his bed a strong box containing 12,000 sequins, against the day the call for action in England might come.[122] By this time, too, he was all but impotent; he later accused Louise of having accepted a drug from Sir Horace Mann that would drain his sexual vigour.[123]

No amount of remonstration from physicians made any impact on the prince. He redoubled his alcoholic frenzy. When he went to the theatre, he took a little bottle of Cyprus wine in his pocket. His inebriation led to minor scandals. On one occasion, at a masked ball, he insisted on dancing a minuet with a young lady, but came close to collapse on the ballroom floor and had to be supported by count Spada.[124] Such incidents further increased the contempt in which the prince was held by Florentine society.

By 1779, even allowing for the likely exaggerations by Horace Mann and his agents, it is clear that the prince was in a deplorable state of physical and mental health. Mann summed it up as follows: a declared ulcer, great sores in his legs, insupportable in stench and temperature. The piles from which he had suffered for years now became augmented to the point where he had almost permanent pain in his bowels.[125]

The strain on Louise, already considerable from carrying on a clandestine love affair with Alfieri, was close to breaking point. It is doubtful whether she had ever loved her husband, but now she hated him. The hatred was reciprocated. About this time Charles Edward penned his most revealing comments on women, proving beyond doubt that a true relationship with them had always been beyond him. He told a story of a man whose mistress had been unfaithful in order to get revenge. Was that revenge on the man because he had loved too much or too little, the prince queried; in other words, there was no pleasing women. The prince reckoned himself a reasonable judge of men (which he was not); but as for women, he went on: 'I have always thought a study of their sex useless, as they are much more wicked and impenetrable.'[126] Written at a time when he was almost certainly impotent, the last word must suggest a classic Freudian slip.

37

'A Man Undone'

(1780–4)

Events now moved rapidly towards the collapse of Charles Edward's marriage. Tired of the drunkenness, the beatings and the demand for sexual variations,[1] Louise laid contingency plans for absconding. She had some powerful allies. Her chief help was her lady-in-waiting and confidante Mlle de Maltzam.[2] She had the secret assistance of count Spada, who carried messages from Louise to Alfieri at the poet's home, and enjoyed sitting with her lover and denigrating the prince. Yet Spada covered his tracks well. It was a full year after Louise's departure before Charles Edward discovered his treachery. Even then, it came to light only after a heated altercation when Spada refused to accompany his master to the theatre.[3]

The other allies who played a key role in Louise's flight were Madame Orlandini and Mr Geoghan. Madame Orlandini was a scion of the Ormonde family; she was the daughter of a Jacobite general in the service of Austria and had made a military marriage to a Florentine general. Now widowed, Madame Orlandini lived secretly with an Irishman, Charles Geoghan.

Geoghan was typical of the adventurers attracted to the exiled Stuart court. After offending his father and being cut off without a penny he came to Italy in search of easy pickings. His handsome face enabled him to live well as a gigolo; it was in this capacity that he snared the wealthy widow Orlandini. The couple even went through a form of marriage, which could not be publicly divulged, lest Madame Orlandini forfeit her rights to her late husband's fortune according to the terms of his will.[4]

This, then, was the unsavoury quartet that plotted Louise's deliverance and the prince's downfall; a supposed Jacobite widow, an Irish gigolo, a treacherous private secretary and a woman (Mlle de

Maltzam) who seems to have been animated by a quite singular hatred of the prince.[5] They took soundings from the Grand Duke of Tuscany as to his attitude in the event of a separation in the Stuart household. The duke, who had never liked the prince, intimated broadly that Louise would have his tacit support.[6]

The speed with which events unfolded, once the prince fell into the trap that had been laid for him, demonstrates clearly that Louise's flight was no spontaneous, unpremeditated affair. The fatal night was 30 November 1780, St Andrew's Day. This was a day that the prince always liked to celebrate, but it had painful associations for him, since it reactivated his feelings of guilt about the clansmen he had destroyed in the '45.

The prince drank even more heavily than usual that day.[7] When he came to bed that night, he was already on the high seas of rage, his inevitable reaction to excessive guilt. Louise must have said the wrong thing at the wrong time. The prince went berserk. He beat her around the head, tore out chunks of her hair, and kicked her out of the bed.[8] Scrambling after her, he then attempted to strangle her. By this time her screams had aroused the whole household. The drunken prince, by now totally beside himself, was dragged off his wife.[9]

That disgraceful episode clinched matters for Louise. She gave orders to her fellow conspirators to put the escape plan into operation. Nine days after the assault, on Saturday 9 December, they lured the prince into a well-concealed trap.[10]

That morning Madame Orlandini came to breakfast at the Palazzo Guadagni. Casually she mentioned that she was going that day to the convent of the Bianchette to view some needlework done by the white nuns; would the count and countess like to come?[11] Suspecting nothing, Charles entered the carriage with the two women for the short drive to the convent on the via Mandorlo (now via Giusti). On arrival at the outside of the convent they 'by chance' came upon Geoghan. The two ladies nimbly ran up the steps and pulled the bell on the convent door. The lame and dropsical prince, supported on Geoghan's arm, followed slowly and painfully, some way behind.[12]

By prearrangement Louise and Madame·Orlandini were immediately admitted. To the prince's astonishment, the door was closed before he got to it. Angrily he banged on the door with his stick. The nuns milked his rage for all it was worth. After an infuriatingly long interval, the Mother Superior came to the grille at the door. She announced that Louise had sought sanctuary from a brutal husband and that it had been granted.[13]

After further futile angry antics, the prince returned to the Palazzo Guadagni. Now discerning something of the truth, he told his dinner companions that night that he would give half his fortune to see Geoghan shot.[14] On being told of this, the young roué had the effrontery to ask for satisfaction.[15] He ran little risk that his challenge would be accepted from an old man who suffered from dropsy, asthma and apoplexy! Geoghan justified his treachery — for the prince had always been fond of him and treated him well — by claiming that a male accomplice was necessary for the convent escape, since Charles Edward always carried a brace of pistols on his person.[16]

While the prince vainly sought redress by sending count Spada to remonstrate with the Grand Duke (double jeopardy!), Louise sought Cardinal York's blessing on the desperate course she had taken. Henry replied that her news came as no surprise; he had foreseen something like this for years.[17] He conferred with the Pope. Pius VI agreed that she had served her time in the vale of tears with the prince.[18] The upshot was an invitation to reside in the same convent (and the very same apartment) in which Clementina Sobieska had taken refuge forty-five years before.[19] To this end the Pope was prepared, provided the Grand Duke of Tuscany did the same, to approve her immediate departure for Rome.

On the night of 27 December 1780 Louise left for Rome. Elaborate precautions were taken to prevent the insensate prince from abducting her. Both Alfieri and Geoghan accompanied her part of the way; Alfieri then returned to Florence to avoid scandal.[20]

The prince meanwhile sat stunned in the Palazzo Guadagni. At first he thought of making difficulties over the clothes Louise requested him to send on, then thought better of it.[21] He was now in possession of the full facts regarding his wife and Alfieri. Over the dinner table he poured out his bitterness against the Piedmontese poet. Emboldened by the prince's lack of response to his earlier bravado, Geoghan claimed to be outraged by the imputations that the 'noble Count Alfieri' was a seducer, and sent a second challenge to a duel.[22] For double-dyed humbug and cowardice, allied to his general depravity, this Irish adventurer took some beating.

But very soon the focus of the prince's rage shifted from Alfieri to his own brother. There was certainly something peculiar about the gusto with which Henry took up his sister-in-law's case. Notions of sibling rivalry spring to mind. This was Henry's unconscious revenge for the snubs and humiliations he had received over the years at the prince's hands. That there was something unseemly about the avidity with which Henry supported Louise's uncorroborated assertions was noticed by Horace Mann. With his usual prurience, he remarked sneeringly: 'Are they Jews enough, if the Count should die, to uncanonise the cardinal, and make him raise up issue for his brother, which the brother could not do for himself?'[23]

Henry's actions lent a specious plausibility to such a scenario. As soon as Louise arrived in Rome, he arranged an audience with the Pope. Thereafter Louise was a frequent visitor to the cardinal's palace at Frascati. He even offered to let her have the use of his town house in Rome at his expense, but she declined, saying she did not want to remain in Italy.[24] She did, however, accept the offer from Cardinal Conti of the loan of his villa at Frascati for the month of July.[25]

Throughout 1781 the relationship between Cardinal York and the 'Queen of Hearts' continued warm. By now a supremely accomplished coquette, Louise's tactic with Henry was to lay it on with a trowel.[26] Still protesting that her relationship with Alfieri was entirely platonic, she sent the cardinal a new copy of Virgil, using her poet-lover as messenger, and alleging that he just happened to be dining with her at the time![27]

It was not just in dealing with Henry that Louise showed herself to be a skilled politician. Unerringly, she made herself agreeable to Charles Edward's arch-enemy Cardinal Bernis.[28] To cap all, the Pope assigned her half of the papal pension of 12,000 crowns that he paid to the prince.[29]

In addition, Louise persuaded the queen of France to assign her a pension of 20,000 crowns (£5,000) a year for life.[30] This was over and above the personal allowance of 4,000 crowns that Henry paid her plus the expenses of a sumptuous apartment with a fine equipage and servants.[31] It has to be remembered that all this time Louise was carrying on her affair with Alfieri in secret and joking with him about the fatuousness of Cardinal York, as she later admitted. For Louise had not remained long in the Ursuline convent. She cajoled and pleaded with Henry to allow her a more worldly existence. Within a month she transferred to the Palace of the Cancelleria, where she remained until the summer of 1784.[32] Once Alfieri heard that she had exchanged her sacred sanctuary for a 'profane' one, he left Florence secretly to join her in Rome.

The more Charles Edward heard of his wife's financial prosperity and her cosy relationship with his brother, while he himself struggled in Florence to make ends meet on a reduced pension, the more angry and depressed at his brother's treachery he became. His wife's extravagances, he claimed, had already brought him close to ruin.[33]

Now she was being encouraged to commit further follies in Rome while his own pension was being cut to accommodate this.

His letters were divided between expressions of indignation at his wife's conduct and stupefaction at Henry's reaction to it.[34] At first he was inclined to quit Florence. He spoke of going to Venice for the 1781 festival and then settling in Genoa.[35] Then he decided to stay and fight. Initially his position was that he was prepared to have his wife back provided she repented publicly.[36] As this looked increasingly unlikely, he turned to tougher strategies. In November 1781 he wrote to the bishop of Florence to have his case put before an ecclesiastical court.

The stubborn, streetfighting Charles Edward is still in evidence in this letter. He asked how it was that an adulterous woman could find sanctuary in a Florentine convent, then proceed to Rome without let or hindrance from the ecclesiastical authorities, and finally stay in the house of his own brother, a cardinal. I had always thought, he concludes sardonically, that the Catholic religion supported the rights of the husband in such cases.[37] Since the Pope had extended his personal protection to Louise, it is not surprising that the prince's application was unsuccessful. Bishop Antonio Martini simply referred the matter to Henry, with a request for guidance. The appeal to the bishop of Florence thus became one more futile appeal to Cardinal York.[38]

As 1782 opened, the tenor of Charles Edward's complaints against his brother for treachery became increasingly shrill. 'It is impossible that such a man can be a brother,' he concluded despairingly. 'How can my brother be so blind?'[39]

Charles decided to send his gentleman of the bedchamber, Sgr Cantini, to Rome to lay the full facts before Henry. Cantini had taken over Spada's duties after the latter's dismissal in 1781. Cantini was to stress particularly that it was the prince, not Cardinal York, who suffered from Louise's extravagances.[40] The halving of his pension continued to be a festering wound; how could the prince doubt that his brother was now his prime enemy?[41]

As 1782 progressed, Charles Edward continued to inveigh against his monster of a brother. He alleged that Henry's treatment of him had turned him into the laughing-stock of Florence. The humiliation over Louise was compounded by desperate money shortages. The Palazzo Guadagni was in urgent need of repair after a recent earthquake; he was down to two good horses and could afford no more.[42] His only consolation was that some of the Florentine nobility were so shocked by Henry's unbrotherly behaviour that they went out of their way to be seen in the prince's company.[43]

Part of the prince's trouble was that he had no one of sufficient *gravitas* to go to Rome and plead his case before the Pope. That defect was partly remedied by the unexpected arrival of the duke of Fitzjames on an Italian tour.[44] At once Charles deputed him to lay his version of events before the Vatican.[45] Meanwhile, the prince took advantage of the Austrian emperor's visit to his brother the duke of Tuscany to lobby *him* for support.[46]

When Fitzjames arrived in Rome, he sought out Prince Bartolomeo Corsini, a long-time supporter of Charles Edward.[47] Together Fitzjames and Corsini sought and obtained an audience with the Pope and explained Charles's position. They asked for three things: the return of the prince's wife; the banishment of Alfieri from Rome; and the payment of the entire papal pension to the prince without deductions.[48]

Pius VI was sufficiently disturbed by what he heard to call in Henry for further consultations. Unfortunately, Henry was still disposed to accept at face value Louise's protestations of innocence in her dealings with Alfieri.[49] He described her conduct during 1781 and 1782 as 'impeccable' and declared that hers was the clearest right to asylum he had ever encountered.[50]

Prince Corsini then came into the firing line from three directions. The Pope censured him for having accepted such a commission. The Grand Duke of Tuscany rebuked him for acting contrary to Florentine interests – since the decline in Charles Edward's income kept him at home and away from the city's casinos and theatres.[51] Finally, Henry weighed in by writing Corsini an open letter on the subject. He dealt firmly with his brother's arguments. Quite apart from the fact that Charles Edward's expenses must now be less, on his own admission since his 'extravagant' wife had left him, the papal pension the prince received was entirely a grace and favour matter at Henry's discretion; the papal pension had been left to Henry in James's will.[52]

The mission ended in catastrophe. Fitzjames, whose track-record of work for the prince was singularly disastrous, found his failure so humiliating that he did not even deign to visit Charles on the return journey. He merely wrote a few lines from Genoa to advise the prince that all hopes of getting his wife back were vain.[53] Then he hurried on to the calmer pastures of France.

Yet, just when it seemed that Louise had won a final victory and that her position was unassailable, the tide turned against her in dramatic fashion. Suddenly the prince fell seriously ill. The dropsy on his chest made breathing even more difficult and painful. He appeared to be coming to his last gasp. Extreme unction was administered and Henry was sent for.[54]

The prince's illness was grave. His left leg was now in the throes of elephantiasis, his entire body was swollen, he struggled for every breath. The prince cried out in agony to his doctors during the worst crisis. His chief physician, sixty-four-year-old Natalis Joseph Palucci, bathed his legs twice a day in a bath of milk and applied poultices to raise blisters on the skin.[55]

Meanwhile Cardinal York sped northwards in his famed fast-horse carriages, the dread and envy of the Campagna. At Siena he paused and sent on an emissary, expecting to hear that his brother had already died. But that admirable constitution had secured the prince a reprieve. Although his fever increased and he was subject to dreadful attacks of diarrhoea, he was saved once again by the suppurating leg. Once this began to discharge, the swelling in his thighs and on his chest lessened. For the moment Charles Edward was out of danger.[56]

When Henry arrived in Florence, on 29 March 1783, the two brothers were in that mood of dispassionate lucidity often induced by a brush with death. After finding lodgings at a convent near his brother's house, Henry spent Sunday 30 March at his bedside.[57] That day Charles told the cardinal the full story of Louise's liaison with Alfieri, adding the kind of circumstantial detail that put the gist of his story beyond doubt. At last Henry's eyes were opened. He began to realise how deeply he had been duped by the Queen of Hearts. With his anger fuelled by self-contempt at having been so ingenuously gullible, the cardinal sped back to Rome to settle accounts.[58]

He secured an immediate audience with Pius VI, put the full facts before him, and demanded Alfieri's immediate expulsion from the papal domains. Pius shared Henry's bitterness at having been duped. He gave the order for the expulsion: Alfieri was to leave Rome within fifteen days.[59]

Even then Louise claimed a moral victory. She wrote to Henry to say that she had 'advised' Alfieri to quit Rome because of rumours about her 'blameless' conduct, and chided the cardinal for mentioning the matter to the Pope before discussing it with her.[60] Nevertheless, on Alfieri's own admission, the expulsion order came as a crushing blow to Psiphio and Psiphia (the onomatopoeic names, significant of kissing, by which the two lovers styled themselves).[61] The parting from his lady was so poignant for Alfieri that he records the exact date of his departure from Rome: 4 May 1783.[62]

The only satisfaction the pair could take was from Roman public opinion. Rome was a city of libertinism and lubricity, for which emotional Catholicism provided a glittering cloak. Henry made the great mistake of having the details of the Alfieri affair published. Instead of being scandalised, Roman society felt instinctive sympathy for the story-book lovers.[63] Henry's reputation, never high outside the corridors of power in the Vatican, plummeted further.

Charles Edward meanwhile made a miraculous recovery. By September he was so far on the mend that he was making little excursions to the towns in Tuscany to watch horse races and other local spectacles. He also spent a week in Siena.[64] Once his energies were restored, he began again to lobby the French court. On 26 September, he wrote to the comte de Vergennes, renewing the plea that Louis XVI undertake his restoration and adding (doubtless with the loss of the American colonies in mind), 'the moment was never more favourable'.[65] He also reminded the French that the pension promised at the time of his marriage had still not been paid.

The expulsion of Alfieri and the recovery of his own health seemed to suggest that Charles was on a winning streak (albeit a minor one). This impression was reinforced in the autumn of 1783 when the prince at last began to receive the royal treatment he so craved. His benefactor was King Gustav III of Sweden, then travelling in Italy under the name of count Haga.[66] When Gustav came to the baths at Pisa to nurse a broken arm, he heard the sad story of the prince's misfortunes. He expressed an interest in meeting Charles.[67] Chevalier de Tours, Gustav's friend, who also had Jacobite connections through his marriage to the Irish aristocrat Lady St George, was sent to Florence as go-between.[68]

The prince invited Gustav to stay with him. To his great delight, the Swedish king agreed to do so. For Charles this was an unprecedented honour. Protocol had hitherto prevented him (as the count of Albany) from receiving sovereigns. The duke of Tuscany had never graced the Palazzo Guadagni with a visit.[69]

Gustav was in Florence throughout December 1783.[70] The prince laid on a series of lavish dinners for him. Over the first meal Charles Edward poured out to Gustav all his bitterness about France. He doubted that Vergennes had even shown his recent letter to Louis XVI. He asked Gustav for help to get him the 240,000 livres a year pension that James used to receive from Versailles. Gustav agreed to help; there had been times in his own life, he confided, when he had been close to the financial straits the prince was now in.[71]

As mutual confidence grew, Gustav put it to Charles Edward that he should accept that all hopes of a Stuart restoration were vain. Kingly dignity was best served by a patient submission to the caprices of fate; after all, Gustav argued, it was the lot of kings to be less happy than other men.[72] Charles seemed to give tacit consent. At any rate, he asked Gustav to find a final solution to his affairs: 'I agree completely to a total separation from my wife and to her no longer bearing my name.'[73]

The appearance of the Swedish king at the Palazzo Guadagni predictably threw the neurotic fusspot Sir Horace Mann into a dither of uncertainty. There had been serious disturbances in Ireland in 1782–3 and Mann feared that the coming of Gustav presaged some new Jacobite scheme on the Celtic fringes.[74] At first he reacted by writing dismissively of Gustav. Then his attitude changed. After suborning the chevalier de Tours, he learned there was nothing to fear. De Tours assured him the prince's ambitions were for money and money alone.[75] Charles Edward had told the Swedish king that the French had deceived him once too often. Nowadays, nothing less than a solemn invitation from England with signatures, like that sent to William of Orange in 1688, plus 70–80,000 crack French troops, would induce him to go to Britain again.[76]

Mann was content. He was indifferent to the 'Pretender's' applications to foreign courts for money. From now on he received detailed verbatim reports from the chevalier de Tours of every conversation between him or Gustav and the prince, plus copies of every letter sent to Versailles. He was thus able to gloat over the fate of Stuart representations to Louis XVI.

Gustav and Tours drafted a financial remonstrance to the French king in Charles's name. Vergennes wrote back at once to say that he could not forward the papers to Louis as they were signed 'Charles, Roi'. In any case, it was beneath the dignity of His Most Christian Majesty to take notice of a domestic quarrel between the Stuart pretender and his wife.[77]

Gustav then tried to persuade the prince to liquidate his other assets. The great ruby of the crown of Scotland, held in the Monte di Pieta, was mentioned. This would find a ready buyer in Czarina Catherine of Russia. Charles Edward rejected the idea with indignation: he would never part with the ruby, since he intended to add it to the crown of England when he was restored.[78]

Since Gustav seemed even now not to have understood the dimensions of the problem, the prince explained it patiently to him. As far as France was concerned, there were two considerations. Because of the actions of various comptroller-generals, the interest on the funds held by the Stuarts in the Hôtel de Ville at Paris had declined from an annual yield of 80,000 livres to just 36,000. Much more important, France had broken a solemn promise, made in 1771 by the duc d'Aigullon, that if the prince married, he would receive the same annual pension as his father (240,000 livres).[79]

Seeing the scope of the problem, Gustav wrote again to the French court. To avoid delays, he sent the letter in his own hand to his minister in Paris. He also wrote to the Spanish court. To tide Charles Edward over immediate problems, he advanced him 4,000 rix dollars (about £1,000). But first he extracted a promise from Charles Edward that he would accept whatever sum the French awarded him. In his letter to Louis XVI, Gustav shrewdly refrained from mentioning any definite amount of money.[80]

The prince was delighted with the way Gustav treated him. Here was a fellow-monarch accepting him as a king, pressing his claim with the hated French, giving him all the consideration he had always sought in vain.[81] Charles was so euphoric that he hardly noticed when Gustav casually revealed the ulterior motive behind his generosity and altruism. But to make sense of this motive we have to go back more than fifty years, to the early days of the Jacobite movement.

The primary impetus for the rise of freemasonry in the first quarter of the eighteenth century came from the Jacobites. The great names of early freemasonry were all partisans of the House of Stuart: the duke of Wharton, the earl of Derwentwater, the chevalier Ramsay (Charles Edward's tutor in 1724). The first lodges in England, France, Spain and Italy were extended Jacobite clubs.[82] Many of James Stuart's closest advisers – the duke of Ormonde, Earl Marischal, even the Anglican clergyman in the Palazzo Muti, Ezekiel Hamilton – were masons. As the 1730s opened, the list of names lengthened to include many of the best-known personalities of the '45, such as Kilmarnock and Murray of Broughton.

But this decade also saw the infiltration of the masonic lodges by British intelligence. Freemasonry ceased to be a Jacobite secret society and seemed likely instead to become a Hanoverian fifth column. Alerted by James Stuart, Clement XII began to invoke the papal Inquisition against the masons.

The lodges kept a low profile and waited for the storm to blow over.[83] It did not. Almost certainly the principal motive for Clement XII's dramatic action in 1738 was that the Hanoverians had secured an important victory in the anti-Jacobite espionage battle by bringing the lodges under anti-Stuart leadership.[84] But whatever his reasons,

Clement issued an edict in that year excommunicating freemasons. In the opinion of his successor Benedict XIV, this was Clement's worst political error.[85]

Outside the papal states the edict had little effect. In Florence the 30,000 or so masons were simply driven underground.[86] And in France Louis XIV and Fleury made sure the ordinance was not published – *lex non promulgata non obligat*, a law not promulgated has no force – so that the masonic movement there did not even have to break step. Most of the great names of eighteenth-century France occupied one or other grade in the lodges: Noailles, Conti, Saxe, Choiseul. French masons like Montesquieu and the duc de Bouillon were among Charles Edward's most important contacts.[87]

With so many friends and associates in the movement it might be thought that Charles Edward, especially with his penchant for secrecy, would be a natural choice as mason. And it is true that at the time of Clement XII's interdiction, he showed great interest in this secret organisation.[88] But his father's unyielding opposition and that of the influential Jesuit Cordara (who wrote a history of the prince's adventures in the '45), prevented him from advancing beyond simple curiosity. The many stories about lodges allegedly founded by the prince turn out to be so many myths.[89]

Now we confront one of the many curious aspects of freemasonry. It was a persistent legend among freemasons that Charles Edward Stuart was the secret head of the entire masonic order. Some said that he was the 'conscious' head and as such, dressed as a masked knight, had inducted many new members into the recondite secrets of the masons. This Lohengrin-like aspect of Charles Edward was plausible, since it fitted both his role as Nietzschean hero and his love of secrecy and disguises.[90]

Others maintained that the head of the Stuart family was the hereditary Grand Master of the Order, whether he realised it or not, since the hereditary principle was integral to masonic beliefs – a curious inverted gloss on the doctrine of indefeasible right. This was supposed always to have been the case, ever since the days of inchoate masonry under Charles II.[91]

It was to clear up these mysteries that Ferdinand, duke of Brunswick, sent his envoy Baron Wachter to Italy in 1777. The principal object of his mission was to find out if Charles Edward Stuart really was the secret Grand Master of all masonic lodges.

Wachter interviewed the prince at Florence on 21 September 1777. Charles Edward told him that he had never belonged to the organisation and therefore, presumably, could not be its Superior.[92] Most of the names mentioned by Wachter were unknown to him. Kilmarnock he knew purely from his activities in the '45. Nevertheless the prince, at the time in acute financial straits, saw a chance to turn matters to his advantage. He told Wachter that if the masons were convinced that he had an hereditary right to the title of Grand Master, he would be happy to accept it. It did not take excessive insight to see that both money and political influence could accrue to the holder of such a position. Wachter promised to promote the prince's cause with the German masons. Charles Edward in turn signed the envoy's affidavit.[93]

When Wachter returned to Germany, he wrote encouragingly to the prince about a Prussian proposal to land 6,000 troops in Scotland provided the prince raised the clans.[94] Charles was non-committal, suspecting (rightly) that Wachter was merely sweetening him up prior to revealing his real intentions.[95]

Next Wachter asked for details of James's movements in the 1740s that would clinch the issue of possible secret links between Jacobites and masons *after* the papal interdiction. The prince replied that James had deposited a large number of his papers in a 'safe house' to prevent their coming into his son's hands.[96]

For the next three years Wachter and the prince fenced with each other.[97] Predictably, without James's papers, the German masons made no further mention of the Prussian project. The prince, too, had learned cunning. When Wachter sent an envoy to Florence to make a casual request for old Jacobite papers, Charles rebuffed him on the grounds that, since he had made no mention of freemasonry, he could not be a bona fide agent of Wachter's![98]

It was at this stage that the Swedes started to steal the Germans' masonic thunder. Gustav III's diplomats encouraged Charles Edward to believe that the difficulties the Germans were making over giving him the title of Grand Master were spurious. In Stockholm the prince's right was fully accepted.[99]

Charles would have done well to remember these straws in the wind when Gustav appeared in Florence, but it is likely that his mental faculties had been severely affected by his near-fatal illness in the spring of 1783. It is abundantly clear that Gustav's real purpose in visiting the prince in December that year was to secure a formal transfer of the title of Grand Master.[100] Gustav was already head of Swedish masonry. What he wanted, and obtained, from Charles Edward, was a patent proclaiming him Grand Master of the entire Templar order. Even if the prince had fully realised what Gustav was up to, it is likely that he would have sold the title in return for the immediate advance of 4,000 rix dollars and the promise of more to come. As it was, the prince got a better deal than that. In exchange for a financial settlement, including the divorce of his wife, Charles gave Gustav a clear title as Grand Master once he died. The prince signed a document making the Swedish king coadjutor in the masons and his eventual successor.[101]

At the eleventh hour the German masons realised that they had been too clever by half. They sent Wachter on another urgent mission to Italy. But he did not arrive until April 1784, by which time Gustav had the transfer patent in his pocket.[102] The sequence of events after Gustav's departure from Florence at the end of December 1783 takes on an entirely different hue once we realise what his true purpose was. The fact is that Gustav III came close to securing the bargain of the century with the *quid pro quo* negotiated in the Palazzo Guadagni.

The Swedish king had been shocked by Charles's general state of health. The prince was bent forward and decrepit and walked only with great pain. His mental faculties were deserting him. After a quarter of an hour he would repeat identical anecdotes told earlier. Clearly he was hanging by a thread during Gustav's visit and sustaining himself with the 'honour' a fellow-monarch was paying him.

No sooner had Gustav departed than Charles Edward fell seriously ill again. This time the prince was thought certain to die. At first he lost all power of speech. His physicians thought he had suffered an apoplectic stroke, then changed the diagnosis to inflammation in the brain. For two days Charles lay speechless and insensible. Then for a short time he recovered consciousness but not the power of speech. Next day he had just two hours of mental lucidity, again with no speech. Just when his doctors were despairing of him, he recovered.[103]

Meanwhile in Rome Gustav's mission ran into a hitch. From Louise of Stolberg and her champion Cardinal Bernis the Swedish king heard a quite different version of events. According to them, Charles Edward was a rich miser who neither needed nor deserved financial assistance.[104] There is some evidence that Gustav half believed them, but he was now firmly committed out of fear that the prince might otherwise repudiate his masonic succession, especially with Wachter in Italy.

Gustav counterattacked. Calmly he agreed with Louise but pointed out certain facts of life. Did she really want to remain forever in a Roman limbo, tied to the strings of the capricious Cardinal York, when she could obtain a favourable divorce settlement, giving her the freedom to live anywhere and be with Alfieri?[105] The argument was irresistible. With the acquiescence of Henry and the Pope, Gustav hammered out a financial agreement. Louise was to give up her 4,000 crowns of the papal pension and the 15,000 livres pin money in return for the freedom to reside wherever she liked. On formal separation she would receive a pension of 60,000 livres from France plus an annual payment of 6,000 crowns on the prince's death. Charles Edward received the full papal pension of 10,000 crowns plus uncontested rights to the effects in the Palazzo Muti and to his share of the Sobieski jewels.[106]

Louise was agreeable in principle, but she wanted more binding guarantees, in particular a written statement from Charles Edward that the two of them were living apart by mutual consent. This Charles Edward duly provided: 'We give our free and voluntary consent to this separation and agree that she should live in Rome or whatever other town seems agreeable to her.'[107]

The divorce settlement was a great diplomatic triumph for Gustav III. Louise wrote profuse letters of thanks to him and his minister Baron Sparre.[108] By, in effect, getting France to foot the bill for the sundering of the unhappy Stuart couple, he gained his patent as Grand Master of Freemasons at an outlay of just 4,000 rix dollars. The cunning Swedish fox had instructed his Florentine banker to use the excuse of the prince's illness not to pay the second instalment of rix dollars.[109] He then 'assumed' that his particular financial agreement with the prince was now subsumed in the general divorce settlement. Quitting Rome in mid-April 1784, Gustav lost no time in shaking the dust of Italy from his heels.[110]

Only when the Swedish king was gone did it occur to Cantini and other financial managers in the prince's household to examine the situation. On application to Gustav's Florence banker, they learned that the king had indeed left a verbal order to pay Charles Edward 50,000 French livres a year for life, but had declined to put the order in writing! When the prince's accountants applied to Vergennes, it transpired that Gustav had not tied up the French end of things either.[111] Fortunately, perhaps, for the prince, he was too ill fully to take in the implications of Gustav's double-dealing. He was saved by illness from knowledge of this last in a long line of betrayals.

Yet at least the knot binding Charles Edward and Louise was severed. She was free to pursue an itinerant life with Alfieri. Her 'special relationship' with Henry, already in abeyance after the 1783 Alfieri revelations, gradually ground to a halt. The adulterous relationship with the poet totally changed Henry's view of her.[112] She continued to write to him as if to a friend,[113] but his reply was cold.

He used his intense irritation about the divorce settlement to mask his hostility towards her. 'It is a piece of insolence . . . on my brother's part, this disposing of money which is mine, as though it were his own, and without my knowledge.'[114] He ended by asking her not to write to him again, as her marital business adversely affected his health.

Louise showed her true opinion of the 'friend' she had flattered for years. She promoted the rumour that Henry ran a puritanical regime in his See at Frascati, which he aspired to turn into a secular monastery; 'a comic figure', she summed him up savagely.[115]

So ended the ill-starred marriage of Charles Edward Stuart. A final assessment seems in order. Louise of Stolberg claimed that in nine years the prince made her the most miserable person that ever existed and that only Christian charity stopped her hating him. Her protestations of virtue sound somewhat hollow alongside her frequent denunciations of her husband: unlivable with, repository of all the vices, possessing the sensibility of a lackey, these are merely the mild criticisms. 'An old walking relic,' 'Useless people never die,' 'It would be a good thing to deliver the world of his weight, with which it has been overcharged too long,'[116] these are some of the epistolary comments of this exemplar of Christian charity.

Louise of Stolberg presents more than usually difficult problems of biographical interpretation. Opinions on her have been wildly divergent. Proto-feminist writers have seen her as the classical emancipated woman yet condemned to be the victim of a drunken, loutish husband. Bonnie Prince Charlie hagiographers have viewed her as low, mean-minded and contemptible. The truth, as so often, lies somewhere between these two extremes. It *is* true that by the 1770s the prince was impossible. His drunken rages and physical violence fully justified Louise's departure in 1780. But it would be a mistake to deduce from this alone that Louise was a simple avatar of sweetness and light. She was a cold, unsentimental, ruthless woman, one of those people with a much higher opinion of herself than was warranted by any wit or wisdom she produced.

She could be charming and delightful but, like most charmers, she calculated the effects to a nicety. She was a consummate coquette but, as with most coquettes, sex was not the spur. She had pretensions as a blue-stocking, but was not in the same class even as a Madame du Deffand or Lady Wortley Montagu, to say nothing of the far superior Madame de Stael. She lacked the wit and accomplishment of the Princesse de Talmont or the spontaneous sexual passion of the duchesse de Montbazon.

Moreover, the indictment against Louise must show that she systematically deceived her brother-in-law out of a mercenary desire not to suffer the financial consequences that would normally have flown from her adultery. The idea of Louise of Stolberg as a woman who would sacrifice everything for love is too wildly at variance with the facts to be taken seriously. She was an accomplished liar, cold, cynical and egotistical.

What she did have was a certain aesthetic sense that allowed her to appreciate the gifts of Bonstetten, Fabre, Alfieri and others. She was an aesthete rather than an intellectual. She was either bored or contemptuous in the company of statesmen or soldiers; a less satisfactory choice as wife for a warrior prince could scarcely be imagined. Moreover, the prince's heavy drinking was peculiarly calculated to elicit a distaste in such a woman. No woman would have relished Charles Edward's drunkenness, but the evidence suggests that Clementina Walkinshaw feared the violence it engendered. What seems to have hurt Louise most was the lack of 'style' involved; the prince behaved like a lackey.

When to the considerable difference in their ages and the basic disharmony between their temperaments is added the mutual disappointment over the marriage, with both parties feeling that in some sense it had been contracted under false pretences, one can only be surprised that the relationship lasted as long as it did. In this connection it is fascinating to observe that both Clementina and Louise of Stolberg endured a little over eight years of the prince before decamping to convents. Cohabitation with Charles Edward, it seemed, produced not so much a seven-year itch as an eight-year frenzy.

38

The Duchess of Albany

(1784–8)

Apart from the divorce and departure of Louise of Stolberg, 1784 brought two more highly significant developments in Charles Edward's life. The first was a partial resolution of his financial difficulties. The second was the reappearance of his daughter Charlotte.

The financial resolution showed Henry in his least favourable light. With Louise out of the picture, both brothers felt able to bring the Sobieski monies out into the open. Liquidating these assets would have put all money worries behind the prince. But Henry was afraid that, when the statute of limitations on Polish redemption of the Sobieski rubies expired, Charles Edward would sell them off to the highest bidder.[1] Since the disposal of the assets in the Monte di Pietà required the signature of both brothers, Henry got what he wanted by refusing to sign. This was completely contrary to the 1742 agreement, which explicitly stated that the disposal of these jewels was Charles Edward's prerogative.[2]

Henry, who had huffed and puffed over his own technical rights during Gustav III's financial settlement, was unwilling to concede his brother's much clearer rights in this instance. He compounded his hypocrisy in 1786 by having the great Sobieski ruby set in his bishop's mitre.[3] And in 1796 he did what he had so denigrated his brother for having supposedly wanted to do: he sold a ruby from the collection, described as 'as large as a pigeon's egg' for some £60,000.[4]

To palliate his poor treatment of his brother, Cardinal York offered him the rest of the Sobieski jewels without argument. This was no hardship to Henry. In contemporary terms he was a millionaire. His annual income from land and church benefices was in excess of 600,000 French livres. And he had just received the arrears from his Mexican benefices, whose payment had been suspended during the

north American war. This amounted to 180,000 Roman crowns
(£45,000).[5] The charge of avarice and miserliness and love of money,
so often brought against Charles Edward, ought rather to have been
laid at his brother's door.

The freeing of his assets in Rome from any further claims from
Louise of Stolberg also enabled the prince to improve his living
standards in other ways. Further items of furniture were brought up
to Florence from the Palazzo Muti.[6] The prince went so far as to ask
the Grand Duke of Tuscany if he could place a canopy with a cloth
of state over his box at the theatre. This was refused, but permission
was given the prince to line the box as he pleased. In one of the
Florentine theatres he furnished his box with crimson damask and
cushions laced with gold. In the other theatre box the same process
was repeated, except for the substitution of yellow damask.[7]

Yet this increased material prosperity was insignificant compared
with Charles's reconciliation with his daughter Charlotte.[8] Even after
the humiliating rebuff in Rome in 1773, Charlotte refused to take no
for an answer. She had all her father's dogged stubbornness. Using
her friend Abbé Gordon, in 1774 she threatened to marry some
unknown commoner unless Charles did something for her. Angry at
being threatened like this, the prince warned her that she could be
cast into anathema for ever if she took such a step.[9] Baulked in this
tactic, Charlotte then bombarded the French court with memoranda,
lamenting her own and her mother's plight.[10] She won the powerful
support of the duc de Richelieu and the duc de Bourbon.[11]

Charles Edward would have done well at this stage to silence his
daughter by promising her something, for Charlotte's appeals to
Versailles cut across Charles Edward's own lobbying of the French
court (this was just after 1774 when the prince was writing to
Maurepas and Vergennes). Faced with competing claims, Louis XVI
decided that Clementina Walkinshaw and Charlotte had the more
deserving case. Their suit would also be cheaper to settle. 'Pouponne'
and her mother were awarded a small pension.[12]

Charlotte meanwhile kept plugging away at her father, undeterred
by his refusal to answer her letters.[13] In 1774 she found a new ally.
Doctor Mahony, James's personal physician, appealed on her behalf,
explaining to Charles Edward about the obstruction in her liver and
the pain it produced.[14] The prince's reply to this was shockingly
callous. He simply reiterated his warning that if she again strayed
out of France for any reason, she would lose all hope of any future
advantage or protection.[15] No amount of special pleading about the

prince's worries about the succession can mitigate the lack of compassion in that letter.[16]

Gordon and Caryll, Charlotte's great champions, were left to shake their heads in disbelief at her father's coldness. This lack of paternal feeling for a seriously ill young woman certainly played its part in Caryll's decision to quit the prince's service in 1775. Gordon was particularly disgusted at Charles's 'dog in the manger' attitude to his daughter. He would neither offer her a word of encouragement nor allow her to marry someone with enough money to keep her, 'since she is at present of a proper age, and if she were to wait much longer, it is probable she would find none'. All her doctors were agreed that her spirits were dashed by Charles Edward's uncompromising posture, and that this depression augmented the organic symptoms in her liver. After all, as Gordon pointed out, 'she was only six years old when carried off that night. She ought not to be utterly ruined for a fault of which her age hindered to be any ways partner.'[17]

Yet as soon as she recovered from that buffet, Charlotte kept up the steady drip-drip of pressure on her father.[18] She hinted that if forbidden to marry, she would join a mendicant order of nuns. How she fused secular and religious ambitions will shortly appear. And, to the prince's fury, his new Paris agent (a replacement for the ageing Gordon) took up the refrain. William Cowley, Prior of the English Benedictines in Paris, started to press her case, repeatedly referring to her bad health and the ominous swelling in her side.[19]

These representations must have kept Charlotte at the back of the prince's mind. Nevertheless, his action in June 1784 surprised a lot of people. No sooner was the ink dry on Gustav III's divorce settlement than the prince announced that he was recognising Charlotte as his legitimate daughter and heiress. This would entitle her to the appellation 'duchess of Albany'.[20] The prince then asked her to come with all speed to Florence.[21]

In the act of legitimation the prince referred to himself as 'grandson of James II, king of Great Britain'. He then wrote to Vergennes to get his solemn deed of recognition registered with the Paris Parlement and to renew the call for the money Gustav was supposed to have negotiated out of Versailles.[22]

As with everything Charles Edward touched, problems of protocol immediately arose. Louis XVI recognised Charlotte as the 'Pretender's daughter' by letters patent of August 1784, registered by the Parlement of Paris the following month, but refused to accept the title of the duchess of Albany.[23]

Armed with this patent, the prince tried to browbeat the court of Tuscany. He asked for his daughter's recognition as duchess, alleging that the French king had already allowed this. The Grand Duke knew the true situation. He allowed the act of legitimation to be published in Florence, but deleted all references to 'the Duchess of Albany'.[24]

Nevertheless, this was a great achievement for Charlotte. All her highest hopes had come to fruition, thanks to her patient and dauntless perseverance. But why did the prince come round so dramatically, after years of cold and callous disregard? The answer is to be sought in his psychology rather than his emotions. There was little of the light on the road to Damascus here.

The delayed shock of Louise's departure took time to make its full impact felt. But after 1781 it is safe to say that there are signs of senility in Charles Edward. His rapturous reception of Gustav III was significant. Having previously displayed a capacity for relatively mature functioning, the prince in the last phase of his life entered a period of regression. Characteristically, this psychological condition involves cleaving to people who will treat the subject as a favoured only child, and holding at arm's length those who will not accord him that status.

In short, Charles Edward's seemingly magnanimous actions towards his daughter in 1784 are far more likely to have reflected his own needs than spontaneous emotion for the once much-loved Pouponne.

Charlotte was indifferent to such nuances. She had achieved her life's ambition. In high excitement she made ready to leave the convent of St Marie in Paris. She wrote to Henry in rather vainglorious style, presuming to address him as uncle now that she was legitimate daughter and heiress of the prince.[25] Then, on 18 September 1784, she started south for Florence.[26]

At the beginning of October she arrived in the Tuscan capital.[27] The prince tried to arrange for her to be presented to the Grand Duchess, but this ploy failed since Charlotte had no letter of recommendation from the French queen.[28] But her coming did cause a minor sensation in Florence, as Mann reluctantly conceded, though granting Charlotte only the status of curiosity value:

she is allowed to be a good figure, tall and well-made, but that the features of the face resemble too much those of her father to be handsome. She is gay, lively and very affable, and has the behaviour of a well-bred French woman, without assuming the least distinction among our ladies on account of her new dignity.[29]

The fashionable ladies of Florence flocked to leave their cards at the Palazzo Guadagni. Charlotte, who was a good administrator, set about organising the household. She made sufficiently rapid progress to be able to take Charles Edward on a tour of Tuscany two weeks after her arrival.

Clearly the condition in which she found her father deeply shocked her. She decided he needed fresh air and an escape from the tedious Florentine routine in which he had become ossified for the past decade. They headed west to Lucca to see a much-praised opera.[30] On the way there the prince gave ample proof that he needed round-the-clock nursing. At Pistoya he was convulsed with an apoplectic fit that lasted four hours. But Charlotte persisted with the excursion. They proceeded to the theatre at Lucca.[31]

The coming of the prince's daughter seemed to change his luck. There had been a long silence from Versailles since Gustav's intervention.[32] Suddenly word came that Vergennes had granted a pension of 60,000 livres a year to the prince, with a reversionary payment to Charlotte of 10,000 livres a year to her on his death.[33] To clear up any doubts about Charlotte's eligibility to bequests on his death, the prince made a solemn declaration that Charlotte was his only child and that he had no others, especially not with Louise of Stolberg.[34]

The other piece of good fortune was the Pope's recognition of Charlotte as duchess of Albany. Pius VI had received reports that Charlotte had brought about a miraculous transformation in the prince's temper and bearing. As a reward, he granted her the title that neither France nor the duchy of Tuscany were prepared to concede.[35]

This papal recognition left Cardinal York out on a limb. Furious both about Charlotte's legitimation, on which he was not consulted, and with her 'impertinence' in writing to him in an over-familiar tone, he had resisted her blandishments.[36] When he protested to the prince, Charles Edward coldly told him that it was not his business, nor was it for him to cavil where the Pope and the French court had raised no difficulty; since he did not dispute Henry's rights, Cardinal York ought not to dispute his.[37]

Henry always squirmed under the lash of his brother's rebukes. He looked around for a means of petty vengeance. Thinking that Louise of Stolberg had now renounced Alfieri for ever, he began to soften towards her. There was a brief resumption of their correspondence. Louise, now in Bologna and jealous of Charlotte's 'usurpation' did not waste the opportunity to pour out her bile:

> The king continues to do a thousand absurdities in Florence, although he can scarcely move from one room to another by means of his swollen legs. His illness does not, however, prevent him bestowing the order of St. Andrew at the end of a banquet on his daughter and on a certain lord who attends him. It is all very ridiculous.[38]

Ridiculous was an epithet better applied to the situation Cardinal York now found himself in. It took the acidulous Walpole to put his finger on the central absurdity: 'So the Pope, who wouldn't grant the title of king to the Pretender, allows his no-Majesty to have created a Duchess! And the Cardinal of York, who is but a ray of the Papacy, and who must think his brother a king, will not allow her title!'[39]

In what was left of 1784 Charlotte had no time to conciliate her uncle. Her hands were full with the ailing prince. By now his health had declined to the point where he no longer took the air in his coach twice daily, as accustomed. He complained of being permanently in great pain and of a feeling of suffocation in his chest.[40] Mann continually remarked that Charlotte would not have to wait long to reap her inheritance.

Charlotte did her best to amuse and distract him. The French traveller Dupaty praised her work as nurse in the most glowing terms.[41] Private balls were held at the house three times a week. The prince would watch Charlotte's lady friends dancing for a while, then gradually doze off.[42]

With the position in the Palazzo Guadagni stable at the beginning of 1785, Charlotte set out to achieve a reconciliation with Cardinal York. On 23 and 30 April she sent Henry two humble and deferential letters, in which she spoke of the grief that prevented her writing at greater length; she hinted also at the disease in her liver. Henry was obviously moved. On 4 May he came round to her decisively. 'Since you appear so anxious for my friendship and my confidence, which greatly pleases me, I can assure you sincerely that you have both.'[43] Henry then wrote to the Pope to say that although certain aspects of the legitimation process had been offensive to him, he now accepted Charlotte unreservedly both as niece and duchess.[44]

The seal of amity was set on this relationship during a tour of Tuscany. In May 1785 Charlotte and her father were in Pisa for the waters. The prince was very ill; but for the duchess the doors of the Pisan nobility were all open.[45] Encouraged by her reception there,

Charlotte set out for a more extended progress around Tuscany in the autumn.[46] It was at Monte Freddo village near Perugia in October 1785 that she and the prince met Henry. Careful diplomacy had prepared all three for this summit conference. It was a complete success. The two brothers claimed to have regained their childhood love for each other. The cardinal was even more charmed by Charlotte than he expected to be.[47] The two of them agreed that the interests of Charles Edward's health were best served by a removal to Rome. They made plans to quit Florence.

Meanwhile, along with her strategy of achieving a total *rapprochement* with the cardinal, Charlotte had been encouraging the two brothers to co-operate in the second of her two grand aims: the humbling of Louise of Stolberg. After her release from Rome in July 1784, Louise was reunited with Alfieri at Colmar. This was risky. If it was found that the recently divorced countess of Albany was living in sin, her pensions both from the Pope and the prince were likely to be stopped. In mid-October 1784, the lovers parted again, he to Pisa, she to Bologna. Then in May 1785 Louise appeared in Paris.

Charlotte had by this time collected enough incriminating evidence against Louise to damage her badly. When the full details of Louise's continuing affair were laid before him, Henry was outraged. For a second time he had trusted her and for a second time she had made a fool of him. Henry wrote to Charles Edward, suggesting strong measures against an 'object' like Alfieri, who had besmirched the Stuart family name.[48]

The prince was happy to oblige. He decided to renege on the financial side of the settlement negotiated by Gustav III. Since he had contracted the marriage in the first place only on a false promise from France, it was for France to bail out the 'Queen of Hearts', if that was Louis XVI's desire.[49]

But the joint remonstrance Charles and Henry sent to Vergennes was designed to ensure that such would not be the French king's desire. Warning the court not to be gulled by the adulterers, the brothers asked Louis XVI to stop her pension if she persisted in living in sin with Alfieri.[50] A full recital of facts and dates relating to the liaison was provided. Henry juxtaposed intelligence reports of the couple's cohabitation in Rome, Baden and Colmar with Louise's letters to him on the same dates, letters full of pious humbug. Other details of her financial chicanery were included.[51] All in all, it was a damning document.

When Louise arrived in Paris, she found she had a tough fight on her hands to save any of her pension. For the next year she was involved in interminable wrangling with Versailles.[52] The French saw the force of the Stuart memorandum, but as they had been the prime movers behind the marriage in 1772, Louis XVI's credibility would have suffered if he had cut Louise adrift.

Charles and Henry were also adamant that they wanted Louise cut out of the Stuart will entirely, so that their joint fortunes would devolve on Charlotte.[53] The brothers were fortified by a legal opinion that the 1772 covenant regarding the jointure and pin money had been subsumed in the 60,000 francs pension Louise obtained from France in 1776.[54] Another favourable opinion held that the jointure was invalid under French law, since no particular property of the prince's had been charged with it.

A good deal of hard bargaining now took place. Finally, in September 1786, a face-saving compromise was reached. Charles Edward's advocate M. Vulpian signed an agreement with Louise's lawyer Busoni before the chancellor of the French consulate in Rome, which stipulated an annual pension of 20,000 livres from Stuart monies (Louise had asked for 40,000) in addition to the 60,000 francs French pension. There were two conditions. One was that the jointure was redeemable after Charles Edward's death for a capital sum of 200,000 livres. The other was that Louise had to sign a statement absolving the Stuarts from all further liability, agreeing that the settlement was a grace and favour matter and involved no responsibility of any kind, and accepting that thenceforth she and her ex-husband would be complete strangers to each other.[55] At the very least, this was a victory on points for the Stuarts. Given the arduous wrangling Louise had to endure at Versailles to achieve even that much, one can reasonably conclude that Charlotte had finally outfoxed the fox.

Gradually Charlotte became a great favourite of Cardinal York's. Apart from the demonstrations of obeisance she had made him, and her skill in putting Louise in her place, what certainly attracted Henry to Charlotte was his assumption that, like him, she was a virgin.[56] After the worldly cynicism of Louise of Stolberg, who had posed as an *ingénue* while being the most practised intriguer, Charlotte seemed innocence itself. Once again, Henry was hopelessly at sea, though neither he nor Charles Edward ever realised their misapprehension.

In fact, Charlotte had long been the mistress of the archbishop of Cambrai (Prince Ferdinand de Rohan-Guémèné). She had borne him three children, the last, a son, just before she set out for Rome. One can only imagine how Henry, who claimed to be scandalised by his brother's mere acceptance of her existence early in 1784, would have reacted had he known the full facts about his beloved niece. Charlotte, it turned out, was every bit as insincere in her attitude to Cardinal York as Louise had been, and even more cunning. Not only had she outmanoeuvred Louise and put herself in line to inherit £100,000 from her father,[57] but unlike Louise, she had managed to cover up all traces of her clandestine affair.

The other fascinating aspect of Charlotte's secret liaison is that once again we see the long arm of the Rohan-Guémèné family enveloping the Stuarts. Charlotte's lover was a younger brother of that Guémèné prince whom Charles Edward had cuckolded in 1747–8. French aristocratic circles were such a small world that it is sometimes hard to remember that eighteenth-century France had a population of twenty millions.

Final arrangements were now made for the return to Rome. The prince realised that he would still be known to the Pope as the count of Albany, but the solidarity of family reconciliation with his brother and daughter seemed to make up for that. The journey was delayed because of the prince's illness but finally, after spending his last St Andrew's Day in Florence, he and his party departed southwards on 1 December 1785, intending to travel twenty miles a day. Rather surprisingly, the prince stood up well to the trip, even after twelve hours a day sitting in a carriage.[58] At Viterbo Henry came out to meet them. He accompanied them back to Rome and then took both Charles and Charlotte to a private audience with the Pope.[59] So it was that the prince returned to the Palazzo Muti, where he had been born sixty-five years before.

That Charlotte now had a special place in Cardinal York's affections became clear when he made over to her all the Sobieski jewels, except the one he had set in his bishop's mitre. Significantly, this time he handed over the great ruby, confident at last that his brother was in responsible hands.[60]

Further steps were taken to put the Stuart finances on a sound footing. The negotiations on the 'Fund of Ohlau' were still dragging on, but this was clearly a hopeless cause. More hopeful, in the light of the English government's virtual admission in 1784 that the Jacobite scare was a thing of the past, was the money due from Mary of Modena's jointure. The arrears on this sum, which England promised to pay by the terms of the 1697 Treaty of Ryswick but never did, amounted to two and a half million pounds by the time of Mary's death in 1718. By the mid-1780s they had grown to an incalculably greater sum.[61]

Through Charlotte's good offices, Lord Caryll was restored to the prince's favour after ten years of disgrace and commissioned to lobby the court at Versailles for assistance in pressing the Stuart demand for satisfaction on the unpaid jointure.[62] This suit fared no better than the various attempts to turn the 'Fund of Ohlau' into hard cash. After much prevarication, the English government finally issued a categorical statement in 1787, repudiating the debt.[63]

In theory, something could be done about money. It was otherwise with the prince's health. Both Charlotte and Henry agreed that the prince could not last long. In March 1786 Cardinal York was summoned from Frascati to administer the viaticum. The prince was seized with an epileptic fit, which continued for long enough to be mistaken for apoplexy. But the 'man of iron', as Louise of Stolberg had dubbed him, pulled through once again.[64]

This was not altogether welcome to Charlotte. She matched her father in the unsentimentality of her real motives for the *rapprochement*. She was prepared to spend a certain amount of time on the cross as Charles Edward's nurse as the price for securing his money for her three children. But she had underrated his staying power and began to realise that she could be in for a long haul. This was both irritating to her and more profoundly distressing, as it increasingly looked as though she was in a race against time. She was aware that her own days were possibly numbered, and at times was just as seriously ill as her patient. Surely the 'man of iron' would not manage to outlive her?[65]

Her mind must have been set at rest by the prince's steep decline at Rome in 1786–7. He now exhibited terminal symptoms of decay. He was often seen, by Goethe among others, struggling out of the theatre, dressed even in summer in a velvet greatcoat and a cocked hat, the sides of which were half drawn up with gold twist.[66] And there was the inevitable Garter, as if the prince constantly needed to remind himself who he was.

The overdressing, even in the summer heat, was made necessary by his declining health. There were times when his leg swelled up to half the size of his body. But nothing would induce him to give up drink. Charlotte made little attempt to stop him. The combination of alcohol and great pain made lucid moments increasingly rare. The Lutheran theologian Friedrich Munter tried to engage him in conversation about freemasonry, but found his mental faculties too far decayed.[67]

Occasionally, if there was company in the Palazzo Muti, Charlotte would try to correct his worst alcoholic excesses. On one such occasion, the prince in a cracked voice addressed an English visitor, one Bertie Greathead (an empty-headed, callow youth) in the following terms: 'I will speak to my subjects in my own way, and I will soon speak to you, sare [sic], in Westminster Hall.' Faced with this outburst, Charlotte simply shrugged her shoulders.[68]

It was the same Greathead, apparently, who stirred Charles Edward's deepest feelings by foolishly getting him to reminisce about the '45. Overwhelmed by mixed, cross-cutting emotions of grief, regret, nostalgia and guilt, the prince was in a wretched tearful state when Charlotte arrived to break up the poignant scene and reprimand the interlocutor.[69]

In the summer of 1786 the Stuart family retired to Albano where, on a whim, the prince revived the practice of touching for the King's Evil.[70] When he returned to Rome, he learned that his old enemy Sir Horace Mann had died. Whatever his infirmities, the prince was managing to outlast most of those who were with him in his great days: Louis XV, Frederick the Great, Earl Marischal were all dead. So too were most of his companions in the great adventure of 1745: Lord George Murray and every single council member save Lord Ogilvy (Elcho died in 1787); all Seven Men of Moidart; John Holker apart, virtually every individual of the Jacobite officer class. Many of the prince's ladies were gone too: the duchesse d'Aiguillon in 1772, the Princesse de Talmont in 1773, Louise de Montbazon in 1781. That the prince had outlived his own era was made clear by the final restitution of the forfeited estates in 1784 to the heirs of the 'rebels' of 1745.[71]

From the autumn of 1786 the prince was in steep decline. The end came shortly after his sixty-seventh birthday. A severe stroke in January 1788 left him semi-paralysed. This time he did not recover. Henry rushed in from Frascati to request a king's burial in St Peter's. But even in death the Pope would not acknowledge Charles III. Henry made plans to bury him in Frascati.[72]

On the morning of 30 January 1788 the end came. Henry administered the last rites of the Catholic Church, that institution the prince so despised. Charles Edward died in his daughter's arms shortly after 9 a.m. Henry became the Cardinal King *in partibus*.[73]

Altars were erected in the ante-chamber and masses said for the repose of the prince's soul. After thirty hours' keening by Irish Franciscan monks, a plaster cast was taken of the prince's face and the body was moved to Frascati. On 3 February Henry conducted the funeral service in the cathedral there. Overcome with emotion, the Cardinal King faltered his way through the office of the dead. Charles

Edward's body was temporarily interred by the central west door of the cathedral.[74] Much later, it was buried in the vaults of St Peter's.

Charlotte inherited an immediate £3,000 per annum on her father's Italian revenues and an indeterminate amount on his French holdings.[75] But she never lived to see the final resolution of the Byzantine wranglings at Versailles about exactly how much France owed her as beneficiary of Charles Edward's will.[76] It was almost as though destiny had reserved her solely for the purpose of easing her father through his last painful years. The cancer in her liver now returned in even more virulent form. On 17 November 1789 she died in Bologna.[77] So passed the last woman for whom the prince had even vestigial affection.

Even in death the prince managed to win a symbolic victory. As if to illustrate that he departed just on the cusp of a new historical era, the first Australian colonists landed at Botany Bay a few days before his demise. One of the first oaths the new governor Arthur Philip had to take was that he would not attempt to restore Charles Edward Stuart to the English throne.[78] The terror of the prince's name lived on. The legend of 'Bonnie Prince Charlie' was already in the making.

Conclusion

Any assessment of Charles Edward must attempt to winnow the historical wheat from the legendary chaff and then examine their interplay. 'Bonnie Prince Charlie' is a creature of myth in more ways than one. The approach suggested by Robert Graves in *Homer's Daughter* is a fruitful one. In order to bring Homer's hero into sharper focus, he disentangles the 'historical' Odysseus from the mythical Ulysses. A similar operation has to be performed with the prince. There is the historical Charles Edward Stuart, long regarded as of little importance to serious scholars. And there is the legendary 'Bonnie Prince Charlie', the archetypal hero suffused in a golden halo, swathed in the nimbus of the imperishable memory of the '45.

With the recent revival in Jacobite studies, we are at last able to appreciate the deadly threat to the regime posed by the 1745 rising.[1] Some of the finest young historians at work today now rate the 'mixed' phenomenon of domestic rebellion and foreign invasion threat, as in 1779, 1798 and, most clearly, 1745, as more important threats to the social and economic order than the much trumpeted 'revolutions' of the 1640s and 1688.[2]

The mind that conceived and carried out the 1745 rising was more than a mere adventurer's. It was that of a man with real strategic flair. The problem was that the prince's qualities did not fit easily into the eighteenth-century context. It is not just in his disdain for organised religion and his contempt for conventional forms of authority that the prince impresses as a 'modern' figure. The impatience and dislike for people who tried to 'give him laws' extended into the military sphere. Lord George Murray and his followers were 'by the book' conventional commanders. Murray was a very fine specimen of that genus to be sure, but he never transcended the limitations of blinkered eighteenth-century thinking: the slow, ponderous build-up; the slogging, murderous set-piece battles of Malplaquet, Laffeld and Minden.

The prince was not hidebound in this way. He understood that the great exploits of human history were all 'impossible' until someone actually did them. He had the intuitive military flair of a Montrose (but without his tactical ability); he possessed the panache of a great cavalry commander like Murat. It was no accident that the prince was a great hunter. He thought of making war in terms of the chase: rapidity of movement, lightning thrusts, economy, sudden death.[3]

That such qualities can coexist with tactical myopia and ineptitude in the world of day-to-day politics has, I hope, been made sufficiently clear. We should not, however, be seduced into overstating the case. Charles Edward Stuart did not conquer Scotland simply on the basis of an ineffable magnetism that led important leaders of Scottish clan and feudal society into lemming-like suicide against their own interests. There was a pre-existing dynamic of social conflict at work in Scotland that Charles Edward was able to energise. Unless we admit this, we shall be nudged dangerously close to the more extreme version of the 'great man' theory of history. If the Scottish clan system was, as some historians claim, a peacefully evolving organism with decades of life left in it, which was convulsed by the thunderbolt arrival of the prince as if from outer space, then Charles Edward must indeed be one of the great figures of world history.[4]

Such a view, even if arrived at by implication, is a gross exaggeration. But we must never forget Charles Edward's real achievement in the '45 and how close he came to success. Paradoxically the danger of forgetting this is especially acute for the prince's biographer. In the forest of detail, including much that is detrimental to the prince's reputation, through which he must hack, there is a risk that by being too close to him the biographer will omit the aerial view. But for historians and general readers alike, Charles Edward's claim to fame must always stand or fall on his achievements in 1745–6. The biographer is at fault if he does not give this fact due weight.

The transition from historical figure to creature of legend can be charted only if the decline in the real Charles Edward is first traced. At his peak, the prince was handsome, intelligent, deeply compassionate, with great charm and affability, and possessed of a powerful personal magnetism. He enjoyed superb natural health and had tuned himself to concert pitch as a warrior. He was a crack shot and a fine horseman. His energy and charisma in the first four months of the '45 laid deep foundations for the later legend of the Bonnie Prince. He seemed to lack none of the qualities of the 'parfait, gentil knight'.

At the nadir of his career the prince was depressive, paranoid, alcoholic, reclusive, prickly and aggressive. His health had deteriorated to an alarming point. He was chronically asthmatic and dropsical. Less than thirty years separates the crest from the trough. Such a steep decline suggests a profoundly unbalanced personality, lacking any middle range of psychic activity.

The old view of the prince as a man unable to deal with failure because of mental feebleness will not stand up to scrutiny. A close study of Charles Edward reveals him as highly intelligent, even if the intelligence was often of the divergent or 'lateral' type. His poor spelling and punctuation is a red herring, assiduously peddled by those who cannot see that 'intelligent' and 'academic' are very far from matching complements. More pertinently, the prince, unlike his father who wrote letters of impeccable orthography and sentiments, never wrote a boring sentence, apart perhaps from the ubiquitous 'My health is perfect', whose significance through reiteration was precisely an unconscious intimation that his *mental* health was far from perfect. The prince habitually uses a medley of unusual (even eccentric) arguments, wit, irony and imagery that give even his most self-pitying letters a peculiar richness, contrasting strikingly with the dryness of James's writing.

Appropriately for one who was himself destined to become a creature of legend, Charles Edward Stuart possessed the attributes of a primitive sun god. Waxing strong, he climbed steadily to the meridian of Derby, then waned, the pace of his decline accelerating.

Every individual thrives on success and languishes in failure, but most are capable of finding a viable equilibrium between the two. No one ever needed to succeed more desperately than Charles Edward Stuart. The ability to achieve the golden mean was beyond him. It had to be spectacular success or abject failure. *Aut Caesar aut nihil* was his motto, self-confessedly.

But whereas the path to success was always likely to be hard-won, the descent into failure was likely to be even steeper, and peculiarly so in the special milieu into which the prince had been born.

The odds against the prince at birth were immeasurably increased by the damage done to him in his early years. His experiences with two well-meaning but singularly disastrous parents left him traumatised and crippled, with particular vulnerabilities of depression, rage, guilt and paranoia.

His relationship with his father left him despising all forms of authority. His relations with possible father-substitutes reinforced that feeling. It was a great tragedy for the prince that the 2nd duke of Berwick (Liria) died young. He was the only one of James's generation who possessed the ability to bring out the best in the prince.

The contempt for authority led by extension to a profound hatred for France, the one nation-state capable of realising his ambitions. As always with the prince, his attitude contained both rational and irrational elements. Even when France was being sincere in its desire to restore the Stuarts, the sincerity was always attenuated by French desire to attempt the task in their own circumspect, calculating way. From his own vantage point the prince was fully justified in feeling badly let down by Louis XV and his ministers, especially in the periods 1744–5 and 1746–8.

On the other hand, the prince exaggerated both the degree and nature of the French 'betrayal'. Because his father collaborated with the French, and they with him, over Henry's cardinalate, Clementina Walkinshaw's flight and (most seriously) the prince's expulsion in 1748, Charles Edward built up an image in his own mind of an oppressive two-headed demon of authority, one head being Louis XV, the other his father.

Yet, arguably, his mother's legacy was even more disastrous. It has often been noted that successful men need to reach adulthood with the driving force of a competent, active mother behind them. Clementina's early and tragic death removed an all-important prop and may in some sense have caused the prince always unconsciously to 'fail'. The unconscious guilt Charles felt over her demise probably produced an internal saboteur ready to exaggerate the negative influences of his life.

Were Charles alive today, his stoical response to his mother's death would not be taken as a sign (as it was) that he had weathered the storm. Rather, we might see it as a repression of all his fears and deeper anguish. We cannot know what he felt: the documents are silent. But that, in an age when calm in the face of disaster was normal conduct, should not surprise us. In human terms it seems likely that the death of Clementina affected Charles more profoundly than any around him suspected.

One effect of this sudden deprivation can be seen in his difficulties with forging long-term relationships with any woman. Clementina Walkinshaw, Marie Louise de Bouillon, the Princesse de Talmont, and his wife, Louise of Stolberg, all served for a while, only to be discarded in anger once they had outlived their function. We cannot plunge too deeply into the prince's hidden character, but some conclusions are too plain to ignore. His mother's death arrested his development, robbing him of the possibility in his later years of developing a sustaining bond with any woman.

The fragile identity produced by this inadequate parenting, reinforced by the peculiar problems of being a 'Pretender', led the prince to be forever at the mercy of a fragmenting self, where there was no equilibrium, where the centre did not hold. This explains the prince's violent mood swings, his oscillation between rage and charm, his pattern of arrant defiance followed by meek submission.

Rage is the most obvious symptom of the fragmenting self, just as depression is the obvious reflex action to guilt. Depression makes one particularly vulnerable to political defeats and issues of self-esteem. The prince experienced more reverses than were good for a man in his psychological condition. The result was paranoia and cold reserve, a morbid fear of intimacy. Possibly the only person the prince ever trusted was his valet John Stewart. Intimate relations with people of his own rank would have meant risking a deeply wounding familiarity.

Depression can be arrested by qualities of wisdom and empathy but only if the depression is not too deeply rooted. The failure of the prince to use his intellect to overcome his irrationality is no argument for his lack of cerebral powers; it suggests, rather, that self-destructive tendencies were too deeply embedded in his mind for intellect to override them. Yet even in severely depressed individuals, the storm of irrationality can be ridden out by the exercise of creativity or humour. The prince, alas, did not possess creative talents of the first order. He had considerable qualities of aesthetic appreciation, but the demon that drove him was political ambition not creative self-realisation.

As for humour, this was certainly the most important defence mechanism in Charles Edward's armoury. No one reading his correspondence or collecting the anecdotes that surround him could fail to notice the humorous tinge to many of his *obiter dicta*. Significantly, we find no record of this aspect of his personality after his marriage in 1772, almost as though the self-destructive cancer had by then destroyed all the positive impulses.

The most interesting cases of paranoia are always those where the dividing line between illusion and reality is very thin. The prince often lamented his singular ill-fortune in hyperbolic terms, but it is important to be clear that there *was* an objective basis for his laments.

The decision at Derby, his brother's becoming a cardinal (especially given the underhand way it was done), the arrest at the Opera and the expulsion from France, these were all events that would have shaken a much stronger man than the prince.

After 1748 Charles had two further crosses to bear. Despite James's saintly protestations, he did not abdicate and hand over his regal status to his son. The prince was thus left as leader of the Jacobite movement – for by becoming a cardinal with James's collusion Henry had virtually announced that in his and his father's opinion Jacobitism was a fantasy – yet without the powers and prerogatives James had commanded when active leader. In such circumstances, the never very wide gap between 'Pretender' and inhabitant of a world of illusion narrowed still further.

After 1766 there was a further dimension to the prince's limbo. This was something that would have brought a much tougher character close to madness, unless the Stuart claim was abandoned altogether. From being Prince of Wales and then king *in partibus*, Charles Edward became, as a result of the Pope's refusal to accept his title, that ultimate absurdity, a Pretender *in partibus*. Nobody who fails to understand the alienating effect of such a status on one whose identity was already shaky can have any hope of understanding Charles Edward Stuart.

The prince was a significant historical personality for less than a year – the duration of the 1745 Jacobite rising. Yet he has become one of history's legendary figures. How is this to be explained? Is it another example of the 'Captain Scott syndrome' – that peculiar British fascination for gallant losers? And does not the interest attaching to Charles Edward refute the old saw that history is about winners?

I would like to suggest that the answer is more complex. For a variety of reasons, which I have tried to unravel above, Charles Edward was uniquely placed to fit into a mythical niche. Along with King Arthur and Robin Hood (also in their pristine state real historical figures), 'Bonnie Prince Charlie' was able to transcend the limitations of 'mere history' to enter a mystical pantheon. It is not the fact of losing so much as the manner of it that guarantees membership of this exclusive club, as the example of the historical Arthur shows.

There is also the question of the unique interplay between historical and legendary subjects. How far, for example, does the transcendent reputation of George Washington derive from his (rather feeble) historical performance and how far from his position as American monument? Charles Edward after his death became the focus for a number of convergent themes: Scottish nationalism, romantic nostalgia for a vanished Eden, even what George Borrow called 'a rage for gentility'. Robert Burns, Sir Walter Scott, even George IV, were key figures in creating the legend of 'Bonnie Prince Charlie'. Even those who affect to disdain this kind of Jacobitism need to explain why Charles Edward Stuart was chosen as the recipient of these posthumous favours. Why not his father, why not Earl Marischal, both of whom were keen to parade an alternative, compromising Jacobitism?

Paradoxically, it seems that it was the very dogged stubbornness that proved so self-destructive in life that won the prince a final victory in death. Who now remembers the victor of Culloden except as 'butcher Cumberland?' Yet the vanquished Charles Edward lives on as the subject of a hundred romances and fantasies. The heroic morality of strenuousness that destroyed the prince's life and turned him into an alcoholic wreck was the same quality that has enabled him to survive in the imagination of humanity. Anyone who has followed the prince through sixty-seven unhappy years in the vale of tears will surely not begrudge him that final victory.

Abbreviations

Add. MSS	Additional Manuscripts, British Library
AD, Nancy	Archives Departmentales de Meurthe et Moselle
AECP	Archives Etrangères, Correspondance Politique, French Foreign Ministry Archives, Quai d'Orsay
AEMD	Archives Etrangères, Mémoires et Documents, French Foreign Ministry Archives, Quai d'Orsay
AGN, Simancas	Archivo General de la Nación (Estado), Simancas
AN	Archives Nationales, Paris
ASV	Archivio Segreto Vaticano (Vatican Archives)
Browne	James Browne, *A History of the Highlands and of the Highland Clans*, 4 vols (Glasgow, 1832–3)
CP	*Cumberland Papers*, ed. H. R. Duff (1815)
FO	Foreign Office Reports, Public Record Office

Guerre	Archives du Ministère de la Défense Nationale, Château de Vincennes
HMC	Reports of the Historical Manuscripts Commission
LM	*The Lyon in Mourning*, ed. Henry Patton, 3 vols (Edinburgh, Scottish Historical Society, 1895)
LP	*Lockhart Papers*, ed. A. Aufrere, 2 vols (1817)
Mahon	*History of England from the Peace of Utrecht*, 7 vols (1858)
Marine	Archives du Ministère de la Marine, Archives Nationales
Marville-Maurepas	Feydeau de Marville, *Lettres au ministre Maurepas*, ed. A. de Boislisle, 3 vols (Paris, 1896)
MP	Maurepas Papers, Cornell University, Ithaca, New York
MCP	*More Culloden Papers*, ed. Duncan Warrand, 5 vols (Inverness, 1923–30)
Morelli	Emilie Morelli, *Le lettere di Benedetto XIV a Tencin*, 2 vols (Rome, 1955)
RA	Royal Archives, Windsor Castle
SE	Sigmund Freud, Standard Edition of the Complete Psychological *Works*, ed. James Strach (1953)
SP	State Papers, Public Record Office
Vat. Lib.	Vatican Library
WO	War Office Papers, Public Record Office

Notes

INTRODUCTION

1 Claude Nordmann, 'Louis XIV and the Jacobites', Ragnild Hatton, ed., *Louis XIV and Europe* (Ohio, 1976) pp.82–111.

2 For two good assessments of Jacobitism in the reign of Queen Anne see Edward Gregg, *Queen Anne* (1980) and D. Szechi, *Jacobitism and Tory Politics 1710–14* (Edinburgh, 1984).

3 For the 1715 Jacobite rising see A. and H. Tayler, *1715: The Story of the Rising* (1936); J. Baines, *The Jacobite Rising of 1715* (1970).

4 For the moving Jacobite court see Marchesa Nobili Vitelleschi, *A Court in Exile*, 2 vols (1902).

5 There is no completely satisfactory life of James, the 'Old Pretender'. Martin Haile, *James Francis Edward. The Old Chevalier* (1907) and Andrew Lang and A. Shield, *The King over the Water* (1907) are dated but still useful. Peggy Miller's *James* (1972) is perceptive and insightful but cursory.

6 HMC Stuart I, pp.484–507.

7 HMC Stuart IV, pp.457–8,468,516.

8 HMC Stuart V, pp.234–5.

9 For John Sobieski see Gabriel-François Coyer, *History of John Sobieski. King of Poland* (1762).

10 HMC Stuart VI, p.95.

11 For full details see Peggy Miller, *A Wife for the Pretender* (1965).

12 See in addition to Miller, op. cit., the details in Add. MSS (Gualterio) 20,313.

13 For the 1719 rising see W. K. Dickson, ed., *The Jacobite Attempt of 1719* (Edinburgh, 1895).

14 Sir John T. Gilbert, *Narratives of the Detention, Liberation and Marriage of Maria Clementina Sobieska styled Queen of Great Britain and Ireland by Sir Charles Wogan and others* (Dublin, 1894), pp.104–5.

CHAPTER ONE

1 R A Stuart 50/30.

2 R A Stuart 50/43.

3 R A Stuart 50/58.

4 Cardinals invited to the confinement were Albani, Astalli, Acquaviva, Barberini, Gualterio, Imperiali, Ottaboni, Pamfilio, Paulani and Saurapanti. R A Stuart 50/138.

5 R A Stuart 51/22.

6 Cf. James to Ormonde on 19 December 1720: 'She is extreme big and will not, I believe, pass this month' (R A Stuart 50/84).

7 R A Stuart 50/131.

8 R A Stuart 51/23.

9 Add. MSS 30,090.

10 Vatican Library, Borgia MSS 565 ff.50–1.

11 R A Stuart 51/2–16 contains the letters. The first ruler to be informed that the new prince's name was Charles Edward was the duke of Lorraine (R A Stuart 51/10).

12 To the duke of Ormonde (11 January 1721) he remarked: 'The Queen . . . has had the most favourable lying-in that ever woman had' (R A Stuart 51/38).

13 Lovers of dramatic irony will savour the reply from Earl Marischal Keith (Madrid, 21 January 1721) – later Charles Edward's most bitter enemy – referring to a 'time of universal joy to all your faithful subjects' (R A Stuart 51/37).

14 R A Stuart 52/2, 15.

15 R A Stuart 52/37.

16 This point was made explicit in a letter from Paris by the Jacobite George Lansdowne to James (R A Stuart 50/100).

17 For the impact of the South Sea Bubble and Jacobite reactions to it cf. R A Stuart 51/53, 76, 80; 52/53, 76, 91, 137.

18 R A Stuart 52/27, 33, 79.

19 Jean Héroard, *Journal sur l'enfance et la jeunesse de Louis XIII* (Paris, 1868) is the classic source for the childhood of princes in this era. For a recent popular survey of the topic from William the Conqueror to the House of Windsor see Charles Carlton, *Royal Childhoods* (1986).

20 Héroard has to be used with care as an inferential source: 'The observations Héroard made cannot be uncritically generalised even to princely or aristocratic milieus of the time,' Elizabeth Mirth Marvick, 'Nature versus Nurture' in Erik de Mause, *The History of Childhood* (1976), p.262.

21 T. G. H. Drake, 'The Wet Nurse in the Eighteenth Century', *Bulletin of the History of Medicine* 8 (1940), pp.934–48.

22 De Mause, *History of Childhood*, op. cit., pp.265,268.

23 R A Stuart 51/38.

24 R A Stuart 52/88, 118.

25 R A Stuart 63/168.

26 'Almost one half of the human species perish in infancy by improper management or neglect', William Buchan, *Domestic Medicine* (Philadelphia, 1809), p.8.

27 'My son is in a very good way, we have got a good, quiet nurse, and all is well looked after now' (R A Stuart 52/125). Cf. James's plaudits for Francesca Battaglia in a glowing reference in 1726 (R A Stuart 97/107).

28 W. B. Blaikie, *Origins of the Forty-Five* (Edinburgh, 1916), p.445.

29 Cf. Philippe Ariès, *L'Enfant et la vie familiale sous l'Ancien Régime* (Paris, 1960).

30 See Locke's 'Some Thoughts concerning Education' (1693).

31 For the practice of cold bathing see Rousseau, *Emile* (Pléiade edition, Paris, 1969), pp.277–8; *Letters and Works of Lady Mary Wortley Montagu* (1861), I, p.209. For its universal acceptance see John Floyer, *The History of Cold Bathing* (1732); Bishop Fleetwood, *Six Useful Discourses on the Relative Duties of Parents and Children* (1749); Anon, *The Common Errors in the Education of Children and their Consequences* (1744).

32 R A Stuart 54/18.

33 R A Stuart 59/11.

34 R A Stuart 53/28; 56/64; 57/93. Louis XIII in the early seventeenth century was twenty-five months at full weaning, but most recorded eighteenth-century cases hovered around the 4–6 months mark (De Mause, op. cit., p.36).

35 R A Stuart 53/44.

36 State Papers, Italian States 14 f.38.

37 R A Stuart 54/18.

38 R A Stuart 64/93.

39 R A Stuart 60/57. This is undoubtedly the source of the typical Walton hyperbole of 5 January 1723 (SP Italian States 14 f.219) when he reports that Charles Edward's legs are so bandy that it is doubtful he will ever be able to walk.

40 R A Stuart 60/82.

41 R A Stuart 61/142.

42 R A Stuart 64/148. Walton described this as a fever caused because his teeth were starting to come through (SP Italian States 14 f.214).

43 R A Stuart 66/148. His remarks to Sir Peter Redmond in June were even more fulsome: 'I wish you could see our little friend, for I am sure he would be to your liking, being in all respects as I could wish' (R A Stuart 67/83).

44 R A Stuart 67/146.

45 R A Stuart 71/74.

46 R A Stuart 74/84.

47 SP Italian States 14 f.23.

48 R A Stuart 76/32.

49 For Ramsay see G. D. Henderson, *Chevalier Ramsay* (1952); A. Cherel, *Un Aventurier religieux au XVIIIe siècle, André-Michel Ramsay* (Paris, 1926); E. Brault, *Le Mystère du chevalier Ramsay* (Paris, 1973); P. Chevallier, *La première profanation du Temple maçonnique* (Paris, 1968) and *Les Ducs sous l'Acacia* (Paris, 1964).

50 Edward Gregg, 'The Jacobite Career of the Earl of Mar' in Eveline Cruickshanks, ed. *Ideology and Conspiracy. Aspects of Jacobitism 1688–1759* (Edinburgh, 1982).

51 R A Stuart 84/4, 12, 23.

52 As the work of Freud shows, nothing is more difficult to disentangle than fact and fantasy in the area of infantile seduction. But Bernis's testimony, whether reality or fantasy, is worth quoting to illustrate the real fears entertained by aristocratic parents on this issue: 'Nothing is too dangerous for morals and perhaps for health as to leave children too long under the care of chambermaids, or even of young ladies brought up in the chateaux. I will add that the best among them are not always the least dangerous. They dare with a

child that which they would be ashamed to risk with a young man' (Bernis, *Mémoires*, ed. F. Masson (Paris, 1878) I, p.9).

53 R A Stuart 53/84. James was quite certain the queen was with child: 'As yet we do not speak of her big belly, although it is already visible' (12 May 1721, R A Stuart 53/98. Cf. also S P Italian States 14 ff.83,506).

54 S P Italian States 14 f.205.

55 R A Stuart 61/45.

56 While the royal couple were at Lucca in 1722, overall responsibility for Charles Edward seems to have devolved on the Abbé (later Cardinal) Tencin, who visited the young prince on a regular basis two or three times a week. S P Italian States 14 ff.89,124.

57 R A Stuart 53/98, 160.

58 R A Stuart 57/118.

59 R A Stuart 64/58.

60 Philippe Ariès, *L'Enfant et la vie familiale*, op. cit., pp.134–42.

61 S P Italian States 15 ff.194,206.

62 *Ibid.*, ff.314,339,378–80,392.

63 R A Stuart 87/65.

64 R A Stuart 91/63.

65 Such an elementary insight was beyond the denizens of the Palazzo Muti. Hence the bland reportage at the time of Henry's birth: 'The Prince is very fond of his brother' (James to Ormonde, 10 March 1725, R A Stuart 80/140).

66 S P Italian States 15 f.339.

67 R A Stuart 86/70.

68 R A Stuart 86/138; S P Italian States 15 f.438.

69 S P Italian States 15 f.451.

70 R A Stuart 87/65.

71 R A Stuart 87/64.

72 Historical Manuscripts Commission 10, I, p.161.

73 R A Stuart 87/64.

74 H M C 10, vi, p.217.

75 S P Italian States 15 f.490.

76 R A Stuart 89/32.

77 R A Stuart 87/81.

78 S P Italian States 14 f.257.

79 Add. MSS (Gualterio) 20,304 f.13; 20,322 f.136.

80 R A Stuart 89/58.

81 S P Italian States 15 f.497.

82 R A Stuart 87/154.

83 R A Stuart 80/117.

84 R A Stuart 89/20.

85 In a letter to Clementina on 27 June 1726. R A Stuart 95/18.

86 For these cf. S P Italian States 14 f.318; 15 f.16.

87 S P Italian States 15 f.520.

88 Add. MSS 21, 896 f.11.

89 S P Italian States 15 f.504.

90 Such as to the Academy of Architecture, Painting and Sculpture on the Capitoline Hill on 11 December 1725 (S P Italian States 15 f.515).

91 R A Stuart 88/136.

92 S P Italian States 16 ff.71,73.

93 R A Stuart 92/82,84; 93/5.

94 S P Italian States 16, f.34.

95 R A Stuart 97/23.

96 R A Stuart 91/63.

97 S P Italian States 16 f.65; R A Stuart 95/60.

98 R A Stuart 97/23.

99 S P Italian States 16 f.104.

100 R A Stuart 90/137; 91/21; S P Italian States 16 f.57.

101 R A Stuart 89/32.

102 S P Italian States 15 f.518; 16 f.65.

103 S P Italian States 16 f.145.

104 R A Stuart 95/130.

105 R A Stuart 91/63.

106 R A Stuart 98/74.

107 R A Stuart 97/106,127; 98/16.

108 S P Italian States 16 f.154.

109 R A Stuart 98/18,66,74.

110 R A Stuart 98/101.

CHAPTER TWO

1 Helen Catherine Stewart, 'The Exiled Stewarts in Italy', *Miscellany of the Scottish Historical Society*, VII, 2nd series (35), Edinburgh, 1941, p.76.

2 R A Stuart 98/153.

3 R A Stuart 98/18.

4 S P Italian States 15 f.137.

5 R A Stuart 95/103.

6 See Aeneas MacDonald's testimony. R. Forbes, ed., *The Lyon in Mourning*, 3 vols (Edinburgh, 1896), I, p.384.

7 S P Italian States 15 f.422.

8 R A Stuart 108/14–17.

9 R A Stuart 105/29.

10 See Liria's diary in *Documentos ineditos para la historia de España* 93 (Madrid, 1889), pp.13–17.

11 S P Italian States 16 ff.237,241,251.

12 'He could ride and fire a gun. He was so good a shot that I have seen him kill birds on the roof with a crossbow and split a rolling ball with a bolt ten times in succession ... I have never seen a more perfect prince in all my life.' *Documentos ineditos*, op. cit., p.18.

13 R A Stuart 107/88,119.

14 R A Stuart 107/118; 109/15; S P Italian States 16 f.281.

15 R A Stuart 108/54.

16 R A Stuart 108/54; 109/109.

17 R A Stuart 108/162; 109/32; 110/3,70,83.

18 Add. MSS 32,752 f.80.

19 S P Italian States 16 f.325.

20 R A Stuart 111/71.

21 R A Stuart 111/19.

22 S P Italian States 16 f.325.

23 R A Stuart 113/30.

24 Add. MSS 20,661 f.120. A similar anodyne greeting in January 1729 is at f.122.

25 R A Stuart 114/116.

26 Unbound letter in RA, Windsor Castle. James replied that his son's letters were a great source of comfort to him in his tribulation at Rome.

27 R A Stuart 115/110; S P Italian States 16 f.372.

28 R A Stuart 116/81.

29 R A Stuart 116/8.

30 R A Stuart 116/14.

31 R A Stuart 117/38,64.

32 R A Stuart 117/83,88.

33 R A Stuart 117/128.

34 R A Stuart 119/11. News of the miscarriage was kept secret. Walton remarked in December 1728 that according to his reckoning Clementina must now be twelve months pregnant! (S P Italian States 16 f.476.)

35 S P Italian States 16 f.467; R A Stuart 121/25,86.

36 R A Stuart 120/100.

37 R A Stuart 120/91. Stafford was given the same terms as Sheridan: board, lodging and one hundred livres a month (R A Stuart 120/102).

38 R A Stuart 120/103.

39 R A Stuart 120/143.

40 At a salary of 2,500 livres a year (R A Stuart 121/35).

41 R A Stuart 122/127,142; 124/18; 122/126.

42 R A Stuart 124/24.

43 R A Stuart 122/27.

44 R A Stuart 124/18.

45 R A Stuart 124/119.

46 R A Stuart 124/156.

47 R A Stuart 125/17.

48 R A Stuart 125/31,75.

49 R A Stuart 125/102.

50 H. Tayler, The Stuart Papers at Windsor (1939), p.83; cf. Charles Edward to James, 12 April 1729: 'I am mighty glad to hear that you are so well and that I shall soon have the happiness to see you. I shall endeavour to be good, that you may always be pleased with me. My brother is grown well again, and my cough is almost gone' (R A Stuart 126/152).

51 R A Stuart 125/35.

52 R A Stuart 126/1; 126/25.

53 R A Stuart 126/137.

54 R A Stuart 127/84.

55 Archivio Segreto Vaticano, Principi 226 f.6 (1 May 1729).

56 Anyone interested in the minutiae of Charles Edward's early life could build up a detailed, almost day-by-day picture from the comprehensive (and even over-comprehensive) reports filed in the State Papers, Tuscany. There are more than 600 folios for the period 1730–3 alone (S P Tuscany 32).

57 R. Shackleton, Montesquieu (Oxford, 1961), p.105; cf. also J. G. Keysler, Travels through Germany, Bohemia, Hungary, Switzerland, Italy and Lorraine (1756–7), II, p.46.

58 S P Tuscany 32 ff.55,122,303. A report from Dunbar in January 1733 is typical: 'Their highnesses were last Sunday at a noble ball given by Count Bolognetti and the appearance they made so charmed everybody that nothing has been talked of in Rome ever since. The truth is, that I never in my life saw anything comparable to the beauty and grace with which the Prince appeared that evening, and there were some English Whigs who could not conceal their emotion on that occasion' (R A Stuart 158/104).

59 S P Tuscany 32 ff.303,345,389.

60 R A Stuart 127/107,109,112,128.

61 R A Stuart 127/155. Whether through backwardness in reading or because of the illegibility of Clementina's hand is not entirely clear. Certainly Clementina's handwriting is singularly dreadful.

62 R A Stuart 128/95.

63 R A Stuart 129/12.

64 S P Italian States 16 f.548.

65 R A Stuart 130/48; 131/144,152.

66 R A Stuart 132/11.

67 R A Stuart 131/7–8; 133/86.

68 S P Italian States 16 ff.537,571–2.

69 R A Stuart 131/143.

70 R A Stuart 131/95. There is a very revealing juxtaposition of the way of life of father and son in a letter from James to Clementina in May 1730: 'Carluccio is just going to kill a buck in the Park of Marino, and I am going to Benediction where I shall not fail to pray for you' (R A Stuart 136/155).

71 R A Stuart 134/103; 135/84.

72 R A Stuart 138/45.

73 R A Stuart 138/54,148.

74 R A Stuart 137/83.

75 R A Stuart 142/19,27.

76 R A Stuart 144/105.

77 R A Stuart 143/154; 144/145; 145/34.

78 R A Stuart 138/163; 139/79; S P Tuscany 32 f.104.

79 S P Tuscany 32 ff.134,142,167.
80 R A Stuart 140/38,104.
81 R A Stuart 140/88.
82 S P Tuscany 32 ff.215,273,285.
83 R A Stuart 145/73,78,119–20,129. On 26 May James wrote to Charles Edward that he and Edgar had been on a trip to Vesuvius, from which he would bring back 'a number of stinking stones for you and Henry' (R A Stuart 145/138).
84 On 13 June 1731 she tells him it will be 'hart' (sic) for him to understand her English, but praises his correspondence with her. 'Your letter has done me more pleasure being by your own composition than if it had been of another' (R A Stuart 146/34).
85 R A Stuart 146/141; 147/103.
86 James to Clementina, 19 September 1731, R A Stuart 148/149.
87 R A Stuart 148/149; 150/157.
88 R A Stuart 151/67.
89 R A Stuart 151/68.
90 R A Stuart 151/124. The narrator concludes sententiously: 'A moralist might hence observe that even the greatest people are born with just sentiments of natural liberty, which are never stifled in them by flattery.'
91 R A Stuart 147/103.
92 R A Stuart 92/3.
93 S P Tuscany 32 f.399.
94 S P Russia 10. f.152.
95 R A Stuart 157/33.
96 R A Stuart 157/155.
97 R A Stuart 157/169.
98 R A Stuart 157/190.
99 Archives Etrangères, Correspondance Politique, Angleterre 376 ff.247–73; 377 ff.126–31; 380 ff.205–7. Cf. also Horace Walpole, *Memoirs of the Reign of George II*, 3 vols (1846), I, p.73.
100 R A Stuart 158/138.
101 R A Stuart 158/122.
102 There is a good example in May 1732 (R A Stuart 153/18). Cf. also R A Stuart 155/165; 161/167.
103 R A Stuart 158/104.
104 R A Stuart 155/24; 156/163.
105 R A Stuart 155/159. 'He has made a progress in two months such as many don't do in as many years who gain their bread by it.'
106 S P Tuscany 32 f.577.
107 S P Tuscany 32 f.488; R A Stuart 155/165.
108 S P Tuscany 32 f.588.
109 S P Tuscany 32 ff.265,267.
110 R A Stuart 168/87,194.
111 James to Inverness, 1 June 1734, R A Stuart 170/151.
112 R A Stuart 158/104.

CHAPTER THREE

1 SP Tuscany 37 f.22.
2 *Ibid.*, f.24.
3 R A Stuart 168/118,126,137,143.
4 S P Tuscany 37 f.24.
5 R A Stuart 168/32; 169/25,55.
6 R A Stuart 169/41.
7 R A Stuart 170/77. Charles Edward bounced back from his privations with his usual élan. Cf. James to Clementina, 20 May 1734: 'Carluccio has won six crowns at *buoco* and is very full at present of swallow shooting' (R A Stuart 170/97).
8 R A Stuart 170/15.
9 R A Stuart 170/92.
10 R A Stuart 170/51.
11 R A Stuart 170/159,179.
12 S P Tuscany 37 f.52; R A Stuart 171/28.
13 R A Stuart 171/33.
14 R A Stuart 171/38.
15 S P Tuscany 37 ff.105,119,127.
16 R A Stuart 171/162–3.
17 S P Tuscany 37 ff.137–8.
18 R A Stuart 172/14; S P Tuscany 37 ff.141–3.
19 R A Stuart 172/10. 'I cannot, my dear child, let this day pass without sending my blessing with all the tenderness I am capable of.... You will, I hope, be one day both a great and a good man, which I pray God to make you' (James to Charles Edward, 30 July 1734, R A Stuart 172/17).
20 R A Stuart 172/47.
21 Tayler, *Stuart Papers at Windsor*, op. cit., p.90.
22 R A Stuart 172/51.
23 Add. MSS 38,851 f.139.
24 Stowe MSS 158 f.187.
25 R A Stuart 172/55.
26 R A Stuart 172/56.
27 Stowe MSS 158 f.187.
28 R A Stuart 172/56.
29 R A Stuart 172/92.
30 R A Stuart 172/86.
31 R A Stuart 172/114.
32 Add. MSS 38,851 f.139; Stowe MSS 158 f.187.
33 *Ibid.*
34 James's letter to Charles Edward on 7 August, before he had heard from Dunbar, is instructive: 'Have a particular care for your diet, for it would be a foolish and vexatious thing should you fall ill there by eating trash' (R A Stuart 172/58).
35 R A Stuart 172/149.
36 Spain used the fiction of Charles

Edward's incognito to counter this (R A Stuart 172/128).

37 R A Stuart 172/73.

38 H M C 15, ii, p.236.

39 S P Tuscany 37 f.165.

40 R A Stuart 172/106,129. Berwick went so far as to praise the prince's education 'which does Lord Dunbar and Sir Thomas no small honour' (R A Stuart 172/88).

41 R A Stuart 172/133–4.

42 R A Stuart 172/166.

43 For Bolingbroke's last throw of these particular dice see R A Stuart 169/26. Nor could Charles's cause have been helped in his father's eyes by Bolingbroke's encomium for the prince's behaviour at Gaeta (R A Stuart 173/178).

44 R A Stuart 171/46.

45 S P Tuscany 37 f.142.

46 'Your late indisposition will, I hope, contribute to make you more temperate in your diet' (R A Stuart 173/22). Cf. also HMC 15, ii, p.237; Add. MSS 38,851 f.139.

47 R A Stuart 172/149.

48 S P Tuscany 37 f.164.

49 *Ibid.*, f.165.

50 R A Stuart 173/166.

51 HMC 10, vi, p.279.

52 S P Tuscany 37 f.165.

53 R A Stuart 173/68–9.

54 R A Stuart 173/114; 174/13. 'The Duke ... promises yet more than the Prince' (22 September 1734).

55 'The Duke was a little too cunning for the Prince' (R A Stuart 175/107).

56 R A Stuart 174/128.

57 R A Stuart 175/10.

58 R A Stuart 176/2.

59 R A Stuart 176/67.

60 R A Stuart 176/22.

61 R A Stuart 176/143,150.

62 R A Stuart 177/1.

63 R A Stuart 177/2.

64 S P Tuscany 37 f.199.

65 R A Stuart 177/10.

66 R A Stuart 177/23.

67 R A Stuart 177/24.

68 R A Stuart 177/49.

69 This is the area where, *par excellence*, the methodological limitations of trying to retrieve the past from documents alone become clear.

70 The *locus classicus* is of course Freud's essay, 'Mourning and Melancholia', *SE* 14, pp.239–58. The subject has recently been examined in great detail in the third volume of John Bowlby's monumental *Attachment and Loss*: J. Bowlby, *Loss, Sadness and Depression* (1980).

71 R A Stuart 179/18.

72 Alastair Smart, *The Life and Art of Allan Ramsay* (1952), p.27.

73 R A Stuart 181/142,149; 182/108,134.

74 R A Stuart 186/82.

75 R A Stuart 182/103.

76 S P Tuscany 37 ff.269,273,304.

77 R A Stuart 183/60,81; 185/188. 'I believe he could fatigue already as much as most people here' (James to Marischal, 23 January 1736, R A Stuart 185/91).

78 S P Tuscany 37 ff.227,229,277. On his many canters in the Villas Barberini and Ludovici Charles Edward sustained frequent falls from his horse from which he emerged unscathed.

79 R A Stuart 185/100; 187/2,38.

80 R A Stuart 192/2; 192/85. 'As for the Prince, I believe there are few people of his age more strong and healthy, and I think he has grown more than usual of late' (James to Inverness, 31 October 1736, R A Stuart 191/11).

81 R A Stuart 191/122,126. At one *caccia* at Valmontone 19 hares, 21 cocks and 12 partridges were taken in one day by the prince's party (R A Stuart 191/39). On another four-day shooting expedition Charles Edward bagged 10 of the 45 cocks culled by the party (R A Stuart 192/66). His best feat was 20 quails in one morning (R A Stuart 179/70).

82 'He continues still wonderfully thoughtless for one to his age' (James to Inverness, 11 January 1736, R A Stuart 185/47). Cf. James to Ormonde, 20 February 1736: 'He is, I thank God, very hearty and strong and has naturally a great deal of vivacity and penetration but is other ways [sic] a little backward for his age both in mind and body.'

83 R A Stuart 192/49.

84 When Cardinal Tencin mentioned Charles Edward's financial problems in early 1745, Pope Benedict XIV drew attention to the many papal benefices the prince had received from Clement XII (Benedict to Tencin, 28 July 1745, Morelli, I, p.257). For Clement XII's generosity to the prince cf. also S P Tuscany 37 ff, 180,202,273,307,353,384.

85 R A Stuart 174/52.

86 R A Stuart 177/63.

87 R A Stuart 177/137,142.

88 R A Stuart 178/73,142.

89 R A Stuart 178/137.

90 R A Stuart 179/49,56.

91 R A Stuart 182/108. Jacobite sights had been set on the siege of Mantua and all the prince's equipment, horses and post-

chaises were ready to depart at a moment's notice (S P Tuscany 37 f.260).

92 R A Stuart 184/112.

93 R A Stuart 193/41,60.

94 R A Stuart 193/133.

95 R A Stuart 193/155.

96 James to O'Rourke, 9 February 1737, R A Stuart 194/33.

97 R A Stuart 194/84.

CHAPTER FOUR

1 S P Tuscany 41 f.40; R A Stuart 196/2.

2 S P Tuscany 41 f.38.

3 R A Stuart 196/19.

4 R A Stuart 196/12.

5 R A Stuart 196/23.

6 'If Your Majesty could have seen with what gravity the Prince heard all the compositions, I'm sure it would have diverted you' (Dunbar to James, 4 May 1737, R A Stuart 196/23).

7 'Nor did any other gentleman sit at supper except the Bishop of Pesaro and Farno, who made a grotesque figure among so many women' (R A Stuart 196/23).

8 S P Venice 63 f.346; R A Stuart 196/49.

9 S P Tuscany 41 f.46.

10 'In conversation the Prince displayed a gravity and attention that would have been proper in someone of thirty' (Dunbar to James, 7 May 1737, R A Stuart 196/50).

11 H M C, 10, i, p.268; R A Stuart 196/50,53.

12 S P Tuscany 41 f.46.

13 R A Stuart 196/64.

14 *Ibid.*

15 R A Stuart 196/73.

16 R A Stuart 196/105.

17 S P Venice 63 f.348.

18 R A Stuart 196/133.

19 S P Tuscany 41 ff.53–4.

20 R A Stuart 197/41.

21 S P Tuscany 41 ff.57–8.

22 S P Venice 63 f.350.

23 R A Stuart 197/41.

24 S P Venice 63 ff.352–3; 'The Doge seemed a mighty genteel and yet good-natured old gentleman' (Dunbar, R A Stuart 197/41).

25 S P Venice 63 ff.352–3.

26 H M C, Denbigh, pp.220–1.

27 'All he [the prince] said was in a lively, civil, respectful manner, but at the same time with an air of superiority that was remarked by everybody' (Dunbar to James, 3 June 1737, R A Stuart 197/92).

28 S P Venice 63 ff.354–5. But not before the prince had toured the entire arsenal on foot 'which in this heat is a tour of

some fatigue' (Dunbar, R A Stuart 197/72).

29 R A Stuart 197/146.

30 *Ibid.*

31 S P Venice 63 f.355. For the eccentric Lady Wortley Montagu's denial of this obvious fact see *Walpole Correspondence*, W. S. Lewis, ed., *The Yale Edition of Horace Walpole's Correspondence*, 39 vols (New Haven, 1937–74), 17, p.98.

32 S P Venice 63 f.356.

33 H M C, 14, ix, p.8.

34 S P Venice 63 f.355.

35 R A Stuart 197/146.

36 R A Stuart 198/29. Cf. also Dunbar to James, 3 June 1737, R A Stuart 197/92 recommending that the prince be kept in the 'grande [sic] monde' so that he could become accustomed to proper behaviour 'which he never will acquire amongst a few of his own people at Rome with whom he has constantly lived and who give him no manner of constraints' (a palpable hit at Sheridan). Also: 'I cannot but tell Your Majesty that in private we might make the same complaints as formerly and that he gives us rather more unease when he travels. But this is only a trouble to his own people and particularly to me who go in the chair with him' (*ibid.*).

37 Apart from tiresome homilies (James to Charles Edward, 31 May, 197/62 contains a very good example of the pettifogging James style), James constantly lectured his son on how he *ought* to respond during the tour: 'I reckon you will be tired of Venice before you leave it, and I hope you will remember our agreement about games of hazard and what I said to you about your eating' (James to Charles Edward, 24 May, R A Stuart 196/60).

38 R A Stuart 198/60.

39 *Ibid.*

40 R A Stuart 198/88. In a pathetic attempt to sugar this pill, Dunbar adds: 'However, I can assure Your Majesty that he never was in better health than at present and I believe you will find him considerably fatter and taller than he was when he left Rome.'

41 S P Tuscany 41 f.62.

42 R A Stuart 198/155.

43 R A Stuart 198/117,155,160; S P Tuscany 41 f.64.

44 For Dunbar's own reluctant testimony as to Charles Edward's personal magnetism see R A Stuart 196/23, 133. Dunbar agreed with the assessment of Cardinal Davia and the Elector of Bavaria that the

prince could already be presented with distinction at any court in Europe (R A Stuart 197/62).

45 R A Stuart 345/162.

46 R A Stuart 185/47.

47 R A Stuart 196/23.

48 R A Stuart 196/89.

49 R A Stuart 196/70; 197/110.

50 R A Stuart 198/39.

51 R A Stuart 199/43.

52 For James's jealousy of Sheridan as father surrogate see below p.313. Since Berwick was (apart from Sheridan) the other obvious rival as father-figure, it is possible that the idea might have been planted unconsciously by Berwick's informing him in June that he had cut off all hair on medical advice (R A Stuart 197/39).

53 'The Prince's hair being very troublesome to him was to his great joy cut off the other day and the wig H.R.H. wears becomes him very well' (R A Stuart 199/181). It will be noted that not even James claimed that his son would be pleased with the haircut.

54 R A Stuart 207/65.

55 Sir Bruce Seton, ed., *Commentary on the Expedition to Scotland made by Charles Edward Stuart, Prince of Wales, by Padre Giulio Cesare Cordara, Miscellany of the Scottish History Society*, 3rd series, IX (1926), p.18.

56 *LM*, ii, p.102.

57 Benedict XIV to Tencin, 24 November 1745, Morelli, I, p.291.

58 Any view expressed by so careful a scholar as Professor L. L. Bongie merits respect, but I cannot accept his thesis that the prince had taken a formal vow of chastity which was not broken until his liaison with Louise de Montbazon in late 1747 (L. L. Bongie, *The Love of a Prince. Bonnie Prince Charlie in France 1744–1748* (Vancouver, 1986), pp.176–7). For one thing, the prince took Clementina Walkinshaw as his mistress as early as January 1746. For another, his brother Henry was complaining of 'orgies' long before the duchesse de Montbazon appeared on the scene. Finally, the prince's own account of his liaison as quoted by Bongie does not suggest a sexual innocent ('he was accustomed in his own country to being extremely cautious in affairs of the heart', Bongie, op. cit., p.10).

59 For details see R A Stuart 203/48,110; 206/44,87; 211/65; 212/129,140; 215/107,118; 218/89,133; 228/162,167; 236/144; 238/82,108; 239/61; 245/193,224; 246/88.

60 Typical 'bags' include: 100 woodcocks and 'cartloads of stags, roes and wild boars' in December 1737 (R A Stuart 203/82); '100 animals, 199 cocks and a great deal of small game' in January 1741 (R A Stuart 230/67); '250 woodcock killed in a week, of which the Prince shot half' in December 1741 (R A Stuart 238/143); 'The Prince killed in one day 70 wild ducks at Fogliano and another day at Cisterna 60 woodcocks' in January 1742 (R A Stuart 239/183); '100 woodcocks killed, most of them by the Prince' in December 1742 (R A Stuart 246/6). Cf. also Elcho, *Short Account*, p.26 with details of a shooting party in December 1740. On the first day 250 woodcocks were killed, on the second 25 deer, and on the third 600 wild ducks. Whatever reservations Charles Edward had about life in Rome, he certainly shared the Italian mania for *la caccia*.

61 H. Tayler, *Jacobite Miscellany* (Edinburgh, 1948), p.113.

62 R A Stuart 216/120; 217/175. The growth, it seems, was not all one way. On 2 January 1740 Edgar reported: 'HRH is now near as fat as the king' (R A Stuart 219/104).

63 Elcho, *Short Account*, p.23. Elcho, typically, protested that the comparison was unfair since the prince was nearly a year older.

64 R A Stuart 214/154; 215/169; 216/14. Even on this occasion James could not resist censoriousness: '[the prince] has not the strongest stomach. I believe the Carnival did him no good, for as to keeping meagre days, that is regulated by the doctors.' In other words, James was determined that his beloved Lenten fasts were not going to be blamed!

65 R A Stuart 223/40; 225/181; 235/139. Although the Elector of Bavaria's servant is said to have called at the Palazzo Muti to enquire about the prince's health in June 1742. *Walpole Correspondence*, op. cit., 17, p.445.

66 In June 1742, when the entire upper social echelon at the Palazzo Muti succumbed to a cold virus, the prince was unscathed (R A Stuart 242/151).

67 R A Stuart 210/26.

68 R A Stuart 210/20, 76; 218/53. Yet even music took second place to hunting: 'HRH loves and understands music very well, yet notwithstanding he prefers the exercise and diversion of shooting to the

fine opera we have at this season' (Edgar, January 1742, R A Stuart 239/71).

69 Charles de Brosses, *Lettres d'Italie* (Dijon, 1927), 2 vols, ii, pp.73–4.

70 R A Stuart 213/97.

71 A. De Angelis, *Nella Roma Papale. Il Teatro Aliberti o delle dame 1717–1863* (Tivoli, 1973), pp.162–3. Cf. S P Tuscany 41 ff.139,246,262; S P Tuscany 46 f.169.

72 Vernon Lee, *Studies in the Eighteenth Century in Italy* (1907), pp.202–3.

73 S P Tuscany 46 f.171.

74 R A Stuart 213/103,129.

75 R A Stuart 213/97.

76 *Walpole Correspondence*, op. cit., 13, p.217.

77 *Letters of Thomas Gray*, ed. Duncan C. Tovey, 3 vols (1900), i, p.68.

78 S P Tuscany 43 f.146.

79 *Letters of Gray*, op. cit., i, p.74.

80 Pierre de Segur, 'Madame du Deffand et sa famille', *Revue des Deux Mondes*, 1917, No. 37, p.837.

81 R A Stuart 239/183. This was the full Highland dress sent as an admiring gift to the prince by the duke of Perth (later lieutenant-general in his armies) in February 1738 (R A Stuart 205/16).

82 S P Tuscany 43 f.139.

CHAPTER FIVE

1 See, for example, Eveline Cruickshanks, *Lord Cornbury, Bolingbroke and a Plan to restore the Stuarts 1731–35* (Royal Stuart Society Series No. 27, 1986).

2 R A Stuart 208/76.

3 R A Stuart 208/145. This despite great admiration for Charles Edward at the Spanish court. Montemar, Berwick's co-commander in 1734, told the Jacobite Colonel Brett in May 1740 that Charles was the most promising and amiable prince he had ever seen. R A Stuart 222/147.

4 F. J. McLynn, 'Issues and Motives in the Jacobite Rising of 1745', *The Eighteenth Century*, 23 (1982), pp.97–133.

5 F. J. McLynn, 'Ireland in the Jacobite Rising of 1745', *Irish Sword*, 13 (1979), pp.339–52.

6 John Stevenson, *Popular Disturbances in England 1700–1870* (1979).

7 See Eveline Cruickshanks, *Political Untouchables. The Tories and the '45* (1979), esp. pp.4–6.

8 For a full discussion of England as 'ancien régime' and the modifying role of Jacobitism see J. C. D. Clark, *English Society 1688–1832* (Cambridge, 1985).

9 See Jeremy Black, *British Foreign Policy in the Age of Walpole* (Edinburgh, 1985), pp.138–55.

10 W. B. Blaikie, *Origins of the Forty-Five* (Edinburgh, 1916), p.xxv.

11 R A Stuart 219/152.

12 For the dithering over Charles Edward's rumoured trip to Spain see S P Tuscany 41 ff.334,337,338; S P Tuscany 42 ff.200,206; S P Tuscany 43 ff.25,33.

13 S P Tuscany 41 f.348.

14 R A Stuart 221/41,127,148; 222/16,75,146.

15 D'Argenson, Marquis, *Journal et mémoires*, ed. E. J. B. Rathery, 9 vols (Paris, 1859–67), ii, p.413; iii, p.59; cf. also Add. MSS 39,476 f.189; H M C, 14, ix, p.48.

16 S P Tuscany 44 ff.79,168.

17 S P Tuscany 43 f.35.

18 R A Stuart 220/153.

19 S P Tuscany 43, f.62.

20 *Ibid.*, f.68.

21 R A Stuart 235/172.

22 S P Tuscany 44 f.526; cf. also *Walpole Correspondence*, 17, pp.202–3.

23 S P Tuscany 43 ff.99, 123.

24 C. Jean Sareil, *Les Tencin* (Geneva, 1969).

25 S P Tuscany 41 f.273.

26 R A Stuart 225/181.

27 R A Stuart 226/30.

28 S P Tuscany 43 ff.134,137–9.

29 *Ibid.*, ff.141–2,148,160.

30 *Ibid.*, f.195.

31 S P Tuscany 46 f.206.

32 S P Tuscany 41 f.340; S P Tuscany 46 ff.229,237.

33 S P Tuscany 43 ff.99,123,172,199; S P Tuscany 46 ff.22,26.

34 R A Stuart 235/186; 236/9.

35 S P Tuscany 46 ff.37,71,132; cf. *Walpole Correspondence*, 18, p.201.

36 H M C 14, ix, p.82.

37 RA Stuart 243/113.

38 Benedict XIV to Tencin, 11 March 1744, Morelli, op. cit., i, p.156.

39 The title given him by his only English biographer. Renée Haynes, *Philosopher King, Pope Benedict XIV* (1970).

40 S P Tuscany 43 ff.84,96,144,158–9,168; S P Tuscany 46 ff.41,55,95,135,149, 192.

41 S P Tuscany 43 f.118.

42 S P Tuscany 46 ff.63,69.

43 See Biblioteca Angelica MSS 1613.

44 S P Tuscany 43 f.213; S P Tuscany 46 ff.20,149,178.

45 S P Tuscany 46 ff.4,14.

46 For exhaustive detail see R A Stuart 302/102–5.

47 Cf. the judgment passed on him in 1749: ' 'Tis true his education has not been in every particular such as a person of his rank is supposed generally to have, yet by a good fund of sense people will see that nature has supplied whatever may

have been wanting in care and industry'
(R A Stuart 302/134).

48 See, for example, the totally banal and
uncommunicative letter to the Dillon
family in 1736 (H M C II, p.33) or the
series of letters from Charles Edward to
Cardinal Gualterio during 1735–42
(Add. MSS 20,661 ff.124–36).

49 J. C. O'Callaghan, History of the Irish
Brigade (1870), p.340.

50 Stosch's report in February 1741 (S P
Tuscany 43 ff.141–2) speaks of Charles
Edward's observed fondness for women.
But it is perhaps significant that Stosch,
who was prepared to invent a string of
bogus mistresses for James, giving names
and places of assignation, provides no
such list for the prince.

51 Lord Elcho writes in his diary that
Charles Edward was interested in
nothing but hunting and music, had no
conversational power, and was not very
intelligent. But Elcho is a notoriously
hostile and unreliable witness in everything concerning the prince.

52 Stowe MSS 158 f.191.

53 Tayler, Stuart Papers at Windsor, pp.106–9.

54 R A Stuart 234/12; S P Tuscany 43 f.207;
S P Tuscany 46 f.171.

55 R A Stuart 245/46.

56 Cf. Bulkeley's remarks on the aftermath
of the 1737 tour: 'When he was driven
back to his prison of Rome (for as such
he always considered it), his high mind
bore with difficulty the depression [italics
mine] of his situation' (R A Stuart
345/162).

57 This section is heavily based on the work
by Heinz Kohut, especially The Search for
the Self. Selected Writings of Heinz Kohut
1950–1978, ed. Paul H. Orenstein, 2 vols
(New York, 1978); cf. also Arnold Goldberg, ed., The Psychology of the Self.A case
book written with the collaboration of Heinz
Kohut (New York, 1978).

58 R A Stuart 298/143. Naturally this secret
correspondence was psychologically
'overdetermined', for unconscious resentment and contempt for his father must
have played a part.

59 S P Tuscany 46 f.17.

CHAPTER SIX

1 Cruickshanks, Political Untouchables, op.
cit., p.38.

2 F. J. McLynn, France and the Jacobite Rising
of 1745 (Edinburgh, 1981), p.16.

3 Walpole Correspondence, 17, p.306. There
was even talk of reviving the trip to Spain
as one of the options (R A Stuart
252/137).

4 James to Tencin, 30 May, 27 June 1743,
R A Stuart 250/47; 251/40.

5 R A Stuart 251/179,210,212; 252/49.

6 R A Stuart 252/82.

7 R A Stuart 252/77.

8 R A Stuart 252/39.

9 R A Stuart 248/115.

10 After the failure of the invasion, Louis
XV told Philip V that the débâcle was
due to a number of factors, but principally the precipitate arrival of the Stuart
prince (AECP, Espagne 478 f.158).
Tencin, too, disingenuously tried to shift
the responsibility for the failure from
French shoulders on to James and
Charles Edward (AECP, Espagne 478
f.101).

11 For this see McLynn, France and the '45,
op. cit. Cf. also J. Colin, Louis XV et les
Jacobites. Le projet de débarquement en
1743–44 (Paris, 1901).

12 R A Stuart 248/136.

13 R A Stuart 250/91; 250/190; 252/39;
254/151.

14 Tayler, Jacobite Miscellany, op. cit., p.14.

15 R A Stuart Box 1/188A. The journey was
also considered dangerous because of the
English agents. Louis XV advised
Balhaldy to take three or four servants
with him on the journey through Switzerland (John Murray, Memorial of John
Murray of Broughton, ed. R. F. Bell
(Scottish History Society 27, Edinburgh
1898), p.87).

16 R A Stuart 254/91–9.

17 R A Stuart 247/43.

18 Here is a typical report from Edgar in
May: 'The Prince, that he might not lose
a whole day's shooting, after supper on
Sunday night put on his garters, and in
his riding coat slept in a chair till after
one o'clock and went away at 2 a.m. to
Palo' (R A Stuart 249/134).

19 Padre Giulio Cesare Cordara, Commentary
on the Expedition to Scotland made by Charles
Edward Stewart, Prince of Wales, Sir Bruce
Seton, ed., Miscellany of the Scottish History
Society, 3rd series, IX (1926), p.25.

20 Jean Sareil, Les Tencin (Geneva, 1969),
p.343.

21 Colin, op. cit., p.46.

22 R A Stuart 257/164.

23 Cordara, op. cit., pp.27–8. Two days
before Christmas, James sent a
supplementary note to Louis XV and
Amelot, informing them that his son
would be departing on 12 January.
Meanwhile he was sending the requested
declarations with Balhaldy (Murray of
Broughton, op. cit., pp.493–5).

24 R A Stuart Box 1/188.

25 R A Stuart 256/43.
26 S P Tuscany 48 f.48; Tayler, *Jacobite Miscellany*, p.15; Amelia C. M. MacGregor, *History of the Clan Gregor* (Edinburgh, 1901), ii, p.361.
27 Tayler, *Jacobite Miscellany*, p.18.
28 This consisted of M. Gaudine, steward to the Bailli de Tencin, and Duncan Buchanan, clerk to the banker Aeneas MacDonald.
29 Tayler, *Jacobite Miscellany*, p.16.
30 S P Tuscany 48 ff.47–8; S P Tuscany 49 f.20.
31 For this nephew of Cardinal Tencin see *Repertorium der diplomatischen Vertreter aller Lander*, ed. Friedrich Hausmann (Zurich, 1950), ii, p.16.
32 Cordara, p.32.
33 S P Tuscany 48 f.47.
34 S P Tuscany 49 ff.24, 48.
35 S P Tuscany 49 f.24.
36 S P Tuscany 49 f.37.
37 The Gaetani were not in on the secret. S P Tuscany 49 f.48.
38 Tayler, *Jacobite Miscellany*, p.24.
39 R A Stuart Box 1/190–3.
40 Tayler, *Jacobite Miscellany*, pp.28–30; R A Stuart 255/80.
41 Cordara, p.41.
42 The deception held Mann's network at bay for eleven days. After that his agents were in full cry on the prince's track (*Walpole Correspondence*, 18, pp.373–9).
43 Cordara, p.42.
44 R A Stuart M.11 (O'Heguerty's account), p.22.
45 Cordara, p.42.
46 Tayler, *Jacobite Miscellany*, p.30; Cordara, p.42.
47 This consequence had been foreseen by James. In a letter to Sempill on 16 January he wrote: 'I hope the French Court will have dispatched immediately to Antibes upon Balhaldy's arrival, for if that governor is not prepared for the Prince's coming, it may be of inconvenience on account of nobody's being even admitted to make a quarantine there' (R A Stuart 255/60).
48 Tayler, *Jacobite Miscellany*, p.32; Cordara, p.43.
49 R A Stuart 255/93.
50 *Murray of Broughton*, op. cit., pp.495–6.
51 Cordara, p.43.
52 R A Stuart 255/91.
53 R A Stuart 255/92; Tayler, *Jacobite Miscellany*, p.32.
54 AEMD, Angleterre 86 f.337; 87 f.20.
55 *Murray of Broughton*, pp.497–8.
56 *Ibid*.
57 R A Stuart 255/127.

58 Cordara, p.44.
59 R A Stuart 255/134.
60 AEMD, Angleterre, 91 f.299; R A Stuart 255/163.
61 For day-by-day details see AEMD, Angleterre, 87 ff.7–19.
62 Mann to Walpole, 4 February 1744, *Walpole Correspondence*, 18, p.385.
63 S P Tuscany 48 ff.25,48,53; cf. also *Walpole Correspondence*, 18, pp.378–9.
64 S P Tuscany 48 f.61; *Walpole Correspondence*, 18, p.396. This was a wild inference based on the fact that Charles Edward had met the Imperial Minister Baron Scarlatti in Rome on a number of occasions since 1742 (S P Tuscany 48 f.53).
65 S P Tuscany 48 f.61.
66 S P Tuscany 48 f.106; *Walpole Correspondence*, 18, p.427.
67 R A Stuart 255/30; Morelli, op. cit., i, pp.144–7. Benedict XIV added that even if he had known, he would not have tried to stop the prince (Morelli, i, p.146).
68 Benedict XIV to Tencin, 8 August 1744, Morelli, i, p.187.
69 Canilliac to Amelot, 25 January 1744, AECP, Rome, 794 f.44.
70 ASV, Francia 483 ff.579,584.
71 R A Stuart 255/163.
72 So strict was French concern for security that an embargo was placed on all English shipping in the Pas de Calais, under the pretext of an anti-smuggling drive (Archives de la Guerre, A1/3034 f.43).
73 Archives Nationales, Marine, B3/421 ff.71–2.
74 Cruickshanks, *Political Untouchables*, p.53.
75 Guerre A1/3034 f.19.
76 AEMD, Angleterre, 90 f.324.
77 Cruickshanks, p.57.
78 S P Tuscany 48 f.381; S P Tuscany 49 f.41; *Walpole Correspondence*, 18, ff.374–5,404.
79 Cruickshanks, pp.57–8.
80 *Walpole Correspondence*, 18, pp.415–16.
81 Tencin to Canilliac, 11 February 1744, AECP, Rome, 794 f.46.
82 S P France 229 ff.143,155–60.
83 This decision had been taken by the French court as soon as it was known that the prince was definitely *en route* to France. Cf. James to Sempill, 13 February 1744: 'Your letter of the 27th January gives me no small astonishment and concern, for how can I reconcile all that has been advanced to me of late with the neglect and indifference which now appears in relation to the Prince's coming into France?' (R A Stuart 255/177).

84 Tayler, *Jacobite Miscellany* (Elcho's Diary), p.132.
85 Guerre A1/3034 f.19.
86 *Murray of Broughton*, p.69.
87 Add. MSS 34,522 f.65; AEMD, Angleterre, 87 f.275; 88 f.73.
88 HMC II, p.88.

CHAPTER SEVEN

1 See, for example S P Tuscany 49 f.41.
2 A S V, Francia 483 f.598; Add. MSS 23,816 ff.196–7.
3 Cruickshanks, *Political Untouchables*, pp.59–61.
4 *Murray of Broughton*, pp.498–9.
5 A E M D, Angleterre, 83 f.176.
6 As Sempill later wrote: 'The stupidity of Read's coming over or being suffered to without knowing how to address himself or to whom is inconceivable but like a madman . . . he wrote to the Comte de Saxe for Mr. MacGregor through Dunkirk. His whole letter is of a piece, equally nonsense and contradictory. I should not be surprised if he has hanged himself instead of returning' (A E M D, Angleterre, 83 ff.179–80).
7 *Lettres et mémoires du marechal de Saxe*, ed. P. H. Grimoard, 5 vols (Paris, 1794), i, p.64.
8 For Prussian alarm at Louis XV's efforts on behalf of the Stuarts see *Politische Correspondenz. Friedrich's der Grosser* (Berlin, 1882), iii, pp.60–1,74,219.
9 Add MSS 33,004 ff.59–61.
10 A S V, Francia 483 ff.570–1; R A Stuart 256/135.
11 For details see Duc de Luynes, *Mémoires sur la cour de Louis XV* (Paris, 1862), v, pp.325–6; Colin, *Louis XV et les Jacobites*, op. cit., pp.147–51; Admiral Sir H. W. Richmond, *The Navy in the War of 1739–1748* (1920), 3 vols, ii, pp.75–8; Albert, duc de Broglie, *Frederic II et Louis XV* (Paris, 1885), ii, p.199.
12 Saxe to Charles Edward, 9 March 1744, R A Stuart 256/104.
13 Guerre A1/3034 f.91.
14 A E M D, Angleterre, 83 f.175.
15 Guerre A1/3034 f.113.
16 R A Stuart 256/63–71.
17 A E M D, Angleterre, 83 f.174.
18 R A Stuart 256/93.
19 R A Stuart 256/96.
20 Charles Edward to Saxe, 11 March, R A Stuart 256/121.
21 Charles Edward to Marischal, 11 March, R A Stuart 256/119.
22 'I cannot but own to you my vexation that they should have so sillily let Norris slip them from Portsmouth without the least resistance' (*ibid.*).
23 Saxe to Charles Edward, 13 March, R A Stuart 256/122.
24 Charles Edward to Saxe, 13 March, R A Stuart 256/124.
25 Saxe to Charles Edward, 16 March, R A Stuart 256/125.
26 'All the world complains that an expedition so well conducted hitherto should have been endangered by Roquefeuil's failing in what was so long and so easily in his power' (Charles Edward to James, 13 March, R A Stuart 256/127).
27 Marischal to Charles Edward, 5 March 1744, A E M D, Angleterre, 91 f.306; Charles Edward to Marischal, 5 March 1744, R A Stuart 256/93; R A Stuart 256/94.
28 'I shall be glad that M. de Roquefeuil judge proper to attack Norris, but what influence is it possible I can have to engage him to it? The Comte de Saxe, as well as others, knows that I am so little in the secret or concert, that I have not so much as had the least answer from the Minister to my demands. I am no seaman, I do not know the force of Norris' (Marischal to Charles Edward, 13 March, R A Stuart 256/126; cf. also A E M D, Angleterre, 91 f.309).
29 A E M D, Angleterre, 83 f.172.
30 R A Stuart 256/132; A E M D, Angleterre, 91 f.315; R A Stuart 256/134.
31 A E M D, Angleterre, 91 f.306.
32 This story can be followed at A E M D, Angleterre, 83 ff.172,178,181,185; 91 ff.302,306.
33 A E M D, Angleterre, 83 f.181.
34 A E M D, Angleterre, 91 ff.311–14.
35 Plus 80,000 livres for pay and a quantity of broadswords with which to arm the Highlanders (R A Stuart 256/131).
36 Marischal said that he had heard from Amelot that the French meant to persist in a Scottish expedition 'but I am most fully convinced that none can be made at present into that country but for its destruction, though perhaps it might make a useful diversion for the interest of France, I am resolved immediately to leave this place' (R A Stuart 256/139).
37 For Buchanan's mission see A E M D, Angleterre, 83 ff.189,192,196–7.
38 R A Stuart 256/185.
39 R A Stuart 302/130–1. Cf. also R A Stuart 345/162.
40 Add. MSS 34,522 f.53.
41 R A Stuart 256/141,155,175.
42 Benedict XIV to Tencin, 8 April 1744, Morelli, i, p.161. Significantly the Pope

added that not only had the French expedition not succeeded; according to his intelligence, it never could have.

43 'I have learned from you how to bear with disappointment, and I see it is the only way, which is to submit oneself to the will of God and never to be discouraged' (Charles Edward to James, 25 March, R A Stuart 256/169). This was formulaic pap. Not only did the prince *never* learn to deal with disappointment, but nothing could have been more alien to his true temperament than the sentiments expressed.

44 R A Stuart 256/180.

45 *Murray of Broughton*, op. cit., pp.500–1.

46 *Ibid.*, p.501.

47 Colin, op. cit., p.182.

48 H M C 14, ix, p.92.

49 S P France 229 ff.165–6,169,171.

50 R A Stuart 256/185.

51 *Ibid.*

52 R A Stuart 256/186.

53 'What has happened is a misfortune, it is true, but I am far from thinking it an irretrievable one, except we should make it so ourselves by pursuing precipitate and desperate measures, and undertake some rash and ill-concerted project, which would only end in your ruin and that of those who would join you in it' (James to Charles Edward, 15 April, R A Stuart 256/194).

54 R A Stuart 256/189.

55 A E M D, Angleterre, 83 f.185; A S V, Francia 483 f.611.

56 Charles Edward to James, 16 April, R A Stuart 256/197.

57 R A Stuart 256/201; 257/13,22.

58 R A Stuart 257/29.

59 Charles Edward to James, 11 May, R A Stuart 257/34.

60 R A Stuart 257/34,48,95.

61 R A Stuart 257/116,120.

62 A E M D, Angleterre, 83 f.204; R A Stuart 257/131.

63 As James remarked (19 June 1744): 'His preferring his present confinement to his going to the Prince of Conti's army was the choice of a wise more than a young man and is much approved by me' (R A Stuart 257/128).

64 R A Stuart 257/165.

65 R A Stuart 258/19,71,85.

66 R A Stuart 258/122.

67 R A Stuart 258/146.

68 R A Stuart 258/22,71,87,116.

69 R A Stuart 258/165.

70 R A Stuart 259/145.

71 R A Stuart 259/127.

72 R A Stuart 259/148.

73 R A Stuart 260/1.

74 R A Stuart 260/2.

75 For James's attitude see R A Stuart 258/13.31 and especially 258/133 (August 1744): 'I don't see what end this incognito answers that can be for our advantage, for it cannot be supposed but that all the world knows that the Prince is somewhere in the French dominions . . . the Prince has manifestly been made a sacrifice of on this occasion.'

76 R A Stuart 257/106; 258/6.

77 R A Stuart 257/58. 'I cannot but remark that the Prince's being actually sent for from Gravelines was just after M. Amelot's removal and that the Prince arrived at Paris immediately after the king set out for the army' (R A Stuart 257/76).

78 R A Stuart 257/58.

79 R A Stuart 258/118.

80 R A Stuart 258/170.

81 R A Stuart 261/11.

82 *Ibid.*

83 R A Stuart 261/30.

84 R A Stuart 258/150. Cf. Sempill to James, 7 December 1744 (R A Stuart 260/11) on France's German allies: 'the most part of whom would probably be pleased to see the duke of Hanover destroyed, but will not venture to concur in the attempt nor even seem to countenance it, because the head of their people would be scandalised at it on account of religion.'

85 *Murray of Broughton*, pp.373–4.

86 'I have taken a house within a league of this town where I am like a hermit. It is situated upon a hill and has an admirable prospect with a little garden, so that I enjoy at least the fresh air of the country' (Charles Edward to James, 1 June, R A Stuart 257/68).

87 R A Stuart 257/166.

88 R A Stuart 259/45,87.

89 *Murray of Broughton*, pp.374–5.

90 R A Stuart 259/141.

91 R A Stuart 260/18.

CHAPTER EIGHT

1 R A Stuart 259/75.

2 R A Stuart 257/114; 258/13.

3 R A Stuart 258/155.

4 R A Stuart 261/12.

5 R A Stuart 260/149.

6 H M C, 10, vi, p.218.

7 For the Monte di Pietà see David Silvagni, *La corte e la societa romana nei secoli xviii e xix* (Florence and Rome, 1885), i, p.340. Cf. also Joseph-Jerome le Français

de Lalande, *Voyage d'un Français en Italie* (Venice, 1769), iv, pp.172–4.

8 H M C, 10, vi, p.221.

9 *Ibid.*, p.219.

10 There is a complete list of the jewels and effects pledged at the Monte di Pietà in the Denys Bower MSS (Year 1742).

11 *Murray of Broughton*, op. cit., pp.371–3.

12 R A Stuart 257/68.

13 R A Stuart 257/95.

14 Cf. Sempill to James, 29 June: 'I have already told you how much the Prince has received from the French Court, which is such an inconsiderable sum that the Court ought to be ashamed of it, but though the Prince has to do with the most tenacious cashier that ever was entrusted by any dealer of spirit, yet this cashier is forced to own that he is directed to supply all the Prince's occasions, so that there is no reason to believe that the Prince will be under the necessity of troubling you' (R A Stuart 257/170).

15 R A Stuart 258/44; 259/77.

16 S P Dom, 106 f.12.

17 R A Stuart 258/107.

18 R A Stuart 259/157.

19 R A Stuart 261/11.

20 'You may imagine how I must be out of humour at all these proceedings, when, for comfort, I am plagued out of my life with tracasseries from our own people who, as it seems, would rather sacrifice me and my affairs than fail in any private view of their own' (Charles Edward to James, 30 November 1744, Lord Mahon, *History of England 1713–1783* (1838), iii, p.ix).

21 R A Stuart 259/118; 260/75.

22 R A Stuart 259/36.

23 Cf. Mézières to Maurepas, 29 August 1744, Maurepas Papers.

24 R A Stuart 257/103,164.

25 R A Stuart 259/145,148.

26 R A Stuart 259/58.

27 R A Stuart 257/34; 258/16.

28 R A Stuart 257/34; 258/85.

29 R A Stuart 257/105.

30 R A Stuart 257/86.

31 S P Tuscany 48 f.120; 49 f.63.

32 R A Cumberland Box 1/253. In view of later bibulous developments, it is ironical to note that the prince's diet sheet is virtually a disguised temperance tract.

33 R A Stuart 257/103.

34 R A Stuart 258/13.

35 R A Stuart 258/16,27.

36 R A Stuart 258/16,86.

37 R A Stuart Box 1/194; 258/96,116.

38 Add. MSS 34,523 f.77.

39 R A Cumberland 2/302. He suffered from fainting fits and headaches as a result.

40 R A Stuart 259/111.

41 R A Stuart 259/127.

42 R A Stuart 259/144; 260/1–2.

43 Charles Edward to James, 1 November, R A Stuart 260/34.

44 R A Stuart 257/41.

45 For Kelly's meteoric rise see R A Stuart 258/16,27; 259/87,145.

46 *Murray of Broughton*, pp.375–6; R A Stuart 259/88,127.

47 R A Stuart 259/171.

48 R A Stuart 258/132,134,150. Marischal's strictures on the pair also influenced James (R A Stuart 259/142).

49 R A Stuart 258/22,41,160.

50 R A Stuart 258/87.

51 A E M D, Angleterre, 85 ff.111–13; 86 f.344; R A Stuart 258/122,165; 259/145.

52 R A Stuart 257/164. Cf. also James Browne, *A History of the Highlands* (Edinburgh, 1853), ii, p.465.

53 R A Stuart 259/98.

54 *Murray of Broughton*, pp.88–91; R A Stuart 259/101. Murray of Broughton's mission had its moments of high comedy, with Murray revealing the extent of Balhaldy's and Sempill's double-dealing to the prince, while Balhaldy was in the next room trying to overhear the conversation (*Murray of Broughton*, pp.94–5).

55 A E M D, Angleterre, 86 f.341.

56 R A Stuart 258/78.

57 The news of the final settlement of the French pension was greatly welcomed in Rome. Benedict XIV reported that for the first time, James, who had sunk daily in spirits ever since his son left, showed signs of an emergence from melancholia (Benedict to Tencin, 23 January, 13 March 1745, Morelli, i, pp.222,232).

CHAPTER NINE

1 Blaikie, *Origins*, op. cit., pp.xliv–xlvi; R A Stuart 258/164.

2 *Murray of Broughton*, op. cit., p.90.

3 S P Dom, 86/69. Sheridan on arrival in France found the prince taller than he remembered him in Rome. He attributed this to his now wearing shoes of normal size instead of with artificially low heels (Tayler, *Stuart Papers*, p.112).

4 *Murray of Broughton*, p.90; R A Stuart 259/75.

5 *Murray of Broughton*, p.91.

6 R A Stuart 259/88.

7 R A Stuart 259/98.

8 Elcho, *Short Account*, p.234; *Murray of Broughton*, p.428. Cf. Charles Edward to Murray of Broughton, May 1745: 'I am

now resolved to be as good as my word and to execute a resolution which has never been out a moment out of my thoughts since I first took it in your presence' (R A Stuart 265/72).

9 R A Stuart Box 1/199.

10 R A Stuart Box 1/200.

11 H M C 11, vii, p.76. The English spies reported: 'His gait is ungracious and his knees appear stiff, but he is otherwise a well-made personage.'

12 R A Stuart Box 1/201.

13 R A Stuart 257/156.

14 R A Stuart 258/139.

15 R A Stuart 259/64.

16 R A Stuart 261/39.

17 S P Tuscany 48 f.114; 49 f.60; Browne, ii, p.452; R A Stuart 261/90. But James continued to insist that any French landing should be in England (R A Stuart 262/30).

18 A E M D, Angleterre, 83 f.213.

19 R A Stuart 261/109; Mahon, iii, p.x.

20 Browne, ii, pp.467–8; *Murray of Broughton*, p.389; R A Stuart 262/1,2,46.

21 R A Stuart 261/170.

22 R A Stuart 261/118; 262/30. But Sheridan hit back at Tencin, calling him 'a tyrant in business' who, if he had his way, would have dispatched the prince to the other side of the Alps. The choice, said Sheridan, was an instant resolution of the debts or a retreat to Avignon.

23 R A Stuart 261/109; Mahon, iii, p.ix.

24 R A Stuart 262/133.

25 R A Stuart 261/107,145,155; 262/43,121.

26 L. L. Bongie, *The Love of a Prince*, op.cit. p.112.

27 R A Stuart 262/41,51.

28 R A Stuart 264/101.

29 R A Stuart 262/173.

30 Philippe d'Albert duc de Luynes, *Mémoires du duc de Luynes sur la cour de Louis XV*, L. Dussieux et E. Souliné, 17 vols (Paris, 1860–6), vi, p.355.

31 Hence the absurdity of Walpole's statement (Walpole to Mann, 24 December 1744, *Walpole Correspondence*, 18, p.552) that Charles Edward had been acknowledged in France as Prince of Wales, and that the Bourbon princes of the blood had been to visit him under that name. In fact the duke of Orléans asked for permission to meet Charles Edward and was refused (R A Stuart 261/11).

32 R A Stuart 263/119.

33 He even visited Butler, the master of horse, at Versailles, wearing a mask and had a close-up view of the royal family (R A Stuart 262/160).

34 Luynes, vi, pp.355–6; R A Stuart 263/51A.

35 R A Stuart 262/2.

36 Feydeau de Marville, *Lettres au ministre Maurepas*, ed. A. de Boislisle (Paris, 1896), 3 vols, ii, p.42; Mahon, iii, p.x; Tayler, *Stuart Papers*, p.117; R A Stuart 263/24.

37 R A Stuart 263/124,125,170; 264/32. News of the prince's low credit rating led Parisian tradesmen to refuse to deliver to him when in Paris (Tayler, *Stuart Papers*, pp.118–19).

38 Browne, ii, pp.453,455,456–7,459.

39 R A Stuart 263/133,166.

40 R A Stuart 264/66,68; Mahon, iii, p.xii.

41 R A Stuart 264/173.

42 R A Stuart 263/200.

43 R A Stuart 264/38,150. The prince's snub was not the only slight received by the Berwick family at this time. Furious with himself for having given so much away to the bishop of Soissons in August 1744, during the famous 'deathbed confession', Louis VX vetoed Soisson's elevation to the purple in April 1745 (R A Stuart 264/97).

44 The French were even more reluctant to meet the cost of providing arms than of sending troops (Mahon, iii, pp.xi-xii).

45 Not that the prince was exactly practising rigid economies. Sheridan's accounts for February 1745 show an expenditure of £470 12s. Included in this is £24 for four opera tickets plus considerable expenditure on wines: 12 bottles of Malaga, 2 of Burgundy, 4 unnamed vintages and 3 bottles of liqueur (R A Cumberland 2/305).

46 Mahon, iii, pp.xi-xii; R A Stuart 263/51.

47 *Murray of Broughton*, pp.390–2.

48 R A Stuart 263/121.

49 Browne, ii, p.458; R A Stuart 264/14.

50 R A Stuart 261/169; 262/64. The first mention of O'Sullivan is in January 1745. He was soon put in charge of the prince's financial affairs (R A Stuart 262/43,160).

51 R A Stuart 261/153; 262/116; 263/94; Browne, ii, pp.456–7,459; *Murray of Broughton*, pp.396–7. Charles Edward responded with bitter and sometimes gloating attacks on the duo (R A Stuart 264/32; *Murray of Broughton*, pp.392–4; Tayler, *Stuart Papers*, p.125).

52 R A Stuart 262/131.

53 Szechi, *Jacobitism and Tory Politics*, op.cit., p.18.

54 Charles Edward to Edgar, 12 June 1745, Denys Bower MSS.

55 For details see R A Cumberland 2/328–31,337,340,342–4; 1,800 broad-

swords were sent in one consignment in May 1745 alone (R A Cumberland, 2/364).

56 Denys Bower MSS.

57 Gaston Martin, *Nantes au dix-huitième siècle* (Toulouse, 1928), esp.pp.240–3; Henri Malo, *Les derniers corsairs 1715–1815* (Paris, 1925).

58 La Tremouille, *Une famille royaliste Irlandaise et Française 1689–1789* (Nantes, 1901), pp.8–18.

59 A and H Tayler, *1745 and After* (1938), pp.46–7 (O'Sullivan's account), pp.46–7; R A Stuart M11 p.34.

60 R A Stuart 263/118.

61 R A Stuart 263/132.

62 R A Stuart 264/97.

63 Charles Edward to Edgar, 12 June 1745, Denys Bower MSS.

64 La Tremoille, op.cit., pp.18–19.

65 R A Stuart 264/151.

66 Tayler, *Stuart Papers*, pp.118–20,122.

67 For a detailed argument on this point see F. J. McLynn, *France and the '45*, op.cit., pp.32–4. Another interesting pointer is that lieutenant of police Marville's reports to Maurepas at this time are a tissue of confusion. See *Marville-Maurepas*, ii, pp.113–15,126–8.

68 For O'Sullivan's career see A and H Tayler, *1745 and After*, op.cit. (hereinafter cited as O'Sullivan).

69 R A Stuart 265/197; Tayler, *Stuart Papers*, p.118.

70 R A Stuart Box 1/212; 264/40; *Murray of Broughton*, p.395; Tayler, *Stuart Papers*, p.124.

71 R A Stuart 265/72.

72 *L M*, i, pp.201,282.

73 For MacDonald see Tayler, *Jacobite Miscellany*, esp.pp.61–6.

74 R A Stuart 261/82.

75 R A Stuart 259/101.

76 For Lord Lovat's devious Jacobite plotting see Bruce Lenman, *The Jacobite Clans of the Great Glen 1650–1784* (1984), pp.132–48.

77 R A Stuart 264/152.

78 R A Stuart 264/123–4; Mahon, iii, pp.xvii–xix; *Murray of Broughton*, pp.396–7.

79 The memoir written to Charles Edward by Sir Hector Maclean and John Roy Stewart on 2 December 1744 (R A Stuart 260/86) makes it plain that the prince's idea of a rising *first* to entice the French was well grounded in the advice he was receiving from the Scottish Jacobites.

80 R A Stuart 265/72.

81 A E M D, Angleterre, 83 f.228; 87 f.173.

82 Add. MSS 34,523; Tayler, *Stuart Papers*, pp.118–20.

83 R A M.10/2 (Sir John MacDonald's account), p.1.

84 *Ibid.*, p.3.

85 R A Stuart 265/201; Browne, iii, p.429.

86 R A Stuart 265/133; Tayler, *Stuart Papers*, p.128.

87 *L M*, i, p.281.

88 R A Cumberland 4/297.

89 R A Stuart M 10/2, p.3.

90 Chevalier de Johnstone, *A Memoir of the Forty-Five* (1820), p.2; La Tremouille, p.21.

91 R A Stuart 266/86; Mahon, iii, p.xx; Tayler, *Stuart Papers*, p.132.

92 'I have been a little sea-sick and expect to be more so, but it does not keep me much a-bed, for I find the more I struggle with it, the better' (Charles Edward to Edgar, 12 July 1745, R A Stuart 266/102; Mahon, iii, p.xxi).

93 R A Stuart M 10/2, p.4; La Tremouille, p.22.

94 R A Stuart 266/102; Tayler, *Stuart Papers*, p.133.

95 R A Cumberland 3/358; 4/301.

96 *L M*, i, pp.285,287.

97 A E M D, Angleterre, 91 f.375. The prince pointedly did not write to Tencin, Orry or Noailles.

98 Cf. Charles Edward to James, 4 August: 'The worst that can happen to me, if France does not succour me, is to die at the head of such brave people as I find there . . . the French Court must now necessarily take off the mask or have an eternal shame on them' (R A Stuart 266/174; Mahon, iii, p.xxii).

99 R A Stuart 265/129.

100 R A Stuart 265/72; Tayler, *Stuart Papers*, pp.118–20.

101 Another literary conceit: Charles Edward was like the *Pequod* in *Moby Dick*, obliged to crowd on sail in the Sunda Straits both to catch up with the whale armada *and* to throw off the pursuing Malay pirates.

102 Browne, iii, pp.440–1; R A Stuart 266/196–7. Cf. also James to Sempill, Browne, iii, pp.430–1.

103 Browne, iii, pp.445–6; R A Stuart 267/86.

104 S P Tuscany 50 f.217.

105 Benedict to Tencin, 25 August and 15 September 1745, Morelli, i, pp.266,273–4.

106 The most recent statement of this oft-repeated charge is in Lenman, *Jacobite Clans of the Great Glen*, op.cit., esp.pp.148–76.

107 See Karl Popper, *The Open Society and its Enemies*, 2 vols (1945).

108 For a detailed analysis of this see F. J. McLynn, *France and the '45*, op.cit.
109 See the chapters on the '45 in Bruce Lenman, *The Jacobite Risings in Britain 1689–1746* (1980).
110 For a lengthier treatment of this topic see McLynn, *The Jacobites* (1985), pp.63–77.
111 R A Stuart 265/175; Browne, iii, p.429; Tayler, *Stuart Papers*, p.129.

CHAPTER TEN

1 *L M*, i, p.285
2 R A Stuart M 10/2, p.5.
3 *L M*, i, pp.203,286–7; O'Sullivan, pp.50–1; La Tremouille, p.23; H M C, 14, ix, pp.130–1; Tayler, *Stuart Papers*, pp.136–7.
4 *London Gazette*, 20–23 July 1745.
5 R A Stuart 267/5.
6 R A Stuart M 10/2, pp.6–7.
7 *L M*, i, p.288.
8 *Ibid.*
9 O'Sullivan, p.50.
10 *L M*, i, p.288.
11 R A Stuart M 10/2, p.7.
12 *Ibid.*, p.8.
13 For the everyday life of the clansmen at the time see Edward Burt, *Letters from a Gentleman in the North of Scotland* (1818).
14 *L M*, i, p.205.
15 *L M*, i, p.289. This was not the prince's only *faux-pas* that night. Having examined the bed, he declared he would stay up all night and give the bed to Sheridan. Taking this as an aspersion on the cleanliness of his sheets, MacDonald, with unconscious irony, expostulated that they were fit for a prince to sleep on (*ibid*).
16 R A Stuart M 11, pp.38–9.
17 Ranald MacDonald of Clanranald, 'Account of Proceedings from Prince Charles's landing to Prestonpans', *Scottish Historical Society Miscellany* IX (Donald Nicholas, ed., 1958), p.206.
18 *L M*, i, p.205.
19 G. Lockhart, *The Lockhart Papers* (1817) (hereinafter *L P*), ii, p.440; *L M*, i, p.148.
20 R A Stuart M 10/2, p.9.
21 *L M*, i, p.289; R A Stuart M 10/2, p.9.
22 R A Stuart M 11, p.39.
23 *Ibid.*, p.40.
24 R A Stuart M 10/2, p.9; La Tremouille, p.28.
25 R A Stuart Box 1/213.
26 Andrew Lang, ed., *The Highlands of Scotland in 1750* (Edinburgh, 1898), pp.67–8.
27 *L M*, ii, p.198.
28 *Ibid.*
29 *L P*, ii, p.479; Clanranald's account, loc.cit., p.204.

30 Clanranald's account, p.206; Denys Bower MSS.
31 *L P*, ii, p.481; H. R. Duff, *Culloden Papers* (1815) (hereinafter *C P*), pp.203–4.
32 R A Stuart M 11, p.41; O'Sullivan, pp.54–5.
33 *L M*, iii, p.50.
34 *L M*, iii, p.51.
35 R A Stuart M 11, p.43.
36 *Murray of Broughton*, p.154.
37 John Home, *The History of the Rebellion in the Year 1745* (1802) (hereinafter Home's *History*), pp.39–40.
38 R A Stuart M 10/2, p.9.
39 'Lochgarry's narrative' in W. B. Blaikie, *The Itinerary of Prince Charles Edward Stuart* (Edinburgh, 1897), p.113; *L M*, i, p.206; R A Stuart M 11, p.43.
40 *L M*, iii, p.52.
41 R A Stuart M 10/2, p.11.
42 Home's *History*, p.44.
43 Not even Bruce Lenman, who used the Lochiel correspondence at Achnacarry house, has been able to penetrate any further into the mystery. *Jacobite Clans of the Great Glen*, op.cit., p.159.
44 R A Stuart M 11, pp.44–7.
45 R A Stuart M 10/2, p.11.
46 R A Stuart M 10/1, pp.28–9.
47 *Ibid.*, p.29.
48 *L M*, iii, p.120.
49 *Ibid.*, p.121.
50 No one can be certain of the mixture of motives that persuaded Lochiel to come out. But Home's story (*History*, p.44) that he was shamed into it is absurdly unconvincing. It is interesting to note that Victorian sentimental Jacobites refused point-blank to accept that Lochiel's decision could have been based on hard-headed interest. For a wilful and badly argued refusal to face facts see Andrew Lang, *Prince Charles Edward*, op.cit., pp.99–100.
51 R A Stuart M 11, p.47; 266/174; 74; Mahon, iii, p.xxi; La Tremouille, p.34.
52 *L P*, ii, p.480.
53 *L P*, ii, p.482.
54 R A Cumberland 4/310.
55 *L P*, ii, p.483; *L M*, i, p.207.
56 *L M*, i, p.292.
57 R A Stuart M 10/2, pp.12–13.
58 S P Scotland 25 Nos 47, 51; *C P*, p.245.
59 S P Scotland 25 Nos 49,53,77,79,82; *C P*, p.246.
60 For his career see G. Menary, *The Life and Letters of Duncan Forbes of Culloden* (1936).
61 For Lovat's relationship with Forbes see Lenman. *Jacobite Clans of the Great Glen.*, op.cit., pp.101–45.
62 See below pp.176–81.

63 *C P*, p.370.
64 *C P*, p.252.
65 *C P*, pp.400–1,409.
66 R A Cumberland 4/311.
67 *The Report of the Proceedings and Opinion of the Board of General Officers on their Examination into the conduct, behaviour and proceedings of Lieutenant-General Sir John Cope* (1749) (hereinafter *Cope*), p.19; *L M*, i, p.352; *C P*, p.406.
68 Lochgarry's narrative, loc. cit., p.113; *L P*, ii, p.483; *L M*, i, p.36; *Murray of Broughton*, pp.165–6; Home's *History*, p.46.
69 R A Stuart 10/1, p.30.
70 *Scots Magazine*, 1747, p.107.
71 *London Gazette*, 3–6 August 1745.
72 *C P*, p.447.
73 *L M*, i, p.207.
74 *L P*, ii, p.484.
75 R A Cumberland 4/311; Clanranald's account, loc.cit., p.208.
76 R A Stuart M 10/2, pp.13–14.
77 S P Scotland 25 Nos 87 and 99; R A Stuart M 11, p.50.
78 *L P*, ii, p.484.
79 *Murray of Broughton*, p.168.
80 Clanranald's account, p.209.
81 R A Stuart M 10/2, p.15.
82 For Cope's situation see the detailed account in R. C. Jarvis, *Collected Papers on the Jacobite Risings* (Manchester, 1972), 2 vols, i, pp.3–24.
83 Clanranald's account, p.210.
84 R A Stuart M 10/2 pp.14–15.
85 *L P*, ii, p.442.
86 *Scots Magazine*, 1747, p.626. After a protest at his levity from the chiefs, the prince was prevailed on to raise this to a matching £30,000.
87 R A Cumberland 4/324; *L M*, i, p.207.
88 *L M*, i, p.207.
89 R A Stuart M 10/1, pp.58–9.
90 O'Sullivan, pp.62–3.
91 *L M*, i, p.207.
92 *L P*, ii, p.442.
93 Home's *History*, p.117.
94 *L P*, ii, p.442.
95 *Cope*, p.116
96 H M C 15, ii, p.245.
97 *Cope*, p.45. Cope's route from Stirling had been through Amulree, Aberfeldy, Trinifur and Dalnacardoch.
98 Clanranald's account, p.211.
99 S P Scotland 25 No. 100.
100 See the Jacobite order of march for 27 August in R A Cumberland 4/328.
101 *L P*, ii, p.443; R A Cumberland 4/329–31.
102 This was the correct decision: Cope reached Ruthven on the 27th, Dalrachny

on the 28th and Inverness on the 29th (*Cope*, p.47).
103 *Murray of Broughton*, p.184.
104 Duncan Warrand, ed., *More Culloden Papers* (Inverness, 1930), 5 vols (hereinafter *M C P*), iv, pp.15,235; *Cope*, pp.43–4; O'Sullivan, p.65; *L M*, i, p.294.
105 R A Cumberland 4/327.
106 *C P*, p.391; *L P*, ii, p.440; O'Sullivan, pp.66–7.
107 *L M*, iii, p.121.
108 *C P*, p.412. For an analysis of Cluny's ambivalence see Lenman, *Jacobite Clans*, op.cit., pp.155–6.
109 *L M*, i, pp.208,294,353. The prince regarded Robertson as an important target. See R A Cumberland 4/319,332,335,339.
110 *L M*, i, pp.208,294.
111 Allardyce Papers, 2 vols (New Spalding Club, Aberdeen, 1895–6), ii, p.368; R A Cumberland 5/246.
112 *Caledonian Mercury*, 3 September 1745.
113 *L M*, i, p.208.
114 *Walpole Correspondence*, 19, p.206.
115 S P Scotland 26 No.3.
116 *L M*, i, p.208.
117 *L P*, ii, p.443.

CHAPTER ELEVEN

1 R A Stuart M 11 p.61.
2 James Maxwell of Kirkconnell, *Narrative of Charles, Prince of Wales's expedition to Scotland in the year 1745* (1841), p.31.
3 R A Stuart M 10/1, p.42.
4 R A Stuart M 11, p.64.
5 Elcho, *Short Account*, op.cit., p.255; Tayler, *Jacobite Miscellany* ('Elcho's Diary'), p.145.
6 Clanranald and Keppoch were given the Dundee assignment (*L P*, ii, p.486); Glenbucket was sent farther afield, to the north-east, on the same mission (R A Cumberland 5/427).
7 R A Stuart M 10/2, p.20.
8 Maxwell of Kirkconnell, op.cit., p.31; Chevalier de Johnstone, *A Memoir of the 'Forty-Five* (1820), p.10.
9 Clanranald's account, p.213.
10 For Murray's career see K. Tomasson, *The Jacobite General* (Edinburgh, 1958).
11 Atholl, 7th duke of, *Chronicles of the Families of Atholl and Tullibardine*, 5 vols (1908), iii, pp.81–2.
12 R A Stuart 10/2, pp.19–20; O'Sullivan, p.68.
13 Chevalier de Johnstone, p.12.
14 R A Cumberland 5/249.
15 Maxwell of Kirkconnell, p.32; R A Stuart 10/1, p.42.
16 Tomasson, op.cit., p.31.

17 *Murray of Broughton*, p.186.
18 *L M*, i, p.208.
19 Maxwell of Kirkconnell, p.33.
20 R A Cumberland 5/253, p.267.
21 *Murray of Broughton*, p.190.
22 Again, this was almost certainly the correct decision. Leaving Inverness, Cope reached Nairn on 4 September, Elgin on the 5th, Fochabers on the 6th, Cullen 7th, Banff 8th, Turriff 9th, Old Meldrum 10th and Aberdeen on the 11th (*Cope*, p.33).
23 *L M*, ii, pp.58–61.
24 *L M*, i, p.209; Maxwell of Kirkconnell, p.33.
25 *Caledonian Mercury*, 16 September 1745; *Murray of Broughton*, p.191. On this day's march the prince once again showed his infallible instinct for showmanship. Between Dunblane and Doune he halted and took a glass of wine while sitting on horseback, reportedly dazzling the local ladies with his regal aura (*L P*, ii, p.486).
26 *L P*, ii, p.489.
27 Lord George Murray, 'Marches of the Highland Army' in R. Chambers, ed., *Jacobite Memoirs of the Rising of 1745* (1834), p.35; *L P* ii, p.486.
28 *Cochrane Correspondence regarding the affairs of Glasgow 1745–46* (Maitland Club, 1830), p.105; S P Scotland 26, No.36.
29 *L M*, i, p.209.
30 O'Sullivan, pp.69–70; R A Stuart M 11, p.68.
31 R A Stuart 10/1, p.44.
32 Lord George Murray, 'Marches', loc.cit., p.36; Maxwell of Kirkconnell, p.33; O'Sullivan, p.70; *Murray of Broughton*, p.132.
33 R A Stuart M 11, p.68.
34 Home's *History*, p.82.
35 S P Scotland 26 ff.47–50.
36 S P Dom 76 ff.245–7.
37 T. B. Howells, *A Collection of State Trials*, 34 vols (1828), 18, pp.863–1070.
38 S P Scotland 26 f.79.
39 R A Stuart M 11, p.71.
40 *L M*, i, p.249; Home's *History*, p.93.
41 R A Cumberland 5/282; Clanranald's account, p.215.
42 R A Stuart 10/1, p.46.
43 R A Stuart M 11, p.75; R A Stuart 10/1, p.48.
44 Woodhouselee MSS (ed. Steuart, 1907), p.25.
45 *L P*, ii, p.488.
46 R A Stuart M 11, pp.73–4.
47 Home's *History*, p.99.
48 Tayler, *Jacobite Miscellany*, p.145.
49 Home's *History*, p.99.
50 *Ibid.*, p.100.

51 Elcho, pp.257–8; O'Sullivan, p.73.
52 Charles Edward reciprocated their affection; he always had a strong feeling for the underdog (cf. *L M*, i, p.214).
53 R A Stuart M 11, p.76; R A Stuart M 10/1, p.49.
54 Elcho, pp.258–9; Tayler, *Jacobite Miscellany*, p.39.
55 *L M*, i, p.214.
56 Elcho, p.259.
57 'At night there came a great many ladies of fashion, to kiss his hand, but his behaviour to them was very cool. He had not been much used to women's company and was always embarrassed while he was with them' (Elcho, p.261).
58 S P Scotland 26 No.24; *L M*, ii, p.209; Maxwell of Kirkconnell, p.38.
59 Woodehouselee MSS, p.32; Elcho, p.262.
60 *L M*, ii, p.209; Maxwell of Kirkconnell, p.39; Home's *History*, Appendix, p.31.
61 Elcho, p.262.
62 *Cope*, p.48.
63 Allardyce Papers, i, p.172; *Caledonian Mercury*, 23 September 1745.

CHAPTER TWELVE

1 K. Tomasson and F. Buist, *Battles of the Forty-Five* (1962), pp.47–8.
2 O'Sullivan, p.83.
3 *Cope*, p.49; *M C P*, iv, p.45.
4 Blaikie, *Origins*, p.405; *Murray of Broughton*, p.198.
5 O'Sullivan, p.75.
6 Lord George Murray, 'Marches', op.cit., p.36.
7 S P Scotland 26 No.31.
8 'The last sheaves having been carried in the night before', A. Carlyle, *The Autobiography of Dr. Alexander Carlyle* (London and Edinburgh, 1910), p.123.
9 Home's *History*, p.113.
10 Lord George Murray, 'Marches', p.36; O'Sullivan, p.76.
11 O'Sullivan, p.76.
12 *Gentleman's Magazine*, 1745, p.520.
13 R A Stuart M 11, p.80.
14 Blaikie, *Origins*, p.407.
15 R A Stuart M 11, p.81.
16 Elcho, p.269.
17 Tomasson and Buist, op.cit., p.61.
18 Blaikie, *Origins*, p.407.
19 Home's *History*, p.118.
20 R A Stuart M 11, pp.82–3.
21 R A Stuart M 10/1, pp.51–3.
22 A. Henderson, *History of the Rebellion 1745–46* (1753), p.87.
23 Home's *History*, p.122.
24 R A Stuart M 11, p.83; Lord George Murray, 'Marches', p.40.
25 Add. MSS 35,451 f.10; H. Tayler, ed.,

Anonymous History of the Rebellion in the Years 1745 and 1746 (1944), p.64.

26 Carlyle, op. cit., p.15; W. A. S. Hewins, ed., *The Whitefoord Papers* (Oxford, 1898), p.58; *C P*, p.224.

27 Mahon, iii, p.xxiv; R A Stuart 269/173.

28 R A Stuart M 11, p.83; Blaikie, *Origins*, p.407.

29 *Murray of Broughton*, p.205.

30 R A Stuart M 10/1, pp.53–4.

31 R A Cumberland 5/290–1; H M C Denbigh, p.187.

32 *Cope*, p.43.

33 For a full analysis of English reactions see W. A. Speck, *The Butcher* (1981), pp.53–87.

34 R A Stuart M 11, pp.92–3.

35 *Ibid.*, p.85.

36 *Caledonian Mercury*, 23 September 1745; *Scots Magazine*, 1745, p.441.

37 R A Stuart M 11 p.93.

38 Elcho, pp.277–9.

39 Maxwell of Kirkconnell, p.43; *Murray of Broughton*, p.212.

40 R A Stuart M 11, p.88.

41 Maxwell of Kirkconnell, p.54.

42 For the requisitioning and provision of shoes for the various regiments see R A Cumberland 5/310,322; 6/168,176,177.

43 *C P*, p.226.

44 For the fate of John Hickson, the messenger in question see F. J. McLynn, *The Jacobite Army in England 1745* (Edinburgh, 1983), p.30.

45 O'Sullivan, p.86.

46 *Ibid.*

47 Tomasson, *The Jacobite General*, op.cit., pp.56–7.

48 Tayler, *Jacobite Miscellany* ('Elcho's Diary'), p.148.

49 In psychological terms, it is fascinating to observe that the 'bad' father surrogate, Lord George Murray, was regarded with the same intense suspicion by the 'good' father-figure Liria (later Berwick). Liria, who met Lord George in the '15, described him as having 'plenty of intelligence and bravery but he is false to the last degree and has a very good opinion of himself' (A. J. Youngson, *The Prince and the Pretender* (1985), pp.105–6).

50 R A Stuart M 11, p.111.

51 Elcho, p.289.

52 R A Stuart M 11, pp.109–10.

53 *Ibid.*, p.110.

54 Lord George Murray, 'Marches', p.45.

55 R A Stuart M 11, p.97.

56 Stowe MSS 158 f.199.

57 *Caledonian Mercury*, 30 September 1745; *Murray of Broughton*, p.220.

58 Elcho, p.291.

59 *Daily Advertiser*, 11,14 October 1745; *Walpole Correspondence*, 19, p.133.

60 R A Stuart M 10/1, p.62.

61 Elcho, p.292.

62 *Scots Magazine*, 1745, pp.442–4.

63 R A Stuart M 11, p.99.

64 Preston's actions were endorsed by the Cabinet Council on 30 September (Add. MSS 33,004 f.92). Horace Walpole actually had the moral effrontery to boast of the castle garrison's actions (*Walpole Correspondence*, 19, p.126). But to the Jacobites, Preston's behaviour was that of the barbarous Turk (R A Stuart M 11 p.98).

65 R A Stuart M 11, pp.93–5.

66 R A Cumberland 6/204–5.

67 *M C P*, iv, p.103; *Murray of Broughton*, p.277.

68 *M C P*, iv, p.107.

69 Pelham MSS (University of Nottingham) Ne.1839.

70 *L M*, i, pp.146–7.

71 Home's *History*, Appendix, p.xviii.

72 SP Scotland 26 No.36; Elcho, p.281. There could be no prevaricating longer, but the Glaswegians bargained shrewdly. Hay settled for £5,000 in cash and £500 in goods (*Cochrane Correspondence*, p.123; *London Gazette*, 5–8 October 1745).

73 S P Scotland 26 Nos 44,47,48.

74 R A Cumberland 6/178–9,234.

75 R A Cumberland 6/265.

76 R A Cumberland 6/221.

77 R A Cumberland 6/228,248–9,250,251,265,274,275.

78 Maxwell of Kirkconnell, p.53.

79 R A Stuart M 11, pp.103–4; Maxwell of Kirkconnell, p.45; Elcho, pp.297–8. Often the review was held under the admiring gaze of the Edinburgh ladies, even the Whig ones (Tayler, *Jacobite Miscellany*, p.40).

80 H M C, Various Colls, viii, p.115; Elcho, p.297.

81 R A Stuart M 11, p.91; O'Sullivan, p.88.

82 Maxwell of Kirkconnell, p.53.

83 For a detailed account of the prince at Holyrood in October 1745 see *Miscellany of the Scottish Historical Society* I (1893), p.540; H M C Hamilton (Supplement), pp.175–6; H M C, 10, i, pp.92–3; Elcho, pp.306–7.

84 *C P*, p.294. Cf. the following testimony from a young Whig lady of a review at Duddingstone: 'The ladies made a circle round the tent and after we had gazed our fill at him, he came out of the tent with a grace and majesty that is unexpressible. He saluted all the circle with an air of grandeur and affability capable of charming the most obstinate Whig . . .

indeed in all his appearances he seems to be cut out for enchanting his beholders and carrying people to consent to their own slavery in spite of themselves' (Tayler, *Jacobite Miscellany*, p.40).

85 O'Sullivan, p.88.

86 Cordara, op.cit., pp.69–70.

87 Add. MSS 36,526 f.16.

88 H M C 8, iii, p.11; R A Cumberland 6/206.

89 Tomasson, *The Jacobite General*, op.cit., p.60.

90 Allardyce Papers, ii, p.480; *Caledonian Mercury*, 4 October 1745; Home's *History*, p.128.

91 *Caledonian Mercury*, 7 October 1745.

92 R A Stuart M 11, p.100; Tayler, *Jacobite Miscellany*, p.40.

93 *Caledonian Mercury*, 14 October 1745.

94 *Caledonian Mercury*, 25 October 1745.

95 *Caledonian Mercury*, 16 October 1745.

96 H M C, 10, i, pp.128–9; R A Cumberland 6/170,258.

97 *Caledonian Mercury*, 30 October 1745.

98 *C P*, p.486; *M C P*, iv, pp.78–9.

99 *Caledonian Mercury*, 21 October 1745.

100 *M C P*, iv, p.111.

101 He was not to do so until the beginning of December, when Charles Edward's army seemed to be sweeping all before it in England (*C P*, pp.302–3).

102 *London Gazette*, 23–26 November 1745.

103 Sir James Fergusson, *Argyll in the '45* (1952), p.42.

104 R A Stuart M 11, pp.99–100; *Caledonian Mercury*, 16 October 1745.

CHAPTER THIRTEEN

1 The most sceptical foreign observer was, paradoxically, Sir Horace Mann, usually a monomaniac where the Stuarts were concerned. See S P Tuscany 50 f.231. Cf. also Mann to Walpole, 9 November 1745, *Walpole Correspondence*, 19, p.140. As late as January Mann persisted in his delusion that Charles Edward was not in Scotland, that he was being impersonated by an imposter (*Walpole Correspondence*, 19, pp.198–9).

2 A S V, Inghilterra, 25 ff.277–80. On papal interest in Charles Edward see also P. Richard, 'Origines et développement de la secrétaire d'état apostolique 1417–1823', *Revue d'histoire ecclésiastique* 11 (1910), p.748.

3 A S V, Inghilterra, 21 f.281.

4 S P Tuscany 50 f.217.

5 A sum of 50,000 crowns (*Walpole Correspondence*, 19, p.170).

6 For full details of the Pope's financial transactions with the Stuarts at this time see Biblioteca Angelica MSS 1618.

7 S P Tuscany 51 ff.22–3.

8 Morelli, i, pp.282–300.

9 Benedict to Tencin, 29 December 1745, Morelli, i, p.301. 'Digitus dei hic est', was the Pope's comment when he heard of the invasion of England (*ibid.*).

10 See, for example, the duc de Bouillon's lobbying. *L M*, iii, pp.142–3.

11 The entire question of French support for the Jacobites is examined exhaustively in F. J. McLynn, *France and the Jacobite Rising of 1745*, op.cit.

12 *Ibid.*

13 *Caledonian Mercury*, 11–25 October 1745.

14 R A Cumberland 6/250.

15 R A Cumberland 6/235.

16 McLynn, *France and the '45*, op.cit., Chapter Four.

17 See F. J. McLynn, *The Jacobite Army in England 1745*, pp.8–10 for the prince's arguments.

18 Maxwell of Kirkconnell, p.54; cf. also the extreme difficulties experienced by MacLachlan of MacLachlan in collecting the land tax (R A Cumberland 5/303; 6/174,210).

19 *Murray of Broughton*, p.213.

20 Tomasson, *Jacobite General*, p.66.

21 R A Stuart Box 1/265.

22 Tayler, *Jacobite Epilogue*, pp.252–4.

23 Eveline Cruickshanks, *Political Untouchables. The Tories and the '45* (1979), pp.36–54.

24 Romney Sedgwick, ed., *The History of Parliament. The House of Commons 1715–1754*, 2 vols (1970), ii, p.545.

25 *Ibid.*, i, p.585.

26 Cruickshanks, *Political Untouchables*, op.cit., pp.60–1.

27 Sedgwick, *House of Commons*, op.cit., i, p.441.

28 Tomasson, *Jacobite General*, p.66.

29 R A Stuart Box 1/265.

30 There is no exact record of the voting but we can hazard a reconstruction. Sheridan, O'Sullivan, Tullibardine, Kilmarnock, Murray of Broughton, Perth, Elcho and Lord Nairne almost certainly voted for the prince. Glenbucket and lords Pitsligo, Ogilvy and Lewis Gordon were away raising men. Lord George Murray was almost certainly backed by Lochiel, Clanranald, Keppoch, Ardshiel, Glencoe and Lochgarry. The vote would thus have been 8–7.

31 F. J. McLynn, *The Jacobite Army in England 1745* (Edinburgh, 1983), p.19.

32 S P Domestic 70/37.

33 See John Roy Stewart's lament in 1747:

'The authors and projectors of that unaccountable scheme (for I must call it so) have much to answer for, to God, the King, the Prince and the Country. I was not then admitted to their councils and was the only colonel debarred, and for no reason I could ever imagine but that I spoke perhaps too manly against such a step to John Murray and Sir Thomas Sheridan whom I found both bent on it to my great surprise. But that did not hinder me from representing upon knees and with tears in my eyes against it' (R A Stuart Box 1/265.)

34 *London Gazette*, 28 September–1 October 1745.

35 *Scots Magazine*, 1745, p.489.

36 *London Gazette*, 29–31 October 1745.

37 *London Gazette*, 19–22 October 1745.

38 *London Gazette*, 15–19 October 1745.

39 *London Gazette*, 26–29 October 1745.

40 Some Whigs were already coming to this conclusion as the only explanation for the Jacobites' 'inexplicable inactivity' at Edinburgh. See Walpole to Mann, 21 October 1745, *Walpole Correspondence*, 19, p.137.

41 See F. J. McLynn, 'Sea Power and the Jacobite Rising of 1745', *Mariner's Mirror* 67, No.2 (1981), pp.163–70.

42 By his own admission, Hitler invaded the USSR in 1941 to remove England's last hope on the Continent and because he feared an attack from the Soviet Union. At the same time the conquest had to be achieved quickly before the USA entered the war on Britain's side (Joachim R. Fest, *Hitler* (1973), Book Seven, Chapter One).

43 Elcho, pp.303–5.

44 His arguments are set out at length in McLynn, *Jacobite Army*, op.cit., pp.11–12.

45 R A Cumberland 6/175,273.

46 *L P*, ii, p.472.

47 McLynn, *France and the '45*, op.cit., p.75.

48 For the motivation of these ideologues of the north-east see A. and H. Tayler, *Jacobites of Aberdeenshire and Banffshire in the '45* (Aberdeen, 1928); *Jacobite Letters to Lord Pitsligo 1745–46* (Aberdeen, 1930). Cf. also Pitsligo's own *Thoughts concerning Man's Condition* (1854). For Lord George Murray see *Chronicles of Atholl*, op.cit., iii, pp.81–2; Tomasson, *Jacobite General*, op.cit., pp.8–10

49 For this point see Annette M. Smith, *Jacobite Estates of the Forty-Five* (Edinburgh, 1982).

50 Lenman, *Jacobite Risings*, op.cit., pp.245–6.

51 *Murray of Broughton*, p.443; G. Harris, *Life of Lord Chancellor Hardwicke*, 2 vols (1847), ii, p.160.

52 Lenman, *Jacobite Clans of the Great Glen*, op.cit; pp. 150–7.

53 *Transactions of the Gaelic Society of Inverness* 21, p.422; Donald Nicholas, *Intercepted Post* (1956), p.30; Home's *History*, p.113.

54 Lenman, *Jacobite Risings*, p.255.

55 The Clanranalds were a particularly devout clan; their chaplain Allan MacDonald accompanied them to Derby and back (S P Dom 96 f.185).

56 Blaikie, *Origins*, p.99.

57 *Chronicles of Atholl*, op.cit., iii, p.44.

58 Harris, *Hardwicke*, op.cit., ii, p.244.

59 *Murray of Broughton*, pp.424,445,456–7.

60 Tayler, *Jacobite Epilogue*, p.xiv.

61 'Lochgarry's narrative' in Blaikie, *Itinerary*, pp.116–18.

62 Andrew Lang, *Pickle the Spy* (1897). The accusation of treachery against Lochgarry himself was revived by the marquis d'Eguilles on his return to France (D'Eguilles to Maurepas, 27 June 1747, MP).

63 See Add. MSS 35,446 ff.151–5; H M C, Polwarth, v, pp.183–242.

64 G. H. Jones, *Mainstream of Jacobitism* (Harvard, 1954), p.241.

65 Though not clan chiefs, the Lowland lairds were moved by similar considerations. The earl of Airlie sent out his son David Ogilvie to head the Airlie tenants. Lord Lewis Gordon, second son of Alexander, 2nd duke of Gordon, to some extent fulfilled the same role. See Sir James Fergusson, *Lowland Lairds* (1949).

66 Lady Anne Mackintosh raised her husband's clan for the prince against the husband's wishes (Blaikie, *Origins*, p.101).

67 A E M D, Angleterre, 79 f.235.

68 Cruickshanks, *Political Untouchables*, op.cit., p.100.

69 There is good supporting evidence for this in W. A. Speck, *The Butcher*, op.cit., pp.184–5: 'Measured in wealth rather than numbers, the government had the more prosperous clans on its side. Scoto-Britanus writing in the *Caledonian Mercury* claimed that "the yearly income of the clans which brought the 4,000 Highlanders to Perthshire does not exceed £1,500, which divided equally among them is only 7s.6d. a year each, not a farthing a day." The Young Pretender, although his army virtually conquered Scotland, never enjoyed mass support. By and large he appealed to those parts of the country which had not benefited economically since the Union.'

70 S P Dom 96 f.154; *Murray of Broughton*, p.223.
71 Sir James Fergusson, *Argyll in the '45*, pp.196,201.
72 Sir Bruce Gordon and Jean Arnot, *The Prisoners of the '45* (Scottish History Society, 3rd series, 13–15, 1928–9), 3 vols.
73 H M C, Various Colls, viii, p.111.
74 Lord Rosebery and Rev. Walter Macleod, *List of Persons concerned in the Rebellion* (Scottish History Society, Edinburgh, 1890), pp.359–62.
75 For a full picture of the army see A. Livingstone, C. W. H. Aikman and B. S. Hart (eds), *Muster Roll of Prince Charles Edward Stuart's Army 1745–46* (Aberdeen, 1984).

CHAPTER FOURTEEN

1 *L M*, ii, p.115.
2 R A Cumberland 6/288.
3 R A Cumberland 6/295.
4 *Chronicles of Atholl*, iii, pp.81–2.
5 R A Cumberland 7/377–9.
6 F. J. McLynn, *The Jacobite Army in England 1745* provides a detailed diary of the activities of the Jacobite army during the period 8 November–20 December 1745 (OS).
7 R A Cumberland 7/387; R A Stuart M 11, p.137.
8 R A Cumberland 7/446.
9 For the siege of Carlisle see W. O. 71/19 ff.286–308; G. C. Mounsey, *Carlisle in 1745* (1846).
10 Add. MSS 34,523 f.79.
11 McLynn, *Jacobite Army*, p.50.
12 Tomasson, *Jacobite General*, pp.76–83.
13 R A Stuart M 11, pp.127–9.
14 This was particularly unpalatable to his brother Tullibardine (R A Stuart M 11, pp.127–9).
15 McLynn, *Jacobite Army*, p.51.
16 R A Stuart M 11, pp.118–19.
17 R A Cumberland 7/416.
18 R A Stuart M 11 p.119.
19 McLynn, *Jacobite Army*, p.65.
20 R A Cumberland 7/430.
21 Blaikie, *Origins* ('John Daniel's account'), p.168.
22 McLynn, *Jacobite Army*, pp.80–1.
23 Jarvis, *Jacobite Risings*, i, p.87.
24 Historical Manuscripts Commission, III, pp.255–6.
25 R. C. Jarvis, *Collected Papers on the Jacobite Risings* (Manchester, 1972), 2 vols, ii, pp.85 *et seq*.
26 David, Lord Elcho, *Short Account of the Affairs of Scotland in 1744–1745 and 1746*, ed. E. Charteris (1907), p.330; James

Maxwell of Kirkconnell, *Narrative of Charles, Prince of Wales's expedition to Scotland in the Year 1745* (1841), p.70.
27 S P Dom 82 ff.62–8; Add. MSS 35,886 ff.82,100.
28 Jarvis, *Jacobite Risings*, ii, pp.237–54.
29 H. Talon, *John Byrom: selections from his journals and papers* (1950), pp.227–44.
30 Elcho, pp.331–2.
31 McLynn, *Jacobite Army*, p.99.
32 H. M. Vaughan, 'Welsh Jacobitism', *Transactions of the Honourable Society of Cymmrodorion* (1920–1), pp.11–39.
33 Lord George Murray, 'Marches', loc.cit., pp.52–3.
34 R A Cumberland 7/453.
35 For Cumberland's movements see Speck, *The Butcher*, op.cit., pp.87–8.
36 Duncan Forbes's letter to Macleod on 13 December shows that all Scotland was holding its breath over the supposedly imminent encounter (R A Cumberland 8/177).
37 McLynn, *Jacobite Army*, pp.113–19.
38 There is a detailed account of the council meeting at Derby in McLynn, *Jacobite Army*, pp.124–32.
39 The prince's own arguments are given at length in the memoir of the '45 he collaborated on with Pierre André O'Heguerty (R A Stuart M 11, pp.142–3).
40 R A Stuart 310/139.
41 L. Eardley Simpson, *Derby and the Forty-Five* (1933), pp.190–2.
42 Jarvis, *Jacobite Risings*, ii, pp.100–1.
43 Home's *History*, p.324.
44 Jarvis, *Jacobite Risings*, ii, pp.100–1.
45 Tomasson, *Jacobite General*, p.114.
46 *The Life and Adventures of Captain Dudley Bradstreet* (1755), pp.126–7.
47 Cruickshanks, *Political Untouchables*, op.cit., pp.92–3.
48 Jarvis, *Jacobite Risings*, op.cit., ii, p.209.
49 *Walpole Correspondence*, 19, pp.109–10.
50 S P Dom 76/50; Add. MSS 32,705 f.409; *Chronicles of Atholl*, ii, p.100.
51 S P Domestic 76/53,56,57,58,59.
52 A. J. Youngson, *The Prince and the Pretender*, op.cit; p.115.
53 This is acknowledged even in Speck's 'pro-Hanoverian' *The Butcher*, pp.88–9.
54 R A Cumberland 9/179.
55 R A Stuart 310/139.
56 McLynn, *Jacobite Army, passim*: cf. also Cruickshanks, *Political Untouchables*, Chapter Six.
57 George II to Maria Teresa, December 1745, MP.
58 See McLynn, *France and the '45*, op.cit.

59 See F. J. McLynn, *Invasion: From the Armada to Hitler 1588–1945* (1987).

60 Bitterness on this point never ceased to rankle with the Jacobites. Cf. R A Stuart 299/162.

61 F. J. McLynn, *France and the Jacobite Rising of 1745* (Edinburgh, 1981), pp.164–87.

62 R A Stuart M 11, p.148.

63 See Cruickshanks, *Political Untouchables*, pp.70,84.

64 R A Stuart M 11, p.150.

65 For Wade see McLynn, *Jacobite Army*, *passim*; cf. also Speck, *The Butcher*.

66 Marine B4/82 f.299.

67 Sir John Clapham, *The Bank of England* (Cambridge, 1945), i, pp.233–4.

68 W. Marston Acres, *The Bank of England from Within* (Oxford, 1931), i, p.181.

69 Marine B4/82 ff.36 *et seq.*

70 On this point see also Choiseul, *Mémoires*, p.55.

71 For a conclusive argument on this point see Max Weber, *Gesammelte aufsätze zur Wissenschaftslehre* (Tubingen, 1951), pp.266–90; for counterfactuals in general see N. Goodman, *Fact, Fiction and Forecast* (1954).

72 Mahon, iii.

73 R A Stuart Box 1/454.

74 'How could they *in that state of mind* [italics mine] have gone on to take London?' (Youngson, *Prince and Pretender*, op.cit., p.22).

75 Lord George Murray, 'Marches', p.57.

76 Allardyce Papers, i, pp.287–93.

77 Tayler, *Jacobite Miscellany* ('Elcho's Diary'), p.151.

78 R A Cumberland 7/444.

79 S P Dom 77/60,118.

80 S P Domestic 77/60.

81 S P Domestic 76/118

82 Maxwell of Kirkconnell, pp.78–9.

83 R A Stuart M 11, p.151.

84 McLynn, *Jacobite Army*, p.148.

85 Speck, *The Butcher*, p.97.

86 McLynn, *Jacobite Army*, p.148.

87 Elcho, p.345.

88 Speck, *The Butcher*, pp.97–8.

89 Elcho, p.346.

90 McLynn, *Jacobite Army*, pp.168–70.

91 Chevalier de Johnstone, p.84.

92 Maxwell of Kirkconnell, p.84.

93 McLynn, *Jacobite Army*, pp.175–81.

94 For Oglethorpe's movements see W. O.71/19 ff.196–282.

95 R A Stuart M 11, pp.161–3; R A Cumberland 8/190.

96 Lord George Murray, 'Marches', p.65.

97 Elcho, pp.348–9.

98 McLynn, *Jacobite Army*, pp.187–9.

99 Speck, *The Butcher*, p.99.

100 R A Cumberland 8/209; O'Sullivan, p.110; Maxwell of Kirkconnell, p.87.

101 R A Cumberland 8/211; Speck, *The Butcher*, pp.99–102.

102 Chevalier de Johnstone, pp.95–7.

103 The prince later came to realise this himself (R A Stuart M 11, p.166).

CHAPTER FIFTEEN

1 Lord George Murray, 'Marches', p.74; Maxwell of Kirkconnell, p.89.

2 *L M*, ii, p.124; O'Sullivan, p.112.

3 *L P*, ii, p.499.

4 *L M*, ii, p.124.

5 *L P*, ii, p.499; Murray, 'Marches', p.77; *London Gazette*, 28–31 December 1745.

6 Maxwell of Kirkconnell, p.89.

7 R A Cumberland 9/164,166. Glasgow was required to produce 12,000 shirts plus 6,000 each of bonnets, waistcoats, shoes and stockings (*Cochrane Correspondence*, p.62).

8 *Cochrane Correspondence*, pp.79,84.

9 RA Cumberland 8/222; Chevalier de Johnstone, p.76; Maxwell of Kirkconnell, p.90.

10 *L P*, ii, p.498.

11 Elcho, p.379.

12 Spalding Club Miscellany, I (1841), pp.337,413.

13 *L M*, iii, p.55.

14 Sir William Fraser, *The Earls of Cromarty* (Edinburgh, 1876), ii, pp.383 *et seq.*

15 *Scots Magazine*, 1745, p.589.

16 *L M*, ii, p.344.

17 R A Cumberland 9/170; *L M*, ii, p.344; Maxwell of Kirkconnell, p.91.

18 *M C P*, iv, pp.167–8.

19 McLynn, *France and the '45*, op.cit., p.133.

20 R A Cumberland 7/432,454,456.

21 Elcho, pp.361–2.

22 S P Scotland 27 Nos 6 and 8.

23 Murray, 'Marches', p.77.

24 Maxwell of Kirkconnell, p.94.

25 Home's *History*, p.159.

26 Chevalier de Johnstone, p.82.

27 *L M*, ii, p.195; Chevalier de Johnstone, p.82.

28 *L M*, ii, p.126.

29 *Cochrane Correspondence*, p.63.

30 Blaikie, *Origins* ('John Daniel's account'), pp.191–2; *L M*, iii, p.125.

31 Elcho, pp.355–6.

32 Elcho, p.363; Tayler, *Jacobite Miscellany*, p. 154. It has sometimes been disputed that Clementina became his mistress at this point but, Elcho's testimony apart, the circumstantial evidence for this is overwhelming. See Compton Mackenzie, *Prince Charlie and his Ladies* (1934), p.204.

33 *Memoirs of Strange and Lumisden*, ii, p.319.

34 Blaikie, *Itinerary*, pp.73–4.

35 *Ibid.*, pp.74–5.

36 Chevalier de Johnstone, p.83; Fraser, *Earls of Cromarty*, op.cit., pp.383,390.

37 *L M*, ii, p.196; H M C, Various Colls, viii, p.162; *Scots Magazine*, 1746, pp.32–4.

38 Elcho, pp.364–7.

39 Tayler, *Jacobite Miscellany* ('Elcho's Diary'), p.155.

40 S P Scotland 27 Nos 11,18.

41 R A Cumberland 9/196,199; R A Stuart M 11, p.180; O'Sullivan, pp.112–13; Elcho, p.367.

42 Elcho, p.367.

43 For detail on Mirabel see R A Cumberland 7/450; 9/157, 172,253. For his incompetence see O'Sullivan, p.121; Chevalier de Johnstone, p.84.

44 R A Cumberland 9/252.

45 R A Cumberland 9/212.

46 R A Cumberland 9/262.

47 Cordara, op.cit., p.103.

48 R A Stuart M 11, p.181; Elcho, p.368.

49 R A Cumberland 9/210.

50 R A Stuart M 11, p.182.

51 Murray, 'Marches', p.79; Elcho, p.369.

52 S P Scotland 27 Nos 25,28; *Scots Magazine*, 1746, p.35.

53 Murray, 'Marches' p.79; Blaikie, *Origins* ('John Daniel's account'), p.194.

54 Elcho, p.370; Tayler, *Jacobite Miscellany* ('Elcho's Diary'), p.155.

55 Murray, 'Marches', p.79.

56 R A Stuart M 11, p.185.

57 *C P*, p.270.

58 Home's *History*, p.167.

59 Maxwell of Kirkconnell, p.99.

60 R A Stuart M 11, p.186.

61 Tomasson and Buist, *Battles of the '45*, op.cit., pp.112–13.

62 Tayler, *Jacobite Miscellany*, p.63

63 Home's *History*, p.169.

64 R A Stuart M11, p.188.

65 R A Cumberland, 9/234.

66 Hawley's own reports to London shed no light on the matter (S P Scotland 27, Nos 29,33,34,37–9).

67 H M C, Hastings, iii, p.54.

68 H M C, 14, ix, pp.139–40; H M C, Various Colls, viii, pp.162–3; Tayler, *Jacobite Miscellany*, p.63.

69 Tomasson and Buist, op.cit., p.105.

70 R A Cumberland 10/298,313.

71 Elcho, p.372 *et seq.*

72 O'Sullivan, p.118.

73 Home's *History*, pp.172–4.

74 Tomasson, *Jacobite General*, pp.142–52.

75 R A Stuart M 11, p.190.

76 Tomasson and Buist, op.cit., pp.122–3.

77 R A Stuart M 11 p.194; Home's *History*, p.176; Elcho, p.377.

78 R A Stuart M 11, pp.190–1.

79 *Ibid.*, p.192.

80 *Ibid.*, p.193.

81 *Ibid.*, pp.194–5.

82 Tomasson and Buist, op.cit., p.126.

83 Tomasson, *Jacobite General*, p.156.

84 O'Sullivan, p.119.

85 Blaikie, *Itinerary* ('Lochgarry's account'), p.119; Tayler, *Jacobite Miscellany*, p.64

86 Alexander Mackenzie, *History of the MacDonalds* (Inverness, 1881), pp.350–3; cf. also *Walpole Correspondence*, 19, p.208.

87 R A Stuart M 11, p.195.

88 Maxwell of Kirkconnell, p.106; Chevalier de Johnstone, pp.134–6.

89 *L M*, ii, p.163.

90 Chevalier de Johnstone, p.89.

91 Fraser, *Earls of Cromarty*, op.cit., p.384.

92 Murray, 'Marches', p.96.

93 Elcho, p.382.

94 *Ibid.*, p.381.

95 S P Scotland 27 No.40.

96 Maxwell of Kirkconnell, p.111.

97 R A Stuart M 11, pp.203–4.

98 Home's *History*, Appendix, p.xxxix.

99 Elcho, p.384.

100 Tomasson, *Jacobite General*, p.163.

101 R A Stuart M 11, pp.202–3.

102 McLynn, *Jacobite Army*, p.25.

103 R A Cumberland 9/249,262.

104 R A Stuart M 11, p.205.

105 For the true nature and extent (much less than Lord George Murray imagined) of the desertions see *Albemarle Papers*, pp.247–59; Tayler, *Anonymous History*, pp.48–9; Fergusson, *Argyll in the '45*, p.93. One of the reasons Murray may have been misled was that the desertion rate was particularly high among the Athollmen (see *Jacobite Correspondence of the Atholl Family* (Edinburgh, Abbotsford Club, 1840), pp.196–200).

106 The lack of direction and sense of purposelessness comes through clearly in Jacobite correspondence of this period (see R A Cumberland 9/235–78).

107 For an interesting discussion of this point see Youngson, *The Prince and the Pretender*, op.cit., pp.237–9.

108 Tomasson, *Jacobite General*, p.165.

109 O'Sullivan, p.122.

110 Home's *History* ('Hay of Restalrig's account'), p.355.

111 Blaikie, *Itinerary*, pp.76–7. It is very significant that Lord Elcho, always a hostile witness to the prince and inclined to give Lord George Murray the benefit of every doubt, agreed with the prince on this point (Elcho, p.385).

112 Exactly what he did claim! (S P Scotland

28 No.3; cf. also *Walpole Correspondence*, 19, pp.207–8.)
113 Blaikie, *Itinerary*, p.77.
114 The prince later reproached himself for not making a more forceful reply, incorporating these points (R A Stuart M 11, pp.206–7).
115 Maxwell of Kirkconnell, p.112.
116 Tomasson, *Jacobite General*, p.164.
117 Blaikie, *Itinerary*, p.78.
118 Home's *History*, Appendix, p.xl.

CHAPTER SIXTEEN

1 O'Sullivan, p.123.
2 Elcho, p.385.
3 Tomasson, *Jacobite General*, p.166.
4 R A Stuart M 11, p.209.
5 R A Cumberland 10/331.
6 R A Stuart M 11, p.210.
7 Maxwell of Kirkconnell, p.114.
8 Home's *History*, pp.187–92.
9 Elcho, p.386; S P Scotland 28 No.1.
10 Tomasson, *Jacobite General*, p.170.
11 R A Stuart M 11, p.211.
12 *Daily Advertiser*, 7 February 1746.
13 Tomasson, *Jacobite General*, p.167.
14 *L M*, i, pp.17,83; *L M*, ii, p.132.
15 R A Cumberland 69/11.41.18.
16 O'Sullivan, p.124; Elcho, p.386.
17 O'Sullivan, p.125.
18 Maxwell of Kirkconnell, p.115.
19 *L M*, ii, p.32.
20 R A Stuart M 11, pp.211–12.
21 Maxwell of Kirkconnell, p.115.
22 Tomasson, *Jacobite General*, p.173.
23 R A Cumberland 10/337.
24 Tomasson, *Jacobite General*, p.174.
25 Lord George Murray, 'Marches', p.100.
26 O'Sullivan, p.127.
27 *Ibid*.
28 Lord George Murray, 'Marches', p.100; Maxwell of Kirkconnell, p.116.
29 The retreat from Stirling made this contingency even more remote. D'Eguilles was now disillusioned, convinced he was with a demoralised and defeated army (Add. MSS 34,523 ff.79–80).
30 Tomasson, *Jacobite General*, p.175.
31 *L M*, i, p.84.
32 R A Cumberland 69/11.41.18.
33 R A Stuart M 11, p.212.
34 *Spalding Club Miscellany* I (1841), p.434.
35 W. Cheyne-MacPherson, *Chiefs of Clan MacPherson* (1948), pp.101–2.
36 Murray, 'Marches', p.100.
37 *L M*, ii, p.132.
38 *Scots Magazine*, 1746, p.87. The prince's column proceeded by Taybridge and Tummel Bridge to Dalnacardoch. His artillery was taken to Blair Atholl via Dunkeld.

39 S P Scotland 28 No.20.
40 *Scots Magazine*, 1746, p.48.
41 *Scots Magazine*, 1746, pp.81–9.
42 Speck, *The Butcher*, p.113.
43 R A Cumberland 10/340,350.
44 R A Cumberland 10/353.
45 R A Cumberland 10/357.
46 R A Cumberland 10/362,366.
47 R A Stuart 273/21.
48 R A Cumberland 10/358.
49 Elcho, p.388.
50 *Scots Magazine*, 1746, p.89; Elcho, p.389.
51 *L M*, ii, p.134; R A Cumberland 10/374.
52 O'Sullivan, p.131.
53 R A Cumberland 10/356.
54 *L M*, ii, p.134.
55 For a sketch of Lady Anne Mackintosh see Compton Mackenzie, *Prince Charlie's Ladies*, op.cit., pp.49–69.
56 See Conway to Walpole, 7 May 1746: 'She was said to be the first in the good graces of the young gentleman but I believe had only the name of it, for he is generally reckoned quite indifferent to women, and I believe a true Italian in all respects' (*Walpole Correspondence*, 37, pp.244–5).
57 Tayler, *Jacobite Miscellany*, p.65.
58 *M C P*, v, pp.4–5.
59 *Scots Magazine*, 1746, p.91.
60 Chevalier de Johnstone, p.145.
61 *L M*, ii, p.134.
62 Chevalier de Johnstone, p.146.
63 O'Sullivan, p.130.
64 *L M*, ii, p.246.
65 *M C P*, v, p.5.
66 *London Gazette*, 1–4 March 1746.
67 *London Gazette*, 8–11 March 1746.
68 *M C P*, v, p.5.
69 Add. MSS 34,523 f.81.
70 *M C P*, v, p.5.
71 Maxwell of Kirkconnell, p.118.
72 *L M*, ii, p.138; *Scots Magazine*, 1746, p.91.
73 R A Cumberland 11/41; *M C P*, v, pp.6–8.
74 *M C P*, v, p.17.
75 *M C P*, v, p.42.
76 R A Stuart M 11, p.215; *M C P*, v, pp.8,17.
77 *Scots Magazine*, 1746, p.92.
78 R A Cumberland 10/371,376.
79 Blaikie, *Origins* ('John Daniel's account'), p.203.
80 R A Cumberland 10/376,385.
81 Murray, 'Marches', p.103; R A Cumberland 11/281.
82 R A Cumberland 11/281–2,292,310.
83 *Spalding Club Miscellany* I (1841), p.380.
84 Maxwell of Kirkconnell, p.121.
85 S P Scotland 28 No.26.
86 Speck, *The Butcher*, p.122.

87 R A Cumberland 10/131.
88 Chevalier de Johnstone, p.159.
89 R A Cumberland 11/12.
90 When the Prince of Hesse arrived in Brussels and Hawley did not 'wait on' him, the prince sent to know if Hawley expected the first visit. Hawley replied: 'He always expected that inferior officers should wait on their commanders, and not only that, but he gave his Highness but half an hour to consider of it' (*Walpole Correspondence*, 19, p.206).
91 *Marchmont Correspondence* (Miscellany of the Scottish History Society V, 1933), p.343.
92 It is curious that Cumberland's egregious treatment of the Prince of Hesse receives no mention in Speck's, *The Butcher*. Perhaps the episode does not create quite the impression the author wants for his hero!
93 R A Cumberland 10/370; 11/297.
94 Tayler, *Jacobite Miscellany* ('Elcho's Diary'), pp.160–1.
95 Maxwell of Kirkconnell, p.130.
96 R A Stuart M 11, p.234. Cf. Walpole to Mann, 6 March 1746: 'The rebellion has fetched breath' (*Walpole Correspondence*, 19, p.221).
97 Maxwell of Kirkconnell, p.119.
98 R A Stuart M 11, pp.216–17; S P Scotland 29 No.14.
99 R A Cumberland 11/234.
100 *Scots Magazine*, 1746, p.139.
101 R A Stuart M 11, p.217.
102 Fergusson, *Argyll in the '45*, op.cit., p.142; Speck, *The Butcher*, p.123.
103 R A Cumberland 11/326.
104 Maxwell of Kirkconnell, p.121.
105 The problem with the prince's lungs 'was one of the great reasons of his staying so much at Inverness afterwards, to the great detriment of his affairs in other places' (*L M*, ii, p.269).
106 R A Cumberland 11/315.
107 *L M*, ii, p.139.
108 *M C P*, v, p.7.
109 *M C P*, v, p.27.
110 *L M*, i, p.355; Murray, 'Marches', p.103.
111 *Scots Magazine*, 1746, p.91; *L M*, i, p.358.
112 Maxwell of Kirkconnell, p.128; *Scots Magazine*, 1746, p.144.
113 Murray, 'Marches', p.111; Fraser, *Earls of Cromarty*, p.390.
114 Maxwell of Kirkconnell, p.128; *M C P*, v, p.39.
115 *M C P*, v, pp.41–4.
116 *M C P*, v, pp.42–7; *L M*, ii, p.270.
117 *L M*, i, p.356.
118 Murray, 'Marches', p.107.
119 *L M*, ii, pp.91–2.

120 *London Gazette*, 29 March–1 April 1746.
121 *Scots Magazine*, 1746, p.142; Home's *History*, p.204.
122 R A Cumberland 12/404.
123 S P Scotland 29 No.26; R A Cumberland 12/405; Elcho, p.404.
124 R A Cumberland 12/418.
125 Murray, 'Marches', p.110.
126 Elcho, p.404.
127 Tomasson, *Jacobite General*, p.198.
128 *Ibid*.
129 Elcho, p.406.
130 *Ibid*., pp.406–7.
131 Lord George Murray's enemies later insinuated that he had not pressed the siege of Blair hard enough, for fear of damaging his brother's property (Elcho, p.406). Cf. also R A Stuart M 11, p.238.
132 *Atholl Correspondence*, op.cit., p.214.
133 Cf. Walpole to Mann, 21 March 1746: 'The Duke complains extremely of the *loyal* Scotch, says he can get no intelligence in an enemy's country than when he was warring with the French in Flanders' (*Walpole Correspondence*, 19, p.228).
134 *Walpole Correspondence*, 19, pp.221–2.
135 Murray, 'Marches', p.110.
136 Maxwell of Kirkconnell, p.122.
137 *Scots Magazine*, 1746, p.145.
138 *Daily Advertiser*, 26 March 1746; *L M*, ii, p.214.
139 R A Stuart, M 11, pp.221–2.
140 R A Stuart M 11, pp.224–5.
141 Elcho, p.401.
142 R A Stuart M 11, pp.225–6.
143 Maxwell of Kirkconnell, p.125.
144 R A Cumberland 12/374,400.
145 *L M*, ii, pp.213 *et seq*.
146 Elcho, p.402.
147 R A Stuart M 11, p.228.
148 *Scots Magazine*, 1746, p.145; *L M*, ii, p.216.
149 R A Stuart M 11, p.229; *L M*, ii, p.217; Elcho, p.402.
150 R A Cumberland 13/312.
151 *L M*, ii, pp.91–2.

CHAPTER SEVENTEEN

1 Elcho, p.398.
2 *Scots Magazine*, 1746, p.137; Murray, 'Marches', p.106.
3 Warren to James, 9 May 1746, R A Stuart 274/60.
4 O'Sullivan, p.146.
5 A S V, Avignone, 111 f.24.
6 It is interesting that Charles Edward himself seems to have had a conscious glimmering of all this. When he got up against his doctor's advice, he declared himself a firm believer in psychosomatic

causation: 'people were sick only when they believed themselves to be' (O'Sullivan, p.146).

7 R A Stuart 274/60; *M C P*, v, p.46.

8 R A Cumberland 12/249.

9 Elcho, p.414.

10 Chevalier de Johnstone, p.70; Maxwell of Kirkconnell, p.121; O'Sullivan, p.114.

11 *L M*, i, p.356; *Scots Magazine*, 1746, p.140.

12 *L M*, ii, p.270; *Scots Magazine*, 1746, p.183; Elcho, pp.412–13.

13 R A Cumberland 13/311; Elcho, p.398.

14 R A Stuart M 11, pp.235–6.

15 Elcho, p.398; Maxwell of Kirkconnell, p.130.

16 R A Cumberland 12/362.

17 R A Cumberland 12/401.

18 R A Cumberland 12/438; Elcho, p.414.

19 *Memoirs of Strange and Lumisden*, i, p.51.

20 R A Cumberland 13/360.

21 Elcho, p.394.

22 R A Cumberland 12/328,360.

23 R A Cumberland 12/376–9.

24 O'Sullivan, pp.255–6.

25 Maxwell of Kirkconnell, p.135.

26 *L M*, i, p.350; ii, p.271; *Daily Advertiser*, 16 April 1746.

27 Murray, 'Marches', p.113; R A Cumberland 13/313.

28 R A Stuart M 11, pp.241–3.

29 *L M*, ii, pp.271–5.

30 Elcho, p.419.

31 *L M*, i, pp.86,260.

32 Murray, 'Marches', p.122.

33 Murray of Broughton's efficiency can be gauged from the fact that, following his illness, his duties were divided between Sheridan (as the prince's personal secretary) and Hay of Restalrig (as secretary to the army). Both Hay and Sheridan were disastrous failures.

34 Maxwell of Kirkconnell, pp.141–2.

35 R A Cumberland 13/326,366.

36 R A Stuart M 11, p.244.

37 R A Cumberland 13/351.

38 O'Sullivan, p.149.

39 Maxwell of Kirkconnell, p.136; Elcho, p.414.

40 R A Stuart M 11, p.244.

41 R A Cumberland 11/323.

42 Elcho, pp.417–18.

43 Murray, 'Marches', p.118.

44 R A Cumberland 13/355.

45 R A Stuart M 11, p.245.

46 *L M*, i, p.359.

47 *L M*, ii, p.273.

48 R A Cumberland 13/351.

49 *Ibid.*

50 R A Cumberland 13/371.

51 Blaikie, *Origins*, pp.159–60.

52 Speck, *The Butcher*, p.131.

53 O'Sullivan, pp.148–9.

54 Chevalier de Johnstone, p.170.

55 *L M*, ii, p.274; R A Cumberland 12/441.

56 R A Cumberland 13/360.

57 His own explanation to O'Heguerty is completely unconvincing, being a mere rehash of O'Sullivan's arguments (R A Stuart M 11, p.248).

58 R A Stuart M 11, pp.248–9; *L M*, ii, p.275; Blaikie, *Origins*, p.415.

59 *Scots Magazine*, 1746, p.184.

60 R A Cumberland 13/387.

61 R A Stuart M 11, p.251.

62 Elcho, p.421; *Spalding Club Miscellany* I (1841), p.343.

63 R A Cumberland 13/294.

64 *L M*, i, p.66.

65 R A Cumberland 13/404.

66 Elcho, pp.422–3.

67 R A Stuart M 11, p.251.

68 *Ibid.*, p.253.

69 *L M*, ii, p.275.

70 R A Cumberland 69/11.41.18.

71 *L M*, ii, p.257.

72 R A Stuart M 11, p.258.

73 R A Cumberland 68/11.37.22.

74 *Ibid.*

75 R A Stuart M 11, p.256.

76 *L M*, i, p.256.

77 R A Cumberland 68/11.37.22.

78 Tomasson, *Jacobite General*, p.206.

79 *L M*, ii, p.275.

80 Tayler, *Jacobite Miscellany* ('Elcho's Diary'), p.162.

81 *L M*, i, p.360.

82 Elcho, p.427.

83 R A Cumberland 69/11.41.18.

84 R A Cumberland 68/11.37.22.

85 O'Sullivan, p.155.

86 *Ibid.*, p.156.

87 Elcho, p.427.

88 R A Cumberland 68/11.37.22.

89 *L M*, i, p.258.

90 R A Cumberland 68/11.37.22.

91 *Ibid.*

92 *L M*, i, p.258.

93 *L M*, i, p.264.

94 *L M*, i, pp.258–9.

95 *Ibid.*

96 *L M*, ii, p.276.

97 Tomasson, *Jacobite General*, p.211.

98 R A Cumberland 68/11.37.22.

99 O'Sullivan, p.157.

100 R A Cumberland 68/11.37.22.

101 *Ibid.*

102 *L M*, i, p.260.

103 Speck, *The Butcher*, p.135.

104 According to Sir John MacDonald, Lord George rebuked him and O'Sullivan for the excessive noise their horses were making (Tayler, *Jacobite Miscellany*, p.66).

105 *L M*, i, p.260.
106 R A Cumberland 68/11.37.22.
107 R A Cumberland 69/11.41.18.
108 *L M*, i, p.67.
109 R A Cumberland 69/11.41.18.
110 *L M*, ii, p.276.
111 *Ibid.*, pp.276–7.
112 R A Cumberland 69/11.41.18.
113 *Ibid.*
114 *L M*, ii, p.276.
115 R A Stuart M 11, p.262.
116 R A Cumberland 69/11.41.18.
117 R A Stuart M 11, p.258.
118 *L M*, i, p.102.

CHAPTER EIGHTEEN

1 Tomasson, *Jacobite General*, p.217.
2 R A Cumberland 69/11.41.18.
3 O'Sullivan, p.159.
4 Murray, 'Marches', p.123.
5 Elcho, p.429.
6 R A Stuart M 11, p.265.
7 R A Cumberland 68/11.37.22.
8 Murray, 'Marches', p.123.
9 R A Cumberland 68/11.37.22.
10 Elcho, p.428.
11 It is possible to speculate that Charles Edward's morbid fear of being besieged was an overdetermined process, triggered both by the débâcle at Carlisle and by the childhood impression inculcated at Gaeta that he was always to be the besieger, never the besieged. The Gaeta experience would also help to explain the pointless insistence on besieging Stirling Castle.
12 Elcho, p.430.
13 R A Cumberland 68/11.37.22.
14 Blaikie, *Origins*, p.lxviii.
15 *Ibid.*, p.lxvix.
16 R A Stuart M 11, p.263.
17 *L M*, i, p.266.
18 Home's *History*, p.368.
19 The prince admitted to O'Heguerty that for the first time ever, on the morning of 16 April, he regarded his affairs in an utterly hopeless light (R A Stuart M 11, p.265).
20 Tomasson and Buist, *Battles of the '45*, op.cit., p.144.
21 R A Stuart M 11, pp.266–7.
22 *L M*, ii, p.277.
23 *L P*, ii, p.509.
24 R A Stuart M 11, pp.267–8.
25 O'Sullivan, p.160. The prince later claimed that he was forced to accede to Murray's demand for the place of honour for fear of treachery if he refused (R A Stuart M 11, pp.268–9).
26 Tomasson and Buist, op.cit., p.148.
27 R A Cumberland 68/11.37.22.

28 Tomasson and Buist, p.155.
29 Elcho, p.431.
30 R A Stuart M 11, p.270.
31 R A Cumberland 68/11.37.22.
32 R A Stuart M 11, pp.271–2.
33 Tayler, *Jacobite Epilogue*, p.63.
34 Maxwell of Kirkconnell, p.151; Elcho, pp.431–2.
35 R A Stuart M 11, p.273.
36 R A Cumberland 69/11.41.18.
37 S P Scotland 30 No.19.
38 S P Scotland 30 No.21.
39 Home's *History*, p.229.
40 O'Sullivan, p.161.
41 *Ibid.*, p.162.
42 R A Stuart M 11, p.271.
43 *L M*, ii, p.278.
44 *L M*, ii, p.225.
45 R A Cumberland 69/11.41.18.
46 *L M*, ii, p.225.
47 Blaikie, *Origins*, p.239.
48 *L M*, i, p.362.
49 Tomasson and Buist, p.167.
50 S P Scotland 30, No.21.
51 Blaikie, *Origins*, p.418.
52 Tomasson and Buist, p.170.
53 Speck, *The Butcher*, p.143.
54 R A Stuart M 11, p.273.
55 R A Cumberland 69/11.41.18.
56 *Ibid.*
57 R A Cumberland 68/11.37.22.
58 Stowe MSS 158, ff.211–14.
59 John Prebble, *Culloden* (1961), pp.88–91.
60 Tomasson and Buist, p.175.
61 H M C, 10, i, p.443.
62 R A Stuart M 11, p.274.
63 R A Cumberland 68/11.37.22.
64 Home's *History*, p.233.
65 R A Stuart M 11, p.275; Home's *History*, p.233.
66 S P Scotland 30 No.21.
67 R A Cumberland 69/11.41.18.
68 Elcho, pp.432–3.
69 R A Cumberland 69/11.41.18.
70 R A Stuart M 11, p.275.
71 Prebble, *Culloden*, pp.105–6.
72 H M C, 10, i, p.444.
73 R A Stuart M 11, p.277.
74 Home's *History*, pp.234–5.
75 R A Cumberland 69/11.41.18.
76 R A Stuart M 11, p.277.
77 R A Cumberland 69/11.41.18.
78 O'Sullivan, p.164.
79 Blaikie, *Origins* ('John Daniel's account'), p.214.
80 R A Cumberland 69/11.41.18.
81 *Ibid.*
82 O'Sullivan, p.164.
83 *Ibid.*
84 Elcho, p.434.
85 H M C, Laing, ii, p.367.

86 R A Stuart 307/173.
87 Blaikie, *Origins*, p.227.
88 Prebble, *Culloden*, pp.114–17.
89 Elcho, p.436.
90 *L M*, i, p.190.
91 Tomasson and Buist, pp.194–5.
92 O'Sullivan, p.167; Tayler, *Jacobite Miscellany*, p.185.
93 As Murray pointed out bitterly in his acrimonious letter to the prince on 17 April (see Tayler, *Jacobite Epilogue*, p.63).
94 R A Cumberland 69/11.41.18.
95 R A Stuart M 11, p.276.
96 Tomasson and Buist, p.190.
97 Maxwell of Kirkconnell, p.151.
98 R A Stuart M 11, pp.264–5.
99 *L M*, ii, pp.278–9.
100 R A Stuart M 11, p.285.
101 Tomasson, *Jacobite General*, p.252.
102 R A Stuart 307/173.
103 Bruce A. Rosenberg, *Custer and the Epic of Defeat* (Pennsylvania, 1974), pp.1–2.
104 Blaikie, *Origins*, p.228.
105 Cordara, p.130; Elcho, p.436.
106 W. C. Mackenzie, *Simon Fraser, Lord Lovat*, op.cit., pp.330–1. Lovat at first urged the prince to fight on in the spirit of Robert the Bruce but could see no future in guerrilla warfare.
107 R A Cumberland 68/11.37.22.
108 Maxwell of Kirkconnell, p.158.
109 *L M*, i, p.363; *Spalding Club Miscellany* I (1841), p.43.
110 Tomasson and Buist, p.204.
111 Tayler, *Jacobite Epilogue*, pp.63–4. Compton Mackenzie described Lord George's letter as 'contemptible'. The historian Bruce Lenman states (*Jacobite Clans of the Great Glen*, op.cit., p.164): 'Alas it was mostly plain fact.' Both views lack psychological subtlety. 'Contemptible' is not a helpful characterisation of a man's actions in the heat of the moment. But equally, only Wallace Stevens's 'logical lunatic' produces statements of 'plain fact' at such a traumatic moment.
112 Elcho, p.437.
113 Chevalier de Johnstone, p.148.
114 R A Stuart 273/117.
115 Chevalier de Johnstone, p.148; Tomasson, *Jacobite General*, p.251.

CHAPTER NINETEEN

1 Blaikie, *Origins*, p.228.
2 *L M*, i, p.68.
3 *L P*, ii, p.540.
4 *L M*, i, p.321; O'Sullivan, p.168.
5 *L M*, i, p.321.
6 *L M*, i, p.191.
7 R A Stuart 307/173.

8 R A Cumberland 69/11.41.18.
9 *L M*, i, p.69.
10 *L M*, i, p.91.
11 *L M*, i, p.322.
12 Blaikie, *Origins*, p.229.
13 *L M*, iii, p.376.
14 O'Sullivan, p.169.
15 *L M*, i, pp.161–2.
16 *L M*, i, p.69.
17 Blaikie, *Origins*, p.230.
18 Browne, *History of the Highlands*, op.cit., iii, p.263; *L M*, i, pp.103,368.
19 Cordara, p.133; O'Sullivan, p.169.
20 O'Sullivan, p.172.
21 *L M*, i, p.163.
22 Add. MSS 34,526 f.66.
23 *L M*, i, p.163.
24 *L M*, i, p.104.
25 R A Stuart 280/19.
26 R A Stuart 307/173.
27 Tayler, *Jacobite Miscellany*, p.115.
28 R A Stuart M 11, p.296.
29 Add. MSS 34,526 f.66; O'Sullivan, p.175.
30 *L M*, i, p.165.
31 Add. MSS 34,526 f.67.
32 R A Stuart 307/173.
33 *Ibid.*
34 *L M*, i, p.69.
35 *L M*, i, p.304.
36 R A Stuart 307/173.
37 O'Sullivan, p.178.
38 *Ibid.*
39 *L M*, i, p.323.
40 R A Stuart M 11, pp.292–4.
41 O'Sullivan, p.173.
42 R A Stuart M 11, p.295.
43 Blaikie, *Origins*, p.233; *L M*, i, p.69.
44 Add. MSS 34,526 f.67.
45 O'Sullivan, p.179.
46 Tayler, *Jacobite Miscellany*, p.115; *L M*, i, p.166.
47 R A Stuart 307/173.
48 *L M*, i, p.193.
49 R A Cumberland 69/11.41.18.
50 R A Stuart 307/173; Add. MSS 34,526 f.68.
51 O'Sullivan, p.180; *L M*, i, p.167.
52 *L M*, i, pp.169,191.
53 Blaikie, *Origins*, p.234; O'Sullivan, p.180.
54 *L M*, i, p.325.
55 Charles Edward claimed to have pre-empted this possibility by stating that he had a large party of clansmen with him (R A Stuart 307/173).
56 *L M*, i, p.369.
57 Add. MSS 34,526 f.68.
58 O'Sullivan, p.181.
59 R A Stuart M 11, p.300.
60 R A Stuart 280/20.
61 O'Sullivan, p.182.
62 *L M*, i, pp.192,325.

63 *L M*, i, p.172.
64 Stowe MSS 158 f.221.
65 Blaikie, *Origins*, pp.236–7.
66 R A Stuart M 11, p.303.
67 O'Sullivan, p.183.
68 See below p.274.
69 R A Stuart M 11, p.304.
70 O'Sullivan, pp.183–4.
71 *L M*, i, p.193.
72 R A Cumberland 69/11.41.18.
73 *L M*, i, p.173.
74 *L M*, i, pp.170,173,193.
75 R A Stuart 307/175.
76 O'Sullivan, p.184.
77 Cordara, p.146.
78 O'Sullivan, p.184.
79 *L M*, i, p.326.
80 *Albemarle Papers*, op.cit., i, pp.69,74; Blaikie, *Origins*, p.239.
81 Blaikie, *Origins*, p.239.
82 *L M*, i, p.370.
83 *L M*, i, p.327.
84 *L M*, i, p.194.
85 O'Sullivan, p.187.
86 *L M*, i, p.194.
87 For this story see Eric Linklater, *The Prince in the Heather* (1965), pp.42–4.
88 Blaikie, *Origins*, p.241.
89 The sojourn at Borrodale is particularly rich in detail. Apart from the prince's own account (R A Stuart 307/175), there is Neal MacEachain's memoir (Blaikie, *Origins*, op. cit.), O'Sullivan's history and the testimony of O'Neill (Stowe MSS 158; *Albemarle Papers*, i, pp.71–6).
90 Blaikie, *Origins*, p.241.
91 R A Stuart 307/175. The prince's memories of this episode look even more curious when we recall that it was almost certainly *Murray of Broughton*, not Lord George Murray, who sent this message (cf. O'Sullivan, p.188). The psychological explanation is almost certainly that the prince conflated the two Murrays in his mind as traitors (Murray of Broughton turned king's evidence to save his own skin when captured by the Hanoverians). This is an interesting example of failure to distinguish illusion from reality. Murray of Broughton was certainly a traitor; Lord George was not.
92 Blaikie, *Origins*, p.241.
93 Add. MSS 34,526 f.70.
94 R A Stuart 307/175.
95 Browne, op.cit., iii, p.445.
96 Blaikie, *Origins*, p.241.
97 For a full account see Prebble, *Culloden*, op.cit., Chapter Four.
98 Home's *History*, p.384; *L M*, i, p.88.
99 H M C, Various Colls, viii, p.167; H M C, 14, ix, p.145.

100 R A Cumberland 69/11.38.12.
101 *M C P*, v, p.70; H M C, Laing, ii, p.367.
102 *Scots Magazine*, 1746, p.238.
103 McLynn, *France and the '45*, op.cit., p.221; Elcho, pp.441–2.
104 R A Cumberland 14/427.
105 John Gibson, *Ships of the '45* (1967), pp.36–41.
106 See above p.271.
107 McLynn, *France and the '45*, op.cit., pp.221 *et seq.*
108 Morelli, i, pp.311–12,338.
109 R A Stuart 275/150,175; Tayler, *Stuart Papers*, p.181.
110 Benedict to Tencin, 13 April 1746, Morelli, i, pp.331–2.
111 Benedict to Tencin, 9 February 1746, Morelli, i, p.313.
112 Benedict to Tencin, 6 June 1746, Morelli, i, p.345.
113 S P Scotland 31 No.25.
114 S P Scotland 32 No.4.
115 For details of the hunt for the prince from the Whig point of view see H M C, 10, i, p.290; H M C, II, p.24; IV, p.81; 12, v, p.198; H M C, Hastings, iii, p.57.
116 Fergusson, *Argyll in the '45*, op.cit., p.180.
117 *L M*, i, p.328.
118 R A Stuart 307/175; R A Stuart M 11, p.318.

CHAPTER TWENTY

1 *L M*, i, p.268.
2 *L M*, i, p.162.
3 *L M*, i, p.370.
4 *L M*, i, p.268.
5 R A Stuart 307/175; Add. MSS 34,526 f.72.
6 O'Sullivan, p,189; McLynn, *France and the '45*, op.cit., p.214.
7 O'Sullivan, pp.190–1.
8 *L M*, i, p.195.
9 *L M*, i, p.268.
10 O'Sullivan, pp.191–2.
11 *L M*, i, p.268.
12 Blaikie, *Origins*, p.247.
13 *L M*, i, p.209.
14 R A Stuart M 11, p.322.
15 *L M*, i, p.196.
16 *Scots Magazine*, 1746, p.336.
17 R A Stuart 307/175.
18 R A Stuart M 11, p.324.
19 Blaikie, *Origins*, p.249.
20 'The bread in these parts is not made of wheat but of barley and is very little cooked. It was, in fact, a kind of raw dough, smelling a good deal and tasting badly, disgusting to anyone of refined upbringing' (Cordara, op.cit., p.151).
21 Cordara, p.150.

22 Add. MSS 34,526 f.73.

23 O'Sullivan, p.193.

24 For a portrait see *Albemarle Papers*, i, p.11.

25 R A Stuart M 11, p.323.

26 *Albemarle Papers*, i, p.75; Cordara, p.152; Tayler, *Anonymous History*, p.268; Tayler, *Jacobite Miscellany*, p.100.

27 O'Sullivan, p.194.

28 R A Stuart M 11, pp.324–5.

29 Blaikie, *Origins*, pp.249–50.

30 *L M*, i, p.196.

31 *L M*, i, p.296.

32 Blaikie, *Origins*, p.250.

33 R A Stuart M 11, p.328.

34 *L M*, i, p.371.

35 R A Stuart 307/175.

36 Add. MSS 34,526 f.74.

37 Blaikie, *Origins*, p.252.

38 R A Cumberland 69/11.41.18.

39 Blaikie, *Origins*, p.253.

40 *Ibid.*, pp.253–4.

41 R A Stuart M 11, p.329.

42 Blaikie, *Origins*, p.254.

43 *Ibid.* The prince's own account is very different. It makes him the intrepid hero of the piece, inwardly fearful but full of the outward qualities of leadership (R A Stuart M 11, p.330).

44 R A Stuart M 11, pp.330–1.

45 Blaikie, *Origins*, p.255.

46 *Ibid.*, pp.255–6.

47 *Ibid.*, p.257.

48 *Ibid.*

49 *Ibid.*

50 *Ibid.*, p.258.

51 *L M*, i, p.327.

52 *L M*, i, p.372.

53 R A Stuart M 11, pp.331–2.

54 *L M*, i, p.372.

55 R A Cumberland 69/11.41.18.

56 Blaikie, *Origins*, p.260.

57 *L M*, i, p.146.

58 *Scots Magazine*, 1746, p.341.

59 *L M*, i, p.298. For criticisms of O'Neill see *L M*, i, p.157. At one point O'Neill's spirits were said to have been so low that the prince actually had to cheer *him* up (*L M*, i, p.108).

60 Stowe MSS 158 f.122.

61 *L M*, i, p.373.

62 *L M*, iii, p.22.

63 *L M*, i, p.329.

64 Compton Mackenzie, *Prince Charlie's Ladies*, op.cit., p.88. The relationship of the prince with Flora MacDonald has always intrigued those interested in the flight in the heather. Among the works dealing with this episode in Flora MacDonald's life are: Alexander Mackenzie, *History of the MacDonalds* (Inverness, 1981), pp.267–71; Home's *History*,

pp.373–6. The most recent assessment is A. MacLean, *A MacDonald for the Prince* (Stornoway, 1982).

65 R A Stuart 280/20.

66 *L M*, i, p.305.

67 *I. M*, i, p.111.

68 Blaikie, *Origins*, p.261.

69 *Ibid.*

70 R A Stuart M 11, p.333.

71 Tayler, *Jacobite Miscellany*, p.186.

72 R A Cumberland 69/11.41.18.

73 *L M*, i, p.301.

74 *C P*, pp.290–1.

75 R A Stuart 280/20.

76 *M C P*, v, p.122.

77 See *Walpole Correspondence*, 30, p.103; 37, pp.251–2.

78 Blaikie, *Origins*, p.265.

79 Stowe MSS 158 f.218.

80 *L M*, i, pp.117–19.

81 *L M*, i, p.119.

82 *L M*, i, p.76.

83 *L M*, i, p.120.

84 *L M*, i, p.121.

85 *L M*, i, p.81.

86 R A Cumberland 69/11.41.18.

87 *L M*, i, pp.76,302.

88 *L M*, ii, p.21.

89 *L M*, ii, p.20.

90 *L M*, ii, p.22.

91 *L M*, i, pp.130,302.

92 *I. M*, ii, p.23. There was a similar incident a little later when the prince paid for his eleven-shilling bill with a guinea and again had to be prompted to insist on his change (*L M*, ii, p.24).

93 Tayler, *Jacobite Miscellany*, p.118.

94 *L M*, ii, p.25.

95 R A Stuart M 11, p.314; *L M*, ii, p.75.

96 'A miserable hut so low that he could neither sit nor stand up but was obliged to lie on the bare ground, having only a bundle of heath for his pillow' (R A Cumberland 69/11.41.18).

97 *L M*, ii, p.74.

98 *L M*, ii, p.75.

99 *Ibid.*

100 R A Cumberland 69/11.41.18.

101 *L M*, i, p.133.

102 *L M*, i, p.134.

103 'The worst roads in Europe' (R A Cumberland 69/11.41.18).

104 *L M*, i, p.139.

105 As the 'master', Macleod would have taken on two of them, and the prince one (R A Cumberland 69/11.41.18).

106 There is a lot of detail on the prince's stay in Elgol in *L M*, i, pp.139,152,177.

107 R A Cumberland 69/11.41.18.

108 *L M*, i, p.140.

109 *L M*, ii, pp.31,81.

110 *L M*, ii, p.186.

CHAPTER TWENTY-ONE

1 For Fergusson's depredations in the islands see *L M*, iii, pp.85–8.
2 R A Cumberland 14/58.
3 The hunt can be followed in H M C, 11, iv, pp.361–2; 12, v, p.198; Hastings, iii, p.57; Du Cane, p.126.
4 H M C, Du Cane, p.129.
5 *M C P*, v, pp.97,107.
6 *Albemarle Papers*, i, p.11.
7 Fergusson, *Argyll in the '45*, p.228.
8 S P Scotland 32 No.53.
9 S P Scotland 32 No.52.
10 See for details of their interrogation and later fate *Albemarle Papers*, i, pp.71–6; S P Scotland 32 No.49; *L M*, i, pp.103,144; Fergusson, *Argyll in the '45*, pp.225–7.
11 H M C, Townshend, p.362.
12 *C P*, p.336.
13 Denis Diderot, *Correspondance*, ed. Georges Roth (Paris, 1957), iii, p.228.
14 See the discussion in Blaikie, *Itinerary*, op.cit., p.109.
15 *Boswell's Life of Johnson*, edited by G. B. Hill, revised by C. F. Powell, 6 vols (Oxford 1934), Vol.v (*Tour to the Hebrides*), pp.193–4.
16 J Doran, ed., *Mann and Manners*, op.cit., i, p.236. Cf. Mann to Walpole, 19 October 1746: 'He should be made a sacrifice of. It would cure them from making any more attempts and would discredit France to the greatest degree. The Pope would make a martyr, and in time, a saint of him, but I had rather he should be prayed to by those fools in heaven than adored in Scotland or England, where in time he would make martyrs of us all' (*Walpole Correspondence*, 19, p.131).
17 *L M*, ii, p.251.
18 R A Stuart M 11, p.337.
19 R A Cumberland 69/11.41.18.
20 *L M*, ii, p.251.
21 *L M*, iii, p.183.
22 *L M*, i, p.332.
23 *L M*, iii, pp.185–6.
24 *L M*, ii, p.252.
25 *L M*, ii, p.252.
26 *L M*, iii, p.187.
27 *L M*, iii, p.188.
28 *L M*, iii, p.189.
29 *L M*, ii, p.252.
30 Both were taken prisoner next day, the chief at Morar and Captain John when he arrived at Elgol (*L M*, ii, p.253). It was on parting from the Mackinnons at Borrodale that, according to the unverified story, the prince gave them the recipe that became the Drambuie liqueur.
31 R A Stuart M 11, p.337.
32 *L M*, i, pp.333–4.
33 *L M*, iii, p.337.
34 R A Cumberland 69/11.41.18.
35 R A Stuart M 11, p.337.
36 *L M*, iii, p.377.
37 *L M*, i, p.334.
38 'Visibly saw the whole coast surrounded by ships of war and tenders, as also the country by other military forces' (*L M*, i, p.335).
39 *L M*, iii, p.377.
40 *L M*, i, p.335.
41 *L M*, i, p.338.
42 *L M*, ii, p.364.
43 R A Stuart M 11, pp.338–9.
44 *Ibid.*, p.339.
45 *L M*, iii, p.377.
46 R A Cumberland 69/11.41.18.
47 *Ibid.*
48 *L M*, i, p.338.
49 *L M*, i, p.339.
50 R A Stuart M 11, pp.341–2.
51 Tayler, *Jacobite Miscellany*, pp.119–20.
52 R A Cumberland 69/11.41.18.
53 *L M*, i, p.339.
54 R A Stuart M 11, p.343.
55 *L M*, ii, p.363.
56 *L M*, i, p.318.
57 R A Cumberland 69/11.41.18.
58 *L M*, ii, pp.363–4; iii, p.91.
59 R A Stuart M 11, pp.343–4.
60 *L M*, iii, p.378.
61 R A Stuart M 11, p.342.
62 *L M*, i, p.340.
63 *L M*, iii, p.378.
64 R A Stuart M 11, p.345.
65 *L M*, iii, p.378.
66 Home's *History*, p.252.
67 Blaikie, *Itinerary* ('Lochgarry's account'), pp.122–3.
68 *L M*, i, p.372.
69 *L M*, iii, p.379.
70 *L M*, i, p.343.
71 Blaikie, *Itinerary* ('Lochgarry's account'), p.123.
72 There were in fact eight of them. Their names were Patrick Grant, John MacDonald, Alexander MacDonnell, Gregor MacGregor and (three brothers) Donald, Alexander and Hugh Chisholm (*L M*, iii, p.202).
73 *L M*, iii, pp.7,97–8.
74 *L M*, iii, p.110.
75 *L M*, iii, pp.111,117.
76 Cf. the description given in Blaikie, *Itinerary*, p.61: 'a cavern formed by the great masses of rock at the bottom of a talm from the hill above – in fact a cavity in

a cairn of stones. The roof of the cavity is formed by a peculiarly shaped mass resembling three-quarters of an umbrella, resting on a spur of rock. The floor of the cave takes a crescent form, the entrance being at the south west, and coming round by the north to the south-east. About the centre was what appeared to be a hearth, and the south-west would have formed the bed. The bottom of the cavern was of gravel, and a pure rivulet of water passed close under the east side of the cave.'

77 *L M*, i, p.344; iii, p.381.
78 *L M*, iii, p.111.
79 R A Stuart M 11, p.347.
80 *L M*, i, p.124.
81 *L M*, iii, p.104.
82 *L M*, i, p.344; iii, p.99.
83 *L M*, i, p.345.
84 *L M*, iii, pp.99–100.
85 *L M*, iii, p.99.
86 *L M*, i, p.346.
87 H. Malo, *Les derniers corsairs. Dunkerque 1715–1815* (Paris, 1925), p.29.
88 Gibson, *Ships of the '45*, op.cit., pp.76–9.
89 H M C 8, iii, p.11.
90 *L M*, iii, p.105.
91 By all accounts the prince's sojourn in Fasnakyle, when he was provisioned by the local farmer John Chisholm, was a bibulous time for him (*L M*, iii, pp.102–3).
92 R A Cumberland 68/11.37.48.
93 S P Scotland 32 No.57.
94 For examples see *Albemarle Papers*, i, pp.228–30, 239.
95 *Albemarle Papers*, i, p.231.
96 R A Cumberland 18/265.
97 S P Scotland 33 No.9.
98 *Scots Magazine*, 1746, p.393.
99 *Ibid.*, p.374.
100 Fergusson, *Argyll in the '45*, p.241.
101 H M C, Denbigh, p.152.
102 Fergusson, op.cit., p.242.
103 *L M*, iii, p.104.
104 They were now ten in number: the prince, Glenaladale, his brother John, young John of Borrodale and six of the Glenmoriston men.
105 *L M*, i, p.347.
106 *L M*, i, p.348.
107 *L M*, i, p.96.
108 R A Stuart M 11, pp.349–50.
109 R A Stuart M 11, p.350.
110 *L M*, i, pp.96,348.
111 R A Cumberland 69/11.41.18.
112 *L M*, iii, p.39.
113 Blaikie, *Itinerary* ('Lochgarry's account'), p.124.
114 *L M*, i, pp.96,349.
115 *L M*, i, pp.98,349.
116 *L M*, iii, p.102.
117 Gibson, *Ships of the '45*, op.cit., pp.114–16.
118 *L M*, i, p.349; iii, p.382.
119 *L M*, i, pp.99–100.
120 R A Cumberland 69/11.41.18.
121 *L M*, i, p.100.
122 R A Cumberland 69/11.41.18.
123 *Ibid*.
124 *Ibid*.
125 *L M*, i, p.101.
126 *L M*, iii, p.39.
127 *L M*, iii, p.102.
128 *L M*, iii, p.182.
129 *L M*, iii, p.140.
130 *L M*, iii, p.39.
131 *L M*, iii, p.41.
132 R A Stuart M 11, p.352; Blaikie, *Itinerary* ('Lochgarry's account'), p.125.
133 *L M*, ii, pp.376–9.
134 *L M*, iii, p.42.
135 See the description in Blaikie, *Itinerary*, p.69.
136 *L M*, ii, pp.376–7.
137 *Daily Advertiser*, 5 August 1746. See also *Walpole Correspondence*, 19, p.295.
138 For statements on the prince's physical health during the flight in the heather see *L M*, i, p.165; iii, p.190.
139 *L M*, ii, p.103.
140 *L M*, i, p.120; ii, p.99.
141 There is a good example cited in *Boswell's Life of Johnson*, op.cit., v, p.193.
142 *Ibid.*, v, p.192.
143 R A Cumberland 69/11.41.18.
144 *Boswell's Life of Johnson*, v, p.196.
145 See the two statements, one critical, the other showing understanding, at *L M*, i, p.35 and *L M*, i, p.80 respectively.
146 *L M*, iii, p.104; i, p.209.
147 *L M*, i, p.209.
148 See *L M*, i, p.170. At Glencanna the prince invited all to join in a toast to her health. He told them her hair was as black as a raven's, that she was a very agreeable, sweet-natured and humble lady, that he loved her and was sure she had a high regard for him (*L M*, iii, p.109).
149 R A Stuart M 11, p.354.
150 *L M*, iii, p.44.
151 *L M*, iii, p.45.
152 *Ibid*.
153 Cordara, p.170.
154 McLynn, *France and the '45*, op.cit., p.230.
155 For a detailed account of Warren's voyage see Leon Lallement, *Le maréchal de camp Warren*, op.cit., pp.48–57.
156 This point was later confirmed with great

bitterness by Albemarle (S P Scotland 33 Nos 31 and 35).

157 *L M*, i, p.319.
158 *L M*, ii, pp.377–8.
159 *Gentleman's Magazine*, 1746, p.554.
160 Certainly neither the Jacobite clans nor the authorities in London. Both expected the prince to come again (S P Scotland 34 Nos 9 and 13).

CHAPTER TWENTY-TWO

1 A S V, Francia, 490 f.444; R A Stuart M 11, p.355; Cordara, pp.171–2.
2 R A Stuart 277/127,130; Mahon, iii, p.xxxi; Browne, iii, p.463; *Daily Advertiser*, 15 October 1746.
3 R A Stuart 345/162.
4 Add. MSS 20,662 f.121.
5 Add. MSS 28,691 f.15; H M C, Kenyon, p.474; *L M*, iii, pp.253–4.
6 Frederick to Andrie, 24 April 1746, *Frederick the Great, Politische Correspondenz*, op.cit., v, p.69. In 1745, Charles's *annus mirabilis*, Baron Franz Trenck (1711–49) had come close to capturing Frederick for ransom.
7 Add. MSS 20,662 f.121.
8 *L M*, i, pp.54–5.
9 *L M*, i, p.25.
10 *L M*, i, p.46.
11 See *Boswell's Life of Johnson*, op.cit., v, p.193.
12 *Ibid.*, v, p.192.
13 R A Stuart 345/162.
14 In 1771 Catherine the Great, in a letter to Voltaire, compared a famous Russian wanderer to the prince in the heather (*Voltaire Correspondence*, ed. Theodore Besterman, 80, p.14).
15 *Oeuvres complètes d'Helvetius*, 5 vols (Paris, 1795), ii, pp.237–8.
16 Luynes, vii, p.453.
17 Luynes, vii, p.456.
18 R A Stuart 277/168; Mahon, iii, pp.xxxi-xxxii; Browne, iii, pp.465–6.
19 R A Stuart 277/165.
20 Luynes, vii, p.462.
21 R A Stuart 278/1.
22 Luynes, vii, pp.460–1.
23 R A Stuart 278/25; Luynes, vii, p.462.
24 R A Stuart 278/41.
25 R A Stuart M 11, p.356; 278/62; Barbier, iii, p.498.
26 R A Stuart 278/3–4.
27 Luynes, vii, p.463.
28 R A Stuart 278/72.
29 R A Stuart 278/118.
30 R A Stuart 278/64. The prince also sent an angry letter of protest to the marquis d'Argenson (R A Stuart 278/113; Tayler, *Stuart Papers*, pp.186–7).
31 R A Stuart 278/169.
32 Tayler, *Stuart Papers*, pp.146–8.
33 'Providence has begun the work. He took Strickland from you in Scotland and Sir Thomas here, at the time he was just returning to you. This you ought to look upon as a manifest call from heaven for you to finish the work and to rescue yourself ·out of such hands' (R A Stuart 279/44). A close reading of this long letter from James (28 November 1746) provides powerful circumstantial evidence for the theory of James's unconscious motivation towards Sheridan that I have advanced here.
34 R A Stuart 279/44,52,55.
35 R A Stuart 278/169; 279/9.
36 Luynes, vii, pp.466–7; R A Stuart 279/18,22.
37 R A Stuart 278/153.
38 R A Stuart 279/124.
39 R A Stuart 280/97.
40 R A Stuart Box 1/242.
41 Browne, iii, pp.476–7; R A Stuart 280/96.
42 R A Stuart 279/171.
43 R A Stuart 279/38.
44 R A Stuart 280/31.
45 R A Stuart Box 1/245.
46 R A Stuart 279/167.
47 R A Stuart 280/57,89.
48 A E M D Angleterre 83 f.336.
49 *Ibid.*, f.328.
50 Sometimes there were 35 '*maitres*' at dinner and 20 at supper plus a singular collection of wines (R A Stuart 279/95).
51 A E M D Angleterre 83 f.341.
52 Pietro Bindelli, *Enrico Stuart* (Frascati, 1982), p.69.
53 R A Stuart 279/171.
54 R A Stuart 280/1A.
55 R A Stuart 279/97.
56 A S V Francia 490 f.457.
57 A S V Francia 490 f.461; R A Stuart 279/34,154.
58 A S V Francia 490 f.469.
59 A S V Francia 490 f.475; R A Stuart 279/169.
60 Browne, iii, pp.474–5; R A Stuart 280/67.
61 A S V Francia 490 f.496; R A Stuart 280/89.
62 R A Stuart 280/89 B.
63 R A Stuart 280/49.
64 R A Stuart 280/38.
65 R A Stuart 279/163.
66 Browne, iii, p.472; R A Stuart 279/114,116.
67 Browne, iii, pp.475–6; R A Stuart 280/73.
68 Browne, iii, pp.485–6; R A Stuart 281/70.
69 Browne, iii, pp.479–83; R A Stuart 281/32. There were other letters in the same vein. On 20 January James told

O'Brien that he thought the prince was living in a world of illusion (R A Stuart 280/105). On the same date he urged his son to try the diplomatic round with France once more: 'We cannot hope to get any good from them by haughtiness and dryness' (R A Stuart 280/101).

70 R A Stuart 280/118.

71 R A Stuart 280/132.

72 R A Stuart 281/26.

73 The prince arrived in Avignon on 1 February (Browne, iii, p.483; R A Stuart 281/28).

74 Browne, iii, p.484; R A Stuart 281/67.

75 R A Stuart 281/29.

76 Browne, iii, pp.486–7; R A Stuart 281/101.

77 Tayler, *Jacobite Epilogue*, pp.135–8; Browne, iii, pp.489–91.

78 A E M D Angleterre 76 f.373.

79 Benedict to Tencin, 22 February 1747, Morelli, i, p.399.

80 Luynes, viii, p.91.

81 *Marville-Maurepas Correspondence*, iii, p.171.

82 S P Tuscany 52 f.88; 53 f.17.

83 A S V Francia 490 f.526.

84 R A Stuart 281/116.

85 Browne, iii, p.488; R A Stuart 281/143.

86 Mahon, iii, pp.xxxviii-xli.

87 R A Stuart 282/40.

88 S P Tuscany 52 f.97; R A Stuart 282/40.

89 R A Stuart 282/40.

90 *Ibid*.

91 Mahon, iii, p.xli.

92 Browne, iii, pp.491–2; R A Stuart 282/11.

93 R A Stuart 282/40.

94 *Walpole Correspondence*, 7, p.288.

95 Charles Edward to Carvajal, March 1747, A G N, Simancas (Nacional, Historico), Legajo 4823.

96 Browne, iii, pp.492–3; R A Stuart 282/38–9.

97 Charles Edward to Carvajal, 13 March, A G N, Simancas, Legajo 4823.

98 Browne, iii, p.493; R A Stuart 282/52.

99 A E M D Angleterre 83, f.325.

100 R A Stuart 282/67.

101 R A Stuart 282/69.

102 R A Stuart 282/126,131.

103 R A Stuart Box 1/274.

104 *Walpole Correspondence*, 19, p.355.

105 *Ibid*., 19, p.393.

106 R A Stuart 280/127; 282/96.

107 *Marville-Maurepas Correspondence*, iii, p.197.

108 Charles Edward to Maurepas, 27 March 1747, M P; to comte d'Argenson, 26 March, R A Stuart 282/90; to Louis XV, R A Stuart 282/93.

109 R A Stuart 279/114,116.

110 R A Stuart 278/179.

111 S P Tuscany 51 ff.298–9; *Daily Advertiser*, 1 November 1746.

112 Browne, iii, pp.472,494–7; R A Stuart 283/7.

113 R A Stuart 282/128.

114 Browne, iii, pp.499–500; R A Stuart 283/60. James anyway thought the idea unwise at a personal level: 'Such a match, if it really could effect your restoration, would, no doubt be desirable, though it is not without its objections, even in respect to you as well as to her, were she otherwise well disposed towards us' (Browne, iii, pp.497–8; R A Stuart 283/33).

115 R A Stuart 283/7.

116 R A Stuart 283/44,47.

117 R A Stuart 283/138; 284/1.

118 Dated 3 January 1747, M P.

119 A E M D Angleterre, 86 ff.373–4.

120 'Il n'a pas assez la parole à la main pour pouvoir raisonner sur les plus simples' (R A Stuart 284/1).

121 Browne, iv, pp.26–9; R A Stuart 289/146.

122 'His behaviour during last winter had appeared at first such as could not be reconciled with the heroism he had shown in the enterprise he had undertaken and became at last offensive' (A E M D Angleterre, 86 f.370).

123 A E M D Angleterre, 86 f.374.

124 *Ibid*., f.370.

125 *Ibid*.

126 D'Eguilles to Maurepas, 27 June 1747, M P.

127 A E M D Angleterre, 86 f.373.

CHAPTER TWENTY-THREE

1 R A Stuart 281/67.

2 R A Stuart 281/22, 50.

3 A S V Francia 490 f.502.

4 R A Stuart 279/114, 116; 280/49.

5 R A Stuart 281/60.

6 R A Stuart 281/50.

7 R A Stuart 279/130, 168.

8 S P Tuscany 46 ff.132–3.

9 R A Stuart 283/3.

10 R A Stuart 283/80, 105.

11 *Murray of Broughton*, pp.399–400; R A Stuart 283/5–6.

12 R A Stuart 283/7.

13 R A Stuart 283/99. For conclusive proof that Tencin and O'Brien colluded in the secret project see R A Stuart, Box 1/258; Box 2/289.

14 A S V Francia 490 f.555.

15 D'Argenson, *Journal et Mémoires*, op,cit., v, pp.98–9.

16 Browne, iii, pp.498–9; R A Stuart 283/45.

17 A S V Francia, 490 ff.549, 555.

18 R A Stuart 283/171.
19 R A Stuart 283/183.
20 Morelli, i, pp.428–9.
21 R A Stuart 283/126.
22 A E C P, Rome, 796 f.95.
23 See La Rochefoucauld to Puysieux, 9 June 1747, A E C P Rome, 801 f.50.
24 Benedict also advised Henry to clear his journey to Rome secretly through the French court. Cf. Henry's note to Louis XV, A E C P, Rome 801 f.9.
25 Morelli, i, pp.428–9.
26 R A Stuart 283/117.
27 R A Stuart 283/141.
28 R A Stuart 284/100.
29 R A Stuart 284/101.
30 R A Stuart 284/105; 285/40.
31 D'Argenson, v, pp.98–9.
32 R A Stuart 284/62.
33 R A Stuart 284/200.
34 R A Stuart 285/49.
35 R A Stuart 284/103.
36 R A Stuart 285/104.
37 Barbier, iv, pp.256–7; D'Argenson, v, pp.98–9; R A Stuart 285/202.
38 Browne, iv, pp.13–14; Tayler, *Stuart Papers*, pp.210–12; R A Stuart 285/126–7.
39 R A Stuart 285/78.
40 Browne, iv, pp.10–11.
41 R A Stuart 367/89.
42 See for example R A Stuart 286/111. His apology in January 1748 is a classic of non-argument: 'As to his becoming a cardinal, you know in your conscience that you have no reason to complain of either him or me for that step having been taken' (R A Stuart 289/82). James was a great one for interpreting other people's consciences to them. The combination of a total lack of *cogent argument*, allied to sanctimoniousness, must have been particularly irritating to the prince.
43 A S V Francia 491 f.24; Morelli, i, p.439; R A Stuart 285/144.
44 A S V Francia, 491 f.15.
45 Barbier, iii, p.19.
46 D'Argenson, v, pp.98–9.
47 Benedict to Tencin, 17 August 1747, Morelli, i, p.444.
48 Morelli, i, p.455.
49 R A Stuart 285/143.
50 R A Stuart 285/66.
51 A S V Francia, 490 f.518.
52 A S V Francia, 491 ff.7, 23.
53 R A Stuart 285/79, 144.
54 R A Stuart 282/73, 145.
55 R A Stuart 283/36, 51, 64.
56 Tayler, *Stuart Papers*, p.190; R A Stuart 282/156.
57 R A Stuart 281/26; 284/50.
58 Browne, iv, p.12; R A Stuart 285/119.

59 R A Stuart 316/225.
60 Browne, iv, p.17; R A Stuart 286/109, 144.
61 Browne, iv, p.17; R A Stuart 287/48.
62 R A Stuart 286/4, 8.
63 A S V Francia, 491 f.23.
64 *Ibid.*, f.8.
65 *Ibid.*, f.24.
66 *Ibid.*, ff.23, 29, 35, 47.
67 R A Stuart 287/116, 122.
68 Browne, iv, pp.19–20.
69 For an unravelling of the complex kinship relationships of the great Jacobite families, as well as a brilliant scholarly reconstruction of the love affair under discussion see L. L. Bongie, *The Love of a Prince. Bonnie Prince Charlie in France 1744–1748* (Vancouver, 1986).
70 *Recueil dit de Maurepas*, 6 vols (Leyden, 1865), vi, p.34. One of the problems Bongie identifies in his book is a confusion of the referend of Princesse de Rohan (Bongie, op, cit., p.281). The problem does not end there. Many contemporaries (Maurepas among them) also referred to Louise as the Princesse de Guémené. As Bongie points out, this usage properly relates to her mother-in-law, Louise-Gabrielle-Julie de Rohan-Soubise.
71 Leon Lallement, *Le Maréchal de Camp Warren* (Vannes, 1893), p.42.
72 Bongie, p.184. Andrew Lang long ago noted: 'there are traces also of an affair with Madame de Montbazon' (*Prince Charles Edward*, op. cit., p.344). And scholars have long known that Louise's letters to the prince were among the Stuart Papers (R A Stuart 316/3–91). But the task of transcribing, dating and making sense of them has always seemed too daunting. It was left to Professor Bongie – in an intellectual voyage comparable in terms of Jacobite studies to Stanley's 1874–7 journey through the Dark Continent – to achieve this.
73 Bongie, p.184.
74 *Ibid.*
75 *Ibid.*, pp.178–83.
76 R A Stuart 287/76. The prince later retracted the offer, claiming that his father had misunderstood what he was saying (R A Stuart 288/72).
77 Marc de Germiny, *Les Brigandages maritimes de l'Angleterre*, 3 vols (Paris, 1925). *Sous le règne de Louis XV*, i, p.71.
78 R A Stuart 345/162.
79 Bongie, op.cit., pp.7, 190.
80 Bongie, p.190.
81 *Ibid.*, pp.5, 193.
82 *Ibid.*, pp.195–7.

83 So dominant was the Princesse de Guémené that when observers saw her, Louise and Charles Edward together, they assumed that Louise was a front and that it was the mother-in-law, then aged forty-three, who was the prince's real mistress. See the report by Nuncio Durini on 18 December after the prince had moved into his new home in Paris: 'At the Rohans his constant companions are the Duchesse de Montbazon and the Princesse de Guémené. *The former is his spiritual companion, the latter his carnal one'* (italics mine) (A S V, Francia 491 f.78).

84 Bongie, pp.193-8.

85 *Ibid.*, p.199.

86 *Ibid.*, p.202.

87 *Ibid.*, p.203.

88 *Ibid.*, pp.204-7.

89 This view receives support from the autobiographical fragment in which the prince speaks obliquely of his affair with Louise (Bongie, pp.9-10, 396-7).

90 Bongie, pp.209-10.

91 *Ibid.*, pp.224-5.

92 *Ibid.*, pp.237-9; 271-2.

93 *Ibid.*, pp.282-5.

94 Albemarle to Holderness, 18 December 1753, S P France 248 f.288.

95 Pelham MSS. Ne. 2086.

96 Bongie, op.cit., pp.212-16.

97 R A Stuart Box 4/1/1/94, 95, 102, 104.

98 Amazingly Pickle the Spy stated that the Princesse de Guémené was one of Charles Edward's favourites! (Pelham MSS. Ne. 2087 (6).) Again we see the confusion between the two women. Clearly he meant the duchesse de Montbazon.

99 D'Argenson, v, p.232.

100 R A Stuart 290/107.

CHAPTER TWENTY-FOUR

1 Egerton MSS 1,609 f.33.

2 Browne, iv, pp.43-4; R A Stuart 294/169.

3 For full details of rank and pay see A E M D, Angleterre 80 ff.51-2; D'Eguilles's character sketches of the recipients and other Jacobites are at *ibid.*, 80 ff.56-62.

4 A E M D Angleterre 80 ff.11-12.

5 *Ibid.*, ff.6, 8-9.

6 R A Stuart 289/82, 167.

7 R A Stuart 345/162. It was Tencin who proposed the prince for the Polish throne. See Frederick the Great, *Politische Correspondenz*, op.cit., v, p.114.

8 For the duchesse d'Aiguillon in general and her relationship with Montesquieu in particular see Robert Shackleton, *Montesquieu*, op.cit., pp.180-5.

9 André Masson, ed., *Oeuvres complètes de Montesquieu* (Paris, 1950), ii, pp.407, 412.

10 Rohan Butler, *Choiseul* (Oxford, 1981), p.479.

11 R A Stuart Box 4/1/105, 107, 110.

12 R A Stuart Box 1/275.

13 R A Stuart Box 2/136A.

14 R A Stuart Box 4/1/113.

15 R A Stuart Box 2/135.

16 R A Stuart Box 4/1/109.

17 Bulkeley to Montesquieu, 14 August 1748, *Correspondance de Montesquieu*, ed. F. Gebelin (Paris, 1914), ii, pp.42-3.

18 *Ibid.*, pp.26-7.

19 *Ibid.*, pp.29-30.

20 Browne, iv, pp.37-8; R A Stuart 293/31.

21 R A Stuart Box 1/286.

22 *Correspondance de Montesquieu*, op.cit., ii, p.61.

23 *Ibid.*, pp.77, 100, 136, 547.

24 *Ibid.*, p.194.

25 R A Stuart Box 1/302.

26 Barbier, iii, p.45. The Princesse de Talmont was born in 1701.

27 *Correspondance de Voltaire*, ed. Besterman, op.cit., 79, p.109.

28 Duc de Tremoille, *Les Tremoilles pendant cinq siècles* (Nantes, 1896), 5 vols, v, pp.78, 94-5.

29 D'Argenson, ix, p.243.

30 *Lettres de la marquise du Deffand à Horace Walpole* (Paris, 1824), iii, pp.47-9.

31 *Marville-Maurepas*, op.cit., iii, p.117.

32 See the copious letters of the Princesse de Talmont to Maurepas during 1746-7 housed among the Maurepas papers at Cornell University.

33 Maupeou to Maurepas, 1 November 1746, 10 March 1747, M P.

34 Maurepas to Stanislas, 12 March 1747, M P.

35 Bongie, *Love of a Prince*, op.cit., pp.222-3.

36 Almost certainly Madame du Deffand.

37 *Walpole Correspondence*, 8, pp.57-8.

38 D'Argenson, v, p.278.

39 A E M D Angleterre 83 f.295.

40 *Ibid.*, ff.296-7.

41 Add. MSS 32,812 f.377.

42 Barbier, iii, p.31. 'For Charles Edward, going to the Opera was like ruling over a fantasy kingdom', Bongie, op.cit., p.222.

43 R A Stuart 290/97.

44 R A Stuart 290/98.

45 Frederick the Great, *Politische Correspondenz*, vi, p.125; R A Stuart 291/75, 114, 153.

46 R A Stuart 292/13.

47 R A Stuart 292/84, 105, 117, 155.

48 R A Stuart 292/181.

49 R A Stuart 292/183; 293/1.

CHAPTER TWENTY-FIVE

1 For their protests see Add. MSS 15,870 f.205; A E M D Angleterre 80. f.32; Browne, iv, pp.32–4; R A Stuart 292/1–5.
2 Add. MSS 32,813 f.158; A E M D Angleterre 80 ff.46–8.
3 A E M D Angleterre 80 f.44.
4 Add. MSS 32,812 f.417.
5 The letter also contained a long complaint about the prince's personal attitude to his sovereign and father (Browne, iv, p.37; R A Stuart 293/10).
6 Browne, iv, pp.38, 49–51; R A Stuart 293/32.
7 Browne, iv, pp.38–9; R A Stuart 293/38.
8 Luynes, ix, p.260.
9 Browne, iv, p.49.
10 A E M D Angleterre 80 f.71.
11 Ibid., f.65.
12 Add. MSS 32,814 ff.161, 169.
13 Add. MSS 32,813 ff.198, 326.
14 Add. MSS 32,814 ff.163–5.
15 Add. MSS 32,814 f.167.
16 Browne, iv, p.43; R A Stuart 294/131.
17 Barbier, iii, pp.40–1; Add. MSS 34,523 f.82; A E M D, Angleterre, 80 ff.82–3.
18 Browne, iv, p.49.
19 D'Argenson, v, p.284.
20 R A Stuart Box 1/287.
21 A E M D, Angleterre 80 f.85.
22 Ibid., f.84.
23 Ibid., f.85; Browne, iv, pp.44–5; R A Stuart 294/176, 189.
24 Luynes, ix, p.123.
25 R A Stuart 294/73.
26 A E M D, Angleterre, 80 ff.78–9.
27 See also Luynes, ix, p.263.
28 A E M D, Angleterre, 80 ff.80–1.
29 Frederick the Great, Politische Correspondenz, vi, pp.271, 295.
30 Ibid., vi, p.304. He did, however, admit that he was curious to learn how the cliff-hanger ended.
31 Benedict to Tencin, 5 June, 22 November 1748, Morelli, ii, pp.56, 101.
32 For the day-to-day unfolding of the crisis, up to and beyond the arrest on 10 December, see Daily Advertiser, 18 November–26 December; St James's Evening Post, 29 November–20 December 1748.
33 A E M D, Angleterre, 80 ff.126–31.
34 D'Argenson, v, p.289.
35 Compton Mackenzie, Prince Charlie's Ladies, op.cit., p.168.
36 A E M D, Angleterre, 80 ff.88, 92–3.
37 Ibid., f.91.
38 Ibid., f.107.
39 D'Argenson, v, p.277.
40 Luynes, ix, pp.136, 259.

41 R A Stuart Box 1/292.
42 R A Stuart Box 1/287.
43 Luynes, ix, p.259.
44 D'Argenson, v, p.284.
45 A S V, Francia, 491 ff.220–1.
46 Luynes, ix, p.257.
47 D'Argenson, v, p.284.
48 Luynes, ix, p.258.
49 D'Argenson, v, p.288.
50 A S V, Francia, 491 f.223.
51 A E M D, Angleterre, 80 ff.105–6.
52 Ibid., ff.101–4; R A Stuart 295/34.
53 Barbier, iii, p.51.
54 Luynes, ix, p.263.
55 A E M D, Angleterre, 80 f.114.
56 Ibid., f.110.
57 Luynes, ix, p.265.
58 Bibliothèque Arsenal MS 7464 f.29.
59 A S V, Avignone, 111 f.158.
60 R A Stuart 296/8.
61 Barbier, iii, pp.40–1; D'Argenson, v, pp.278, 285, 296–7.
62 A S V, Avignone, 111 f.74.
63 Ibid.
64 Tencin to Belle-Isle, 9 December 1748. Guerre A1/3313 f.80.
65 A S V, Avignone, 111 f.25.
66 Ibid., f.75.
67 Ibid.
68 A E M D, Angleterre, 80 ff.95–6.
69 A S V, Avignone, 111 f.163.
70 D'Argenson, v, p.317.
71 A S V, Avignone 111 f.26; D'Argenson, v, pp.319, 367.
72 A E M D, Angleterre, 80 f.117.
73 Luynes, ix, p.142.
74 A S V, Francia, 491 f.187.
75 Ibid., ff.182, 196–7, 200; D'Argenson, v, p.236; Luynes, ix, p.123.
76 D'Argenson, v. p.297.
77 R A Stuart 345/162.
78 The plans are set out in exhaustive detail in A E M D, Angleterre, 82 ff.226–44.
79 Luynes, ix, p.149.
80 A S V, Francia 491 f.229.
81 R A Stuart 295/104.
82 R A Stuart 295/182.
83 Luynes, ix, p.149.
84 R A Stuart 295/104.
85 Luynes, ix, p.149.
86 Add. MSS 32,717 ff.504–5.
87 'Réellement, c'est une belle chose que vous faites. C'est magnifique. Si j'avais mes montagnards vous ne m'oseraiez me prendre si facilement . . . si braves gens employés à une telle ministre. . . .' 'They had the insolence to tell me I should fear no hurt. I looked at them with indignation and contempt' (R A Stuart 295/182).
88 R A Stuart 295/104.

89 D'Argenson, v, p.313.
90 *Ibid.*, p.310.
91 R A Stuart 295/104.
92 R A Stuart 296/7.
93 R A Stuart 295/182.
94 R A Stuart 295/104.
95 A E M D, Angleterre, 80 ff.133–4.
96 D'Argenson, v, p.313.
97 Luynes, ix, p.150.
98 R A Stuart 295/104.
99 R A Stuart 296/7.
100 R A Stuart 295/182.
101 Luynes, ix, p.152.
102 R A Stuart 295/104.
103 R A Stuart 295/163.
104 R A Stuart 295/104.
105 *Ibid.*
106 Luynes, ix, p.151.
107 R A Stuart 295/104.
108 A E C P, Angleterre, 425 f.17.
109 R A Stuart 295/104.
110 *Ibid.*
111 R A Stuart Box 1/293–4.
112 Bibliothèque Arsenal MS 11658 ff.174–226 contains exhaustive detail on Berryer's search of the prince's house and the arrest of his followers.
113 D'Argenson, v, p.518.
114 A E M D, Angleterre, 80 f.145.
115 *Ibid.*
116 Luynes, ix, p.155; R A Stuart 295/122.
117 A E C P, Angleterre Supplement, 10 f.242.
118 A E M D, Angleterre, 80 ff.16–69.
119 *Ibid.*, f.172.
120 *Ibid.*, f.173.
121 *Ibid.*, f.172.
122 *Ibid.*, ff.150, 153.
123 *Ibid.*, f.175.
124 *Ibid.*, ff.156–7.
125 *Ibid.*, ff.181–2.
126 *Ibid.*, ff.178, 183.
127 *Ibid.*, f.180.
128 E. C. Mossner, *Life of David Hume* (Edinburgh, 1954), pp.218–19.
129 A E M D, Angleterre, 80,f.200.
130 *Ibid.*, f.205.
131 *Ibid.*, f.219.
132 *Ibid.*, ff.224–30.
133 A E C P, Angleterre, Supplement, 10 f.242.

CHAPTER TWENTY-SIX

1 A S V, Avignone, 111 f.75; D'Argenson, v, p.312.
2 D'Argenson, v, p.313.
3 *Journal inédit du duc de Croy*, ed. Grouchy and Cottin, 4 vols (Paris, 1906), i, pp.113–15.
4 F. Masson, ed., *Mémoires et lettres de Cardinal Bernis* (Paris, 1878), i, p.119.

5 A S V, Avignone, 111 f.27; D'Argenson, v, p.316.
6 Frederick to Chambrier, 21 December 1748, *Politische Correspondenz*, vi, p.324. He asked Chambrier to write to him no more about the prince.
7 A E C P, Rome, 803 f.178.
8 D'Argenson, v, p.315.
9 Tencin to Belle-Isle, 19 December 1748, Guerre A1/3313 f.116.
10 Barbier, iii, p.52.
11 Bibliothèque d'Arsenal MS, 3128 f.347; Maurice Tourneux, ed., *Correspondance littéraire, philosophique et critique par Grimm, Diderot, Raynal, Meister, etc.* (Paris, 1877), i, p.257; D'Argenson, v, pp.371–2. Some good examples are reproduced in Bongie, *Love of a Prince*, op.cit., pp.263–5.
12 S P Tuscany 56 f.275.
13 A S V, Avignone, 111 f.29. Walpole did his dubious best to pour scorn on all this. 'What a mercy that we had not him here! With a temper so impetuous and obstinate as to provoke a French government when in their power, what would he have done with an English government in his power' (*Walpole Correspondence*, 20, pp.8–9).
14 For a long dispatch, illustrating this in detail see A S V, Avignone, 111 ff.164–7.
15 D'Argenson, v, p.317.
16 *Ibid.*, pp.319–20.
17 *Ibid.*, v, p.368.
18 Luynes, ix, p.151.
19 A E C P, Angleterre, Supplement 10 f.242.
20 Browne, iv, p.52; R A Stuart 295/198.
21 S P Tuscany 56 f.273; Morelli, ii, pp.115–16.
22 Morelli, ii, pp.121–2.
23 MS 2572 Bibliothèque du Musée Calvet, quoted in H. Tayler, 'Jacobite Papers at Avignon', *Scottish Historical Society*, 3rd series, XXI, Miscellany V (Edinburgh, 1933), pp.309–11.
24 MS 2825, Bibliothèque du Musée Calvet, quoted in Tayler, loc.cit., p.309.
25 A S V, Avignone, 194 ff.65, 67.
26 Benedict XIV to Tencin, 21 January 1749, Morelli, ii, pp.121–2.
27 A S V, Avignone, 194 f.67.
28 Benedict XIV to Tencin, 1 January 1749, Morelli, ii, pp.115–16.
29 The Pope shrewdly predicted that the prince was merely pretending to settle in Avignon as a prelude to a mysterious disappearance (Morelli, ii, pp.120–2).
30 A S V, Avignone, 111 ff.30–1, 33–4, 40, 45.
31 Morelli, ii, p.120.
32 R A Stuart 296/171–2.

33 The Pope had a genuine affection for James, who was in despair over his son's conduct. Benedict told Tencin that James's sorrow had never been so great, not even when Charles Edward was in Scotland and his father daily expected to hear of his death or capture (Morelli, ii, pp.122–3).

34 Morelli, ii, pp.134–5.

35 Tayler, *Jacobite Miscellany*, p.5.

36 A S V, Avignone, 111 f.46.

37 Morelli, ii, p.127.

38 S P Tuscany 53 f.212. For the personalities and career of the cardinals involved see C. Berton, *Dictionnaire des Cardinaux* (Paris, 1857), p.1127; Michael Ranfft, *Merkwurdige Lebesgeschichte aller Cardinale* (Regensburg, 1773), iii, p.348. For Benedict's poor opinion of Riviera, Lanti and Corsini, respectively cardinal protectors of England, Scotland and Ireland, see Benedict to Tencin, 29 January 1749, Morelli, ii, pp.122–3.

39 Morelli, ii, pp.120–2.

40 A S V, Avignone, 111 ff.19–21, 55–6, 63, 65, 68–9.

41 Add. MSS 32, 816 ff.144, 165.

42 A S V, Francia, 491 ff.237, 239.

43 *Ibid.*, ff.241, 243.

44 *Ibid.*, f.245.

45 P. Vaucher, ed., *Recueil des Instructions aux Ambassadeurs: Angleterre 1688–1791* (Paris, 1965), iii, p.329.

46 Add. MSS, 32,816 f.165.

47 *Ibid.*, ff.233–4.

48 For the sustained English pressure on France see S P France 232 ff.20, 33, 94.

49 Morelli, ii, pp.141–2. As the Pope explained to Tencin on 5 February, whereas Louis XV had a treaty with George II and had had to act against the prince, he did not and did not feel like expelling him. To invite others to do it would be too much like cowardice and would be a blot on his conscience (Morelli, ii, pp.124–5). Benedict's best-case scenario was that the prince would move to one of the papal states. The Pope would then be free of French pressures, but still able to claim that he had resisted English pressure (Benedict to Tencin, 2 April 1749, Morelli, ii, p.142).

50 A S V, Avignone, 111 ff.62, 64.

51 A S V, Avignone, 194 ff.69–74.

52 Tayler, 'Jacobite Papers', loc.cit., pp.297–8.

53 A S V Avignone, 111 ff.80–6.

54 S P Tuscany 53 f.218.

55 A S V, Avignone, 111 f.97.

56 In a cold rage he remarked to Tencin on 26 February that Charles Edward seemed to think that because the Vatican had traditionally supported the Stuarts, he was compelled to indulge the caprices of a prince who had not even written him a single line, yet accepted all favours done for him as his due (Morelli, ii, p.131).

57 Morelli, ii, p.131.

58 A S V, Avignone, 111 ff.102–4.

59 *Ibid.*, ff.23–9, 74–7, 157–67.

60 Morelli, ii, pp.128–9.

61 Morelli, ii, pp.121–2, 131–2.

62 A S V, Avignone, 111 ff.111–12.

63 A S V, Avignone, 194 ff.72, 74–6.

64 *Ibid.*, f.76.

65 S P France 232 f.73.

66 Morelli, ii, pp.131–2.

67 A S V, Acignone, 111 ff.124–5.

68 *Ibid.*, ff.131–2.

69 *Ibid.*, ff.120–2. The story soon reached England. Cf. Add. MSS 32,816 f.229.

70 A S V, Avignone, 111 f.133; Morelli, ii, pp.135–6.

CHAPTER TWENTY-SEVEN

1 A S V, Francia, 491 f.256.

2 A S V, Francia 491 f.267; Morelli, ii, p.140.

3 The Princesse de Talmont pined away during their separation. She said her carnival had been a sad affair. She had been to no balls, avoided all society, and spent Mardi Gras in her 'cage'. She mentions having seen the duchesse de Montbazon: 'I spoke today with a woman who loves you to madness' (R A Stuart Box 4/1/63). For further letters from her to the prince in Avignon see Box 4/1/62–5.

4 Henri Lion, *Le président Hénault 1685–1770* (Paris, 1903), pp.77–8.

5 For confirmation of the prince's stay from the Stuart Papers see Box1/310; Box 4/1/86. Writing in January 1750, Elisabeth Ferrand tried to tempt him back to Paris by saying that the nuns would endeavour to make his stay at the convent more comfortable than last season (R A Stuart Box 4/1/23).

6 Maurice Tourneur, ed., *Correspondance de Grimm, Diderot, Raynal, Meister* (Paris, 1882), xii, p.343.

7 Lucien Percy, *Le président Hénault et Madame du Deffand* (Paris, 1893), p.301.

8 David Daiches, *Charles Edward Stuart* (1973), p.282. Cf. also Bongie, *Love of a Prince*, op.cit., pp.273, 315. A definitive study of the relationship between the two ladies will be provided by Professor Bongie in his next book.

9 Tourneur, *Correspondance de Grimm, Diderot, etc.*, op.cit., xii, p.343.

10 R A Stuart 298/8.

11 R A Stuart 298/32; Box 4/1/85.

12 R A Stuart 298/61.

13 R A Stuart 298/152. The prince's illicit presence in Paris at this time was widely suspected. Cf. S P France 105/309 ff.91, 96.

14 R A Stuart 316/101.

15 R A Stuart 298/152. James immediately wrote to tell his son that it was inconceivable that he would be allowed to stay in Venice (R A Stuart 298/73).

16 Morelli, ii, pp.161–2. Cf. A S V, Francia, 491 f.301. For the nuncio's explicit statement of personal sympathy see Morelli, ii, p.153. Once again, it seems, the prince had exercised his famous charm.

17 Morelli, ii, pp.161–2.

18 *Ibid.*, ii, p.164.

19 R A Stuart 298/74.

20 R A Stuart 298/62, 75.

21 Morelli, ii, pp.167–8; A S V, Francia 491 f.303.

22 R A Stuart Box 1/305.

23 Browne, iv, p.60; R A Stuart 298/106.

24 Morelli, ii, pp.161–2, 167–8.

25 R A Stuart 311/95.

26 G. Maugras, *La cour de Lunéville au 18ᵉ siècle* (Paris, 1904), p.398; cf. also Maugras, *Dernières Années du roi Stanislas* (Paris, 1906); Pierre Boye, *La cour Polonaise de Lunéville 1737–1766* (Nancy, 1926).

27 For the letter see R A Stuart 298/77. For the circumstances of its delivery and reception see Butler, *Choiseul*, op.cit., pp.811–12.

28 R A Stuart 303/131.

29 See S P Tuscany 56 ff.367, 374; S P France 233 f.299; Morelli, ii, p.200.

30 R A Stuart 298/178.

31 R A Stuart 298/134; 299/44.

32 R A Stuart Box 2/114; S P Tuscany 53 f.230.

33 R A Stuart 298/106.

34 R A Stuart 300/83; 316/207.

35 R A Stuart 299/87.

36 Letters in the Stuart Papers definitely place him in Paris on 9 and 17 November 1749 (R A Stuart 301/30).

37 D'Argenson, v, p.481.

38 R A Stuart 301/30.

39 S P France 232 f.261; 233 ff.73–7.

40 Luynes, ix, p.430.

41 S P Tuscany 56 f.312.

42 D'Argenson, vii, pp.279–80.

43 Frederick the Great, *Politische Correspondenz*, vi, pp.559, 572; A S V Francia 491 f.283; S P 105/309 f.85; Morelli, ii, pp.141–2, 149.

44 A S V, Francia 491 f.275; Morelli, ii, pp.156–7; D'Argenson, v, p.483.

45 S P France 233 f.206; S P 105/309 f.91; Morelli, ii, pp.141–2, 156–7.

46 A S V, Francia 491 ff.285, 291.

47 Browne, iv, pp.57, 63; R A Stuart 297/41.

48 A S V, Francia 491 ff.260, 291; S P France 232 f.217; 245 F.135.

49 Princess Radziwill later married Count Ignacy Morawski in 1764 (C.F. Jacobi, *Europäische Genealogisches Handbuch* (Leipzig, 1800), i, p.533).

50 Morelli, ii, p.479; S P Tuscany 53 f.244.

51 For the rumour's many manifestations see A S V, Francia 491 f.275; Add. MSS, 34,445 f.98; S P France 244 f.179; S P 105/309 f.98; D'Argenson, v, p.444.

52 A S V, Francia 491 f.265; D'Argenson, vi, p.386.

53 R A Stuart 306/8; D'Argenson, vi, p.37.

54 The title Andrew Lang gives to his survey of the prince's mythical adventures during the 'obscure years' (Lang, *Pickle the Spy*, pp.44–66).

55 Barbier, iii, p.141.

56 D'Argenson, vi, p.37.

57 S P France 232 f.192; 246 f.119; S P Tuscany 58 f.135; *Walpole Correspondence*, 20, p.168.

58 Add. MSS 33050 f.126.

59 Add. MSS 32,868 f.394; Morelli, ii, pp.168–9; D'Argenson, v, p.492.

60 S P France 241 ff.148, 220, 279; 249 ff.190, 192.

61 S P France 241 f.178.

62 Heeckeren, *Benoit-Tencin Correspondance*, ii, p.273.

63 R A Stuart Box 3/147.

64 See S P France 248 ff.304, 309–11.

65 S P France 237 ff.68, 72; 241 f.178.

66 Add. MSS 32,854 f.254.

67 R A Stuart 282/123.

68 R A Stuart 315/106; 316/106, 117.

69 R A Stuart Box 4/1/61.

70 R A Stuart Box 4/1/69–70.

71 R A Stuart 316/122.

72 R A Stuart 316/121.

73 R A Stuart Box 4/1/15.

74 R A Stuart Box 4/1/54, 56.

75 See the following examples: (1) Talmont to the prince. 'You're destroying me. You're killing me. I'm in a rage. I'm unworthy of your madness and cruelty' (R A Stuart Box 4/1/52). 'You've outraged my heart which you never truly knew' (R A Stuart 316/100). 'You are opinionated, indomitable and closed to justice.' (2) The prince to Talmont. 'I'm astonished at your coldness' (R A Stuart Box 4/1/54). 'If you want to be in my

life, everything must change on your side'
(R A Stuart 315/105).

76 The princess threatened to stay away
until Charles Edward became more
docile and *submitted to her will* (italics
mine) R A Stuart Box 4/1/56.

77 R A Stuart 305/118.

78 R A Stuart 316/109, 120.

79 R A Stuart 315/103.

80 See the princess's autobiographical fragment written to Goring (R A Stuart Box
4/1/79).

81 R A Stuart 305/117.

82 R A Stuart 316/118.

83 R A Stuart 315/107.

84 R A Stuart Box 4/1/79.

85 R A Stuart 306/13.

86 R A Stuart 306/91.

87 R A Stuart Box 4/1/74.

88 R A Stuart Box 4/1/79A.

89 R A Stuart 307/177.

90 R A Stuart Box 4/1/74.

91 R A Stuart Box 2/133; Box 4/1/54.

92 Stowe MSS 158 f.248.

93 She often complained that he would
never confide in her the secrets of his
'great affairs' (R A Stuart Box 4/1/55).

94 R A Stuart 309/90–1.

95 R A Stuart 316/98.

96 R A Stuart Box 4/1/68, 79, 80.

97 R A Stuart 315/105.

98 R A Stuart Box 1/324.

99 R A Stuart 310/30.

100 R A Stuart Box 1/323.

101 R A Stuart 311/32.

102 R A Stuart 312/164; Box 4/1/78.

103 R A Stuart Box 4/1/1.

104 R A Stuart Box 4/1/4.

105 R A Stuart Box 4/1/7–8.

106 R A Stuart Box 4/1/37–9.

107 Ferrand and Vassé found it hard to
understand the prince's violent mood
swings and ascribed his behaviour to
rank ingratitude (R A Stuart Box
4/1/7–8, 13).

108 In *Pickle the Spy*, Andrew Lang identifies
'*le philosophe*' as Montesquieu. In *The
Companions of Pickle*, he changes his mind
and identifies him as Condillac, on the
basis of Elisabeth Ferrand's friendship
with the founder of Sensationalism. Both
conjectures are wrong. As R A Stuart Box
4/1/1 clearly shows, '*le philosophe*' always
denoted Helvetius.

109 R A Stuart 316/225.

110 Some examples of the doggerel, written
in French and English:

Hier j'ai pris un émétique sévère
Et demain je me purge par derrière
Pour le soir je prends un ver de bière

Je me fou de L'univers
Et du ciel et de la terre

I never sit down
But will on a throne
To shite or to prone

(all at R A Stuart 316/190).

111 R A Stuart Box 2/112–13. The prince's
remarks on religion always display the
utmost cynicism. Cf. 'The only religion I
know is my sword' (Luynes, ix, p.264).

112 R A Stuart 311/45. The quarrel was
patched up in November through
Goring's mediation. For once the prince
acted contrite (R A Stuart 312/151).

113 R A Stuart Box 1/324.

114 For details see R A Stuart Box 4/1/80–2.

115 R A Stuart Box 4/1/79.

116 R A Stuart 298/28, 52.

117 R A Stuart Box 4/1/79A.

118 *Ibid.*

119 *Ibid.*

120 R A Stuart 318/151.

121 R A Stuart 319/6.

122 R A Stuart 319/141.

123 R A Stuart Box 4/1/83.

124 R A Stuart Box 4/1/79A.

125 R A Stuart 320/16, 65, 120; 321/35.

126 R A Stuart Box 4/1/79A.

127 *Ibid.*

128 R A Stuart 316/129.

129 R A Stuart 322/125; 323/15.

130 *Lettres de la marquise du Deffand à Horace
Walpole* (Paris, 1824), iii, pp.47–9.

131 Browne, iv, pp.64–5; R A Stuart 301/63;
302/55.

132 R A Stuart 324/124.

133 R A Stuart 326/74.

134 R A Stuart 326/168.

135 R A Stuart 327/20.

136 R A Stuart 327/142.

CHAPTER TWENTY-EIGHT

1 Pelham MSS Ne.2086.

2 For confirmation that these were the
prince's target groups see R A Stuart 300/
37.

3 Cf. Mézières to Maurepas, 29 August
1744, 3 June 1746, M P.

4 R A Stuart 301/97.

5 R A Stuart 308/14.

6 A E C P, Angleterre, 429 ff.157–9.

7 R A Stuart 306/142.

8 R A Stuart 304/55; 306/88.

9 H M C, 15, ii, p.250; R A Stuart 309/13;
310/13. James could not resist the opportunity of a lecture. 'As to the new power
of Regency you want, you must be sensible that you have acted towards me, for
these five years past, in a manner which
noways deserves so great a mark of trust
and kindness, but far be it from me to

act, especially towards you, by pique or resentment. It is true the treatment you give me is a continual heartbreak to me, but it excites my compassion more than my anger . . . if you seem to forget that you are my son, I can never forget I am your father' (Browne, iv, p.73).

10 This was quickly picked up by Sir Horace Mann (Mahon, *The Decline of the Last Stuarts. Extracts from Despatches* (1843, Roxburghe Club), p.9.

11 R A Stuart 310/69.

12 Lang, *Pickle the Spy*, op. cit., p.104.

13 R A Stuart 308/84. For the Pelhams' fear of a Cumberland regency see R A Stuart 320/66.

14 R A Stuart 310/116.

15 R A Stuart 316/221; 318/136.

16 R A Stuart Box 3/1.

17 Louis Dutens, *Mémoires d'un voyageur qui se repose* (London, 1806), 5 vols, II, pp.119–25.

18 For Holker's career see André Remond, *John Holker, manufacturier et grand fonctionnaire en France au XVIIIᵉ siècle* (Paris, 1946).

19 R A Stuart Box 3/1.

20 R A Stuart 310/116.

21 J. Y. T. Greig, ed., *Letters of David Hume* (Oxford, 1932), ii, p.272.

22 William King, *Political and Literary Anecdotes* (1819), p.196; Mahon, *Last Stuarts*, op. cit., p.96.

23 R A Stuart Box 2/264A.

24 Mahon, *History*, op. cit., iv, pp.7–9.

25 Martin Haile, *James Francis Edward* (1907), p.372.

26 Dutens, *Mémoires*, op. cit., iii, p.48.

27 For the prince's own statement on this point and his confirmation of the abjuration see R A Stuart Box 1/454B.

28 Fitzmaurice, *Life of Shelburne*, i, p.272; *Walpole Correspondence*, 22, pp.324–5. The exact church in which the ceremony took place is disputed, but the most likely candidate is St Mary-le-Strand.

29 King, *Anecdotes*, op. cit., p.199.

30 *Ibid.*, p.201.

31 *Ibid.*, p.199.

32 R A Stuart Box 3/1.

33 R A Stuart 310/116.

34 R A Stuart Box 3/1.

35 For further references to the prince's 1750 visit to London see R A Stuart 349/68 and 350/42.

36 R A Stuart Box 1/326; 312/151; 313/65.

37 R A Stuart 311/32.

38 There is no direct record of the Berlin meeting in the Stuart Papers (which are very thin for this period), but for confirmation see SP France 233 f.400; 235 f.17;

240 f.126. Cf. also Edith Cuthell, *The Scottish Friend of Frederick the Great. The last Earl Marischal* (1915), 2 vols, i, p.241.

39 Add. MSS 33050 f.199.

40 R A Stuart Box 1/333.

41 R A Stuart 321/58.

42 R A Stuart 320/176.

43 R A Stuart 320/171.

44 The shrewdest observers saw that unless George II died too, the passing of Frederick alone, with five sons to succeed him, was not especially favourable for the Jacobite cause (Benedict XIV to Tencin, 28 April 1751, Morelli, ii, p.381).

45 R A Stuart 324/61,86.

46 S P France 242 ff.41,44.

47 S P France 233 f.354.

48 S P France 241 f.104; 242 f.46.

49 William Coxe, *Memoirs of the Administration of the Rt Hon. Henry Pelham* (1829), 2 vols, ii, p.404.

50 R A Stuart Box 1/337.

51 R A Stuart Box 1/336.

52 R A Stuart 323/37.

53 R A Stuart 323/35.

54 R A Stuart 325/5,17; 326/63.

55 Romney Sedgwick, ed., *The History of Parliament; the House of Commons 1715–1754* (1970), 2 vols, i, pp.287–8.

56 R A Stuart 398/89.

57 Add. MSS 33050 f.197.

58 Sir Charles Petrie, 'The Elibank Plot 1752–53', *Royal Historical Society Transactions*, 4th series, 14, pp.175–96.

59 R A Stuart 348/94.

60 'Two Fragments of Autobiography of Earl Marischal Keith', *Miscellany of the Scottish History Society*, V, 3rd series (1933), p.367.

61 Sedgwick, *House of Commons*, op. cit., ii, pp.121–2.

62 Add. MSS 33050 f.199.

63 *Ibid.*, ff.196–7, 387.

64 A E C P, Angleterre, 431 ff.4–10; A E M D, Angleterre, 40 ff.222–37.

65 R A Stuart 318/123.

66 Add. MSS 33050 f.373.

67 *Ibid.*, f.196.

68 R A Stuart 347/70.

69 H M C, 11, vii, p.44. The Irish proposed embarking their men at Dublin, Drogheda, Rush and Sherrish and either landing them in six hours in North Wales or within twenty-four hours in Scotland (Add. MSS 33050 f.389).

70 Add. MSS 33050 f.381.

71 R A Stuart 333/39.

72 R A Stuart 330/141.

73 R A Stuart 332/145.

74 See below p.420.

75 For Pickle's role in the Elibank Plot see Lang, *Pickle the Spy*, pp.145 *ets eq.*

76 R A Stuart 330/1041.

77 R A Stuart 340/106.

78 R A Stuart 334/49,103; 335/90; 336/3.

79 R A Stuart 334/139,158; 335/14,18.

80 Her letter to James on 17 March 1752 contains not a word about the plot (R A Stuart 330/89).

81 S P France 245 f.144.

82 Add, MSS 32,840 f.268.

83 R A Stuart 337/31.

84 R A Stuart 334/118,150,166; cf. S P Tuscany 58 ff.162–3.

85 R A Stuart 340/32.

86 Add. MSS 3050 f.199.

87 S P France 245 f.11.

88 Pelham MSS Ne.2097.

89 R A Stuart 348/94.

90 *Ibid.*

91 Add. MSS 33050 ff.389–90.

92 Pelham MSS Ne.2101.

93 Pelham MSS Ne.2199b; 2122–3b; 2200b.

94 Lang, *Pickle the Spy*, p.201.

95 Pelham MSS Ne.2122.

96 Stowe MSS 158 ff.204–10.

97 Add. MSS 32,844 f.104; *Daily Advertiser*, 12, 17, 19 April; 1 May 1753.

98 *Gentleman's Magazine*, 1753, p.292; Walpole, *Memoirs of the Reign of George II*, i, pp.333, 353–4.

99 Add. MSS 33050 f.196.

100 Pelham MSS Ne.2132–7. This is of course the famous episode immortalised in R. L. Stevenson's *Kidnapped*. For confirmation of Alan Breck Stewart as the assassin (he received an increase in his Jacobite pension for the exploit), see R A Stuart Box 1/374A.

101 Marischal to Frederick, 16 February 1753, *Politische Correspondenz*, ix, pp.356–7.

102 Same to same, 7 May 1753, *Politische Correspondenz*, ix, pp.436–8.

103 S P France 248 ff.273,283.

104 Frederick to Michell, 16 June 1753, *Politische Correspondenz*, ix, pp.447–8.

105 See the exhaustive Jacobite analysis at R A Stuart 341/69.

106 S P France 240 ff.149,168,176.

107 S P France 241 ff.220, 279.

108 S P France 244 f.179. The rumour reached Rome where it was once again loftily dismissed by James (Morelli, ii, p.479).

109 Add. MSS 33050 f.409.

110 'Had you entered into the view I formerly gave you, you had been probably at this time the father of a family, with a wife whom it would not have been beneath you to have married had you been in England. . . . I could almost say I would rather see you married to a private gentlewoman than that you should not be it at all. . . . If this letter has the same fate with many others I have writ to you, I might have saved myself the trouble of writing it' (James to Charles Edward, 30 December 1750, R A Stuart 314/125; Browne, iv, pp.77–8).

111 King, *Anecdotes*, op. cit., p.201.

112 *L M*, iii, pp.132–5; R A Stuart 341/58.

CHAPTER TWENTY-NINE

1 R A Stuart Box 2/136.

2 A brave but unconvincing attempt is made by Sir Compton Mackenzie in *Prince Charlie's Ladies*, op. cit., pp.194–200.

3 R A Stuart 321/109.

4 Browne, iv, p.88; R A Stuart 323/159.

5 R A Stuart 327/115.

6 R A Stuart 310/116.

7 R A Stuart 324/43.

8 R A Stuart 326/63; 327/123.

9 Donald MacIntosh to Edgar, 6 February 1754, R A Stuart 346/142.

10 R A Stuart 330/61; 331/80.

11 R A Stuart 331/105.

12 A E M D Angleterre 81 f.94.

13 For full details see C. Leo-Berry, *The Young Pretender's Mistress* (1977).

14 *Memoirs of Strange and Lumisden*, op. cit., ii, p.319.

15 *Walpole Correspondence*, 10, pp.46–7.

16 H M C, 11, vii, pp.50, 151–2.

17 Stowe MSS 158 f.224.

18 *L M*, i, pp.314–15.

19 R A Stuart Box 1/344.

20 A E M D Angleterre 81 f.71.

21 R A Stuart 316/113.

22 Some, but not all, of the subsequent correspondence can be followed in Tayler, *1745 and After* ('O'Sullivan's account'), op. cit., pp.240–5.

23 R A Stuart Box 1/345.

24 R A Stuart 332/51.

25 R A Stuart Box 1/346.

26 R A Stuart 332/65.

27 From 1768–72 she was a bedchamber woman at £200 p.a. See *Royal Kalendar*, 1768, p.90; *Court and City Register*, 1772, p.91.

28 R A Stuart Box 1/349.

29 R A Stuart 332/139.

30 R A Stuart Box 1/347.

31 Leo-Berry, op. cit., p.44.

32 R A Stuart 332/139; 333/18,58.

33 R A Stuart 333/58,80.

34 R A Stuart 333/150.

35 R A Stuart 333/5,17.

36 R A Stuart 338/141.

37 R A Stuart 334/169; 337/49,67,145.
38 R A Stuart 337/155,174; 338/32,98.
39 R A Stuart 340/32.
40 R A Stuart 340/140.
41 Browne, iv, p.111; R A Stuart 342/162.
42 R A Stuart Box 1/355.
43 King, *Anecdotes*, op. cit., p.205.
44 Marischal, 'Two Fragments', loc. cit., p.368.
45 R A Stuart 340/64.
46 *Ibid.*
47 R A Stuart 340/129.
48 R A Stuart 340/165.
49 R A Stuart Box 1/359; Lang, *Pickle the Spy*, p.187.
50 R A Stuart 340/122.
51 R A Stuart 340/165; 341/159.
52 R A Stuart 341/1.
53 R A Stuart 341/33.
54 R A Stuart 341/52.
55 R A Stuart 341/110.
56 R A Stuart 341/159.
57 R A Stuart 341/188.
58 R A Stuart 341/151.
59 R A Stuart Box 1/367.
60 R A Stuart 341/87.
61 R A Stuart 343/17.
62 R A Stuart 343/176.
63 A E M D Angleterre 81 f.96.
64 A E M D Angleterre 81 ff.71–2.
65 R A Stuart 344/161.
66 R A Stuart 343/17.
67 R A Stuart 344/152; Lang, *Pickle the Spy*, p.229.
68 Sir Compton Mackenzie, *Prince Charlie's Ladies*, p.204.
69 *Ibid.*
70 Leo-Berry, op. cit., pp.52–4.
71 *Memoirs of Strange and Lumisden*, op. cit., ii, pp.214–15.
72 Oliver MacAllester, *A Series of Letters* (1767), i, p.39. MacAllester's information was later endorsed by the Abbé John Gordon (R A Stuart 403/74).
73 Tayler, *1745 and After*, op. cit., pp.252–3.
74 R A Stuart 332/65.
75 R A Stuart 332/145.
76 R A Stuart 344/202.
77 R A Stuart 346/18.
78 R A Stuart 347/42,71.
79 R A Stuart 347/128.
80 R A Stuart Box 1/376.
81 R A Stuart 348/18.
82 *Ibid.*
83 R A Stuart Box 1/388.
84 R A Stuart 348/197.
85 R A Stuart 348/18.
86 R A Stuart 348/139,171.
87 R A Stuart 348/18.
88 R A Stuart 348/182.
89 R A Stuart 348/19.

90 R A Stuart Box 1/384.
91 R A Stuart 341/17.
92 R A Stuart 341/110,125.
93 R A Stuart 343/2.
94 R A Stuart 337/31.
95 R A Stuart 337/147.
96 R A Stuart 344/152.
97 R A Stuart 346/46. Most of the letter is reproduced in Lang, *Pickle the Spy*, pp.255–62.
98 *Ibid.*
99 R A Stuart 346/65.
100 Marischal explicitly endorsed Goring's comments about Dumont and the money in a letter to the prince on 8 January (R A Stuart 346/36).
101 R A Stuart 346/65.
102 R A Stuart 346/89.
103 R A Stuart 347/42.
104 R A Stuart 347/128.
105 Browne, iv, pp.119–20; R A Stuart 347/130.
106 R A Stuart 348/40.
107 R A Stuart 348/79.
108 R A Stuart 348/51.
109 Browne, iv, pp.120–1; R A Stuart 348/81.
110 R A Stuart 348/80.
111 R A Stuart 348/88.
112 Browne, iv, p.121; R A Stuart 348/89.
113 R A Stuart 347/31.
114 R A Stuart 347/75.
115 R A Stuart 347/78.
116 R A Stuart 349/131. Cf. Charles's similar memo to R A Stuart 349/148: 'My courage will never fail, but my health and my body suffer from the terrible situation I am in.'
117 R A Stuart 347/128; 348/122,143; 349/4.
118 R A Stuart 350/58,114,192.
119 R A Stuart 348/139,177; 349/4.
120 For Charlotte's progress see R A Stuart 348/171,195.
121 R A Stuart 350/117.
122 H M C, III, p.421; Browne, iv, p.122; R A Stuart 350/94.

CHAPTER THIRTY

1 R A Stuart 350/192.
2 R A Stuart 352/49,107.
3 R A Stuart 353/59.
4 Robinson to Villettes, 28 May 1756, S P Switzerland 35.
5 R A Stuart 353/58.
6 'I would not turn away a cat to please those scoundrels,' MacAllester, *Series of Letters*, op. cit., i, p.128.
7 R A Stuart 356/193.
8 R A Stuart 355/15.
9 The prince's furious reactions can be followed at R A Stuart 351/62; 352/32,82; 353/58,133; 354/54.

10 R A Stuart 353/59.

11 R A Stuart 353/59D.

12 R A Stuart 353/92.

13 R A Stuart 355/108.

14 R A Stuart 358/90.

15 R A Stuart 354/55.

16 Add. MSS 32,847 f.261; S P France 248 f.304.

17 S P France 249 f.263.

18 S P France 249 f.274.

19 H M C, III, p.141.

20 S P France 250 ff.206,312.

21 H M C, Hastings, iii, p.108.

22 S P France 249 f.190.

23 H M C, III, p.141.

24 S P France 250 f.326.

25 R A Stuart 358/18,59,61.

26 For details see R A Stuart 353/58,93–108; 357/85; 359/56.

27 R A Stuart 353/59.

28 Lady Primrose gave Mittie £150 and eagerly listened to his tales of the prince's depravity (R A Stuart 359/190; 362/51).

29 R A Stuart 360/12.

30 R A Stuart 356/148.

31 R A Stuart 357/42.

32 R A Stuart 356/193.

33 R A Stuart 357/70.

34 R A Stuart 357/84.

35 R A Stuart 357/103,158.

36 R A Stuart 357/85.

37 R A Stuart 358/28.

38 R A Stuart 357/152.

39 R A Stuart 357/135.

40 R A Stuart 358/87.

41 R A Stuart 357/134.

42 R A Stuart 357/162.

43 Some idea of the unconscious forces inherent in such a father–son exchange can be formed from a reading of Alan Valentine, ed., *Fathers to Sons. Advice without Consent* (Oklahoma, 1963).

44 R A Stuart 352/77.

45 R A Stuart 352/183.

46 R A Stuart 355/102.

47 R A Stuart 355/102. This request was repeated on 21 July 1755 (R A Stuart 357/75) and on 18 August 1755 (R A Stuart 357/144).

48 R A Stuart 358/135.

49 R A Stuart 359/41.

50 R A Stuart 360/110.

51 R A Stuart 359/141.

52 R A Stuart 360/184.

53 R A Stuart 360/6.

54 R A Stuart 360/87.

55 R A Stuart 361/111.

56 R A Stuart 362/33.

57 R A Stuart 363/38.

58 R A Stuart 359/57–8.

59 R A Stuart 360/91.

60 R A Stuart 358/129.

61 R A Stuart 363/75,165.

62 R A Stuart 363/93.

63 R A Stuart 364/17.

64 R A Stuart 363/89,112.

65 R A Stuart 363/85–7.

66 R A Stuart 364/128.

67 R A Stuart 365/55.

68 R A Stuart 365/91.

69 R A Stuart 364/157.

70 R A Stuart 365/91.

71 R A Stuart 366/101.

72 R A Stuart 366/155.

73 R A Stuart 366/154.

74 R A Stuart 366/163.

75 R A Stuart 367/84.

76 R A Stuart 368/175.

77 R A Stuart 372/63.

78 The prince noted in his own hand in contemptuous amusement the rumour that Clementina hated him so much that he had to chain her to the bed every night to prevent her running away (R A Stuart 363/139).

79 R A Stuart 364/117.

80 R A Stuart 364/113.

81 R A Stuart 364/116.

82 R A Stuart 370/66,158; 371/91; 374/23.

83 R A Stuart 364/67; 365/91,98.

84 R A Stuart 372/2–3.

85 R A Stuart 371/69.

86 R A Stuart 374/85.

87 Even so, what follows is a severe compression of the material, with many purple passages ignored or excluded.

88 R A Stuart 364/56.

89 R A Stuart 364/72.

90 R A Stuart 364/116.

91 R A Stuart 366/8.

92 R A Stuart 366/126.

93 R A Stuart 366/135.

94 R A Stuart 366/140.

95 R A Stuart 366/141.

96 R A Stuart 366/131.

97 R A Stuart 367/30.

98 R A Stuart 366/160; 367/34.

99 R A Stuart 368/109.

100 R A Stuart 370/15.

101 R A Stuart 370/158.

102 R A Stuart 371/126.

103 R A Stuart 372/1.

104 R A Stuart 373/61.

105 R A Stuart 373/128.

106 R A Stuart 374/7.

107 R A Stuart 374/91.

108 R A Stuart 374/43.

109 R A Stuart 374/151.

110 R A Stuart 376/78.

111 R A Stuart 377/20.

112 R A Stuart 379/124.

113 R A Stuart 380/136.

114 R A Stuart 381/84.
115 R A Stuart 383/61,107,141.

CHAPTER THIRTY-ONE

1 R A Stuart 379/125–6; 381/84.
2 R A Stuart 386/61.
3 R A Stuart 383/74; 384/64.
4 R A Stuart 386/2.
5 R A Stuart 384/77.
6 R A Stuart 384/126.
7 R A Stuart 382/50; 383/61.
8 R A Stuart 386/31.
9 R A Stuart 386/56.
10 R A Stuart 386/112.
11 R A Stuart 387/19.
12 R A Stuart 387/137.
13 Claude Nordmann, 'Choiseul and the last Jacobite attempt of 1759', in Eveline Cruickshanks, ed., *Ideology and Conspiracy* (Edinburgh, 1982), pp.201–17.
14 R A Stuart 389/118; 390/69.
15 R A Stuart 390/60.
16 Charles Edward to Belle-Isle, 30 January 1759, R A Stuart 390/69.
17 R A Stuart 390/114.
18 R A Stuart 390/135,138. The meeting is also described in L. Dutens, *Mémoires d'un voyageur*, op. cit., ii, pp.124–5. Cf. also Sir N. W. Wraxall, *Historical Memoirs of my own Time* (London, 1818), pp.308–10. Wraxall erroneously places the meeting in 1770.
19 For the French desire to see Charles Edward land in Ireland see A E M D Angleterre 54 ff.93–4.
20 R A Stuart 390/132; 392/67; 394/108.
21 R A Stuart 390/161.
22 R A Stuart 390/172; 391/13.
23 A E C P Angleterre 442 ff.136–8.
24 *Ibid.*
25 R A Stuart 393/36.
26 R A Stuart 390/151.
27 A E C P Angleterre 442 ff.174–80.
28 Nordmann, loc. cit., p.209.
29 R A Stuart 391/69.
30 R A Stuart 391/49.
31 R A Stuart 391/37.
32 R A Stuart 392/75,90,102.
33 R A Stuart 391/36.
34 R A Stuart 392/81.
35 R A Stuart 393/4.
36 R A Stuart 392/33.
37 See above p.199.
38 R A Stuart 395/168.
39 A S V, Francia, 513, f.41.
40 R A Stuart 393/157.
41 R A Stuart 493/59.
42 R A Stuart 393/168,174.
43 R A Stuart 393/166; 397/98.
44 R A Stuart 393/58.
45 R A Stuart 391/7.

46 R A Stuart 393/120.
47 R A Stuart 393/121.
48 R A Stuart 398/31.
49 R A Stuart 399/99.
50 R A Stuart 399/122.

CHAPTER THIRTY-TWO

1 R A Stuart 405/187.
2 R A Stuart 398/98.
3 R A Stuart 399/114; 401/18,86–7; 402/54,69,89,117.
4 R A Stuart 402/9.
5 R A Stuart 414/88.
6 R A Stuart 403/43. Cf. also *Walpole Correspondence*, 26, pp.46–7.
7 A E M D Angleterre 81 f.96.
8 Mackenzie, *Prince Charlie's Ladies*, op. cit., pp.213–14.
9 R A Stuart 404/172.
10 Add MSS 39,923 f.148.
11 R A Stuart 402/144.
12 R A Stuart 402/142.
13 R A Stuart 402/143.
14 R A Stuart 402/150.
15 R A Stuart 402/155.
16 *Ibid.*
17 R A Stuart 402/161,169.
18 R A Stuart 402/153.
19 R A Stuart 402/165,178.
20 R A Stuart 402/167.
21 R A Stuart 402/162,170,171.
22 R A Stuart 402/175,191,192,204,208.
23 R A Stuart 402/179,204,216; 403/74,96.
24 R A Stuart 402/216.
25 R A Stuart 402/184–8.
26 R A Stuart 402/206.
27 R A Stuart 403/25,139.
28 R A Stuart 403/3.
29 R A Stuart 404/17.
30 A E C P Angleterre 442 ff.405–7.
31 R A Stuart 403/43.
32 R A Stuart 403/5.
33 R A Stuart 404/17,94.
34 R A Stuart 402/204; 403/8.
35 R A Stuart Box 1/510.
36 R A Stuart 403/8.
37 R A Stuart 404/179; 403/8.
38 R A Stuart 404/173.
39 R A Stuart 402/198.
40 R A Stuart 403/35,52,157.
41 R A Stuart 402/151,181; Box 1/507,
42 R A Stuart 403/59.
43 R A Stuart 403/68.
44 R A Stuart 403/119.
45 R A Stuart 404/173.
46 R A Stuart 409/215.
47 R A Stuart 413/166.
48 H M C, 11, vii, p.44.
49 S P France 251 ff.78, 178.
50 S P France 258 f.263.

51 *Correspondance de Voltaire*, op. cit., 51, p.237.

52 *Ibid.*, 49, pp.179–80.

53 R A Stuart 403/82. Sholto Douglas, brother of Sir John Douglas, visited the prince as representative of the English Jacobite party in September 1760 (R A Stuart 403/83,89,98).

54 Tayler, *Stuart Papers*, op. cit., pp.249–50. This is a bad misreading of a document (original at R A Stuart 398/159). The address at the top of the letter is clearly that of the addressee.

55 Other sources for the George III coronation story are *Scots Magazine*, 1788, pp.209–11; *St. James's Chronicle*, 1–3 May 1788; *Hume's Letters*, op. cit., ii, p.484; *Walpole Correspondence*, 11, p,296.

56 Even the jittery duo, Horace Walpole and Horace Mann, accepted the truth of this. Cf. *Walpole Correspondence*, 22, p.90.

57 *London Chronicle*, 11–13 November 1762.

58 R A Stuart 406/118.

59 R A Stuart 411/24.

60 R A Stuart 413/58.

61 S P Tuscany 68 ff.93,98.

62 *Walpole Correspondence*, 22, p.90.

63 S P France 254 ff.12–13.

64 S P 105/315 ff.312–14; *Walpole Correspondence*, 22, p.255.

65 R A Stuart 409/52.

66 R A Stuart 409/159.

67 R A Stuart 414/88,168. This ploy was sometimes combined, illogically, with the argument that the prince was not safe at Bouillon (R A Stuart 414/102).

68 R A Stuart 412/14; 414/2. After being initially refused all access to the prince, Caryll had an interview with Thibault at Bouillon in March 1762 (R A Stuart Box 1/521–7).

69 R A Stuart 413/111.

70 R A Stuart 411l/111.

71 La Tremouille, *Une Famille royaliste*, op. cit., p.71.

72 For Lady Webb and her correspondence with the prince see R A Stuart 412/180,187; 413/6.

73 R A Stuart 412/179.

74 R A Stuart 413/8,26.

75 R A Stuart 417/9.

76 R A Stuart 415/90.

77 Lady Webb's comments are interesting in this respect: 'I have knowledge enough to know that your preservation is a miracle of divine providence. You think you have, and it is true, a very good constitution, but you don't eat enough to support it. The quantity of wine you drink continally heats your blood to such a degree that the least inflammation

would carry you off in a few hours. I observed once that the blood worked up and surrounded your neck; which frightened me to such a degree lest it should seize your head that I was ready to scream out in your presence' (R A Stuart 427/82).

78 R A Stuart 430/106.

79 Boswell, *Life of Johnson*, op. cit., v, p.196. Of course the reason is clear. As we have stressed before, because of the vast reservoir of *unconscious* guilt, the prince's mind could not allow him to absorb the *conscious* guilt for the post-Culloden sufferings.

80 *Walpole Correspondence*, 7, pp.274–5.

81 R A Stuart 420/47.

82 *Ibid.*

83 R A Stuart 422/60; 425/101; 428/135–6,199; 429/13.

84 R A Stuart 429/14.

85 R A Stuart 420/213.

86 R A Stuart 421/1.

87 R A Stuart Box 1/535.

88 R A Stuart 421/61.

89 R A Stuart 421/37.

90 R A Stuart 421/3.

91 R A Stuart 420/213A.

CHAPTER THIRTY-THREE

1 R A Stuart 429/47.

2 R A Stuart 427/118; 428/59.

3 R A Stuart 424/71.

4 R A Stuart 425/86.

5 R A Stuart 425/117.

6 R A Stuart 426/38.

7 R A Stuart 426/63,109.

8 R A Stuart 426/110.

9 R A Stuart 427/64; 429/7.

10 R A Stuart 429/32.

11 R A Stuart 429/99.

12 R A Stuart 429/132.

13 R A Stuart 429/162.

14 R A Stuart 429/179.

15 Matthias Buschkuhl, *Great Britain and the Holy See 1746–1870* (Dublin, 1982), pp.17–18.

16 A S V Inghilterra 25 f.73; A S V Principi 254 f.8.

17 A S V Principi 233 ff.343–8,353,358.

18 A S V Principi 233 ff.367–70.

19 A S V Inghilterra 25 ff.68–9; A S V Principi 233 f.258.

20 Benedict to Tencin, 11 November 1750, Morelli, ii, p.329.

21 Same to same, 23 December 1750, 3 February 1751, Morelli, ii, pp.341,354.

22 Benedict to Tencin, 26 July 1752, Morelli, p.495.

23 Benedict to Tencin, 6 November 1754,

Heeckeren, *Benoit-Tencin*, op. cit., ii, p.370.

24 Same to same, 18 July 1753, Heeckeren, ii, p.279.

25 Same to same, 19 November 1755, Heeckeren, ii, p.155.

26 R A Stuart 381/119,153.

27 R A Stuart 382/50.

28 R A Stuart 383/107; 385/119.

29 R A Stuart 385/137.

30 R A Stuart 402/62.

31 R A Stuart 415/153.

32 R A Stuart 415/157.

33 R A Stuart 416/92.

34 R A Stuart 418/85.

35 R A Stuart 429/22.

36 R A Stuart 429/89.

37 A S V Instrumenta Miscellanea 7596 f.1; Biblioteca Angelica MS 2293 f.151; Add. MSS 34,638 f.293.

38 A S V Instrumenta Miscellanea 7596 f.1; Add. MSS 34,638 f.296.

39 R A Stuart 429/162.

40 S P Tuscany 70 f.188.

41 A S V Inghilterra 25 ff.179–80; Biblioteca Angelica MS 2293 f.151.

42 A S V Inghilterra 25 f.180; Biblioteca Angelica MS 2293 f.153.

43 S P Tuscany 71 ff.63–4.

44 Biblioteca Angelica MS 2293 ff.156–7.

45 *Ibid.* f.155; A S V Inghilterra 25 ff.180–1.

46 R A Stuart 430/42.

47 R A Stuart 429/143,145,160.

48 R A Stuart 430/80.

49 R A Stuart 431/104–5,118.

50 R A Stuart 431/42.

51 R A Stuart 431/114.

52 R A Stuart 430/170,178; 431/7.

53 R A Stuart 431/24–5.

54 R A Stuart 431/82.

55 *Memoirs of Lumisden and Strange*, op. cit., ii, pp.77–9.

56 R A Stuart 432/18.

57 A S V Instrumenta Miscellanea 7596 ff.2–10; A S V Inghilterra 25 ff.161–77.

58 Biblioteca Angelica MS 2293 ff.194–5.

59 *Memoirs of Lumisden and Strange*, ii, pp.82–3.

60 Henri-Joseph Bouchard d'Esparber de Lussan, marquis d'Aubeterre (1714–88), had been French ambassador in Spain from 1757 to 1763. From 1763 to 1769 he served in the same capacity in Rome (Du Deffand, op. cit., ii, p.244).

61 *Memoirs of Lumisden and Strange*, ii, p.84.

62 S P Tuscany 71 ff.63–4.

63 A S V Inghilterra 25 ff.182–5.

64 Biblioteca Angelica MS 2293 f.159.

65 *Memoirs of Lumisden and Strange*, ii, pp.80–1.

66 For Alessandro Albani's spying activities at this time see S P Tuscany 71 f.18; S P 105/317 f.29.

67 Biblioteca Angelica MS 2293 f.161.

68 S P Tuscany 71 ff.33–45.

69 A S V Inghilterra 25 f.102.

70 A S V Inghilterra 25 ff.194–200.

71 Biblioteca Angelica MS 2293 f.162.

72 A S V Inghilterra 21 ff.76–7.

73 Biblioteca Angelica MS 2293 f.171.

74 *Ibid.*, f.172.

75 A S V Inghilterra 21 ff.76–91.

76 *Walpole Correspondence*, 22, p.386. This was in fact one of the options being considered by Mann at the time.

77 A S V Inghilterra 25 f.99.

78 Biblioteca Angelica MS 2293 ff.174–6.

79 *Ibid.*, ff.176–7.

80 A S V Inghilterra 25 f.101.

81 *Ibid.*

82 Biblioteca Angelica MS 2293 f.173.

83 *Ibid.*, ff.163–4.

84 A S V Inghilterra 25 f.99.

85 Mann had earlier raised this exact point (*Walpole Correspondence*, 22, p.384).

86 The duke of Richmond was already trying to discredit Aubeterre with the duc de Praslin (H M C, Bathurst, pp.691–2).

87 H M C, III, p.130.

88 Biblioteca Angelica MS 2293 f.161.

89 A S V, Instrumenta Miscellanea 7596 f.10. Cf. also Instrumenta Miscellanea 6680.

90 R A Stuart 431/82.

91 *Memoirs of Strange and Lumisden*, ii, p.87.

92 R A Stuart 433/27.

93 *Memoirs of Strange and Lumisden*, ii, pp.88–90.

94 S P 105/317 f.44.

95 *Ibid.*, f.48.

96 R A Stuart 433/123.

97 *Memoirs of Strange and Lumisden*, ii, pp.74–6.

98 R A Stuart 433/158.

99 *Memoirs of Strange and Lumisden*, ii, p.86.

100 R A Stuart 433/28,117,119.

101 *Walpole Correspondence*, 22, p.399.

102 Doran, *Mann and Manners*, op. cit., ii, pp.164–5.

103 For details of the abortive Serrant mission see La Tremoille, *Une Famille royaliste*, op. cit., pp.72–6. Cf. also R A Stuart 433/195,198; 434/12,42,84,116.

104 Walpole attributed this to the spectre of 1759: 'The Pope dare not acknowledge the Pretender while Mr Pitt lives' (*Walpole Correspondence*, 30, p.216).

105 *Mann and Manners*, op. cit., ii, p.162.

106 Mahon, *Last Stuarts*, op. cit., p.26.

107 S P 105/317 ff.59,61.

108 *Walpole Correspondence*, 22, pp.392–3; *Mann and Manners*, ii, p.163.

109 For Orsini see Friedrich Hausman, ed., *Repertorium der Diplomatischen Vertreter aller Lander* (Zurich, 1950), ii, p.239.
110 S P 105/317 f.57.
111 R A Stuart 434/197; Mahon, *Last Stuarts*, p.31.
112 *Walpole Correspondence*, 22, pp.392–3.
113 Mahon, *Last Stuarts*, p.31.
114 *Walpole Correspondence*, 22, p.408.

CHAPTER THIRTY-FOUR

1 James's will, signed on 21 November 1760, is at A S V Inghilterra 25 ff.109–12. The king later tried to simplify some of the provisions of his will in a codicil dated 26 May 1762 (A S V Inghilterra 25 ff.28–9).
2 A S V Inghilterra 25 f.110.
3 The Sempills knew the right cards to play. After condoling with the prince on the death of James, the new Lord Sempill (Francis, the prince's *bête noire*, had died in 1748) claimed that his family had suffered financial hardship because of the enmity of the Lismores (O'Briens) and Tencin – just the right mixture to evoke a sympathetic response from the prince had he really possessed a fortune (A E M D Angleterre 93 ff.153,163–4).
4 For Mann's exaggerated estimate of the prince's wealth see *Walpole Correspondence*, 22, pp.385,387. But Lumisden estimated that when debts and annuities were paid, Charles Edward's yearly income was no more than three thousand English guineas (*Memoirs of Strange and Lumisden*, ii, p.104).
5 R A Stuart 433/130.
6 *Memoirs of Strange and Lumisden*, ii, p.102.
7 *Ibid.*, pp.103–4.
8 *Ibid.*, p.93.
9 Mahon, *Last Stuarts*, op. cit., p.33.
10 R A Stuart 434/71.
11 R A Stuart 433/130; 434/2.
12 R A Stuart 434/11.
13 *Ibid.*
14 R A Stuart 435/43.
15 For confirmation see Serrant's reports from Paris (R A Stuart 435/182; 437/84).
16 R A Stuart 433/201.
17 R A Stuart 434/188; 435/6,31,56.
18 R A Stuart 435/29,31,56,75; 436/168.
19 R A Stuart 436/90.
20 R A Stuart 436/31.
21 R A Stuart 437/92.
22 'Deprived by the cruelty of this government of the pleasure of society, 'tis the same to His Majesty whether he is here or at Rome. He says that he is like one on shipboard; he converses only with his own little crew' (*Memoirs of Strange and Lumisden*, ii, p.97).
23 R A Stuart 437/59.
24 R A Stuart 437/59,102,112.
25 R A Stuart 437/172.
26 *Memoirs of Strange and Lumisden*, ii, p.97; R A Stuart 437/94.
27 La Tremoille, *Une Famille royaliste*, p.77.
28 *Memoirs of Strange and Lumisden*, p.98; R A Stuart 438/87.
29 R A Stuart 438/122.
30 R A Stuart 439/58.
31 R A Stuart 439/84.
32 *Memoirs of Strange and Lumisden*, ii, p.98.
33 Doran, *Mann and Manners*, ii, p.174.
34 H M C, III, pp.137–8.
35 *L M*, iii, p.222.
36 H M C, III, p.421.
37 R A Stuart 440/155.
38 R A Stuart Box 1/549.
39 A D, Nancy, H.77 (August 1767).
40 R A Stuart 442/17,36; 443/8.
41 H M C, III, p.421.
42 *Memoirs of Strange and Lumisden*, ii, pp.106,109.
43 A E M D Angleterre, 93 f.155.
44 *Memoirs of Strange and Lumisden*, ii, p.107.
45 In November 1766 Charles Edward was reported by Mann to have 'committed in the last week some great outrages against some of his own people in a drunken fit, by drawing his sword and pursuing them, so that they narrowly escaped being killed' (Mahon, *Last Stuarts*, p.34).
46 *Memoirs of Strange and Lumisden*, ii, pp.109–10.
47 R A Stuart 442/140.
48 *L M*, iii, p.224.
49 R A Stuart 445/116.
50 *L M*, iii, pp.222–3.
51 *Memoirs of Strange and Lumisden*, ii, pp.111–13.
52 *Ibid.*, pp.119–20.
53 *Ibid.*, p.119. However, as Lumisden said: 'But how is it possible to conceal what has been seen by so many?'
54 *L M*, iii, p.232.
55 Thomas W. Copeland, ed., *Correspondence of Edmund Burke*, 10 vols (Cambridge and Chicago, 1978), ii, p.283.
56 R A Stuart 446/187.
57 *L M*, iii, p.234; Mahon, *Last Stuarts*, pp.34–5.
58 R A Stuart 446/188. The prince's closing remarks seem particularly hypocritical. Claiming that he would now be king of England if he had rejected Catholicism, he went on: 'it was proposed to me several times and thank God I always rejected it'(!!!).
59 R A Stuart 447/9,15.

60 'For God's sake, dear brother, reflect seriously on all this and at least in the meanwhile do not put your foot in Rome, for that would blow up everything' (R A Stuart 447/20).

61 R A Stuart 447/9,20.

62 See the snobbishness evinced by Dunbar on the new Pope: 'His low birth and education give me pain' (R A Stuart 447/40).

63 Mahon, *Last Stuarts*, pp.35–6.

64 R A Stuart 447/40.

65 Mahon, *Last Stuarts*, p.36.

66 R A Stuart 447/182.

67 R A Stuart 448/113.

68 R A Stuart 448/107.

69 How bad the situation was can be inferred from the fact that in 1768 the prince ceased to take the English newspapers for reasons of economy. When Lord Caryll took over Lumisden's duties, he received board and lodging only (*Memoirs of Strange and Lumisden*, ii, p.105).

70 R A Stuart 449/5.

71 R A Stuart 449/95,142.

72 R A Stuart 450/33; 451/99.

73 *L M*, iii, p.223.

74 R A Stuart 449/139–41. Princess Maria Anna Sapieha (born 1728) was the second wife of Prince Johann Cajetan Jablonowski and sister-in-law of the Princesse de Talmont. She was also distantly related to Charles Edward through the Sobieskis, since her husband was grandnephew of King John Sobieski's wife.

75 R A Stuart 450/110.

76 R A Stuart 450/144.

77 R A Stuart 450/150; S P Tuscany 75 f.108.

78 S P Tuscany 75 f.108.

79 *Walpole Correspondence*, 23, pp.225–6.

80 There were also four servants out of livery, two ordinary footmen and two ancillary footmen (S P Tuscany 75 f.124).

81 S P Tuscany 75 f.140.

82 Mahon, *Last Stuarts*, p.39.

83 R A Stuart 450/160,167.

84 R A Stuart 450/204.

85 S P 105/320 f.213.

86 Mahon, *Last Stuarts*, pp.39–40.

87 R A Stuart 451/13.

88 R A Stuart 451/196.

89 R A Stuart 451/99.

90 Giulini G. Sepegni, ed., *Carteggio di Pietro e Alessandro Verri* (Milan, 1926), v, pp.46–8.

91 Lady Anne Miller, *Letters from Italy*, 3 vols (1776), ii, pp.194–8.

92 *Ibid.*, p.199.

93 *Ibid.*, p.198.

CHAPTER THIRTY-FIVE

1 R A Stuart 452/107.

2 R A Stuart Box 1/568; 452/127.

3 R A Stuart Box 1/574.

4 R A Stuart Box 1/573.

5 *L M*, iii, pp.353–4 for these and other details of Caryll's career.

6 R A Stuart 452/119.

7 H M C, 10, vi, p.224; R A Stuart 454/116.

8 R A Stuart Box 1/569; 454/80.

9 R A Stuart 453/117.

10 R A Stuart 453/114; 454/119.

11 R A Stuart 454/132,140,149.

12 H M C, 10, vi, p.224.

13 S P Tuscany 76 ff.147–51.

14 *Walpole Correspondence*, 23, pp.318–19.

15 cf. Mann to Walpole, 17 September 1771: 'You will laugh at me perhaps for being solicitous about so pitiful an object as the Pretender now is, but though advanced in years, and either drunk or half asleep, he may still be made use of to do mischief' (*Walpole Correspondence*, 23, p.324).

16 S P Tuscany 76 f.160.

17 Walpole thought that Spain had invited the prince to Madrid to launch him against Scotland. In typical Walpole fashion he could not resist a jibe at Mann's expense over the 'disappearance': 'I am sorry that so watchful a cat should have let its mouse slip at last, without knowing into what hole it has run' (*Walpole Correspondence*, 23, p.328).

18 See Baron de Viomenil, *Lettres sur les affaires de Pologne en 1771 et 1772* (Paris, 1808). For Charles Edward's reflections on events in Poland see R A Stuart Box 1/575.

19 *Walpole Correspondence*, 5, p.111.

20 S P Tuscany 76 f.153.

21 Du Deffand, op. cit., iii, p.111.

22 S P Tuscany 76 f.157.

23 H M C, 10, vi, p.223.

24 *Ibid.*

25 Hence the laments of Parisian Jacobites that they had not seen their leader during his stay in the capital (R A Stuart 445/86,135,145; 456/97).

26 H M C, 10. vi, p.224.

27 *Ibid.*, p.225.

28 Ryan's first target was to be the Princess of Salm. If his bid proved unsuccessful, he was to proceed to other princesses (eighteen-year-old Princess Marie Isabelle de Mansfeld was mentioned), and thereafter he was to scour the Empire, in Brussels, Cologne, Mannheim and else-

where until he found a suitable bride (H M C, 10, vi, p.223).

29 *Ibid.*, pp.223–5.

30 *Ibid.*, pp.223–4.

31 *Walpole Correspondence*, 23, p.343.

32 S P 105/295 f.133.

33 Horace Mann, as usual, tried to make propaganda out of the most trivial incident: 'He was in great danger . . . on which occasion he expressed the utmost fear and consternation' (Mahon, *Last Stuarts*, p.44). It was an abiding aim of Whig propaganda to call Charles Edward's physical courage – the one attribute that could not actually be doubted – into question. Cf. the nonsense about his cowardice during the '45 retailed by David Hume (Add. MSS 34,516 f.4).

34 S P Tuscany 76 f.208; R A Stuart 455/136. Mann next tried to discredit the prince on the alleged 'absurdity' of his trip. 'Not only by the cardinals but by the common people he was hooted at for having made so much mystery about so insignificant a journey' (*Walpole Correspondence*, 23, p.343).

35 H M C, 10, vi, p.225.

36 *Walpole Correspondence*, 23, p.351 provides some pointers.

37 H M C, 10, vi, p.225.

38 R A Stuart 456/123–4.

39 R A Stuart 456/14. High hopes had evidently been entertained for this marriage. Her itinerary to Marseilles and on by sea to Civitavecchia had already been worked out (H M C, 10, vi, pp.225–6).

40 The Princess of Salm that the prince bade for was Marie-Louise de Rhingrave, daughter of Philipe-Joseph, Prince of Salm-Kyrbourg and Marie-Thérèse Josephe de Hornes. The mother of Charles Edward's first prospective bride, in other words, was the sister of Louise of Stolberg's mother (C. F. Jacobi, ed., *Europäisches Genealogisches Handbuch* (Leipzig, 1800), p.397). For Louise of Stolberg's genealogy see H M C, 8, iii, p.7.

41 R A Stuart 456/123,135.

42 R A Stuart 456/168; 457/14.

43 R A Stuart 457/15.

44 P. Sirven, *Vittorio Alfieri* (Paris, 1938), iii, pp.347–72 analyses this early period of Louise's life. Cf. also Carlo Pellegrini, *La Contessa d'Albany e il Salotto del Lungarno* (Naples, 1951), p.13.

45 H M C, 10, vi, p.226.

46 These can be found at R A Stuart 458/18,19,33.41.

47 H M C, 10, vi, p.229.

48 R A Stuart 458/44.

49 R A Stuart 457/161.

50 H M C, 10, vi, p.229.

51 R A Stuart 458/103.

52 R A Stuart 458/104.

53 H M C, 10, vi, pp.226–7.

54 *Ibid.*, p.228.

55 *Ibid.*, p.230.

56 *Ibid.*, pp.227–8.

57 R A Stuart 458/157.

58 A. Theiner, *Geschichte des Pontificats Clemens XIV*, 2 vols (Leipzig, 1853), ii, p.153 (also translated in Paris in the same year as *Histoire du Pontificat de Clement XIV*).

59 S P Tuscany 76 ff.187–8.

60 Bushkuhl, *Great Britain and the Holy See*, op. cit., pp.19–20.

61 R A Stuart 458/122.

62 R A Stuart 458/103.

63 R A Stuart 458/104,123.

64 R A Stuart 458/125,135,138.

65 R A Stuart 458/143.

66 Also present were the duke of Berwick and the marquis of Jamaica (Du Deffand, iii, 218; H M C, 10, vi, p.230).

67 R A Stuart 458/150,156.

68 It was even stipulated that, except in an emergency, no stop was to be made in Mantua (H M C, 10, vi, p.226).

69 For Marefoschi see Charles Breton, *Dictionnaire des cardinaux* (Paris, 1857), p.1187.

70 R A Stuart 458/159.

71 R A Stuart 459/23.

72 R A Stuart 459/40.

73 R A Stuart 459/45.

74 H M C, 10, vi, p.231; R A Stuart 459/66.

75 R A Stuart 459/66.

76 H M C, 10, vi, p.231.

77 R A Stuart 459/67.

78 *Daily Advertiser*, 14 May 1772.

79 See the extended comments in the *London Chronicle*, 2–4 April 1772; *St James's Chronicle*, 16–18 April 1772.

80 *Politische Correspondenz*, op. cit., 32, pp.119,154,

81 S P Tuscany 77 ff.42,44; H M C, 10, vi, p.232.

82 S P Tuscany 77 f.48; Theiner, op. cit., ii, p.160.

83 *L M*, iii, p.324.

84 Theiner, op. cit., ii, p.161.

85 H M C, 10, vi, p.233.

86 R A Stuart 461/84.

87 See below p.537.

88 See the analysis in P. Sirven, *Alfieri*, op. cit., iii, pp.347–72.

89 R A Stuart 457/115.

90 R A Stuart 457/14.

91 R A Stuart 458/156.

92 R A Stuart Box 1/577.
93 *Souvenirs de Charles Victor Bonstetten* (Paris, 1832), pp.61–9.
94 G. Charvet, *Une correspondance inédite de la Comtesse d'Albanie* (Nimes, 1878), p.13.
95 R A Stuart 463/142; 464/88.
96 Bower MSS; H M C, 10, vi, pp.232–3; R A Stuart 462/157,160; 464/151.
97 R A Stuart 461/55; 462/66.
98 R A Stuart 464/150.
99 H M C, 10, vi, p.234.
100 For the three diversions mentioned (apart from Louise) see respectively R A Stuart 462/45; 461/149; 461/159.
101 R A Stuart 422/131–2.
102 See H. Tayler, *Prince Charlie's Daughter* (1950), p.31; F. J. A. Skeet, *Charlotte Stuart, Duchess of Albany* (1932), pp.31–2.
103 R A Stuart 446/63.
104 R A Stuart 448/51–2.
105 A E M D Angleterre, 81 ff.97–8.
106 R A Stuart 459/75.
107 R A Stuart 461/57.
108 The sequence of events can be followed in R A Stuart 462/67; 463/117.
109 A E M D Angleterre, 81 ff.71–5.
110 R A Stuart 467/73,106,118; 468/70–1.
111 H M C, 10, vi, p.234.
112 *Ibid.*
113 R A Stuart 469/33.
114 R A Stuart 467/15.
115 Bruno Bassi, 'Vittorio Alfieri e la Suezia', *Annali Alferiani* (1943), II, p.15.
116 Mahon, *Last Stuarts*, p.46.
117 R A Stuart 470/32.
118 *L M*, iii, p.281.
119 Ernst Emmerling, *Pompeo Batoni* (Darmstadt, 1932), pp.35–6. There is an excellent description of the painting (this is the author's forte) in James Lees-Milne, *The Last Stuarts* (1983), p.107.
120 *Walpole Correspondence*, 24, p.102.
121 Bonstetten, *Souvenirs*, op. cit., pp.61–9.
122 *Walpole Correspondence*, 24, p.94.
123 A considerable amount of attention has been given to Louise of Stolberg. The most scholarly work on her is by Leon G. Pelissier: *Lettres et ecrits divers de la Comtesse d'Albany* (Paris, 1901); *Le Portefeuille de la Comtesse d'Albany* (1902); *Lettres inédites de la Comtesse d'Albany*, 3 vols (1904–15). A. Reumont, *Die Gräfin von Albany* (Berlin, 1860) is still useful. There are a number of works in English of varying worth: Margaret Crosland, *Louise of Stolberg, Countess of Albany* (1962); Margaret Michiner, *No Crown for the Queen* (1937); H. M. Vaughan, *The Last Stuart Queen* (1910); Vernon Lee, *The Countess of Albany* (1884). Far the best one-volume appraisal is by Carlo Pellegrini, *La Contessa d'Albany e il Salotto del Lungano* (Naples, 1951).

CHAPTER THIRTY-SIX

1 R A Stuart 473/191; 474/8.
2 R A Stuart 474/33–4.
3 The French court had successfully stalled Fitzjames by introducing the smoke-screen of a proposed Franco-Spanish subsidy (R A Stuart 474/38).
4 The answer from Spain, received on the eve of d'Aiguillon's resignation, was less than encouraging (R A Stuart 474/78).
5 Charles Edward to Maurepas, 20 July 1774, A E M D Angleterre, 81 f.89.
6 R A Stuart 474/192. Charles Edward excused himself on the grounds that he had to act fast, and at the time no ministers had been appointed. But it was another case of his jumping the gun.
7 R A Stuart 475/169; 476/154.
8 A E M D Angleterre 81 f.103.
9 R A Stuart 474/194; 475/83,132.
10 R A Stuart 475/169.
11 R A Stuart 474/188.
12 R A Stuart 475/176.
13 R A Stuart 476/24.
14 R A Stuart 476/69.
15 R A Stuart 477/88. Cf. R A Stuart 477/167: 'My distress is inconceivable for lack of money.'
16 R A Stuart 477/178.
17 R A Stuart 477/179. Gordon replied that the only chance of getting anything was to settle for a reduced sum (R A Stuart 479/32).
18 R A Stuart 479/24.
19 R A Stuart 479/56.
20 R A Stuart 479/97.
21 R A Stuart 479/188.
22 R A Stuart 479/99,206.
23 A E M D Angleterre 81 f.247.
24 Money was probably the most cogent factor, but Mann stressed the continuing non-recognition by the Pope in a Holy Year as the crucial determinant (Mahon, *Last Stuarts*, p.47).
25 R A Stuart 461/161; 471/40.
26 R A Stuart 474/194.
27 R A Stuart 474/188,202,205.
28 R A Stuart 475/39,83.
29 R A Stuart 474/178; 475/164.
30 R A Stuart 475/175,181,197.
31 R A Stuart 476/13,133. 'My intention is to stay at Siena some time, as I do not think of going to Rome before a Pope is chosen' (Charles Edward to Gordon, 1 November 1774, R A Stuart 476/155).
32 S P Tuscany 79 f.141.
33 Walther Limpburger, *Die Gebäude von Florenz* (Leipzig, 1910), p.41.

34 R A Stuart 477/164.

35 Mahon, *Last Stuarts*, p.48.

36 For the Borgia links with Marefoschi see Vatican Library, Fondo Borgia, 812 ff.48,66–7,71–8. For Borgia links with Henry see Fondo Borgia, 792 ff.54–6.

37 R A Stuart 477/113.

38 For details see A E C P, Rome, 872 ff.137–46.

39 R A Stuart 478/63.

40 Roda to Wall, 22 January, 12 February 1761, A G N, Simancas, Legajo 4966.

41 Bindelli, *Enrico Stuart*, op. cit., p.107.

42 Pastor, *History of the Popes*, op. cit., 39, pp.16–17.

43 A E C P Espagne 574 f.217.

44 Bushkuhl, *Great Britain and the Holy See*, op. cit., p.22.

45 R A Stuart 479/205,207.

46 R A Stuart 480/77.

47 R A Stuart 480/82.

48 R A Stuart 481/174.

49 R A Stuart 481/190.

50 For further bitter protests against 'a low submission to the Hanoverian government' see R A Stuart 482/44–6.

51 Mann reported that when the prince was still hopeful that his brother might become Pope, Caryll and count Spada had to attend him while he went in for some very noisy boasting in the public casino (Mahon, *Last Stuarts*, p.49).

52 *L M*, iii, p.352.

53 *L M*, iii, p.361; R A Stuart 480/73,104,110.

54 R A Stuart 480/46.

55 *Walpole Correspondence*, 24, p.94.

56 *L M*, iii, p.338.

57 Doran, *Mann and Manners*, op. cit., ii, p.278; Moore, *Letters from Italy*, ii, p.393.

58 For Bonstetten in the Palazzo Corsini see Bonstetten, *Souvenirs*, op. cit., pp.61–9.

59 R A Stuart Box 3/129.

60 R A Stuart 481/43.

61 *L M*, iii, pp.364–5.

62 R A Stuart 481/44.

63 *Walpole Correspondence*, 24, p.118.

64 R A Stuart 481/44.

65 R A Stuart Box 2/124. For the medical jottings and frequent requests for medical books see R A Stuart 484/18; 485/157; 489/55,88.

66 *Walpole Correspondence*, 24, pp.136–7; Doran, *Mann and Manners*, ii, p.279.

67 Mahon, *Last Stuarts*, p.54; Doran, ii, p.98.

68 Mahon, *Last Stuarts*, p.52.

69 *Ibid.*, p.49.

70 *Walpole Correspondence*, 24, pp.244–5.

71 R A Stuart 481/43.

72 Mahon, *Last Stuarts*, p.50.

73 Emilio Bertana, *Alfieri* (Turin, 1904),

p.171. For Bonstetten's career see Marie L. Herking, *Bonstetten 1745–1832* (Lausanne, 1921).

74 Carlo Pellegrini, *La Contessa d'Albany e il Salotto del Lungano*, op. cit., p.21.

75 R A Stuart Box 1/578.

76 R A Stuart Box 3/128.

77 Mahon, *Last Stuarts*, p.51.

78 *Ibid.*

79 Giulini G. Seregni, ed., *Carteggio di Pietro a Alessandro Veri* (Milan, 1926), viii, pp.147–8.

80 Mahon, *Last Stuarts*, p.50.

81 R A Stuart 481/136; 484/180; 485/83.

82 'A house belonging to an Englishman who keeps three houses for English and other travellers was proposed to him . . . but upon further examination they did not find the house proper for them' (S P Tuscany 80 f.143).

83 S P Tuscany 81 f.119.

84 Walther Limpburger, *Die Gebaude von Florenz* (Leipzig, 1910), p.46.

85 *Walpole Correspondence*, 24, pp.244–5.

86 Doran, ii, p.279.

87 For the financial scurrying prior to the house purchase and the removal of effects see R A Stuart 485/5,10,25,40,84,96,102,131. Cf. also Add. MSS 34,638 ff.307–9.

88 H M C, 15, ii, p.251.

89 R A Stuart Box 3/130. Cf. also Archives of Douai, IL/D Stuart No.3.

90 A. Von Reumont, *Die Grafin von Albany*, 2 vols (Berlin, 1860), i, p.148.

91 Doran, ii, p.298.

92 On Alfieri see Emilio Bertana, *Vittorio Alfieri* (Turin, 1904); P. Sirven, *Vittorio Alfieri* (Paris, 1938).

93 Vittorio Alfieri, *Vita . . . scitta da esso*, ed. V. Branca (Milan, 1983), pp.193–5.

94 *Ibid.*, pp.195–7.

95 R A Stuart Box 3/130. For other books ordered by Louise in this period see H M C, 15, ii, p.251.

96 P. Sirven, *Alfieri*, op. cit., iv, pp.89 *et seq.*

97 Alfieri, *Vita*, op. cit., p.202.

98 R A Stuart 490/57.

99 Vat. Lib. Fondo Borgia, 894 ff.265–8.

100 Dutens, *Mémoires d'un voyageur qui se repose*, op. cit., pp.30–1.

101 H M C, 14, App.x, 2, pp.368–9.

102 H M C, 14, App.x, 2, p.326; *Walpole Correspondence*, 9, p.160.

103 R A Stuart 481/42.

104 R A Stuart Box 1/586.

105 R A Stuart 491/160.

106 R A Stuart 500/121; 501/77. Among other papers Cowley sent the prince were city plans of Boston and New York (R A Stuart 503/16).

107 R A Stuart Box 1/590.
108 Archives of Douai. IL/D Stuart No.6.
109 R A Stuart 497/119.
110 R A Stuart 307/88; 314/113.
111 See the checklists of his reading at R A Stuart 316/175,185,275.
112 R A Stuart 482/162.
113 R A Stuart Box 3/113–14.
114 Add. MSS 34,638 f.393 provides a partial catalogue.
115 R A Stuart Box 2/122.
116 Dutens, *Mémoires*, op. cit., iii, pp.32–3.
117 For representative instances of 'pure' bibliophilia (i.e. an obsession with the artefact itself rather than its contents) see R A Stuart 461/171; 463/78,122; 467/209,211; 471/26.
118 For some pointers see Freud, 'Creative Writing and Day Dreaming', S.E.ix, pp.143–53.
119 R A Stuart 487/83; 494/94.
120 Mahon, *Last Stuarts*, p.56.
121 *Walpole Correspondence*, 24, pp.479–80. On Louise: 'her beauty is vastly faded of late. She has paid dearly for the dregs of royalty' (Doran, ii, p.351).
122 Mahon, *Last Stuarts*, p.55.
123 *Walpole Correspondence*, 25, pp.100–2.
124 Mahon, *Last Stuarts*, p.56.
125 S P Tuscany 82 f.348.
126 Mahon, *History*, iii, p.xlvii.

CHAPTER THIRTY-SEVEN

1 Mann refers archly on the infamous night of 30 November to the prince's having 'committed the most nauseous and filthy indecencies from above and below upon her' (*Walpole Correspondence*, 25, pp.100–2).
2 R A Stuart 500/154.
3 R A Stuart 502/96.
4 Dutens, *Mémoires*, op. cit., ii, pp.253–5.
5 See her vitriolic letter to the prince (R A Stuart 500/78).
6 Dutens, ii, p.252.
7 Add. MSS 35,520 f.68.
8 *Ibid.*, f.169.
9 S P 105/287 f.210. For confirmation cf. also Mlle Maltzam's account given to Father Cowley (Archives of Douai, IL/D Stuart, Nos 5 and 8).
10 Alfieri, *Vita*, op. cit., p.206.
11 Dutens, ii, p.255.
12 Egerton MSS 2641 f.115; Add MSS 35,520 ff.169–70.
13 Dutens, ii, p.255.
14 Add. MSS 35,520 f.170.
15 R A Stuart 500/14.
16 S P 105/287 f.211; Marchesa Nobili Vitelleschi, *A Court in Exile*, 2 vols (1902), ii, pp.438–9.
17 For Henry's reply (15 December 1780) see *Revue des Deux Mondes*, 15 January 1861 (2nd Series, 31, pp.227–9). Cf. Reumont, *Die Gräfin von Albany*, i, pp.219–22.
18 Reumont, *Die Gräfin*, op. cit., i, pp.222–3.
19 *Walpole Correspondence*, 25, p.115.
20 S P 105/287 f.226.
21 R A Stuart 500/56. This did not, however, prevent Mann from the categorical but false statement that the prince refused to send on her clothes (Mahon, *Last Stuarts*, p.59).
22 R A Stuart 500/154.
23 *Walpole Correspondence*, 25, p.115.
24 Mahon, *Last Stuarts*, p.61.
25 Add MSS 34,634 f.35.
26 *Ibid.*, ff.23–5,33.
27 *Ibid.*, f.29.
28 *Ibid.*, f.23. For Charles Edward's hatred of Bernis see Charles Edward to Gordon, 5 August 1772, Bower MSS.
29 R A Stuart Box 1/593; Mahon, *Last Stuarts*, p.60.
30 S P 105/288 f.61.
31 D Silvagni, *La corte e la società romana nei secoli XVIII e XIX* (Florence, 1885). i, p.366.
32 R A Stuart Box 1/592.
33 Archives of Douai, IL/D Stuart No.7. The prince claimed that his wife was a spendthrift and during her years in Florence had spent 600,000 francs without his knowledge (Sirven, *Alfieri*, iii, p.394).
34 R A Stuart 501/31; 502/96; Add MSS 34,634 ff.1,5.
35 Mahon, *Last Stuarts*, p.60.
36 A Reumont, 'Gli ultimi Stuardi, la Contessa d'Albany e V. Alfieri', *Archivio Storico Italiano*, IV, vol.8 (1881), p.71.
37 R A Stuart 502/106.
38 Reumont, 'Gli ultimi Stuardi', loc. cit., pp.71–2.
39 R A Stuart 502/149.
40 R A Stuart 503/111.
41 R A Stuart 503/163; 504/23.
42 R A Stuart 502/149.
43 R A Stuart 504/118.
44 R A Stuart 504/6,151.
45 R A Stuart 505/19.
46 R A Stuart 504/6,104.
47 R A Stuart 505/19.
48 R A Stuart Box 1/597.
49 R A Stuart 505/20,46.
50 A. D. Perrero, 'Gli ultimi Stuardi e V. Alfieri sul fondamento di documenti inediti 1782–83', *Rivista Europea*, 24 (1881), p.697.
51 Mahon, *Last Stuarts*, pp.62–3.
52 *Ibid.*, pp.63–4.
53 R A Stuart Box 1/598.

54 F O 79/3 f.285.
55 *Walpole Correspondence*, 25, pp.394–5.
56 Mahon, *Last Stuarts*, pp.65–6.
57 F O 79/3 f.289.
58 F O 79/3 ff.297–8.
59 Mahon, *Last Stuarts*, p.67.
60 Add. MSS 34,634 f.51.
61 Emilio Bertana, *Alfieri*, op. cit., pp.195–7.
62 Alfieri, *Vita*, p.218.
63 Doran, *Mann and Manners*, ii, p.400.
64 Mahon, *Last Stuarts*, p.68.
65 A E M D, Angleterre, 81 f.145.
66 For Gustav III in general see *Collection des écrits politiques, littéraires et dramatiques de Gustav III* (Stockholm, 1805). For his Italian journey see Baron de Nenno, *Gustav III, Roi de Suède et Anckarstroem 1746–92* (Paris, 1876), p.168. The best modern study of Gustav III's reign is in Claude Nordmann, *Grandeur et liberté de la Suède 1660–1792* (Paris, 1971).
67 F O 79/3 ff.369–71.
68 F O 79/3 f.374.
69 Mahon, *Last Stuarts*, p.73.
70 R A Stuart 506/151,164,172.
71 F O 79/3 f.374.
72 Seregni, *Carteggio*, op. cit., v, pp.48–9; Reumont, *Die Grafin*, op. cit., i, p.241.
73 R A Stuart 502/189; *Walpole Correspondence*, 25, ff.441–2.
74 Doran, ii, p.402.
75 For Chevalier de Tours and Mann's stranglehold on him see F O 79/3 f.352.
76 S P 105/299 f.73.
77 F O 79/3 f.360.
78 *Ibid.*, f.361.
79 Mahon, *Last Stuarts*, p.75.
80 F O 79/3 f.392.
81 The prince referred to Gustav as 'his very dear brother' (R A Stuart 507/49).
82 For freemasonry in eighteenth-century France see P. Chevallier, *Les ducs sous l'Acacia* (Paris, 1964); *La première profanation du temple maçonnique* (Paris, 1968). For the Jacobite role in Spain see J. A. F. Benimeli, *La masonería española en el siglo 18* (Madrid, 1974), esp. pp.48–65. For Italy see Carlo Francovich, *Storia Massoneria in Italia* (Florence, 1974).
83 S P Tuscany 42 ff.131,137–8; cf. also R. G. Gould, *History of Freemasonry* (1887), iii, p.300; Giuseppe Leti, *Carboneria e masoneria nel risorgimento italiano* (Genoa, 1925), pp.37–40; Eugen Lennhoff, *Freemasons* (New York, 1934), pp.139–40.
84 Alec Mellor, *La charte inconnue de la franc-maçonnerie chretienne* (Tours, 1965), pp.119–20. This is also the principal thesis in Mellor's *Nos frères séparés les Francs-Maçons* (Paris, 1961).
85 S P Tuscany 46 ff.182–3.

86 R A Stuart 198/130.
87 Gustave Bord, *La franc-maçonnerie en France* (Paris, 1908).
88 R A Stuart 203/163.
89 D. Ligon, ed., *Dictionnaire universal de la Franc-maçonnerie* (Paris, 1974), i, p.74.
90 Frankovich, op. cit., p.220.
91 *Ibid.*, pp.228–9,258.
92 R A Stuart 491/123.
93 P Maruzzi, 'Notizie e documenti sul liberi muratori a Torino ne secolo XVIII', *Bollettino storico-bibliografico subalpino* 30 (1928), pp.207–10.
94 R A Stuart 493/19.
95 R A Stuart 493/95,152,
96 R A Stuart 493/179.
97 R A Stuart 494/43; 498/189.
98 R A Stuart 498/188.
99 R A Stuart 498/188,248.
100 This is confirmed by the best recent study of Gustav's reign (Nordmann, *Grandeur et liberté de la Suède*, op. cit., p.424,
101 A. Geffroy, *Gustav III et la Cour de France*, 2 vols (Paris, 1867), ii, p.16.
102 R A Stuart 506/130.
103 *Walpole Correspondence*, 25, pp.467–8; Doran, ii, pp.403–4.
104 F O 79/4 f.35.
105 Baron Sparre handled the detailed negotiations. Since he was very fond of Louise, it was easier for the Swedes to convince her. For a full survey of Louise's relations with Gustav III and Sparre see Bruno Bassi, 'Vittorio Alfieri y la Suezia', *Annali Alferiani*, 2 (1943), pp.1–16.
106 F O 79/4 ff.67–8.
107 Reumont, *Die Grafin*, op. cit., i, pp.242–3.
108 Bassi, loc. cit., pp.16,19; Pellegrini, op. cit., p.55.
109 F O 79/4 f.35.
110 R A Stuart 507/49.
111 Mahon, *Last Stuarts*, pp.82–4.
112 Henry's reflections on Alfieri as '*origo mali*' both in the breakdown of his brother's marriage and his own relationship with Louise are at Add. MSS 30,478 ff.207–10.
113 Add. MSS 34,634 ff.63,67.
114 *Ibid.*, f.65.
115 Reumont, 'Gli ultimi Stuardi', loc. cit., pp.70–1; cf. also A. Ademollo, 'Il Diario del Cardinale Duca di York', *Nuova Antologia*, 1 July 1880, pp.27–8; Pellegrini, op. cit., pp.74–5.
116 Here is Louise's version of her life with Charles Edward as told to one English traveller: 'He was constantly and madly drunk and seldom had a moment of reason. He was ever talking about his restoration or abusing the French and the Pope. He was equally covetous and

extravagant. His own table was always sumptuously provided, but he would grudge the countess a little mutton broth in the morning. She acknowledged he had one good quality – he never betrayed a secret, and never disclosed who belonged to his party until after their death; nor would he listen to any ill-natured things said of people' (*Autobiography of Miss Cornelia Knight* (1861), pp.79–80). Louise's acknowledgment of his 'one good quality' is particularly illuminating in the light of Earl Marischal's accusations (see pp.430–1 above).

CHAPTER THIRTY-EIGHT

1 F O 79/4 f.100.
2 F O 79/5 f.5.
3 *Ibid.*, f.6.
4 F. A. Skeet, *H.R.H. Charlotte Duchess of Albany* (1932), p.150.
5 Mahon, *Last Stuarts*, pp.82–3.
6 F O 79/4 f.100.
7 F O 79/4 f.103.
8 For Charlotte, apart from the above-cited work of hagiography by Skeet see Susan Buchan, *The Funeral March of a Marionette* (1933) and (best of all) H. Tayler, *Prince Charlie's Daughter* (1950).
9 R A Stuart 473/55.
10 Archives Nationales, Series K,1303 f.105; A E M D Angleterre 81 f.109.
11 A E M D Angleterre 81 ff.121–7; R A Stuart 473/152,162.
12 A E M D Angleterre 81 ff.115,120.
13 R A Stuart 474/154; 475/66.
14 R A Stuart 475/178.
15 R A Stuart 475/181.
16 This is the 'justification' offered by the arch-hagiographer of Charles Edward, Sir Compton Mackenzie in *Prince Charlie's Ladies*, op. cit.
17 R A Stuart 480/48.
18 R A Stuart 481/23,131; 482/20.
19 R A Stuart 485/64,171; 496/83.
20 H M C, 10, vi, p.235.
21 R A Stuart 507/55.
22 F O 79/4 ff.85–6.
23 A E M D Angleterre 81 ff.152–92.
24 F O 79/4 ff.100,110,112–13.
25 Add. MSS 34,634 ff.77–8.
26 Pelissier, *Portefeuille de la Comtesse d'Albany*, op. cit., pp.61,83.
27 Add. MSS 34,634 ff.79–80.
28 F O 79/4 ff.108–9.
29 *Walpole Correspondence*, 25, p.535.
30 Mahon, *Last Stuarts*, p.87.
31 *Ibid*.
32 By now the prince was having his doubts about Gustav. 'He has doubts that the king of Sweden has complied with the promise he made to speak to His Majesty in his favour' (F O 79/4 ff.85–6).
33 H M C, 10, vi, pp.235–6.
34 H M C, 10, vi, p.236; Reumont, *Die Gräfin von Albany*, op. cit., ii, p.317.
35 H M C, 10, vi, p.235.
36 Add. MSS 34,638 f.341.
37 Add. MSS 34,634, f.9. Charles Edward was very bitter about his brother's attitude. Cf. Mann in December 1784: 'The faculties of his mind are as weak as his body. They are always employed when awake in abusing the cardinal, his brother, for refusing to adopt his niece' (*Walpole Correspondence*, 25, pp.549–50).
38 Add. MSS 34,634 f.70. Cf. an earlier letter in the same month (December 1784) from Louise to Henry: 'As to your brother, nothing surprises me in his behaviour. I know him so well that I consider him capable of going to any lengths of absurdity' (*ibid.*, f.68).
39 *Walpole Correspondence*, 25, pp.552–3.
40 F O 79/4 f.153.
41 C. M. J. D. Dupaty, *Lettres sur Italie en 1785* (Paris, 1788), i, pp.151–3.
42 F O 79/4 f.155.
43 See Add. MSS 34,634 ff.79–81 for the correspondence.
44 H M C, 10, vi, p.237.
45 Add. MSS 34,634 f.15; Mann, *Last Stuarts*, p.90.
46 Add. MSS 34,634 f.15.
47 Charles Edward to Cowley, 7 October 1785, Archives of Douai, IL/D Stuart No.11.
48 Add. MSS 34,638 f.345.
49 Add. MSS 34,634 f.12.
50 A E M D Angleterre 81 ff.192–3.
51 Add. MSS 34,638 f.347.
52 A E M D Angleterre 81 ff.198–200; 222–30.
53 Archives of Douai, IL/D Stuart No.10; A E M D Angleterre 81 ff.211–12.
54 H M C, 10, vi, p.238.
55 *Ibid.*, ff.237–8.
56 Henry was not alone in making this foolish assumption. See Compton Mackenzie, *Prince Charlie's Ladies*, p.279.
57 *Walpole Correspondence*, 33, p.450.
58 Tayler, *Prince Charlie's Daughter*, p.79.
59 Mahon, *Last Stuarts*, pp.91–2.
60 F O 79/5 ff.5–6.
61 A E M D Angleterre 81 ff.218–21; Add. MSS 34,638 ff.86–98.
62 R A Stuart 507/10.
63 Add. MSS 34,638 ff.173–4.
64 F O 79/5 f.36.
65 Tayler, *Prince Charlie's Daughter*, pp.72,73,75,76,81,87,88,92,100

66 N. W. Wraxall, *Historical Memoirs of my own Times*, 5 vols (1884), i, p.211.

67 F. Munter, *Aus den Tagebuchern Friedrich Munters wanderund lajahre eines Danisken gelehrten*, 3 vols (Copenhagen and Leipzig, 1937), ii, p.232.

68 A. Hayward, ed., *Autobiography of Mrs. Piozzi*, 2 vols (1861), i, p.331.

69 Lang, *Prince Charles Edward Stuart*, p.449.

70 Mahon, *Last Stuarts*, p.93.

71 Annette M. Smith, *The Jacobite Estates of the Forty-Five* (Edinburgh, 1982). Walpole wrote at the time of the restitution: 'If the Count [sc. Charles Edward] himself has any feelings left, he must rejoice to hear that the descendants of many of his martyrs are to be restored to their forfeited estates in Scotland by an act just now passed' (*Walpole Correspondence*, 25, p.521).

72 Mahon, *Last Stuarts*, p.94.

73 There were still some Jacobites left who sincerely mourned his passing. Cf. this lament from Isabella Strange: 'I do assure you grief has much affected me. None can feel the loss of a beloved friend more than I do that of the first man who drew my attention into actual life. My head and heart has now no more to do with vain wishes. I hope my friend is much happier now than this world could make him. He now views with a smile the littleness of all the pursuits of this world' (*Memoirs of Strange and Lumisden*, ii, p.216).

74 R A Stuart 515/70. Cf. also Henry to Walker, 9 March 1788, Archives du Nord (Lille), 18 H.67.

75 For full details of Charles Edward's legacies to Charlotte see Archivio di Stato (Roma), *Miscellanea Famiglie*, Busta 170, Nos 18–19; Busta 171 No.3. For the French monies see A E M D Angleterre 81 ff.234–6 for details.

76 For details see A E M D Angleterre 81 ff.238–48.

77 Archives du Nord, 18H 67.

78 Manning Clark, *Short History of Australia* (Sydney, 1963), p.25.

CONCLUSION

1 'The '45 was the greatest crisis that affected the eighteenth-century British state' Jeremy Black, *Britain in the Age of Walpole* (1984), p.20. See also the remarks in J. C. D. Clark, *Revolution and Rebellion. State and Society in England in the Seventeenth and Eighteenth Centuries* (Cambridge, 1986) p.153: 'Was the '45 a last despairing, romantic hopeless gamble? Or was it the mishandled (but still extremely dangerous) culmination of widespread resentment against Hanoverian rule?' The author leaves us in no doubt of his preference for the latter interpretation.

2 Clark, *Revolution and Rebellion*, op. cit., pp.41–2.

3 My view is strongly at variance with that of the latest scholar to write on the military dimension. See James Michael Hill, *Celtic Warfare* (Edinburgh, 1986).

4 Since Bruce Lenman in his *Jacobite Clans of the Great Glen*, op. cit. argues for the 'evolutionary' theory of the Scottish clans, disrupted only by the advent of Charles Edward in 1745 (see especially p.149), it is startling to find this assessment of the prince in his earlier book: 'lacked military ability', 'obstinate, insensitve egotism', 'the temper of a despot' (Lenman, *Jacobite Risings in Britain*, op. cit., pp.240,287,288 respectively). It is possible, just, to maintain that Charles Edward was a blockhead who got a lucky break and tapped by pure chance into the latent contradictions of Scottish society. But if the clan system was *not* inevitably doomed to demise, then Charles Edward's destruction of it must rank as a truly Nietzschean achievement, ahead even of anything Napoleon was able to bring about.

Bibliography

I MANUSCRIPT SOURCES

England

Royal Archives, Windsor Castle
  Stuart Papers
  Cumberland Papers
Public Record Office
  Foreign Office Reports, Series 79
  War Office Papers, Series 71
  State Papers: Domestic, Scotland, France, Switzerland, Russia, Venice, Tuscany,
    Italian States, Archives of various embassies
British Library, MSS Dept.
  Additional MSS (various)
  Stowe MSS
  Egerton MSS
Senate House Library, University of London
  Denys Bower MSS (microfilms)
University of Nottingham Library
  Pelham MSS
Douai, Berkshire
  Archives of Douai Abbey

France

Archives Nationales
  Series K,B2,B3,B4 (Marine)
Bibliothèque de l'Arsenal
Vincennes, Archives de la Guerre, Series A1
Ministère des Affaires Etrangères, Quai d'Orsay
  Archives Etrangères, Correspondance Politique: Angleterre, Rome, Espagne
  Archives Etrangères, Mémoires et Documents, Angleterre
Lille, Archives du Nord
Nancy, Archives Departmentales de Meurthe-et-Moselle

Rome

Archivio di Stato
  Carte Famiglie, Stuart
Biblioteca Angelica

Vatican City

Vatican Library
  Borgia MSS (Latin)
Archivio Segreto Vaticano
  Lettere di Principi
  Instrumenta Miscellanea
  Nuncios' reports: Avignone, Francia, Inghilterra

Spain

Archivo General de Simancas (Estado)

USA

Cornell University
  Maurepas MSS

2 NEWSPAPERS AND PERIODICALS

CALEDONIAN MERCURY
DAILY ADVERTISER
GENTLEMAN'S MAGAZINE
LONDON CHRONICLE
LONDON GAZETTE
REVUE DES DEUX MONDES
ST JAMES'S CHRONICLE
ST JAMES'S EVENING POST
SCOTS MAGAZINE

3 PUBLISHED PRIMARY SOURCES (COLLECTIONS OF DOCUMENTS, MEMOIRS, CORRESPONDENCE, ETC)

ALBEMARLE PAPERS, ed. C. S. Terry (Aberdeen, 1902).
ALFIERI, VITTORIO, *Vita . . . scritta da esso*, ed. V. Branca (Milan, 1983).
ALLARDYCE PAPERS, 2 vols (New Spalding Club, Aberdeen, 1895–6).
ARGENSON, PIERRE, COMTE D', *Correspondance du comte d'Argenson*, ed. Maurice d'Argenson (Paris, 1922).
ARGENSON, PIERRE, COMTE D', *Correspondance du comte d'Argenson. Lettres des Maréchaux de France* (Paris, 1924).
ARGENSON, RENÉ, MARQUIS D', *Journal et mémoires*, 9 vols, ed. E. J. B. Rathery (Paris, 1859–67).
ATHOLL FAMILY, *Jacobite Correspondence of* (Edinburgh, Abbotsford Club, 1840).
ATHOLL, 7TH DUKE OF, *Chronicles of the Families of Atholl and Tullibardine*, 5 vols (1908).
BARBIER, E. J. F., *Journal historique et anecdotique du régne de Louis XV* (Paris, 1847).
BERNIS, FRANÇOIS JOACHIM, CARDINAL, *Mémoires et lettres*, ed. F. Masson (Paris, 1878).

BLAIKIE, W. B., *Origins of the Forty-Five* (Edinburgh, 1916).

BONSTETTEN, CHARLES VICTOR, *Souvenirs* (Paris, 1832).

BOSWELL, JAMES, *Life of Samuel Johnson*, ed. G. B. Hill (revised by C. F. Powell), 6 vols (Oxford, 1934).

BRADSTREET, D., *The Adventures of Captain Dudley Bradstreet* (1755).

BROSSES, CHARLES DE, *Lettres familières écrites d'Italie*, 2 vols (Dijon, 1927).

BUCHAN, WILLIAM, *Domestic Medicine* (Philadelphia, 1809).

BURKE, EDMUND, *Correspondence*, 10 vols, ed. Thomas W. Copeland (Cambridge and Chicago, 1978).

BURT, EDWARD, *Letters from a Gentleman in the North of Scotland* (1818).

CARLYLE, A, *The Autobiography of Dr. Alexander Carlyle* (London and Edinburgh, 1910).

CHAMBERS, R., ed., *Jacobite Memoirs of the Rising of 1745* (1834) (containing Lord George Murray's 'Marches of the Highland Army').

CHARVET, G., *Une correspondance inédite de la Comtesse d'Albanie* (Nîmes, 1878).

CHATEAUROUX, MADAME DE, *Correspondance avec le duc de Richelieu* (Paris, 1806).

CHESTERFIELD, PHILIP DORMER STANHOPE, *Private Correspondence of Chesterfield and Newcastle* (Royal Historical Society, Camden Series, xliv, 1930).

CHEVERNEY, COMTE DUFORT DE, *Mémoires sur les régnes de Louis XV et Louis XVI*, 2 vols (Paris, 1909).

CHOISEUL, DUC DE, *Mémoires, 1719–1785* (Paris 1904).

CLANRANALD, RANALD MACDONALD OF, 'Account of Proceedings from Prince Charles's Landing to Prestonpans', *Scottish Historical Society Miscellany 9*, ed. Donald Nicholas (1958).

Cochrane Correspondence regarding the affairs of Glasgow 1745–46 (Maitland Club, Edinburgh, 1830).

COPE, LIEUTENANT GENERAL SIR JOHN, *The Report of the Proceedings and Opinion of the Board of General Officers on thier examination into the conduct, behaviour and proceedings of* (1749).

CORDARA, PADRE GIULIO CESARE, *Commentary on the Expedition to Scotland made by Charles Edward Stuart, Prince of Wales*, Sir Bruce Seton, ed. *Miscellany of the Scottish History Society*, 3rd series, IX (1926).

Court and City Register 1772.

COXE, WILLIAM, *Memoirs of the Administration of the Right Honourable Henry Pelham*, 2 vols (1829)

COYER, GABRIEL-FRANÇOIS, *History of John Sobieski, King of Poland* (1762).

CROY, DUC DE, *Journal inédit 1718–1784*, 4 vols (Paris, 1906).

Culloden Papers, ed. H. R. Duff (1815).

DICKSON, W. K., ed., *The Jacobite Attempt of 1719* (Edinburgh, 1719).

DIDEROT, DENIS, *Correspondance*, ed. Georges Roth (Paris, 1957).

DORAN, J. *Mann and Manners at Florence 1740–1786*, 2 vols (1876).

DU DEFFAND, MARIE CHAMROND, MARQUISE DE, *Correspondance complète*, ed. St Aulaire, 3 vols (Paris, 1866).

DUPATY, C. M. J. D., *Lettres sur Italie en 1785* (Paris, 1788).

DUTENS, LOUIS, *Mémoires d'un voyageur qui se repose*, 2 vols (1806).

ELCHO, LORD, *A Short Account of the Affairs of Scotland in 1744, 1745 and 1746*, ed. E. Charteris (1907).

FLEETWOOD, BISHOP, *Six Useful Discourses on the Relative Duties of Parents and Children* (1749).

FLOYER, JOHN, *The History of Cold Bathing* (1732).

FREDERICK THE GREAT, *Politische Correspondanz* (Berlin, 1879–82).

GRAY, THOMAS, *Letters*, ed. Duncan C. Tovey, 3 vols (1900).

GUSTAVUS III, king of Sweden, *Collection des écrits politiques, littéraires et dramatiques de Gustav III* (Paris, 1805).

HAUSMANN, FRIEDRICH, *Repertorium der diplomatischen Vertreter aller Lander* (Zurich, 1750).

HEECKEREN, EMILE DE, *Correspondance de Benoit XIV avec Tencin*, 2 vols (Paris, 1912).

HELVETIUS, CLAUDE ADRIEN, *Oeuvres complètes*, 5 vols (Paris, 1795).

HÉNAULT, PRÉSIDENT CHARLES, *Mémoires* (Paris, 1855).

HENDERSON, A., *History of the Rebellion 1745–46* (1753).

HÉROARD, JEAN, *Journal sur l'enfance et la jeunesse de Louis XIII* (Paris, 1868).

Historical Manuscripts Commission, Second, Third, Fifth, Seventh, Eight, Tenth, Eleventh, Twelfth, Thirteenth, Fourteenth, Fifteenth Reports; Stuart, Hastings, Denbigh, Laing, Bathurst, Lothian, Du Cane, Egmont, Portland, Various Collections.

HOME, JOHN, *The History of the Rebellion in the Year 1745* (1802).

HOWELLS, T. B., *A Collection of State Trials*, 34 vols (1828).

HUME, DAVID, *Letters*, ed. J. Y. T. Greig (Oxford, 1932).

JOHNSTONE, CHEVALIER DE, *A Memoir of the Forty-Five* (1820).

LALANDE, JOSEPH-JÉROME LE FRANÇAIS DE, *Voyage d'un Français en Italie* (Venice, 1769).

KEYSLER, J. G., *Travels through Germany, Bavaria, Hungary, Switzerland and Lorraine* (1756–7).

KING, WILLIAM, *Political and Literary Anecdotes* (1819).

KNIGHT, CORNELIA, *Autobiography* (1861).

LALLEMENT, LÉON, *Le Maréchal de Camp Warren* (Vannes, 1893).

LA TREMOUILLE, DUC DE, *Les Tremouilles pendant cinq siècles*, 5 vols (Nantes, 1896).

LA TREMOUILLE, CHARLES, DUC DE, *Une famille royaliste, irlandaise et française* (Paris, 1901).

LIRIA, DUQUE DE, *Diario del viaje a Moscovia del dùque de Liria y Xerica* (*Documentos ineditos para la historia de Espana*) (Madrid, 1889).

Lockhart Papers, ed. A. Aufrere, 2 vols (1817).

LUYNES, ALBERT, DUC DE, *Mémoires sur la cour de Louis XV*, ed. Dussieux and Soulie (Paris, 1860–6).

The Lyon in Mourning, ed. Henry Patton, 3 vols (Edinburgh, Scottish History Society, 1895).

MACALLESTER, OLIVER, *A Series of Letters*, 2 vols (1767).

MAHON, LORD, *Decline of the Last Stuarts. Extracts from Despatches* (Roxburghe Club, 1843).

MARISCHAL, GEORGE KEITH, hereditary earl, 'Two Fragments of Autobiography', ed. J. Y. T. Greig, *Miscellany of the Scottish History Society*, 3rd series (1933).

Marchmont Correspondence, Miscellany of the Scottish History Society (1933).

MARVILLE, FEYDEAU DE, *Lettres au ministre Maurepas*, ed. A. de Boislisle, 3 vols (Paris, 1896)

MAUREPAS, COMTE DE, *Recueil dit de Maurepas*, 5 vols (Leyden, 1865).

MAXWELL OF KIRKCONNELL, JAMES, *Narrative of Charles Prince of Wales's expedition to Scotland in the year 1745* (Edinburgh, 1841).

MILLER, LADY ANNE, *Letters from Italy*, 3 vols (1776).

Miscellany of the Spalding Club (1841).

MONTAGU, LADY WORTLEY, *Letters and Works* (1861).

MONTESQUIEU, CHARLES-LOUIS DE SECONDAT, BARON DE, *Correspondance*, ed. F. Gebelin (Paris, 1914).

MONTESQUIEU, CHARLES-LOUIS DE SECONDAT, BARON DE, *Oeuvres complètes* (Paris, 1950).

More Culloden Papers, ed. Duncan Warrand, 5 vols (Inverness, 1923–30).

MORELLI, EMILIO, *Le lettere di Benedetto XIV a Tencin*, 2 vols (Rome, 1955).

MURRAY OF BROUGHTON, JOHN, *Memorials*, ed. R. F. Bell (Scottish History Society 27, 1898).

NOAILLES, ADRIEN, DUC DE, *Mémoires politiques et militaires*, ed. Millot (Paris, 1777).

PELISSIER, LÉON G., *Lettres et écrits divers de la comtesse d'Albany* (Paris, 1901).

PELISSIER, LÉON G., *La portefeuille de la comtesse d'Albany* (Paris, 1902).

PELISSIER, LÉON G. *Lettres inédites de la comtesse d'Albany*, 3 vols (Paris, 1904–15).

PIOZZI, MRS, *Autobiography*, ed. A. Hayward, 2 vols (1861).

PITSLIGO, ALEXANDER FORBES, lord, *Thoughts concerning Man's Condition* (1854).

RICHELIEU, DUC DE, *Mémoires authentiques*, ed. Boislisle (Paris, 1918).

ROUSSEAU, JEAN-JACQUES, *Emile* (Pleïade edition, Paris, 1969).

Royal Kalendar, 1768.

SAXE, MAURICE, COMTE DE, *Lettres et mémoires du maréchal de Saxe*, ed. Grimoard, 5 vols (Paris, 1794).

STRANGE, SIR ROBERT and ANDREW LUMISDEN, *Memoirs*, ed. J. Dennistoun, 2 vols (1855).

TALON, H., *John Byrom: selections from his journals and papers* (1950).

TAYLER, A. and H., *Jacobites of Aberdeenshire and Banffshire in the '45* (Aberdeen, 1928).

TAYLER, A. and H., *Jacobite letters to Lord Pitsligo* (Aberdeen, 1930).

TAYLER, A. and H., *1745 and After* (containing 'O'Sullivan's account') (1938).

TAYLER, HENRIETTA, *The Stuart Papers at Windsor* (1939).

TAYLER, HENRIETTA, *Jacobite Epilogue* (1941)

TAYLER, HENRIETTA, *Anonymous History of the Rebellion in the Years 1745 & 1746* (1944).

TAYLER, HENRIETTA, *Jacobite Miscellany* (Edinburgh, 1948).

TOURNEUX, MAURICE, ed., *Correspondance de Grimm, Diderot, Raynal, Meister etc.* (Paris, 1882).

VALORI, MARQUIS DE, *Mémoires* (Paris, 1820).

VAUCHER, P. ed., *Recueil des instructions aux ambassadeurs. Angleterre 1688–1791* (Paris, 1965).

Vernon Papers (Navy Records Society XCIX, 1958).

VERRI, *Carteggio di Pietro e Alessandro*, ed. Giulini G. Sepegni (Milan, 1926).

VIOMENIL, BARON DE, *Lettres sur les affaires de Pologne en 1771 et 1772* (Paris, 1808).

VOLTAIRE, FRANÇOIS MARIE AROUET, *Oeuvres complètes*, ed. Moland (Paris, 1877–85).

VOLTAIRE, FRANÇOIS MARIE AROUET, *Précis du siècle de Louis XV*, ed. Beuchot (Paris, 1888).

VOLTAIRE, FRANÇOIS MARIE AROUET, *Correspondance*, ed. Besterman (Geneva, 1953–67).

WALPOLE, HORACE, *Correspondence*, ed. W. S. Lewis (New Haven, 1937–74).

WALPOLE, HORACE, *Memoirs of the Reign of George II* (1846).

Whitefoord Papers, ed. W. A. S. Hewins (Oxford, 1898).

Woodhouselee MSS., ed. Steurat (1907).

WRAXALL, N. W., *Historical Memoirs of My Own Time* (1818).

4 BOOKS AND ARTICLES CITED

ACRES, W. MARSTON, *The Bank of England from Within* (Oxford, 1931).

ANGELIS, A. DE, *Nella Roma Papale. Il Teatro Aliberti o delle dame 1717–1863* (Tivoli, 1973).

ARIÈS, PHILIPPE, *L'enfant et la vie familiale sous l'Ancien Régime* (Paris, 1960).

BAINES, J., *The Jacobite Rising of 1715* (1970).

BASSI, BRUNO, 'Vittorio Alfieri e la Suezia', *Annali Alferiani*, II (1943).

BENIMELI, J. A. F., *La masoneria española en el siglo 18* (Madrid, 1974).

BERTANA, EMILIO, *Alfieri* (Turin, 1904).

BERTON, C., *Dictionnaire des cardinaux* (Paris, 1857).

BINDELLI, PIETRO, *Enrico Stuart* (Frascati, 1982).

BLACK, JEREMY, ed., *Britain in the Age of Walpole* (1984).

BLACK, JEREMY, ed., *British Foreign Policy in the Age of Walpole* (Edinburgh, 1985).

BLACK, JEREMY, ed., *'Natural and Necessary Enemies', Anglo-French Relations in the 18th Century* (1986).

BLAIKIE, W. B., *Itinerary of Prince Charles Stuart from his landing in Scotland July 1745 to his departure in September 1746* (Edinburgh, 1897).

BLOS, PETER, *On Adolescence. A Psychoanalytic Interpretation* (New York, 1962).

BONGIE, L. L. *The Love of a Prince. Bonnie Prince Charlie in France 1744–1748* (Vancouver, 1986).

BORD, GUSTAVE, *La Franc-maçonnerie en France* (Paris, 1908).

BOWLBY, JOHN, *Attachment and Loss*, 3 vols (1980).

BOYE, PIERRE, *La Cour Polonaise de Lunéville 1737–1766* (Nancy, 1926).

BRAULT, E., *Le Mystère du chevalier Ramsay* (Paris, 1973).

BROGLIE, ALBERT, DUC DE, *Frédéric II et Marie-Thérèse* (Paris, 1883).

BROGLIE, ALBERT, DUC DE, *Frédéric II et Louis XV*, 2 vols (Paris, 1885).

BROGLIE, ALBERT, DUC DE, *Marie-Thérèse imperatrice* (Paris, 1888).

BROGLIE, ALBERT, DUC DE, *Maurice de Saxe et le Marquis d'Argenson* (Paris, 1891).

BROGLIE, ALBERT, DUC DE, *La Paix d'Aix la Chapelle* (Paris, 1891).

BROWNE, JAMES, *A History of the Highlands and of the Highland Clans*, 4 vols (Glasgow, 1832–3).

BUCHAN, SUSAN, *The Funeral March of a Marionette* (1933).

BUSHKUHL, MATTHIAS, *Great Britain and the Holy See 1746–1870* (Dublin, 1982).

BUTLER, ROHAN, *Choiseul* (Oxford, 1981).

CARLTON, CHARLES, *Royal Childhoods* (1986).

CHEREL, A., *Un aventurier religieux au 18ᵉ siècle. André-Michel Ramsay* (Paris, 1926).

CHEVALLIER, P., *Les Ducs sous l'Acacia* (Paris, 1964).

CHEVALLIER, P., *La première profanation du temple maçonnique* (Paris, 1968).

CLAPHAM, SIR JOHN, *The Bank of England* (1945).

CLARK, J. C. D., *English Society 1688–1832* (Cambridge, 1985).

CLARK, J. C. D., *Revolution and Rebellion. State and Society in the Seventeenth and Eighteenth Centuries* (Cambridge, 1986).

CLARK, MANNING, *A Short History of Australia* (1963).

COLIN, JEAN, *Louis XV et les Jacobites. Le projet de débarquement en Angleterre en 1743–44* (Paris, 1901).

CROSLAND, MARGARET, *Louise of Stolberg, Countess of Albany* (1962).

CRUICKSHANKS, EVELINE, *Political Untouchables. The Tories and the '45* (1979).

CRUICKSHANKS, EVELINE, ed., *Ideology and Conspiracy. Aspects of Jacobitism 1688–1759* (Edinburgh, 1982).

CRUICKSHANKS, EVELINE, *Lord Cornbury, Bolingbroke and a Plan to Restore the Stuarts 1731–1735* (Royal Stuart Papers 27, 1986).

CUTHELL, EDITH, *The Scottish Friend of Frederick the Great. The Last Earl Marischal*, 2 vols (1915).

DRAKE, T. G. H., 'The Wet Nurse in the Eighteenth Century', *Bulletin of the History of Medicine* (1940), pp. 934–48.

EMMERLING, ERNST, *Pompeo Battoni* (Darmstadt, 1932).

ERIKSON, ERIK, *Young Man Luther* (New York, 1958).

ERIKSON, ERIK, *Childhood and Society* (New York, 1963).

ERIKSON, ERIK, *Identity and Crisis* (New York, 1964).

ERIKSON, ERIK, *Insight and Responsibility* (New York, 1964).

FERGUSSON, SIR JAMES, *Lowland Lairds* (1949).

FERGUSSON, SIR JAMES, *Argyll in the '45* (1952).

FITZMAURICE, LORD, *Life of William, Earl of Shelburne* (1912).

FRANKOVICH, CARLO, *Storia Massoneria in Italia* (Florence, 1974).

FRASER, SIR W., *The Chiefs of Colquhoun* (Edinburgh, 1869).

FRASER, SIR W., *The Earls of Cromartie* (Edinburgh, 1876).

FRASER, SIR W., *The Chiefs of Grant*, 3 vols (Edinburgh, 1883).

FREUD, SIGMUND, *Standard Edition of the Complete Psychological Works of*, ed. James Strachey (1953).

GEFFROY, A., *Gustav III et la cour de France*, 2 vols (Paris, 1867).

GERMINY, MARC DE, *Les Brigandages maritimes de l'Angleterre*, 3 vols (Paris, 1925).

GIBSON, JOHN, *Ships of the '45. The Rescue of the Young Pretender* (1967).

GOLDBERG, ARNOLD, *The Psychology of the Self. A Case Book written with the collaboration of Heinz Kohut* (New York, 1978).

GOULD, R. F., *History of Freemasonry* (1887).

GREGG, EDWARD, *Queen Anne* (1980).

HAILE, MARTIN, *James Francis Edward. The Old Chevalier* (1907).

HARRIS, G., *Life of Lord Chancellor Hardwicke*, 2 vols (1847).

HAUSSMAN, FRIEDRICH, *Repertorium der diplomatischen vertreter aller Lander* (Zurich, 1950).

HAYNES, RENÉE, *Philosopher King. Pope Benedict XIV* (1970).

HENDERSON, G. D., *Chevalier Ramsay* (1952).

HERKING, MARIE L., *Bonstetten 1745–1832* (Lausanne, 1921).

JACOBI, C. F., *Europäische Genealogisches Handbuch* (Leipzig, 1800).

JARVIS, R. C., *Collected Papers on the Jacobite Risings*, 2 vols (Manchester, 1972).

JONES, G. H., *The Mainstream of Jacobitism* (Harvard, 1954).

KOHUT, HEINZ, *The Analysis of the Self. A Systematic Approach to the Psychoanalytic Treatment of Narcissistic Personality Disorders* (New York, 1971).

KOHUT, HEINZ, *The Restoration of the Self* (New York, 1977).

KOHUT, HEINZ, *The Search for the Self. Selected Writings of Heinz Kohut 1950–1978*, ed. Paul H. Orenstein, 2 vols (New York, 1978).

LANG, ANDREW, *Pickle the Spy* (1897).

LANG, ANDREW, *The Companions of Pickle* (1898).

LANG, ANDREW, *The Highlands of Scotland in 1750* (1898).

LANG, ANDREW, *Prince Charles Edward Stuart* (1903).

LANG, ANDREW (with A. Shield), *The King over the Water* (1907).

LEE, VERNON, *The Countess of Albany* (1884).

LEE, VERNON, *Studies in the Eighteenth Century in Italy* (1907).

LEES-MILNE, J., *The Last Stuarts* (1983).

LENHOFF, EUGEN, *Freemasons* (New York, 1934).

LENMAN, BRUCE, *The Jacobite Risings in Britain 1689–1746* (1980).

LENMAN, BRUCE, *The Jacobite Clans of the Great Glen 1650–1784* (1984).

LEO-BERRY,C., *The Young Pretender's Mistress* (1977).

LETI, GIUSEPPE, *Carboneria e massoneria nel risorgimento italiano* (Genoa, 1925).

LIGON, D., *Dictionnaire universel de la Franc-maçonnerie* (Paris, 1974).

LIMPBURGER, WALTHER, *Die Gebaude von Florenz* (Leipzig, 1810).

LINKLATER, ERIC, *The Prince in the Heather* (1965).

LION, HENRI, *Le president Hénault 1685–1770* (Paris, 1903).

LIVINGSTONE, A., AIKMAN, C. W. H. and HART, B. S., eds, *Muster Roll of Prince Charles Edward Stuart's Army 1745–46* (Aberdeen, 1984).

MACGREGOR, AMELIA C., *History of the Clan Gregor* (Edinburgh, 1901).

MACKENZIE, ALEXANDER, *History of the MacDonalds* (Inverness, 1881).

MACKENZIE, COMPTON, *Prince Charlie's Ladies* (1934).

MACKENZIE, W. C., *Simon Fraser, Lord Lovat* (1908).

MACKENZIE, W. J. M., *Politics and Social Science* (1967).

MACLEAN, A., *A MacDonald for the Prince* (Stornoway, 1982).

MCLYNN, F. J., *France and the Jacobite Rising of 1745* (Edinburgh, 1981).

MCLYNN, F. J., *The Jacobite Army in England 1745. The Final Campaign* (Edinburgh, 1983).

MCLYNN, F. J., *The Jacobites* (1985).

MCLYNN, F. J., *Invasion: from the Armada to Hitler 1588–1945* (1987).

MACPHERSON, W. CHEYNE, *Chiefs of Clan MacPherson* (1948).

MAHON, LORD, *History of England from the Peace of Utrecht*, 7 vols (1858).

MALO, HENRI, *Les derniers corsairs. Dunkerque 1715–1815* (Paris, 1925).

MARTIN, GASTON, *Nantes au dix-huitième siècle 1714–74* (Toulouse, 1928).

MARUZZI, P., 'Notizie e documenti sul liberi muratori e Torino ne secolo XVIII', *Bolletino storico-bibliografico subalpino*, 30 (1928).

MAUGRAS, G., *La Cour de Luneville au 18e siècle* (Paris, 1904).

MAUGRAS, G., *Dernières années du roi Stanislas* (Paris, 1906).

MAUSE, ERIK DE, *The History of Childhood* (1976).

MELLOR, ALEC, *Nos frères séparés les Francs-Maçons* (Paris, 1961).

MELLOR, ALEC, *La charte inconnue de la franc-maçonnerie chretienne* (Tours, 1965).

MENARY, G., *The Life and Letters of Duncan Forbes of Culloden* (1936).

MICHINER, MARGARET, *No Crown for the Queen* (1937).

MILLER, PEGGY, *A Wife for the Pretender* (1965).

MILLER, PEGGY, *James* (1972).

MOSSNER, E. C., *Life of David Hume* (Edinburgh, 1954).

MOUNSEY, G. C., *Carlisle in 1745* (1846).

MUNTER, F., *Auf den Tageburchen Friedrich Munters Wanderund Lejahre eines Danisken gelehrten* (Copenhagen and Leipzig, 1937).

NENNO, BARON DE, *Gustav III, Roi de Suède et Anckarstroem 1746–92* (Paris, 1876).

NICHOLAS, DONALD, *Intercepted Post* (1956).

NORDMANN, CLAUDE, *Grandeur et liberté de la Suède 1660–1792* (Paris, 1971).

O'CALLAGHAN, J. C., *History of the Irish Brigade in the Service of France* (Glasgow, 1870).

PASTOR, LUDWIG, *History of the Popes* (trans. 1949).

PELLEGRINI, CARLO, *La contessa d'Albany e il salotto del lungarno* (Naples, 1951).

PEREY, LUCIEN, *Le président Hénault et Madame du Deffand* (Paris, 1893).

PERRERO, A. D., 'Gli ultimi Stuardi e V. Alfieri sul fondamento di documenti inediti 1782–83', *Rivista Europea*, 24 (1881).

PETRIE, SIR CHARLES, 'The Elibank Plot 1752–53', *Royal Historical Society Transactions*, 4th Series 14 (1931), pp.175–96.

POPPER, SIR KARL, *The Open Society and its Enemies*, 2 vols (1945).

PREBBLE, JOHN, *Culloden* (1961).

RANFFT, MICHAEL, *Merkwurdige Lebesgeschichte aller Cardinale* (Regensburg, 1773).

REMOND, ANDRÉ, *John Holker, manufacturier et grand fonctionnaire en France au XVIIIe siècle* (Paris, 1946).

REUMONT, A., *Die Grafin von Albany*, 2 vols (Berlin, 1860).

REUMONT, A., 'Il principe e la principesa de Craon e i primi tempi della regenza lorense in Toscana', *Archivio Storico Italiano*, III, vol. 15 (1877).

REUMONT, A., 'Gli ultimi Stuardi, la contessa d'Albany et V. Alfieri', *Archivio Storico Italiano*, IV, vol. 8 (1881).

RICHARD, P., 'Origines et developpement de la secrétaire d'état apostolique 1417–1823', *Revue d'histoire ecclésiastique*, 11 (1910).

RICHMOND, ADMIRAL SIR H. W., *The Navy in the War of 1739–1748*, 3 vols (Oxford, 1920).

ROSEBERY, LORD and MACLEOD, REV. WALTER, *List of Persons concerned in the Rebellion of 1745* (Edinburgh, 1890, Scottish History Society).

ROSENBERG, BRUCE A., *Custer and the Epic of Defeat* (Pennsylvania, 1974).

SAREIL, JEAN, *Les Tencin* (Geneva, 1969).

SEDGWICK, ROMNEY, ed., *The History of Parliament: the House of Commons 1715–1754*, 2 vols (1970).

SEGUR, PIERRE DE, 'Madame du Deffand et sa famille', *Revue des Deux Mondes*, no. 37 (1917).

SETON, SIR BRUCE and ARNOT, JEAN, *The Prisoners of the '45*, 3 vols (Edinburgh, Scottish History Society, 3rd series 13–15, 1928–9).

SHACKLETON, R., *Montesquieu* (Oxford, 1961).

SILVAGNI, DAVID, *La corte e la società romana nel secoli XVIII e XIX* (Florence and Rome, 1885).

SIMPSON, LLEWELLYN EARDLEY, *Derby and the Forty-Five* (1933).

SIRVEN, P., *Vittorio Alfieri* (Paris, 1938).

SKEET, J. A., *Charlotte Stuart, Duchess of Albany* (1932).

SMART, ALASTAIR, *The Life and Art of Allan Ramsay* (1952).

SMITH, ANNETTE, M., *Jacobite Estates of the Forty-Five* (Edinburgh, 1982).

SPECK, W. A., *The Butcher: the duke of Cumberland and the suppression of the Forty-Five* (Oxford, 1981).

STEWART, HELEN M., 'The Exiled Stewarts in Italy', *Miscellany of the Scottish Historical Society*, VII, 2nd Series, 35 (Edinburgh, 1941).

SZECHI, D., *Jacobitism and Tory Politics 1710–14* (Edinburgh, 1984).

TAYLER, A. and H., *1715: The Story of the Rising* (1936).

TAYLER, HENRIETTA, *Prince Charlie's Daughter* (1950).

THEINER, A., *Geschichte des Pontificats Clemens XIV*, 2 vols (Leipzig, 1853).

THEINER, A., *Histoire du Pontificat de Clement XIV* (Paris, 1853).

TOMAN, WALTER, *The Family Constellation* (New York, 1976).

TOMASSON, KATHERINE, *The Jacobite General* (Edinburgh, 1958).

TOMASSON, KATHERINE and BUIST, F., *Battles of the '45* (1962).

VALENTINE, ALAN, ed., *Fathers to Sons. Advice without Consent* (Oklahoma, 1963).

VAUGHAN, H. M., *The Last Stuart Queen* (1910).

VITELLESCHI, MARCHESA NOBILI, *A Court in Exile*, 2 vols (1907).

WEBER, MAX, *Gesammelte aufsatze zur Wissenschatslehre* (Tubingen, 1951).

YOUNGSON, A. J., *The Prince and the Pretender* (1985).

Index